Max Planck Institute for Innovation and Competition

For further volumes/weitere Bände:
http://www.springer.com/series/7760

MPI Studies on Intellectual Property and Competition Law

Volume 22

Edited by

Josef Drexl
Reto M. Hilty
Joseph Straus

Reto M. Hilty • Kung-Chung Liu
Editors

Compulsory Licensing

Practical Experiences and Ways Forward

Springer

Editors
Reto M. Hilty
Max Planck Institute for Innovation and Competition
Munich
Germany

Kung-Chung Liu
Institutum Iurisprudentiae Academia Sinica
Taipei
Taiwan

ISSN 2191-5822 ISSN 2191-5830 (electronic)
ISBN 978-3-662-51516-7 ISBN 978-3-642-54704-1 (eBook)
DOI 10.1007/978-3-642-54704-1
Springer Heidelberg New York Dordrecht London

Printed on acid-free paper

Springer is part of Springer Science+Business Media (www.springer.com)

Contents

Introduction

Reto M. Hilty and Kung-Chung Liu

Contents

A group of 20 scholars gathered at the Fifth Conference on European and Asian Intellectual Property: Compulsory Licensing (CL) held on 3–5 December 2012 in Taipei under the auspices of the Max Planck Institute for Intellectual Property and Competition Law (Max Planck Institute for Innovation and Competition since 2014) and Institutum Iurisprudentiae, Academia Sinica, an event jointly sponsored by the National Science Council (Ministry of Science and Technology since March 2014), Fair Trade Commission, Institute of Law for Science & Technology, National Tsing Hua University, Institute for Information Industry, and National Taiwan University Law School in Taiwan. Their goals were to study the CL experiences made in India, Latin America, Thailand, Taiwan, Germany, and the European Union—particularly related to medical concerns and competition

R.M. Hilty is Professor of Law and Director of the Max Planck Institute for Innovation and Competition. K.-C. Liu is Professor of Law.

R.M. Hilty
Max Planck Institute for Innovation and Competition, Munich, Germany
e-mail: hilty@ip.mpg.de

K.-C. Liu
Institutum Iurisprudentiae Academia Sinica, Taipei, Taiwan, Republic of China
and School of Law, Singapore Management University, Singapore
e-mail: liukc@gate.sinica.edu.tw; kcliu@smu.edu.sg

R.M. Hilty and K.-C. Liu (eds.), *Compulsory Licensing*, MPI Studies on Intellectual Property and Competition Law 22, DOI 10.1007/978-3-642-54704-1_1,

issues—and to analyse the legal framework of international IP conventions, including the provisions of the Paris Convention, the TRIPS Agreement, and the Doha Declaration on the TRIPS Agreement and Public Health. The overall aim was to explore the CL-related doctrinal groundwork in order to make CL a better workable mechanism that would facilitate a balance of interests, notably the speedy use and dissemination of patents and other IP rights.

This book is composed of three parts: I—Practices Across Jurisdictions, II—The Operation of Compulsory Licensing Regime, and III—Doctrinal Discussions.

1 Part I

The first chapter by N.S. Gopalakrishnan and Madhuri Anand explores the emergence of compulsory licence provisions in general and its evolution in India. A brief analysis of the pre-TRIPS provisions in the Indian Patent Act 1970 is attempted to find out its use by the Indian industries. An elaborate study of the post-TRIPS provisions of the Indian Patent Act, along with the analyses of its interpretations by judicial authorities, is also undertaken to examine its effectiveness in the new context. Further, a brief attempt is made to find out the attitude of Indian industries in using these provisions.

The second chapter by Carlos M. Correa studies the law and practices in Latin America. CL and government use are provided for in Latin American countries' patent legislation, but so far only two countries (Brazil and Ecuador) have made effective use of this flexibility to improve access to patented medicines. While the consistency with the provisions of TRIPS on CL was questioned in two cases under the WTO dispute settlement mechanism, such challenge did not lead to changes in legislation. Notably, one of such cases seems to confirm the compatibility with that Agreement of CLs based on the lack of effective working of a patent in the country of grant.

The chapter by Jakkrit Kuanpoth looks at Thailand's experiences with the use of CL to increase access to medicines. It highlights the use of CL in the context of a range of public health responses. It first discusses the use by Thailand of the compulsory government-use licensing to increase access to medicines. It also examines international rules on CL. Finally, the chapter discusses various legal issues under the Thai Patent Act regarding the CL provisions. It also highlights the possible impact, in a broad sense, of the use of legal mechanisms such as CL, which aims to effectively maintain fair market competition and dilute the monopoly power of the patent holder.

The chapter by Kung-Chung Liu discusses CL and government use in Taiwan. It points out that the Taiwanese Patent Act foresaw from its inception in 1944 CL and government use. The provisions on the former have been amended several times, moving away from the Paris Convention model, while provisions on the latter were revised once, only to narrow its scope. Overall speaking, the regime on CL and government use is in regress and fails to fulfil its function of balancing public and private interests. Thus far in Taiwan, two CL have been granted and implemented, with the second being annulled later, and only one government use has been granted and yet not implemented due to its precondition not being satisfied. The Fair Trade Commission has not yet seen CL as one of the "necessary corrective measures" of the Fair Trade Act, although it did find violation of the Fair Trade Act in the Philips CD-R case.

In the next chapter, Philipp Maume focuses on Germany, where the discussion of CLs under competition law is of particularly high relevance. The chapter shows that German competition law obliges the holder of a patent, which is essential in a standard to grant a licence on terms that are fair, reasonable, and non-discriminatory (FRAND). Users of such patents can also raise a so-called competition law defence against imminent injunction orders. The German courts' approaches to this defence have become more and more sophisticated over the last years, trying to close a number of structural gaps in the Federal Supreme Court Ruling Orange Book Standard. However, it remains unclear if or to what extent the defence complies with European law. To clarify, the District Court Düsseldorf in March 2013 submitted the case to the European Court of Justice for a preliminary ruling under Art. 267 Treaty on the Functioning of the European Union (TFEU). This chapter suggests a streamlined, simplified approach to competition-law-based defences.

The chapter by Matthias Lamping discusses the special cases under European law, in which an intellectual property right will constitute an "essential facility" and therefore enable the right holder to control access to, and thus competition in, the market. In such cases, a refusal to licence may lead to an abuse of market dominance within the meaning of Art. 102 TFEU. Depending on the circumstances of the case, the abuse may consist in a discrimination of trading partners, an unjustified foreclosure of competitors, a negligence of market needs, or an expansion of market power to another related market. However, a CL will not always be the appropriate remedy to stop the established abuse, its anti-competitive effects, and its recurrence. In principle, the European Commission asks the dominant company to cease and desist from the abusive conduct, but it does not grant CLs.

2 Part II

The chapter by Susy Frankel and Jessica C. Lai explores recognised and appropriate grounds for CLs. It analyses whether patent law's social contract is a reason in favour of CL and finds that CL is worthy of thorough consideration in order to promote competition. However, whether competition is promoted will be fact specific, technology specific, market specific, and timing specific. The chapter concludes that just as the social contract of patent law requires balance, so too does the use of CL. Consequently, CL deserves greater attention as a means to contribute to rebalancing patent law's social contract.

The next chapter, by Xiuqin Lin, ponders on prior negotiation and remuneration for patent CL. It contends that Art. 31 of the TRIPS Agreement leaves great flexibilities for WTO Members to qualify the requirement for "prior negotiation". Moreover, the TRIPS Agreement does not specify the meaning of "adequate remuneration" for CL. WTO Members enjoy great flexibilities to determine the adequate remuneration and the purpose of CL, as opposed to other circumstances, which deserve particular consideration. Also the rules and procedures for setting remuneration for CL should be easy to predict. It is advisable for WTO Members to adopt specific rules on determining the "reasonable commercial terms" and "reasonable period of time". This chapter further examines the existing methods to assess the remuneration for CL of pharmaceutical patents, arguing that the well-recognised guidelines proposed by the United Nations Development Programme and the WHO could serve as guidance for setting the CL royalty in developing countries.

The chapter by Richard Li-dar Wang reflects on ancillary orders of CL and their compatibility with the TRIPS Agreement. It concludes that for a CL to work effectively, three conditions must be met: competent licensees with sufficient capacities, adequate market size, and access to necessary know-how. If the third condition is missing, the authority granting such licences may issue a know-how transfer order to fill in the gap. Given that no exception to the protection of undisclosed information is expressly acknowledged in the TRIPS Agreement, there are some not-well-founded doubts about the know-how transfer orders' compatibility with TRIPS. Ancillary orders may also direct non-voluntary licensees to address specific harms to public interest, ensuring the attainment of their policy goals. In addition, the granting authority can issue a side effect averting order to alleviate unnecessary impact that the licence may impose on the patent or copyright holders. Orders requiring local manufacturing are likely to violate the principle of non-discrimination between imports and local production, as enshrined in Art. 27.1 of the TRIPS Agreement.

The chapter by Ida Madieha bt. Abdul Ghani Azmi takes on the issue of scope and duration of CL. Her study reveals that the TRIPS Agreement provides significant flexibility to Members to determine the scope and duration of CLs issued by them. TRIPS mandates, however, that the scope and duration of the licence must not go beyond the purpose for which the licence is issued. For countries that have never invoked CLs before, the lack of detailed provision on this offers little guidance on how to invoke such licences. This chapter examines national experiences on CLs and draws lessons from them by identifying the relevant criteria in setting the scope and duration of CLs. From these experiences, several observations were made. It is essential that the terms of such non-voluntary licences address the harm to be alleviated. The terms of the licences must be relevant, effective, and proportionate to the harm to be alleviated. The chapter ends by suggesting that national authorities have broad discretion in terms of the scope of the licences. However, such licence must be carefully crafted to reach the specific purpose for which the licence is issued or to cure the harm it seeks to remedy.

The chapter by Matthias Leistner looks at the requirements for compulsory dependency licence by learning from the transformative use doctrine in copyright law. Essentially, the chapter argues in favour of a functional and relative approach to the interpretation of the main condition of Art. 31 (l) TRIPS, i.e. that "(i) the invention claimed in the second (dependent) patent shall involve an important technical advance of considerable economic significance in relation to the invention claimed in the first patent". The chapter draws on copyright law doctrine of transformative use to argue that both substantive conditions of Art. 31 (l) (i) TRIPS should be interpreted consistently with regard to the relation to the primary patent, i.e. a lower threshold should apply if the primary patent embodies only an incremental technical advance.

In the next chapter Burton Ong asks whether competition law can facilitate access to essential medicines. While the TRIPS Agreement has been amended, through the introduction of the Art. 31bis system, to enable patented pharmaceuticals manufactured under a CL to be exported to patients in less-developed countries upon satisfaction of specific criteria, it is unclear whether this mechanism provides a satisfactory legal framework to enable sufficient life-saving drugs to reach those who are unable to pay the full prices charged by the major pharmaceutical companies in their home markets. This chapter examines the possibility of relying, as an alternative, on another exception within the TRIPS Agreement—the Art. 31 (k) provision, which permits compulsory patent licences to be granted to remedy anti-competitive practices—to facilitate access to essential medicines by enabling generic versions of patented drugs to be exported to, and imported by, less-developed countries without having to seek the prior consent of the relevant pharmaceutical patent proprietors. It is submitted that, in the hands of courageous and inventive competition authorities who are able to surmount various tricky political, jurisdictional, and doctrinal hurdles, competition law principles may be able to provide the means of facilitating such an endeavor.

The chapter by Ichiro Nakayama and Yoshiyuki Tamura is about denial of injunctive relief on grounds of equity in the U.S. and Japan. In common law nations, injunctions are categorised as remedies in equity, and theoretically they are supposed to be an exceptional remedy that courts may grant in their discretion in cases where remedies like damages fail to provide effective protection. Nonetheless, the courts in the U.S. had automatically granted injunctions until the 2006 Supreme Court decision in eBay, which has dramatically changed the landscape. While the ratio of denial of injunctive relief has drastically increased after the eBay case, the Federal Trade Commission in 2011 provides useful framework in discussing whether to grant injunction: ex ante transaction versus ex post transaction. Based on this analytical tool, FTC proposes insightful recommendations to modify some court practices. On the other hand, in Japan, the patentee has the "right" to seek injunction and the Japanese courts rarely deny the injunction. However, since the exclusivity of patents is merely a means to achieve the prosperity of industry, a patent "right" after the examination and registration by the Patent Office could be conceived as a provisional one, a mere transit point within the broader process in which the requirements for excluding others from using the invention are reviewed step by step.

The chapter by Chung-Lun Shen and Jyh-An Lee concerns the review of granted CLs. Based on their arguments about exceptions and limitations, the granting of a

CL should be tested by the criteria provided under Art. 30 TRIPS Agreement to secure its justification, after which limited exceptions can be allowed in patent law provided that they "do not unreasonably conflict with a normal exploitation of the patent and do not unreasonably prejudice the legitimate interests of the patent owner, taking account of the legitimate interests of third parties". They opine that "a normal exploitation" and "the legitimate interests" of the patent should be subject to the substitution effects of the products made under CL, and the legitimate interests of third parties should be measured by whether such interests benefit the ultimate goal of patent law. When the infringing acts have no substitution effects, "a normal exploitation" and "the legitimate interests" of the patent are not negatively impacted.

3 Part III

The chapter by Lionel Bently and Brad Sherman deals with limiting patents. Drawing on the 2010 WIPO Study into patent exclusions and exceptions, the chapter examines the limits that are placed on patents in different countries around the world. After looking at some of the problems that arise in undertaking a global study of this nature, it then looks at some of the key reasons given for the existence of different exclusions and exceptions. This is followed by a wide-ranging historical account of the fate of exclusions and exceptions over the last century. The chapter ends by speculating on possible future developments and a plea to ensure that the flexibility in international law is not constrained unnecessarily.

The chapter by Hanns Ullrich dwells on mandatory licensing under patent law and competition law and their different concerns, complementary roles. The thesis of this contribution is that each of patent law's CL rules does (and ought to) follow its own distinct rationale. Their common denominator is that they are specific to the systematic operation of patent protection as an incentive mechanism for innovation. By contrast, competition law constitutes part of the framework regulation of the market. Where its application results in imposing licensing obligations on patentees, it does so in order to correct an unjustified restriction of competition. This remedial function of antitrust-related licensing obligations is complementary to, but different from, patent law's rules on CL. The different functions of system-supportive or system-intrinsic mandatory licensing rules and competition-related obligations also mean that before introducing new or broadening existing provisions on CLs, a proper diagnosis has to be made of the ill that they are supposed to cure.

The chapter by Reto M. Hilty discusses legal remedies against abuse, misuse, and other forms of inappropriate conduct of IP right holders. It argues that the abuse (or misuse) defence against various forms of dysfunctional enforcements of IP rights appears to be, at first glance, an efficient remedy, which surely entails faster effects than the lengthy prosecution of a CL. At a closer look, however, the legal consequences of an abuse defence are quite unclear. International law does not offer guidance. Furthermore, it's questionable whether approaches of equity, primarily known in common law countries, provide convincing results—apart from the fact that civil law systems mostly lack such approaches anyway. What is needed is rather an intermediate solution between unrestricted enforcement and non-injunction. Particularly, more balance may be achieved through monetary compensation to the right holder: in case enforcement of an IP right proves to be abusive, this right should be downgraded to a "liability regime". Indeed, CL permits usage against payment to the right holder. If the current conception of abuse defence is deemed to be too complex in practice, and if it is illusory that it constitutes a convincing alternative, the legal setting of CL should be modified.

The chapter by Celeste C. Yang trails Crown use and government use. This chapter first looks into the legislative history and provisions both in the U.K. and the U.S. and further introduces some landmark case laws in these two countries that shape the rules respectively. In the conclusion, this chapter differentiates Crown use from government use and finds that legal theories supporting the rules are different and the U.S. is much more relaxed in terms of the scope of use and method recognised for authorisation. This chapter also points out the procedural difference between the civil law CL with the Crown use and government use.

The chapter by Geertrui Van Overwalle explores fair use as a workable concept in European patent law. The study shows that the US fair use concept may inspire the European legislator in designing institutional and legal responses to monitor the exercise of patent rights in an attempt to safeguard an adequate balance between private and public interests and operationalise the 'social contract' in the post-grant phase. However, the application of the US fair use concept in one contentious real life case, namely the Myriad (breast cancer genes) case, is not very helpful in remedying restrictive and exorbitant licensing behaviour. Further research is needed to explore the extent to which the limited conclusion holds when testing the US fair use concept in other technological sectors, such as ICT or telecom. At first sight, these sectors seem to be less prone to restrictive licensing behaviour. Due to the nature of the products, and to the importance of interoperability and compatibility, there is a recurrent need among companies to (cross-)licence their patents. The fair use concept might prove to be a valuable instrument in dealing with the exact scope and level of FRAND licensing terms in the context of standard essential patents.

The last chapter by Yugank Goyal gauges the economic and procedural constraints of CLs for medicines. It reveals that there is no conclusive evidence for causal relationship between issuance of CL for medicines and fall in innovation or foreign direct investment inflow. Various other factors such as predictability and market potential need to be taken into account, for understanding the after-effects of the grant of CL.

4 Looking Beyond

Countries less developed in terms of IP and besieged by a hostile international environment are certainly deterred from perceiving CL and government use as legitimate and integral components of a balanced patent system and are constantly, more unconsciously than consciously, narrowing down the scope of CL and government use. Taiwan typifies such countries. To avoid this from reoccurring in other Members of the WTO, some measures would be worth exploring.

As a first step, a generalised doctrine such as this volume and the "Declaration on Patent Protection—Regulatory Sovereignty under TRIPS (Patent Declaration)", spearheaded by the Max Planck Institute for Innovation and Competition,[1] are striving for would significantly help reinstate CL and government use and enable Members to avail themselves of CL and government use in confidence to remedy IP abuse (such as not working) and anti-competitive conduct and to satisfy legitimate domestic needs, whether developmental, technological, or societal. As the Patent Declaration rightly points out, "In order to accommodate important public interests and confine exclusivity within reasonable limits during the entire life-time of a patent, states must be able to adjust the scope of exclusive rights even after the patent has been granted (para. 27)". "The discretion of states to make use of CLs as regulatory instruments is ensured by the fact that neither Art. 31 of the TRIPS Agreement nor Art. 5A of the Paris Convention contains any restriction with regard to the grounds on which a CL may be issued (para. 28)", and therefore "states may reverse the burden of proof concerning the existence of an obligation to licence, and they may give immediate effect to a compulsory licence pending administrative or judicial review (para. 32)".

In addition, the correct recognition and utilisation of the flexibilities of the TRIPS Agreement by individual Members can also be of help. In the same vein, the Patent Declaration advocates that "Articles 7 and 8 of the TRIPS Agreement recognize that the patent system is embedded in a framework of policy controls. Within the ambit of these provisions, states should possess a high degree of discretion in regulating domestic innovation markets while pursuing public interest goals (para. 5)".

Last but not the least, the TRIPS Council can play a critical role by issuing guidelines to Members for substantive grounds for CL and government use. "In this connection, it bears emphasising that Art. 1(1) of the TRIPS Agreement expressly grants WTO Members the freedom to determine the appropriate method of implementing the provisions of the Agreement in their own legal systems and practice (Patent Declaration para. 5)."

Looking beyond the realm of patent, the rules on compulsory patent licence and government use are at least equally, if not more, needed in copyright law, which also involves multiple facets of public interest.

---

[1] Available at http://www.ip.mpg.de/files/pdf2/Patent_Declaration1.pdf.

Part I
Practices Across Jurisdictions

Compulsory Licence Under Indian Patent Law

N.S. Gopalakrishnan and Madhuri Anand

Contents

Abstract Compulsory licence provisions in patent law are always hailed as an effective mechanism to curb the abuse of exclusive rights by the patent holder. This is also projected as a tool to facilitate access to patented products at affordable cost. This age-old belief has to be relooked into with the changes in the industry practices. The attempt in this chapter is to explore the emergence of compulsory licence provisions in general and its evolution in India. A brief analysis of the pre-TRIPS provisions in the Indian Patent Act 1970 is attempted to find out its use by the Indian industries. An elaborate study of the post-TRIPS provisions of the Indian Patent Act, along with the analyses of its interpretations by judicial authorities, is also undertaken to examine its effectiveness in the new context. A brief attempt is also made to find out the attitude of Indian industries in using these provisions.

N.S. Gopalakrishnan is Director of the Inter University Centre for IPR Studies. M. Anand is Research Officer at the HRD Chair on IPR.

N.S. Gopalakrishnan • M. Anand
School of Legal Studies, Inter University Centre for IPR Studies, Cochin University of Science and Technology, Cochin, Kerala, India
e-mail: gopalakrishnan.n.s@gmail.com; madhurianand23@gmail.com

R.M. Hilty and K.-C. Liu (eds.), *Compulsory Licensing*, MPI Studies on Intellectual Property and Competition Law 22, DOI 10.1007/978-3-642-54704-1_2,

1 Introduction

The post-TRIPS period witnessed considerable tension in the functioning of patent systems all over the world.[1] Increased competition in the globalised trading environment compels the owner of a patent to use the exclusive rights to prevent competition, particularly in areas where patents play an important role. Abuse of exclusivity by the owner of a patent, particularly non-working of the invention in the territory in which protection was granted, on many occasions results in defeating the very purpose for which patent was granted. Patent being a monopoly privilege granted by the state for achieving certain definite purposes, the failure of the owner to perform his fundamental obligations and the lethargic attitude of the state to adequately monitor and control the abuse of exclusivity effectively are harmful to the progress of science, access to goods, and the industrial and economic development of the nation as a whole. This creates a situation that necessitates and authorises limiting and suspending its existence, either temporarily or till the expiry of patent rights. The monopoly privileges have, from early days, been granted so that the invention shall be worked in the nation granting the privilege, to boost innovation, to promote industrialisation, and to help the nation.[2] Patent is granted for the encouragement of trade and in consideration of the disclosure of such inventions to the public.[3] The holder of the right is expected to exercise the entitlement in such a way that it does not contradict the purpose sought to be attained by the grant of the right.

Compulsory licence is a mechanism for superseding the exclusivity associated with patents in case of failure on the part of the patent owner to perform his obligations. It is a system whereby the government or government agency allows third parties (other than the patent holder, typically the competitor) to produce and market a patented product or process without the consent of the patent owner.[4] This mechanism enables timely intervention by the government to achieve equilibrium between two objectives of rewarding inventions and in case of need, making them available to the public during the term of the patent. Through such an intervention mechanism, the government balances the rights of the patent holder with his obligations to ensure working of patents, availability of the products at a reasonable

---

[1] See, generally, "The Scenarios for the Future", European Patent Office (2007); "To Promote Innovation: The Proper Balance of Competition and Patent Law and Policy", FTC Report 2003; Bessen (2003); Ayres and Parchomovsky (2007).

[2] See, generally, Sathe (2012).

[3] Hatschek's Patent [1909] 26 R.P.C. 228.

[4] Regarding the compulsory licence, the Indian Controller of Patents and Designs in *Natco Pharma Limited v. Bayer Corporation* available at http://www.ipindia.nic.in/iponew/compulsory_license_12032012.pdf observed thus: "involuntary contract between a willing buyer and an unwilling seller".

price, promotion and dissemination of technological invention, and protection of public health and nutrition.[5]

The successful functioning of compulsory licence regime depends mainly on two factors, viz. availability of manufacturing capabilities of the potential users of compulsory licence and the government's ability to monitor the impact of patents on access to patented products. Further, there should be straightforward, transparent, and fast procedures for the governance of compulsory licence. This chapter is an attempt to examine the balance maintained by the compulsory licence provisions available under the Indian Patent Act and its possible enjoyment to facilitate affordable patented products to the consumers of India.

2 The Emergence of Compulsory Licence in General and Its Incorporation in India

The emergence of compulsory licence can be traced back to the UK Statute of Monopolies in 1624, which insists on the working of the invention in the territory.[6] The UK Patent Act of 1883 recognised compulsory licensing,[7] and the grounds, *inter alia*, included that the patent was not being worked in the UK,[8] the reasonable requirements of the public were not satisfied, or any person was prevented from working or using an invention. This provision had a great influence on patent laws in other countries, as well as in the development of the International Convention for the Protection of Industrial Property (Paris Convention).[9]

[5] Discussion paper on compulsory licensing, available at www.dipp.nic.in/English/Discussion_Papers, visited on 20th July 2013. Justice R. Ayyangar, quoting Akerman, observed: "the compulsory license has acquired a positive function in serving the general interest of the community in itself and independently of an abuse on the part of the patentee. The concession of a license is no longer the sanction for the failure of the patentee to live up to his obligations but the form under which the community expresses its right over the invention", *Report on revision of patent law*, Government of India, (1959), para 138.

[6] Section 6 reads: "(a) Provided also, that any declaration before mentioned shall not extend to any letters patents (b) and grants of privilege for the term of fourteen years or under, hereafter to be made, of the sole working or making of any manner of new manufactures within this realm..."

[7] Section 22 reads: "If the patentee refuses to grant licenses on reasonable terms, the Board of Trade may order him to grant licenses upon such terms as the Board may deem just upon the petition of any person interested and proof of either the following facts: (a) that in consequence of such refusal the invention is not being worked in the United Kingdom; (b) that in consequence of such refusal the reasonable requirements of the public cannot be supplied; (c) that in consequence of such refusal anyone is prevented from working or using an invention of his own to the best advantage".

[8] Levenstein's Petition [1989] 15 RPC 732 at 732–737.

[9] Article 5(A)(2) of the Paris Convention stipulated the 'working requirements' for patents to prevent the abuses that might result from the exercise of the exclusive rights conferred by the patent, for instance failure to work, and added compulsory licensing as the means of exploiting

Being a British colony, India's initial patent laws were based on those of its colonial masters, and no earlier domestic recognition of patents has been reported. The first Act regarding patent rights in India was passed in 1856 (Act VI of 1856) as a result of the recommendations of the Lord Macaulay Law Commission.[10] It was modelled on the same lines as the British Patents Act of 1852. The Act of 1856 was repealed in 1857 because it had not received the consent of the Council of Directors of the East India Company. This Act was re-enacted with modifications under the Act of 1859. Thus, the real legislative history of patent rights in India begins with the "Act for granting exclusive privileges to inventors" of 1859. The 1859 Act was followed by the Patents and Design Protection Act of 1872. This was replaced by the Invention and Design Act of 1883, which included the main features of the Paris Convention. One was the introduction of compulsory licences where the 'exclusive privileges' were not being worked to the best advantage or at all in India or where the reasonable requirements of the public were not being met.

3 Working of Compulsory Licensing Provisions in India Before TRIPS

The Patents and Designs Act of 1911 replaced all the previous Acts in this regard. During this period, India was under the control of British rulers, and this Act was also passed to accommodate the interests of the colonial British Empire at the expense of India.[11] The 1911 Act recognised product patents and also had provisions for issuing compulsory licences.[12] It provided for compulsory licence in

patents in the Hague revision. Since then, to grant compulsory licensing as a measure to combat misuse or abuse of monopoly rights has gradually become a legal obligation for countries.

[10] See Jain and Biswas (1999), at 1.1–.6.

[11] See Raghavan (2006), p. 279.

[12] Section 22 reads: "(1) At any time after the expiration of three years from the date of the sealing of the patent, a person interested may apply to the Controller upon any one or more of the grounds specified in subsection (2) for a license under the patent. (2) The grounds upon which an application under sub-section (1) may be made as are follows, that is to say: (a) that the patented invention, being capable of being commercially worked in India, has not been commercially worked therein or is not being so worked to the fullest extent that is reasonably practicable; (b) that a demand for the patented article in India is not being met to an adequate extent or on reasonable terms, or is being met to a substantial extent by importation of the patented article from other countries; (c) that the commercial working of the invention in India is being prevented or hindered by the importation of the patented article from other countries; (d) that by reason of the refusal of the patentee to grant a license or licences on reasonable terms — (i) a market for the export of the patented article manufactured in India is not being supplied, or (ii) the working or efficient working in India of any other patented invention which makes a substantial contribution to the establishment or development of commercial or industrial activities in India is unfairly prejudiced; (e) that by reason of conditions imposed by the patentee upon the grant of licences under the patent, or upon the purchase, hire or use of the patented article or process, the manufacture, use or sale of materials not protected by the patent or the establishment or development of commercial or

case of misuse or abuse of patent rights. But the provisions were not so effective. One of the drawbacks was the absence of a provision to fix a reasonable period for negotiation with the patentee for a voluntary licence, failing which one can apply for a compulsory licence. As a result of this, the patentee used to drag this process for years to make futile such negotiation.[13]

After independence, the Indian government felt that a patent regime that had been devised under British rule needed substantial restructuring to bring it in line with the aspirations of an independent country. In 1948, the government appointed a committee to "review the patent laws in India with a view to ensure that the patent system was more conducive to national interests".[14] The committee reported that "the Indian patent system has failed in its main purpose, namely to stimulate inventions among Indians and to encourage the development and exploitation of new inventions for industrial purposes in the country so as to secure the benefits thereof to the largest section of the public".[15] The committee found that foreign patentees did misuse or abuse their patents by importing the patented product rather than manufacturing it in India, fixing the prices at a high level, or not allowing others to manufacture the product even when they were not engaged in manufacturing.[16] The committee submitted its interim report in 1949, suggesting the use of compulsory licences to address this problem. For this, the committee suggested that application for compulsory licence could be made after 3 years to the Comptroller General on the ground that the industry or commerce in India was affected, export of that item was not taking place, and the manufacture or market of other patented products was adversely affected.[17] The government accepted some of these recommendations and amended Sections 22, 23, and 23A to 23G of the 1911 Act (*vide* Act 32 of 1950) to include rules regarding working of inventions, compulsory licence,

---

industrial activities in India is unfairly prejudiced. (3) An application under this section may be made by any person notwithstanding that he is already the holder of a license under the patent; and no person shall be esteemed from alleging any of the matters specified in sub-section (2) by reason of any admission made by him, whether in such a license or otherwise, or by reason of his having accepted such a license. (4) In this section the expression "patented article" includes any article made by a patented process".

[13] For example, a government research institute (Haffkine Institute) applied for a compulsory licence. It sent a notice to the patentee in this regard, and the patentee responded by saying that it was willing to give the licence voluntarily on the basis of the royalties to be fixed through negotiations. At first, it demanded a high rate of 25 %, and it took more than 4 years to reduce it to 10 %. But by that time, the institute decided to abandon the project. See Chaudhuri (2002), p. 30.

[14] The committee is known as the Patents Enquiry Committee and was headed by Dr. Bakshi Tek Chand, a retired judge of the High Court and a member of the Constituent Assembly. The main task of the committee was to examine the then existing patent legislation in India and the working of the same. It was also asked to suggest measures for improving the Indian patent system so that national interest could be encouraged by invention and its commercial development could be fostered.

[15] See Dr. Bakshi Tek Chand, Patents Enquiry Committee, Interim Report, p. 156, quoted in R. Ayyangar, 'Report on the Revision of the Patent Law', September 1959, para 25.

[16] *Supra* note 15, p. 29.

[17] Dhavan et al. (1990), pp. 434–435.

and revocation. The amendment in 1952 laid the foundation of other provisions relating to automatic endorsement of patent with the words 'license of right' on an application by the government so that the Controller could grant licences in respect of inventions relating to food, medicine, and drug.[18]

All these recommendations and changes made to the Act did not prove to be very effective, as the provisions were fairly cumbersome when it came to their actual application. This is evident from the very limited compulsory licence applied and granted during this period.[19] Hence, the Indian government appointed another committee headed by Justice Rajagopala Ayyangar. The committee submitted its final report, 'Report on the Revision of the Patent Law', in 1959. The report recommended that the patent system be improved, *inter alia*, by providing remedies for the evils that India, in common with other countries, experiences from foreigner-owned patents that are not worked in the country but rather held either to block the industries of the country or to secure monopoly of importation.[20]

The Patent Act of 1970 was enacted mainly to accommodate the recommendations of the two committees mentioned above, even though minor amendments

[18] See Section 23C, which was introduced by the Act (LXX) of 1952.

[19] Status of compulsory licence applications during 1950–1957 (Report of the Revision of the Patent Law 1959)

Year	Kind of invention	No. of applications	Nationality of patentee	Nationality of applicant	Result Accepted	Rejected	Other
1950	Agricultural machinery	4	Indian	Indian	2	2	–
1951	Textile (4) Pharma. (1)	5	(4) U.K. (1) Indian	Indian	–	–	–
1952	Engineering	2	(2) U.K.	Indian	2	–	–
1953	–	–	–	–	–	–	–
1954	–	–	–	–	–	–	–
1955	Engineering	1	U.S.	Indian	–	–	Pending
1956	Watch (1) Dyeing (2)	3	German	Indian	–	–	Pending
1957	Watch (1) House fitting (1) Medicine (1)	3	(2) U.K., German	Indian	–	–	Pending

[20] See Justice N. Rajagopala Ayyangar, 'Report on the Revision of Patent Law', 1959, para 182. Identifying the fact that the abuse of patent rights has been a matter of common concern for many countries, the committee observed: "India is not unique in having to face this problem of patents for vital inventions being owned by foreigners who evince no desire to work them within the country. The problem is common to all under developed countries which have adopted the patent system of awarding inventors. Two means for redressing this handicap have generally been adopted, namely compulsory working with revocation of the patent in the event of non working and compulsory licensing on terms of royalty settled by an outside authority where the parties do not agree". *Ibid.*, para 125.

were made previously. Keeping in mind the conclusion of the report of 1959 identifying that foreigners held 80–90 % of the patents in India and were exploiting the system to achieve monopolistic control of the market, the framers jotted down the general principles applicable to working of patented inventions[21] that remain even today the basic principles of patent protection in India. The main aim was to ensure that patents do not lead to monopoly by foreign companies or result in high prices for patented goods. Special attention was given to medicines and food items. The 1970 Act provided only process patent for food, medicines, drugs, and substances produced by chemical process for a short period of time.[22] These inventions were also subjected to special compulsory licence.[23] One of the interesting provisions in the Act is Section 83, which talks about the general principles applicable to the working of patented inventions, beginning with a wide *non obstante clause*. It is evident from this provision that the owner of patent has an obligation to commercially exploit the invention in India and not to enjoy market monopoly by importing the patented article.

The 1970 Act envisaged two forms of compulsory licences. The first one was a general compulsory licence applicable to all inventions, and the second was especially designed for drugs known as "license of right". While the general compulsory licence was available only after the expiry of 3 years of grant of patent on a case-by-case basis on specific request,[24] the "licenses of right" were a provision to facilitate automatic licence to all patents issued under the Act where the reasonable requirements of the public are not satisfied.[25] Regarding the process patents issued for drugs, the licences of right were deemed to have been endorsed on expiration of 3 years from the date of sealing of the patent.[26] The deemed licences of right were

[21] Section 83 reads: "Without prejudice to the other provisions contained in this Act, in exercising the powers conferred by this Chapter, regard shall be had to the following general considerations, namely: (a) that patents are granted to encourage inventions and to secure that the inventions are worked in India on a commercial scale and to the fullest extent that is reasonably practicable without undue delay; and (b) that they are not granted merely to enable patentees to enjoy a monopoly for the importation of the patented article".

[22] Section 53 (a) gives the duration of protection as 5 years from the date of sealing of patent or 7 years from the date of filing the patent application, whichever period is shorter.

[23] See Section 87, which provides that every patent in force at the time of commencement of this Act in respect of inventions relating to (1) substances used or capable of being used as food or as medicine or drug (2) the methods or processes for the manufacture or production of any such substance as is referred to in sub-clause (1); (3) the methods of processes for the manufacture or production of chemical substances (including alloys, optical glass, semiconductors and intermetallic compounds), shall be deemed to be endorsed with the words "Licenses of right" from the commencement of the Act or from the expiration of 3 years from the date of sealing of the patents.

[24] Section 84(1).

[25] Section 88(1) reads: "Where a patent has been endorsed with the words "Licenses of right", any person interested in working the patented invention in India may require the patentee to grant him a license for the purpose on such terms as may be mutually agreed upon, notwithstanding that he is already the holder of a license under the patent".

[26] See Section 87.

introduced to ensure the availability of pharmaceutical products based on process patent at an affordable price through multiple sources. Compulsory licence and licences of right can be issued if the reasonable requirements of the public have not been met. The phrase "reasonable requirement of the public" is very open ended, even though some guidelines were provided in the Patent Act itself. The Act in Section 90 specifically identified the circumstances in which it is considered that reasonable requirements of the public have not been met.[27]

There were not many compulsory licences issued based on this provision. It was pointed out that in spite of these wide-ranging provisions, it is difficult to assert with confidence that the public interest has been satisfied.[28] It was also observed that even though the Patents Act contains provisions for addressing the issues raised by monopoly, practical applications of these provisions were contingent on a number of intervening events.[29] These intervening events made it incredibly hard to actually break the monopoly or correct the asymmetry that any patent right may bring into the economy. But as noted by the Ayyangar Committee,[30] even though there were not many takers for compulsory licence, these provisions could have acted as a deterrent factor for the patentee to refuse voluntary licence of the patent.

---

[27] Section 90 reads: "For the purposes of Sections 84, 86 and 89, the reasonable requirements of the public shall deemed not to have been satisfied (a) if by reason of the default of the patentee to manufacture in India to an adequate extent and supply on reasonable terms the patented article which is necessary for its efficient working or if, by reason of the refusal of the patentee to grant a license or licenses on reasonable terms, *i*) an existing trade or industry or the development thereof or the establishment of any new industry in India or the trade or industry of any person or classes of persons trading or manufacturing in India is prejudiced; or (ii) the demand for the patented article is not being met to an adequate extent or on reasonable terms from manufacture in India; or (*iii*) a market for the export of the patented article manufacture in India is not being supplied or developed; or (*iv*) the establishment or development of commercial activities in India is prejudiced; or (b) if, by reason of conditions imposed by the patentee (whether before or after the commencement) upon the grant of licenses under the patent or upon the purchase, hire or use of the patented article or process, of any trade or industry the manufacture, use or sale of materials not protected by the patent, to the establishment or development of any trade or industry in India, is prejudiced; or (c) if the patented invention is not being worked in India on a commercial scale to an adequate extent or is not being so worked to the fullest extent that is reasonably practicable; or (d) if the demand for the patented article in India is being met to a substantial extent by importation from abroad by (i) the patentee or persons under him; or (ii) persons directly or indirectly purchasing from him; or (iii) other persons against whom the patentee is not taking or not taken proceedings for infringement; or (e) if the working of the patented invention in India on a commercial scale is being prevented or hindered by importation from abroad of the patented article by the patentee or the other persons referred to in the preceding clause".

[28] Read, *generally*, Dhavan et al. (1990).

[29] *Ibid.*

[30] See *supra* note 20, para 140.

4 The Scenario After TRIPS

The Indian Patents Act was amended in 1999, 2002, and 2005 to satisfy the TRIPS obligations. Utilising the flexibilities in TRIPS and the Doha Declaration on the TRIPS Agreement and Public Health, the amendments in 2002 and 2005 brought many changes in the provisions dealing with compulsory licence. The effective utilisation of TRIPS flexibilities depends on various factors, mainly the incorporation of corresponding flexibilities in Indian domestic law and the political will to use these flexibilities. The existence of a vibrant and dynamic domestic industry (in the public or private sector) is essential to make use of the flexibilities contained in the domestic patent law. The amended provisions have in general broadened the grounds for seeking compulsory licences and also re-emphasised some of the basic principles behind the inclusion of such provisions in the Act. The amendments are therefore a combination of policy statements and a set of substantive augmentation of the earlier provisions on compulsory licences.

One of the major outcomes of the amendment is the deletion of the provisions dealing with "licenses of right". It is argued that these provisions are outside the scope of the TRIPS mandate. The provision of 'licenses of right' was introduced in 1970 for enabling interested parties to use the patented invention straight away without giving the patent holder an opportunity of being heard.[31] According to this section, the central government is authorised to make an application to the Controller for an order to endorse any patent with the words 'licenses of right'. The grounds for the central government to make such an application are the same as that of a general compulsory licence. The final decision of endorsing the patent with 'licenses of right' was left to the Controller.[32] The owner of patent is bound to give licence to such patents on such terms and conditions agreed by the parties, and in case of failure to agree the terms will be fixed by the Controller of Patent and the royalty and other remuneration shall not exceed 4 % of the net ex-factory sale price in bulk of the patented article.[33] It was felt that these conditions go against the conditions laid down in Article 31(a) and (b) of the TRIPS Agreement.

---

[31] Section 86, as it was introduced in 1970, reads: (1) At any time after the expiration of 3 years from the date of the sealing of the patent, the Central Government may make an application to the Controller for an order that the patent may be endorsed with the words "Licenses of right" on the ground that the reasonable requirements of the public with respect to the patented invention have not been satisfied or that the patented invention is not available to the public at a reasonable price. (2) The Controller, if satisfied that the reasonable requirements of the public with respect to patented invention have not been satisfied or that the invention is not available to the public at a reasonable price may make an order that the patent be endorsed with the words 'Licenses of Right'. This provision was deleted by the Patents (Amendment) Act 2002.

[32] See Section 86(2).

[33] Section 88(5), as introduced in 1970, reads: "...the royalty and other remuneration reserved to the patentee shall in no case exceed four percent of the net ex-factory sale price in bulk of the patented article (exclusive of taxes levied under any law for the time being in force and any commissions payable)..."

Another change is the expansion of Section 83, the general principles applicable to the working of patented inventions, to include several new conditions.[34] The most significant are the ones dealing with the obligation to ensure public health, transfer of technology, and availability of patented invention at a reasonably affordable price to the public. If grant of patent does not result in achieving any of the purposes mentioned in the general principles, the government can grant compulsory licences so that these patents could be worked to ensure the same. There are three different types of compulsory licence provisions that are available after the amendments. In addition to the broadening of the existing general compulsory licence provisions, there is now special compulsory licence for meeting emergency needs, including public health crisis, and compulsory licence for export to countries with no manufacturing capabilities.

4.1 General Compulsory Licence

International agreements do not have any guiding principle on identifying the grounds for compulsory licence. The Paris Convention only mentions 'failure to work' as an example of abuse of right by the patentee. So it is entirely upon the discretion of individual nations to identify the grounds. Article 31 of the TRIPS Agreement also does not place any restriction on the grounds for compulsory licensing and thereby left member nations to list out the grounds. The Doha Declaration further clarifies that 'Each member has the right to grant compulsory license and the freedom to determine the grounds upon which such licenses are granted'.[35]

Section 84 of the Indian Patents Act deals with the grounds for compulsory licences, which include the following:

(a) that the reasonable requirements of the public with respect to the patented invention have not been satisfied, or

[34] The new clauses introduced through the Patents (Amendment) Act 2002 in Section 83 are ".... (c) that the protection and enforcement of patent rights contribute to the promotion of technological innovation and to the transfer and dissemination of technology, to the mutual advantage of producers and users of technological knowledge and in a manner conducive to social and economic welfare, and to a balance of rights and obligations; (d) that patents granted do not impede protection of public health and nutrition and should act as instruments to promote public interest specially in sectors of vital importance for socio-economic and technological development of India; (e) that patents granted do not in any way prohibit Central Government in taking measures to protect public health; (f) that the patents right is not abused by the patentee or person deriving title or interest on patent from the patentee, and the patentee or a person deriving title or interest on patent from the patentee does not resort to practices which unreasonably restrain trade or adversely affect the international transfer of technology; and (g) that patents are granted to make the benefit of the patented invention available at reasonably affordable prices to the public".

[35] Paragraph 5(b) of Doha Declaration on the TRIPS Agreement and Public Health.

(b) that the patented invention is not available to the public at a reasonably affordable price, or
(c) that the patented invention is not worked in the territory of India.

All applications for compulsory licence must fall under any one of the grounds mentioned above. Of course, these grounds are overlapping, and it is very difficult to interpret these terms or adduce evidence. However, one can resort to Sections 83, 84(6), and 84(7) for some guidance in this regard. It is important to note that the grounds for issuing a general compulsory licence are separated by the disjunctive 'or', and therefore even if one of the conditions is satisfied, the Controller will be well within his rights to order compulsory licence.

The first ground is that reasonable requirements of the public have not been met by the patentee. Section 84(7) of the Patents Act identifies a list of circumstances that will result in reasonable requirements of the public being deemed not to have been satisfied.[36] These circumstances include (a) refusal of the patentee to give licence resulting in prejudice to the industrial activity, demand for the article not being met, and failure to develop an export market; (b) unreasonable conditions resulting in prejudice to the development of trade and industry; (c) imposition of exclusive grand back conditions and prevention to challenge the validity of patent or coercive package licences; (d) case of not working on a commercial scale to an adequate extent or to the fullest extent reasonably possible; and (e) case of working on a commercial scale being prevented by importation of the patented article from abroad. It is the failure to establish trade and industry and the lack of availability of the patented articles that are the major concerns addressed in this ground. The Intellectual Property Appellate Board (IPAB) had the opportunity to discuss this ground in the *Natco* case.[37]

On March 9, 2012, the Indian Controller of Patents and Designs issued the country's first compulsory licence after the amendments in the case of *Natco Pharma Ltd. v. Bayer Corp.*[38] to the domestic pharmaceutical manufacturer Natco Pharma for a patent owned by the German pharmaceutical manufacturer Bayer Corporation. The patent concerned Bayer's drug marketed under the name Nexavar®, or Sorafenib Tosylate in chemical nomenclature, which is used to treat renal cell carcinoma (RCC), a form of kidney cancer, and heptacellular carcinoma (HCC), a form of liver cancer. The Controller found Natco eligible for compulsory licensing on all the three grounds and held that (a) Bayer had made its drug available to only a small percentage of eligible patients, which did not meet the reasonable requirements of the public; (b) the price of close to rupees 280,000/- per

---

[36] This section is substantially the same as the earlier Section 90 of the Act. See *supra* note 27. One additional clause included through the amendment is "if the patentee imposes a condition upon the grant of licence under the patent to provide exclusive grant back, prevention to challenges to the validity or coercive package licensing".

[37] *Bayer Corporation v. Union of India, The Controller of Patents and Natco Pharma Limited*, MANU/IC/0016/2013.

[38] Available at http://www.ipindia.nic.in/iponew/compulsory_license_12032012.pdf.

month was not reasonably affordable to the purchasing public; and (c) Bayer's patent was not being worked in India as Nexavar was not being manufactured in India.

Regarding the first ground, the Controller, relying on the GLOBOCAN 2008 report,[39] concluded that the number of potential patients in India afflicted with kidney cancer and liver cancer for a year would be significantly higher than Bayer's estimation, namely 8,842 patients. Nevertheless, even if Bayer's figure for patients per year were accepted, the quantity of drugs that Bayer imported in 2011 would have only catered to the therapeutic needs of 2 % of the assumed 8,842 patients. Further, the Controller found that only an insignificant quantum of the drug was made available to the public during 2009 and 2010, after the grant of the patent in 2008. The Controller further held that in this case Section 84(7)(a)(ii) is also invoked beyond doubt. Accordingly, he held that the reasonable requirements of the public with respect to the patented invention have not been satisfied. On appeal, the IPAB confirmed this and also observed that "the failure to meet the demand on reasonable terms must logically mean both quantity and price".[40] The Board concluded that "the Controller was right in holding that the sales of the drug by the appellant at the price of about rupees 280,000/per month was alone relevant for the determination of public requirement and he was also right in considering the purchasing capacity of the public and the evidence available to conclude that the invention was not reasonably affordable to the public".[41] It is felt that the decision goes in tune with the general principles and the provisions of the Act.

The second ground on which a compulsory licence can be sought under Section 84 is 'that the patented invention is not available to the public at a reasonably affordable price'. The statute provides no guidance to the Controller to determine what constitutes a 'reasonably affordable price'. The obvious conclusion is to take into account the circumstances of each case, such as the purchasing power of the Indian public, the costs of production incurred by the patentee, the nature of the end-users of that particular patented product and their purchasing power, and also the availability and affordability of any substitute. The Controller in *Natco* addressed this ground in detail. He stated that "the word 'reasonable' necessarily means [sic] affordable to patients, which necessarily is relative *vis-a-vis* the paying capacity of the patient".[42] He further observed that the word 'reasonable' has to be considered in reference to both the public, i.e. patients, and the patentee as well. If the word is not construed in this manner, the word would have no effect.

---

[39] A publication by GLOBOCAN project of the World Health Organization. The aim of the project is to provide contemporary estimates of the incidence of mortality, prevalence, and disability-adjusted life years (DALYs) from major types of cancers, at the national level, for 184 countries. For details, refer to http://globocan.iarc.fr/.

[40] *Supra* note 37, para 38.

[41] *Ibid.*, para 44.

[42] *Supra* note 38, p. 31.

Therefore, the Controller opined that the cost both of R&D and of manufacture have to be taken into account while considering the 'reasonably affordable price'.[43]

The Controller also provided guidance for interpreting the term 'affordability'. He explains that it is the capacity to pay, and different sections of the public have vastly different capacity to pay. What may be 'affordable' for one class or section may not be 'affordable' for another class or section. The phrase 'available to the public at a reasonably affordable price' therefore must be so interpreted to mean that the payment as a whole is 'affordable' for a particular class or section.[44] On appeal, affirming this the IPAB further clarified that the reasonably affordable price necessarily has to be fixed from the view point of the public, and the word 'affordable' itself indicates the public can afford to buy the drug. The Board confirms that price is definitely a factor that will determine whether the public will reach out for a particular invention. The Board rejected the philanthropic activities[45] taken up by the patentee as a measure to ensure affordability of the drug. According to the Board, in determining the affordability of a particular drug, regard has to be given to the market price of the drug and not the price of the drug at any other subsidised programme. In order to ensure availability and affordability of the drug, the Board went to the extent of considering 'import' as one of the ways of working the invention. But the Board suggested that the criteria should be import of products on a commercial scale to an adequate extent and sold at a reasonably affordable price.[46]

The Controller has determined that the price of the drug required for one month's treatment shall not exceed rupees 8,880/-. This price has been suggested by the compulsory licence applicant. One important question is whether the Controller is required to look into the affordability of the drug even at this price. The Patents Act does not mandate the Controller to fix the price suggested by the applicant. Under Section 90 of the Patents Act, the Controller, in settling the terms and conditions of the compulsory licence, shall endeavour to secure that the patented inventions are made available to the public at reasonably affordable prices.[47] The very inclusion of such a provision in the Act means that the Controller has a definite role in fixing the price rather than going by the price suggested by the applicant. The Controller can examine the affordability of the drug in relation to the price suggested by the applicant. The yardstick used to assess affordability of patentee's drug can also equally be applied in this case. In determining the affordability of the patentee's drug, the Controller obviously relies upon expert opinion, per capita income, etc., and the same method can be used to fix the price of the drug to be sold by the applicant. It is disappointing to note that there was no effort on the part of the

[43] *Ibid.*, p. 34.

[44] *Ibid.*, p. 35.

[45] Bayer, the patent holder in this case, was supplying drugs through a Patient Assistance Programme (PAP) where the price is lower than the commercial price.

[46] *Supra* note 37, para 41.

[47] Section 90(1)(iii).

Controller to find out whether the price suggested by the applicant was the lowest possible, taking into consideration the cost of production and distribution, the royalty to be paid to the owner of patent, and the marginal profit of the applicant. Before finalising the price, the Controller ought to have checked the basis for fixing the price.[48]

The third ground on which compulsory licence under Section 84 can be issued is that the patented invention is not worked in the territory of India. There is no explanation for the word 'work' anywhere in international agreements dealing with patent protection. Domestic working requirements were first employed by many developed countries in the 1800s as protectionist measures to stem the outflow of national wealth associated with the granting of patents to foreigners.[49] Working of patent remained a contentious issue during the negotiations of the Paris Convention. Since countries maintained different meanings for this word, it was finally left to countries to decide.[50] The term 'work' needs to be interpreted in line with the objective sought to be achieved by the grant of patent.[51] If the objective is to ensure access to patented product at an affordable price, as well as the promotion of industrialisation of the country and transfer and dissemination of technology, the interpretation of 'work' does not need be confined to 'importation'.

The term 'work' has always caused disputes internationally since it is liable to different interpretations. In the dispute between the USA and Brazil,[52] the two countries had completely different interpretations of 'work'. Brazil argued that 'work' would be interpreted as 'to manufacture', to manufacture sufficiently patented products, or to use the patented methods in Brazil; accordingly, to import, to sell, and to offer to sell are not considered 'work'. But the US argued that as long as the patented products are 'imported' from any member of the WTO, the patent has

---

[48] It is interesting to note that immediately after the issue of compulsory licence, M/s Cipla Ltd., which was manufacturing and selling the same drug at rupees 30,000/- based on the judgment of the Delhi High Court, reduced the price of the same drug to rupees 6,840. See Kulkarni (2012).

[49] Mueller (2007). Also see Carl Moy (1993), pp. 457, 475–476.

[50] Lin Xiuqin mentioned the following facts with regard to this: in the Rome Meeting in which all Paris Convention members participated in 1896, as all countries had different interpretations on the word 'work', the meeting finally adopted the compromise opinion that the word 'work' has different meanings and every member country has the right to interpret the term 'work' themselves. The Conventions that followed the Paris Convention do not change this position. Another IP scholar, Ladas, also mentioned that the meaning of the term 'work' under the Paris Convention had not been clearly described in the Convention and could be interpreted by the member countries. See Xiuqin (2003), quoted by Liu (2009), p. 118.

[51] Read, *generally*, Michael (1997).

[52] The Unites States filed a complaint against Brazil in the WTO on the ground that Article 68 of the Brazilian Patent Law is inconsistent with the obligations of Brazil under Article 27 of the TRIPS Agreement. Article 68 of the Brazilian Patent Act requires the patent holder to manufacture the subject matter of the patent within the territory of Brazil, within 3 years of obtaining a patent, unless the patent holder can show that local production is not economically feasible or reasonable, failing which the Brazilian companies may apply for compulsory licence of patent. See Yumy and Kunisawa (2012), chap. 8, p. 297.

been worked in that country. Since the case was withdrawn later by the US,[53] there was no final conclusion on this.

In order to ascertain the meaning of 'work' in the Indian law, it is worth looking at the debates of the UK Parliament during the passage of the Patents Act 1902.[54] Sir William Houldsworth, one of the members of the Parliament, said that the foreign patentee acts as a dog in the manger, sending his patented article to this country but doing nothing to have the patented article manufactured here. He lamented that "our industries are, under our own law, starved in the interests of the foreigner".[55] Further, Sir Robert Reid, supporting the necessity of revoking patents granted in the UK to foreigners who do not work them, said that "nothing can be more absurd or more outrageous than that a foreign patentee can come here and get a patent and use it, not for the purpose of encouraging the industries of this country, but to prevent our people from what they otherwise would do". Similarly, Mr. Cripps, another member of the Parliament, opined that "nothing could be worse for this country than that foreign patentees should be protected in this country while the industry is carried on abroad".[56] These observations had considerable influence on the use of the term 'work' in the Indian law.

The Indian patent regime places significant importance on the "working" of a patent. The context in which the word "work" is used in different sections of the Act makes it clear that it means actual manufacture of the patented article in India. Section 83 clarifies that patents "are not granted merely to enable patentee to enjoy a monopoly for the importation of the patented article".[57] Similarly, Section 84(7)(e) makes it clear that if the working of the patented invention on a commercial scale is prevented or hindered by the importation of the patented article from abroad by the patentee, then this is a ground for issuing compulsory licence based on reasonable requirements of the public not being satisfied.

A detailed examination of the term working of patents had been done in the *Natco* case, both by the Controller and the IPAB. The Controller observed that since the term 'worked in the territory of India' has not been defined in the Act, we have to locate its meaning from various international conventions, agreements, and provisions contained in our own Act and its legislative history. The Controller, after an extensive study on the provisions of the Paris Convention, TRIPS Agreement, and the Patents Act 1970, especially Section 83, came to the conclusion that 'worked in the territory of India' implies manufactured in India to a reasonable

[53] The United States withdrew the complaint due to the counterclaim filed by Brazil challenging US law requiring local working by the patentee in certain instances. See WT/DS224/1, G/L/437, IP/D24, G/TRIMS/D/18, available at http://www.worldtradelaw.net/cr/ds224-1(cr).pdf, visited on 20th July 2013.

[54] This Act for the first time introduced the principle of revocation of a patent for abuse of the monopoly by non-working of the patented invention for 3 years from the sealing of the patent. See Section 3(5).

[55] See Rajagopala Ayyangar, *supra* note 20, pp. 51–53.

[56] *Ibid.*

[57] See Section 83(b).

extent so that the principles enumerated in Section 83 can be brought into effect. In the absence of manufacturing in India, Section 83 would be a dead letter. The Controller further supplements his conclusion of local working by placing reliance on Section 84(6)(ii) and Section 90(2). He noted that even though these sections refer to the compulsory licence applicant, the same logic can be applied with respect to the patentee too. He concluded his analysis by affirming that 'worked in the territory of India' means 'manufactured to a reasonable extent in India'.[58] On appeal, the Board avoided giving a definition of 'work' in the Order. Rather, it tried to link 'work' with availability and affordability of the product.[59] The Board stated that even if the product is imported, the patentee should ensure that importation must be on a commercial scale to an adequate extent and sold at a reasonably affordable price. Therefore, it seems that the Board is more concerned with the availability and affordability of the drug in this case. The Board, relying on the TRIPS Agreement on this point, stated that the term is a flexible one and is not defined in the Act, so it has to be interpreted on a case-by-case basis. According to the Board, working cannot mean that the requirement of working would be satisfied by having import monopoly for all patented inventions. Therefore, the Board concluded that "working could mean local manufacture entirely, and 'working' in some cases could mean only importation. It would depend on the facts and evidence of each case".[60] It appears that the Board wanted to leave it open rather than give a final interpretation to the term since it was not necessary to decide it in this case.

4.2 *Special Compulsory Licence*

The amendment introduced two sets of provisions to deal with the grant of compulsory licence in case of national emergency, circumstance of extreme urgency, and public non-commercial use. These are based on the flexibilities available under Article 31 of the TRIPS and Doha Declaration. The main provision empowers the Central Government to make a declaration for the grant of compulsory licence by the Controller. The Central Government can exercise this power at any time after the sealing of any patents if it is satisfied that there exists national emergency, extreme urgency, or public non-commercial use.[61] The declaration

[58] See *supra* note 38, pp. 39–44.

[59] See *supra* note 37, para 31.

[60] *Ibid.*, para 52.

[61] Section 92 reads: "(1) If the Central Government is satisfied, in respect of any patent in force in circumstances of national emergency or in circumstances of extreme urgency or in case of public non-commercial use, that it is necessary that compulsory licenses should be granted at any time after the sealing thereof to work the invention, it may make a declaration to that effect, by notification in the Official Gazette, and thereupon the following provisions shall have effect, that is to say — (i) the Controller shall, on application made at any time after the notification by any person interested, grant to the applicant a licence under the patent on such terms and

should be in the nature of inviting interested parties to apply for a compulsory licence. Once the declaration is made, it is presumed that the Central Government is satisfied with the existence of any one of the situations envisaged under the section. It is not mandatory for the Central Government to state in the declaration the specific ground on which it exercised its power. The provision is silent about the procedure to be followed by the Central Government while making the declaration. The term 'is satisfied' means the subjective satisfaction of the Central Government, and therefore it is not required to issue notices and hear parties before being 'satisfied'. But it is also understood that the Central Government is bound to follow the normal procedure that is adopted while issuing orders. It is clear that this provision is applicable to any patent in force in any field of technology and in individual cases. Hence, it is mandatory that the declaration must specifically identify the patent for which compulsory licence can be granted. While making a declaration in the Official Gazette, the Central Government is essentially taking an administrative action that can be challenged in a court of law on grounds of failure to exercise jurisdiction, abuse of discretion, etc.

It is important to note that the Act has not defined national emergency, extreme urgency, and public non-commercial use. These terms are not defined in Article 31 of TRIPS either. In the absence of definition, the general meaning of the term applies.[62] One can resort to Paragraph 5(c) of the Doha Declaration,[63] which states that "each member nation has the right to determine what constitutes a 'national emergency' or 'other circumstance of extreme urgency". So it is left to member nations to define the terms. Emergency or urgency in a patent context refers to a situation in which any of the grounds mentioned in Section 84 must exist and that

---

conditions as he thinks fit; (ii) in settling the terms and conditions of a licence granted under this section, the Controller shall endeavour to secure that the articles manufactured under the patent shall be available to the public at the lowest prices consistent with the patentees deriving a reasonable advantage from their patent rights. (2) The provisions of sections 83, 87, 88, 89 and 90 shall apply in relation to the grant of licences under this section as they apply in relation to the grant of licences under sec. 84. (3) Notwithstanding anything contained in sub-section (2), where the Controller is satisfied on consideration of the application referred to in clause (i) of sub-section (1) that it is necessary in — (i) a circumstance of national emergency; or (ii) a circumstance of extreme urgency; or (iii) a case of public non-commercial use, which may arise or is required, as the case may be, including public health crises, relating to Acquired Immune Deficiency Syndrome, human immune deficiency virus, tuberculosis, malaria or other epidemics, he shall not apply any procedure specified in section 87 in relation to that application for grant of licence under this section:

PROVIDED that the Controller shall, as soon as may be practicable, inform the patentee of the patent relating to the application for such non-application of section 87".

[62] *In Commissioner of Central Excise, New Delhi v. Connaught Plaza Restaurant (P) Ltd., New Delhi*, MANU/SC/1021/2012, the Supreme Court held that in the absence of a statutory definition, a particular term has to be construed in its common parlance understanding to determine its amplitude.

[63] Paragraph 5(c) reads: Each Member has the right to determine what constitutes a national emergency or other circumstances of extreme urgency, it being understood that public health crises, including those relating to HIV/AIDS, tuberculosis, malaria and other epidemics, can represent a national emergency or other circumstances of extreme urgency.

requires immediate intervention from government due to some crisis. While interpreting the terms, the authorities in India have to consider various factors, including the general principles elaborated in Section 83 of the Act. In the absence of definition, it can be safely inferred that these terms refer to serious situations. Thus, emergency refers to unexpected serious circumstances, whereas extreme urgency is the outcome of circumstances that resulted in seriousness.

As a preliminary step to the exercise of jurisdiction under this section, the Central Government must record its satisfaction as to existence of such circumstances. The expression 'emergency', even if understood in its common parlance, would mean an exigent situation.[64] Another definition of emergency is a serious, unexpected, and potential dangerous situation requiring immediate action.[65] Such an emergent case must exist for the purpose of making a declaration. In either of these circumstances envisaged under the section, the urgency must exist, and that emergent situation must be reflected from the records before the Central Government that passed the declaration under this section.

Another ground provided under the section is 'public non-commercial use'. This term is also not defined either in TRIPS or in the Indian Act, giving ample freedom to make use of this ground. When using the term 'public non-commercial use', reference to Section 47 of the Patents Act must be made. This section exempts certain uses from the rights granted to the owner of patent, and one such circumstance is the use or importation of medicine by the government for the purpose merely of its own use or for distribution in any dispensary, hospital, or other medical institution maintained by or on behalf of the government or any other dispensary, hospital, or medical institution that the Central Government may specify in this behalf by notification in the Official Gazette. The instances mentioned in the section are clear instances of public non-commercial use and could be treated as guiding principles in interpreting this term. The term 'public' is generally understood as 'pertaining to people', and 'non-commercial' is an activity that is not for business or profit. Therefore, the ordinary meaning of the term 'public non-commercial use' may be construed as the use of the patented product for the benefit of the public on a non-profit basis. Public non-commercial use focuses on the 'public' nature of the 'use' and not on the public nature of the entity manufacturing the patented product. In other words, even a private party could use this provision, provided it is doing so for public and non-commercial purposes. Comparatively, this provision is wider than the other two, i.e. the existence of either emergency or extreme urgency.

Once the notification is issued, the Controller is bound to issue compulsory licence to any applicant on such terms and conditions as he thinks fit. The Controller is also obligated to ensure that the articles are manufactured in India and made available to the public at the lowest price consistent with the patentees deriving a

---

[64] See Ramlila Maidan Incident v. Home Secretary, Union of India and Others MANU/SC/O313/2012.

[65] Ibid.

reasonable advantage from their patent rights.[66] The normal procedure such as notice to the patentee, hearing to objections, etc. needs to be followed before the grant of compulsory licence.[67] The Act allows[68] the Controller to waive this procedure if he is satisfied "that it is necessary in (i) a circumstance of national emergency or (ii) a circumstance of extreme urgency or (ii) a case of public non-commercial use, which may arise or is required, as the case may be, including public health crises relating to Acquired Immuno Deficiency Syndrome, human immunodeficiency virus, tuberculosis, malaria or other epidemics". In such cases, his only obligation is to inform the patentee of the non-application of the procedure.[69] It is interesting to note that there is an express mention of public health crises in this provision.

It is extremely difficult to appreciate the reasons for asking the Controller to again ascertain whether any of these conditions exist at the time of issuance of compulsory licence because this may lead to delay and even procedural problems. The Act is silent on the procedure to be followed by the Controller for ascertaining this. One reason for mandating the Controller to satisfy the conditions could be the absence of the provision for cancellation of such notification. Once it is issued, it will remain valid even after the circumstances have ceased to exist, and interested parties can make applications at any time. An application for compulsory licence can be filed immediately after the notification or after the lapse of a considerable time. The section gives an impression that the Controller has to conduct an independent inquiry to find out the existence of the conditions in both cases. It appears that in case of applications filed immediately after the notification, the Controller can dispense with his independent inquiry and rely on the fact that the government notified for grant of compulsory licence and waived the procedure. It is strongly felt that his obligation to conduct an independent inquiry arises only where the applications are filed after the lapse of a considerable time. The use of the term "which may arise or is required" in Section 92 makes it clear that this is needed only if he has a doubt as to the existence of the conditions at the time of considering the application. This interpretation also goes in tune with the purpose for which the special compulsory licence provisions are included in the Act. But the still remaining question is who will produce the evidence required for the Controller to assess the existence of any of these conditions. Is there an obligation on the part of the applicant to provide necessary evidence? It may be possible for the Controller to request that such applicant provide sufficient materials before him to determine the continued existence of the circumstance. The government has not yet used this

---

[66] See Section 92 (1)(ii).

[67] See Section 92(2).

[68] See Section 92(3).

[69] See Section 92(3) proviso.

provision, and it is reported that the government is contemplating the same for some cases.[70] One may have to wait and see how the government and courts are going to interpret the provision.

4.3 Compulsory Licence to Export to Countries with No Manufacturing Capabilities

The provision for grant of compulsory licence to export patented products to countries with no manufacturing capabilities was introduced based on the Doha Declaration,[71] which clarified the rule embodied in Article 31(f)[72] of TRIPS. Even though the TRIPS Agreement provides certain flexibilities that are intended to help the member countries to fulfil their obligations to meet the rights and socio-economic interests of their people, the conditions associated with this kept the use of flexibility options away from the developing and least developed countries. Article 31(f) is one such stipulation, which, probably inadvertently, prevents the developing and least developed countries from using the compulsory licensing provisions in a flexible way to facilitate access to patented products, particularly when they are not in a position to manufacture them locally.[73]

The General Council of the WTO, in order to overcome the difficulties that WTO Members with insufficient or no manufacturing capacities in the pharmaceutical sector could face, came up with a solution in August 2003.[74] It permits the

---

[70] Rajagopal (2013).

[71] Paragraph 6 of the Doha Declaration reads: "WTO Members with insufficient or no manufacturing capacities in the pharmaceutical sector could face difficulties in making effective use of compulsory licensing under the TRIPS Agreement. We instruct the Council for TRIPS to find an expeditious solution to this problem and to report to the General Council before the end of 2002".

[72] Article 31(f) reads: "any such use shall be authorized predominantly for the supply of the domestic market of the Member authorizing such use".

[73] There is a view that the term 'predominantly' in Article 31(f) of the TRIPS Agreement suggests that there is some scope for providing for a licence to export, albeit a limited one. See Basheer and Kochupillai (2005).

[74] Civil society groups in both developing and developed nations have identified the problem of lack of access to health care in general and drugs in particular. They have pointed out that more than a third of the world's population has no access to essential drugs. Most of these people live in developing countries. Access to drugs in developing countries is determined by several factors. There are hardly any drugs to combat diseases that are widespread in these countries, and even the existing drugs are often not available to the patients who need them. One of the important determinants of access to drugs is the manufacturing capabilities of the country. This deficiency has been recognised by many academic experts and international organisations that declared that there are apparent conflicts between TRIPS and human rights. Read Sterckx (2007), p. 199.

export of pharmaceutical products to countries with no manufacturing capabilities subject to the satisfaction of certain conditions.[75]

Article 31 of the TRIPS Agreement explains the conditions to be satisfied when a member nation allows for the use of a patent without the authorisation of the right holder. Article 31(f) is especially relevant in the context of Paragraph 6 of the Doha Declaration because it deprives a country with no manufacturing capabilities from using compulsory licence to facilitate access to medicines by way of import from other countries. Paragraph 6 of the Doha Declaration tries to reverse the disadvantage that countries with no manufacturing capacity face and to achieve equality of opportunity in compulsory licensing without regard to whether a country possesses manufacturing capacity or not.[76]

Indian law has incorporated this flexibility by introducing a new Section 92A in the year 2005. Section 92A[77] has to be dealt with separately from other compulsory licences. Compulsory licence can be issued for the sole purpose of manufacturing and exporting the pharmaceutical products to a country having insufficient or no manufacturing capacity in the pharmaceutical sector for the concerned product for public health problems. The compulsory licence will be issued only if such country has granted a compulsory licence to the applicant or by notification or otherwise allowed importation of the patented pharmaceutical products from India. This means that the applicant has to first approach the country with insufficient or no manufacturing capacity for a compulsory licence before he files an application in India under Section 92A. However, this is needed only if the patented product in India is also patented in the county of import. The inclusion of alternate conditions

---

[75] Conditions include an application by the importing country to the WTO, the compulsory licence granted in the exporting country shall also be notified to the WTO and be limited to the amount necessary to meet the needs of the importing country, products shall furthermore be distinguishable through specific labelling and marking, and information must be published on the Internet, etc. Refer to 'Implementation of paragraph 6 of the Doha Declaration on the TRIPS Agreement and public health', available at http://www.wto.org/english/tratop_e/trips_e/implem_para6_e.htm, visited on 22nd July 2013.

[76] Attaran (2003), p. 743. See generally, Correa (2004).

[77] Section 92A of the Patents Act 1970 reads: "(1) Compulsory licence shall be available for manufacture and export of patented pharmaceutical product to any country having insufficient or no manufacturing capacity in the pharmaceutical sector for the concerned product to address public health problems, provided compulsory licence has been granted by such country or such country has, by notification or otherwise, allowed importation of the patented pharmaceutical products from India; (2) The Controller shall, on receipt of an application in the prescribed manner, grant a compulsory licence solely for manufacture and export of the concerned pharmaceutical product to such country under such terms and conditions as may be specified and published by him; (3) The provisions of sub-sections (1) and (2) shall be without prejudice to the extent to which pharmaceutical products produced under a compulsory licence can be exported under any other provision of this Act".

Explanation: For the purposes of this section, 'pharmaceutical products' means any patented product, or product manufactured through a patented process, of the pharmaceutical sector needed to address public health problems and shall be inclusive of ingredients necessary for their manufacture and diagnostic kits required for their use.

"by notification or otherwise", it appears, is to include products patented in India but not protected in the county of import. We can't find such an option in the Doha text, and it is entirely the contribution of Indian legislators. It appears that the intention for such an insertion is to relax the strict rule that forces the applicant to come up with either a compulsory licence issued by that country or a notification. The term 'otherwise' contemplates something other than a compulsory licence or notification. According to this, any legal measures taken by a county with no manufacturing capabilities will enable Indian industries to manufacture that product in India and export it to this country.

Further, it is to be noted that the General Council's decision on Paragraph 6 does not mandate the importing member to mention the name of the country of importation. Section 92A uses the term "notification" without stressing what it should contain. But it is clear from the intention of the section that the notification has to justify the conditions that a country has insufficient or no manufacturing capacity for the concerned product to address public health problem. The term 'public health problem' is defined neither in the Doha Declaration nor in the Indian Patents Act and has to be construed in a general understanding of the term.

The Controller granting a compulsory licence under this provision has to specify the terms and conditions. Even though Section 92A does not explicitly talk about remuneration or royalty to the patentee, the Controller may fix it by taking into account the nature of the invention, the expenditure incurred by the patentee in making the invention or in developing it and obtaining a patent and keeping it in force, and other relevant factors. It is made clear that this will not preclude others from exporting pharmaceutical products produced through other forms of compulsory licence granted in India.

The explanation to Section 92A defines the scope of the pharmaceutical product[78] that comes under the purview of this section: any patented product or product manufactured by a patented process, including all such ingredients that are necessary for manufacturing of such products. The diagnostic kits required for the use of the patented product are also covered.[79] The provision is applicable when a patent covers a product or a manufacturing process. Further, it applies to products "of the pharmaceutical sector" in general without any limitation as to the types of products (e.g., synthesised chemical products or biological products), their characterisation as essential medicines, or the kind of diseases they are intended to treat. It also clarifies that this concept includes "active ingredients necessary for its manufacture".

[78] The Doha Declaration defines the term "pharmaceutical product" as any patented product, or product manufactured through a patented process, of the pharmaceutical sector needed to address the public health problems as recognised in paragraph 1 of the Declaration. It is understood that active ingredients necessary for its manufacture and diagnostic kits needed for its use would be included.

[79] See Explanation to Section 92A.

India is still one of the major international suppliers of generic drugs.[80] Section 92A allows Indian generics makers to continue to reverse engineer, make, and sell drugs to other countries. But it is unfortunate to note that this provision has not yet been used by any Indian company.[81] An attempt was made on 15 September 2007, when Natco Pharma Ltd.[82] filed an application for a compulsory licence under this section before the Controller for the export of 30,000 tablets to Nepal. Natco has offered Roche, the owner of patent, 5 % royalty. Interestingly, the Delhi Patent Office allowed hearing Roche and Pfizer over the issue, which prompted Natco to file an interlocutory petition saying that Roche and Pfizer should not be party to the compulsory licence hearing that takes place between the Patent Office and Natco. Natco's petition was dismissed by the Patent Office. The decision states that even though from a strict reading of the provision a hearing is not required, at the same time denial of such an opportunity to the patent holder would violate the principles of natural justice. The Patent Office felt that such a hearing shall be helpful in deciding the terms and conditions for granting such a licence and in avoiding the abuse of the provisions of Section 92 (A).[83] The Controller identified the following deficiencies in Natco's application: "i) the letter issued by the Government of Nepal, said to be permission for importation of patented pharmaceutical product, is not in the language as recognized by Indian Patent Rules 2003. Therefore, this letter cannot be considered as permission for import by the Nepal government; ii) the requirement for the importation of the patented drug from India has not been notified to the TRIPS Council by the Government of Nepal and iii) Rule 96 (Indian Patent Rules 2003) requires the applicant to set out the terms and conditions of the license which he is willing to accept. The applicant has not complied with this requirement."[84]

Section 92A does not explicitly mention that a hearing will be allowed to the patentee, but that does not exclude the possibility for a hearing. This can further be supported by Rule 97(1) of the Patents Rules 2003.[85] It appears from the news reports that the Nepal notification is mere authorisation from Nepal's drug Controller permitting imports of Natco's generic drug, and this authorisation does not

[80] See, generally, Bera and Mukherjee (2012), pp. 575–587.

[81] The application filed by Natco Pharma Ltd. to export Roche's "Tarceva" and Pfizer's "Sutent" to Nepal has been withdrawn. Refer to Unnikrishnan (2008).

[82] Natco first made an attempt to get a licence under this section before it made the application under the general provision. Reportedly, Natco had a licence from Nepal to import Erlotinib, patented in India by Swiss firm Roche under the brand name Tarceva, and Sunitinib, patented by US firm Pfizer Inc. under the name Sutent. See Basheer (2008).

[83] Read Kumar (2010).

[84] See Basheer (2008).

[85] Rule 97(1) reads: If, upon consideration of the evidence, the Controller is satisfied that a *prima facie* case has not been made out for the making of an order under any of the sections referred to in rule 96, he shall notify the applicant accordingly, and unless the applicant requests to be heard in the matter, within 1 month from the date of such notification, the Controller shall refuse the application.

speak of a public health problem in Nepal, one of the conditions for issuing a compulsory licence under Indian patent law.[86] Regarding notification to the TRIPS Council by the Government of Nepal, the Indian law does not explicitly mention this, even though it may be read into clause (2) of Section 92A, as a condition to be looked into by the Controller. But the question is that if the Controller is satisfied otherwise, should he stay the compulsory licensing application till such time as the WTO notification is made by the importing country? It appears this is needed; otherwise, it may defeat the purpose of this provision. But later it was reported that Natco withdrew its compulsory licensing application.[87] Since this application is withdrawn, one has to wait and see how this provision is going to be useful for Indian industries to continue exploring new processes for the manufacture of generic versions of newly patented products in India.

4.4 Procedure for the Grant of Compulsory Licence

Under the Indian Patents Act, the Controller has the exclusive authority to grant a compulsory licence under the Patents Act, and appeal lies with the Intellectual Property Appellate Board. Any person interested is eligible to make an application for compulsory licence. 'Person interested' has been defined in the Act as to include a 'person engaged in, or in promoting, research in the same field as that to which the invention relates'. This definition is inclusive in nature. As per Section 84(2), a person who is currently the holder of a licence for the patent can also make an application. The licensee is not stopped from alleging the grounds under the Patents Act by the reason of any admission made by the licensee in such a licence. However, not every person interested would be eligible to obtain a compulsory licence. There are other conditions also needing to be satisfied in order to obtain compulsory licence. Every application shall contain a statement setting out the nature of the applicant's interest, together with such particulars as may be prescribed and the facts upon which the application is based. While considering the application, the Controller has to look into the following factors: (a) 'the ability of the applicant to work the invention to the public advantage'[88]; (b) 'the capacity of the applicant to undertake the risk in providing capital and working the invention, if the application were granted'[89]; and (c) 'Whether the applicant has made efforts to obtain a license from the patentee on reasonable terms and conditions, and such

[86] Refer *supra* note 102.

[87] See Unnikrishnan (2008). After this, they made the effort to get the compulsory licence under Section 84.

[88] Section 84(6)(ii).

[89] Section 84(6)(iii).

efforts have not been successful within a reasonable period,[90] i.e. a period not ordinarily exceeding 6 months'.[91]

The above factors are provided to ensure working of the patented invention in India. One of the grounds for the issuance of compulsory licence is non-working of the patented product in India. So while granting a compulsory licence, the Controller has to ensure that the applicant has the capacity (including economic capacity) to manufacture the patented invention to the benefit of the public in a commercial scale without undue delay.[92] The Intellectual Property Appellate Board in the *Natco* case[93] defined the term 'commercial sales' as supply that the patentee makes to the public at the market price. Even though the Board explains the term in reference to the patentee, the same can be applied with reference to the applicant too. It is also possible to infer that Section 84(6)(ii) and (iii) presupposes an existing industry. These conditions can be further strengthened by also assessing the applicants' ability to cure the defect for which the licence was requested. Section 90(ii)[94] shall also be read along with these conditions. It provides that in settling the terms of the compulsory licence, the Controller shall endeavour to secure that patented invention is worked to the fullest extent by the person to whom the licence is granted.

The Controller, in considering the application for a compulsory licence, is required to take into account the measures already taken by the patentee or any licensee to make full use of the invention.[95] This provision echoes the spirit of the Paris Convention, which states that a compulsory licence application may be refused if the patentee justifies his inaction by legitimate reasons.[96] This provision has to be read along with Section 87 of the Patent Act, which deals with the procedure for dealing with applications under Sections 84 and 85 of the Patents

---

[90] Section 84(6)(iv).

[91] Explanation to Section 84(6)(iv) of the Patents Act 1970 as introduced in the 2005 amendment.

[92] Section 89(a).

[93] See *supra* note 37, para 47.

[94] Section 90(ii) reads: "(1) In settling the terms and conditions of a licence under section 84, the Controller shall endeavour to secure — (ii) that the patented invention is worked to the fullest extent by the person to whom the licence is granted and with reasonable profit to him".

[95] Section 84(6)(i) reads: "the nature of the invention, the time which has elapsed since the sealing of the patent and the measures already taken by the patentee or any licensee to make full use of the invention".

[96] Article 5A(4) reads: "A compulsory license may not be applied for on the ground of failure to work or insufficient working before the expiration of a period of four years from the date of filing of the patent application or three years from the date of the grant of the patent, whichever period expires last; it shall be refused if the patentee justifies his inaction by legitimate reasons. Such a compulsory license shall be non-exclusive and shall not be transferable, even in the form of the grant of a sub-license, except with that part of the enterprise or goodwill which exploits such license".

Act.[97] While considering the measures taken by the patentee to make full use of the invention, supply of an alleged infringer can't be considered at all, as settled by the Controller in the *Natco* case.[98]

Clause (iv) of the subclause 6 of Section 84 requires the Controller to check whether the applicant has made efforts to obtain a licence from the patentee on reasonable terms and conditions, and such efforts taken by the applicant have not been successful within a reasonable period of 6 months. This provision was necessary in view of India's commitment to the TRIPS Agreement.[99] The term 'reasonable terms and conditions' is not defined in the Act and has not yet been interpreted by a binding authority. With regard to the term 'reasonable period of time', an explanation to Section 84(6) has been added in the 2005 amendment clarifying the reasonable period to negotiate and obtain a voluntary licence from the patentee as 6 months. The purpose may be to prevent the patentee from unnecessarily extending the process in order to delay the compulsory licensing. The proviso to the section enables the Controller to waive these prior negotiations in certain cases and for certain purposes. This exemption is in line with Article 31(b) of the TRIPS Agreements.

The issue relating to the nature of the negotiations and its failure came up for consideration before the Intellectual Property Appellate Board in the *Natco* case.[100] The Board confirmed that once an effort is made by a party for seeking a voluntary licence and the same was rejected by the patent holder, it is not required to make another request as per the law. The Board further clarified that "the term 'efforts to obtain' in the relevant Section does not mean continued negotiations between the parties, but a single attempt by a party to obtain a voluntary license that would satisfy the requirement under the Section".[101]

Section 84(6) prohibits the Controller from taking into account matters subsequent to the making of the application while deciding a compulsory licence application. But the Intellectual Property Appellate Board took a liberal

[97] Section 87 reads: "(1) Where the Controller is satisfied, upon consideration of an application under section 84, or section 85, that a *prima facie* case has been made out for the making of an order, he shall direct the applicant to serve copies of the application upon the patentee and any other person appearing from the register to be interested in the patent in respect of which the application is made, and shall publish the application in the Official journal; (2) The patentee or any other person desiring to oppose the application may, within such time as may be prescribed or within such further time as the Controller may on application (made either before or after the expiration of the prescribed time) allow, give to the Controller notice of opposition; (3) Any such notice of opposition shall contain a statement setting out the grounds on which the application is opposed; (4) Where any such notice of opposition is duly given, the Controller shall notify the applicant, and shall give to the applicant and the opponent an opportunity to be heard before deciding the case".

[98] See *supra* note 38, pp. 20 and 21.

[99] See Article 31(a).

[100] In *Bayer v. Union of India and Others*, the compulsory licence applicant, Natco, has sent a request letter to the patent holder, Bayer, for a licence, and the same was not appreciated by Bayer.

[101] See *supra* note 37, paras 10–16.

interpretation to this section.[102] It states that since the compulsory licence proceedings themselves are in the public interest, there is no ban on taking the efforts of the patentee subsequent to the making of the application. So the Board is giving absolute priority to the welfare or interest of the public rather than the interests of the compulsory licence applicant. It restates that the intention behind granting a compulsory licence application is for making the patented product available and affordable to the public, and it hardly matters whether the invention is made easily available on a reasonably affordable price by the patentee himself pending the proceedings so long as the Controller is assured that the high price will not be restored. The decision of the Board finally concludes that the words at the end of Section 84(6) are not an absolute taboo to prevent the inventor from bringing down the price and making his invention available to the public.[103] The Board took support of Section 94[104] to justify its above conclusion.

In settling the terms and conditions of compulsory licence under Sections 84 and 92,[105] the Controller shall determine the royalty and other remuneration payable to the patentee. The IPAB's order reminds us that the compulsory licence proceedings are in the public interest and are neither against the inventor nor in favour of the compulsory licensee. Therefore, the interpretation of the terms in Sections 84 and 92 should be in such a way as to achieve public interest.

The application has to be filed in the prescribed form.[106] The procedure dealing with a compulsory licence application is set out in Section 87[107] of the Act. On receiving the application, the Controller considers the evidence therein to determine

[102] The Controller, while deciding the application, was of the opinion that Section 84(6) (i) of the Patents Act bars the Controller from considering any measures taken by the patentee subsequent to the making of the compulsory licence application. *Ibid.*, p. 54.

[103] *Ibid.*, paras 42 and 43.

[104] Section 94 reads: "(1) On an application made by the patentee or any other person deriving title or interest in the patent, a compulsory licence granted under section 84 may be terminated by the Controller, if and when the circumstances that gave rise to the grant thereof no longer exist and such circumstances are unlikely to recur: PROVIDED that the holder of the compulsory licence shall have the right to object to such termination. (2) While considering an application under sub-section (1), the Controller shall take into account that the interest of the person who had previously been granted the licence is not unduly prejudiced".

[105] By virtue of Section 92(2), this provision is applicable to compulsory licences issued under Section 92 also in normal circumstances.

[106] See Form 18, Schedule II of the Patent Rules 2003.

[107] Section 87 reads: "(1) Where the Controller is satisfied, upon consideration of an application under section 84, or section 85, that a *prima facie* case has been made out for the making of an order, he shall direct the applicant to serve copies of the application upon the patentee and any other person appearing from the register to be interested in the patent in respect of which the application is made, and shall publish the application in the Official journal. (2) The patentee or any other person desiring to oppose the application may, within such time as may be prescribed or within such further time as the Controller may on application (made either before or after the expiration of the prescribed time) allow, give to the Controller notice of opposition. (3) Any such notice of opposition shall contain a statement setting out the grounds on which the application is opposed. (4) Where any such notice of opposition is duly given, the Controller shall notify the

whether a *prima facie* case is made out on the basis of the facts disclosed in the application. If on a perusal of the application the Controller is convinced that a *prima facie* case is made out, he shall direct the applicant to serve copies of the application upon the patentee and any other person who, from the entries made in the Register of Patents, appears to be a 'person interested' in the patent in respect of which the application is made. The application is also published in the Official Journal.

In case a *prima facie* case is not made out, the Controller notifies the applicant accordingly. The applicant may thereafter request a hearing. Such a request must be made within 1 month from the date of notification. After hearing the applicant, the Controller determines whether to continue with the application or to refuse it. In the *Natco* case, one of the grounds for the appeal is that under Section 87(1), where the Controller has arrived at *prima facie* satisfaction that a case has been made out without giving an opportunity to be heard to the appellant.[108] For this, the Board answered thus: "At the stage of Section 87(1), the Controller has two options. Even on the face of it, he may decide that the compulsory licence cannot be granted. This may be for various obvious reasons like, the application having been made before the lapse of the three years mandated by law. The Controller has another option. On the face of it, he may decide that this is a matter where the parties have to be heard before a decision is arrived at. It does not mean that the Controller has decided one way or the other. It means only that on going through the application and considering the facts alleged, he is of the opinion that the other side should be heard. Therefore, he directs the applicant to serve copies on the other side. It is clear from Section 87(1) that *prima facie* satisfaction precedes the direction to issue notice to the patentee or other persons. Therefore, it is futile to contend that for arriving at *prima facie* satisfaction, the other side should be heard. The hearing of the other side arises only after notice of opposition is filed and Section 87(4) stage is reached. After hearing both parties, the Controller again has two options. He may reject the application for licence or he may grant the licence. At the stage of 87(1) no such determination of rights is contemplated and all that is contemplated at that stage is whether this application deserves to be granted a hearing. Therefore, this ground is rejected".[109] The Board is correct in making this interpretation.

If the Controller decides to continue with the application, the patentee or any other person desiring to oppose the application may, within 2 months from the date of publication of the application in the official journal, send a notice of opposition to the Controller in the prescribed form.[110] The notice of opposition is required to contain a statement setting out the grounds of opposition,[111] along with the

---

applicant, and shall give to the applicant and the opponent an opportunity to be heard before deciding the case".

[108] See *supra* note 37, para 9.

[109] *Ibid.*, para 9.

[110] See Form 14, Schedule II of the Patent Rules 2003.

[111] See Section 87(3), read with Rule 98 of the Patent Rules 2003.

evidence in support thereof. The notice must also state the terms and conditions of the licence, if any, the opponent is prepared to grant the applicant.[112] On receiving the notice of opposition in the prescribed format, the Controller notifies the applicant.[113] The opponent is required to serve a copy of the notice of the opposition, along with the evidence in support thereof, to the applicant. The fact of service must be brought to the notice of the Controller.[114] After the notice of opposition has been duly served upon the applicant, the Controller fixes a date and time for hearing[115] of the case. No additional or further evidence or statements can be delivered by either party to the Controller (after the notice of opposition has been served) without seeking leave to do so from the Controller, unless the Controller requisitions the same.[116]

It appears that the Act follows a fair and transparent procedure for the grant of compulsory licence by keeping in mind the interests of the owner of patent and the public. But one of the major problems with this is the failure of the law to fix a time period within which the procedure must be completed. Given the detailed procedure to be followed by the Controller, this may result in delaying the grant of compulsory licence. The parties have the right to appeal to the IPAB. The Board is also expected to follow fair procedure before deciding the case. There is no time period fixed for the completion of the appeal either. But it may be noted to the credit of the Controller that the first compulsory licence on Natco's case was decided within a period of 8 months[117] from the filing of application and appeal with the Board within 10 months[118] of the filing of the appeal. It is expected that this trend will be followed even in the future.

5 Conclusion

The analysis of the compulsory licence provisions in the Indian law clearly reflects the efforts made by the legislators to ensure balance between the conflicting interests while granting compulsory licence, particularly protecting the public interest in making the patented products available at affordable cost. But the uncertain meanings, evidentiary requirements, and considerable expenses with little

[112] See Rule 98(2) of the Patent Rules 2003.

[113] See Section 87(4), read with Rule 98 of the Patent Rules 2003.

[114] See Rule 98(3) of the Patent Rules 2003.

[115] The procedure specified in sub-rules 2–5 of Rule 62 of the Patent Rules 2003 shall apply wherever relevant.

[116] See Rule 98(4) of the Patent Rules 2003.

[117] Natco Pharma Limited filed the compulsory licence application on 29.07.2011, and the Controller rendered his decision on 09.03.2012.

[118] Bayer Corporation filed an appeal against the Controller's decision before the IPAB on 04.05.2012, and the ruling was made on 04.03.2013.

prospect of gauging the possible success of an application are factors that may discourage a potential applicant. Rather, these thresholds appear as a barrier to a potential applicant and undermine any incentive the provision might hold for a patent holder to licence and work the invention sooner. It is important to note that there are not many compulsory licence applications pending before the Controller even after the issue of compulsory licence to Natco in a time-bound manner. One of the reasons assigned by the Swan Committee[119] in England for the paucity of compulsory licence applications was that few inventions could be worked commercially with the description and instruction contained in the patent specification without the knowledge of the technical know-how, and as the patentees were not inclined and could not be compelled to impart the know-how, the compulsory licensing provisions were rendered ineffective.[120] Justice Ayyangar observed that this factor is obviously of greater significance for India due to its lack of technological know-how.[121] But Justice Ayyangar concluded that it was not a feasible option to compel the patentee to impart the secret information regarding the patent.[122] Ayyangar's report also stated that it got representations from Indian licensees of patents held by foreigners that Indian industrialists were unwilling to make applications for compulsory licences for fear of causing displeasure of the foreign patentees, which might take retaliatory action in those fields in which they were collaborating. These observations assume significance even today.[123] Thus, the policy question at issue is whether these limitations might be redressed so that compulsory licensing is a real threat to licence and inventions are worked sooner. If the Indian industry is not going to exploit the compulsory licence system, it will become extremely difficult to argue that it is an effective tool to balance the monopoly created by the patent system and public interest. The whole argument that introducing compulsory licence into the patent system would effectively check the monopolistic practices of the patent holder is bound to fail if Indian industries are going to find comfort zones working with the owners of patent.

[119] A Departmental Committee under the chairmanship of Sir Kenneth R. Swan appointed by the Board of Trade of the U.K. in April 1944 to consider and report the changes to be brought in the Patents and Designs Act and in the practice of the Patent Office and the courts.

[120] See Justice N. Rajagopala Ayyangar, 'Report on the Revision of Patent Law', 1959, para 156, quoting from the Interim Report of Swan Committee of the U.K.

[121] *Ibid.*

[122] *Ibid.*

[123] An example is the new trends in the Indian pharma industry resulting in merger, takeover, contract research, etc. of Indian industries with MNC's. For details, see generally Gopakumar and Santhosh (2012), pp. 9–14; Dabade (2013); and Chaudhari (2012).

References

Attaran A (2003) Assessing and answering paragraph 6 of the Doha Declaration on the TRIPS Agreement and public health: the case for greater flexibility and a non justifiability solution. Emory Int Law Rev 17:743

Ayres I, Parchomovsky G (2007) Tradable patent rights: a new approach to innovation. http://papers.ssrn.com/sol3/papers.cfm?abstract_id=1020276

Basheer S (2008) Breaking news: Natco withdraws "Doha" compulsory licence application. Spicy IP, 28 September 2008. http://spicyipindia.blogspot.in/2008/09/breaking-news-natco-with draws-doha.html. Visited 22 July 2013

Basheer S, Kochupillai M (2005) The 'Compulsory Licence' regime in India: past, present and future. A report submitted to Japanese Patent Office. http://ssrn.com/abstract=1685129. Visited 5 Aug 2013

Bera A, Mukherjee A (2012) The importance of generic drugs in India. Int J Pharm Chem Biol Sci (IJPCBS) 2(4):575–587. http://www.ijpcbs.com/files/2106-22.pdf. Visited 22 July 2013

Bessen J (2003) Patent thickets: strategic patenting of complex technologies. http://papers.ssrn.com/sol3/papers.cfm?abstract_id=327760

Carl Moy R (1993) The history of the patent harmonization treaty: economic self-interest as an influence. J Marshall Law Rev 26:457, 475–476

Chaudhari S (2012) Multinationnals and monopolies: pharmaceutical industry in India after TRIPS. Economic and Political Weekly, 24 March 2012

Chaudhuri S (2002) TRIPS Agreement and the amendment of patents act in India. Economic and Political Weekly, 10 August 2002, p 30

Correa CM (2004) Implementation of the WTO general council decision on paragraph 6 of the Doha Declaration on the Trips Agreement and public health. University of Buenos Aires, April 2004. http://apps.who.int/medicinedocs/pdf/s6159e/s6159e.pdf at p. 11. Visited 20 July 2013

Dabade G (2013) With 100% FDI in pharma, medicines may soon cost more. Deccan Herald. http://www.deccanherald.com/content/215612/with-100-fdi-pharma-medicines.html. Visited 22 July 2013

Dhavan R, Harris L, Jain G (1990) Whose interest? Independent India's patent law and policy. J Indian Law Inst 32:434–435

Gopakumar KM, Santhosh MR (2012) An unhealthy future for the Indian pharmaceutical industry? Third World Resurgence, No. 259, March 2012, pp 9–14

Jain R, Biswas R (1999) Law of patents: procedure & practice. V:1.1–1.6. www.twinside.org/sg/title2/resurgence/2012/259cover03.htm

Kulkarni K (2012) India Cipla slashes generic price of Bayer's Nexavar, 3 May 2012. http://www.reuters.com/article/2012/05/03/india-cipla-bayer-idUSL4E8G35OT20120503. Visited 5 Aug 2013

Kumar S (2010) Compulsory licensing provision under TRIPS: a study of Roche vs Natco case in India vis-à-vis the applicability of the principle of Audi Alteram Partem. SCRIPTed (J Law Technol Soc) 7(1). http://www2.law.ed.ac.uk/ahrc/script-ed/vol7-1/kumar.asp. Visited 20 July 2013

Liu X (2009) A study on patent compulsory license system in China—with particular reference to the drafted 3rd amendment to the patent law of the P.R. of China. In: Amicorum L, Straus J (eds) Patents and technological progress in a globalized world. Springer, Heidelberg, p 118

Michael H (1997) Regulating patent holders: local working requirements and compulsory licenses at international law. Osgoode Law J 35(2)

Mueller JM (2007) The Tiger awakens: the tumultuous transformation of India's patent system and the rise of Indian pharmaceutical innovation. Univ Pittsburgh Law Rev 68:491

Raghavan S (2006) Of the unequals of the Uruguay round. Intellect Prop Law Rev 10:273

Rajagopal D (2013) Compulsory license likely for three cancer drugs. The Economic Times, 14 January 2013. http://articles.economictimes.indiatimes.com/2013-01-14/news/36331897_1_compulsory-licence-indian-patent-act-patent-controller. Visited 5 Aug 2013

Sathe MV (2012) Compulsory licensing in knowledge economy—it is now or never—what, why and when about CL. Satyam Law International, New Delhi

Sterckx S (2007) The WTO–TRIPS patent regime after DOHA: promises and realities (chap. 11). In: Torremans P, Shan H, Eraum J (eds) Intellectual property and TRIPS compliance in China; Chinese and European perspectives. Edward Elgar Publishing Limited, Cheltenham, p 199

Unnikrishnan CH (2008) Natco withdraws plea on making patented drugs. Live Mint & The Wall Street Journal, 28 September 2008. http://www.livemint.com/Companies/ptTTNsQ4InCP8Y8avJ305J/Natco-withdraws-plea-on-making-patented-cancer-drugs.html. Visited 22 July 2013

Xiuqin L (2003) Legal thoughts for local implementation of patent. Legal Stud (5) [quoted by Xiaohai Liu, "A study on patent compulsory license system in China—with particular reference to the drafted 3rd Amendment to the Patent Law of the P.R. of China" in Liber Amicorum and Joseph Straus, Patents and Technological Progress in a Globalized World, Springer, 2009, p. 118]

Yumy V, Kunisawa M (2012) The Brazilian patent system: challenges for the future (chap. 8). In: Shimanami R (ed) The future of patent system. Edward Elgar Publishing Limited, p 297

The Use of Compulsory Licences in Latin America

Carlos M. Correa

Contents

Abstract Compulsory licences and government use are provided for in Latin American patent legislation, but so far only two countries (Brazil and Ecuador) have made effective use of this flexibility, in both cases in order to improve access to patented medicines. While the consistency with the provisions of TRIPS on compulsory licensing was questioned in two cases under the WTO dispute settlement mechanism, such challenge did not lead to changes in legislation. Notably, one of such cases seems to confirm the compatibility with that Agreement of compulsory licences based on the lack of effective working of a patent in the country of grant.

C.M. Correa is Director of the Centre of Interdisciplinary Studies on Industrial Property and Economics. Special Advisor on Intellectual Property and Trade, South Centre, Geneva, Switzerland.

C.M. Correa
Law Faculty, Centre of Interdisciplinary Studies on Industrial Property and Economics, University of Buenos Aires, Buenos Aires City, Argentina
e-mail: quiess@gmail.com

R.M. Hilty and K.-C. Liu (eds.), *Compulsory Licensing*, MPI Studies on Intellectual Property and Competition Law 22, DOI 10.1007/978-3-642-54704-1_3,

1 Introduction

Compulsory licensing is one of the important 'flexibilities' recognised under Article 31 of the Agreement on Trade-related Aspects of Intellectual Property Rights (the TRIPS Agreement).

Since January 1995—the general date of entry into force of the TRIPS Agreement—at least[1] 11 developing and least developed countries (LDCs)[2] have granted compulsory licences (CLs) or decided the public non-commercial use (hereinafter 'government use') of patents.[3] The great majority of CLs/government use involved drugs for HIV/AIDS. Only a few related to drugs for other communicable or non-communicable diseases: cancer (Thailand and India), cardiovascular disorders (Thailand). Taiwan also granted CLs, one in connection with a medicine for avian flu and another one in relation to patents unrelated to the pharmaceutical field.[4]

Latin American countries have used the policy space left by the TRIPS Agreement to design national legislation on intellectual property (IP) to a different extent.[5] So far, only two countries (Brazil and Ecuador) have threatened or made effective use of CL/government use provisions.

Complaints under the Dispute Settlement Understanding (DSU) of the WTO based on the alleged inconsistency of national provisions on CLs with the TRIPS Agreement were submitted against two countries in the region (Argentina and Brazil), in both cases by the USA. These complaints, however, did not lead to changes in legislation.

This chapter examines, first, the modalities for CLs/government use available in Latin American legislation and addresses its relationship with the provisions relating to test data protection. Second, it describes cases in which the TRIPS consistency of the provisions on CLs was questioned in the context of the WTO rules. Third, it considers cases in which the possibility of the grant of a CL led to price reductions of the concerned products; the case of an unsuccessful request for a

---

[1] This figure does not include cases where government use has been implemented through simple procurement letters addressed by the competent authorities to medicine suppliers, such as UNICEF. See t'Hoen (2009), p. 60.

[2] This is despite the fact that, in accordance with the TRIPS Council decision of 27 June 2002 (IP/C/25), LDC WTO Members will not be obliged to implement or apply Sections 5 and 7 of Part II of TRIPS or enforce rights under those provisions until 1 January 2016 with regard to pharmaceutical products.

[3] See Khor (2007); See Beall and Kuhn and Sampat (2014).

[4] Taiwan granted in 2004 a CL on patents held by Phillips relating to the manufacture of recordable compact discs (CD-Rs). The CL was later revoked by a court on the ground that the applicant had failed to provide sufficient and convincing evidence that the terms and conditions proposed to obtain a voluntary licence were reasonable. In addition, Taiwan granted in 1978 a CL against a Japanese company (Nippon Soda Co. Ltd.) to work its method patent and to produce patented products (farm chemical called "Topsin", patent number 5644). For more details, see the chapter "Compulsory Licence and Government Use in Taiwan: A Regress" by Kung-Chung Liu, in this volume.

[5] See, e.g., Correa (2007b).

CL is also mentioned. Fourth, the CLs/government use granted in the region is briefly reviewed. Fifth, the status of implementation of the WTO Decision of August 30, 2003, in the Latin American region is examined. Finally, some conclusions are drawn from the previous analysis.

2 Provisions on CLs and Government Use

Patent legislation in Latin America provides for different grounds for the granting of compulsory licence, as well as for the possibility of ordering the government use of any patent. An illustrative list of such grounds is provided in the Table below.

Grounds for granting CLs and government use in Latin American legislation[6]

Grounds for issuing CLs	Countries were these grounds are provided for
Failure to exploit a patent	Andean Community, Argentina, Brazil, Dominican Republic, Honduras, Mexico, Chile, Uruguay, Costa Rica
Public interest	Andean Community, Brazil, Dominican Republic, Honduras, Mexico, Chile, Uruguay, Guatemala, Costa Rica
National emergency and other circumstances of urgency	Andean Community, Argentina, Brazil, Dominican Republic, Honduras, Mexico, Chile, Uruguay, Guatemala, Costa Rica, El Salvador
Remedy for anti-competitive practices	Andean Community, Argentina, Brazil, Dominican Republic, Chile, Uruguay, Guatemala, Costa Rica
Failure to obtain a licence under reasonable terms	Argentina, Dominican Republic, Honduras, Uruguay
Dependent patents (when a patent cannot be exploited without using another patent)	Andean Community, Argentina, Brazil, Dominican Republic, Honduras, Chile, Uruguay, Costa Rica

While a number of Latin American countries have signed free trade agreements (FTAs) with the USA and the European Union, such agreements have not introduced limitations on the possible grounds for CLs. This is possibly the result of the unambiguous confirmation by the Doha Declaration on the TRIPS Agreement and Public Health[7] (hereinafter 'the Doha Declaration') of the WTO Members' right to determine the grounds for CLs.[8]

[6] Updated from Oliveira et al. (2004).

[7] See http://www.wto.org/english/thewto_e/minist_e/min01_e/mindecl_trips_e.htm. Some FTAs and bilateral IPR agreements signed by the US with some countries (e.g., Jordan, Sri Lanka) before the Doha Declaration limited the grounds for the granting of compulsory licences.

[8] See, e.g., Correa and Matthews (2011).

As a result of such FTAs, however, the execution of CLs may be impeded if test data are subject to exclusive rights. Although the TRIPS Agreement only requires, under Article 39.3, to protect such data against unfair competition,[9] the FTAs with the USA and the European Union impose the so-called data exclusivity, which, under certain conditions, prevents a generic company from using or relying on the data developed by another company to obtain marketing approval of a medicine containing the same chemical entity. In these situations, while a CL may allow the use of a patent, the compulsory licensee may not be able to obtain the required marketing approval for its own product.

Although in an imprecise manner, some FTAs have attempted to clarify the relationship between CLs and test data protection through 'side letters' that state that the FTA would not prevent the parties from taking measures to protect public health.[10]

In the case of the FTA between the USA, the Central American countries, and Dominican Republic (CAFTA-DR), an "Understanding Regarding Certain Public Health Measures" states that "[T]he implementation of provisions of Chapter 15 of the Agreement does not affect the ability of either Party to take necessary measures to protect public health by promoting access to medicines for all. This will concern, in particular, cases such as HIV/AIDS, tuberculosis, malaria and other epidemics as well as circumstances of extreme urgency or national emergency". This wording is clearly limitative as it refers to cases where a measure is 'necessary' (a concept generally interpreted narrowly under WTO law) and to particular diseases.[11]

In order to overcome the ambiguities in the relationship between data exclusivity provisions and CLs, the Chilean regulation on test data has clarified that such protection "shall not apply, when: . . . the pharmaceutical or agrochemical product is subject to a compulsory licence, as established in this Law" (consolidated text, Industrial Property Law, No. 19.996, Article 91). This clause provides a good model for countries where a conflict between data exclusivity and CLs may arise.[12]

[9] Argentina, Brazil, Bolivia, Ecuador, Uruguay, and Venezuela follow this approach and do not recognise data exclusivity.

[10] See Roffe and Santa Cruz (2007).

[11] However, in response to the concerns of some US lawmakers, the U.S.T.R. sent a "clarifying" letter to the US Congress on July 19, 2004, regarding the interpretation of a side letter on public health attached to the U.S.—Morocco FTA. In the letter, the General Counsel to the U.S.T.R. stated that data exclusivity provisions would not "stand in the way" of compulsory licences necessary to protect public health and to effectively utilise the WTO Decision of August 30, 2003.

[12] See also Correa (2009a).

2.1 Consistency of CL Provisions with the TRIPS Agreement

2.1.1 Lack or Insufficient Working of a Patent

The obligation to work a patent—understood as the local manufacturing of a patented product or the industrial use of a patented process—was provided for in a large number of national laws in the nineteenth century.[13] During the twentieth century, however, most industrialised countries relaxed or eliminated such an obligation in order to ensure patent holders the option of exploiting their patents merely through importation and thereby facilitate transborder activities in an increasingly globalised world market.

During the Uruguay Round negotiations, there was an intense North–South debate on the admissibility of CLs for lack of or insufficient working of a patent.[14] Developing countries wanted to ensure that a future Agreement did not restrict the possibility of granting CLs on those grounds, as allowed by Article 5A of the Paris Convention. The divergences on this issue remained unsettled until the very final stage of the negotiations in December 1991, when a compromise was reached on the basis of wording incorporated into Article 27.1 of the Agreement:

> ...patent rights shall be enjoyable without discrimination...whether the products are imported or locally produced.

Many commentators and policymakers have read this provision as the death sentence of working obligations for patent owners. In fact, although some national

---

[13] Some patent laws, such as the French law of 1844, provided for the revocation of patent in case of lack of local exploitation. The Argentine patent law No. 111 of 1864, for instance, adopted this approach. The Paris Convention for the Protection of Industrial Property (hereinafter 'the Paris Convention') did not disallow revocation in those cases but made it conditional upon failure of a prior compulsory licence (Article 5A of the Paris Convention).

[14] *See, e.g.*, Negotiating Group on Trade-Related Aspects of Intellectual Property Rights, including Trade in Counterfeit Goods, *Meeting of Negotiating Group of 2, 4 and 5 April 1990*, Note by the Secretariat MTN.GNG/NG11/20, April 24, 1990, ¶34; Negotiating Group on Trade-Related Aspects of Intellectual Property Rights, Including Trade in Counterfeit Goods, *Existence, Scope and Form of Generally Internationally Accepted and Applied Standards/Norms for the Protection of Intellectual Property*, Note Prepared by the International Bureau of WIPO, MTN.GNG/NG11/W/24, May 5,1988, p. 2; Negotiating Group on Trade-Related Aspects of Intellectual Property Rights, including Trade in Counterfeit Goods, *Meeting of Negotiating Group of 11, 12 and 14 December 1989*, Note by the Secretariat, MTN.GNG/NG11/17, January 23, 1990, ¶41; Negotiating Group on Trade-Related Aspects of Intellectual Property Rights, including Trade in Counterfeit Goods, *Meeting of Negotiating Group of 11–12 May 1989*, Note by the Secretariat, MTN.GNG/NG11/12, June 13, 1989, ¶5; Negotiating Group on Trade-Related Aspects of Intellectual Property Rights, including Trade in Counterfeit Goods, Meeting *of Negotiating Group of 11–12 May 1989*, Note by the Secretariat, MTN.GNG/NG11/12, June 13, 1989, ¶36; Negotiating Group on Trade-Related Aspects of Intellectual Property Rights, including Trade in Counterfeit Goods, *Meeting of Negotiating Group of 30 October–2 November 1989*, Note by the Secretariat, MTN.GNG/NG11/16, December 4, 1989, ¶24; Negotiating Group on Trade-Related Aspects of Intellectual Property Rights, including Trade in Counterfeit Goods, *Meeting of Negotiating Group of 12–14 July 1989*, Note by the Secretariat, MTN.GNG/NG11/14, September 12, 1989, at 75, 83.

laws have maintained or specifically provided for the granting of CLs for lack of or insufficient working, after the adoption of the TRIPS Agreement such provisions are not so common as before. In some cases, 'working' is interpreted broadly so as to encompass the importation of the patented product or of the product manufactured with a patented process. This obviously dilutes the working obligation as a tool to promote local manufacturing.[15]

A proper interpretation of Article 27.1, in accordance with Articles 31 and 32 of the Vienna Convention on the Law of Treaties, however, suggests that the granting of compulsory licences due to the lack or insufficient working is TRIPS consistent.[16] In effect, Article 27.1 of the Agreement does not specify whether the products that are "imported or locally produced" are those of the patent owner or third parties' infringing products. The "patent rights" referred to in Article 27.1 are defined in Article 28.1 of the Agreement, which only requires the granting of *negative* rights with regard to the exploitation of the invention, that is, the right to prevent third parties from using in various forms (without authorisation) the patented invention. Hence, an interpretation of Article 27.1, read in conjunction with Article 28.1, suggests that the products mentioned in Article 27.1 are *infringing* products, not the products of the patent owner himself, since patents only confer exclusionary rights in relation to the former. In other words, Article 27.1 forbids discrimination between *infringing* imported and *infringing* locally made products, but it does not prevent the establishment of differential obligations with regard to products made or imported by the patent owner or with his/her consent.

Thus, the non-discrimination clause of Article 27.1 applies in cases where the rights enjoyed by patent owners are different (substantially or procedurally) depending on the foreign or domestic origin of the third parties' products. For instance, Section 337 of the U.S. Tariff Act was found inconsistent with the GATT in *United States—Section 337 of the Tariff Act of 1930* since it accorded less favourable treatment to imported products challenged as infringing U.S. patents than the treatment accorded to similarly challenged products of United States origin.[17]

It should also be noted that Article 5(A)(2) of the Paris Convention—incorporated into the TRIPS Agreement via its Article 2—provides that each party to the Convention "shall have the right to take legislative measures providing for the grant of compulsory licenses to prevent the abuses which might result from the exercise of the exclusive rights conferred by the patent, for example, *failure to work*" (emphasis supplied). In accordance with international law principles, there is a presumption against treaty conflict; that is, the Paris Convention and the TRIPS

[15] See, e.g., Article 60 of Decision 486 of the Andean Community: 'For the purposes of this Chapter. . .[E]xploitation shall also be understood to mean the importation of the patented product, including its distribution and marketing, where this is done on a scale sufficient to satisfy the demands of the market. Where the patent refers to a process that does not result in a product, the requirements for marketing and distribution shall not be enforced'.

[16] See e.g., Correa (2007c).

[17] See Haedicke (2000), p. 774.

Agreement need to be read in a manner that reconciles their respective provisions.[18] Notably, the latter does not explicitly ban or otherwise refers to CLs for failure to work. If the TRIPS Agreement drafters would have intended to restrict the use of such licences, they could have excluded the applicability of Article 5A of the Paris Convention, as they did with the provisions on CLs contained in the Washington Treaty on Intellectual Property in respect of Integrated Circuits (Article 6.3).[19]

Finally, Article 7 of the TRIPS Agreement makes it clear that one of the objectives of the Agreement is to promote technology transfer, which may be ensured, in some circumstances, by means of compulsory licences for non-working.

In January 2001, the US brought a complaint against Brazil arguing that the Brazilian law's authorisation to grant compulsory licences when patents were not worked was TRIPS inconsistent.[20] In accordance with Article 68 of the Brazilian law:

> (1) The following may also be grounds for a compulsory licensing:
> I - failure to exploit the object of the patent within the Brazilian territory or failure to manufacture the product or failure to fully use a patented process, except in case of economic unfeasibility, in which case importing shall be admitted; or
> II - marketing that does not satisfy the needs of the market.

While Brazil and the USA failed to clarify the issue at the consultation stage of the WTO dispute settlement procedures and the USA was, hence, entitled to request the establishment of a panel, the USA withdrew the complaint on the basis of an agreement reached with the Brazilian government. In accordance with this agreement, without prejudice to their respective positions, the United States and Brazil agreed to enter into bilateral discussions before Brazil makes use of Article 68 against a U.S. patent holder.[21] This agreement does not prevent Brazil from granting a CL based on Article 68 but only requires it to enter into bilateral discussions; Brazil may subsequently decide to grant a CL. It may be speculated that the USA withdrew the complaint against Brazil because of fears that an adverse ruling in the WTO could set a negative precedent—from the US perspective—on the interpretation of Articles 27.1 and 31 of the TRIPS Agreement. The fact is that the TRIPS compatibility of CL provisions for non-working has never been raised again under the DSU, despite the fact that several national laws contain provisions allowing for compulsory licences in such cases.[22]

---

[18] See, in this regard, para. 6.66 of *United States—Section 110(5) of the US Copyright Act*, Report of the Panel, WT/DS160/R, 15 June 2000, where the panel argued for a harmonious interpretation of the TRIPS Agreement and the Berne Convention.

[19] See Article 35 of the TRIPS Agreement.

[20] *See Brazil—Measures Affecting Patent Protection*, Request for the Establishment of a Panel by the United States, January 9, 2001, WT/DS199/3.

[21] See *Brazil—Measures Affecting Patent Protection*, Notification of Mutually Agreed Solution, WT/DS199/4, G/L/454, IP/D/23/Add.1, July 19, 2001.

[22] See, e.g., Article 84(1) of the Patents Act of India, Section 48 of the UK Patents Act 1977, Section 70(2) of the Patents Act 1992 of Ireland, Article 75 of the Indonesian patent law of 2001. On March 12, 2012, the Indian Patent Office issued a compulsory licence in favour of the local

2.1.2 CLs as a Remedy for Anti-competitive Practices

The US questioned, in 2000, the consistency with the TRIPS Agreement Article 31 (k) of the provisions of the Argentine patent law No. 24.481 regarding the availability and granting of compulsory licences to remedy anti-competitive practices. The US objection concerned the process for the granting of such licences, as it wanted to make it clear that a prior determination of the existence of anti-competitive practices by the competition authority was required. The US and Argentina reached an agreement on the matter[23] on the basis of the joint reading of the law and its implementing regulation (Decree 260/96). The agreement confirmed that 'in order to justify the granting of a compulsory licence. . .a prior decision must have been handed down by the National Commission on the Defense of Competition (or the body that might substitute it in the future) analyzing the practice in question based on Law No. 25.156 (Law of Defense of Competition). According to this law, the existence of an abuse of a dominant position in the market must be established in order for a practice to be considered anti-competitive'.[24]

2.2 CLs as a Tool for Price Reduction

The number of CLs/government use granted worldwide has been low.[25] This does not mean, however, that the provision of CL in national laws may not contribute to mitigating the effects of the exclusive rights granted to title-holders. A credible threat of a CL can discipline title-holders, particularly in respect of prices charged for protected products.

A good example of this situation is provided by the price reductions for two anti-retrovirals that the Brazilian government was able to secure after indicating that CLs could otherwise be granted. The Ministry of Health made HIV/AIDS medicines available free of charge to all citizens under the National STD/AIDS Program. In 2001, the Ministry was able to obtain price reductions of 40–70 % for nelfinavir and efavirenz, on which Roche and Merck, respectively, held patents. The bargaining position of the Ministry was strengthened by the fact that Brazil already had manufacturing capacity in pharmaceuticals. Farmanguinhos, the main

company Natco Pharma for an anti-cancer medicine (sorafenibtosylate) patented by Bayer, based on Article 84(1) of the Patents Act. See 'India Grants First Compulsory Licence, For Bayer Cancer Drug', 12 March 2012, available at http://www.ip-watch.org/2012/03/12/india-grants-first-compulsory-licence-for-bayer-cancer-drug/.

[23] See WTO documents WT/DS171/3, WT/DS196/4, IP/D/18/Add.1, IP/D/22/Add.1. 20 June, 2002.

[24] Ibid.

[25] USA is an exception, given its extensive recourse to CLs as a remedy for anti-competitive practices, in addition to the government use of patents. See, e.g., Reichman and Hasenzhal (2003).

government drug producer, was able to produce several anti-retrovirals at low cost, as well as to reverse engineer and realistically estimate production costs for the drugs of interest to the Ministry of Health. This capacity was probably the key in conveying to Roche and Merck the message that the threat of CLs was real.

Another case that led to a reduction of the price of a combination of anti-retrovirals, but in this case without issuing a CL, was triggered in Colombia by a request by non-governmental organisations[26] in 2008 for the grant of a CL on Abbott's patented combination of lopinavir and ritonavir (Kaletra). This product was sold by Abbott at several thousand dollars per person per year. However, the Ministry of Social Protection declined to issue a declaration of public interest and a CL. An "Acción Popular" (a type of class action lawsuit that can be filed when collective fundamental rights are violated or limited) was filed before the competent court. The court held that Abbott had violated a 2009 government pricing order and directed the Ministry to initiate procedures for the application of sanctions against it. On appeal, the Administrative Tribunal of Cundinamarca upheld in part the lower court's decision in September 2012. While it also declined to grant a compulsory licence, it found that the Ministry of Social Protection had violated the collective right to health by not enforcing price regulations on Kaletra.[27]

In response to the lawsuit, the government ordered reductions initially of around 54–68 % of the price. The price control measures generated savings in 2009–2012 of about 100 billion Colombian pesos. It has been argued, however, that taking the price of generic alternatives into account, savings could have been 100 % higher if a CL had been granted.[28]

In another case, a request for a CL submitted to the competent authority in the Dominican Republic has reportedly been dismissed. It referred to the drug clopidogrel (Plavix) marketed by Bristol Myers Squibb and Sanofi Aventis, a French company. The French embassy was reported to have written to the Secretary of State of the Dominican Republic to voice opposition to the compulsory licence request.[29]

3 CLs Granted in the Region

As noted, two Latin American countries, Brazil and Ecuador, have granted so far CLs, which are analysed below.

[26] IFARMA, Misión Salud, la Mesa de Organizaciones con Trabajo en VIH/SIDA and RECOLVIH.

[27] See, http://www.citizen.org/actions-colombia.

[28] Ibid.

[29] Radhakrishnan and Amin (2014).

3.1 Brazil

Brazil granted, in May 2007, a compulsory licence regarding efavirenz, an antiretroviral patented by Merck Sharp & Dohme ('Merck') under the so-called *pipeline* mechanism (which allowed retroactive protection for products that would have otherwise been in the public domain in Brazil). A total of 77,000 patients, equivalent to 42 % of the total number of patients under the HIV/SIDA governmental program, were treated with efavirenz.

Prior to the grant, the Brazilian government engaged in negotiations with the patent holder for a price reduction. The government noted that

a) Merck was selling Efavirenz at cheaper prices in countries at the same development level but with fewer people in need of treatment than Brazil;
b) Indian generic versions (supplied by Cipla, Ranbaxy, and Aurobindo) were much cheaper than Merck's product, as cheap as US$0.45/pill or an annual cost of US$164.25/patient.[30]

In negotiations prior to the CL, Merck offered a price reduction from US$1.59 to 1.10 per dose, which was deemed unsatisfactory by the Brazilian government. Presidential Decree No. 6.108 (4 May 2007) decided the "compulsory license, on the ground of public interest, of Efavirenz's patents, for public non-commercial use" for a period of 5 years (renewable for the same period[31]) and a royalty fee for the patent owner of 1.5 % of the finished product.

Initially, the CL covered the importation of generic versions from India at a third of the price offered by Merck. Farmanguinhos, the official pharmaceutical laboratory of the Oswaldo Cruz Foundation, produced the first batch of efavirenz in January 2009 at 45 % of the price set by Merck before the CL.[32] Due to the lack of sufficient technical information in the patent specifications, Farmanguinhos had to perform its own research activities in order to reverse engineer the product and to import small quantities of efavirenz from India; a preliminary injunction filed by Merck to stop the importation was rejected by the Brazilian courts.[33]

The CL allowed the Ministry of Health to save around 58 % (US$103.5 million) of the resources otherwise needed for the period 2007–2012.[34]

The pharmaceutical company reacted negatively against the granted CL. The president of Merck's Latin American division was reported to state that "the perception of Brazil will not be the same" and that the company was reviewing

---

[30] See Chaves and Reis (2014).

[31] Renewal of the CL was ordered by Decree 7723 (04/May/2012).

[32] Ibid.

[33] 'Compulsory Licensing of Efavirenz in Brazil', Summary of the presentation of J.M. do Nascimento Júnior, Ministry of Health, Brazil, Access to Pharmaceuticals Rio meeting February 23, 2010, available at http://www.accesstopharmaceuticals.org/case-studies-in-global-health/efavirenz-brazil/.

[34] da Silva et al. (2012).

its investment plan in the country.[35] A Merck spokesperson said that "[T]his expropriation of intellectual property sends a chilling signal to research-based companies about the attractiveness of undertaking risky research on diseases that affect the developing world, potentially hurting patients who may require new and innovative life-saving therapies".[36] In a statement of 4 May 2007, the US Chamber of Commerce said that the '...[Brazilian] government has made a major step backward. Breaking off discussions with Merck and seizing its intellectual property sends a dangerous signal to the investment community. Merck researchers invested hundreds of millions of dollars to develop this ground-breaking medicine. Clearly, there was room to negotiate a solution acceptable to both parties...'.[37]

Although the United States Trade Representative (USTR) had expressed concerns in the 2007 Special 301 Trade Report (drafted before Brazil issued its compulsory licence) because Brazil had indicated consideration of the use of CLs on patented pharmaceutical products, no trade sanctions were pursued against Brazil after the granting of the efavirenz CL, nor was an out-of-cycle review of Brazil's IP regime carried out.

3.2 Ecuador

Article 363 (7) of the Constitution of Ecuador provides that, for the attainment of the good living regime (*el regimen de buen vivir*), it is an obligation of the State to "guarantee availability and access to medicines of quality that are safe and efficacious, to regulate their commercialization, and to promote the national production and the use of generic medicines that correspond to the epidemiological needs of the population".

The granting of CLs in Ecuador has been based on Article 2 of Presidential Decree 116 of November 16, 2009, issued in accordance with Article 61 of Decision 486 of the Commission of the Andean Community and Article 154 of the Law of Intellectual Property, which, taken together, establish that a compulsory licence can be granted at any time for reasons of public interest, emergency, or national security.[38]

Presidential Decree No. 118 of November 16, 2009, declared "of public interest, access to medicines used for the treatment of diseases that affect the population of Ecuador and that are priorities for public health". It specified that compulsory

---

[35] See http://citation.allacademic.com/meta/p_mla_apa_research_citation/2/4/2/4/9/pages242498/p242498-16.php. On the diplomatic and other pressures exerted in relation to CLs, see Smith et al. (2009), pp. 684–691.

[36] See Alcorn (2007).

[37] See http://lists.essential.org/pipermail/ip-health/2007-May/011111.html.

[38] Article 154 of the Law of Intellectual Property requires a decision by the President of the Republic to grant CLs.

licences could be issued for patents protecting medicines for human use that are necessary for the treatment of such diseases. This Decree opened the way for the granting of CLs on any patent relating to medicines considered to be a priority from a public health perspective.

In addition, Article 8 of Resolution No. 10-04 P-IEPI (Instituto Ecuatoriano de la Propiedad Intelectual) of January 15, 2010, provided guidelines for issuing compulsory licences on pharmaceutical patents. It provided that "[O]nce the documentation is examined and the patent holder is notified, IEPI, through the National Office of Intellectual Property (Dirección Nacional de Propiedad Industrial, DNPI), will request the Ministry of Public Health to indicate whether the object of the request is a medicine that is used for humans for the treatment of diseases that affect the Ecuadorean population and are a priority for public health".

On April 14, 2010, the government of Ecuador granted a CL for ritonavir, an anti-retroviral drug, to Eskegroup SA, the local distributor of CIPLA, a generic company from India. The royalty (4 %) was determined on the basis of the WHO/UNDP-recommended 'Tiered Royalty Method (TRM)'.[39] Eskegroup was obligated to pay $0.041 in royalties to Abbott for every 100 mg ritonavir capsule and $0.02 per lopinuine (combination of ritonavir and lopinavir). The CL led to a reduction of the prices charged by Abbott and to the importation of generic products, with savings on the order of 30 % of the original price.[40]

The US Emergency Committee for American Trade (a business coalition) criticised the granting of the CL, arguing that Ecuador's decision appeared to be 'contrary' to the TRIPS Agreement, and qualified it as an effort "to nullify the protection of intellectual property".[41] However, the reaction of the pharmaceutical companies directly affected by the measure was quite moderate.[42] Although they emphasised the 'exceptional' nature that, in their view, CLs should have, they did not question the government's decision: 'We realize that the interests of public health are not subordinated to rights of any kind, especially in circumstances of particular gravity. And, consistent with our principle of compliance with and

[39] See Love (2005).

[40] See Icaza (2012).

[41] See Submission for the Record by Peter Maybarduk, Staff Attorney, Public Citizen, www.wcl.american.edu/pijip/download.cfm?downloadfile. In accordance with leaked cables, 'the U.S. Ambassador warned officials in Ecuador's Ministry of Foreign Affairs of the "IPR eligibility requirements" of trade benefit programs including the Andean Trade Promotion and Drug Eradication Act, implying that compulsory licensing could jeopardize Ecuador's eligibility' (Public Citizen, Leaked Cables Show U.S. Tried, Failed to Organize Against Ecuador Compulsory Licensing, available at http://www.citizen.org/leaked-cables-show-US-tried-failed-to-organize-against-ecuador-compulsory-licensing), May 10, 2011.

[42] It is interesting to note that after Thailand granted a CL regarding Kaletra (lopinavir and ritonovir), Abbott Laboratories announced that it would not introduce new medicines in the country and withdrew applications for the registration of a new formulation of Kaletra, the painkiller Brufen, an antibiotic called Abbotic, the blood-clotting medicine Clivarine, arthritis drug Humira, high-blood pressure medication Tarka, and kidney disease drug Zemplar (see http://www.taipeitimes.com/News/world/archives/2007/03/22/2003353350).

enforcement of laws, we democratically accept the decision of the President to make legal use of this exceptional mechanism...'.[43]

A second CL was requested of the government of Ecuador, on June 15, 2012, by Acromax Laboratorio Quimico Farmaceutico S.A. regarding the combination of the anti-retrovirals lamivudine+abacavir, protected by patent PI-08-1913 held by the Glaxo Group Ltd. The patent application, filed on May 14, 1998, had been granted on January 5, 2007 (Patent No.: PI-08-1913, "Una Nueva Sal"). The CL was granted by IEPI, after confirmation by the Ministry of Public Health that abacavir+ lamivudine was a priority medicine, on November 12, 2012. The CL is non-exclusive, for non-commercial public use. It can be executed through importation or local production until the expiry of the patent, on May 14, 2018. In determining the royalty rate, Ecuador also used the TRM. It was set as 11.7 cents per capsule.[44] The government's aim is to reduce the cost of the medicine by 75 %.[45]

4 Implementation of the Decision of August 30, 2003

The Decision of August 30, 2003, established a mechanism, based on the waiver of paragraphs (f) and (h) of Article 31 of the TRIPS Agreement, to allow the export of patented pharmaceutical products under a compulsory licence to countries without manufacturing capacity in pharmaceuticals. WTO members decided to transpose this Decision into an amendment to the Agreement through the incorporation of a new article, 31bis. Approval by the WTO members of this amendment is still pending, 6 years after the General Council's adoption.

No Latin American country has notified the Council for TRIPS of its interest in using the mechanism established by the Decision as an eligible importing country. No Latin American country has amended its legislation either to specifically change provisions that exclude (in line with Article 31(f) of the TRIPS Agreement) the possibility of granting a CL for exports only.[46] The WTO Decision mechanism has never been used in the region.

Nine Latin American countries have approved the amendment to the TRIPS Agreement so far:

---

[43] Statement by the Industria Farmacéutica de Investigación (IFI), 27.10.09.

[44] See http://keionline.org/node/1589.

[45] See 'IEPI: Emitimos segunda licencia obligatoria para medicamentos. Acceso a medicamentos, esencial al interés público' (2012), available at http://www.iepi.gob.ec/module-contenido-viewpub-tid-4-pid-184.html.

[46] Article 197.3 of the FTA signed between the EU, Peru, and Colombia provides that '[T]he Parties shall contribute to the implementation and respect the Decision of the WTO General Council of 30 August 2003 on Paragraph 6 of the Doha Declaration on the TRIPS Agreement and Public Health, as well as the Protocol amending the TRIPS Agreement, done at Geneva on 6 December 2005'.

El Salvador (19 September 2006)
Mexico (23 May 2008)
Brazil (13 November 2008)
Colombia (7 August 2009)
Nicaragua (25 January 2010)
Argentina (20 October 2011)
Panama (24 November 2011)
Costa Rica (8 December 2011)
Honduras (16 December 2011)

The reasons explaining the low interest shown in the region regarding the use of the WTO Decision need to be further explored. A possible explanation is the perception that the system created by the Decision is cumbersome and does not generate sufficient incentives for potential suppliers of low-cost pharmaceutical products.[47]

5 Conclusions

As examined above, the threat of CLs/government use has been effective in leading to price reductions for pharmaceuticals in some Latin American countries, while such licences have only been granted in three cases, all of them relating to anti-retroviral drugs.

In comparison with other regions, Latin America has made a limited use so far of CL/government use provisions. This is despite the fact that national laws provide for different modalities of CLs, in line with Article 31 of the TRIPS Agreement, and that domestic pharmaceutical companies control a significant segment (around 42 % in value) of the regional market.[48] The reasons for this limited use need to be further researched. They may relate to the fact that many drugs under patent in developed countries did not receive protection in Latin America in the pre-TRIPS era, and, hence, the need for CLs/government use may have not been so pressing. Another reason may be the lack of expertise of health authorities in IP matters and on the ways to implement CLs/government use to address public health needs[49] and the limited weight of such authorities in decisions that may affect the country's relations with major trade partners. The fact that some patent offices have started to apply more rigorously the patentability standards may have also helped to avoid the need for CLs/government use.[50]

---

[47] See, e.g., Correa (2003).

[48] See Juan Manuel Santa María y María Laura Devoto (2012).

[49] For some practical recommendations for issuing CLs/government use in the area of public health, see Correa (2009b).

[50] For instance, through Joint Resolutions 118/2012, 546/2012, and 107/2012 from the Ministry of Health, the Ministry of Industry, and the National Institute of Industrial Property (INPI), the

Importantly, CLs may be granted to address any public interest. For instance, a CL grounded on the lack or insufficient exploitation of a patent may be conferred to allow a for-profit activity in the country of grant in order to foster local manufacturing, incorporate technologies, and create jobs. It is often wrongly assumed that CLs can only be used in cases of emergencies or public health crises or that their use should be exceptional and always for non-profit. Nevertheless, CLs are an integral part of the patent system, and they can be implemented where the generation of alternative supplies is necessary or convenient for national interests, including of an economic nature.[51] In fact, the TRIPS Agreement leaves ample room to determine the grounds of CLs/government use; it only provides in Article 31 for a number of *conditions* that need to be met.

Similarly, it is sometimes believed that the government use cannot involve the participation of private entities. However, the TRIPS Agreement clearly allows the intervention of contractors without distinction of whether they are private or public.[52] The experience of the USA shows that private companies have been normally involved in and benefit from the execution of such use.[53]

In some cases, the information provided in the patent specifications is not sufficient to implement the protected invention, and complementary know-how is necessary. CLs/government use may include, where needed, an obligation to transfer such know-how, to enable the effective use of the patent. Precedents of

---

Argentine government adopted 'Guidelines for Patentability Examination of Patent Applications on Chemical and Pharmaceutical Invention' (2/5/2012), which provide for scientifically based, rigorous criteria to assess the patentability requirements.

[51] For instance, Article 48A.-(1) on compulsory licensing of the UK Patent Act provides that '[I]n the case of an application made under section 48 above in respect of a patent whose proprietor is a WTO proprietor, the relevant grounds are -

(a) where the patented invention is a product, that a demand in the United Kingdom for that product is not being met on reasonable terms;
(b) that by reason of the refusal of the proprietor of the patent concerned to grant a licence or licences on reasonable terms -
(i) the exploitation in the United Kingdom of any other patented invention which involves an important technical advance of considerable economic significance in relation to the invention for which the patent concerned was granted is prevented or hindered, or
(ii) the establishment or development of commercial or industrial activities in the United Kingdom is unfairly prejudiced;
(c) that by reason of conditions imposed by the proprietor of the patent concerned on the grant of licences under the patent, or on the disposal or use of the patented product or on the use of the patented process, the manufacture, use or disposal of materials not protected by the patent, or the establishment or development of commercial or industrial activities in the United Kingdom, is unfairly prejudiced'.

[52] TRIPS Agreement, Article 31(b): '...In the case of public non-commercial use, where the government *or contractor*, without making a patent search, knows or has demonstrable grounds to know that a valid patent is or will be used by or for the government, the right holder shall be informed promptly' (emphasis added).

[53] See, e.g., Correa (1999) and Reichman and Hasenzhal (2003).

this kind can be found in US court decisions.[54] There are no limitations under the Latin American legislation to impose this kind of requirement, which is not banned by the TRIPS Agreement.

The national laws of several Latin American countries should be amended in order to allow a broader application of CL/government use, including in some cases an expansion of the grounds that can be invoked, a stricter definition of working requirements, and a simplification of procedures.

Concerns about possible negative reactions from developed countries' governments and their implications for trade or political relations may also be a factor explaining the relatively low number of CLs/government use of patents in Latin America. Such concerns may, however, be exaggerated, as shown by the case of Ecuador and—outside the region—Indonesia, which has recently granted seven CLs without any known negative repercussions.[55] Importantly, no complaint has been submitted against countries that granted CLs/government use under the WTO dispute settlement rules. This is a strong indicator that the legitimacy of the CLs and government use under the TRIPS Agreement is out of discussion, particularly after the clear confirmation by the Doha Declaration in this regard. This should provide sufficient comfort to governments facing situations of high pricing or lack of access to certain technologies or products and should encourage them to consider CLs/government use as an ordinary measure they can adopt. CLs/government use should not be viewed as 'exceptional' mechanisms but as one of the instruments, inherent to the IP system, that governments can normally implement to address national needs and attain their objectives in areas such as industrialisation, agricultural development, environmental protection, education, and public health.

Although CLs/government use can be applied in relation to patents in any field of technology, public health concerns are likely to continue to be the leading cause for their granting, particularly to the extent that governments elaborate IP strategies that fully integrate IP measures into their national policies on public health and that it is feared that high prices of patented medicines, particularly, anti-retrovirals, may have 'devastating' effects in the region.[56]

Importantly, notwithstanding the efforts that the US government made during the negotiation of the WTO Decision of August 30, 2003, to limit the use of CLs to certain infectious diseases, CLs/government use can be applied to *any* medicines. Moreover, as illustrated by the case of Taiwan—and indeed of the USA[57]—CLs/ government use can be implemented to ensure access to other technologies outside

[54] For instance, in *FTC v. Xerox Corporation*, a consent decree was issued according to which the patent and know-how barriers to competition developed by Xerox were eliminated by requiring Xerox to license some of its patents free of royalty, and the rest at low royalties, and to offer all of its office copier know-how royalty free to U.S. patent licensees.

[55] See, e.g., Velázquez (2012).

[56] ITPC (2012), p. 26.

[57] In the USA, CLs/government use has not only been extensively used by the federal government, but CLs on a great variety of products and technologies are granted through court decisions that deny permanent injunctions in cases of proven infringement of patents. Following the US Supreme

the pharmaceutical field, for instance technologies necessary to address climate change adaptation or mitigation.

Finally, it will be important for competition authorities in the region to better understand the relationship between IP and competition law and to use CLs as a remedy in cases of anti-competitive practices, including refusal to grant a voluntary licence on reasonable commercial terms when access to an essential patented technology is precluded. The CL issued by the Italian competition authority with regard to a pharmaceutical product[58] provides a telling example of the space available in this regard. Competition authorities may also consider developing specific guidelines to address this relationship.[59]

References

Alcorn K (2007) Brazil issues compulsory license on efavirenz, 7 May 2007. http://www.aidsmap.com/Brazil-issues-compulsory-license-on-efavirenz/page/1427206/

Beall R, Kuhn R (2012) Trends in compulsory licensing of pharmaceuticals since the Doha Declaration: a database analysis. http://www.plosmedicine.org/article/info%3Adoi%2F10.1371%2Fjournal.pmed.1001154

Chaves GC, Reis R (2014) Country case study: Brazil. In: Correa C (ed) Pharmaceutical innovation, incremental patenting and compulsory licensing. South Centre, Geneva

Coco R, Nebbia P (2007) Compulsory licensing and interim measures in Merck: a case for Italy or for antitrust law? J Intellect Prop Law Pract 2(7):452–462

Correa C (1999) Intellectual property rights and the use of compulsory licenses: options for developing countries, trade-related agenda, development and equity, working papers, South Centre, Geneva

Correa C (2003) TRIPS and access to drugs: toward a solution for developing countries without manufacturing capacity? Emory Int Rev 17(2):389–406

Correa C (2007a) Intellectual property and competition law: exploring some issues of relevance to developing countries. ICTSD, Geneva

Correa C (2007b) Public health and the implementation of the TRIPS Agreement in Latin American. In: Blouin C, Heymann J, Drager N (eds) Trade and health: seeking common ground. McGill-Queen's University Press, Montreal

Correa C (2007c) Trade related aspects of intellectual property rights, (Volume VI of commentaries on the GATT/WTO Agreements). Oxford University Press, Oxford

Correa C (2009a) A model law for the protection of undisclosed data. In: Melendez-Ortiz R, Roffe P (eds) Intellectual property and sustainable development: development agendas in a changing world. Edward Elgar, Oxford

decision in *eBay Inc v. MercExchange LLC*, permanent injunctions were denied in those circumstances by district courts in 54 cases. See www.patstats.org/patstats2.html.

[58] Coco and Nebbia (2007). A decision of the South African Competition Commission regarding anti-retrovirals is also relevant. See, e.g., Correa (2007a).

[59] See, for instance, *Antitrust Guidelines for the Licensing of Intellectual Property Issued by the U.S. Department of Justice and the Federal Trade Commission*, April 6, 1995, and the guidelines relating to the incorporation of patents into standards issued by the Korean Fair Trade Commission in http://berkeleyantitrust.blogspot.com.ar/2012/04/recent-korea-fair-trade-commission.html.

Correa C (2009b) Guide for the application and granting of compulsory licences and authorization of government use of pharmaceutical patents. WHO, Geneva, http://apps.who.int/medicinedocs/documents/s19902en/s19902en.pdf
Correa C, Matthews D (2011) Discussion paper. The Doha Declaration ten years on and its impact on access to medicines and the right to health, UNDP. http://www.undp.org/content/dam/undp/library/hivaids/Discussion_Paper_Doha_Declaration_Public_Health.pdf
da Silva FVN, Hallal R, Guimarães A (2012) Compulsory license and access to medicines: economics savings of Efavirenz in Brazil. Submission to the XIX – international AIDS conference, Washington, July 2012. pag.aids2012.org/. . ./cl%20efv%20final.pptx
Haedicke M (2000) U.S. imports, TRIPS and section 337 of the Tariff Act of 1930. Int Rev Ind Prop Copyright Law 31(7/8):774
Icaza A (2012) Experiencia Ecuatoriana en la aplicación de los ADPIC para acceso a medicamentos. Submitted at the UNDP-UNAIDS workshop on 'intellectual property rights and access to treatment: challenges and opportunities in select Latin American and Caribbean countries, Havana, 20–22 November
ITPC (2012) Estudio Comparativo de Precios de Medicamentos (ARVs) y Factores Relacionados en 6 Paises de Latinoamerica. Bolivia, Ecuador, Honduras, Guatemala, Nicaragua y Peru, Guatemala. http://www.portalsida.org/Article_Details.aspx?ID=13274
Juan Manuel Santa María y María Laura Devoto (2012) Perspectivas del Mercado Farmacéutico Mundial, Latinoamericano y Argentino. IMS, Buenos Aires
Khor M (2007) Patents, compulsory licences and access to medicines: some recent experiences. TWN, Penang
Love J (2005) Love. Remuneration guidelines for non-voluntary use of a patent on medical technologies. UNDP and World Health Organization. Health economics and drugs, TCM Series No. 18
Oliveira MA, Bermudez JAZ, Chaves GC, Velázquez G (2004) Has the implementation of the TRIPS Agreement in Latin America and the Caribbean produced intellectual property legislation that favours public health? Bull World Health Organ 82(11):811–890
Radhakrishnan P, Amin T (2014) Strengthening patent standards: an alternative route to compulsory licensing for low and middle income countries. In: Correa C (ed) Pharmaceutical innovation, incremental patenting and compulsory licensing. South Centre, Geneva
Reichman JH, Hasenzhal C (2003) Non-voluntary licensing of patented inventions: historical perspective, legal framework under TRIPS, and an overview of the practice in Canada and in the USA. UNCTAD-ICTSD, Geneva
Roffe P, Santa Cruz M (2007) Intellectual property rights and sustainable development: a survey of major issues. http://www.eclac.org/publicaciones/xml/7/32167/W161.pdf
Sampat P (2014) Promoting local pharmaceutical capacity in developing countries: a discussion on inventive step and compulsory licensing. In: Correa C (ed) Pharmaceutical innovation, incremental patenting and compulsory licensing. South Centre, Geneva
Smith RD, Correa C, Oh C (2009) Trade, TRIPS, and pharmaceuticals. Lancet 373:684–691, http://policydialogue.org/files/publications/Trade_Agreements_and_Health_Stiglitz.pdf
t'Hoen E (2009) The global politics of pharmaceutical monopoly power, drug patents, access, innovation and the application of the WTO Doha Declaration on TRIPS and public health. AMB Publishers, Diemen
Velázquez G (2012) Indonesia Government Granted 7 compulsory licences to promote access to HIV-related medicines. South Bulletin, South Centre, Geneva

Compulsory Licences: Law and Practice in Thailand

Jakkrit Kuanpoth

Contents

Abstract When the WTO/TRIPS Agreement entered into force in 1995, around 100 countries had adopted compulsory licensing under national intellectual property law. The compulsory licensing measure can be effective in dealing with situations inhibiting access to medicines, for example when a patent holder fails to use the patent in the granting country or when he or she maintains artificially high prices for patented articles. Despite the significant international development, it remains to be seen how the flexibility margins provided by the TRIPS provisions can be used as safeguards to protect public health interests of the poor countries. Effective mechanisms are also required to support countries that are unable to make effective use of compulsory licensing due to the inefficiency of manufacturing capacity. This chapter examines the problem of using the legal mechanism of compulsory licensing by developing countries. It looks at Thailand's experiences with the use of compulsory licensing to increase access to medicines. Since the

J. Kuanpoth is Associate Professor and Head of Postgraduate Studies.

J. Kuanpoth
Faculty of Law, University of Wollongong, Wollongong, NSW, Australia
e-mail: jakkrit@uow.edu.au

R.M. Hilty and K.-C. Liu (eds.), *Compulsory Licensing*, MPI Studies on Intellectual Property and Competition Law 22, DOI 10.1007/978-3-642-54704-1_4,

majority of compulsory licences issued around the world are related to pharmaceutical patents, the chapter highlights the use of compulsory licensing in the context of a range of public health responses. It first discusses the use by Thailand of the compulsory government use licensing to increase access to medicines. It also examines international rules on compulsory licensing, including the provisions of the Paris Convention, the TRIPS Agreement, and the Doha Declaration on the TRIPS Agreement and Public Health. Finally, the chapter discusses various legal issues under the Thai Patent Act regarding the compulsory licensing provisions. It also highlights the possible impact, in a broad sense, of the use of legal mechanisms such as compulsory licensing, which aims to effectively maintain fair market competition and dilute the monopoly power of the patent holder.

1 Introduction

Essential medicines are those that satisfy the health care needs of the majority of the population; they should therefore be available at all times in adequate amounts and in the appropriate dosage forms and at a price that individuals and the community can afford. Essential medicines save lives and improve health only if they are available, affordable, and properly used. Nowadays, despite the potential health impact of essential medicines, and despite substantial spending on medicines borne by either the government or the patient, lack of access to essential medicines remains a serious public health problem in many developing countries. Over one-third of the population in developing countries in Asia and Africa still do not have regular access to needed medicines. It is even more tragic that most leading causes of death and disability in many developing countries can be prevented, treated, or alleviated with effective essential medicines.

Affordable prices are fundamental for improving access to medicines. Although the prices of essential medicines have significantly decreased in many cases, compared with local purchasing power in many developing countries, they remain too high. The high level of medicine prices stems from several factors, including lack of price competition, a non-transparent markup system, taxes and tariffs on medicines, the preference of health professionals and consumers for branded products instead of cheaper generics, and the lack of alternative sources for patented medicines.[1] Patent protection for pharmaceuticals is the main factor that leads to the restricted supply and overpricing of an essential product. Stricter patent protection has allowed firms to increase market share and charge high prices. The question of constraints as regards pharmaceutical patenting has been a subject of serious concern and has been intensely debated in the WTO meetings, which led to the adoption of the Doha Declaration on the TRIPS Agreement and Public Health at

[1] Kuanpoth (2006), pp. 31–36.

the WTO Ministerial Conference in Doha in November 2001.[2] The Declaration was an important step forward in improving access to medicines. It affirms that the TRIPS Agreement can and should be interpreted and implemented in a manner supportive of the WTO members' right to protect public health and that mechanisms, such as compulsory licensing, can be used to improve access to medicines for all.[3]

Compulsory licensing is a non-voluntary licence issued by the State authorising a third party to perform acts covered by the patents against the will of the patent holder. When the TRIPS Agreement entered into force in 1995, around 100 countries had adopted compulsory licensing under national intellectual property law.[4] This measure can be effective in dealing with situations inhibiting access to medicines, for example when a patent holder fails to use the patent in the granting country or when he or she maintains artificially high prices for patented articles. Despite the significant international development, it remains to be seen how the flexibility margins provided by the TRIPS provisions can be used as safeguards to protect public health interests of the poor countries.[5] Effective mechanisms are also required to support countries that are unable to make effective use of compulsory licensing due to the inefficiency of manufacturing capacity.

The aim of the chapter is to examine the problem of using the legal mechanism of compulsory licensing by developing countries. It will take a close look at Thailand's experiences with the use of compulsory licensing to increase access to medicines. Since the majority of compulsory licences issued around the world are related to pharmaceutical patents, this chapter will focus on the use of compulsory licensing in the context of a range of public health responses. The chapter is organised and divided into three major sections. First, it discusses the use by Thailand of the compulsory government use licensing to increase access to medicines. The second part examines international rules on compulsory licensing, including the provisions of the Paris Convention, the TRIPS Agreement, and the Doha Declaration on the TRIPS Agreement and Public Health. Third, the paper discusses various legal issues under the Thai Patent Act regarding the compulsory licensing provisions. It also highlights the possible impact, in a broad sense, of the use of legal mechanisms such as compulsory licensing, which aims to effectively maintain fair market competition and dilute the monopoly power of the patent holder.

---

[2] WTO Ministerial Conference (2001); See also Abbott (2005), pp. 317–358.

[3] Scherer and Watal (2002), pp. 913–939.

[4] Lybecker and Fowler (2009), pp. 222–239.

[5] Scherer and Watal (2002), p. 317.

2 Government Use Licensing in Thailand on Patented Heart Disease and HIV/AIDS Medicines

In November 2006 and January 2007, the Thai Ministry of Public Health issued government use licences against patents over three medicines: (1) efavirenz, Merck's anti-HIV drug (branded 'Stocrin'); (2) lopinavir/ritonavir (branded 'Kaletra'), an ARV distributed by Abbott Laboratories; and (3) clopidogrel, an anti-clotting drug sold by Sanofi-Aventis and BMS. Clopidogrel, which is sold under a brand name 'Plavix', is one of the world's biggest selling heart disease medicines, with annual sales of US$6 billion. It was estimated that around 200,000 Thai patients were suffering from heart conditions and blood clotting problems that could be treated with the drug. Although the past decade has seen a number of developing countries granting compulsory licences,[6] Thailand was the first developing country that issued a government use licence for a non-HIV medicine. The grant of a compulsory licence over a non-HIV drug reflected Thailand's view that the compulsory licensing can be used for patented medicines treating all sorts of ailments, not only HIV/AIDS.

As for drugs required for the treatment of HIV/AIDS, the Ministry of Public Health claimed that only around 20,000 infected people were able to access the HIV treatment.[7] The Thai Government pointed to high drug prices as the main factor for its inability to provide health care coverage. In the 2007 fiscal year, for example, public health accounts for 9.5 % of the total public expenditure, which is equivalent to 4,373 million baht (about US$112 million).[8] With this amount, the Government claimed that it could afford to provide medicines to one-fifth of the total 500,000 of the Thai people living with HIV/AIDS at the companies' price. The issuance of compulsory licences would allow the Ministry of Public Health to treat many more patients because it could switch to a generic version of the drugs that costs, on average, only one-seventh to one-tenth the prices of the patented and branded products, cutting the drug bill by two-thirds.[9]

HIV/AIDS is one of the leading causes of death in Thailand. Approximately, 300,000 have already died from HIV/AIDS-related illnesses since Thailand's first case of HIV/AIDS was reported in 1984.[10] The Thai Government started its

[6] The developing countries that have issued compulsory licences for patents on essential drugs include the following: Zimbabwe (April 2003: all ARV medicines), Malaysia (October 2003: didanosine, zidovudine, and FDC didanosine), Zambia (September 2004: FDC lamivudine+stavudine+nevirapine), Indonesia (October 2004 and March 2007: lamivudine and nevirapine, and efavirenz; September 2012: efavirenz, abacavir, didanosine, lopinavir, ritonavir, tenofovir, tenofovir/emtricitabine, and tenofovir/emtricitabine/efavirenz), Thailand (November 2006 and January 2007: efavirenz and lopinavir/ritonavir), Brazil (May 2007: efavirenz).

[7] Ministry of Public Health and National Health Security Office (2007), pp. 5–8.

[8] *Id.*

[9] Yamabhai et al. (2011), p. 28. See Baron (2008).

[10] WHO/UNAIDS/UNICEF (2007).

HIV/AIDS campaigns in the early 1990s with emphasis on prevention, which has subsequently proved to be remarkably successful in slowing down the rate of HIV infections.[11] In 1992, the Ministry of Public Health shifted its HIV/AIDS policy from prevention to the subsidisation of anti-retroviral (ARV) treatment and the introduction of locally produced, low-cost ARVs.[12] At the beginning of the campaigns, only mono-ARV therapy (i.e., AZT or zidovudine) was prescribed free of charge for a small number of selected HIV patients. However, drug resistance occurred as the virus evolved to escape the inhibitory effects of the drug, requiring a change of medication. The Ministry was forced to switch to the combination therapy of using two or three drugs, which is more potent in suppressing the virus but also more expensive than a single therapy, to treat HIV/AIDS.

In its early stage, the national health insurance scheme, which was introduced in 2002, did not cover ARV treatment, due to the high cost of drugs and limited public budgets, despite the fact that the Government was committed to providing universal access to all treatments, including ARVs. Many HIV/AIDS patients who received treatment under the national HIV/AIDS campaigns were forced to discontinue their treatment due to the limitations on the capacity of health systems. Since it was clear that the cost of ARVs far exceeds personal and national budgets, the Thai Government felt that it had no choice but to take different approaches to bring down the cost of ARVs, ranging from local manufacture or importing of generic medicines to coercive government use of patented drugs.

The Government instructed the Government Pharmaceutical Organisation (GPO), a state enterprise under the Ministry of Public Health, to carry out research and development in order to manufacture off-patent medicines. This led to the successful production of an ARV cocktail called GPO-vir (i.e., a fixed-dose combination of stavudine, lamivudine, and nevirapine), which costs US$31 per patient per month, compared to US$490 per patient per month for the imported brand-name drugs.[13] The issued government use licences authorised the Ministry of Public Health to import generic versions of the patented medicines from the countries where the prices are lower. In fact, a licence granted in November 2006 permitted the Ministry to import a batch of 66,000 bottles of generic efavirenz from India at half the price offered by Merck, increasing access to life-saving drugs for an additional 20,000 patients.

These strategies have increased Thailand's ability to provide basic health care services to its people. They have also made treatment with selected ARV medications available for all Thais under the national health care system since October 2005. There are several success factors contributing to the improvement of access to medicines in Thailand, including the country's relatively good health care and reliable supply systems, and the Public Health Ministry's policy that enhances

[11] Piot and Seck (2001), pp. 1106–1112.

[12] United Nations Development Programme (2004), pp. 13–18.

[13] The comparative prices quoted here refer to the prices offered by the GPO and the multinational companies during 2000–2002.

rational selection and use of drugs. The existence of a significant local capacity to manufacture generic drugs and capacity to research and manufacture affordable medicines is also critical to ensure accessibility, particularly over the longer term. The GPO is currently producing most of the first-line regimens of ARVs required for the local market. It also exports ARVs it produces to other developing countries at affordable prices. Finally, a combination of domestic capacities and the use of appropriate strategy such as the use of the non-voluntary licensing, among other factors, have increased the Thai Government's bargaining power in negotiations with brand-name companies over price discounts.

It is interesting to note that the use of the compulsory licensing by the Thai Government has attracted a variety of reactions.[14] The owners of the affected drugs expressed their concerns about the process of compulsory licensing. They maintained that the compulsory use of the patents by Thailand violated WTO/TRIPS rules. The arguments against the use of compulsory licensing by the Thai Government can be summarised as follows[15]:

- The Thai government did not engage in negotiations with the patent holder before issuing a compulsory licence.
- Thailand had not declared an emergency before announcing the licence.
- The Thai compulsory licensing does not meet the requirement of "public non-commercial use". The compulsory licences were issued to the GPO, a state enterprise under the Ministry of Public Health that operates on a for-profit basis.
- The royalty rate of 0.5 % of the total sale value to be paid to the patent holder is considered arbitrary and too low.
- The use of the compulsory licensing would reduce the patent owner's profits, thereby decreasing the incentive to continue research and development.

Thailand refers to the rules available in the WTO/TRIPS to justify its action on compulsory licensing. The Ministry of Public Health also contended that it was engaged in extensive discussion with the right holders for more than 2 years before it finally decided on government use licensing.[16] The use of the drugs by the State, according to the Ministry, would not affect the patented market, as the medicines distributed under the non-voluntary licensing scheme would be for those unable to pay, most of whom are already covered by the universal coverage. After the licences were granted, the two parties held several rounds of dialogue. The compulsory licensing had led the pharmaceutical companies to seek serious discussions with the Ministry, in which they finally agreed to lower their prices.

The move by the Thai Government brought an angry response from the Office of the United States Trade Representative (USTR).[17] In its 2007 and 2008 reviews, the

---

[14] United States Government Accountability Office (2007).

[15] PReMA (2007).

[16] Intellectual Property Watch (2007).

[17] Bangkok Post (2008).

USTR exerted extraordinary pressure on Thailand by placing Thailand on the Priority Watch List (PWL) under Special 301 of the Omnibus Trade and Competitiveness Act of 1988. It also threatened to revoke the trade privileges it grants to Thailand under the Generalised System of Preferences. The leverage, which was previously successfully applied by the United States on Thailand in 1992, causing Thailand to amend its patent law to protect pharmaceuticals,[18] is clearly pressure to discourage government use licensing. Furthermore, the fear of compulsory licensing has caused the United States to limit and prevent the compulsory licensing scheme under the bilateral Free Trade Agreement (FTA) it has negotiated with Thailand since 2003. The United States intends to use the bilateral platform to negotiate change in the patent law of Thailand on compulsory licences. In the FTA negotiations, it demanded Thailand to implement stricter laws concerning the licensing scheme, including, *inter alia*, narrowing the situations in which non-voluntary licences can be issued.[19]

So far, this chapter has provided a background on the case of non-voluntary licensing in Thailand. The next sections will present a theoretical and practical analysis of the international and national rules regarding the compulsory licensing mechanism.

3 International Law on Compulsory Licensing

A compulsory licence allows a government to authorise itself or a third party to perform acts covered by the patent exclusive rights (e.g., manufacturing, selling, or importing the patented product). The TRIPS Agreement does not mention the term 'compulsory (or non-voluntary) licence' throughout its text. It only authorises 'other use[s] of the subject matter of a patent without the authorisation of the right holder'. TRIPS Article 31 establishes the conditions under which WTO Members may grant a compulsory licence but does not limit the grounds upon which such licence can be granted. This provision, in conjunction with Article 2.1 of TRIPS and Article 5A(2) of the Paris Convention for the Protection of Industrial Property 1883, authorises the granting of compulsory licences in a wide variety of contexts, including non-working of patents, public non-commercial use, anti-competitive practices, etc.

[18] Sell (2002), pp. 500–501.

[19] Kuanpoth (2006), p. 17.

3.1 Compulsory Licensing to Enforce the Working Requirement

3.1.1 The Paris Convention

The function of the modern patent system is based on reciprocity between the granting state and the patent owner. Patent law of many countries requires the patent holder to work his/her invention within the country. Paris Union members may adopt measures to compel local working of patents subject to certain conditions. According to Article 5A of the Paris Convention, the member states cannot revoke patents they have granted by relying on the ground that the patentee has exploited his/her patent by means of importing the patented articles manufactured abroad into the country. This provision effectively recognises the monopoly power of the patentee to import a patented product. At the same time, it discourages local production of the patented products where a patent holder can import finished and lower cost products into the country.

Although the Paris Convention does not explicitly stipulate that patents must be effectively exploited in the granting state, the parties are entitled to enforce local working for national benefits.[20] As authorised by Article 5A, each member has a right to adopt legislative measures to prevent abuses of a patent holder's exclusive rights. The legal measures mentioned in the provision include compulsory licensing and forfeiture of patents. Paris Union members have a right to issue a compulsory licence to a third party for the prevention of patent abuses resulting from the exclusive right under a patent. An example of the abuses is provided in Article 5A(2), namely 'failure to work'. However, the term 'failure to work' in this provision is not clearly defined by the Convention. The lack of a definition may create uncertainty in the parties who are considering applying for a compulsory licence.

In addition to compulsory licensing, members of the Paris Union may impose forfeiture of the patents they have granted. But under Article 5A(3), the right to forfeit is subject to two conditions. First, a member state may prescribe forfeiture of the patent only in cases where a compulsory licence has already been granted and such a licence is inadequate to prevent the non-working or the insufficient working. Second, the forfeiture shall not be applied before the expiration of 2 years from the grant of the first compulsory licence. These requirements have made forfeiture of patents a secondary measure, subject to the condition that the use of compulsory licensing has proved to be ineffective.

It may be noted that some countries, particularly the United States, are dissatisfied with the existence of this provision. They take the view that allowing States to expropriate private proprietary rights is unfair and might lead to serious distortions of legitimate trade. At the Washington Conference in 1911 and the third and the

[20] Roffe (1974), pp. 15–26.

fourth sessions of the Diplomatic Conference on the Revision of the Paris Convention (held in 1982 and 1984, respectively), the United States and its allies proposed to prohibit the use of the compulsory licensing for local working. However, Paris Union members failed to reach an agreement on amending Article 5 of the Paris Convention.[21]

3.1.2 The TRIPS Agreement

While the Paris Convention recognises that local working may be required by the patent-granting state, the TRIPS Agreement does not address the issue of local working. Article 27.1 of the TRIPS Agreement requires equal treatments for both imported and locally manufactured products and so seems to prohibit the imposition of local working requirements.[22] However, there are several reasons to believe that TRIPS does not totally ban local working of patents. First, TRIPS does not limit the right of countries to establish compulsory licensing on grounds other than those explicitly mentioned in the Agreement. Second, the patent-granting country might impose working obligations in accordance with Article 5A of the Paris Convention, which is incorporated into TRIPS by virtue of Article 2.1 of the TRIPS Agreement.[23] Third, as Article 27.1 is a provision containing general rules of patentability, it is subject to specific rules under Article 28 (Rights conferred) and Article 31 (Other use without authorisation of the right holder) of the TRIPS Agreement.[24] According to a general rule of treaty interpretation under the Vienna Convention on the Law of Treaties, when general principles are in conflict with a specific provision, the specific rule shall take precedence. The particular or specific provision on compulsory licensing such as Article 31 will therefore take precedence over a conflicting general provision of Article 27.1.

Professor Carlos Correa contends that the Article 27.1 text must be read in conjunction with Article 28.1 and that the requirement of non-discriminatory treatment will apply to infringing products only, not the products coming from the patent owner. According to Correa, the provision "forbids discrimination between infringing imported and infringing locally made products, but it does not rule out the establishment of differential obligations with regard to non-infringing imported and locally-made products (i.e. products made or imported by the patent owner or with his/her consent)".[25] It is interesting to note that patent laws of most developed countries still continue to regard the local working obligation as an

[21] Bodenhausen (1991), pp. 30–34.

[22] Doane (1994), p. 465; Adelman and Baldia (1996), p. 507; Foster (1998), p. 283.

[23] Correa (2005), pp. 227–256.

[24] Champ and Attaran (2002), p. 365.

[25] See *supra* note 23, p. 243.

essential element to balance the patent system. Accession to the TRIPS Agreement has not led those countries to change their local working provisions.[26]

3.2 Government Use Licensing

The non-voluntary licensing for government use derived from 'Crown use' under English common law. By granting exclusive rights to the patent holder, the Crown reserved the right to use patented inventions without the consent of or paying compensation to the patent holder.[27] The government use provision is considered necessary and in the larger public interest and incidental to sovereign powers and functions of the State. Although the Paris Convention provisions are silent on the issue of government use,[28] this licence regime can be found in the law of many countries, including United States patent law (35 USC 181; 28 USC 1498), United Kingdom Patents Act 1977 (ss. 55–59), Australia Patents Act 1990 (ss. 163–169), etc. Countries, both developed and developing, implement such powers in the widest terms to cover all possibilities, particularly those involving national security, emergencies, defence, and public needs such as health care, environment, and other matters of necessity. For example, section 56 of the UK Patents Act 1977 provides for the use of patented inventions by the Crown in cases of supply for foreign defence purposes, production or supply of drugs and medicines, and production or use of atomic energy or research considered by the government agency to be necessary or expedient.

The government use provision is of special interest and a significant tool to achieve social and economic functions of the patent system. Articles 7, 8, and 31 of the TRIPS Agreement clearly intend to extend the social benefits of patents to other areas than the provisions of the Paris Convention. The Doha Declaration on the TRIPS Agreement and Public Health reaffirms that each country has the right to determine what constitutes a ground for government use, such as national emergency or other circumstances of extreme urgency. In fact, a government use provision covers all uses of a patent by the State for either public non-commercial or commercial purposes. It may also be issued in the public interest (e.g., the protection of the environment, public health, nutrition, and concerns of basic importance to the technological, social, and economic development of the country). TRIPS Article 31(f) stipulates that the use of a compulsory licence must be made predominantly for the supply of the domestic market, and the products produced under a compulsory licence may not be exported to another country. But the term "predominantly" is tantamount to "largely" or "mainly" (i.e., more than 50 %), and the export of drugs produced under the compulsory licence is

[26] *Id.* p. 240.

[27] *Feather v R* (1865), 6 B&S 257.

[28] Gontijo (2005), pp. 7–9.

not completely prohibited. This interpretation has been confirmed by the Doha Declaration on TRIPS and Public Health, in particular the decision of the TRIPS Council of 30 August 2003 on the export of drugs to WTO Members with insufficient or no manufacturing capacities in the pharmaceutical sector.

4 Compulsory Licensing Under Thai Law

The Thai patent law provides for the grant of a compulsory licence in four situations, including

(1) non-working or inadequate working of patents so as to meet the local demand for the patented products (section 46);
(2) use for working of dependent patents (sections 47 and 47bis);
(3) public non-commercial use of patented substances for meeting the public needs (section 51);
(4) use for public interest due to war or national emergency (section 52).

Under Thai law, the system of compulsory licensing is envisaged as a mechanism to encourage local working and improve free competition [i.e., situations (1) and (2), respectively] and to authorise the use of patented article for public interest [i.e., situations (3) and (4)]. While in the former situations a compulsory licence is granted to a private competitor, the compulsory licensing in the latter circumstances allows the State agency to authorise the use of patented substances for meeting public needs.

4.1 Thai Law on Local Working Requirement

Compulsory licensing for local working is stipulated in sections 46–50 of the current patent law of Thailand, the Patent Act B.E. 2522 (1979). According to section 46, non-working of the patent within the national economy is regarded as an abuse that would justify the grant of a compulsory licence. Although the term "working" is not clearly defined, the provision comprises both the manufacture of the product or the import of the patented product into Thailand. The patent may be worked either by the patentee or with his consent. Thai law considers non-working in two particular circumstances. First, section 46 explicitly states that the failure to work arises when a patented product has not been produced or the patented process has not been applied for manufacture in Thailand. Second, non-working also arises when the patentee charges a high price for a patented product and the latter is not available (i.e., affordable) in sufficient quantities to meet domestic demand.

In the above circumstances, any person seeking a compulsory licence must submit an application to the Director General of the Department of Intellectual Property (DIP) upon showing that a request for authorisation to use the patented invention on reasonable terms and an appropriate amount of royalty had been made by him to the patentee but no agreement was concluded with the patentee within a reasonable period of time.[29] In addition, the applicant has to show that, within the specified time, the patented product has not been produced or the patented process has not been applied, in the country without any legitimate reason, or no product produced under the patent is sold in the domestic market or such a product is sold but at an unreasonably high price or does not meet the public demand without any legitimate reason.[30]

Proving abuse by non-working and the absence of reasons to justify such conduct is up to the applicant, which does not look justified in light of the fact that under the Paris Convention an obligation to work the invention in the granting country is placed on the patent holder. The patentee should thus have the duty to present evidence to justify his inaction,[31] the more so since justifying reasons for the inaction will be known foremost to the patentee. The current allocation of the burden of proof makes the Thai compulsory licensing system rather impractical. There has been no application for a licence, and no compulsory licence for exploitation of a patent on the grounds of non-working or insufficient working has been granted since the Patent Act B.E. 2522 entered into force in 1979.

4.2 *Thai Law on Government Use Licensing*

Sections 51 and 52 of the Patent Act B.E. 2522, in compliance with TRIPS Article 31, provide for non-voluntary government use licensing. Thai law also lays down procedural and substantive rules to be fulfilled prior to exercising government use licensing, including the following conditions.

4.2.1 Grounds for Government Use Licensing

Section 51 of the Patent Act provides for compulsory licensing for public non-commercial use, including for public consumption, defence, conservation of environment and natural resources, prevention of shortage of food or medicines, etc. Section 52 authorises the use of patented products in cases of a national emergency, e.g. health-related emergencies due to an insufficient availability of drugs on HIV/AIDS, anthrax, SARS, and bird flu. In these and other circumstances (e.g., war, epidemics, a natural catastrophe, etc.), the State agency may issue an

[29] Patent Act B.E. 2522, section 46, para. 3.

[30] Ministerial Regulations No. 6, B.E. 2524, clause 14(1). The Royal Gazette, Special Issue, 98 (196), 17 November 1981.

[31] Paris Convention, Article 5A(4) states: "... it should be refused if the patentee justifies his inaction by legitimate reason".

authorisation to use the patented substance at any time during that national emergency on terms and conditions as the State may deem fit.

4.2.2 Consultation with the Patent Holder

Although Thailand, as a WTO member, can use various public health safeguards in line with international rules to promote access to affordable generic medicines, it is important for the Thai Government to ensure that its act is in full compliance with all the requirements of the TRIPS Agreement, particularly the condition that the State undertakes a consultation with the patent holder prior to granting a compulsory licence. This condition can however be waived when a compulsory licence is granted: (1) to remedy anti-competitive practices, (2) in a national emergency or other circumstances of extreme urgency, or (3) for public non-commercial use.[32]

Sections 47 and 47bis of the Thai Patent Act do not require the prospective licensee to show that it has attempted but failed to obtain a voluntary licence from the patentee. However, the State agency is required to notify the patentee in writing without delay after a licence has been issued, but the law is silent on the details and content of this notification. Since the issuance of the government use licences on the patented medicines by Thailand was aimed for non-commercial purposes and for public interests (i.e., carrying out a service for public consumption), the Thai authorities may not be required to enter into prior consultation with the patent holder as permitted under Article 31(b).

4.2.3 Remuneration

As far as the rate of remuneration is concerned, TRIPS requires the government agency to pay adequate compensation to the patent holder, but it does not specify what amount of remuneration is adequate.[33] The ambiguity of the term ‘adequate remuneration’ allows the granting country to compulsorily exploit the patent in exchange for the fee considered by the State to be reasonable.[34] In the United States, a reasonable royalty refers to “the amount that a person desiring to manufacture [or use] a patented article . . . would be willing to pay as a royalty and yet be able to make [or use] the patented article, in the market at a reasonable profit”.[35] Therefore, the fees can be either a fixed sum per unit sold or a percentage of the net sale price of the product produced by the licensee (e.g., normally between 1 and 5 %). Other factors may also be taken into consideration to determine a reasonable royalty: expected volume of production, price under the non-voluntary licence,

[32] TRIPS, Article 31(b).

[33] TRIPS, Article 31(h).

[34] Love (2005), p. 18.

[35] *Wright v United States*, 53 Fed. Cl. 466, 469 (Ct. Cl. 2002).

potential market price and profit margin, R&D and related legal costs, advertising and administrative expenses, possible substitutes, risks undertaken in first producing the invention, evidence of bad faith or anti-competitive practices, the country's economic and health situation such as evidence of how the public interest would be served by the invention, and so on.[36]

Section 51 of the Patent Act requires the licensing authority to offer the amount of remuneration and conditions for the granting of a compulsory licence to the Director General of the DIP. No guidelines are provided as to what is the reasonable remuneration. The law only requires both parties to enter into negotiations to evaluate the rate of the royalty. If the parties fail to reach an agreement within the period prescribed by the Director General, the Director General will make a decision as to the royalty and conditions. Parties may appeal the decision to the Board of Patents and, further, to the Intellectual Property and International Trade Court within 60 days.[37] The appeal provisions were adopted in order to comply with TRIPS Article 31(i) and (j), which requires that any decision relating to the authorisation of such use and the remuneration "shall be subject to judicial review or other independent review by a distinct higher authority in that Member". It may be noted that the patentee can only appeal the terms of the licence but has no right to appeal the grounds for the decision to grant the licence. In addition, the appeal by the patent holder will not suspend the execution of the order and will not delay the issuance of the licence.

4.2.4 Supply of Domestic Market and WTO Decisions 2003 and 2005

The significance of the compulsory licensing to improve access to essential medicines may be minimised when a country does not have capacity to manufacture the required drugs.[38] The problem is exacerbated by the fact that the products cannot be imported, as the newly invented drugs are likely to be under patent protection in the countries where they are manufactured. A couple of the TRIPS provisions permit production for export. First, under Article 31(k), the product produced under a compulsory licence that is issued to combat anti-competitive practices may be exported to other countries. Second, TRIPS Article 31(f) stipulates that the use of a compulsory licence must be made predominantly for the supply of the domestic market. This can be interpreted as meaning that less than half of the production authorised by a compulsory licence can be exported. Paragraph 6 of the Doha Declaration and the decisions of the WTO General Council of 2003 and 2005 reaffirm that WTO Members may issue a compulsory licence to produce and export generic medicines to countries with insufficient or no manufacturing capacity in the

[36] See *supra* note 34, p. 21.

[37] Patent Act B.E. 2522, sections 50 and 51.

[38] Harrelson (2001), p. 192.

pharmaceutical sector.[39] The 2005 Decision also waives the payment requirement in the eligible importing Member.[40]

The current law of Thailand does not implement the Decisions adopted by WTO. Thailand may wish to adopt a provision permitting import of medicines that it lacks manufacturing capacity to produce. Since there are large generic producers in Thailand, like the GPO, it may consider incorporating into the national patent law provisions enabling the export of pharmaceutical products manufactured under the compulsory licensing.

5 Conclusion

The non-voluntary or compulsory licensing system appears in the Paris Convention, the TRIPS Agreement, and many patent laws of both developed and developing countries. Patent rights are granted based on reciprocity between the inventor and society. The compulsory licensing is the very cornerstone of the patent system. While the law grants exclusive rights, the system ensures that such rights will not be abused by the patentee. When the patent holder fails to fulfil his legal obligation, it is justifiable for the State to intervene and allow another person to make essential products available to the public.

Although the compulsory licensing provisions under the patent law of Thailand looks promising, the failure or the success of the system depends upon a strong political will of the Government. The case of Thailand has proved that government action is essential to protect patients by offsetting the patentee's power to extract excessive prices. The non-voluntary licensing encourages private patent owners to negotiate with the government agency in order to provide medicines at a more reasonable price. It is also likely to lead to an increase in the production or import of the generic version of the drug. States, whether developed or developing, generally use legal measures to facilitate the domestic production of patented inventions and at the same time prevent a single company from dominating the market and creating barriers to entry for potential competitors. There is no reason why developing countries like Thailand should not continue to use these legal mechanisms to achieve the aim of guaranteeing public interests. It is therefore strongly recommended that the relevant authorities of developing countries should instigate employing this available mechanism against those patents that are failing to meet domestic demand.

[39] World Trade Organisation (2005).

[40] Abbott (2005), pp. 317–358.

References

Abbott FM (2005) The WTO medicines decision: world pharmaceutical trade and the protection of public health. Am J Int Law 99:317–358

Adelman MJ, Baldia S (1996) Prospects and limits of the patent provision in the TRIPS Agreement: the case of India. Vanderbilt J Transnatl Law 29:507–533

Bangkok Post (2008) Thai traders urge 'Extreme Caution' on CL. 14 February

Baron D (2008) Compulsory licensing, Thailand, and Abbott Laboratories. Stanford Graduate School of Business Case P-66

Bodenhausen GCH (1991) Guide to the application of the Paris Convention for the protection of industrial property as revised at Stockholm in 1967. WIPO Publication No. 611 (E), Geneva

Champ P, Attaran A (2002) Patent rights and local working under the WTO TRIPS Agreement: an analysis of the US–Brazil patent dispute. Yale J Int Law 27:365–393

Correa CM (2005) Can the TRIPS Agreement foster technology transfer to developing countries? In: Maskus KE, Reichman JH (eds) International public goods and transfer of technology under a globalized intellectual property regime. Cambridge University Press, Cambridge, pp 227–256

Doane M (1994) TRIPS and intellectual property protection in an age of advancing technology. Am Univ J Int Law Policy 9:465–479

Foster G (1998) Opposing forces in a revolution in international patent protection: the US and India in the Uruguay round and its aftermath. UCLA J Int Law Foreign Aff 3:283–298

Gontijo C (2005) Changing the patent system from the Paris Convention to the TRIPS Agreement: the position of Brazil. The Heinrich Böll Foundation, Global Issue Paper No. 26, Berlin. http://fdcl-berlin.de/fileadmin/fdcl/Publikationen/GIP_Gontijo-Patente.pdf. Accessed 2 Aug 2012

Harrelson JA (2001) Note: TRIPS, pharmaceutical patents, and the HIV/AIDS crisis: finding the proper balance between intellectual property rights and compassion. Widener Law Symp J 7:175–201

Intellectual Property Watch (2007) Thailand presents report on compulsory licensing experience. http://www.ip-watch.org/2007/03/12/thailand-presents-report-on-compulsory-licensing-experience/?res=1024&print=0. Accessed 1 Nov 2012

Kuanpoth J (2006) Harmonisation of TRIPS-plus IPR policies and potential impacts on technological capability: a case study of the pharmaceutical industry in Thailand. ICTSD-UNCTAD project on IPRs and sustainable development, Geneva. http://www.iprsonline.org/unctadictsd/regional_research.htm. Accessed 15 July 2012

Love J (2005) Remuneration guidelines for non-voluntary use of a patent on medical technologies. World Health Organisation, WHO/TCM/2005.1, Geneva

Lybecker KM, Fowler E (2009) Compulsory licensing in Canada and Thailand: comparing regimes to ensure legitimate use of the WTO rules. J Law Med Ethics 37:222–239

Ministry of Public Health and National Health Security Office (2007) Facts and evidences on the 10 burning issues related to the government use of patents on three patented essential drugs in Thailand. Document to support strengthening of social wisdom on the issue of drug patent, Bangkok. www.moph.go.th/hot/Second_white_paper_on_the_Thai_CL_%5BEN%5D.pdf. Accessed 14 Nov 2012

Piot P, Seck AMC (2001) International response to the HIV/AIDS epidemic: planning for success. Bull World Health Organ 79:1106–1112

PReMA (2007) Statement from the President of the Pharmaceutical Research and Manufacturers' Association of Thailand (PReMA). Press Release, Bangkok

Roffe P (1974) Abuses of patent monopoly. World Dev 2:15–26

Scherer FM, Watal J (2002) Post-TRIPS options for access to patented medicines in developing nations. J Int Econ Law 5(4):913–939

Sell SK (2002) TRIPS and the access to medicines campaign. Wis Int Law J 20:481–522

United Nations Development Programme (2004) Thailand's response to HIV/AIDS: progress and challenges. UNDP, Bangkok

United States Government Accountability Office (2007) Intellectual property: U.S. trade policy guidance on WTO declaration on access to medicines may need clarification. GAO-07-1198. http://www.gao.gov/assets/270/267763.html. Accessed 14 Nov 2012

WHO/UNAIDS/UNICEF (2007) Towards universal access: scaling up priority HIV/AIDS interventions in the health sector. http://www.who.int/hiv/mediacentre/universal_access_progress_report_en.pdf. Accessed 28 July 2012

WTO Ministerial Conference (2001) 4th session, Doha, 9–14 November 2001. WT/MIN(01)/Dec/2, 20 November 2001

World Trade Organisation (2005) Implementation of paragraph 11 of the General Council decision of 30 August 2003 on the implementation of paragraph 6 of the Doha Declaration on the TRIPS Agreement and Public Health. Council for trade-related aspects of intellectual property rights, IP/C/41. www.wto.org/english/news_e/pres05_e/pr426_e.htm. Accessed 12 July 2012

Yamabhai I et al (2011) Government use licenses in Thailand: an assessment of the health and economic impacts. Global Health 7:28. http://www.globalizationandhealth.com/content/7/1/28. Accessed 25 Mar 2013

Compulsory Licence and Government Use in Taiwan: A Regress

Kung-Chung Liu

Contents

Abstract The Taiwanese Patent Act foresaw from its inception in 1944 compulsory licence (CL) and government use. The provisions on the former have been amended several times, moving away from the Paris Convention model, while provisions on the latter were revised once, only to narrow its scope. Overall speaking, the regime on compulsory licensing and government use is in regress and fails to fulfil its function of balancing public and private interests. Thus far in Taiwan, two CL have been granted and implemented with the second being annulled later, and only one government use has been granted and yet not implemented due to its precondition not being satisfied. The Fair Trade Commission has not yet seen CL as one of the "necessary corrective measures" of the Fair Trade Act, although it did find violation of the Fair Trade Act in the Philips CD-R case.

K.-C. Liu is Professor of Law.

K.-C. Liu
Institutum Iurisprudentiae Academia Sinica, Taipei, Taiwan, Republic of China
and School of Law, Singapore Management University, Singapore
e-mail: liukc@gate.sinica.edu.tw; kcliu@smu.edu.sg

R.M. Hilty and K.-C. Liu (eds.), *Compulsory Licensing*, MPI Studies on Intellectual Property and Competition Law 22, DOI 10.1007/978-3-642-54704-1_5,

1 Introduction

CL in the broader sense includes CL (in the stricter sense) and government use. However, for conceptual clarity, this chapter treats CL and government use separately. CL is different from government use in that its grantee is a non-government entity, while the grantee in government use is a government or entities working for the government.

Modelled after Article 5A(2) of the Paris Convention, without however mentioning the term "to prevent the abuses" of patent rights, the Taiwanese Patent Act foresaw from its inception in 1944 CL and government use. The provisions on compulsory licensing have been amended several times, moving away from the Paris Convention, while provisions on government use were revised once, only to narrow its scope. Overall speaking, the regime on compulsory licensing and government use is in regress and fails to fulfil its function of balancing public and private interests.[1]

In addition to the Patent Act, the Fair Trade Act can, at least also be applied in order to result in CL. This chapter will first discuss in theory, the Patent Act then the Fair Trade Act (Sects. 2 and 3) in Taiwan. This chapter would not be complete without mentioning the latest provision on compulsory licencing for pharmaceuticals to export, therefore the concluding remarks are reserved for that purpose (Sect. 4).

2 The Patent Act

2.1 Compulsory Licence

Two CL have been granted thus far in Taiwan. Both were put into practice, yet the second one was later annulled by the Taiwan Intellectual Property Office (TIPO).

2.1.1 Half a Century of Good Old Days: 1944–1994

The Law in Books

The 1944–1994 Patent Act clearly saw patent not as an end in itself but rather as an instrument for the satisfaction of domestic needs and the incremental nature of technological improvement that is usually based on prior inventions.

[1] About the general need for and legitimacy of compulsory licensing, see Liu (2012), pp. 679–699. About the economic merits of compulsory licensing, see Antonelli (2013), pp. 157–174.

It was provided in Article 9 that a later invention that was based on a prior invention could still apply for invention patent or utility model patent (dependent patent). However, the dependent patentee shall provide the first patentee with appropriate monetary compensation or an offer of joint production, which the first patentee shall not refuse without justifiable reason. This was in fact an implicit CL provision.

Article 67 stipulated that not or insufficient working of a patent can lead to its rescission or compulsory licensing: The Patent Office can rescind the patent ex officio or issue CL upon application of interested parties when the patentee has not worked or not appropriately worked the patent 3 years after the patent grant without justifiable reasons. The Patent Office shall notify the patentee before deciding. The grantee of the CL shall provide the patentee with monetary compensation, which in case of dispute shall be decided by the Patent Office.[2]

Article 68 defined what would constitute "not appropriately working the patent": 1. The patented product has not been produced in large scale without sufficient reason while it is possible to use the product in the country; 2. The patentee produces the patented products entirely or for the most part in foreign countries and imports them into domestic market; 3. The patentee of an dependent invention fails to reach a voluntary licensing agreement under reasonable terms and conditions with the first patentee upon whose patent the dependent patent was based; 4. Parts have been imported and are only to be assembled domestically. In addition, where a patented product, which would fill an important need in the country, has not been sufficiently supplied despite being appropriately worked, the Patent Office may order the patentee to expand his supply within designated time limit (Article 70). If, however, the expansion fails to lead to sufficient supply, a further case of "not appropriately working the patent" will be constituted, which would result in a CL.[3]

Article 69 obliged the grantee to work the patent at issue appropriately: where the grantee of the CL according to Article 67 fails to work the patent appropriately, the Patent Office may rescind the compulsory licence upon application or ex officio.

The Practice: The Nippon Soda Topsin Case

There had been only one case in which a CL was issued by the Central Bureau of Standards (CBS, predecessor of the TIPO) under the Ministry of Economic Affairs (MOEA) during 1944–1994. It took almost 7 years of legal back and forth before

[2] The CL regime seemed only natural to the most authoritative commentator of that time, Yu-Fong Nin (who also served as head of the Patent Office). In his well-known thesis, Industrial Property Rights Law (in Chinese, 1st ed. 1972, p. 202 and again 3rd ed. 1982, p. 202), he just recited Article 67 without elaborating on it.

[3] Chen (1995), pp. 186–187.

the CL was finally confirmed. Presumably, the CBS was not familiar with the raison dětre of compulsory licence, and the patentee and the Japanese government had exerted much pressure on the CBS and the MOEA.

On 23 July 1976, a local company filed with the CBS an application for CL against a Japanese company (Nippon Soda Co. Ltd.) to work its method patent and to produce patented products (a farm chemical called "Topsin", patent number 5644). After more than 1 year, on 14 February 1978, the CBS issued a CL on the following grounds: while it is possible to use the patented product domestically, the patentee made no large-scale manufacture, importing only a small quantity for test sales purposes. According to the manufacturing plans of the applicant and the alleged licensee (a local company), the manufacturing technology required is rather simple, the facilities needed very limited, and the investment needed to produce the patented products small. By the time the patentee signed the draft licensing agreement (25 October in 1974) with the licensee, 3 years had elapsed since the patent grant, and the draft agreement was not yet formalized. In addition, the manufacturing plan proposed by the applicant was concrete and feasible, and its manufacturing method identical to the one contained in the patent descriptions. Taking the aforementioned into consideration, the CBS concluded that the patentee had not worked the patent 3 years after the patent grant without justifiable reasons. The CBS issued a CL without specifying its duration and ordered that the patentee be rewarded with compensation to be negotiated by the parties and that it be notified of the agreement reached.[4]

In the application for the CL, the applicant mentioned that a post note of NT$60 was included in the application. But no record can be found in the archive of the CBS on whether the parties had reached consensus on the compensation and how much it was.

On appeal, the case was annulled by the MOEA on the ground that the issued compulsory licence was limited to the use of claims 1 and 2 and did not include the use of claims 20–23 of the patent, which were necessary for producing the patented products; as such, the CL was obviously inappropriate.[5] The case was remanded back to the CBS, which simply confirmed on 25 February 1980 that the licence lost its validity with immediate effect.[6] The applicant appealed the decision to the MOEA, which was of the opinion that the CBS should substantially review the case rather than just reiterating the decision the MOEA made on 13 April 1979.[7] Upon the second remand, the CBS again granted a CL to use the patent, however including claims 1 and 2 and 20–23.[8] After being rejected by the MOEA[9] and the

[4] CBS (66) Tai Zhuan Cheng Er Tze 65589 (14 February 1978).

[5] MOEA (68) Gi 11239 (13 April 1979).

[6] CBS (69) Tai Zhuan Cheng Yi Tze 104993 (25 February 1980).

[7] MOEA (70) Su 14582 (17 April 1981).

[8] CBS (70) Tai Zhuan Cheng Yi Tze 126940 (6 November 1981).

[9] MOEA (71) Su 18908 (2 June 1982).

Executive Yuan,[10] the patentee brought appeal to the Supreme Administrative Court, which concurred with the CBS. The court's decision focused exclusively on confirming that the patentee had "not appropriately worked the patent"[11]: by the time the patentee signed the "enforcement contract (formal contract)" with the licensee, 6 years had elapsed since the patent grant; the 300 kg of "Topsin-M" produced by the plaintiff were "elementary body" and not "product" and therefore did not suffice to be the actual result of working of the patent; the statistics from the Taiwanese Farm-chemicals Association provided by the plaintiff were about the product made domestically and not the product made by the licensee; and the product for test sales was imported from Japan.

2.1.2 The Beginning of Regress: 1994–2012

Based on the misinterpretation of the draft Article 31 (b) of the TRIPS Agreement as allowing only three substantive grounds for compulsory licence,[12] namely national emergency, non-profit use for public interest, and failure of the applicant to reach voluntary licensing agreement with the patentee under reasonable commercial terms within a considerable period of time, in 1994 the TIPO proposed to delete the general clause for CL against not or insufficient working of patent[13] and recognize only four specific grounds for compulsory licensing: (1) national emergencies, (2) not-for-profit use of a patent for the enhancement of public welfare, (3) failure to reach a voluntary licensing agreement with the patentee, (4) remedy against anti-competitive conduct (Article 67 renumbered as Article 78 and as Article 76 in 2003). In addition, a mandatory cross-licensing mechanism was also envisioned to cure the failure of a dependent patentee whose invention was based on the invention of others to reach a voluntary licensing agreement with such other patentees, as well as to cure the failure of a method patentee whose products made with the said method are covered by the product patent to reach a voluntary licensing agreement with such product patentee (Article 80, renumbered as Article 78 in 2003[14]). The proposal was accepted entirely by the Legislative Yuan and became law in 1994.

[10] The Executive Yuan Tai (71) SuTze 17491 (18 October 1982).

[11] The Supreme Administrative Court 1983 Pan-Tze 359 Decision (decided on 7 April 1983).

[12] Document of the Legislative Yuan of 1 January 1994, Second Congress, First Session, 48th Meeting. It has been widely accepted by the international IP community that Article 31 of the TRIPS Agreement imposes only a stringent procedural requirement but leaves Members leeway in deciding the grounds for issuing CL. For more details, see the chapter "The Use of Compulsory Licences in Latin America" by Carlos M. Correa, in this volume.

[13] However, some commentators lauded the provision as more "up to date". See Chen (1997), p. 109.

[14] In 1997, an additional requirement was inserted into this Article: "the dependent invention or the method patent must 'involve an important technical advancement of considerable economic significance in relation to the prior invention or product patent'".

Only two applications had been filed between 1994 and 2012. While the first led to the grant of a CL by the TIPO against Philips ("Philips CD-R case") to remedy failure to reach a voluntary licensing agreement with Philips,[15] the second was later withdrawn by the applicant.[16]

The Philips CD-R Case

Philips, Sony, and Taiyo Yuden have pooled their patents on CD-R together and jointly licensed the pooled patents through a Joint Licensing Agreement (JLA)[17] in 1992 with one royalty formula: 3 % of the net sales price and not lower than ¥10 (Japanese Yen). Philips was designated as the sole contact for licensing the pooled patents. The market price of a CD-R disc at the time the JLA was entered into was approximately ¥300, making 3 % of which almost identical with ¥10. However, the market price of CD-Rs in the meanwhile dropped drastically and made the price floor of ¥10 unbearable. In July 2002, GigaStorage, a Taiwanese CD-R manufacturer and once a licensee of CD-R patents held by Philips, filed with TIPO an application for compulsory licence of the five patents owned by Philips after fruitless negotiation with Philips to reduce the royalty to reflect the falling prices of CD-Rs.

A. The TIPO Granted Compulsory Licence Against Philips

The TIPO came to a decision 2 years later (in 2004) and permitted the applicant the use of Philips's five patents primarily to satisfy the needs of domestic market to the dates when they expired (ranging from 26 January 2007 to 19 December 2009).[18] The TIPO did not touch upon the sensitive issue of appropriate compensation since the object of the application for compulsory licence was limited to the granting of such and did not involve the calculation of compensation. However, no agreement on the calculation of compensation has ever been reached between the two parties. The case was appealed to the Taipei Administrative High Court in August 2006.

B. The TIPO Annulled the Granted Compulsory Licence

GigaStorage and Philips filed separately with the TIPO applications to annul the compulsory patent licence on 23 April and 5 May 2006. Among other reasons,

[15] For more details, see Liu (2011), pp. 83–104.

[16] The unsuccessful fate of the CL against Philips might have played a role in the withdrawal of the application because the applicant was also a local CD-R manufacturer.

[17] The JLA was declared a cartel agreement among competitors and banned by the Taiwanese Fair Trade Commission (TFTC). Accordingly, Philips, Sony, and Taiyo Yuden started to license their own patents separately despite the later Supreme Administrative Court decision that rejected the determination by the TFTC. For more details, see Liu (2011), pp. 86–87.

[18] For more details, see Liu (2011), p. 88.

GigaStorage's main consideration was that it would cease to manufacture CD-Rs in Taiwan on 31 May 2007 and no longer need the CL. Philips's application was based on the ground that the licensee exceeded the limit of "primarily for domestic market" by exporting more than 50 % of its production made under the CL. Philips went further to demand that the licence be retroactively annulled, hoping to eradicate any precedential effect of the TIPO's decision.

On 31 May 2007, the TIPO annulled the CL with immediate rather than retroactive effect as requested by Philips. Its reasoning was twofold: GigaStorage no longer needed the use of the patents and no other public interest was at stake, and evidence provided by Philips could not directly prove that GigaStorage exported more than 50 % of its production made under the CL.[19]

C. The Taipei Administrative High Court Rescinded the TIPO's Decision to Grant Compulsory Licence

Regardless of the fact that the TIPO annulled the CL with immediate effect on 31 May 2007 and that the compulsory licence was granted only to GigaStorage, the Taipei Administrative High Court rescinded the decisions of the TIPO on 13 March 2008, but only on the ground that the TIPO failed to take into consideration factors other than the way royalty is calculated when determining "the reasonable commercial terms". Given the fact that GigaStorage and Philips entered into a settlement agreement on 29 October 2007,[20] the TIPO decided not to appeal the decision, which made the case final.

2.1.3 Race to the Bottom: 2013 Patent Act

Under the TIPO's initiative,[21] the Patent Act was revised on 29 November 2011 by the Legislative Yuan to limit the TIPO's power to grant CL. The amendment took effect on 1 January 2013. The new provision largely closes down the possibility of granting CL upon application to three narrowly defined situations: (1) - non-commercial exploitation for enhancement of public interest, (2) exploitation of dependent patents, (3) commission by a patentee of acts restricting competition or unfair competition acts determined by a court or by the Taiwanese Fair Trade Commission (TFTC).

[19] The TIPO Tzefatze No. 09618600360 (31 May 2007).

[20] For more details, see Liu (2011), p. 89.

[21] The European Union reacted strongly to the TIPO's decision to grant compulsory licence against Philips and demanded that Taiwan revise provisions on compulsory licence and "ensure that precedential effects of the measures are eliminated, including ensuring that the compulsory licenses are revoked in their entirety" within 2 months from the transmission of the report to the TIPO. Under such threat, the TIPO undertook to revise the Patent Act.

Article 87(2) prescribes grounds for compulsory licensing:

> 1. Under any of the following circumstances, for which compulsory patent licensing is necessary, the Specific Patent Agency may, upon request, grant compulsory licensing of a patent: (1) where the patented invention is exploited non-for-profit for the enhancement of public interest; (2) where a later invention or utility model patent cannot be exploited without infringing a prior invention or utility model patent, and where the later invention or utility model patent involves an important technical advancement of considerable economic significance in relation to the prior invention or utility model patent;(3) where a patentee has be found committing acts restricting competition or unfair competition acts by a court or by the TFTC.[22]

Application for CL of a patent covering semiconductor technology shall be filed based on the grounds set forth in Subparagraphs 1 and 3 of the preceding Paragraph (Article 87(3)). Application for CL of a patent in accordance with Subparagraphs 1 through 2 of Paragraph 2 may only be permitted if the requestor for CL has made efforts to obtain authorisation from the right holder on reasonable commercial terms and conditions and such efforts have not been successful within a reasonable period of time (Article 87(4)). In response to a request for compulsory licensing of a patent in accordance with Subparagraph 2 of Paragraph 2, the owner of the prior patent may propose reasonable terms and conditions and seek the grant of CL of the later patent owned by the requestor (Article 87(5)). Article 88 prescribes the procedure, scope, duration, etc. of a CL. Article 89 deals with the termination of a CL.

2.2 *Government Use*

2.2.1 1944–1994: Limitation or Expropriation of Patents for the Military or State-Run Businesses

The Patent Act did not contain a general government use clause but mentioned two specific kinds of government use. Article 72 stipulated that the government may limit or expropriate patents entirely or partially for military purposes or to meet the needs of state-run enterprises, provided that the patentees have been compensated with money. No record or literature shows that this Article had ever been put to use prior to its deletion in 1994.

[22] Theoretically, any violation of the Fair Trade Act, which is composed of antitrust and unfair competition law, would suffice. However, violation of the unfair competition provision alone would hardly justify the grant of a compulsory licence.

2.2.2 1994–2012: Further Narrowing Down Government Use to National Emergency

Replacing Expropriation with Compulsory Licence

The reason for the deletion of Article 72 of the Patent Act was that "the grounds for CL will be limited by this amendment to national emergency, public-interest-enhancing non-profit use and failure to reach licensing agreement under reasonable commercial terms within a reasonable period. In case of national emergency, a much more serious scenario than the military use and with stricter requirements, only compulsory license of patents can be applied for, whereas expropriation of patents can be applied to military use. This seems to be out of balance. As for the expropriation of patents to meet the needs of state-run enterprises, it runs counter to the established policy of privatisation of state-run enterprises. To avoid undue involvement of the public sector in private economic activities, such provision is therefore deleted". The deletion has not aroused much debate even though it is very dubious whether compulsory licensing for national emergency and government use for the military are comparable at all and it is not clear which scenario can be said to be more serious than the other.

The Practice: The Tamiflu Case

On 31 October 2005, the Department of Health (DOH) filed with the TIPO an application for a CL to use a patented drug owned by Gilead Sciences, Inc., USA and exclusively licensed to F. Hoffmann-La Roche Ltd, Switzerland. The application was motivated by the fear that an epidemic of avian flu might break out in Taiwan. In less than 2 months, the TIPO approved conditionally the application for manufacturing such patented capsules until 31 December 2007. Thanks to the fact that the feared epidemic did not break out, the CL was not implemented.[23]

2.2.3 The 2013 Patent Act

The 2013 Patent Act's revision of government use was mainly driven by the need of government authorities to respond to national emergency or other circumstances of extreme urgency immediately without having to file an application for compulsory licence and for the sake of "clearly delineating the division of competence and responsibility between offices" (cited from the legislative reasons). There has not been much parliamentary debate on this revision. According to Article 87 (1), in response to national emergency or other circumstances of extreme urgency, the TIPO shall, in accordance with an Emergency Order or upon notice from the

[23] Liu (2008), p. 67.

competent central government authorities, grant compulsory licence and notify the patentee as soon as reasonably practicable. In other words, the TIPO no longer has to make a decision and will just issue a compulsory licence automatically.

2.3 Assessment of the 2013 Patent Act Regime on Compulsory Licence and Government Use

2.3.1 Compulsory Licence

By and large, the new provisions on compulsory licensing are in regress, rather than progressing, in terms of furthering public interests, mainly because a general clause for compulsory licence is missing (such as Article 67 of the Patent Act between 1949 and 1994), which is common in Germany,[24] Japan,[25] and the UK.[26]

The Legacy of the Philips CD-R Case

The Philips CD-R case was annulled by the TIPO on the ground that it was no longer needed and by the Taipei Administrative High Court for not being inclusive enough in determining reasonable commercial terms and conditions. Notwithstanding, the substantive reasons of the Philips CD-R case remain unchallenged and therefore command precedential or at least guiding effects for the interpretation of the new patent law.

According to the Philips CD-R ruling, the standing of the applicant to file for compulsory licence will not be affected by his/her use of the patent at issue prior to the filing[27]; factors to be taken into consideration when determining the reasonable commercial terms and conditions include the calculation methods for royalty; the benefits to the licensor and licensee; the shared risks; the renown of the technical brand; market demands; the scope, duration, and technology of the licence; horizontal competition; conditions in the licensing market; and the clauses contained in the licensing agreement.[28] It cannot be concluded as reasonable commercial terms and conditions when it is solely based on the calculation methods for royalty proposed by the applicant; "reasonable period of time" shall be determined

[24] See the chapter "Compulsory Licensing in Germany" by Philipp Maume, in this volume.

[25] Masabumi Suzuki/Yoshiyuki Tamura, chapter 5 in Liu and Hilty (2012), pp. 33–60.

[26] For a detailed discussion of the patent law of the UK, see Liu (2012), p. 688.

[27] Liu (2008), p. 67. Whether the alleged infringer of a patent can use CL as a defence against infringement claim only when the TIPO actually granted such licence beforehand remains to be clarified by courts.

[28] Liu (2011), p. 89.

according to general social conceptions and not unilaterally by the length asserted by either the applicant or his/her opposing party.[29]

Depriving the Patentee of Procedural Right to Be Heard Prior to the Grant of Compulsory Licence in Circumstances of Extreme Urgency

It is undoubtedly true that national emergency allows no time for negotiating a voluntary licensing agreement for the needed patent. That's why the second sentence of Article 31 (b) of the TRIPS Agreement waives a prior negotiation requirement as stipulated in the first sentence. However, the basic right of being heard before the handing down of an adverse decision cannot be waived altogether in other circumstances of extreme urgency. In addition, the involvement of the patentee before the competent central government authorities can substantially contribute to the correct evaluation of the case and the outcome of such a compulsory licence.

Abandoning the TIPO's Gatekeeper Role in National Emergency and Circumstances of Extreme Urgency

In case of national emergency and circumstances of extreme urgency, all that is required of the TIPO is to notify the patentee as soon as reasonably practicable. The TIPO no longer has any role to play. Whether the requested patent is the right cure compared to other alternative patents and whether some ancillary orders (such as providing aid or know-how information[30]) are required to work the CL are entirely left with the President or the competent central government authorities, who are unfamiliar with the patent landscape. The TIPO should at least intervene when the President and the competent central government authorities decide on the grant of CL and not abandon its gatekeeper role.

Erroneously Limiting Public Interest Use to Not-for-Profit

The provision on not-for-profit use that would enhance public interest stands out for two reasons. For one thing, it does not elaborate on the meaning or scope of public interest,[31] which provides courts with little guidance on its application. Without clear guidance, courts in Taiwan tend to interpret public interest narrowly. For

---

[29] Liu (2008), pp. 68–70.

[30] For a detailed discussion of ancillary orders that are required to make the issued compulsory licence work, see the chapter "Ancillary Orders of Compulsory Licensing and Their Compatibility with the TRIPS Agreement" by Richard Li-dar Wang, in this volume.

[31] According to Chen (1995), p. 186, public interest should be interpreted broadly to include at least national defence, national health, medicines, food, and environmental protection.

another, it limits such CL to not-for-profit use, a limitation that is in itself infeasible in a market economy and therefore cannot be found in the much looked-up patent law of, say, Germany and the UK.[32] Not-for-profit should not be the precondition for compulsory licence.[33]

Public Non-commercial Use Stricter Than TRIPS[34]

According to Article 87(3), the application for public non-commercial use may only be permitted if the applicant for compulsory licence has made efforts to obtain authorisation from the right holder on reasonable commercial terms and conditions and such efforts have not been successful within a reasonable period of time. However, under Article 31(b) of the TRIPS Agreement, this requirement of prior unsuccessful negotiation may be waived by a Member in cases of public non-commercial use. In comparison, Article 87(3) is stricter than Article 31(b) of the TRIPS Agreement and wrongfully favours patentees' interest over public interest.

The Immediate Determination of Remuneration Runs the Risk of Being Premature and Incorrect

According to Article 88(3), a decision on an application for compulsory licence shall indicate the required remuneration. The legislative reason was that "the current two-stage approach (negotiate first, the TIPO intervenes later when dispute arises) was time-consuming and the patentee cannot be compensated in time". Indeed, in Germany, the remuneration will be decided by the Federal Patent Court when it grants CL and the payment of which is the precondition for such a grant.[35] However, in Germany, one can rather easily draw a good picture of what constitutes reasonable compensation for a specific licensing agreement with help from literature such as "Licensing Rates for Technical Inventions".[36]

In sharp contrast, it would be extremely difficult, if not impossible, for the TIPO to intervene and decide the reasonable remuneration in a void (without external help) and in advance. Only the later and actual development of the market can

---

[32] For a detailed discussion of the patent law of Germany, see Liu (2012), p. 689.

[33] Patent Declaration that "In determining the scope and duration of a compulsory license states should take into account the commercial interests of licensees. A Compulsory licensee should not be deprived of the possibility of obtaining reasonable compensation and an adequate return on investment. Otherwise, he or she will have no incentive to apply for a compulsory license in the first place." (Paragraph 32).

[34] Shieh (2012), p. 49.

[35] Wilhelm in Fitzner/Lutz/Bodewig, PatRKomm, 4th ed., 2012, PatG § 24 Rn. 56; Benkard/Rogge, Patentgesetz, 10th ed., 2006 § 24, Rdnr. 33.

[36] For a detailed discussion, see Liu (2012), p. 696.

better tell. One wonders why the Patent Act would not follow the wisdom of the "Orange Book" decision by the German Supreme Court by requiring the applicant to first pay an amount according to equitable discretion and letting the parties work out the difference later with the assistance from the TIPO.

Unduly Excluding Design Patents from Compulsory Licensing

Article 87(2) mentions only invention patents and utility model patents as the scope of CL and government use, and Article 142 does not apply Articles 87 and 88 mutatis mutandis to design patents. This seems to mismatch the growing importance of design patents in an interconnected world.[37] According to the Copyright, Designs and Patents Act 1988, UK, the government has power to grant CL for both registered and unregistered designs for protection of the public interest.[38] This would be very much needed Taiwan in the foreseeable future.

2.3.2 Government Use

The Legacy of the Tamiflu Case

According to the Tamiflu case, which was not challenged by the parties or courts, what constitutes a national emergency shall be determined by competent national authorities alone; in case of national emergency, the patent at issue needs not be the only or last means to cope with it, and the guarantee by the patentee that he/she will provide the patented drug ahead of the scheduled delivery date cannot dissolve the national emergency in time.[39]

---

[37] However, some are still of the opinion that design patents are not related to public interest at all; see Yang (2003), p. 456.

[38] Section 238 provides: (1) Subsection (1A) applies where whatever needs to be remedied, mitigated or consists of or includes—(a) conditions in licences granted by an unregistered design right owner restricting the use of the design by the licensee or the right of the design right owner to grant other licences, or (b) a refusal of a design right owner to grant licences on reasonable terms. (1A) The powers (by the Secretary of State, the Competition Commission or the Office of Fair Trading) conferred by Schedule 8 to the Enterprise Act of 2002 include power to cancel or modify those conditions and, instead or in addition, to provide that licences in respect of the design right shall be available as of right. (3) The terms of a licence available by virtue of this section shall, in default of agreement, be settled by the comptroller. Section 270 provides the same powers exercisable for protection of the public interest when it comes to registered designs: (1) The registrar may by order cancel or modify any such condition or may, instead or in addition, make an entry in the register to the effect that licences in respect of the design are to be available as of right. (2) The terms of a licence available by virtue of this section shall, in default of agreement, be settled by the registrar on an application by the person requiring the licence; and terms so settled shall authorise the licensee to do everything which would be an infringement of the right in the registered design in the absence of a licence.

[39] Liu (2008), pp. 71–75.

The Scope and Requirement of Government Use Too Narrow and Stringent

The 2013 Patent Act mistakenly limits government use to national emergency and circumstances of extreme urgency, excluding other public interest concerns that might be of lesser gravity yet equally legitimate, such as health care, environment protection, and national defence. The Patent Act further ties national emergency only to an Emergency Order issued by the President, which happened only once after the lifting of Martial Law in 1987.[40] What's really worrying is that the function and legitimacy of government use seem to have gradually faded away from the realm of patent law under the influence of technocrats of the TIPO.

3 The Fair Trade Act

In principle, CL can also be acquired via the application of the Fair Trade Act. However, the TFTC has not yet seen compulsory licence as one of the "necessary corrective measures" of the Fair Trade Act, although it did find a violation of the Fair Trade Act in the Philips CD-R case.

The FTTC found in the Philips CD-R case abuses of a joint monopolistic position by and cartel[41] among Philips, Sony, and Taiyo Yuden and imposed NT $8 million, NT$4 million, and NT$2 million fines, respectively, but in one administrative decision and not three. While the Taipei Administrative High Court upheld the first finding and overruled the second, it found itself unable to render an "affirmed-in-part, vacated-in-part" decision and was compelled to rescind the TFTC's decision as a whole. Both the TFTC and the complainant appealed the case to the Supreme Administrative Court, which was rejected on 4 April 2007.[42]

The case was remitted back to the TFTC, which came to the same conclusion that the following exploitative abuse of monopoly power violated Article 10(2) and (4) of the Fair Trade Act: refusing to renegotiate royalty with licensees while there have been significant changes in the market; refusing to provide licensees with

[40] In 1999, an Emergency Order was issued by the President after a magnitude 7.3 earthquake hit Taiwan.

[41] However, the Taipei Administrative High Court was of a totally different opinion and was guided by the following facts: (1) the TFTC has determined the relevant market to be the "CD-R technology market"; (2) what the TFTC defined as CD-R is products produced in accordance with the standards specified in the Orange Book set up by Philips and Sony; (3) local CD-R manufacturers must use all the patents owned by Philips et al. in order to make CD-Rs; (4) using patents of any one of the three companies would not be sufficient to manufacture CD-Rs; (5) therefore, patents owned by Philips et al. were complementary in nature and every pooled patent was indispensable, which made the patented technology no longer substitutable, and no competition relationship could exist between Philips et al.

[42] The Supreme Administrative Court Pantze 553 of 2007 (4 April 2007).

information about the content, scope, or valid term of the licensed patents; and commanding that licensees not challenge the validity of the licensed patents.[43]

In case the TFTC reaches the finding that an IP owner has abused its monopolistic market power by charging prohibitively high royalty, it is arguably desirable for the TFTC to issue CL thereupon so as to avoid the delay that will ensue when the victim of such abuse has to file with the TIPO an extra application for compulsory licence.

4 Concluding Remarks

Taiwan has accepted the amendment of the TRIPS Agreement proposed by the general council of the World Trade Organization on 31 July 2012. To honor that international commitment the 2013 revision to the Patent Act introduces provisions on Compulsory licensing for pharmaceuticals to export (CLPE). Article 90 prescribes grounds of and procedures for CLPE for assisting countries with insufficient or no manufacturing capacities in the pharmaceutical sector to obtain pharmaceutical product(s) needed in treating HIV/AIDS, tuberculosis, malaria, and other epidemics. Article 91 deals with the export of patented pharmaceutical products made under the compulsory licence and the remuneration for the patentees.

Although CLPE is conceptually similar to government use, it differs from the latter in that it is the result of international human brotherhood and therefore for the use of foreign government rather than for domestic government.

References

Antonelli C (2013) Compulsory licensing: the foundations of an institutional innovation. WIPO J Anal Intellect Prop Iss 4(2):157–174
Chen W-Y (1995) Study of patent regime (in Chinese). Taipei
Chen W-Y (1997) Patent law (in Chinese). Taipei
Liu K-C (2008) IPR enforcement and competition act (in Chinese), 3rd edn, Taipei
Liu K-C (2011) The Taiwanese "Philips" CD-R cases: abuses of a monopolistic position, cartel and compulsory patent licensing, chapter 6. In: Heath C, Sanders A (eds) Landmark intellectual property cases and their legacy. Kluwer Law International, Alphen aan den Rijn
Liu K-C (2012) The need of and justification for a general competition-oriented compulsory licensing. Int Rev Ind Prop Competition Law 43(6):679–699
Masabumi Suzuki/Yoshiyuki Tamura in Liu K-C, Hilty R (eds) (2012) The enforcement of patents. Max Planck Asian intellectual property law series, pp 33–60
Nin Y-F (1972) Industrial Property Rights Law. Taipei
Nin Y-F (1982) Industrial Property Rights Law. Taipei
Shieh M-Y (2012) Comments on and analysis of the newly revised patent act (in Chinese). Taiwan Law Rev (205):44–57
Yang C-S (2003) The theory and application of the patent law (in Chinese). Taipei

[43] The TFTC Tzutze 098156 (29 October 2009).

Compulsory Licensing in Germany

Philipp Maume

Contents

Abstract In the last 20 years, German courts have developed a sophisticated approach to compulsory licensing of patents. Compulsory licences under competition law are of particularly high relevance. In short, German competition law obliges the holder of a patent, which is essential in a standard to grant a licence on terms that are fair, reasonable, and non-discriminatory (FRAND). Users of such patents can also raise a so-called competition law defence against imminent injunction orders. The German courts' approaches to this defence have become more and

P. Maume, Ph.D. (Augsburg), S.J.D. (La Trobe), is Assistant Professor.

P. Maume
TUM School of Management, Technische Universität München, Munich, Germany
e-mail: philipp.maume@tum.de

R.M. Hilty and K.-C. Liu (eds.), *Compulsory Licensing*, MPI Studies on Intellectual Property and Competition Law 22, DOI 10.1007/978-3-642-54704-1_6,

more sophisticated over the last years, trying to close a number of structural gaps in the Federal Supreme Court ruling *Orange Book Standard*. However, it remains unclear if or to what extent the defence complies with European law.

The resonance of the German debate in international scholarly literature has remained relatively low, probably because of the language barrier. Most works merely scratch the surface of the particularly complex issues. This chapter provides an in-depth analysis of the German legal background and the consequences in practice. It suggests a streamlined, simplified approach to competition-law-based defences.

1 Introduction

Compulsory licences under German law have been subject to prolific debate in the last two decades. In particular, three periods can be identified, each related to a Federal Court of Justice decision. First, the discussion focused on sec 24 of the Patent Act (PatG)[1] and its ambit, resulting in the decision *Polyferon* in 1996. Second, facilitated by the debate about compulsory licences under European law, the possibility of patent licences under competition law was clarified in the decision *Standard Spundfass* in 2004. The third and final phase revolved around competition law defences in patent infringement proceedings, resulting in the decision *Orange Book Standard* in 2009.

The importance of compulsory licences under German law transcends national borders and has a significant impact on technology companies all over Europe. Germany is Europe's biggest economy and retail market, and its location makes it essential for the distribution of products throughout the continent. Germany is by far the most important forum for patent litigation in Europe,[2] with non-German companies making use of the technical expertise of the German patent court system.[3] However, the resonance of the German debate in international scholarly literature is relatively low.[4] This is probably caused by the particularities of the German legal system and language barriers. This chapter gives an overview of the development of compulsory licensing in Germany, the leading decisions, and their implications in practice. It argues that although the Federal Court of Justice has introduced a solid legal basis for compulsory licences, the decision *Orange Book*

[1] Patentgesetz (PatG).

[2] A survey conducted by the Council of the European Union in 2007 suggests that German patent courts are dealing with more patent lawsuits (600–700 matters p.a.) than the two next 'biggest' forums, France (450 matters p.a.) and England (150 matters p.a.) combined; see Council of the European Union, Working Document 11622/07 (12 July 2007), at 23–31.

[3] Ann (2009), p. 205.

[4] In this chapter, reference will be given to publications in English whenever possible. However, a lot of relevant sources, in particular on competition law defences, are only available in German.

Standard has failed to establish a simple and transparent procedure for introducing competition-based defences into patent infringement proceedings.

2 Compulsory Licences Under the Patent Law

2.1 Structure and Practical Relevance

The compulsory licence, which can be granted under sec 24 of the PatG, is a classical compulsory licence. The provision was redesigned in 1998 to ensure compliance with the Agreement on Trade Related Aspects of Intellectual Property Rights (TRIPS). Sec 24 addresses use of the patent 'without authorisation of the patent holder' as envisaged by Art 31 of TRIPS.

The licence is granted by the Federal Patent Court in Munich. The licence is non-exclusive, and the patentee needs to be remunerated, taking into account the commercial value of the patent.[5] The grant of the compulsory licence is subject to two conditions. First, prior to the application, the applicant must have sought to obtain a licence from the patent holder on reasonable conditions usual in trade. Second, the grant of the compulsory licence needs to satisfy a public interest test.[6] As set out in sec 24(5), the public interest test is satisfied in the event the patentee does not use the patented invention (or not predominantly in Germany) and the compulsory licence would ensure an adequate supply of the patented product to the domestic market. Sec 24 further sets out two special situations: for compulsory licences in the field of semiconductor technology, the grant is only possible if necessary to remove an anti-competitive practice that has previously been established in judicial or administrative proceedings.[7] For dependency licence, the applicant's invention must exhibit an important technical advance of considerable economic significance in relation to the invention claimed in the first patent.[8]

Between 1923 and 1943, German courts granted a total of 23 compulsory licences.[9] Since its inception in 1961, the Federal Patent Court's reports evidence only 20 applications for a compulsory licence under sec 24.[10] It was only in one case, which will be discussed later, that the Federal Patent Court granted a compulsory licence. One possible reason for these low numbers could be that potential

[5] PatG, Sec. 24(6).

[6] PatG, Sec 24(1).

[7] PatG, Sec 24(4).

[8] PatG, Sec 24(2). See discussion in the chapter "The Requirements for Compulsory Dependency Licences: Learning from the Transformative Use Doctrine in Copyright Law" by Matthias Leistner, in this volume.

[9] Kraßer (2009), para. 34 IV(b).

[10] For an overview, see Benkard (2006), Sec. 24, note 4.

users are more confident to challenge the validity of the patent itself.[11] However, scholars argue that the mere existence of the provision facilitates a patentee's willingness to enter into a licence agreement[12] ('hammer on the wall' argument).

2.2 The Public Interest: Polyferon[13]

The main question under sec 24 is whether the grant of the licence is in the 'public interest'. Due to the low number of court decisions, it was not until 1996 that the Federal Court of Justice could shed light on the meaning of the term. The background of the decision is emblematic for compulsory licences in Germany: Polyferon was a medication against arthritis that was covered by a German patent not held by the manufacturer. The patent holder was planning to apply for an accreditation for his own product but hadn't filed the application yet. The manufacturer of Polyferon had asked the patent holder to grant a licence on reasonable terms. The patent holder had declined and commenced patent infringement proceedings against the manufacturer. The District Court Düsseldorf granted an injunction, prohibiting the distribution of Polyferon by the manufacturer. Thereupon, the manufacturer applied for a compulsory licence under sec 24.

The applicant argued that the patent holder's own product had not been accredited by the German authorities yet and Polyferon was the only available medication to battle a particular kind of arthritis. Thus, a compulsory licence would be in the public interest.[14] The Federal Patent Court granted the compulsory licence because it saw the need for an adequate medication. The licence was then revoked on appeal by the Federal Court of Justice. The Court held that supplying the population with important medication might be in the public interest; however, there was no conclusive evidence that Polyferon was required to supply the population with essential medication.[15] So the Federal Court of Justice applied a strict, narrow understanding of the public interest, which is difficult to meet in practice.

More generally, the Court held that the public interest could have technical, economical, social, or medical aspects.[16] Significantly, this list of possible grounds does not include competition. In addition, the grant of a compulsory licence under sec 24 does not require abusive conduct by the patentee. In other words, potentially anti-competitive conduct by a market dominator (for example, a refusal to grant a

[11] Scheffler (2003), at p. 100.

[12] Kraßer (2009).

[13] Federal Court of Justice, *Polyferon*, File Number X ZR 26/92, 5 December 1995, reported in BGHZ 131, 247. The decision is sometimes also referred to as *Interferon/Gamma*.

[14] Federal Patent Court, 7 June 1991, reported in BPatGE 32, 184.

[15] Federal Court of Justice, supra note 13, at 257 et seq.

[16] Ibid.

licence on reasonable terms) is not a ground to grant a compulsory licence under sec 24, unless the grant of the licence would be in the public interest. The patentee's competitors are unable to 'mask' their business interest in obtaining a licence as public interest. As a result, it is factually impossible for competitors to obtain a compulsory patent licence on competition grounds under sec 24 of the PatG.

3 Compulsory Licences Under Competition Law

3.1 Statutory Basis

After *Polyferon*, the legal debate shifted towards competition law. The approach taken for compulsory licences under competition law differs from compulsory licences under the PatG. Under competition law, it is prohibited to abuse a dominant market position. Under European law, this principle is set out in Art 102 of the Treaty on the Functioning of the European Union (TFEU); the German equivalent is sec 19(1) of the Act against Restraints of Competition (GWB).[17] Assumptions on the relationship between market shares and market powers are set out in sec 19 (2) and (3), and sec 19(4) describes examples of abusive conduct. Sec 19 is flanked by sec 20(1), which sets out that a company in a dominating position may not unduly constrain or discriminate other companies. The provisions are not seen as separate rules but rather as one coherent rule prohibiting market power abuse in Germany.[18] Similar to Art 102 TFEU, typical examples of abuse of a dominant position are overpricing, price fixing, and refusal to deal.[19] The remedies for breaches of the GWB and the TFEU are set out in sec 33 of the GWB. For abuses of market power, the common remedies are compensation under sec 33(3) and, if the misconduct is still going on, abatement under sec 33(1). Importantly, the GWB only addresses abusive conduct in general without referring to intellectual property rights. So the question arose as to whether the 'normal' rules for the abuse of market power applied also to patent holders or whether the courts would need to develop a different approach.

3.2 The Interface Between Patent and Competition Laws

In the 1990s and early 2000s, the debate on the relationship between intellectual property law and competition law was discussed under European law. In the

[17] Gesetz gegen Wettbewerbsbeschränkungen (GWB).

[18] For convenience, the rule will be henceforth referred to as 'sec 20'.

[19] See Loewenheim et al. (2009), Sec. 19 GWB, note 91–106.

decisions *Magill*[20] and *IMS Health*,[21] the European Court of Justice (ECJ) established the obligation of a holder of intellectual property rights to grant licences under Art 82 EC (now Art 102 TFEU) in certain circumstances.[22] Although the decisions dealt with copyrights and protected databases, there was little doubt that the decisions also applied to patents.

The question remained whether compulsory licences were also possible under German competition law and, if so, under which conditions. This debate predates the ECJ decisions and started when the GWB was introduced in 1957. Two main arguments against compulsory licences under competition law were put forward.[23] First, the GWB does not explicitly refer to intellectual property. Conversely, the PatG sets out detailed procedures and prerequisites for compulsory patent licences. Thus, the GWB as the more general statute could not be used to circumvent the more specific PatG. Second, a patent holder who refuses to grant licences does exactly what the patent is allowing him to do. Limiting the patentee's rights on competition grounds would turn the basic principles of intellectual property rights upside down and, eventually, threaten the patent system as such.[24]

3.3 *The Grounds for Compulsory Licences:* Standard Spundfass[25]

3.3.1 Background

The first landmark decision on compulsory licensing and the abuse of market power was *Standard-Spundfass* in 2004. It involves a standardised type of industry drum ('Standard Spundfass', or 'standard tight-head drum'). In the late 1990s, the German Chemical Industry Association (VCI) had called for the submission of proposals for a new kind of drum with an improved draining mechanism. According to the VCI terms, the best proposal would be made the official recommendation, which means it would become the de facto standard in the German chemical industry. The winner would patent the technology and grant royalty-free licences

[20] European Court of Justice, *RTE and ITP v Commission* (C-241/91 P and C-242/91 P) [1995] ECR I-743.

[21] European Court of Justice, *IMS Health v NDC Health* (C-418/01) [2004] ECR I-5039.

[22] For discussion, see the chapter "Refusal to License as an Abuse of Market Dominance: From Commercial Solvents to Microsoft" by Matthias Lamping, in this volume.

[23] For a detailed discussion, see Maume (2010), at pp. 6–13.

[24] Ibid.

[25] The Federal Court of Justice, *Standard Spundfass*, File Number KZR 40/02, 13 July 2004, reported in BGHZ 160, 67. For convenience, reference will be made to the English translation available at 36 IIC 741 (2005).

to the other companies that had submitted proposals. All other manufacturers would be granted licences on reasonable terms.

An Italian manufacturer of industry drums that had not submitted its own design approached the patent holder and demanded a free licence. The manufacturer argued that the patentee was a monopolist and that the refusal to grant a royalty-free licence would be discriminatory because the manufacturer's competitors held such licences. Thus, the patentee would abuse his market power under German competition law. The patentee argued that he was just exercising his rights conferred by the patent.

3.3.2 Obligation to Grant a Licence Under Special Circumstances

The Federal Court of Justice's reasoning laid out the foundations for compulsory licensing in Germany. The Court held in accordance with its ruling in *Polyferon* that sec 24 of the PatG did not provide for a compulsory licence on competition grounds. However, it held that the provision does not rule out that compulsory licences might be granted for other reasons, such as the abuse of market power under sec 20 of the GWB.[26] The two provisions serve different purposes and have different requirements—while the PatG contains a public interest test, the GWB requires the abuse of a dominant market position.[27] Therefore, sec 24 of the PatG is not more specific than sec 20 of the GWB, as the provisions are different in nature.

The Federal Court of Justice also elaborated on market power. The Court followed the idea that a patent grants exclusive rights to the patentee but not automatically a dominant position in a product market. Even if the grant of a patent resulted in a dominant market position, the legal position stemming from the patent requires protection.[28] In particular, the patentee retains a wide discretion as to whether to grant a licence or not and under which conditions. As a result, the scope for objective justification of unequal treatment of would-be licensees is fundamentally broad.

However, stricter requirements for justification might be considered if additional circumstances exist in light of which the unequal treatment endangers the freedom of competition as envisaged in the GWB.[29] Such special circumstances could arise if an industrial standard or a standard-like set of conditions makes using the patent essential to access a downstream product market. The Court emphasised that it does not matter if the patentee initiated, contributed to, or at least approved the standard. It is sufficient that the patentee benefits from the standard. If the patentee exploits this situation to restrict market access by criteria that contradict the freedom of

[26] Ibid, at 744.

[27] Ibid.

[28] Ibid, at 746.

[29] Ibid.

competition, then he is abusing his market-dominating position.[30] The result would be an obligation to grant a licence to ensure the soundness of competition on the product market.

3.3.3 Licence Conditions

The Court acknowledged that the obligation to grant a licence does not strip the patentee of its entrepreneurial freedom. The Court in particular held that the patentee was not required to accept any offers of licensees-to-be, as the pursuit of best conditions and prices by market participants is generally consistent with fair competition.[31] In particular, competition law does not provide any blanket most-favoured-status clause intended to force the dominant undertaking in general to provide the same favourable conditions, especially prices. Even undertakings that dominate a market should not be prevented from reacting differently to different market conditions. Hence, an unequal treatment of licensees is justified as long as the underlying considerations and intentions stem from sound economic and entrepreneurial behaviour. The type and extent of the unequal treatment is the key.[32] In other words, the royalties that can be justified by the patentee need to be assessed for every case separately.

3.3.4 Implications

Broadly, *Standard Spundfass* established an obligation to grant a licence for patents if use of the protected technology is necessary for accessing product markets where the patent is part of an established market standard. More broadly, special circumstances that might justify such an obligation arise when the reward earned by the patent's exclusivity does not result from the invention itself but from external factors (such as standards). Thereby, the Federal Court of Justice followed an approach that is more economics based than the ECJ with its new product rule (as established in *IMS Health*).[33] Although *Standard Spundfass* dealt with a de facto standard, it also applies to consensual standards that were established by market participants or via standard-setting organisations.[34]

---

[30] Ibid.

[31] Ibid, at 747.

[32] Ibid.

[33] European Court of Justice, *IMS Health v NDC Health* (C-418/01) [2004] ECR I-5039, paras. 37–38. See also Leistner (2005), p. 750.

[34] Subsequent court decisions are clear about the fact that the obligation to grant a licence and potential competition law defences apply to de facto and contractual market standards in the same manner; see, e.g., Court of Appeal Düsseldorf, *UMTS Mobilstation*, File Number 4b O 273/10, 24 March 2011, available at http://www.duesseldorfer-archiv.de/?q=node/4426.

Despite covering different issues and setting out different prerequisites for the licence, the thrust of the Federal Court of Justice decision is roughly consistent with the ECJ decisions *Magill* and *IMS Health*. Both courts used arguments that were developed under the essential facilities doctrine.[35] Intellectual property rights grant their owners exclusivity rights but are subject to competition law control. The Federal Court of Justice's reasoning relates to the general relationship between intellectual property rights and competition law. It is noteworthy that patent standards are just given as an example for special circumstances from which an obligation to grant a licence might arise. It is also likely that the doctrine of special circumstances might apply to other intellectual property rights that have become part of a standard. An example could be software code, which is protected by copyright or a *sui generis* right.

Standard Spundfass did not, however, clarify all open questions. The Court's statements on the right licence conditions remain rather general. Although not expressly stated by the Court, it is widely accepted that the conditions need to be 'fair, reasonable and non-discriminatory' (FRAND).[36] This interpretation accords the best practice by standardisation organisations.[37] However, the Court's theoretical approach allowed owners of essential patents to argue that the conditions offered by prospective licensees were insufficient and therefore not FRAND. In practice, the main argument between patentee and licensee shifted away from whether the licence was to be granted towards how the licence was to be granted. Hence, although laying the theoretical foundations, *Standards Spundfass* did not provide a comprehensive sketch for sorting out the practical issues of compulsory licensing in Germany.

4 Competition Law Defences Against Patent Law Claims

4.1 Background

Standard Spundfass established that competition laws could force patentees to grant licences of intellectual property rights under certain circumstances. After 2004, more and more defendants in patent infringement proceedings raised a new kind of defence. They argued that the patentee could not be granted compensation and injunction orders on the basis that it was under an obligation to licence the patent. The patentee could not prevail in court because it would be in breach of competition

[35] Fine (2002), p. 457; Liu (2008), p. 757.

[36] For example, Herr (2009), p. 10; Treacy and Lawrance (2008), p. 22; Zhang (2010), at p. 401; Tapia (2010), at p. 16.

[37] See, for example, Cl 6.1 ETSI IPR-Policy, available at http://www.etsi.org/images/etsi_ipr-policy.pdf.

law. This argument became known as the 'competition law defence' (Zwangslizenzeinwand).[38]

The problem is unique to intellectual property as the defendant does not require the other party's cooperation to use the protected information. For example, under a sale of goods contract, the purchaser needs to rely on the seller for delivery. Similarly, if access to an essential facility was demanded, the market-dominating undertaking was still required to take action to grant the access. If the dominating undertaking did not comply with these obligations, the other side could take legal action in the civil court or try to convince the competition authorities to take administrative action. In contrast, if a patent is at issue, potential users don't need to rely on the patentee—they can simply use the patent.

Because of this unique background, no existing patent law or competition law rules address the issue. Nevertheless, the defence was raised in a growing number of court cases. The courts therefore needed to rely on general law principles to determine whether the competition law defence could be successfully raised in infringement proceedings and what the prerequisites would be.

4.2 Compensation

The first question was whether the defence could be raised against compensation claims under sec 139(2) of the PatG. The main argument was that a patentee would be liable for compensation under sec 33(3) of the GWB if he refused to grant the desired licence. The patentee's claim under sec 139(2) of the PatG and the user's claim under sec 33(3) of the GWB could then be set off against each other.[39] This would effectively limit or even neutralise the patentee's right to be compensated.

The Federal Court of Justice accepted this argument to a certain extent. In the *Standard Spundfass* decision, the Federal Court of Justice held that 'compensation for damages to the patentee resulting from the use ... can in any case only be demanded for the amount to which the plaintiff would have been entitled if it had not illegally refused to grant the defendant . . . a license'. If the defendant had made the patentee an offer on acceptable terms prior to using the patent and if the patentee had refused this offer, the patentee would only be entitled to the royalties set out in the offer. Hence, the infringer's obligation to pay compensation remains untouched. The defence, however, limits the patentee's compensation claim to the equivalent of adequate royalties.[40] Thus, the Federal Court of Justice resolved the problem by

[38] Alternatively, the defence is referred to as 'antitrust defence' or 'antitrust objection'. It seems that an English translation has not yet been established.

[39] Kühnen (2003), at p. 523.

[40] Under German patent law, the patentee can choose from three different methods for calculating damages: (1) the profits lost due to the infringement, (2) licence analogy, meaning an amount of compensation equivalent to adequate royalties under a licence agreement, and (3) disgorgement of profits. For discussion, see Benkard (2006), paras. 61–75a.

applying the existing patent law and followed the idea that compulsory licences require the patentee to be compensated. Due to the small differences between 'normal' patent infringements and an infringement of an essential patent whose owner is under an obligation to grant a licence, the practical importance of a competition law defence raised against compensation claims is rather low.

4.3 *Injunction*

Raising the defence against injunction claims under sec 139(1) of the PatG is of much higher practical relevance. The reason is that an invalid defence would lead to an injunction order. As a result, the defendant would often need to take an established product off the market, with potentially devastating consequences. Despite the landmark decision *Orange Book Standard*, the issue has not been fully clarified yet.

4.3.1 The Arguments

Several arguments were raised in favour of the defence. By refusing to grant the licence, the plaintiff violated sec 20 of the GWB.[41] By granting an injunction order petitioned by the plaintiff, the court would authorise unlawful conduct. If the licence was claimed under Art 102 TFEU, the injunction order would limit the effectiveness of European law (so-called *effet utile*), making the injunction order invalid.

A second argument referred to general civil law principles. According to sec 242 of the Civil Code, parties of a contract are under an obligation to perform in good faith (*Treu und Glauben*). Courts and scholars have extended this contractual rule to a general principle of fairness for the whole civil law system. One of the most important applications of sec 242 is as a procedural defence if the litigant is exercising his rights in an unfaithful way. This is referred to as abuse of rights (*Rechtsmissbrauch*[42]), which also applies to patent law.[43] One example of such abuse is addressed by the *dolo agit* defence. It prescribes that a litigant cannot successfully obtain an item if the defendant would be entitled to demand the item back because of a counterclaim. Such behaviour would be inconsistent with the litigant's obligations and thus abusive under sec 242. Commentators argued that the same applies to a patentee who is under an obligation to grant a licence.[44] Sooner or

[41] Wirtz and Holzhäuser (2004), at pp. 693 et seq.

[42] This should not be confused with the abuse of a dominant market position under competition law, which is the legal basis for the obligation to grant a licence (see above).

[43] Federal Court of Justice, *Weichvorrichtung II*, File Number X ZR 73/95, 5 June 1997.

[44] Kühnen (2003); Wirtz and Holzhäuser (2004); Heinemann (2005), at p. 199.

later, the patentee and the user would enter into a licence agreement, giving the licensee the right to use the patent. Granting an injunction order would ignore the patentee's obligations under competition law and could be addressed by the *dolo agit* defence.

Further, the protection granted to the defendant under competition law is arguably insufficient. If the patentee refuses to grant the licence without justification, he is liable for compensation under sec 33 of the GWB (see above). However, compensation under competition law requires the aggrieved party to quantify its actual losses, which is virtually impossible. Also, being kept from the downstream market has irrevocable consequences—a compensation payment cannot restore lost market shares.[45]

These arguments were criticised by other commentators. The patentee might be under an obligation to grant a licence, but there is no licence agreement yet. Hence, the patentee still has the right to exclude the defendant from using the patent.[46] Sec 139(1) of the PatG does not provide discretion for the judge whether to grant an injunction or not. If the patent is infringed upon, an injunction needs to be granted. As stated in *Standard Spundfass*, the patentee retains a wide discretion in respect of the licence fees. Respective negotiations may be complicated and lengthy. It cannot be expected that the parties reach an agreement in due course. Thus, enforcing the patentee's rights in court is not abusive under sec 242 of the Civil Code.[47]

Further, German laws provide several ways to address anti-competitive conduct. The appropriate way is to initiate proceedings in the cartel court under sec 33 of the GWB. Before using the patent, the defendant should have initiated an action for performance under sec 33(1). If he was successful, the licence would be granted. Alternatively, the defendant could have tried to convince the competition authorities to take action. By using the patent, the defendant ignored these established remedies and exercised an act of vigilantism and therefore cannot rely on the abuse of rights doctrine under sec 242 of the Civil Code, which stems from equitable principles.

Another issue is Art 31 lit a) of TRIPS. The provision prescribes that authorisation (which means authorisation by public authorities such as courts) shall be considered by the individual merits. The admission of a competition law defence would circumvent this requirement because the patent would be used without court authorisation.[48] It might even be used in cases in which the patentee is under no obligation to grant the licence.

---

45 Maume (2010), at p. 64.

46 Jaecks and Dörmer (2006), p. 97.

47 Von Merveldt (2004), p. 19; Rombach (2008), at p. 321.

48 Rombach (2008).

4.3.2 Discussion

The issue is complicated. Overall, the arguments in favour of the competition law defence seem slightly more convincing.[49] Not allowing the defence would be in stark contrast to the guiding theme: the patentee must allow applicants to use the patent under competition law. Rejecting the defence would open the door for further abuses of market power.

On the other hand, it is convincing that the *dolo agit* rule cannot be applied. The patentee might be under an obligation to grant a licence, and the licence agreement might come into force sooner or later, but it is not clear if and when this will happen. A likely change of the contractual situation is not sufficient to constitute an abuse of rights under sec 242 of the Civil Code. However, there are other aspects if the patentee's behaviour might be abusive. It is an established principle under sec 242 that a party cannot benefit from a situation if it deliberately caused the situation.[50] Speaking more generally, a party cannot benefit from its own misbehaviour. A typical example is an heir who unfaithfully caused the death of the deceased and is thus not entitled to the inheritance. This resembles the competition law defence. By declining a reasonable offer, the patentee is actively thwarting the user's efforts to obtain a licence despite being under an obligation to enter into the contract. The patentee retains its rights under sec 139 of the PatG by unfaithful conduct. Sec 242 of the Civil Code suggests that a patentee cannot benefit from this favourable position that he unfaithfully retained, which means he cannot be granted an injunction.

The risks that the competition law defence presents to patentees should not be underestimated. It is certainly correct that a competition law defence might be used for improper purposes. For this reason, it is crucial to find a way to prevent further abuse without weakening the patentee's position excessively. A possible way would be to require the user to deposit a reasonable amount before using the patent.[51] This would prevent patent infringements 'on spec'.

A practical problem was that users found it difficult to ascertain licence conditions that were reasonable in a way that the patentee was not allowed to decline them without breaching the patentee's obligations under competition law.[52] The reason was that the German rules of civil procedure stipulated a strong protection of company know-how,[53] as well as evidence rules that are unfavourable for the plaintiff (for example, no pretrial discovery). So plaintiffs seeking licences had to 'guess' a royalty rate, putting them into a difficult situation. As a result, the

---

[49] For a detailed discussion of all arguments, see Maume (2010), at pp. 69–110.

[50] Ibid, at 106–110.

[51] Ibid, at 134–139.

[52] Ibid, at 129–134.

[53] Licence conditions (in particular, royalties) are usually protected as know-how.

patentee, who is under no obligation to take the initiative and make an offer himself, could in most cases reject the offer as inappropriate.[54]

4.3.3 Orange Book Standard[55]

The approaches taken by the lower patent courts to address the issue were rather diverse. In two decisions, the District Court Mannheim refused to state whether the defences could, in theory, be raised as it was not relevant for the cases.[56] The Court of Appeal Karlsruhe[57] and the District Court Düsseldorf[58] allowed the defence in principle but prescribed different requirements for its use. As a result, the legal situation was unclear, presenting serious legal uncertainty to market participants.

In May 2009, the Federal Court of Justice published its decision *Orange Book Standard*. The Orange Book Standard is part of the 'Rainbow Books', a collection of compact disc specifications. Orange Book relates to CD-R, which means blank CDs upon which material can be recorded by the user only once. The patent in question described the way different recording layers were aligned on the blank CD. The defendant argued that the patentee was under an obligation to grant a licence under the *Standard Spundfass* principles and raised the competition law defence against the patentee's application for an injunction order.

The Federal Court of Justice allowed the competition law defence on two conditions. First, the defendant must have made an offer under fair, reasonable, and non-discriminatory conditions that the patentee could not lawfully refuse.[59] If the patentee refuses to state appropriate conditions or if these conditions seem unreasonable, the defendant is allowed to make an unspecified offer and to request the patentee to determine the amount of royalties owed.[60] This mechanism is known from sec 315 of the Civil Code, which regulates a party's right to unilaterally

---

[54] The Court of Appeal Karlsruhe, for example, required the prospective licensee to make an offer that aligns to the best conditions the patentee could ask without abusing his market power. In other words, the licensee would have to match these hypothetical conditions without having knowledge about other licences granted by the patentee. This was practically impossible, and the competition law defence would have been useless in practice: see The Court of Appeal Karlsruhe, *Orange Book Standard*, File Number 6 U 174/02, 13 December 2006, available at http://openjur.de/u/209900.html.

[55] Federal Court of Justice, *Orange Book Standard*, File Number KZR 39/06, 6 May 2009, reported in BGHZ 180, 312. For convenience, reference will be made to the English translation available at 41 IIC 369 (2010).

[56] District Court Mannheim, File Number 7 O 94/08, 27 February 2009, available at http://openjur.de/u/341036.html, and File Number 7 O 115/05, 9 November 2007, available at http://openjur.de/u/356346.html.

[57] The Court of Appeal Karlsruhe, supra note 54.

[58] District Court Düsseldorf, *MPEG2-Standard*, File Number 4b O 346/05, 30 November 2006, reported in InstGE 7, 70.

[59] The Federal Court of Justice, supra note 55, para. 29.

[60] Ibid, para. 40.

change the terms of the contract, in particular the monies owed. Typical examples are contracts on utilities (water, gas, etc.) that empower the supplier to adjust the fees if necessary. Court control is provided by sec 315(3), allowing the user to challenge the patentee's determination of licence fees if they appear to be excessive. Second, the defendant must act according to the offer that he made, which means the defendant needs to pay or put the royalties that he had offered prior to using the patent into escrow.[61]

The remarkable implication of the Orange Book Standard model is that the Federal Court of Justice changed the nature of the competition law defence. By determining the royalties under sec 315 of the Civil Code, the patentee accepts the user's offer. Henceforth, a binding licence agreement exists. So the *Orange Book Standard* model is not just a defence in infringement proceedings; it is a new way of establishing licence agreements. This effect also resolves any concerns about TRIPS because the patent is not used without the permission of the patentee.

The decision was welcomed by the majority of commentators.[62] Being able to make an unspecified offer rid potential licensees of the onerous task of guessing what adequate royalties might be. On the other hand, it safeguarded the interests of the patentee by requiring the user to pay or deposit royalties. It seemed that the Court had managed to balance the parties' interests successfully.

4.3.4 Open Questions

As time went by, it became obvious that the *Orange Book Standard* principles were difficult to handle because the Federal Court of Justice did not cover all issues of the offer and the deposit that might arise in practice. Patentees and users, usually assisted by specialised high-profile law firms, tried to exploit gaps and ambiguities to gain a competitive advantage over the other side. Four issues will be explained in more detail now.

Application of *Orange Book Standard* to Essential Patents?

The Federal Court of Justice did not distinguish between de facto and consensual standards that have been established under the auspices of standard setting organisations (SSO). Consequently, the courts are applying the competition law defence to patents that are essential in consensual standards.[63] This is criticised by some

[61] Ibid, para. 36.

[62] Nägele and Jacobs (2009), p. 1062; Busche (2009), p. 104; Heinemann (2009), p. 286659; Jestaedt (2009), p. 801; Gärtner and Vormann (2009), p. 440. Some commentators, however, criticised the Court's narrow understanding of competition law (Ullrich 2010a, p. 337) and a misapplication of European law principles, in particular the *effet utile* (de Bronett 2009, p. 899).

[63] The District Court Mannheim, UMTS-Mobiltelefon II, File Number 7 O 100/10, 18 February 2011, available at http://lrbw.juris.de/cgi-bin/laender_rechtsprechung/document.py?Gericht=bw&

German commentators, who argue that the Federal Court of Justice did not take into account the particularities of standardisation agreements.[64] Owners of essential patents are not just earning the rewards for their inventions. They are also rewarded for the popularity of the established market standard. From an economic perspective, the patentee is overcompensated.[65] In addition, by exercising the rights granted by the patent, a single patentee might block the whole standard. This presents a danger for the whole standardisation process. Owners of essential patents usually need to declare that they are willing to grant a licence on fair, reasonable, and non-discriminatory conditions (FRAND declaration).[66] For these reasons, there is considerable substance to the argument that the prerequisites of injunction orders and the amount of royalties that are owed for essential patents need to be approached differently. A possible implication could be that injunction orders are generally unavailable for essential patents.[67] This would also have consequences for the competition law defence and needs to be taken into account by German courts.[68]

Unconditional Offer

The Federal Court of Justice required the potential licensee to make an unconditional offer for a licence agreement. The Court did not specify when the offer needs to be made. In late 2011, the District Court Mannheim ruled that it is sufficient to make the offer during the proceedings.[69] However, the term 'unconditional' was interpreted strictly. The District Court Mannheim required the patent user to accept his liability for compensation for the time he used the patent without permission of the owner. Otherwise, so the Court reasoned, the user would have an advantage over other users that duly paid or deposited royalties, complying with the *Orange Book Standard* principles. In particular, the potential licensee cannot make the offer under the condition that the patent is and remains valid. The licensee must act faithfully and is therefore not allowed to challenge the validity of the patent in

nr=14011; Court of Appeal Düsseldorf, *UMTS Mobilstation*, File Number 4b O 273/10, 24 March 2011, available at http://www.duesseldorfer-archiv.de/?q=node/4426.

[64] Körber (2013), p. 87; Ullrich (2010b), at pp. 52–63.

[65] For an economic analysis, see Ullrich (2010b), at pp. 76–80; Merges and Kuhn, at pp. 7 et seqq.

[66] See, for example, Cl 6.1 ETSI IPR-Policy, available at http://www.etsi.org/images/etsi_ipr-policy.pdf.

[67] Körber (2013), at p. 88; Ullrich (2010b), at pp. 90–93; Maume (2012b), at pp. 245–261.

[68] The District Court Mannheim repeatedly held that FRAND declarations are not legally binding because they lack finality of terms and intention to enter into the contract. As a result, the fact that a patentee has given a FRAND declaration cannot be used as a defence; see, for example, District Court Mannheim, *FRAND-Erklärung*, File Number 7 O 94/08, 27 February 2009, available at http://openjur.de/u/341036.html. The decision was confirmed by the Court of Appeals Karlsruhe, *FRAND-Grundsätze*, File Number 6 U 66/09, 23 March 2011.

[69] The District Court Mannheim, *GPRS-Zwangslizenz*, File Number 7 O 122/11, 9 December 2011, available at http://openjur.de/u/357699.html.

separate proceedings.[70] In the words of the Court of Appeal Karlsruhe, the licensee must waive all possible defences against his obligation to pay royalties and compensation.[71] As a result, the user might be forced into a licence agreement although such an agreement is in fact not necessary.[72] This presents a high risk for the user.

Scope of the Offer

Another problem relates to the territorial ambit of the licence offer. Is it sufficient that the user restrains his or her offer to the national (here: German) patent? Or is the user under an obligation to request licences in respect of other countries as well? A closely related question is whether the user may make an offer in respect of a licence for a single patent or whether the user needs to accept a pool licence, including other patents that the user may not require.

The courts have not clarified this issue yet. The District Court Düsseldorf held that the user does not have the right to claim a pool licence tailored to the user's particular needs. Instead, the Court found it acceptable for the user to accept a worldwide pool licence that was offered by the patentee.[73] The Court of Appeal Düsseldorf, however, felt the need to point out that it was not sure about the territorial ambit of the licence and left the question unanswered.[74] The District Court Mannheim held that the user was not required to make an offer for a worldwide pool licence.[75] This would only be the case if it could be expected that the user would infringe upon other patents held by the patentee.

It is fair to say that the matter causes major legal uncertainty. The majority of commentators seem to share the view taken by the District Court Mannheim.[76] This is convincing. The model established by the Federal Court of Justice is a German particularity. Its aim is to fend off abusive injunction claims for patent infringement in Germany. However, the defence does not replace a proper licence. For that reason, it is irrelevant what the territorial scope of the licenses offered by the patentee would usually be. Legally, the defence does not have any relevance in other jurisdictions. It would be odd to force the user to offer a licence agreement including patents *outside* Germany just to keep his defences against the alleged

---

[70] Ibid.

[71] The Court of Appeal Karlsruhe, *GPRS-Zwangslizenz III*, File Number 6 U 136/11, 13 June 2012, available at http://openjur.de/u/357979.html.

[72] It might, for example, turn out that the patent has been declared essential by the patentee without being an essential part of the standard in truth.

[73] The District Court Düsseldorf, *Videosignalcodierung III*, File Number 4b O 78/07, 11 September 2008, available at http://openjur.de/u/131857.html.

[74] The Court of Appeal Düsseldorf, *Interframe Dropping*, File Number 2 U 131/08, 28 January 2010, available at http://openjur.de/u/143070.html.

[75] The District Court Mannheim, File Number 7 O 65/10, 27 May 2011 (not available online).

[76] Maume (2012a), at pp. 225–227; Körber (2013), at pp. 91–93; Reimann and Hahn (2010), at p. 382; Kühnen (2011), para. 1293. Against that Jestaedt (2009), at p. 804; Hötte (2011), at p. 189.

infringement *inside* Germany available. As a result, the user should have the right to limit his offer to the German patent.

Escrow and 'Sufficient' Royalties

The fourth problem relates to the escrow model. The Federal Court of Justice held that a user who wants to raise the competition law defence must pay or deposit a sufficient amount of royalties (see above). The obvious rationale is that the Court wants to impose certain obligations on the user in order to keep the patentee's financial interests safe. The second rationale is to keep patent infringement proceedings free of difficult considerations about royalties. In practice, the most complicated question that needs clarification by the court is the amount of royalties owed by the user. Determining the appropriate rate is onerous and time consuming. In an effective patent system, infringement proceedings (in particular, preliminary proceedings) need to be as fast and efficient as possible. The Court held that if an amount has been deposited, which in any event is sufficient, the infringement court may, if the other preconditions for defence are satisfied, limit itself to determining whether the patentee is obliged to accept the offer of a licence contract.[77]

The Court's idea is excellent, but, unfortunately, the wording is not. The problem is the phrase 'in any event sufficient' (*jedenfalls ausreichend*). The decision does not elaborate on the meaning of 'sufficient'. The term is not common in patent practice either. The wording suggests that an amount that is 'in any event sufficient' is higher than a 'reasonable' amount. In practice, users would probably be willing to deposit a higher amount if they can be sure that the competition law defence remains available. However, the ongoing 'patent wars' and the series of contested patents might force users to deposit higher royalties in a number of cases simultaneously. In addition, the user would have to make deposits even if the user is of the opinion that the patent has not been infringed but wants to retain the competition law defence as a second option. Such deposits might be a serious strain on a company's cash flow and disadvantage smaller competitors.[78] Therefore, some commentators argue in favour of additional ways to secure the patentee's interests, for example via guarantees.[79]

---

[77] The Federal Court of Justice, supra note 55, para. 40.

[78] Reimann and Hahn (2010), at p. 392.

[79] Wirtz (2011), at p. 1401; Maume and Tapia (2010), at p. 925.

4.3.5 A Flawed Idea or a Flawed Execution?

The Motives

The aforementioned questions result in a high level of legal uncertainty that is, from a practitioner's point of view, unsatisfying. From a scholar's perspective, however, the question remains whether the Federal Court of Justice's approach to the problems was correct and what lessons can be learned from 'the German experience'.

There is no serious doubt that allowing some kind of competition law defence is the right approach. If the technicalities of German civil procedure and competition law make it unreasonably difficult for competitors to obtain the licences to which they are entitled, the rules need to be adjusted to a certain extent. Without a competition law defence, the patentee's obligations under competition law would be rather useless in practice. Moreover, the technical necessity of standardisation would be in danger if a single owner of an essential patent could exercise his exclusivity rights without restraints.

The Court's considerations about the potential licensee's obligations are also convincing. Imposing a duty to pay or deposit royalties is known from copyright law. Under the Act on the Collective Exploitation of Copyrights (Gesetz über die Wahrnehmung von Urheberrechten und verwandten Schutzrechten, UrhWG), copyright owners can join an association that is tasked with the exploitation and the enforcement of copyrights in a certain area. For example, *GEMA* is responsible for copyrights on music, while *VG Wort* is responsible for printed works. These associations negotiate licence agreements and compensation on behalf of their members and distribute the fees among them. The associations have the obligation to grant licences on reasonable terms to any party who is interested in using the protected works, sec 11(1) of the UrhWG. If the association and the user cannot agree on reasonable terms, the user can use the protected work if he pays the uncontested amount of fees and deposits the contested amount. This mechanism was the inspiration for the *Orange Book Standard* model.

The Court's idea to keep the infringement proceedings free of complex deliberations about the correct amount of royalties is smart and demonstrates a good understanding of problems faced by the patent courts in practice. In sum, the Federal Court of Justice's motives appear reasonable. The ideas behind the *Orange Book Standard* principles are sound.

Problems

If the main rationales for the *Orange Book Standard* model are sound, why are practitioners facing a proliferation of problems that make raising the defence hardly possible? The main issue seems to be that the Federal Court of Justice tried to find a solution based on principles that already exist under German law. This is not wrong in itself. However, it results in a number of problems that suggest that the Court's execution of its idea was not optimal. This can be illustrated by the following examples.

Firstly, relying on existing German rules makes the decision bound to German legal intricacies and its application in other jurisdictions unlikely. Commentators warned against German patent law being carried into 'doctrinal and international isolation'.[80] Until now, courts in other European countries have been reluctant to apply the *Orange Book Standard* principles.[81] It might have been a better idea if the Federal Court of Justice had tried to develop a new model that aligns better to practices in other European countries. Sec 242 of the Civil Code would have been an appropriate vehicle as the understanding of the provision is constantly developed and refined by the courts.

Secondly, relying on rules that were not created for this specific situation only works to a certain extent. In comparative law, this is referred to as 'legal irritants', which occur if a rule is transplanted from one legal system to another.[82] However, the same problem may occur if a rule is transplanted from distinct areas of regulation within one jurisdiction. A good example is the application of sec 315 of the Civil Code.[83] Allowing the user to make an unspecified offer deviates from the fundamentals of German contract law. Addressing the problem by applying sec 315 is, at first glance, a good move as the provision is sometimes applied in cases of market power (determination of utility prices by powerful providers, so-called monopoly cases).[84] However, its application for the competition law defence causes contrition. For example, the defendant in patent infringement proceedings generally has the burden of proof for defences.[85] Accordingly, the Court concluded that if the royalties are determined by the patentee and the user wants to challenge this determination in court, the burden of proof must be coherent with the patent infringement proceedings.[86] Hence, the user has the burden of proof that the royalties as determined by the patentee are not reasonable. However, in the aforementioned monopoly cases under sec 315, the burden of proof lies with the monopolist and not with the user. So why did the Federal Court of Justice outline different rules for the burden of proof for comparable situations? The simple answer is that this inconsistency was inevitable because sec 315 was never meant to be

---

[80] Ullrich (2010a), at p. 337.

[81] The Court of The Hague expressly dismissed the approach taken by the German Federal Supreme Court in a comparative case; see Court of The Hague, *Philips Electronics v SK Kassetten*, File Number 316522/HA ZA 08-2522, 17 March 2010, paras. 6.19–6.25, available at http://www.eplawpatentblog.com/eplaw/2010/03/nl-philips-v-sk-kasetten-frand.html. For good overviews of different approaches taken by courts, see Laakkonen (2011), Lundie-Smith and Moss (2013), p. 400.

[82] See, for example, Teubner (1998), p. 11.

[83] Maume (2012a), at p. 230; Jestaedt (2009), at p. 803; Höppner (2010), at p. 420.

[84] Maume and Tapia (2010), at p. 926.

[85] Benkard (2006), Sec 139, note 114.

[86] The Federal Court of Justice, supra note 55, para. 39.

applied in cases of market power abuse and patent infringements. This is a good example for a legal irritant. The practical problem arising from this theoretical background is that courts find it difficult to fill gaps in the *Orange Book Standard* system in a coherent way.

Thirdly, the model moves the user closer to a 'regular' licensee. The Federal Court of Justice pointed out that the user needs to act as if he had been granted the licence.[87] So the Court draws a parallel between the defendant and a hypothetical licensee in a regular licence agreement. The courts therefore try to fill gaps in the *Orange Book Standard* ruling by an analogy to the 'honest licensee' (redlicher Lizenznehmer).[88] This is a dangerous deduction. We have to keep in mind that the background of the *Orange Book Standard* model is a dominating undertaking that is abusing its market powers. In this situation, the equality of bargaining powers that underlies all contractual theory is seriously flawed. It is therefore objectionable to draw parallels between a situation covered by *Orange Book Standard* and a regular licence agreement. In addition, the overall approach is not convincing because an honest licensee might behave in various ways, sometimes even irrationally. Contractual relationships between market participants do not follow simple, objective rules. For example, companies regularly enter into negotiations with offers that are not reasonable. After a lot of bargaining, the parties will come to a compromise that will usually be on reasonable terms. However, the parties' initial proposals might not have been reasonable—does that make them dishonest licensors and licensees? Using an honest licensee as an analogy misconceives the diversity of possible business situations and factually leads to a code of conduct that is set out by judges and not by market participants. It is doubtful that this outcome is desirable.

All these suggest that although the motives for the Federal Court of Justice decision were sound, the execution of the idea was not. The *Orange Book Standard* model results in legal irritants, puts the German laws in danger of international isolation, and forces judges to double guess and prescribe business practices.

Proposal: Back to the Roots

A main lesson that can be learned from the German experience is that the ambit of the competition law defence should not be overstretched. Such a defence should merely prevent the patentee from exercising his rights as long as he is under an obligation to grant a licence. The defence, however, should not replace the licence agreement. The defence is a temporary solution to the issue, while the licence is the final solution. This fundamental distinction, blurred by the Federal Court of Justice, should be the starting point. A first conclusion would be that we need to distinguish between the competition law defence in patent infringement proceedings and a second lawsuit initiated by the user to obtain the licence.

---

[87] The Federal Court of Justice, supra note 55, para. 39.

[88] For example, District Court Düsseldorf, supra note 34; District Court Mannheim, supra note 69.

If the patentee refuses to grant a licence for a standard essential patent, the prospective user pays or deposits a reasonable amount of royalties, plus a premium,[89] and initiates proceedings in the cartel court to obtain the licence. The point is that the offered and deposited amount does not need to be the one appropriate offer that the patentee would be required to accept. It would suffice if the offer and deposit were adequate to safeguard the patentee's financial interests. The offeror could rely on an independent third party for this assessment. If the patentee initiated patent infringement proceedings, the offeror would need to prove that his offer was reasonable and the deposit was adequate to protect the patentee's interests. The Court could limit itself to a summary assessment as to whether the patent was essential and if the amount of royalties was adequate. This would establish a clear rule that leaves no room for interpretation and abuse. The final decision about the royalties would need to be made in separate proceedings in the cartel court.

A downside of this model would be that it would require two separate court involvements instead of one. However, a closer look demonstrates that there would be no substantial differences in practice. Under the *Orange Book Standard* model, the licensee can initiate proceedings if he is of the opinion that the patentee's determination of royalties was not reasonable. It is argued by commentators that many licensees would take this step because the royalties are nearly always contested by the parties. Thus, under the *Orange Book Standard* principles, it is quite likely that the parties will meet again in court anyway.[90] So the apparent advantage of having less involvement of the courts is in fact not as big as it first seems.

4.4 Last Exit: European Court of Justice?

Since the decision *Orange Book Standard* was released in 2009, the patent courts tried to apply the model in practice, filling gaps in the Federal Court of Justice decision if necessary. However, the patent courts did not voice substantial criticism or concern about the model.

This changed in March 2013. Again, the case revolved around a standard in the telecommunications industry. The patent at issue was part of the Long Term Evolution (LTE) Standard. It had been established under the auspices of the European Telecommunications Standards Institute (ETSI) and the patentee that declared its willingness to grant licences on FRAND conditions. The patentee and

[89] Under German civil procedure, a litigant prevailing in first instance can enforce his claim even before it has finally been established by the court of second instance if he deposits a security of 110 % (or sometimes 120 %) of the claim he wishes to enforce, sections 709 and 711 of the Civil Procedure Act (Zivilprozessordnung). Using the patent under the Orange Book Standard principles is comparable with such a preliminary enforcement so that the 110 % rule should be applied here; see Maume (2010), at p. 138.

[90] Hötte (2011), at pp. 231–235; Ullrich (2010a), at p. 350.

the user had been in negotiations between November 2010 and March 2011 but did not exchange formal offers for licence agreements. After the negotiations failed, the patentee applied for an injunction order at the District Court Düsseldorf.

In March 2013, the District Court applied to the ECJ for a preliminary decision under Art 267 TFEU.[91] In Europe, national courts have to initiate these proceedings (1) if they see different possible interpretations of the TFEU and (2) if the outcome of a case depends on this interpretation. The mechanism shall safeguard a consistent interpretation of European law by national courts. The District Court posed the question as to what constitutes an abuse of a dominant undertaking in relation to a patent that is essential to a market standard. In his first question, the District Court suggested two possible answers. Firstly, a patentee who has made a FRAND declaration abuses his market power if he applies for an injunction order although the user has demonstrated his willingness to enter into negotiations. Secondly, the abuse of market power requires the user to make an offer on FRAND conditions, which the patentee could not lawfully refuse. It is obvious that the latter, which is based on *Orange Book Standard*, is much more patentee friendly. In the ensuing questions 2–5, the District Court enquired about details of negotiations and offer, depending on the outcome of question 1. In simpler terms, the District Court is asking about the relationship between the *Orange Book Standard* model and essential patents. The underlying theoretical question is if the model is overburdening users, thereby limiting the effectiveness of European law.[92]

The District Court argued that some conditions set out by the Federal Court of Justice for an effective competition law defence do not appear to be compelling. The District Court particularly expressed unease about the implications of the user's obligation to make an unconditional offer, which includes the prohibition of challenging the validity of the patent in court.[93] The implication would be that essential patents would never be challenged. The Court argued that it is not in the public interest to maintain a patent if it was granted unlawfully.[94] This is a very convincing argument.

An important impetus for the Court's application was an investigation by the European Commission against Samsung for alleged abuse of essential patens in December 2012.[95] The European Commission generally acknowledges the economic benefits of standardisation.[96] However, standardisation agreements also have anti-competitive effects because they factually exclude technologies that are not embedded in the standard from the market.[97] For that reason, it is essential that

---

[91] The District Court Düsseldorf, *LTE-Standard*, File Number 4b O 104/12, 21 March 2013, reported in 2013 GRUR-RR 196.

[92] De Bronett (2009).

[93] The District Court Düsseldorf, supra note 91, at 200.

[94] Ibid.

[95] European Commission (2012).

[96] European Commission (2011), paras. 268, 283.

[97] Ibid, at para. 263.

standardised technologies can be used by all market participants (open access). A patentee who applies for an injunction despite having made a FRAND declaration abuses the market power conveyed by the standard and harms competition.[98] This approach can hardly be accommodated with the German patent courts' reluctant stance towards FRAND declarations.[99]

The District Court's application could be a major turning point for the competition law defence. It is possible that the ECJ follows the approach taken by the European Commission. In this case, European competition law would forbid the exercise of some rights granted by the patent if it was essential for a standard.[100] European law can be applied to abuses of market power in Germany,[101] and the application of European law is given precedence over national laws. As a result, the *Orange Book Standard* principles would become obsolete in cases involving consensual standards. But even if the ECJ approved the approach taken by the Federal Court of Justice, the debate about the competition law defence would be reinvigorated because the District Court enquired about the scope of the user's obligations. This could result in modifications of the *Orange Book Standard* principles.

5 Conclusions

In the last 20 years, the German courts have significantly refined their approach to compulsory licensing. The practical relevance of compulsory licences under patent law is low. The reason is that the Federal Court of Justice developed a strict public interest test that does not allow for licences on grounds of competition law. Compulsory licences under competition law are of much higher relevance in Germany. The Federal Court of Justice confirmed that a patentee's rights granted by the patent are protected even if the patentee is in a dominant market position. However, if the patent is necessary for access to a downstream market because it is part of an established market standard, the patentee may be under an obligation to grant a licence on FRAND conditions.

The Federal Court of Justice also allowed the so-called competition law defence. As a result, owners of essential standard patents will not be granted an injunction

---

[98] European Commission (2012).

[99] See The District Court Mannheim, supra note 68.

[100] The District Court Düsseldorf also asked the question if the same conditions would apply to other rights granted by the patent, for example compensation and account for profit.

[101] Art 102 TFEU can be applied if the undertaking is dominant within an essential part of the internal market. As a standard usually applies to all countries in Europe, and the respective product market usually transcends national borders, the exercise of patent rights will regularly be subject to Art 102; see Maume and Tapia (2010), at p. 929. The German patent courts are also applying the Orange Book Standard principles under European law; see Court of Appeal Karlsruhe, supra note 71; Court of Appeal Düsseldorf, supra note 34.

order if the user complies with his obligations set out in the decision *Orange Book Standard*. That means that the user needs to make an offer on FRAND conditions (or, alternatively, make an unspecified offer and require the patentee to determine the royalties) and pay or deposit sufficient royalties. Unfortunately, these *Orange Book Standard* principles were not comprehensive and left a number of questions open, which need to be answered by the patent courts subsequently. It appears that the Federal Court of Justice's approach was too broad, overstretching the scope of a temporary defence. The result is a model that contains inconsistencies and uncertainties. Courts in other jurisdictions should learn from this 'German' experience and try to allow competition law defences under clear, unambiguous conditions that are easy to handle in practice. The story has not come to an end yet. The next chapter will be written by the European Court of Justice, whose decision will most likely be a major turning point in the debate.

References

Ann C (2009) Verletzungsgerichtsbarkeit – Zentral für jedes Patentsystem und doch häufig unterschätzt. GRUR 205–209

Benkard G (2006) Patentgesetz, 10th edn. Verlag C.H. Beck, Munich

Busche J (2009) Der Einwand der Zwangslizenz im Patentverletzungsverfahren. CIPR 104–107

de Bronett G-K (2009) Gemeinschaftsrechtliche Anmerkungen zum Orange-Book-Standard-Urteil des BGH. WuW 899–908

European Commission (2011) Guidelines on the applicability of Article 101 of the Treaty on the Functioning of the European Union to horizontal co-operation agreements. Off J C 11 of 14.01.2011

European Commission (2012) Antitrust: commission sends statement of objections to Samsung on potential misuse of mobile phone standard-essential patents. In: Press Release IP/12/1448, 21 December 2012. http://europa.eu/rapid/press-release_IP-12-1448_en.htm?locale=FR. Accessed 28 June 2014

Fine F (2002) NDC/IMS: a logical application of essential facilities doctrine. Eur Comp Law Rev 23:457–461

Gärtner A, Vormann T (2009) Der kartellrechtliche Zwangslizenzeinwand im Patentverletzungsstreit – Orange Book Standard und seine Folgen für die Praxis. Mitt 440–446

Heinemann A (2005) Kartellrechtliche Zwangslizenzen im Patentrecht. ZWeR 198–206

Heinemann A (2009) Comment. LMK 286659

Herr J (2009) Patent litigation and industry standards: the compulsory license defence. Intellect Prop Technol Law J 21:10–15

Höppner T (2010) Der kartellrechtliche Zwangslizenzeinwand gegen Ansprüche aus Patent- und Urheberrechten. ZWeR 395–429

Hötte D (2011) Die kartellrechtliche Zwangslizenz im Kartellrecht. Westfälische Wilhelms-Universität Münster Verlag, Münster

Jaecks J, Dörmer T (2006) Der wettbewerbsrechtliche Anspruch auf Lizenzerteilung, die eigenmächtige Nutzung von Immaterialgüterrechten und die prozessualen Folgen. In: Bösche K , Füller J, Wolf M (eds) Variationen im Recht – Festgabe für Franz Jürgen Säcker. Berliner Wissenschaftsverlag, Berlin, pp 97–116

Jestaedt M (2009) Der Lizenzerteilungsanspruch nach der BGH-Entscheidung Orange Book Standard. GRUR 801–805

Körber T (2013) Kartellrechtlicher Zwangslizenzeinwand und standardessentielle Patente. NZKart 87–99
Kraßer R (2009) Patentrecht, 6th edn. Verlag C.H. Beck, Munich
Kühnen T (2003) Der kartellrechtliche Zwangslizenzeinwand und seine Berücksichtigung im Patentverletzungsprozess. In: Keller E, Plassmann C, von Falck A (eds) Festschrift für Winfried Tilmann zum 65. Geburtstag. Carl Heymanns Verlag, Cologne, pp 513–526
Kühnen T (2011) Handbuch der Patentverletzung, 6th edn. Carl Heymanns Verlag, Cologne
Laakkonen A (2011) Defences to patent infringements in a standards context. In: paper presented at the 19th Fordham conference, April 2011. http://fordhamipconference.com/wp-content/uploads/2011/04/Laakkonen.pdf. Accessed 28 June 2014
Leistner M (2005) Comment. Int Rev Intellect Prop Comp Law 36:592–595
Liu K-C (2008) Rationalising the regime of compulsory patent licensing by the essential facilities doctrine. Int Rev Intellect Prop Comp Law 39:757–774
Loewenheim U, Meesen K, Riesenkampf A (2009) Kartellrecht: Deutsches und Europäisches Recht, 2nd edn. Verlag C.H. Beck, Munich
Lundie-Smith R, Moss G (2013) Bard v Gore: to injunct, or not to injunct, that is the question. GRUR Int 400–408
Maume P (2010) Der kartellrechtliche Zwangslizenzeinwand im Patentverletzungsprozess. Carl Heymanns Verlag, Cologne
Maume P, Tapia C (2010) Der Zwangslizenzeinwand ein Jahr nach Orange Book Standard – Mehr Fragen als Antworten. GRUR Int 923–930
Maume P (2012a) Der Zwangslizenzeinwand am Scheideweg. ZGE/Int Prop J 4:216–241
Maume P (2012b) Standardisierungsvereinbarungen – ein erster Schritt zu einem modernen Patentrecht? In: Kreutz P et al (eds) Realitäten des Zivilrechts, Grenzen des Zivilrechts. Boorberg Verlag, Stuttgart, pp 239–261
Merges R, Kuhn J, An Estoppel doctrine for patented standards. Calif Law Rev 97:1–50
Nägele T, Jacobs S (2009) Zwangslizenzen im Patentrecht. WRP 1062–1075
Reimann T, Hahn T (2010) Orange Book Standard – Ratgeber oder Buch mit sieben Siegeln? In: Harmsen C, Jüngst O, Rödiger F (eds) Festschrift für Wolfgang von Meibom. Carl Heymanns Verlag, Cologne, pp 373–394
Rombach P (2008) Die kartellrechtliche Zwangslizenz im Patentverletzungsprozess. In: Müller G, Osterloch E, Stein T (eds) Festschrift für Günter Hirsch zum 65. Geburtstag. Verlag C.H. Beck, Munich, pp 311–322
Scheffler D (2003) Die (ungenutzten) Möglichkeiten des Rechtsinstituts der Zwangslizenz. GRUR 97–105
Tapia C (2010) Industrial property rights – technical standards and licensing practices (FRAND) in the telecommunications industry. Carl Heymanns Verlag, Cologne
Teubner G (1998) Legal irritants: good faith in British law or how unifying law ends up in new divergences. Mod Law Rev 61:11–32
Treacy P, Lawrance S (2008) FRANDly fire: are industry standards doing more harm than good? J Intellect Prop Law Pract 3:22–29
Ullrich H (2010a) Patents and standards – a comment on the German Federal Supreme Court Decision Orange Book Standard. Int Rev Intellect Prop Comp Law 41:337–351
Ullrich H (2010b) Patente und technische Normen: Konflikt und Komplementarität in patent- und wettbewerbsrechtlicher Sicht. In: Leistner M (ed) Europäische Perspektiven des Geistigen Eigentums. Mohr Siebeck Verlag, Tübingen, pp 14-95
Von Merveldt M (2004) Der Ausschluss kartellrechtlicher Einwendungen im Patentverletzungsverfahren. WuW 19–25
Wirtz M, Holzhäuser M (2004) Die kartellrechtliche Zwangslizenz. WRP 683–695
Wirtz M (2011) Der kartellrechtliche Zwangslizenzeinwand nach der Orange-Book-Standard-Entscheidung des BGH. WRP 1392–1405
Zhang L (2010) How IPR policies of telecommunication standard-setting organisations can effectively address the patent ambush problem. Int Rev Intellect Prop Comp Law 41:380–409

Refusal to Licence as an Abuse of Market Dominance: From Commercial Solvents to Microsoft

Matthias Lamping

Contents

Abstract Although intellectual property rights do not automatically confer a dominant market position, they may put the right holder in the position to behave more or less independently of his or her competitors, customers, and ultimately consumers. The extent of the relative immunity from competition depends on a number of factors, from the specific characteristics of the protected subject matter through to the structure of the relevant market. In extreme cases, an intellectual property right will constitute an "essential facility" and therefore enable the right holder to control access to, and thus competition in, the market. In such cases, a refusal to license may lead to an abuse of market dominance within the meaning of Article 102 TFEU. Depending on the circumstances of the case, the abuse may consist in a discrimination of trading partners, an unjustified foreclosure of

---

M. Lamping is Senior Research Fellow.

M. Lamping
Max Planck Institute for Innovation and Competition, Munich, Germany
e-mail: matthias.lamping@ip.mpg.de

R.M. Hilty and K.-C. Liu (eds.), *Compulsory Licensing*, MPI Studies on Intellectual Property and Competition Law 22, DOI 10.1007/978-3-642-54704-1_7,

competitors, a negligence of market needs, or an expansion of market power to another related market. However, a compulsory licence is not always the appropriate remedy to stop the established abuse, its anti-competitive effects, and its recurrence. In principle, the European Commission asks the dominant company to cease and desist from the abusive conduct, but it does not grant compulsory licences.

1 Introductory Remarks

The rights to choose one's trading partners and to freely dispose of one's property are generally recognised principles of law, in many cases with constitutional status. It is assumed to be in the interest of competition and ultimately economic welfare to allow a company to retain for its own use facilities, technologies, or other commodities that it has developed for that purpose. The incentive to invest in these assets would likely be reduced if competitors were, upon a simple request, able to share the benefits. Thus, the mere fact that by retaining property for its own use—or for no use at all—an undertaking gains a competitive advantage over other market participants cannot justify an obligation to contract.[1]

However, things change when the property owner enjoys market power. In order to preserve freedom, there must be restrictions to it.[2] For this reason, Article 102 TFEU prohibits "any abuse by one or more undertakings of a dominant position within the Internal Market or in a substantial part of it". As a result the freedom to contract will decrease with the degree of market power. In principle, there is nothing unlawful about market dominance. But with power comes responsibility. The one who rules a market must answer for its operability. Irrespective of the reasons for which an undertaking has a dominant position—due to superior performance, natural monopoly, or even fraud—it therefore has a "special responsibility"[3] towards residual competition: it must refrain from any behaviour that may unduly prevent other undertakings from entering the market and the remaining market participants from competing on the merits.[4] This means that a dominant company will not enjoy the same freedoms in operating on the market and interacting with competitors as others. It may come into conflict with the law,

[1] AG Jacobs, Case C-7/97, Bronner, 1998 ECR I-7791, para. 56.

[2] See Fikentscher (1997).

[3] Case 322/81, Michelin, 1983 ECR 3461, para. 57; Case C-333/94, Tetra Pak II, 1996 ECR I-5951, para. 21; Case T-65/89, BPB Industries, 1993 ECR II-389, para. 67; Case T-219/99, British Airways, 2003 ECR II-5917, para. 242.

[4] See Eilmansberger (2007), Art. 82, paras. 3 et seqq.; Eilmansberger (2005a), pp. 132 et seq.; Wessely, paras. 59 et seqq.; Lübbig (2005), Art. 82, para. 1; Schröter (2003), Art. 82, paras. 24, 166; Frenz (2006), paras. 1112 et seqq.; European Commission, DG Competition Discussion Paper on the Application of Article 82 of the Treaty to Exclusionary Abuses, 2005, paras. 54 et seqq.

even if the very same behaviour would be perfectly legitimate for any other company that does not enjoy a dominant position.

Over the past 30 years, the European institutions have produced extensive case law on the scope of that "special responsibility" in the context of access to intellectual property. This chapter offers a summary of that jurisdiction and a critical evaluation of the *status quo*.

2 Market Dominance and Its Abuse

European antitrust law protects competition as an institution.[5] The objective of Article 102 TFEU is twofold: preserving competitive market structures and protecting competition as a 'discovery procedure', "whose results are unpredictable and altogether different from what anybody could have consciously aimed for, and whose desired effects are manifested in that it thwarts certain intentions and disappoints certain expectations".[6]

For Article 102 TFEU to apply, it is necessary that three elements are present together:

- the existence of a dominant position on the relevant market,
- the abuse of that position, and
- the possibility that trade between the Member States may be affected thereby.

2.1 *Market Power and the Relevant Market*

Despite its exclusionary effect, an intellectual property right does not automatically confer a dominant position.[7] Competition law secures access to markets, not to property.[8] Market dominance refers to a position of economic strength that enables

[5] See Eilmansberger (2005a), p. 138; Hawk (1988), p. 78; Bishop and Walker (2002), p. 250; Whish (2005), p. 175; Korah (2004), p. 211; van den Bergh and Camescasca (2006), p. 277; Turnbull (1996), pp. 102 et seq.; Temple Lang (2006), p. 612.

[6] Hayek (1968), p. 3; see also Kirzner (1974), pp. 89 et seqq.; Kirzner (1997), pp. 60 et seqq.; Hoppmann (1966), pp. 286 et seqq.; Hoppmann (1967), pp. 251 et seqq.; Kaufer (1966), pp. 481 et seqq.; Kaufer (1967), pp. 242 et seqq.; Schumpeter (1964); Schumpeter (2005), p. 137.

[7] See Case 24/67, Parke, Davis & Co., 1968 ECR 86, 112; Case 78/70, Deutsche Grammophon, 1971 ECR 487, para. 7; Case 258/78, Nungesser, 1982 ECR 2015, para. 28.

[8] For a comprehensive analysis of the relation between intellectual property rights, relevant innovation and technology markets, and market dominance, see Frueh (2012), pp. 37 et seqq.; Eilmansberger (1992), p. 625; Ullrich and Heinemann (2007), paras. 22, 42; Faull and Nikpay (2007), paras. 10.211 et seqq.; Lamping (2010), pp. 155 et seqq.; chapter "Mandatory Licensing Under Patent Law and Competition Law: Different Concerns, Complementary Roles" by Ullrich, in this volume.

its proprietor "to prevent effective competition being maintained on the relevant market by giving it the power to behave independently of its competitors, customers and ultimately of its consumers".[9]

The concept of the relevant market implies that there can be "effective competition between the products or services which form part of it and this presupposes that there is a sufficient degree of interchangeability between all the products or services forming part of the same market in so far as a specific use of such products or services is concerned"[10] (functional or subjective equivalence). The possibilities of competition must therefore be judged from the demand side and "in the context of the market comprising the totality of products which, with respect to their characteristics, are particularly suitable for satisfying constant needs and are only to a limited extent interchangeable with other products".[11] In order to assess the position that the intellectual property owner occupies in the market as a result of his legal right to exclude, it is therefore necessary to determine whether the protected subject matter is at least potentially interchangeable with or substitutable for other subject matter by reason of its characteristics, its price, as well as its intended use.[12]

The extent to which the dominant market position rests on the exclusionary effect of the intellectual property right in question is irrelevant.[13] Whether an intellectual property right constitutes a bottleneck to the market or whether it is only the straw that breaks the camel's back makes no difference for the assessment of market dominance, but it may well be relevant for establishing a violation of Article 102 TFEU and the choice of remedy since this, contrary to the prevailing opinion,[14] requires a causality between dominance and its abuse.[15]

---

[9] Case 27/76, United Brands, 1978 ECR 207, para. 65; Case 85/76, Hoffmann-La Roche, 1979 ECR 461, para. 38; Case 322/81, Michelin, 1983 ECR 3461, para. 30; Case 311/84, CBEM, 1985 ECR 3261, para. 16; Joined Cases C-395/96 P and C-396/96 P, Compagnie Maritime Belge, 2000 ECR I-1365, para. 34; Case T-30/89, Hilti, 1991 ECR II-1439, para. 90; Case T-128/98, Aéroports de Paris, 2000 ECR II-3929, para. 147; Case T-219/99, British Airways, 2003 ECR II-5917, para. 189.

[10] Case 85/76, Hoffmann-La Roche, 1979 ECR 461, para. 28; Case 322/81, Michelin, 1983 ECR 3461, para. 48.

[11] Case 322/81, Michelin, 1983 ECR 3461, para. 37; Case 6/72, Continental Can, 1973 ECR 215, para. 32.

[12] See European Commission, Guidelines on the Application of Article 81 of the EC Treaty to Technology Transfer Agreements, OJ 2004, C 101/2, para. 21.

[13] See Eilmansberger (1992), p. 625; Ullrich and Heinemann (2007), para. 42.

[14] Roth and Rose (2008), para. 10.004; Schröter (2003), Art. 82, para. 166; Möschel (2007), para. 123; Mestmäcker and Schweitzer (2004), § 15, paras. 31 et seqq.; Jung (2008), Art. 82, paras. 28, 118; Dirksen (2006), Art. 82, para. 85; Ritter and Braun (2004), pp. 422 et seq.; Jones and Sufrin (2008), p. 322; Frenz (2006), paras. 1120 et seq.

[15] See Eilmansberger (2007), Art. 82, paras. 124 et seqq.; Eilmansberger (2005a), pp. 140 et seqq.; Eilmansberger (2006), pp. 15 et seqq.; Deringer (1969), Art. 86, para. 30; Vogelenzang (1976), pp. 61 et seqq.; Lamping (2010), p. 165.

An extreme case of market dominance is "essential facilities",[16] *i.e.* assets that are indispensable in order to operate on the market and for which, by reason of their special characteristics—in particular, technical and legal restraints, prohibitive costs, and/or time reasonably required for reproducing them—there are no viable substitutes available to potential competitors that are thereby excluded from the market.[17] Unless there are actual or potential alternatives in existence that enable them to compete on the merits with sufficient prospects of success—even if these alternatives are less advantageous (less effective, less efficient, or more costly) than the facility owned by the dominant undertaking[18]—it must be presumed that competition is foreclosed. As a result, the legal "monopoly" conferred by the intellectual property right degenerates into a true economic monopoly that allows the right holder to behave completely independent of other market participants.

In such an unusual case, where access to somebody else's intellectual property in the form of a licence is indispensable in order to operate on the market (on a par), the ownership over that right automatically confers a dominant position within the meaning of Article 102 TFEU.[19]

---

[16] The term "essential facility" originates in US law: United States v. Terminal Railroad Association of St. Louis, 224 U.S. 383, 411 (1912); Associated Press v. United States, 321 U.S. 1 (1945); Gamco, Inc. v. Providence Fruit & Produce Bldg., 194 F.2d 484 (1st Cir. 1952); Woods Exploration & Producing Co. v. Aluminum Co. of America, 438 F.2d 1286 (5th Cir. 1971); Otter Tail Power Co. v. United States, 410 U.S. 366 (1973); Hecht v. Pro Football, Inc., 570 F.2d 982 (D.C. Cir. 1977); Fishman v. Estate of Wirtz, 807 F.2d 520 (7th Cir. 1986); MCI Communications Corp. v. American Tel. and Tel. Co., 708 F.2d 1081 (7th Cir. 1983); Aspen Skiing Co. v. Aspen Highlands Skiing Corp., 472 U.S. 585 (1985); Verizon Communications Inc. v. Law Offices of Curtis v. Trinko, L.L.P. 540 U.S. 398 (2004); for a closer analysis of the US "essential facility doctrine", see Lamping (2010), pp. 239 et seqq., with further references.

[17] See Case 88/589/EEC, London European—Sabena, 1988 ECR L 317/47; Case 92/213/EEC, British Midland v. Aer Lingus, 1992 ECR L 96/34; European Commission, Report on Competition Policy 1992, para. 219 (Holyhead); Case 94/19/EC, Sea Containers v. Stena Sealink, 1994 ECR L 15/8, para. 66; European Commission, Report on Competition Policy 1993, para. 234; Case 94/119/EG, Rødby, 1994 ECR L 55/52, para. 12; Joined Cases T-374/94, T-375/94, T-384/94 and T-388/9, European Night Services, 1998 ECR II-3141, para. 209; Case C-7/97, Bronner, 1998 ECR I-7791, paras. 41 et seqq.; see also European Commission, Notice on the Application of the Competition Rules to Access Agreements in the Telecommunications Sector, OJ 1998, C 265/2, para. 68.

[18] See Case C-7/97, Bronner, 1998 ECR I-7791, paras. 43 et seqq.

[19] See Desealers (1995), p. 564; Montag (1997), p. 75; Abermann, p. 171; Humpe and Ritter (2005), p. 19; Eilmansberger (2006), p. 27; Eilmansberger (2003), p. 16; Eilmansberger (2007), Art. 82, para. 369; Jung (2008), Art. 82, para. 219; Anderman and Schmidt (2007), p. 45; Lamping (2010), pp. 319 et seqq., with further references.

2.2 *Abuse of a Dominant Position*

Even where the owner of an intellectual property right enjoys a dominant position, he does not automatically commit an abuse by exploiting his right to the possible detriment of others.[20] The finding of a dominant position is not in itself an allegation of unlawful conduct. In contrast to Section 2 of the Sherman Antitrust Act (15 U.S.C.), Article 102 TFEU does not prohibit dominance as such, neither its creation and preservation nor its strengthening,[21] but only its abuse.[22] Such an abuse may, *in particular*, consist in

(a) directly or indirectly imposing unfair purchase or selling prices or other unfair trading conditions;[23]
(b) limiting production, markets, or technical development to the prejudice of consumers;[24]
(c) applying dissimilar conditions to equivalent transactions with other trading parties, thereby placing them at a competitive disadvantage (discrimination);[25]
(d) making the conclusion of contracts subject to acceptance by the other parties of supplementary obligations that, by their nature or according to commercial usage, have no connection with the subject of such contracts (tying and bundling).[26]

These forms of abuse are typically classified into exclusionary abuses, directed at excluding competitors from the market or preventing them from entering it, and exploitative abuses, whereby the dominant undertaking exploits its economic power.[27] Both kinds of abuse may also be carried out through agreements between undertakings, decisions by associations of undertakings, and concerted practices, which are subject to Article 101 TFEU.

As the wording indicates, the list contained in Article 102 is not exhaustive. Abuse is an undefined legal term open to interpretation. The European Court of Justice (ECJ) has defined it as "an objective concept" relating to behaviour "which is such as to influence the structure of a market where, as a result of the very

[20] Eilmansberger (1992), p. 625; Eilmansberger (2007), Art. 82, para. 345; chapter "Mandatory Licensing Under Patent Law and Competition Law: Different Concerns, Complementary Roles" by Ullrich, in this volume.

[21] Case C-250/92, Gøttrup-Klim, 1994 ECR I-5641, para. 49; Case T-17/93, Matra Hachette, 1994 ECR II-595, para. 153.

[22] For a comparative analysis, see Bloch et al. (2005), pp. 325 et seqq.; Fox (1986), pp. 984 et seq.

[23] See Lamping (2010), pp. 184 et seqq., with further references.

[24] Ibid., pp. 236 et seqq.

[25] Ibid., pp. 204 et seqq.

[26] Ibid., pp. 215 et seqq.

[27] On the distinction between both forms of abuse, see European Commission, Guidelines on the Effect on Trade Concept Contained in Articles 81 and 82 of the Treaty, OJ 2004, C 101/81, paras. 73 et seqq.

presence of the undertaking in question, the degree of competition is weakened and which, through recourse to methods different from those which condition normal competition in products and services on the basis of the transactions of commercial operators, has the effect of hindering the maintenance of the degree of competition still existing in the market or growth of that competition".[28] The decisive question therefore is "whether the dominant undertaking has made use of the opportunities arising out of its dominant position in such a way as to reap trading benefits which it would not have reaped if there had been normal and sufficiently effective competition".[29]

3 Refusal to Licence as an Abuse

Exercising the exclusive rights conferred by a patent, a trademark, a copyright, or the like is not abusive on the sole ground that it is the act of an undertaking occupying a dominant position if that right has not been used as an instrument for the abuse of such a position.[30] The right of an intellectual property owner to prevent third parties from manufacturing and selling or importing, without his consent, products incorporating the protected subject matter constitutes "the very essence of his exclusive right".[31] An obligation imposed upon him to grant to third parties a licence, "even in return for a reasonable royalty", would lead to the proprietor "being deprived of the substance of his exclusive right".[32] Consequently, a refusal to grant such a licence cannot in itself constitute an abuse of a dominant position.

However, the conduct of an undertaking in a dominant position, consisting of the exercise of an intellectual property right granted by national law, cannot, by virtue of that fact alone, be exempt from competition law review.[33] The fact that Article 345 TFEU obliges the Treaties to respect "the rules in Member States governing the system of property ownership", which includes intellectual property,[34] does not change this.

---

[28] Case 85/76, Hoffmann-La Roche, 1979 ECR 461, para. 91; Case C-95/04 P, British Airways, 2007 ECR I-2331, para. 66; Case 31/80, L'Oréal, 1980 ECR 3775, para. 27; Case 322/81, Michelin, 1983 ECR 3461, paras. 29, 70; Case C-62/86, AKZO, 1991 ECR I-3359, para. 69; Case 85/609/EEC, ECS/AKZO, 1985 ECR L 374/1, para. 81; European Commission, Report on Competition Policy 1997, para. 62.

[29] Case 27/76, United Brands, 1978 ECR 207, para. 249.

[30] Case 102/77, Hoffmann-La Roche, 1978 ECR 1139, para. 16.

[31] Case 238/87, Volvo, 1988 ECR 6211, para. 8; Case 53/87, Renault, 1988 ECR 6039, para. 16.

[32] Ibid.

[33] Joined Cases C-241/91 P and C-242/91 P, RTE and ITP, 1995 ECR I-743.

[34] AG Roemer, Case 24/67, Parke, Davis & Co., 1968 ECR 86, 120.

3.1 *Specific Forms of Abuse*

Within the scheme of Article 102 TFEU, an abusive refusal to licence can take a number of forms, depending on the circumstances of the case and the behavioural patterns of the right holder.[35] The case is quite clear where the refusal amounts to

- a discrimination of trading partners, putting licensees at a competitive advantage over those who are not granted a licence, or
- an unjustified foreclosure of competitors because the conclusion of the licence is made subject to the purchase of other products or services (tying or bundling).

In both cases, there will usually be a clear violation of Article 102 TFEU because the refusal to license realises an independent and explicit form of abuse. Establishing an abuse is more complicated where the alleged conduct does not fit into the indicative list of Article 102 TFEU, such as

- a refusal to licence otherwise than on terms or conditions that the right holder knows to be unacceptable, including an undue delay in negotiations or in fulfilling contractual obligations (a "constructive refusal"),[36] or
- a refusal to licence at all.

In the last two cases, competition law is pushed to the limits of its regulatory capacities. On the one hand, it is the essence of any intellectual property right to entitle its owner to exclude others from commercially exploiting the protected subject matter. On the other hand, it is the essence of that exclusionary effect to integrate intellectual property into a market-based pricing mechanism.[37] Intellectual property rights convert information into a tradable commodity.[38] Thus, in principle, it should be up to the right holder to choose his trading partners and to

[35] In principle, it makes no difference whether the dominant company refuses to contract with a new business partner (cf. Joined Cases C-241/91 P and C-242/91 P, RTE and ITP, 1995 ECR I-743; Case T-69/89, RTE, 1991 ECR II-485; Case T-70/89, BBC, 1991 ECR II-535; Case T-76/89, ITP, 1991 ECR II-575; Case 89/205/EEC, Magill TV Guide, 1989 ECR L 78/43; Case C-7/97, Bronner, 1998 ECR I-7791; Case T-504/93, Tiercé Ladbroke, 1997 ECR II-923; Case C-418/01, IMS Health, 2004 ECR I-5039) or whether it refuses to extend a current contractual relationship (cf. Joined Cases 6/73 and 7/73, Commercial Solvents, 1974 ECR 223; Case 72/457/EWG, Zoja, 1972 ECR L 299/51; Case 311/84, CBEM, 1985 ECR 3261; Case 27/76, United Brands, 1978 ECR 207). Both cases are equally covered by Article 102 TFEU. See Wirtz (2006), p. 189; Humpe and Ritter (2005), pp. 7 et seqq.; Ritter (2005), pp. 282 et seqq.; arguing for a differentiated assessment: Schröter (2003), Art. 82, para. 252; Möschel (2007), para. 224.

[36] See Case 1999/243/EC, TACA, 1999 ECR L 95/1, para. 553; Case 2001/892/EC, Deutsche Post, 2001 ECR L 331/40, para. 141; see also European Commission, Guidance on the Commission's Enforcement Priorities in Applying Article 82 of the EC Treaty to Abusive Exclusionary Conduct by Dominant Undertakings, OJ 2009, C 45/7, para. 79.

[37] See Bußmann (1977), p. 130; Carvalho (2001), p. 25.

[38] See Arrow (1962), p. 615.

freely dispose of his intellectual property, just as it should be up to him to ask whatever price the market is willing to pay.[39] This, however, holds true only to the extent that there is effective competition in the relevant market that prevents him from fixing prices and terms. Where this is not the case, abandoning the market to its fate would be incompatible not only with the rationale of competition law but also with the role of intellectual property as a "framework regulation for competition on dynamic markets".[40]

3.2 Access to Essential Facilities

3.2.1 Common Ground, Different Practices

An outright refusal to licence will usually attract the attention of competition authorities where it relates to an "essential" or "indispensable facility" and therefore forecloses or is likely to foreclose the relevant market.[41] European case law suggests that a refusal to license an indispensable intellectual property right that is not discriminatory, exploitative, or part of a tying or bundling strategy can only be considered abusive where

(1) this prevents the market from being served with new or more advanced products or services for which there is a potential demand,
(2) the owner of the intellectual property right instrumentalises the exclusionary power conferred thereby in order to protect or strengthen its position in another related market (market leveraging).

Both cases share a common denominator: the abusive conduct originates from an asset to which no actual or potential substitute exists and that therefore confers on its owner a decisive influence on the operation of the relevant market, including pricing and distribution policies, the availability of products and services, and ultimately the entry and exit of competitors. In both cases, the exclusionary effect of intellectual property protection distorts competition since market revenues are distributed not according to market performance[42] but rather according to an

---

[39] See Beier (1991), p. 20 (fn. 11); Anderman (1998), p. 229; Anderman and Schmidt (2007), p. 52; Friden (1989), p. 211.

[40] Ullrich (2012), p. 425; Ullrich (2007a), p. 28; Ullrich (2007b), 94.

[41] See Case T-201/04, Microsoft, 2007 ECR II-3601; Case COMP/C-3/37.792, Microsoft; Case C-418/01, IMS Health, 2004 ECR I-5039; Joined Cases C-241/91 P and C-242/91 P, RTE and ITP, 1995 ECR I-743; Case T-69/89, RTE, 1991 ECR II-485; Case T-70/89, BBC, 1991 ECR II-535; Case T-76/89, ITP, 1991 ECR II-575; Case 89/205/EEC, Magill TV Guide, 1989 ECR L 78/43; Case T-504/93, Tiercé Ladbroke, 1997 ECR II-923; Case 238/87, Volvo, 1988 ECR 6211; Case 53/87, Renault, 1988 ECR 6039.

[42] According to Kantzenbach, this is a fundamental condition for the functionality of competition. See Kantzenbach (1967), pp. 16 et seq.

indirect, artificial allocation of market power based on an exclusive right whose scope—even taking into account possible *ex post* limitations thereto, such as compulsory licences[43]—is essentially determined without any reference to the economic environment where it is supposed to produce, or risks producing, its economic effects.

Despite their common denominator, the cases are of a different nature.[44] The first form of abuse mentioned above is an exploitative abuse. Where a company neglects a market demand and prevents it from being accommodated by competitors, the actual violation of Article 102 TFEU consists in a negligence of the "special responsibility" towards the dominated market. The one who rules the market must not only refrain from any behaviour that may eliminate residual competition. It must also ensure that market needs are adequately accommodated.[45] In principle, even in the complete absence of competition, a dominant undertaking will still have the right to refuse granting a licence. The mere fact that there are no or at least no substantial competitors does not oblige the monopolist to create competition at the expense of its well-acquired market position. However, despite the lack of actual competition, the dominant company will be expected to behave as if it were operating in a perfectly competitive market environment.[46] This includes not only its general responsibility towards satisfying market needs but also its pricing[47] and innovation behaviour. If not only competition by imitation but also competition by substitution is eliminated,[48] as is the case where an intellectual property right constitutes an indispensable facility,[49] it follows that the right holder

[43] On the latter, see chapter "Mandatory Licensing Under Patent Law and Competition Law: Different Concerns, Complementary Roles" by Ullrich, in this volume; chapter "Compulsory Licensing in Germany", by Maume, in this volume; Chapter "The Requirements for Compulsory Dependency Licences: Learning from the Transformative Use Doctrine in Copyright Law" by Leistner, in this volume.

[44] See Venit and Kallaugher (1994), p. 339; Fine (2002), pp. 459 et seq.; Sufrin (2004), p. 26; Hatzopolous (2004), p. 1624; Lévêque (2005), pp. 80, 82 et seqq., 91; Anderman and Schmidt (2007), p. 67; Tritton (2008), p. 1042; Palmstorfer (2008), pp. 564 et seqq.; Eilmansberger (2007), Art. 82, paras. 331, 374; Ullrich and Heinemann (2007), GRUR B, para. 59; Lamping (2010), pp. 282 et seqq., with further references.

[45] For a quantitative perspective, see Ahlborn et al. (2005), p. 1147; for the qualitative dimension, see Desealers (1995), p. 566; Pilny (1995), p. 957; Derclaye (2004), p. 403; Spindler and Apel (2005), p. 137; Leistner (2005), pp. 152, 160 et seq. Höppner (2005), p. 462; Heinemann (2006), pp. 712, 710 (fn. 58); Ohly (2007), pp. 65 et seq. Howarth and McMahon (2008), p. 123; Turney (2005), p. 189.

[46] See Miksch (1949), p. 310.

[47] The fact that a competitor intends to introduce cheaper products or services will however generally not be enough in order to establish an abuse, unless the pricing policy of the dominant company amounts to a violation of Article 102(a) TFEU and therefore to a constructive refusal to license (see Case 1999/243/EC, TACA, 1999 ECR L 95/1, para. 553; see supra fn. 37 for further references).

[48] This constitutes a systemic anomaly in the area of intellectual property protection. See Drexl et al. (2006), p. 566; Drexl (2004), pp. 806 et seq.; Conde Gallego (2006), pp. 27 et seq.

[49] See Lamping (2010), pp. 293 et seqq.

must either himself exploit the market opportunities protected by the intellectual property right or enable others to do so. If he fails on both ends, competition law must intervene.[50]

Market leveraging is a different story. In this case, the dominant company does not simply reap the benefits of a well-acquired market position. It rather illegitimately expands that position into another technically or commercially related but economically self-contained market and thereby gains an unjustified competitive advantage in that market. This makes it a particularly serious form of exclusionary abuse. In order to establish a violation of Article 102 TFEU, both markets must be sufficiently independent from each other so as to warrant the conclusion of an illegitimate expansion of market power, and at the same time they must be sufficiently related[51] so that causality between the dominant position in the upstream market and the distortion of competition in a downstream market can be determined. In the context of intellectual property rights, the decisive question is to which extent the market opportunities created thereby should be reserved to the right holder.[52] Although protection granted by intellectual property law usually relates to all possible uses of the protected subject matter that fall within the scope of the exclusive rights, competition authorities may still determine that some of these uses are more inclusive in the intellectual property right than others.[53] Not each and every follow-on market that is legally reserved to the right holder due to an essential facility or bottleneck situation relates to the "specific subject matter"[54] of the intellectual property right at issue. Some market opportunities reflect the substance of the intellectual property, whereas others are rather incidental consequences of the legal protection afforded thereto.

An example that, in theory, involves both forms of abusive conduct can be found in *Volvo*[55] and *Renault*.[56] The refusal of a car manufacturer to grant a licence for

---

[50] Ibid., pp. 286 et seqq., 324 et seqq.

[51] Mestmäcker and Schweitzer (2004), § 18, para. 20.

[52] See Dreier (2001), pp. 53, 60, 70 et seqq.; Eilmansberger (2003), pp. 21 et seqq.; Schuhmacher (2003), pp. 109 et seq.; Eilmansberger (2005b), p. 338; O'Donoghue and Padilla (2006), p. 437; Eilmansberger (2007), Art. 82, para. 396; Eilmansberger (2005a), p. 162.

[53] See Lamping (2010), pp. 289 et seqq., 336 et seqq.

[54] See Joined Cases C-267/95 and C-268/95, Merck, 1996 ECR I-6285, paras. 30 et seq.; Case 15/74, Centrafarm, 1974 ECR 1147, paras. 9 et seq.; Case 434/85, Allen and Hanburys, 1988 ECR 1245, para. 11; Case 187/89, Merck, 1981 ECR 2063, para. 4; Case C-235/89, Commission v. Italy, 1992 ECR I-777, para. 17; Case C-30/90, Commission v. United Kingdom, 1992 ECR I-829, para. 21; Case C-191/90, Generics and Harris Pharmaceuticals, 1992 ECR I-5335, para. 23; Case 78/70, Deutsche Grammophon, 1971 ECR 487, para. 11; Joined Cases C-92/92 and C-326/92, Phil Collins, 1993 ECR I-5145 para. 20; Joined Cases 55/80 and 57/80, Musik-Vertrieb membran GmbH, 1981 ECR 147, para. 12.

[55] Case 238/87, Volvo, 1988 ECR 6211.

[56] Case 53/87, Renault, 1988 ECR 6039.

"must match" spare parts leads to market leveraging,[57] irrespective of whether these parts are covered by design protection or not.[58] In turn, the decision no longer to produce spare parts for a particular model even though many cars of that model are still in circulation constitutes a failure of the dominant company to accommodate the needs of the dominated market.

3.2.2 Different Practices, Different Rules

Contrary to what the ECJ seems to have claimed in *IMS Health*,[59] a refusal to licence is not only incompatible with Article 102 TFEU if it both "prevents the emergence of a new product for which there is a potential consumer demand"[60] and "excludes any competition on a secondary market".[61] Since an independent form of abuse stands behind each of these restraints of competition, there is no need to require their cumulative presence.[62] On one hand, preventing the market from being served with new or more advanced products is not only abusive where it excludes competition in a "secondary market".[63] On the other hand, market leveraging is not only abusive where it prevents the emergence of such products.[64] A cumulation of both conditions is clearly sufficient to establish a violation of Article 102 TFEU but certainly not necessary for a refusal to license to be considered anti-competitive.[65]

[57] Despite the ECJ's finding that such a refusal can only be considered abusive where it is combined with an arbitrary refusal to supply spare parts to independent repairers (Case 238/87, Volvo, 1988 ECR 6211, para. 9; Case 53/87, Renault, 1988 ECR 6039, para. 16).

[58] On the scope of design protection for spare parts and its antitrust implications, see Drexl et al. (2005), p. 448.

[59] Case C-418/01, IMS Health, 2004 ECR I-5039, para. 38: "[I]n order for the refusal by an undertaking which owns an [intellectual property right] to give access to a product or service indispensable for carrying on a particular business to be treated as abusive, it is sufficient that three cumulative conditions be satisfied, namely, that that refusal is preventing the emergence of a new product for which there is a potential consumer demand, that it is unjustified and such as to exclude any competition on a secondary market."

[60] See Joined Cases C-241/91 P and C-242/91 P, RTE and ITP, 1995 ECR I-743, paras. 29 et seq., 54; Case C-418/01, IMS Health, 2004 ECR I-5039, paras. 48 et seq.

[61] See Joined Cases C-241/91 P and C-242/91 P, RTE and ITP, 1995 ECR I-743, paras. 44, 56; Case C-418/01, IMS Health, 2004 ECR I-5039, paras. 40 et seqq.

[62] See Heinemann (2005), pp. 72 et seqq.; Eilmansberger (2005b), p. 335; Leistner (2005), pp. 150 et seqq.; Eilmansberger (2007), Art. 82, paras. 323, 331; Weiß (2007), Art. 82, para. 40; Monti (2007), p. 229; Conde Gallego and Riziotis (2004), p. 571; Drexl (2004), p. 799.

[63] Fine (2002), pp. 459 et seq.; see also Eilmansberger (2007), Art. 82, para. 365; Heinemann (2005), pp. 72 et seq.; Korah (2005), p. 437; Korah (2006), p. 147.

[64] See Eilmansberger (2007), Art. 82, paras. 331, 374; Mennicke (1996), pp. 653 et seq.; Müller (1998), p. 236; Casper (2002), p. 701.

[65] See Fine (2002), pp. 460 et seq.; Anderman (2004), pp. 13 et seq.; Tremmel (2004), p. 286; Vinje and Dodoo (2005), p. 100; Höppner (2005), p. 460; Temple Lang (2005), p. 64; Anderman and Schmidt (2007), p. 62; Ullrich and Heinemann (2007), GRUR B, para. 59; Körber (2007), p. 1213; Tritton (2008), pp. 1044, 1054; Hartmann-Rüppel and Engelhoven (2008), p. 302.

The secondary market requirement is essentially a relic from the early *Commercial Solvents*[66] and *Télémarketing*[67] decisions, on which the ECJ has erroneously based its subsequent case law involving intellectual property rights. The requirement made perfect sense in the context of these decisions since they related to classic leveraging situations. In *Commercial Solvents*, for example, there was an economically self-contained downstream market for ethambutol, a drug for the treatment of tuberculosis, and a distinct upstream market for products based on nitroparaffins, which includes the raw materials (nitropropane and aminobutanol) needed to manufacture ethambutol. By stopping supplies of these raw materials to its customers, Commercial Solvents, which had a worldwide monopoly in the production and sale of nitropropane and aminobutanol, eliminated all competition in the market for derivatives and consequently ended up being the only producer of ethambutol.

In other cases, such as *Magill*[68] and *IMS Health*,[69] the distinction between an up- and a downstream market is highly artificial. By applying the "two market requirement" developed in the leveraging cases of the 1970s to ordinary essential facility situations, the ECJ had no choice but to consider the essential facility a market in itself, even though it falls short of the economic definition of a market. Apparently, the Court failed to realise that not all refusal to contract cases are equal and that despite the common denominator of an essential facility two forms of abuse must be distinguished. In *IMS Health*, for example, there was no "secondary market" in which competition could have been excluded. It does not appear very convincing to distinguish between an upstream market for a "brick structure", which divides a geographical territory into a certain number of segments or bricks, and a downstream market for pharmaceutical sales data, which is processed and reported according to that brick structure. The fact that customers will not accept sales reports based on a different brick structure makes that structure a *de facto* standard and consequently an essential facility, but it does not create an economically self-contained relevant market. Cases like *Magill* and *IMS Health* are not about leveraging market power but simply about a selective refusal to contract, which reserves to the owner of the essential facility the market opportunities created thereby.

In fact, the ECJ itself seemed to be rather uncomfortable with the conclusion reached in *IMS Health*. Right after finding that a refusal to licence will not be deemed abusive unless it both "prevents the emergence of a new product" and "excludes any competition on a secondary market", the Court literally banishes the

---

[66] Joined Cases 6/73 and 7/73, Commercial Solvents, 1974 ECR 223; Case 72/457/EWG, Zoja, 1972 ECR L 299/51.

[67] Case 311/84, CBEM, 1985 ECR 3261.

[68] Joined Cases C-241/91 P and C-242/91 P, RTE and ITP, 1995 ECR I-743; Case T-69/89, RTE, 1991 ECR II-485; Case T-70/89, BBC, 1991 ECR II-535; Case T-76/89, ITP, 1991 ECR II-575; Case 89/205/EEC, Magill TV Guide, 1989 ECR L 78/43; for a discussion of these decisions, see Lamping (2010), pp. 256 et seqq.

[69] Case C-418/01, IMS Health, 2004 ECR I-5039; for a discussion of this decision, see Lamping (2010), pp. 263 et seqq.

latter requirement into insignificance by stating that "for the purposes of the application of the earlier case-law, it is sufficient that a potential market or even hypothetical market can be identified".[70] According to the Court, "it is determinative that two different stages of production may be identified and that they are interconnected, inasmuch as the upstream product is indispensable for the supply of the downstream product".[71] This could also be read as a cryptic way of suggesting that not all market opportunities protected by an intellectual property are necessarily reserved to its right holder, independent of whether they give rise to a separate product market.

Whereas the secondary market requirement did not fit for *Magill* and *IMS Health*, a strict application of the "new product" requirement would have led to unsatisfactory results in *Microsoft*,[72] which was, just as *Commercial Solvents* and *Télémarketing*, essentially about market leveraging. Microsoft held a dominant position in the market for client PC operating systems. By refusing to disclose and authorise the use of interoperability information for the purpose of developing and distributing products competing with Microsoft's own products on the market for work group server operating systems, it restricted competition on that market. The absence of interoperability had the effect of "reinforcing Microsoft's competitive position on the work group server operating systems market".[73] Such a behaviour is contrary to Article 102 TFEU, independent of whether it prevents the emergence of a new product on the neighbouring market. That also explains why the Court of First Instance encountered difficulties in cumulatively applying the *Magill* criteria, which ultimately prompted it to conclude that "the circumstance relating to the appearance of a new product cannot be the only parameter which determines whether a refusal to license an intellectual property right is capable of causing prejudice to consumers"[74] within the meaning of Article 102 TFEU.[75]

3.3 Objective Justification

A dominant undertaking has the possibility of demonstrating an objective justification for its conduct even if it is *prima facie* an abuse. To be more precise: certain types of conduct on the part of a dominant undertaking do not fall within the

[70] Case C-418/01, IMS Health, 2004 ECR I-5039, para. 44; AG Tizzano, Case C-418/01, IMS Health, 2004 ECR I-5039, paras. 56 et seqq.

[71] Case C-418/01, IMS Health, 2004 ECR I-5039, para. 45.

[72] Case T-201/04, Microsoft, 2007 ECR II-3601; Case COMP/C-3/37.792, Microsoft; for a discussion of these decisions, see Lamping (2010), pp. 256 et seqq., 269 et seqq.

[73] Case T-201/04, Microsoft, 2007 ECR II-3601, para. 422.

[74] Ibid., para. 647.

[75] See also Ullrich.

category of abuse at all if they can be justified on reasonable grounds.[76] A refusal to licence that fulfils the above-mentioned requirements for an abuse may thus be admissible if it

- serves a legitimate public interest objective, such as health or consumer protection,[77] or
- amounts to legitimate business behaviour.

In view of the "more economic approach"[78] that the Commission has been pushing since the early 2000s, a dominant company may eventually also argue that its conduct has produced efficiency gains that outweigh its alleged anti-competitive effects. If at all, such an efficiency defence must however be handled with extreme caution.[79]

The most promising justification that a dominant undertaking can invoke is its right to not be punished for legitimate business behaviour, which encompasses competition on the merits, as well as the protection of legitimate commercial interests.[80] In the context of access to intellectual property, such a defence could refer to the protection of concrete investments made in relation to the protected subject matter and its exclusive exploitation, of trade or business secrets that would need to be disclosed together with a licence, or simply to the fact that the licence petitioner demands unacceptable licence terms or conditions.[81] It should be recalled that Article 102 TFEU does not prohibit dominance as such, neither its creation nor its strengthening,[82] but only its abuse through practices that cannot be considered competition on the merits.[83] After all, abuse is "recourse to methods *different* from those which condition normal competition in products and services".[84,85]

---

[76] AG Jacobs, Case C-53/03, Syfait, ECR 2005, I-4609, para. 72.

[77] Case T-30/89, Hilti, 1991 ECR II-1439, para. 118; Case T-83/91, Tetra Pak I, 1994 ECR II-755, paras. 83 et seq., 139 et seq.

[78] See Drexl (2008), p. 27; Drexl (2007), p. 647; Schmidt and Voigt (2006), p. 1098; Drexl et al. (2011), containing a collection of essays on the foundations of the economic approach in competition law and its normative and institutional limitations.

[79] See Lowe (2004), p. 171; Loewenthal (2005), pp. 464 et seq.

[80] See Loewenthal (2005), p. 464; see also Bergman (2000), p. 63; Eilmansberger (2003), pp. 17 et seqq.; Eilmansberger (2005a), p. 165; Thyri (2005), pp. 397 et seqq.; Eilmansberger (2007), Art. 82, paras. 418 et seqq.; Elhauge (2003), p. 253.

[81] See Tritton (2008), p. 1058.

[82] Case C-250/92, Gøttrup-Klim, 1994 ECR I-5641, para. 49; see supra fn. 21 for further references.

[83] See Faull and Nikpay (2007), paras. 4.154 et seq.; Eilmansberger (2007), Art. 82, paras. 419, 421; Anderman and Schmidt (2007), p. 38.

[84] Case 85/76, Hoffmann-La Roche, 1979 ECR 461, para. 91; see supra fn. 28 for further references.

[85] See also United States v. Aluminum Co. of America, 148 F.2d 416, 430 (2nd Cir. 1945): "A single producer may be the survivor out of a group of active competitors, merely by virtue of his superior skill, foresight and industry. In such cases a strong argument can be made that, although the result may expose the public to the evils of monopoly, the Act does not mean to condemn the

In the context of essential facilities, both the facility as such as well as its essentiality must be attributable to competition on the merits. A legitimate business defence can only be successful if the restriction of competition is in its entirety the result of superior performance. Furthermore, the conduct that is to be justified must be covered by the "intentionality" of the essential facility.[86] The decisive question is whether the essential facility constitutes an independent and purposeful result of the dominant company's supremacy in competition and whether an obligation to share it with competitors would have prevented the company from developing it in the first place. If, on the other hand, the essential facility is just a byproduct or spin-off of other commercial activities (such as television programme[87] or interoperability[88] information) or a result of exceptional market conditions (such as network effects,[89] standardisation,[90] or natural monopoly), its owner should have a hard time arguing that an obligation to contract or disclose information "would amount to an interference with its incentive to innovate".[91] An aspect that could also be of relevance in that context is the extent to which the essential facility is based on third-party investments, such as state aid, open innovation, or consumer involvement.[92] The lower the contribution of the dominant company to the creation and market penetration of the essential facility is, the weaker is its claim to remain the only one on the market exploiting it.

Last but not least, a refusal to license must also be a proportional measure. The alleged conduct must not only serve a legitimate purpose, but it should also not limit competition beyond what is necessary and sufficient to achieve that purpose.

3.4 Conclusion

In conclusion, a refusal to license can be considered abusive within the meaning of Article 102 TFEU if three requirements are met:[93]

resultant of those very forces which it is its prime object to foster: finis opus coronat. The successful competitor, having been urged to compete, must not be turned upon when he wins".

[86] See Lamping (2010), pp. 353 et seq.

[87] See Case 89/205/EEC, Magill TV Guide, 1989 ECR L 78/43, para. 22.

[88] See Case T-201/04, Microsoft, 2007 ECR II-3601.

[89] See Lamping (2010), pp. 304 et seqq.

[90] See Case C-418/01, IMS Health, 2004 ECR I-5039, para. 6; BGH (German Supreme Court) Decision of 13 July 2004, KZR 40/02, Standard Spundfass, GRUR 2004, 968.

[91] See Case T-201/04, Microsoft, 2007 ECR II-3601, paras. 111, 274, 627, 670, 752; Case COMP/C-3/37.792, Microsoft, para. 709.

[92] See Case C-418/01, IMS Health, 2004 ECR I-5039, paras. 5 et seq., 29 et seq.

[93] On the burden of proof, see Lamping (2010), pp. 291 et seq.

(1) The protected subject matter is indispensable in order to compete on the market, and there are no viable actual or potential substitutes to it.[94]
(2) By refusing to grant a licence, the right holder
   - prevents a quantitative or qualitative improvement of the satisfaction of market demands to the prejudice of consumer welfare;[95] *or*
   - expands its dominant position into another economically independent market that is not only a downstream market stage of the essential facility and the market opportunities created thereby.[96]
(3) The refusal to license cannot be justified on reasonable grounds.[97]

As a general rule, market leveraging should be more difficult to justify.[98] From an antitrust perspective, the negligence of a special responsibility towards the dominated market—whether due to inability or reluctance—may be considered less reprehensible than a foreclosure of another market. The objective of the prohibition of abuse of market dominance is to prevent distortions of competition rather than to protect the position of particular market participants. Despite the central role that consumer welfare plays in competition policy,[99] competition law is primarily about open markets, not about happy consumers. It is about protecting competition as an institution. The welfare-enhancing effects of an "open market economy with free competition" (cf. Article 119 TFEU) are naturally part of that

[94] For a comprehensive analysis of the criteria relevant for assessing "indispensability" and "non-duplicability", see Lamping (2010), pp. 293 et seqq., 314 et seqq.

[95] See Lamping (2010), pp. 324 et seqq.

[96] Ibid., pp. 336 et seqq.

[97] Ibid., pp. 343 et seqq.

[98] This may also be concluded from *Commercial Solvents*. In that case, the ECJ did not even bother to undertake an analysis of the downstream market but concluded that an abuse had taken place simply as a result of the company's dominance in the upstream market for nitroparaffins and its subsequent leverage of that dominance into the downstream market for ethambutol (Joined Cases 6/73 and 7/73, Commercial Solvents, 1974 ECR 223).

[99] See European Commission, DG Competition Discussion Paper on the Application of Article 82 of the Treaty to Exclusionary Abuses, 2005, para. 4; European Commissioners tend to put great emphasis on the Commission's devotion to consumer welfare: Italianer, Competition Policy for Consumers' and Citizens' Welfare, speech given on 24 May 2013 at the "European Competition and Consumer Day" in Dublin; Almunia, Competition and Consumers: The Future of EU Competition Policy, speech on 12 May 2010 at the "European Competition Day" in Madrid; Kroes, Consumer Welfare: More than a Slogan, speech delivered on 21 October 2009 at the "Competition and Consumers in the 21st Century" conference in Brussels; Monti, Competition for Consumers' Benefit, speech on 22 October 2004 at the "European Competition Day" in Amsterdam; Lowe, Consumer Welfare and Efficiency—New Guiding Principles of Competition Policy? Speech on 27 March 2007 at the "13th International Conference on Competition and 14th European Competition Day" in Munich; Lowe, The Consumer Interest in Competition Cases, in: Andenas, Hutchings and Marsden, Current Competition Law, 2005, Vol. III, 167; Monti, Competition and the Consumer: What are the Aims of European Competition Policy?, speech on 26 February 2002 at the "European Competition Day" in Madrid.

regulatory goal, but they should not be the centre of attention of the antitrust analysis.

3.5 *Tangible Versus Intangible Property*

The above-mentioned requirements for an abusive refusal to contract should apply equally to all kinds of commodities: movable property (such as raw materials or machines), immovable property (such as infrastructure, distribution, or production facilities), and intangible property (such as intellectual property rights, virtual networks, trade or business secrets).[100] From an antitrust perspective, there is no reason to favour one over the other. In particular, there is no reason to provide for stricter requirements where the "essential facility" is protected by an intellectual property right.[101] Competition law aims at preventing distortions of competition, irrespective of the kind of property that stands in the way of achieving that.

The fact that intellectual property is not more worthy of protection than other kinds of property is not to say that it may not be in need of special consideration.[102] By its very nature, information is more susceptible to expropriation than tangible property. Although exclusive rights are involved in both cases, there is a qualitative difference between granting access to an infrastructure that can only be used under direct control of its owner and granting a licence for a protected technology or disclosing a trade secret. Whenever the competitive advantage of an asset can be detached from its material self, the spillover effects of sharing it with competitors tend to be unmanageable and might well lead to a distortion of competition rather than to its improvement.

---

[100] Eilmansberger (2007), Art. 82, paras. 332, 359.

[101] See US Department of Justice and Federal Trade Commission (1995), p. 3; Easterbrook (1990), pp. 108 et seqq.; Crowther (1995), p. 525; Taylor (1995), p. 101; Ridyard (1996), p. 445; Mennicke (1996), pp. 651 et seq.; Heinemann (2002), pp. 494, 713; Katz (2002), p. 349; Baumol (2002), p. 80; MacKie-Mason (2002), p. 8; Beckmerhagen (2002), p. 329; Eilmansberger (2003), p. 15; Elhauge (2003), pp. 276 et seq., 304; Schuhmacher (2003), p. 109; Genevaz (2004), pp. 743 et seqq.; Eilmansberger (2005b), pp. 335 et seq.; Eilmansberger (2005a), p. 159; Ritter (2005), pp. 290 et seqq.; Heinemann (2005), p. 71; Thyri (2005), pp. 394 et seq.; O'Donoghue and Padilla (2006), pp. 421 et seqq.; Heinemann (2006), p. 710; Eilmansberger (2007), Art. 82, paras. 386 et seqq.; Monti (2007), p. 239; for dissenting opinions, see Kaplow (1984), p. 1817; Montag (1997), p. 75; Lipsky and Sidak (1999), p. 1220; Hovenkamp et al. (2002), pp. 13 et seqq.; Casper (2002), pp. 694 et seqq., 706; Gleklen (2002), p. 10; Schwarze (2003), pp. 25 et seq.; Derclaye (2003), pp. 696 et seqq.; Derclaye (2004), p. 402; Anderman (2004), p. 18; Wirtz and Holzhäuser (2004), p. 685; Jung (2004), p. 391; Temple Lang (2005), p. 59; Merdzo (2005), p. 169; Lévêque (2005), p. 91; Spindler and Apel (2005), p. 137; Forrester (2005), p. 938; Höppner (2005), pp. 460 et seq.; Hovenkamp et al. (2006), pp. 15 et seq.; Anderman (2008), p. 399.

[102] See Eilmansberger (2003), p. 15; Font Galarza (2003), p. 14; Drexl (2004), p. 805; Eilmansberger (2005a), p. 159; Eilmansberger (2005b), p. 336; Lipsky and Sidak (1999), pp. 1218 et seq.; Katz (2002), pp. 345 et seq.; O'Donoghue and Padilla (2006), p. 422.

Indeed, this does not affect the extent to which competition law imposes an obligation to contract. Such an obligation, as well as the prerequisites that need to be fulfilled in order for it to be applicable, arises from competition law. It is a direct effect of the right of other market participants in not being unduly hindered in competition. This right is independent of any trade-offs that may or may have not been done at the time of granting property protection and determining its scope. However, the qualitative difference between tangible property and intangible property may be relevant for the grounds that can be brought forward in order to justify a refusal to contract. This is where competition authorities need to balance the opposing rights of the proprietor and his competitors. This is where they need to reconcile two essentials of the market economy: private property and free competition. Both are indispensable for the operation of markets, but sometimes one needs to step back behind the other.

4 Compulsory Licence as a Remedy

Once a violation of Article 102 TFEU has been established, the Commission may impose a sanction in order to punish the dominant company for the illegitimate conduct and a remedy in order to stop the abuse, its anti-competitive effects, and its recurrence. Remedies must be directed at the concrete restriction of competition, and they must be proportionate. A remedy must therefore always be a direct response to the established abuse.

In the context of a refusal to licence, it must be differentiated between the two forms of abuse discussed above: market leveraging and a negligence of market needs. It is only in the case of an illegitimate expansion of market power that a compulsory licence is the compelling remedy. Here, the refusal to licence is the actual abuse, creating the anti-competitive effects that need to be undone. In the case of an abuse due to an insufficient response to market needs, the situation is different. Here, the refusal to license does not cause the abuse. It merely prevents other market participants from making up for it. A compulsory licence will only come into play where the dominant company is unable or unwilling to live up to its expectations.[103]

It must nevertheless be borne in mind that it is not within the competences of the Commission to grant a compulsory licence. If a violation of Article 102 TFEU is established, the Commission asks the dominant company to cease and desist from the anti-competitive conduct. If such conduct consists in a refusal to license, it will however impose not a compulsory licence but rather an obligation to abstain from refusing a license. It is then up to the parties to conclude the agreement, as well as to

---

[103] In this case, the scope of the compulsory licence may be restricted to what is necessary in order to undo the abuse, *i.e.* accommodate the unsatisfied demand.

negotiate its terms and conditions.[104] Regarding the content of that agreement, the Commission's only interest is to ensure a sufficiently broad scope so that anti-competitive effects are eliminated and no additional abuse takes place (*e.g.*, due to inappropriate terms or conditions or a tie-in of unrelated products or licences). Anything else would force the Commission into the role of a "price commissioner", which is obviously a daunting task for a competition authority.[105] Without the metering function of a competitive market, the determination of a fair and adequate price or royalty is virtually impossible. Unless the Commission is aware of comparable markets and transactions that could be used as a benchmark,[106] it has no other choice but to look into the investments made in connection with the intellectual property at stake[107] and add an adequate amount that reflects the incurred risks, failures, and opportunity costs.[108]

5 Concluding Remarks

Whenever intellectual property rights are involved, courts tend to be awestruck. Competition authorities usually treat intellectual property with kid gloves for fear of getting lost in the complex dynamics of protecting private property as a means of ensuring effective competition. The restrained control of European institutions over anti-competitive uses of intellectual property rights is a clear testimony to this. Both the Commission and the Court should be more daring about these issues. As an integral element of the overall regulation of competitive markets, intellectual

[104] See Ullrich.

[105] See European Commission (1994), para. 207; Möschel (2007), para. 133 et seq.; Bishop and Walker (2002), p. 194; O'Donoghue and Padilla (2006), pp. 627 et seq.; Whish (2005), p. 689; Jung (2008), Art. 82, para. 144; Heinemann (2002), p. 463 (fn. 1054).

[106] The "comparative market" approach is also used in the context of Article 102(a) TFEU in order to assess whether prices charged by the dominant undertaking are excessive or discriminatory. See Case 395/87, Staatsanwaltschaft, 1989 ECR 2521, para. 38; Case 30/87, Bodson, 1988 ECR 2479, para. 31; Joined Cases 110/88, 241/88 and 242/88, Lucazeau, 1989 ECR 2811, para. 25; Case 84/379/EWG, BL, 1984 ECR L 207/11; for further details, see Eilmansberger (2007), Art. 82, paras. 216 et seqq.; Dirksen (2006), Art. 82, para. 98 et seqq.; Jung (2008), Art. 82, paras. 147, 287 et seqq.; Schröter (2003), Art. 82, para. 188 et seqq.; O'Donoghue and Padilla (2006), pp. 614 et seqq.; Lübbig (2005), Art. 82, para. 152 et seqq.

[107] On the calculation of these investments, see Kingston (1994), p. 661; Kingston (2001), p. 419; Merges (1992), p. 73.

[108] See European Commission, Guidelines on the Application of Article 81 of the EC Treaty to Technology Transfer Agreements, OJ 2004, C 101/2, para. 8; O'Donoghue and Padilla (2006), p. 623; Korah (2004), p. 99; Keeling (2003), p. 379; Anderman and Kallaugher (2006), p. 273; Anderman and Schmidt (2007), p. 52; Roth and Rose (2008), para. 10.108; Korah (1988), p. 383.

property protection should not escape antitrust scrutiny, not even within its very substance, its "specific subject matter".[109]

In assessing the abusive character of a refusal to license, one should keep in mind that competition law does not question the intellectual property of the dominant undertaking as such, but only its freedom to contract. Indeed, under exceptional circumstances, a denial of the freedom to contract may well undermine the competitive advantages entailed by intellectual property protection. But in the vast majority of cases, including those discussed above, an obligation to licence will not deprive the right holder of the possibility to gain a fair "reward for his creative effort"[110] that encourages him to continue innovating.

References

Abermann (2003) Ist die Übernahme der Essential Facilities-Doktrin überflüssig? Medien und Recht 171

Ahlborn, Evans, Padilla (2005) The logic & limits of the exceptional circumstances test in Magill and IMS health. Fordham Int Law J 1147

Anderman (1998) EC competition law and intellectual property rights

Anderman (2004) Does the Microsoft case offer a new paradigm for the "Exceptional Circumstances" test and compulsory copyright licenses under EC competition law? Comp Law Rev 1

Anderman (2008) Microsoft v. Commission and the interoperability issue. Eur Intellect Prop Rev 399

Anderman, Kallaugher (2006) Technology transfer and the new EU competition rules

Anderman, Schmidt (2007) EC competition policy and IPRs. In: Anderman (ed) The interface between intellectual property rights and competition policy, p 45

Arrow (1962) Economic welfare and the allocation of resources for invention. In: Nelson (ed) The rate and direction of inventive activity, p 615

Baumol (2002) The free-market innovation machine

Beckmerhagen (2002) Die essential facilities doctrine im US-amerikanischen und europäischen Kartellrecht, p 329

Beier (1991) Missbrauch einer beherrschenden Stellung durch Ausübung gewerblicher Schutzrechte? In: Westermann, Rosener (eds) Festschrift für Quack

Bergman (2000) The Bronner case – a turning point for the essential facilities doctrine? Eur Comp Law Rev 63

Bishop, Walker (2002) The economics of EC competition law

Bloch et al (2005) A comparative analysis of Art. 82 of the EC Treaty and Sec. 2 of the Sherman Act. Zeitschrift für Wettbewerbsrecht (ZWeR) 325

Bußmann (1977) Patentrecht und Marktwirtschaft. GRUR 130

Carvalho (2001) The primary function of patents. J Law Technol Policy 25

Casper (2002) Die wettbewerbsrechtliche Begründung von Zwangslizenzen. ZHR

Conde Gallego (2006) Die Anwendung des kartellrechtlichen Missbrauchsverbots auf "unerlässliche" Immaterialgüterrechte. GRUR Int 27

[109] For a synopsis of the ECJ's jurisdiction on the "specific subject matter" of intellectual property rights, see van der Wal (1994), pp. 230 et seq.

[110] Joined Cases C-267/95 and C-268/95, Merck, 1996 ECR I-6285, paras. 30 et seq.; see supra fn. 55 for further references.

Conde Gallego, Riziotis (2004) Case note. Int Rev Intellect Prop Comp Law 571
Crowther (1995) Compulsory licensing of intellectual property rights. Eur Law Rev 525
Derclaye (2003) Abuses of dominant position and intellectual property rights. World Comp 696
Derclaye (2004) The IMS health decision: a triple victory. World Comp
Deringer (1969) Das Wettbewerbsrecht der Europäischen Wirtschaftsgemeinschaft
Desealers (1995) Die "Essential Facilities"-Doktrin im Lichte des Magill-Urteils des EuGH. EuZW
Dirksen (2006) In: Langen, Bunte (eds) Kommentar zum deutschen und europäischen Kartellrecht, vol 2
Dreier (2001) Primär- und Folgemärkte. In: Schricker, Dreier, Kur (eds) Geistiges Eigentum im Dienst der Innovation
Drexl (2004) Intellectual property and antitrust law. Int Rev Intellect Prop Comp Law
Drexl (2007) Abuse of dominance in licensing and refusal to license: a "More Economic Approach" to competition by imitation and to competition by substitution. In: Ehlermann, Atansiu (eds) Competition law annual 2005: the interaction between competition law and IP law, p 647
Drexl (2008) Is there a "More Economic Approach" to intellectual property and competition law? In: Drexl (ed) Research handbook on intellectual property and competition law, p 27
Drexl, Hilty, Kur (2005) Design protection for spare parts and the commission's proposal for a repairs clause. Int Rev Intellect Prop Comp Law 448
Drexl et al (2006) Comments of the Max Planck Institute for Intellectual Property, Competition and Tax Law on the Directorate-General Competition Discussion Paper of December 2005 on the Application of Art. 82 of the Treaty to Exclusionary Abuses. Int Rev Intellect Prop Comp Law 566
Drexl, Kerber, Podszun (eds) (2011) Competition policy and the economic approach
Easterbrook (1990) Intellectual property is still property. Harv J Law Public Policy 108
Eilmansberger (1992) Der Umgang marktbeherrschender Unternehmen mit Immaterialgüterrechten im Lichte des Art. 86 EWGV. Europäische Zeitschrift für Wirtschaftsrecht (EuZW) 625
Eilmansberger (2003) Abschlusszwang und Essential Facility Doktrin nach Art. 82, Europäisches Wirtschafts- und Steuerrecht (EWS)
Eilmansberger (2005a) How to distinguish good from bad competition under Article 82 EC. Common Mark Law Rev
Eilmansberger (2005b) The essential facilities doctrine under Art. 82. King's College Law J
Eilmansberger (2006) Dominance – the lost child? Eur Comp J
Eilmansberger (2007) In: Hirsch, Montag, Säcker (eds) Münchener Kommentar zum europäischen und deutschen Wettbewerbsrecht, vol 1
Elhauge (2003) Defining better monopolization standards. Stanford Law Rev
European Commission (1994) Report on competition policy
Faull, Nikpay (2007) The EC law of competition
Fikentscher (1997) Die Freiheit und ihr Paradox
Fine (2002) NDC/IMS: a logical application of the essential facilities doctrine. Eur Comp Law Rev
Font Galarza (2003) Interface between antitrust and intellectual property rights. Int Bus Lawyer 14
Forrester (2005) Article 82: remedies in search of theories. Fordham Int Law J 938
Fox (1986) Monopolization and dominance in the United States and the European Community. Notre Dame Law Rev 984
Frenz (2006) Handbuch Europarecht, vol 2
Friden (1989) Recent developments in EEC intellectual property law. Common Mark Law Rev 211
Frueh (2012) Immaterialgüterrechte und der relevante Markt
Genevaz (2004) Against immunity for unilateral refusals to deal in intellectual property. Berkeley Technol Law J 743

Gleklen (2002) Per se legality for unilateral refusals to license IP is correct as a matter of law and policy. Antitrust Source 10
Hartmann-Rüppel, Engelhoven (2008) Kartellrecht und Eigentum. ZWeR 302
Hatzopolous (2004) Case note. Common Mark Law Rev 1624
Hawk (1988) The American (antitrust) revolution. Eur Comp Law Rev 78
Hayek (1968) Der Wettbewerb als Entdeckungsverfahren. Kieler Vorträge
Heinemann (2002) Immaterialgüterschutz in der Wettbewerbsordnung
Heinemann (2005) Compulsory licences and product integration in European Competition Law. Int Rev Intellect Prop Comp Law
Heinemann (2006) Gefährdung von Rechten des geistigen Eigentums durch Kartellrecht? GRUR 710
Hoppmann (1966) Das Konzept der optimalen Wettbewerbsintensität. Jahrbücher für Nationalökonomie und Statistik 286
Hoppmann (1967) Die Funktionsfähigkeit des Wettbewerbs: Bemerkungen zu Kantzenbachs "Erwiderung". JbNSt 251
Höppner (2005) Missbräuchliche Verhinderung "neuer" Produkte durch Immaterialgüterrechte. GRUR Int
Hovenkamp, Janis, Lemley (2002) IP and antitrust
Hovenkamp, Janis, Lemley (2006) Unilateral refusals to license. J Comp Law Econ 15
Howarth, McMahon (2008) Windows has performed an illegal operation. Eur Comp Law Rev 123
Humpe, Ritter (2005) Refusal to deal, college of Europe Global Competition Law Centre Research Paper on the modernization of Article 82 EC
Jones, Sufrin (2008) EC competition law
Jung (2004) Die Zwangslizenz als Instrument der Wettbewerbspolitik. ZWeR 391
Jung (2008) In: Grabitz, Hilf (eds) Das Recht der Europäischen Union, vol 2
Kantzenbach (1967) Die Funktionsfähigkeit des Wettbewerbs
Kaplow (1984) The patent-antitrust intersection. Harv Law Rev 1817
Katz (2002) Intellectual property rights and antitrust policy. J Telecomm. High Technol Law
Kaufer (1966) Kantzenbachs Konzept des funktionsfähigen Wettbewerbs. JbNSt 481
Kaufer (1967) Das Konzept der optimalen Wettbewerbsintensität: Eine Replik. JbNSt 242
Keeling (2003) Intellectual property rights in EU law, vol I
Kingston (1994) Compulsory licensing with capital payments as an alternative to monopoly grants for intellectual property. Res Policy 661
Kingston (2001) Innovation needs patent reform. Res Policy 419
Kirzner (1974) Competition and entrepreneurship
Kirzner (1997) Entrepreneurial discovery and the competitive market process. J Econ Lit 60
Korah (1988) No duty to license independent repairers to make spare parts. Eur Intellect Prop Rev 383
Korah (2004) An introductory guide to EC competition law and practice
Korah (2005) The interface between intellectual property rights and competition in developed countries. SCRIPT-ed 437
Korah (2006) Intellectual property rights and the EC competition rules
Körber (2007) Wettbewerb in dynamischen Märkten zwischen Innovationsschutz und Machtmissbrauch. Wirtschaft und Wettbewerb (WuW) 1213
Lamping (2010) Patentschutz und Marktmacht
Leistner (2005) Intellectual property and competition law. ZWeR
Lévêque (2005) Innovation, leveraging and essential facilities. World Comp 80
Lipsky, Sidak (1999) Essential facilities. Stanford Law Rev 1220
Loewenthal (2005) The defence of "Objective Justification" in the application of Article 82 EC. World Comp 464
Lowe (2004) DG competition's review of the policy on abuse of dominance. In: Annual proceedings of the FCLI, p 171
Lübbig (2005) In: Loewenheim, Meessen, Riesenkampff (eds) Kartellrecht

MacKie-Mason (2002) Antitrust immunity for refusals to deal in (intellectual) property is a slippery slope. Antitrust Source 8
Mennicke (1996) "Magill" – Von der Unterscheidung zwischen Bestand und Ausübung von Immaterialgüterrechten zur "essential facilities"-Doktrin. Zeitschrift für das gesamte Handelsrecht und Wirtschaftsrecht (ZHR) 653
Merdzo (2005) Der Fall "MS Health" und das Spannungsverhältnis zwischen nationalen Immaterialgüterrechten und dem europäischen Wettbewerbsrecht. Zeitschrift für Europarechtliche Studien 169
Merges (1992) Uncertainty and the standard of patentability. High Technol Law J 73
Mestmäcker, Schweitzer (2004) Europäisches Wettbewerbsrecht
Miksch (1949) Die Wirtschaftspolitik des Als-ob. Zeitschrift für die gesamte Staatswissenschaft 310
Montag (1997) Gewerbliche Schutzrechte, wesentliche Einrichtungen und Normung im Spannungsfeld zu Art. 86 EGV. EuZW 75
Monti (2007) EC competition law
Möschel (2007) In: Immenga, Mestmäcker (eds) Wettbewerbsrecht, vol 1
Müller (1998) Die "Essential Facilities"-Doktrin im Europäischen Kartellrecht. EuZW
O'Donoghue, Padilla (2006) The law and economics of Article 82 EC
Ohly (2007) Geistiges Eigentum und Wettbewerbsrecht. In: Oberender (ed) Wettbewerb und geistiges Eigentum, p 65
Palmstorfer (2008) Missbräuchliche, parallelexportbehindernde Lieferbeschränkungen, Wirtschaftsrechtliche Blätter
Pilny (1995) Missbräuchliche Marktbeherrschung gemäß Art. 86 EWGV durch Immaterialgüterrechte. GRUR 957
Ridyard (1996) Essential facilities and the obligation to supply competitors under UK and EC competition law. Eur Comp Law Rev 445
Ritter (2005) Refusal to deal and "Essential Facilities". World Comp
Ritter, Braun (2004) European competition law
Roth, Rose (2008) European community law of competition (Bellamy & Child)
Schmidt, Voigt (2006) Der "more economic approach" in der Missbrauchsaufsicht. WuW 1098
Schröter (2003) In: Schröter, Jakob, Mederer (eds) Kommentar zum Europäischen Wettbewerbsrecht
Schuhmacher (2003) Die Essential Facility Doctrine als Herausforderung für das Urheberrecht. In: Dittrich (ed) Beiträge zum Urheberrecht VII, pp 109
Schumpeter (1964) Theorie der wirtschaftlichen Entwicklung
Schumpeter (2005) Kapitalismus, Sozialismus und Demokratie
Schwarze (2003) Urheberrechte und deren Verwaltung im Lichte des europäischen Wettbewerbsrechts. Zeitschrift für Urheber- und Medienrecht 25
Sufrin (2004) The IMS case. Comp Law J 26
Spindler, Apel (2005) Urheber- versus Kartellrecht. JuristenZeitung 137
Taylor (1995) Copyright versus right to compete. Comp Telecommun Law Rev 101
Temple Lang (2005) The application of the essential facility doctrine to intellectual property rights under European Competition Law. In: Lévêque, Shelanski (eds) Antitrust, patents and copyright
Temple Lang (2006) Anticompetitive abuses under Article 82 involving intellectual property rights. In: Ehlermann, Atanasiu (eds) European competition law annual 2003: what is an abuse of a dominant position, p 612
Thyri (2005) Immaterialgüterrechte und Zugang zur wesentlichen Einrichtung. WuW
Tremmel (2004) Case note. Österreichische Blätter 286
Tritton (2008) Intellectual property in Europe
Turnbull (1996) Barriers to entry, Article 86 EC and the abuse of a dominant position. Eur Comp Law Rev 102

Turney (2005) Defining the limits of the EU essential facilities doctrine on intellectual property rights. North Western J Technol Intellect Prop 189
Ullrich (2007a) The interaction between competition law and intellectual property law: an overview. In: Ehlermann, Atanasiu (eds) Competition law annual 2005: the interaction between competition law and intellectual property, p 28
Ullrich (2007b) National, European and community patent protection. In: Ohly (ed) Geistiges Eigentum und Gemeinfreiheit, p 94
Ullrich (2012) Intellectual property: exclusive rights for a purpose. In: Klafkowska-Waśniowska (ed) Problemy Polskiego e Europejskiego Prawa Prywatnego, p 425
Ullrich H (2014) Mandatory licensing under patent law and competition law: different concerns, complementary roles. In: Hilty RM, Liu KC (eds) Compulsory licensing. Practical experiences and ways forward. Springer, Berlin, Heidelberg
Ullrich, Heinemann (2007) In: Immenga, Mestmäcker (eds) Wettbewerbsrecht, vol 1
US Department of Justice and Federal Trade Commission (1995) Antitrust guidelines for the licensing of intellectual property
van den Bergh, Camescasca (2006) European competition law and economics
van der Wal (1994) Article 86 EC: the limits of compulsory licensing. Eur Comp Law Rev 230
Venit, Kallaugher (1994) Essential facilities: a comparative approach. In: Hawk (ed) Fordham Corporate Law Institute, p 339
Vinje, Dodoo (2005) Microsoft v. EC. CRi 100
Vogelenzang (1976) Abuse of a dominant position in Article 86. Common Mark Law Rev 61
Weiß (2007) In: Callies, Ruffert (eds) EUV/EGV
Wessely (2005) In: Jaeger et al (eds) Frankfurter Kommentar zum Kartellrecht, Art. 82 (Anwendungsgrundsätze)
Whish (2005) Competition law
Wirtz (2006) Europäisches Kartellrecht
Wirtz, Holzhäuser (2004) Die kartellrechtliche Zwangslizenz. Wettbewerb in Recht und Praxis (WRP) 685

Part II
The Operation of Compulsory Licensing Regime

Recognised and Appropriate Grounds for Compulsory Licences: Reclaiming Patent Law's Social Contract

Susy Frankel and Jessica C. Lai

Contents

Abstract This chapter discusses the existing framework of compulsory licensing at the international level and the grounds upon which licences can be granted. The chapter uses that background to analyse whether patent law's social contract is a reason in favour of compulsory licensing. The chapter finds that compulsory licensing is worthy of thorough consideration in order to promote competition. However, whether competition is promoted will be fact specific, technology specific, market specific, and timing specific. The chapter concludes that just as the social contract of patent law requires balance, so too does the use of compulsory licensing. Consequently, compulsory licensing deserves greater attention as a means to contribute to rebalancing patent law's social contract.

S. Frankel is Professor of Law and Director New Zealand Centre International Economic Law.
J.C. Lai is Postdoctoral Researcher.

S. Frankel
Faculty of Law, Victoria University of Wellington, Wellington, New Zealand
e-mail: susy.frankel@vuw.ac.nz

J.C. Lai
University of Lucerne, Lucerne, Switzerland
e-mail: jessica.lai@unilu.ch

R.M. Hilty and K.-C. Liu (eds.), *Compulsory Licensing*, MPI Studies on Intellectual Property and Competition Law 22, DOI 10.1007/978-3-642-54704-1_8,

1 Introduction

Patent law is significantly justified through an incentive theory,[1] which holds that without the incentive of the exclusive rights (currently for at least a 20-year term) there would be less invention (which takes the form of both processes and products) and innovation (including getting the invention to marketable form).[2] This utilitarian theory is premised on the basis that people would be less willing to invest in an invention, and bring a related product to market, if competitors would be able to copy the invention and offer it at a lower price than the innovator. A competitor can usually charge a lower price because a competitor's price is less likely to include the costs of invention and innovation (because the competitor as imitator would not have incurred this cost). The patent system is therefore designed to incentivise the creation of inventions that are new and useful to society.[3] This incentive rationale has at its core a focus on the societal benefits of the invention. That focus has proved to be too narrow, especially, as is discussed below, because there is no obligation whatsoever to work the invention. Consequently, the contribution of the information behind the invention[4] and its disclosure also justifies the patent system. This is a worthy goal because if inventors are not encouraged to publish their invention, they might otherwise keep such information as a trade secret.[5] The patent system, through this disclosure mechanism, also aims for the diffusion of technology and technological transfer.[6] The timing of the disclosure requirement suggests that third parties must have some right to use the invention (or at least the information about the invention that has been disclosed) before the end of the patent term; otherwise, the disclosure would be made public when patents expire.[7] This "social contract"[8] of modern patent systems means that patentees are given a right to exclude others from making, using, offering for sale, selling, or importing their patented inventions for a set amount of time in return for disclosing the invention to the public.[9]

---

[1] Cornish et al. (2010), at paras 3-36–3-48. Note: The incentive theory itself is often challenged, e.g. Moore (2003), pp. 602–630; and Hettinger (1989), at pp. 47–51.

[2] Menell (2000), at pp. 146–147. Of course the distinction between invention and innovation is by no means well delineated. The two usually take place simultaneously. For example, further invention may be required to bring something to market. This further invention may even be patentable.

[3] Chisum et al. (2001), at p. 6; and Cornish et al. (2010), at paras 3-05–3-06 and 3-49–3-51.

[4] Chisum et al. (2001), at p. 15.

[5] Landes and Posner (2003), at pp. 294 and 326–332.

[6] Gervais (2012), at para. 2.113. Disclosure is one method of diffusion; others, although controversial, may include investment.

[7] Eisenberg (1989), at p. 1022.

[8] Drahos (2010), at pp. 27–32. MacQueen et al. (2008), at paras 10.15–10.16. See also chapter 'Fair Use: A Workable Concept in European Patent Law?' by Geertrui Van Overwalle, in this volume.

[9] The international requirements for disclosure are found in the WTO, Agreement on Trade-Related Aspects of Intellectual Property Rights, Marrakesh Agreement Establishing the World Trade Organization, Annex 1C, 1869 UNTS 299; 33 ILM 1197 (adopted on 15 April 1994, entered into force 1 January 1995) ["TRIPS" or "TRIPS Agreement"] Article 29, which provides:

Patent owners have no obligation to exploit their patents, whether for manufacture, use, sale, or importation,[10] but nevertheless are entitled to injunctive relief and damages/royalties against infringers.[11] Unlike with trademarks, patents cannot be removed from the register due to non-use. TRIPS does allow for revocation or forfeiture of a patent so long as it can be challenged through judicial review.[12] The negotiation history shows that such a challenge not only is limited to revocation due to the failure to meet the criteria for grant but could also be on the ground of public interest.[13] Yet few states allow for patent revocation or forfeiture on the ground of lack of exploitation by the owner.[14] That patents are regulated differently from trademarks is because the two forms of intellectual property have different characteristics. Trademarks were traditionally a tool to prevent fraud and protect consumers, developing in the courts within the realm of tort law and competition law, and becoming more property-like in the mid-late nineteenth century.[15] As such, trademark law protects the use of marks in the course of trade and is, thus, primarily interested in public use. There is no analogous trade requirement in patent law,

"Members shall require that an applicant for a patent shall disclose the invention in a manner sufficiently clear and complete for the invention to be carried out by a person skilled in the art and may require the applicant to indicate the best mode for carrying out the invention known to the inventor at the filing date or, where priority is claimed, at the priority date of the application".

[10] As per the exclusive rights under TRIPS, supra note 9, Article 28.

[11] As specifically held by the US Supreme Court in *Continental Paper Bag Co. v Eastern Paper Bag Co.*, 210 U.S. 405 (1908).

[12] TRIPS Agreement, supra note 9, Article 32.

[13] Gervais (2012), at para. 4.424. Gervais also notes that attempts were made during the negotiation of TRIPS to limit revocation to cases where a patent failed to meet the criteria for grant, but these were not successful. The WIPO, Paris Convention for the Protection of Industrial Property, 828 UNTS 303 (adopted on 20 March 1883, entered into force 16 April 1970), as revised at Stockholm (14 July 1967), Article 5.A(1) stipulates that "[i]mportation by the patentee into the country where the patent has been granted of articles manufactured in any of the countries of the Union shall not entail forfeiture of the patent", And Article 5.A(3) states that "[f]orfeiture of the patent shall not be provided for except in cases where the grant of compulsory licenses would not have been sufficient to prevent the said abuses". Articles 1–12 and Article 19 of the Paris Convention are incorporated into TRIPS in Article 2.1. See also Blakeney (1996), at paras 8.19–8.20 and 8.31.

[14] Australia does. However, this is only after a compulsory licence has been granted and the lapse of two years if "the reasonable requirements of the public with respect to the patented invention have not been satisfied" and "the patentee has given no satisfactory reason for failing to exploit the patent" or the patentee is contravening competition law. Patents Act 1991 (Cth), s. 134; and Patents Regulations 1991 (Cth), reg. 12.2(1). Rather contradictory, however, s. 138 of the Patents Act 1991 (Cth) states that revocation can only be made "on one or more of the following grounds, but on no other ground", but the list that follows does not include the revocation ground held in s. 134.

The New Zealand Patents Act 2013 also allows courts to revoke patents if they are "satisfied that the patentee has, without reasonable cause, failed to comply with a request of the government department to exploit the patented invention for the services of the Crown on reasonable terms" [s. 108(1)].

[15] Bently (2008), pp. 3–41; Landes and Posner (2003), at pp. 206–209; and Pulos (2005–2006), pp. 833–869.

which means that patent law assumes that there are public and private domains of use. In other words, though patents may very well be exploited in public, they may not be used at all or only used in private, such as by the patentee for further research. The patentee is not under an obligation to innovate, bring the invention to the public, or allow others to do so.

Daniel Gervais has stated that though there may be a presumption that a patentee may try to exploit the patent for profit, and upon failure to do this try to license or sell the patent, an obligation to work a patent would go a step further.[16] Describing the vision that animated the TRIPS demanders, he noted:

> If one looks at the patent system as an equilibrium between, on the one hand, a limited monopoly (both in time and scope) to reward and "incent" technological innovation and, on the other hand, full disclosure of a new invention and its industrial applicability, forcing a patentee to work the invention within a specific time-frame or exercising a wide-ranging right to issue non-voluntary licences (in the absence of an emergency or other similar situation) may be considered as an additional condition, thus tipping the balance towards the "public interest".[17]

The owners of patents do not seem to be living up to their part of the social contract when they refuse to license their patents without a rational explanation usually linked to orderly commercial exploitation, do not exploit them, or minimise exploitation and licences excessively in order to maintain high prices. This can be with respect to general end-product markets, or research markets, and is particularly a problem with inventions that one cannot reasonably substitute or invent around.

Patents typically create pseudo monopolies. That is, they do not usually create monopolies in the true sense of the word because they do not prevent competitors from offering similar and competing products that do not infringe the patent.[18] There are, for example, many different types of penicillins that compete on the same market and different pharmaceutical companies own the patents. The expansion of patentable subject matter into that which is more fundamental or informational—such as small isolated biological materials or computer programs—creates something closer to a real monopolistic effect. For example, certain biotech patents are often so fundamental in character that they sometimes protect that which is impossible to substitute or invent around.[19] When such inventions are not publically accessible, the social contract has been bypassed.

Exceptions to infringement, such as experimental use, theoretically could contribute to maintaining the balance in the social contract. Such exceptions, however, have not worked very well in most jurisdictions. There is barely an experimental use exception, for example in the United States, and no mandatory international

[16] Gervais (2012), at para. 2.113.

[17] Ibid., at para. 2.113.

[18] See Frankel (2013), at sects 4.2.3(e) and 7.1.3.

[19] Berman and Dreyfuss (2006), at p. 873; Dreyfuss and Evans (2011), at pp. 1368–1370; and Palombi (2009), at p. 388.

rule on this subject.[20] Regulatory review exceptions—which allow competitors of patented pharmaceuticals to perform research and the tests necessary to obtain regulatory approval of their generics before the lapse of the patents so that they can bring the drugs to market as soon as the patent term ends—do work. However, such exceptions are very narrow in application. A question therefore is if a broader exception is needed to maintain the social contract. Would compulsory licensing be more successful than other exceptions have been to date?

This chapter first gives an overview of compulsory licensing at the international level and the grounds upon which such licences can be granted. This is followed by a discussion about whether reclaiming the social contract is a reason in favour of compulsory licensing. The chapter concludes with a discussion about the overall balance.

2 Compulsory Licensing at International Law

2.1 The Paris Convention and the TRIPS Agreement

The possibility of compulsory licensing exists to ensure local working of patents and that consumer demand and public expectation (or reasonable public requirement) can be met.[21] Compulsory licences may also work as a tool to promote competition and increase the affordability of patented inventions[22] and to remedy abuses of unexploited patents that clog the register.[23] The fact that a licence is required suggests that the subject matter must be patentable. Thus, compulsory

[20] See Strandburg (2004), pp. 81–155. Where exceptions do exist, they are usually drafted with vague terminology incorporating nebulous distinctions, leaving both owners and users unsure of their positions. See OECD, 'Genetic Inventions, Intellectual Property Rights and Licensing Practices: Evidence and Policies' (2002), at p. 81. In contrast, copyright law has strong exceptions, the contours of which are regularly contested before courts.

[21] Cornish et al. (2010), at paras 7-40 and 21-22. Compulsory licence regimes are implemented differently in different states; e.g. 28 USC § 1498; Patents Act 1977 (UK), ss 48–50; Patents Act 1953 (NZ), s. 46; Patents Act 1990 (Cth), s. 133; and Agreement Relating to Community Patents—Done at Luxembourg on 15 December 1989, 89/695/EEC, OJ L 401, 30/12/1989 P. 0001–0027, Articles 45–47. Most Commonwealth countries also allow for Crown Use under certain circumstances, which could also be used for the purposes of local working of patents or meeting consumer demand and public expectation, particularly in emergencies, as the provisions usually do not require that attempts to negotiate a licence have already been made; e.g. Patents Act 1953 (NZ), s. 55; Patents Act 1990 (Cth), s. 163; and Patents Act 1977 (UK), s. 55. For discussion on compulsory licences in other jurisdictions, in this volume, see Jakkrit Kuanpoth, 'Compulsory Licences: Law and Practice in Thailand'; Philipp Maume, 'Compulsory Licensing in Germany'; Carlos M. Correa, 'The Use of Compulsory Licences in Latin America'; and Kung-Chung Liu, 'Compulsory Licence and Government Use in Taiwan: A Regress'.

[22] Correa (2000), at p. 93; and Blakeney (1996), at para. 8.29.

[23] Blakeney (1996), at para. 8.19.

licences are an exception to patent infringement rather than exclusion from patentability.[24] This may be relevant to how a compulsory licence is interpreted and what function it is supposed to serve.

The Paris Convention provides that "[e]ach country of the Union shall have the right to take legislative measures providing for the grant of compulsory licenses to prevent the abuses which might result from the exercise of the exclusive rights conferred by the patent, for example, *failure to work*" or *insufficient working*.[25] This means that the patent owner does not make or supply the market for the invention. The granted compulsory licences are non-exclusive and non-transferable (even as sub-licences).[26]

States have utilised this provision differently, not necessarily using the terms "failure to work" or "insufficient working".[27] For example, New Zealand allows for compulsory licences where "a market for the patented invention is not being supplied, or is not being supplied on reasonable terms, in New Zealand".[28] The UK uses the terminology that "a demand is not being met on reasonable terms" or there is a "refusal of the proprietor of the patent concerned to grant a licence or licences on reasonable terms".[29] However, the UK Patents Act also contains terms such as "not being so worked to the fullest extent that is reasonably practicable" and a market "is not being supplied".[30] Australia uses the phrase that "the reasonable requirements of the public with respect to the patented invention have not been satisfied", which includes adequate manufacture, supply on reasonable terms, carrying on of a patented process to a reasonable extent, granting of licences on reasonable terms, unfair conditions on purchase/hire/use of the patented product/process, or if the invention is not being worked in Australia on a commercial scale in Australia, when this is possible.[31]

---

[24] The difference between exclusions and exceptions is explained by Lionel Bently and Brad Sherman, chapter 'Limiting Patents', in this volume. That a compulsory licence is sought or granted is not indicative of there being a valid patent, as it may be that a second or subsequent user would license, whether or not the patent was valid, because it would be cheaper and quicker to obtain a licence (even if compulsory) than challenge the patent.

[25] Paris Convention, supra note 13, Article 5.A(2) (emphasis added). The term "insufficient working" is stipulated in Article 5.A(4). The Paris Convention further states that compulsory licences can only be applied for 4 years after the date of filing or 3 years from the date of grant, whichever period expires last [Article 5.A(4)]. It also states that an application for a compulsory licence "shall be refused if the patentee justifies his inaction by legitimate reasons", which is a broad and liberally interpreted defence [Article 5.A(4)]; Blakeney (1996), at para. 8.20.

[26] Paris Convention, supra note 13, Article 5.A(4).

[27] As noted by Kuanpoth, supra note 21, the term "failure to work" is not defined in the Paris Convention.

[28] Patents Act 1953 (NZ), s. 46(2); and Patents Act 2013 (NZ), s. 164(2).

[29] Patents Act 1977 (UK), s. 48A, which deals with compulsory licences for patentees who are WTO proprietors.

[30] Patents Act 1977 (UK), s. 48B, which deals with compulsory licences for patentees who are non-WTO proprietors.

[31] Patents Act 1990 (Cth), ss 133(2)(a)(ii) and 135.

The different terminology that domestic laws use suggests different policies about the role of compulsory licensing. Being "reasonably supplied" includes both local manufacturing and imports as a means to meet market demand. That imports can be a means to supply would also be an interpretation consistent with globalisation[32] and with the trade-liberalising goal of the World Trade Organization (WTO), which includes the TRIPS Agreement.[33]

Terms such as "worked", "manufacture", and "carrying on of a patented process" are targeted at local manufacture or use of the patented invention. These terms, however, predate the WTO. The Paris Convention working provisions provide the scope for compulsory licences at domestic law; they do not require jurisdictions to have those exceptions. Therefore, in some jurisdictions, the policy could be that importation alone would be sufficient working of the patent and in others that might not be the case.[34] TRIPS now provides that "patents shall be available and patent rights enjoyable without discrimination as to the place of invention, the field of technology and whether products are imported or locally produced".[35] Thus, arguably, importation can satisfy a local working requirement.[36]

The Paris Convention compulsory licensing provisions are incorporated into the TRIPS Agreement.[37] Article 31 of TRIPS covers situations where there is use without the authorisation of the patentee, either by the government or third parties authorised by the government.[38] Other than incorporating the Paris Convention, TRIPS does not expressly refer to the ground of failure to work or insufficient working.[39] Instead, Article 31 of TRIPS implicitly provides other grounds for compulsory licences. It does not specifically or exclusively define the grounds but

---

[32] Correa, 'The Use of Compulsory Licenses in Latin America', who notes that the change in understanding of "working" a patent to include importing the invention was a consequence of globalisation.

[33] TRIPS Agreement, supra note 9.

[34] Correa, 'The Use of Compulsory Licenses in Latin America'.

[35] TRIPS Agreement, supra note 9, Article 27. Michael Blakeney suggests that this means importation does satisfy the Paris Convention working requirement. See Blakeney (1996), at para. 8.22.

[36] Gervais (2012), at para. 2.409. In contrast, see Correa, 'The Use of Compulsory Licenses in Latin America'.

[37] TRIPS Agreement, supra note 9, Article 2.1.

[38] Though Article 31 of TRIPS is clearly the main clause for compulsory licensing, some have argued that such provisions can also come under Article 30, which is the general clause for limiting patentees' exclusive rights. For example, Belgium contends that its provisions for compulsory licensing are justified under Articles 8 and 30. By doing this, they are able to side-step the conditions set out in Article 31. See the discussion by Reichman (2010), at p. 598. Daniel Gervais has stated that according to *lex specialis*, Article 30 cannot cover cases of use by governments or by third parties authorised by governments, as this is covered by Article 31; Gervais (2012), at para. 2.396.

[39] It did in earlier drafts [as 31(n)] but was removed between the Brussels Draft and the Dunkel Draft. See Gervais (2012), paras 2.400–2.408.

refers to certain grounds throughout its explication of the conditions under which use without authorisation of the patentee may take place.

One of the grounds referred to is if the patentee refuses to deal.[40] Refusal to deal is an anti-competitive practice, whereby Party A refuses to deal with (license or supply) Party B so as to maintain or improve its market position or to gain market position in another market. For example, Party A may refuse to sell to Party B a part of a two-part engine that it manufactures unless party B also buys the second part from Party A or at least does not buy it from Party C (a competitor of Party A).

Article 31 of TRIPS also implicitly makes compulsory licences a potential remedy to other anti-competitive practice, depending on the competition laws of Member States.[41] TRIPS additionally provides conditions for compulsory licences for national emergencies (or extreme urgencies),[42] government use,[43] and public interest[44] and when cross-licensing is required.[45]

In TRIPS, no grounds for compulsory licensing are expressly delineated;[46] however, Article 31 contains "strict safeguards".[47] Article 31 stipulates that such licences may only be granted if the granting process considers applications on their individual merits, the licences are of limited duration, scope is limited to the purpose for which the licence was authorised, the licences are non-exclusive and non-assignable, they are for the supply of the domestic market of the Member

---

[40] TRIPS Agreement, supra note 9, Article 31(b) states that a licence may only be granted if efforts have been made to obtain authorisation from the patent owner on reasonable commercial terms and conditions and that such efforts have not been successful within a reasonable period of time.

[41] TRIPS Agreement, supra note 9, Article 31(k). In such cases, conditions (b) and (f) do not have to be satisfied when a judicial or administrative process has permitted use to remedy the anti-competitive practice, i.e. there does not need to be a refusal to deal, and the licence can be for the supply of non-domestic markets. In the US, patent legislation does not specifically allow for compulsory licences; however, they are allowed under US antitrust law; Correa (2000), at p. 95. For a discussion on the relationship between compulsory licences and competition law in Germany, see Maume, 'Compulsory Licensing in Germany'.

[42] TRIPS Agreement, supra note 9, Article 31(b). In a national emergency or other circumstances of extreme urgency, there does not need to be a refusal to deal.

[43] TRIPS Agreement, supra note 9, Article 31(b). In cases of public non-commercial use (i.e. government use), there does not need to be a refusal to deal. See also Blakeney (1996), at para. 8.26.

[44] The "public interest" is not an implied ground for compulsory licensing from Article 31 of TRIPS. However, as will be discussed further, interpretation of TRIPS allows one to take into account the broader concept of the "public interest" from Articles 7 and 8 of TRIPS.

[45] TRIPS Agreement, supra note 9, Article 31(l) provides that when a licence for a first patent is required in order to exploit a second, Members may also authorise compulsory licences if the invention claimed in the second patent involves an important technical advance of considerable economic significance in relation to the invention claimed in the first patent, the first patent owner is entitled to cross-license on reasonable terms, and the licence to the first patent is non-assignable, except with assignment of the second patent.

[46] As also noted by Kuanpoth, 'Compulsory Licences: Law and Practice in Thailand'.

[47] Gervais (2012), at para. 2.409.

authorising such use,[48] they are capable of being terminated if circumstances change, they are subject to adequate remuneration, and the legal decision to licence and remuneration are subject to judicial review.[49]

The relationship between the Paris Convention and TRIPS is complex. The Article that incorporates the Paris Convention into TRIPS states that "[n]othing in Parts I to IV of this Agreement shall derogate from existing obligations that Members may have to each other under the Paris Convention".[50] Therefore, it is reasonable to conclude that both the Paris Convention working requirements and the TRIPS use without authorisation provisions are grounds for compulsory licences. That is not a full picture, however. How the Paris Convention and TRIPS work together is also relevant. TRIPS neither eliminates the Paris Convention nor derogates from it, but the Paris Convention equally cannot be used to defeat the safeguards that TRIPS requires for licences.

2.2 The Few Uses of Compulsory Licences

Compulsory licences are seldom used, and they seem not often explored.[51] For many countries this may be because their use as a mechanism to correct market failures of patent law either has not been seen as commercially important or is seen as contradictory to market-driven economic policies.

One of the key uses of compulsory licences is to access patented inventions. The use of compulsory licences is, however, limited because of their focus on the market. We can ascertain this market focus from the terminology used in national legislation, which makes it clear that compulsory licences exist to ensure that a market is being supplied or demand is being met. Thus, compulsory licences are of little assistance to those who simply wish to research. Accordingly, a related question is whether, rather than having a broad experimental use exception, experimental use should be governed by a compulsory licensing regime. The difference would be that the exception model is an unremunerated model, whereas a licensing model remunerates.

[48] Note: Article 31bis, implemented by the WTO General Council, 'Amendment of the TRIPS Agreement', Decision of 6 December 2005 (WTO Doc. WT/L/641, 2005), to allow developing countries to import pharmaceuticals from other states with compulsory licences when they do not have the capacity to manufacture. However, implementation required that two-thirds of the WTO Members ratify the Article by 1 December 2007, which did not happen. The deadline was extended to 31 December 2009, 31 December 2011 and then to 31 December 2013 (see http://www.wto.org/english/tratop_e/trips_e/amendment_e.htm). Until then, a "Waiver" has been in place since 2003; WTO General Council, 'Implementation of Paragraph 6 of the Doha Declaration on the TRIPS Agreement and Public Health', (WTO Doc. WT/L/540 and Corr.1, 2003). For discussion, see Reichman (2010), at pp. 592–596; and Verma (2010), pp. 623–672.

[49] TRIPS Agreement, supra note 9, Article 31(a) and (c)–(j).

[50] TRIPS Agreement, supra note 9, Article 2.2.

[51] Australian Law Reform Commission (ALRC) (2004), at paras 27.10 and 27.18; and Correa (2000), at p. 97.

The general experience so far in the UK and the US does not put compulsory licensing in a positive light. That experience shows arbitrariness in application and a long expensive process of obtainment.[52] The US has the widest exception for government use (including use by its contractors), and the government is under no obligation to notify patent owners of such use.[53] This has been particularly problematic with US military use or use by its defence contractors and for foreign patent owners who cannot easily detect the use of their patents.[54] The US is renowned for being generally opposed to the concept of compulsory licences, and private parties have no opportunity to seek such,[55] except as a correction for anti-competitive behaviour. As a dominant player in the pharmaceutical, biotech, and software industries, this is of great consequence.

Although the number of compulsory licences that have been granted is not great, the coercive nature of their existence should not be underestimated. The threat of a compulsory licence can often result in voluntary licences.[56] But that coercive nature may not be without ill effect, as it may have an adverse effect on foreign direct investment.[57] As discussed further below, ultimately it is a question of getting the balance right between ensuring a certain level of sanctity of exclusive rights so that there is a great enough incentive for invention and innovation and ensuring the public interest in having access to the invention.

3 TRIPS and the Social Contract as a Ground for Compulsory Licensing

As noted in the introduction of this chapter, part of the theoretical foundation of patent law is a social contract. The TRIPS Agreement embodies aspects of the social contract in its minimum standards, such as requiring that domestic law entails disclosure.[58]

---

[52] Cornish et al. (2010), at paras 7-41–7-42 and 21-19. See also chapter 'Legal Remedies Against Abuse, Misuse and Other Forms of Inappropriate Conduct of IP Right Holders', by Reto M. Hilty, in this volume.

[53] 28 USC § 1498; and Rushing (2012), pp. 879–916. As a TRIPS Agreement matter, this is where Article 44.2 (and Article 73) TRIPS functionally supersede Article 31, which requires notification and remuneration [paras (b) and (h)].

[54] Rushing (2012).

[55] Ibid., at para. 7-43; Berman and Dreyfuss (2006), at p. 907; Resnik (2003), p. 3; and ALRC (2004), at paras 27.21–27.22. See also Kuanpoth, 'Compulsory Licences: Law and Practice in Thailand'.

[56] Correa (2000), at p. 97; and Reichman (2010), at p. 598.

[57] See Gervais (2014). For a different view see Reichman (2010), at pp. 614–618; chapter 'Economic and Procedural Constraints of Compulsory Licenses for Medicines', by Yugank Goyal, in this volume; and discussion in Part IV infra.

[58] See supra notes 8 and 9.

In essence, the social contract is a balance between protection and other public goods. Protection of inventions is not only for the benefit of the inventor but also for the public good because of the connection to encouraging invention. Notions of the public good are not static, and equally so patents law's social contract is not static. When the TRIPS Agreement was negotiated, concerns of developing countries led to the inclusion of Articles 7 and 8, in particular,[59] which articulate balancing factors such as allowing measures to "promote the public interest in sectors of vital importance to their socio-economic and technological development". This is a reflection, and in a sense a TRIPS update, of the social contract.[60]

There have been difficulties with applying Articles 7 and 8 in a dispute settlement context. The role of Articles 7 and 8 in the interpretation of substantive TRIPS provisions was acknowledged by the Panel in *Canada – Pharmaceutical Patents*. It stated that Articles 7 and 8 cannot result in a renegotiation of the wording of other Articles but must be borne in mind when interpreting the object and purposes of provisions in the TRIPS Agreement.[61] The panel did not, however, give a full discussion of the object and purpose of TRIPS, as the Vienna Convention on the Law of Treaties[62] requires.[63] That Articles 7 and 8 are a key to interpretation was underscored in the Doha Declaration.[64] They are a "fundamental principle" of TRIPS, not a stand-alone exception to the other provisions of the Agreement.[65]

---

[59] Gervais (2012), at para. 2.111.

[60] TRIPS Agreement, supra note 9, Article 7 Objectives

The protection and enforcement of intellectual property rights should contribute to the promotion of technological innovation and to the transfer and dissemination of technology, to the mutual advantage of producers and users of technological knowledge and in a manner conducive to social and economic welfare, and to a balance of rights and obligations.

Article 8 Principles

1. Members may, in formulating or amending their laws and regulations, adopt measures necessary to protect public health and nutrition, and to promote the public interest in sectors of vital importance to their socio-economic and technological development, provided that such measures are consistent with the provisions of this Agreement.

2. Appropriate measures, provided that they are consistent with the provisions of this Agreement, may be needed to prevent the abuse of intellectual property rights by right holders or the resort to practices which unreasonably restrain trade or adversely affect the international transfer of technology.

[61] Panel Report, *Canada – Pharmaceutical Patents*, WT/DS114/R, adopted 7 April 2000, at paras 7.25-7.26.

[62] UN, Vienna Convention on the Laws of Treaties, 1155 UNTS 331, 8 ILM 679 (adopted on 23 May 1969, entered into force 27 January 1980).

[63] See Frankel (2006), pp. 365–431.

[64] WTO Ministerial Conference, 'Declaration on the TRIPS Agreement and Public Health', Fourth Session, Doha [WTO Doc. WT/MIN(01)/DEC/2, 2001], at para. 5(a) provides that "In applying the customary rules of interpretation of public international law, each provision of the TRIPS Agreement shall be read in the light of the object and purpose of the Agreement as expressed, in particular, in its objectives and principles".

[65] That Articles 7 and 8 cannot result in exceptions not envisaged during the negotiation of TRIPS is clear from Article 8 and the requirement that any measures taken be "consistent with the

Some of the difficulty rests in how one can interpret balance into the TRIPS Agreement between multiple objectives,[66] including not restricting trade, promoting invention and innovation, ensuring that those who need to can access the invention, and other public interests.[67] Additionally, the TRIPS Agreement recognises that Member States may have to "calibrate"[68] their intellectual property laws for their domestic situation. This is part of the structure of the Agreement and its object and purpose.[69] These calibrations must, however, be in compliance with the TRIPS Agreement. Some of these balancing factors can be found in the justifications, rationales, and enactments of domestic law. Commentators have suggested that looking for an international *acquis* of intellectual property could provide a means to bringing balance between domestic objectives and international objectives into the system.[70]

The WTO has thus far recognised the Berne Convention *acquis*. In *US – Section 110(5) Copyright Act*, the Panel recognised that the TRIPS Agreement incorporated not only the wording of Articles of the Berne Convention but also its accompanying understanding that had developed over its almost 100 years of existence.[71] The negotiating history supported this conclusion.[72] The Paris Convention can be viewed analogously, meaning that the TRIPS Agreement also embodies the overall Paris Convention *acquis*. The Paris Convention *acquis* includes the social contract of patent law, as it is a part of the understanding surrounding the Paris Convention.[73]

As mentioned above, though TRIPS refers to some grounds for the grant of compulsory licences, these are not exhaustive.[74] Article 31 does not delineate any

provisions of this Agreement"; see Gervais (2012), at para. 2.123. See also Van den Bossche (2008), at p. 745, ".... the provision in Article 8 is limited by the requirement that measures falling there under be *consistent* with the provisions of the *TRIPS Agreement*. Thus, rather than creating an exception from *TRIPS* disciplines for measures serving public policy objectives, Article 8 is best seen as enunciating a fundamental principle of the *TRIPS Agreement* to be taken into account, with Article 7, when interpreting and applying its remaining provisions" (italics in original).

66 Consistently with the overall patent *acquis* and Vienna Convention on the Laws of Treaties (supra note 62).

67 See Frankel (2006); and Van den Bossche (2008), at pp. 744–745.

68 On the calibration narrative, see Gervais (2007), pp. 3–59.

69 Frankel (2009), pp. 1023–1065.

70 Dinwoodie and Dreyfuss (2012).

71 WTO Panel, *United States – Section 110(5) of the US Copyright Act*, WT/DS160/R, adopted 27 July 2000, at FN 85.

72 Ibid. See also *Canada – Patent Protection of Pharmaceutical Products*, WT/DS114/R, adopted 7 April 2000, at para. 7.15, which states that "As a consequence of the extended context that has to be taken into account when interpreting provisions of the TRIPS Agreement, the Panel, in considering the negotiating history of the TRIPS Agreement, concluded that interpretation may go beyond the negotiating history of the TRIPS Agreement proper and also inquire into that of the incorporated international instruments on intellectual property".

73 See MacQueen et al. (2008), at paras 10.12–10.13.

74 Correa (2000), at p. 97; and Blakeney (1996), at para. 8.22.

limits as to what can be a ground for the grant of compulsory licences.[75] At the same time, there is no international norm for some of the grounds upon which a compulsory licence may be granted, for example anti-competitive conduct. In other words, though international norms may have formed around exceptions where there is a failure to work or insufficient working of patents from national applications of the ground, for example, there is no general international norm about when unauthorised use may take place (or a compulsory licence may be granted) as a consequence of anti-competitive conduct of the patentee. Jerome Reichman has stated that the existence of the provisions in Article 31 "only magnified the legitimacy of every complying government's right to resort to compulsory licensing *whenever its domestic self-interest so required*",[76] offering an extremely blank canvas for what can constitute a ground. Michael Blakeney has noted that grounds (other than those referred to in Article 31) may be gleaned from Article 8, "which enunciates general principles which are applicable to the TRIPS Agreement as a whole",[77] and that Article 7 may be relied upon by Member States seeking to implement policies for compulsory licensing.[78] Unlike Article 7, Article 8 allows Members to take specific action against the abuse of intellectual property rights.[79] Blakeney writes that the theme of Article 7 is taken up in Article 8.1 through the phrase "to promote the public interest in sectors of vital importance to their socio-economic and technological development", and Article 8.2 supplements this by permitting appropriate measures to prevent "the resort to practices which unreasonably restrain trade or adversely affect the international transfer of technology".[80]

Care must be taken, however, because as discussed above Articles 7 and 8 are not stand-alone exceptions in TRIPS. They inform interpretation of the minimum standard provisions and the object and purpose of the TRIPS Agreement. Therefore, in the compulsory licence context, they can support the policy grounds to have compulsory licences, in accordance with the safeguards of Article 31.

There is, thus, significant leeway for states to implement compulsory licensing provisions on policy grounds one can glean from the objectives and principles of Articles 7 and 8. As Articles 7 and 8 are a reflection of the social contract underlying modern patent law, an appropriate ground for compulsory licensing is the reclaiming of the social contract, for example, in situations when patentees are preventing the flow of information or technology in a manner that upsets the fine balance of the quid pro quo. This gives a considerable deference to goals at a domestic level, provided they are consistent with the TRIPS Agreement.

---

[75] Van den Bossche (2008), at pp. 788–789; and Blakeney (1996), at para. 8.22.

[76] Reichman (2010), at p. 591 (emphasis added).

[77] Blakeney (1996), at para. 8.22. See also Cotropia (2008), at p. 561, who states that "Article 8 of TRIPS sets forth principles that define the situations under which exceptions are acceptable".

[78] Blakeney (1996), at para. 3.08.

[79] Gervais (2012), at para. 2.123.

[80] Blakeney (1996), at para. 3.08.

4 Conclusion: The Overall Balance

It is a common rhetoric that the patent regime currently favours patentees over users, and the overall balance is off kilter. This chapter illustrates that a means to readjust the current balance potentially lies in recognising the reclaiming of the social contract as a ground for granting compulsory licences. However, there are arguments that compulsory licences can discourage research and development, and investment, i.e. invention and innovation.[81] Some claim that compulsory licensing is counter to patent theory. Christopher Cotropia, for example, has said:

> The concept of compulsory licensing runs counter to basic patent theory. The possibility of compulsory licensing and the involuntary breaking of exclusivity can erode the incentive to invent. A would-be inventor can no longer depend on patent exclusivity as a means of recouping costs because of the uncertainty of such exclusivity. As the likelihood that the patent system will bust patents via compulsory license increases, the incentive to create patentable inventions decreases.[82]

In response, all exceptions to exclusive rights run contrary to the exclusive right and the theory that underpins it; that is the nature of an exception. Put differently, the purpose of an exception is to run contrary to the exclusive right; otherwise, an exception would not be needed. What TRIPS does is provide parameters for exceptions, including parameter for uses of compulsory licences.

Cotropia continues:

> Given that compulsory licensing may deter the creation of the very technology the patent system intends to foster, there must be a significant countervailing interest to justify such licensing. There needs to be some overriding "political or social objective" that requires a compulsory license for the objective to be met. [83]

This argument really calls for compulsory licences to be well defined and regulated rather than wide open for any reason. That is exactly what the TRIPS Agreement seeks to do.

To further illustrate, some have said that liberal use of compulsory licences for the purposes of pharmaceuticals may allow for the development of generic companies but at the same time has a negative impact on the establishment or growth of research-based entities.[84] Reichman has counter-argued that there is no clear relationship between the level of intellectual property protection and foreign direct investment,[85] and whether compulsory licences can reduce the incentive to innovate depends on whether the licences target a market that is of significance to the patentee.[86] For example, compulsory licences for pharmaceuticals in developing

---

[81] Correa (2000), at pp. 93 and 100.

[82] Cotropia (2008), at p. 560.

[83] Ibid.

[84] Discussed by Reichman (2010), at p. 603.

[85] See also Goyal, supra note 57.

[86] Ibid., at pp. 614–618.

states may not affect the incentive to innovate at all because pharmaceutical companies are little affected by the loss of those markets. Hence, it is important to look at the exact case at hand. As stated by Gervais:

> Clearly, there are cases (e.g. certain life-saving pharmaceutical products especially in crisis situations) where the public interest is obviously greater. But, it is also important to bear in mind that broad exclusions from patentability or patent protection may reduce the attractiveness of patents if and when they damage significant markets.[87]

Thus, though compulsory licences may serve to reclaim the social contract—and this should be the object and purpose behind compulsory licence regimes—at the end of the day, one cannot forget that the social contract consists of an intricate balance. The concept of the "social contract" is broad and far more imprecise than concepts like a declared national health emergency. As stated in the introduction, flexible exceptions to patent infringement have not proven to function well. We should, thus, delineate what compulsory licensing should cover. Doing so should aim to simultaneously create certainty (for patentees and potential users) and ensure overall balance.

That said, compulsory licences should not be feared. Threats of chill should be taken seriously but can also be overstated. One source of investment could be chilled, but another may step into its place. Compulsory licensing is a delicate balance and is worthy of thorough consideration in order to promote competition. Whether competition is promoted will be fact specific, technology specific, market specific, and timing specific. That is precisely why compulsory licensing deserves greater exploration as a means to contribute to rebalancing the social contract.

References

Australian Law Reform Commission (ALRC) (2004) Genes and ingenuity report: gene patenting and human health. Commonwealth of Australia, Sydney

Bently L (2008) From communication to thing: historical aspects of the conceptualisation of trade marks as property. In: Dinwoodie GB, Janis MD (eds) Trademark law and theory: a handbook of contemporary research. Edward Elgar, Cheltenham, pp 3–41

Berman HM, Dreyfuss RC (2006) Reflections on the science and law of structural biology, genomics, and drug development. UCLA Law Rev 53(4):871–908

Blakeney M (1996) Trade related aspects of intellectual property rights: a concise guide to the TRIPS Agreement. Sweet & Maxwell, Bath

Chisum DS et al (2001) Principles of patent law, 2nd edn. Foundation Press, New York, 2001

Cornish W, Llewelyn D, Aplin T (2010) Intellectual property: patents, copyright, trade marks and allied rights, 7th edn. Sweet & Maxwell, London

Correa C (2000) Integrating public health concerns into patent legislation in developing countries. South Centre, Geneva

[87] Gervais (2012), at para. 2.113.

Cotropia CA (2008) Compulsory licensing under TRIPS and the Supreme Court of the United States' decision in *eBay v. MercExchange*. In: Takenaka T (ed) Patent law and theory: a handbook of contemporary research. Edward Elgar, Cheltenham, pp 557–583
Dinwoodie GB, Dreyfuss RC (2012) A Neofederalist vision of TRIPS: the resilience of the international intellectual property regime. Oxford University Press, New York
Drahos P (2010) The global governance of knowledge: patent offices and their clients. Cambridge University Press, New York
Dreyfuss RC, Evans JP (2011) From *Bilski* back to *Benson*: preemption, inventing around, and the case of genetic diagnostics. Stanford Law Rev 63(4):1349–1376
Eisenberg RS (1989) Patents and the progress of science: exclusive rights and experimental use. Univ Chic Law Rev 56:1017–1086
Frankel S (2006) The WTO's application of "the Customary Rules of Interpretation of Public International Law" to intellectual property. V J Int Law 46(2):365–431
Frankel S (2009) Challenging TRIPS-Plus Agreements: the potential utility of non-violation disputes. J Int Econ Law 12:1023–1065
Frankel S (2013) Intellectual property in New Zealand, 2nd edn. LexisNexis, Wellington
Gervais DJ (2007) TRIPS and development. In: Gervais DJ (ed) Intellectual property, trade and development. Oxford University Press, Oxford, pp 3–59
Gervais DJ (2012) The TRIPS Agreement: drafting history and analysis, 4th edn. Sweet & Maxwell, Croydon
Gervais DJ (2014) TRIPS and development: an update. In: Gervais DJ (ed) Intellectual property, trade and development, 2nd edn. Oxford University Press, Oxford (forthcoming)
Hettinger EC (1989) Justifying intellectual property. Philos Public Aff 18(1):31–52
Landes WM, Posner RA (2003) The economic structure of intellectual property law. Harvard University Press, Cambridge
MacQueen HL, Waelde C, Laurie GT (2008) Contemporary intellectual property: law and policy. Oxford University Press, New York
Menell PS (2000) Intellectual property: general theories. In: Bouckaert B, de Geest G (eds) Encyclopedia of law and economics, vol I, The history and methodology of law and economics. Edward Elgar, Cheltenham, pp 129–188
Moore AD (2003) Intellectual property, innovation, and social progress: the case against incentive based arguments. Hamline Law Rev 26(3):602–630
Palombi L (2009) Beyond recombinant technology: synthetic biology and patentable subject matter. J World Intellect Prop 12(5):371–401
Pulos M (2005–2006) A semiotic solution to the propertization problem of trademark. UCLA Law Rev 53:833–869
Reichman JH (2010) Compulsory licensing of patented pharmaceutical inventions: evaluating the options. In: Correa CM (ed) Research handbook on the protection of intellectual property under WTO rules: intellectual property in the WTO, vol I. Edward Elgar, Cheltenham, pp 589–622
Resnik DB (2003) A biotechnology patent pool: an idea whose time has come? J Philos Sci Law 3
Rushing S (2012) Plugging the leak in § 1498: coercing the United States into notifying patent owners of government use. Vanderbilt J Transnational Law 45:879–916
Strandburg KJ (2004) What does the public get? Experimental use and the patent bargain. Wisconsin Law Rev 1:81–155
Van den Bossche P (2008) The law and policy of the World Trade Organization, 2nd edn. Cambridge University Press, New York
Verma SK (2010) The Doha Declaration and access to medicines by countries without manufacturing capacity. In: Correa CM (ed) Research handbook on the protection of intellectual property under WTO rules: intellectual property in the WTO, vol I. Edward Elgar, Cheltenham, pp 623–672

Prior Negotiation and Remuneration for Patent Compulsory Licensing: Practice, Problem, and Proposal

Xiuqin Lin

Contents

Abstract Opinions vary on the nature of prior negotiation, as well as the meaning of adequate remuneration for CL under Art. 31 of the TRIPS Agreement. A review of the historical negotiating process and current practice in different jurisdictions shows that "prior negotiation", designed as a procedure to protect patent holders, is interpreted differently among WTO members due to the ambiguity of the TRIPS Agreement. Art. 31 of the TRIPS Agreement leaves great flexibilities for WTO members to qualify the requirement for "prior negotiation". Moreover, the TRIPS Agreement does not specify the meaning of "adequate remuneration" for CL. This

X. Lin is Professor of Law.

X. Lin
Intellectual Property Research Institute, Law School, Xiamen University, Xiamen, Fujian Province, P. R. China
e-mail: xqlin@xmu.edu.cn

R.M. Hilty and K.-C. Liu (eds.), *Compulsory Licensing*, MPI Studies on Intellectual Property and Competition Law 22, DOI 10.1007/978-3-642-54704-1_9,

chapter argues that WTO members enjoy great flexibilities to determine the adequate remuneration and the purpose of CL, as opposed to other circumstances, which deserves particular consideration. Also, the rules and procedures for setting remuneration for CL should be easy to predict. It is advisable for WTO members to adopt specific rules on determining the "reasonable commercial terms" and "reasonable period of time". This chapter further examines the existing methods to assess the remuneration for CL of pharmaceutical patents, arguing that the well-recognised guidelines proposed by the UNDP and the WHO could serve as guidance for setting the CL royalty in developing countries.

1 Introduction

Art. 31 of the TRIPS Agreement obligates the applicant of patent compulsory licence (hereinafter "CL") to conduct a prior negotiation before seeking a CL and to pay adequate remuneration to patent holders when a CL is granted: "where the law of a Member allows for other use of the subject matter of a patent without the authorisation of the right holder, including use by the government or third parties authorised by the government, the following provisions shall be respected:

...

(b) such use may only be permitted if, prior to such use, *the proposed user has made efforts to obtain authorization from the right holder on reasonable commercial terms and conditions and that such efforts have not been successful within a reasonable period of time*. This requirement may be waived by a Member in the case of a national emergency or other circumstances of extreme urgency or in cases of public non-commercial use.

...

(h) the right holder shall be paid adequate remuneration in the circumstances of each case, taking into account the economic value of the authorization".

These provisions have generated varied viewpoints about the nature of prior negotiation and the meaning of adequate remuneration. How should prior negotiation be conducted to fulfil the requirement of the TRIPS Agreement? What is adequate remuneration? How should the remuneration be determined? The answers

---

[1] See the chapter "Compulsory Licences: Law and Practice in Thailand" by Jakkrit Kuanpoth, in this volume.

[2] Application for Compulsory Licence under Section 84 (1) of the Patent Act 1970 in Respect of Patent No. 215758, Compulsory License Application No. 1, 2011. For more details, see the chapter "Compulsory Licence under Indian Patent Law" by N.S. Gopalakrishnan and Madhuri Anand, in this volume.

[3] Some unsuccessful attempts have been made to seek a CL related to drugs for hepatitis B, tuberculosis, and AIDS in China. For instance, in 2008, a public interest organisation, Beijing Yirenping Center, together with 1,843 HBV carriers and HIV-infected persons, appealed to the Ministry of Commerce to issue CL for Lamivudine. In July 2011, Shanghai Aurisco Pharmaceutical Limited planned to organise domestic non-governmental organisations to apply for patent CL

to these questions vary substantially. These issues remain contentious and pose serious impediments towards the grant of a CL. For instance, in Thailand, the patentee of the AIDS drug efavirenz argued that the granting of the CL violated WTO Rules/TRIPS since the Thai government did not engage in prior negotiations before issuing a CL.[1] The same argument was brought up by Bayer in the recent CL case in India.[2] To shed some light on those questions, this chapter will examine the provisions and interpretation of "prior negotiation" (Sect. 2) and "adequate remuneration" under Art. 31 of the TRIPS Agreement (Sect. 3) and identify some options and proposals for member states of the WTO to adjust their legislation (Sect. 4). The chapter will pay special attention to CL in India and relevant Chinese law (admittedly, no CLs have ever been granted in China so far),[3] given their economic importance and huge populations.

2 Prior Negotiation: A Puzzling Hurdle to a CL

Art. 31 (b) generally requires that a party seeking a CL first undertake negotiations with the patent holder for a voluntary licence on "reasonable commercial terms and conditions and that such efforts have not been successful within a reasonable period of time". These conditions are designed, upon the insistence of developed countries, to ensure that a patent owner's rights are "not abrogated unjustifiably". However, from the language of the TRIPS Agreement, the nature of prior negotiation is not entirely clear.

2.1 *Nature of Prior Negotiation: A Substantive Ground or a Procedure?*

It has been controversial whether the prior negotiation under Art. 31(b) of the TRIPS Agreement is a substantive ground for granting CL or simply a procedure before an applicant seeks a CL. The "Ground Theory" treats prior negotiation as a ground for CL.[4] In the well-informed document issued by the International Bureau of the World Intellectual Property Organization (WIPO), the "failure to obtain a voluntary license under reasonable terms within a reasonable period" is listed as one of the six most widely adopted grounds for CL in developing countries.[5] Some further maintain that the refusal to license on reasonable commercial terms would

for Tenofovir disoproxil used for AIDS. http://www.chinaipr.gov.cn/newsarticle/news/government/201203/1285090_1.html.

[4] Li et al. (2008), pp. 1034 and 1043.

[5] WIPO CDIP (Committee on Development and Intellectual Property) (2010), p. 15, Sec. 49.

[6] Liu (2009), pp. 115 and 121–122.

hinder technological progress and would constitute an abusive use of patent rights and therefore would trigger the CL. That is to say, as long as a qualified person applies to the patentee with reasonable commercial terms for a licence but the patentee does not grant his consent within a reasonable period, it would constitute a ground for a CL. However, the advocates of the "Procedure Theory" claim that prior negotiation under Art 31 (b) is merely a procedure rather than an independent ground for granting CL. That is to say, the patentee enjoys the right to refuse a voluntary licence even if reasonable commercial terms are offered by an applicant. As a general rule, the applicant who seeks a CL must make efforts to negotiate a voluntary licence with the patentee before he can file an application for CL.[6]

The contention about the nature of prior negotiation is highlighted in the revision history of China's patent law. To be brief, the 1984 Patent Law adopted the "Procedure Theory", Art. 54 of which stated: "any units or individuals who apply for a compulsory licence should furnish proof to show that it or *he has made requests for authorization from the patentee to exploit its or his patent on reasonable terms and conditions*, but failed to conclude a licensing agreement". The law treated "prior negotiation" as a prerequisite procedure. However, the Patent Law, as revised in 1992, took the "Ground Theory" approach. Art. 51 of the 1992 Patent Law stated: "If the entity with the ability to implement the patent has made request for a licence to exploit the invention or utility model patents on reasonable terms and conditions, but had not been successful within a reasonable period of time to obtain the authorization, the Patent Office can, upon the unit's application, grant licence to implement the patent for invention or utility model". The provisions remained unchanged in the 2000 Patent Law.

Nevertheless, the current Patent Law as revised in 2008 adopts the "Procedure Theory". Article 54 provides that "Any entity or individual requesting, in accordance with the provisions of Article 48(1)[7] or Article 51[8] of this Law, a compulsory license for exploitation *shall furnish proof to show that it or he has made requests for authorization from the patentee to exploit its or his patent on reasonable terms and conditions, and such efforts have not been successful within a reasonable period of time*". Moreover, the Chinese Patent Law limits the grounds for requesting a CL to six circumstances: namely, failure to work, existence of qualified dependent patents, national emergency, existence of extreme urgency, public non-commercial use, and adjudicated anti-competitive practice. Such narrow interpretation of the TRIPS Agreement may well contribute to the absence of CLs in China.[9]

Clearly, the nature of "prior negotiation" has undergone substantial changes under China's patent law, and the present Chinese patent law treats it as a

[7] Art. 48 (1) regulates the CL on the ground of "failure to work" a patent.

[8] Art. 51 deals with the CL on the ground of 'dependent patents'.

[9] Lin (2006a, b).

[10] Submission by Japan, Addendum, Patents: Non-Voluntary Licences, MTN.GNG/NG11/W/17/Add. 3, sec. 2 (1).

procedural premise for granting CL. However, at the international level, it is not clear whether the "procedure approach" is the only correct interpretation of Art. 31 (b) of the TRIPS Agreement. The negotiating history of the TRIPS Agreement may shed some light on this point. It shows that the "prior negotiation" clause, which originated from Japan's suggestion, carries specific meaning. In the revised submission on "Patents: Non-Voluntary Licences" dated 8 December 1989, Japan proposed the following provision: "in the granting of a non-voluntary licence, an application for the licence shall be filed with a competent authority only on the following grounds, *provided that the patentee has refused to grant a voluntary licence requested by the same applicant in accordance with normal commercial practices*".[10] Furthermore, the representative of Japan explained that the term "normal commercial practices" in Section 2(1) was intended to refer to negotiations for obtaining voluntary licences conducted as normal and in good faith and where due cooperation and diligence in concluding such contracts within a reasonable period had been shown. The provisions were designed to exclude unreasonably low royalty rates and to be flexible enough to allow for variations in such rates; it was to be expected that normal commercial practices and royalty rates would vary by industry.[11] It is self-evident that Japan treated "prior negotiation" as a procedural safeguard for patent holders. In addition, Switzerland proposed similar provisions on "prior negotiation". It stated that for the reason of an overriding public interest, a CL may be granted "provided that the owner of the patent had refused to grant a contractual licence on terms that are in line with normal commercial practices".[12] However, some Latin American states such as Peru made it a ground for granting a CL if the patent owner refused to grant a contractual licence.[13] Subsequently, the 1990 Draft Agreement on Trade-related Aspects of Intellectual Property Rights, in Art. 26 (3), stated that "Except in the case of a manifest national emergency, a compulsory licence may only be issued after unsuccessful efforts made by the applicant in line with normal commercial practices to negotiate a voluntary licence with the right holder".[14] The final text of Art. 31 (b) of the TRIPS Agreement makes similar provisions. The above historical review shows that the "prior negotiation" under Art. 31 (b) has been designed to be a procedure to protect patent holders, i.e. to make sure the patentee is heard before a CL application is filed. However, the final text of the TRIPS Agreement is different from the Japanese proposition in that the TRIPS Agreement takes a "direct approach" to require the applicant of a CL to make efforts to obtain a voluntary licence from the patentee, while the Japanese position took an "indirect approach" to require the applicant to prove that "the patentee has refused to grant a voluntary licence". For practical reasons, the provisions of the TRIPS Agreement are the better option because it is easier for the

[11] MTN.GNG/NG11/17, p. 18, para. 39. 23 January 1990.

[12] MTN.GNG/NG11/W/32/Rev. 2, p. 100.

[13] MTN.GNG/NG11/W/32/Rev. 2, p. 102.

[14] Draft Agreement on Trade-related Aspects of Intellectual Property Rights, MTN.GNG/NG11/W/68, p. 9, 29 March 1990.

applicant to prove that he had made efforts to obtain a voluntary licence than to prove that the patentee has refused to license. In some cases, the patentee may remain silent after receiving the request for a licence and never directly reject the request for a licence.

2.2 *Interpretation of 'Prior Negotiation'*

"Prior negotiation" here means that the applicant of the CL must have made efforts to obtain a voluntary licence on reasonable terms prior to filing an application for a CL. In the strict sense, the word "negotiation" here is somewhat misleading because Art. 31 (b) of the TRIPS Agreement does not require the two parties, the applicant and the patentee, to talk and discuss with each other in order to try to reach an agreement. It only requires the applicant to make efforts to seek a voluntary licence in good faith. Then how much effort would qualify for a "prior negotiation" in this context? The TRIPS Agreement does not set qualitative and quantitative criteria for the "efforts", although the plural form of "efforts" is used here. Viewing from the negotiating history of the TRIPS Agreement, especially as shown by the Japanese proposition, it does not require continued efforts on the part of the applicant to seek a licence, and thus a single attempt to seek a voluntary licence would satisfy the requirement. As explained by the Japanese representative during the negotiation period, the essence of the "prior negotiation" is to enhance the patentee's position in order to negotiate a favourable voluntary licence when facing the threat of a CL. It does not require continued efforts to obtain a licence. In the *Natco* case, the Indian Intellectual Property Appellate Board (IPAB) took such an approach.[15] The Board opined that once an effort is made by a party to seek a voluntary licence and the same was rejected by the patent holder, it is not required to make another request; a single attempt by the applicant to obtain a voluntary licence would satisfy the requirement.[16]

The next question would be at what time prior negotiation should be conducted. The TRIPS Agreement provides no clear guidance, and Art. 31 (b) simply states that "prior to *such use*, the proposed user has made efforts to obtain. . .." Does 'prior to *such use*' mean that negotiation must precede filing an application for CL or that it must precede granting of a CL? Logically, the answer should be the former because the "prior negotiation" mechanism is designed to provide the patentee with an opportunity to be heard and to prevent a CL. This position is reflected in domestic law of many states. For example, China's "Measures for Implementing

[15] In *Bayer v. Union of India and Others*, the compulsory licence applicant, Natco, had sent a request letter to the patent holder, Bayer, for a licence, and the same was not appreciated by Bayer.

[16] *Bayer Corporation v. Union of India, The Controller of Patents and Natco Pharma Limited*, MANU/IC/0016/2013, paras. 10–16.

[17] Art. 11, 15 March 2012.

Patent Compulsory Licensing", as amended in 2012, require the applicant seeking a CL to provide evidence to prove that it has made efforts to obtain a voluntary licence with reasonable terms and conditions but with no success when he applies for a CL under the grounds of "non-working" and "dependent patents".[17] Thus, the "efforts" to obtain a voluntary licence shall be conducted "prior to" the filing of an application for a CL.

As for the manner of "prior negotiation", it varies by industry. At least, it should be conducted in good faith and in accordance with normal commercial practices. Thus, the general principles of contract law should be observed. In commercial practice, when parties negotiate with a view to making a contract, many preliminary communications may pass between them before a definite deal is made. Then all the preliminary efforts to obtain a patent licence should be deemed as the process of "prior negotiation". However, Art. 31 (b) of the TRIPS Agreement requires that "the proposed user has made efforts to obtain authorization from the right holder *on reasonable commercial terms and conditions*". Thus, to qualify as "prior negotiation", the applicant shall propose "*reasonable* terms and conditions" to the patentee when he requests a voluntary licence. Put in the context of contract law, it should be an offer to make a contract or "an invitation to treat". An offer is an expression of willingness to contract on *specified* terms, made with the intention that it shall become binding as soon as it is accepted by the person to whom it is addressed. An invitation to treat should also contain *specified* terms and conditions. The distinction between an offer and an invitation to treat depends on the criterion of intention to be bound.[18] A letter or expression with no specified terms cannot be regarded as either an offer or an invitation to treat. Not only should the terms be specified, but the TRIPS Agreement further requires that the terms and conditions should be "reasonable".

2.3 Reasonable Commercial Terms and Conditions

Under Art. 31 (b) of the TRIPS Agreement, the applicant for a CL generally needs to prove that it has sought and failed to obtain a voluntary licence from the patent holder on '**reasonable commercial terms and conditions**' before he could apply for a CL. Then what does "commercial terms and conditions" mean? What terms

[18] Treitel (1995), pp. 8–10.

[19] The Controller General of Patents Designs and Trademarks of India ("Controller") granted Natco Pharma Limited ("Natco"), an Indian drug manufacturer, a CL to manufacture Bayer's patent drug—Nexavar (Sorafenib). Bayer appealed, and the Intellectual Property Appellate Board upheld the Controller's decision. Application for Compulsory Licence under Section 84 (1) of the Patent Act 1970 in Respect of Patent No. 215758, Compulsory License Application No. 1, 2011.

[20] MTN.GNG/NG11/W/32/Rev. 2, p. 100.

[21] UNCTAD-ICTSD: Resource Book on TRIPS and Development [M/OL], p. 469, http://www.iprsonline.org.

and conditions are "reasonable"? These provisions could lead to various interpretations, as shown in a recent landmark CL case in India.[19]

From the negotiation history of the TRIPS Agreement as stated above,[20] the "commercial terms and conditions", originated from Japan's submission, should be assessed in accordance with the "normal commercial practice". According to the Resource Book on TRIPS and Development, issued by the UNCTAD ("Resource Book"), a patent licence generally includes the payment of a royalty and other terms,[21] which usually include the following: (1) *Duration of the licence term*. In a voluntary transaction, this is usually negotiated by the patentee and licensee. However, the duration of a CL is usually limited. (2) *Additional technology*. A voluntary license usually states the extent to which the patent holder will aid in the implementation of technological solutions. However, a CL is only limited to the patent covered, and is not extended to the relevant know-how. (3) *Export restrictions*. In a voluntary license, patent owners may or may not impose restrictions on the geographical scope of selling the licensed product; however, the TRIPS Agreement imposes strict restrictions on the export of the products manufactured under the CL.[22] In addition, the patent licence terms often include the scope of use. In a voluntary licence, the patentee may include the terms such as the geographical or product scope of using the licensed technology. However, in a CL, the scope of using the patented technology is restricted to the purpose for which it was authorised. This may limit the ability of the licensee to achieve economies of scale in its production facilities. In the context of Art. 31(b), the "commercial terms and conditions" are those usually shown in a voluntary licence. The word "commercial" here should be interpreted with flexibility for, at least, two reasons. Firstly, there should have existed a situation to be regarded as a ground for filing a CL when an applicant initiated the "prior negotiation". The "efforts" to negotiate is virtually a pre-CL warning to the patentee. Thus, it is different from the "normal commercial" situation. Secondly, it also means that an overriding public interest needs to be served when a "prior negotiation" is conducted.

The TRIPS Agreement does not specify what terms should be included in the licensing proposal made by the applicant, and this may create room for fighting. In the CL case between Bayer and Natco, this issue was under contest. In both proceedings before the Controllers and the IPAB, Bayer submitted that *Natco had not sought a voluntary license on reasonable commercial terms within reasonable period of time*. The fact is that before applying for a CL, Natco served a letter, dated December 6, 2010, upon Bayer to apply for a voluntary licence for the said patent and requested Bayer to respond within 14 days. In response, the counselor for Bayer said: "In view of what has been stated above, our client does not consider it

[22] UNCTAD-ICTSD: Resource Book on TRIPS and Development [M/OL], p. 470. http://www.iprsonline.org.

[23] Application for Compulsory Licence under Section 84 (1) of the Patent Act 1970 in Respect of Patent No. 215758, Compulsory License Application No. 1, 2011, pp. 9–10.

[24] *Ibid.*

appropriate to grant a voluntary licence to manufacture and market the product, Naxaver, to Natco". Bayer argued that the letter of Natco cannot be deemed as a "prior negotiation" in the given context because it didn't specify *what terms and conditions* Natco was willing to accept and that the period of 14 days was not reasonable. Nor is the single, unilateral notice from Natco sufficient to satisfy the requirements of Art. 31(b).[23] The Controller, who didn't address the nature of the letter, held that Bayer "categorically" refused to grant a voluntary licence and that Natco could not have taken further efforts to obtain a voluntary licence, and hence the requirement of prior negotiation had been satisfied.[24]

Interestingly, during the subsequent CL proceeding before the Controller, the applicant, Natco, proposed five terms and conditions, including (1) the geographical scope to manufacture and sell Sorafenib only in India; (2) the patients covered by the licence; (3) royalties as set by the Controller; (4) limitation on the price of Sorafenib under the CL—Rs. 74 per tablet, i.e. not more than Rs. 8,800 per month for therapy; (5) commitment to offer free of charge to at least 600 needy patients per year. Bayer proposed ten terms and conditions, which included (1) the non-exclusiveness of the CL; (2) restrictions on the Applicant's representation of its products manufactured under the CL; (3) limitation on the price of Applicant's products; (4) the Applicant's liability for the products made under the CL; (5) royalty—15 % of net sales; (6) the term of the CL; (7) no implied licences to other patents, no warranties of validity and enforceability; (8) non-challenging of the validity of the patent under the CL; (9) liberty of the patentee to dispose of its residual right, to compete, or to license a third party; (10) other terms normal in the industry (such as bookkeeping, and reporting mechanism).

In the Controller's decision, Mr. Kurian, combining the proposed terms of the Applicant and the Bayer, prescribed 13 terms and conditions: (1) price of the drug covered by the patent—shall not exceed Rs. 8,800 for a pack of 120 tablets, as proposed by the Applicant; (2) the obligation of the licensee to maintain accounts of sale etc. and report to the Controller as well as the Licensor; (3) restrictions on the Applicant to outsource the production; (4) the license is non-exclusive; (5) the license is non-assignable; (6) royalty at the rate of 6 % of the net sales; (7) the license is granted solely for the purpose of making, using, offering to sell and selling the drug covered by the patent for the purpose of treating primary kidney cancer (advanced renal cell carcinoma) and advanced primary liver cancer (hepatocellular carcinoma)in human within the Territory of India. (8) the licensee is obliged to supply the drug free of cost to 600 needy patients per year; (9) restrictions on the licensee to import the drug; (10) the term of license is for the rest of the time period during which the patent remains valid. (11) restrictions on the licensee's representation and packing of its products; (12) licensee's liability for its products and for all associated products; (13) the Licensor's freedom to dispose of its residual patent rights. Clearly, the Controller adopts most terms and conditions

[25] Application for Compulsory Licence under Section 84 (1) of the Patent Act 1970 in Respect of Patent No. 215758, Compulsory License Application No. 1, 2011, pp. 55–62.

submitted by the applicant and the Licensor. Conditions 1, 7, and 8 of the Decision are identical or similar to those proposed by the applicant, while conditions 2, 3, and 10–13 are similar to those submitted by Bayer.[25]

It is worth noting that the above terms and conditions proposed by both Natco and Bayer in the Sorafenib CL proceeding are not the "*commercial* terms" of "prior negotiation" as per Art. 31 (b) of the TRIPS Agreement. Those are the terms and conditions of the CL. The terms and conditions for a CL should be different from those of a voluntary licence. While the commercial terms usually depend on the general commercial practice in the industry and the bargaining power of the parties, the terms and conditions of *a CL* are greatly subject to the discretion of the competent authority. By viewing Art. 31 of the TRIPS Agreement and the essence of "prior negotiation", it would be is sensible to interpret "reasonable commercial terms and conditions" under Art. 31 (b) in a flexible way.

Moreover, the "reasonableness" of the "terms and conditions" should be assessed on a case-by-case basis by taking into account the circumstances of each case. Having said that, there is a minimum requirement for the "reasonable commercial terms and conditions", that is, the terms should be *prima facie* commercially sensible. At least, a proposal made by the applicant shall contain terms on royalty and the scope of the licence. Thus, the single letter without specifying any royalty or other terms served by Natco upon Bayer in the above-cited Indian case could hardly be regarded as "reasonable".

2.4 Reasonable Period of Time

The requirement of negotiating a voluntary licence within the '**reasonable period of time**' under Art. 31 (b) of the TRIPS Agreement was stipulated to prevent tactical delay on the part of the patent holder to grant a patent licence. As noted by the Resource Book, "a patent holder who does not wish to licence its technology, but that also does not wish to see a compulsory licence granted, may well attempt to prolong negotiations using a variety of tactics. Such tactics may include appearing to be engaged in serious negotiations over detailed terms and conditions that do not reach a conclusion".[26] To prevent the tactic of delay, the "reasonable period of time" was added in the TRIPS Agreement, probably upon the insistence of the developing countries, because the original proposition of Japan did not contain the time limit.[27] In practice, the reasonable time period for negotiations may depend on several factors such as the purpose for which the licence is sought. For example, a

[26] UNCTAD-ICTSD: Resource Book [M/OL], p. 470, http://www.iprsonline.org.

[27] Submission by Japan, "Addendum, Patents: Non-Voluntary Licences", MTN.GNG/NG11/W/17/Add. 3, sec. 2 (1).

[28] UNCTAD-ICTSD: Resource Book on TRIPS and Development [M/OL], p. 470, http://www.iprsonline.org.

negotiator seeking to commence production of a life-saving pharmaceutical would be justified in seeking a more rapid conclusion of negotiations than a negotiator seeking to commence production of an improved fishing rod.[28] To serve the need of broad public interest, the TRIPS Agreement allows member states to interpret the 'reasonable period of time' in a flexible manner.

At a domestic level, the 'reasonable period of time' is so essential for the administration of the CL that it should not be left open. It is critical for the parties and the competent authority to determine when a CL application could be filed. That is to say, the triggering point of a CL proceeding depends on the "reasonable time". Thus, the domestic law of WTO members should be clear and specific on this. However, most countries such as China simply adopt the language of the TRIPS Agreement—"reasonable period of time"—and leave it to the competent authorities to determine in accordance with the situations of each individual case. Only a few jurisdictions set some rules on the 'timing' of CLs. For example, in India, an explanation to Sec. 84(6) of the Patents Act has been added in the 2005 amendment to clarify the 'reasonable period' to negotiate and obtain a voluntary licence from the patentee as 6 months. It states that 'for the purposes of clause (iv), "reasonable period" shall be construed as a period *not ordinarily exceeding* a period of six months'.[29] To be noted, the 'reasonable period' under the Indian Patents Act is not fixed at 6 months; rather, it is a period that does '*not ordinarily exceed six months*', leaving room for the Controller to decide in an individual case. In a less direct manner, the Intellectual Property Law of the Dominican Republic provides that "when a potential user has attempted to obtain the granting of a license from the patent holder under reasonable commercial terms and conditions and such attempts have not been effective after a period of **two hundred and ten** (**210**) days, counted from the date on which the respective license was applied for, the General Agency for Industrial Property, after prior hearing of the patent holder, shall be able to issue compulsory licenses relating to that patent".[30] Likewise, the Canadian Patent Act (as amended in 2005) in Sec. 21.04, which is titled "the conditions for granting of authorization", provides:

> (3) The Commissioner shall authorize the use of the patented invention only if:
>
> (c) the applicant provides the Commissioner with a solemn or statutory declaration in the prescribed form stating that the applicant had, **at least thirty days** before filing the application,
> (i) sought from the patentee or, if there is more than one, from each of the patentees, by certified or registered mail, a licence to manufacture and sell the pharmaceutical product for export to the country or WTO Member named in the application on reasonable terms and conditions and that such efforts have not been successful.

[29] Explanation 1, Art. 84 (6)(iv).

[30] Art. 40, Law on Industrial Property No. 20-00 of 18/04/2000, see WIPO CDIP/5/4, Annex I, p. 48, 2010.

[31] Love (2001).

Clearly, neither Dominican Republic nor Canada *directly* defines the "reasonable period of time". Among the three approaches cited above, the Indian approach is more direct and easier to follow, although it still has some uncertainties. Sec. 21.04 of the Canadian Patent Act does frame the minimum time period between *requesting* a voluntary licence and the filing of CL application, and this gives some guidance on when the applicant may file for a CL. By contrast, the Dominican law defines the time period (210 days) between the *requesting* of a voluntary licence and the "*issuing*" of a CL. It leaves the applicant in doubt as to when he may appropriately file an application for a CL. The lack of clear rules on the "reasonable period of time" between requesting a voluntary licence and applying for a CL may create a grey area that may become a battle field and may thus exacerbate the difficulties in resolving a CL case.

To clarify the triggering point for requesting a CL, James Love proposes a guideline to set the "reasonable period of time".[31] It requires the parties to negotiate a voluntary licence within "no more than six months". This proposition is virtually identical to the provisions in the Indian Patents Act and suffers from the same problem of uncertainty. To strike a balance between certainty and flexibility, the domestic law should set a specific time period (e.g., 3 months) between requesting a voluntary licence and seeking a CL, and the time limit can be shortened if the patentee explicitly refuses to grant a licence or the competent authority sees it fit in special circumstances. Meanwhile, the time period can be extended if the parties agree so or the competent authority sees it fit.

2.5 *Waiver of Prior Negotiations*

According to Art. 31 (b) and (k) of the TRIPS Agreement, prior negotiation with the patent holder may be exempted in the following cases:

1. national emergency;
2. other circumstances of extreme urgency;
3. public non-commercial use;
4. anti-competitive conducts.

These provisions leave very broad room for interpretation. During the TRIPS negotiations, member states were not able to reach a consensus on the meaning of the situations of urgency, national emergency, non-commercial public use, and anti-competitive conducts. During the Uruguay Round, a proposal presented by India was accepted to ensure ample freedom for countries to define these expressions.[32]

---

[32] Sun (2003), p. 3.

[33] Nolff (2002), p. 3.

2.5.1 National Emergency

From the language of Art. 31 (b) of the TRIPS Agreement, members of the WTO are free to determine the circumstances that characterise a national emergency, which are extremely important in the public health crises caused by epidemics or pandemics. The Doha Declaration on TRIPS and Public Health in 2001 maintains the flexibility of the TRIPS Agreement, which allows the implementation of public policies that facilitate access to medications.[33] Furthermore, paragraph 5(c) of the Doha Declaration adopted a broad definition of "a national emergency" or "other circumstance of extreme urgency", which are not limited to situations where time is of the essence but include more generally "public health crises".

2.5.2 Other Circumstances of Extreme Urgency

According to the Resource Book, the term "other circumstances of extreme urgency" makes clear that a waiver of the prior negotiation requirement does not depend upon a formal declaration of national emergency. The use of the term "extreme" in connection with "urgency" suggests that it is highly desirable to move quickly to grant a licence. The term "extreme" refers to the far end of the spectrum of urgency, although it is not possible to lay out a general rule as to what differentiates extreme urgency from moderate urgency.[34] As reaffirmed in the Doha Declaration, the WTO member is entitled to determine what constitutes "other circumstances of extreme urgency".

2.5.3 Public Non-commercial Use

"Public non-commercial use" is a flexible concept, leaving WTO members with considerable flexibility in granting CLs without requiring voluntary negotiations in advance. During the TRIPS negotiation, the attempts to introduce criteria to define the content of the expression "public interest" failed because developing nations were uninterested in restraining flexibility to adopt governmental policies to address health concerns. The term "public non-commercial use" has various meanings. For example, the term "public" could refer to use by a government, as opposed to private entity. The term may refer also to the purpose of the use, that is, use for "public" benefit. A private entity could be charged with exploiting a patent for the benefit of the public.[35] "Non-commercial use" may be defined either in relation to the nature of the transaction or in relation to the purpose of the use. Regarding the nature of the transaction, "non-commercial" may be understood as "not-for-profit"

[34] Resource Book, p. 471.

[35] Resource Book, p. 471.

[36] Resource Book, p. 471.

use. A commercial enterprise does not ordinarily enter the market without intending to earn a profit. Regarding the purpose of the use, "non-commercial" may refer to the supply of public institutions that are not functioning as commercial enterprises. The supply of a public hospital operating on a non-profit basis may be a "non-commercial" use of the patent.[36]

2.5.4 Anti-competitive Conduct

Pursuant to Art. 31(k) of the TRIPS Agreement, when CLs are used by governments to remedy adjudicated anti-competitive practices (pursuant to findings by judicial or administrative bodies), there is no requirement of prior negotiations with the patent holders under Article 31(b). The concept "anti-competitive practices" is very flexible and subject to varied interpretations. Presently, the patent law in most jurisdictions states only the general principle that a CL may be granted to remedy anti-competitive practices but provides no clear definition of the concept. Usually, it is for the competition law or anti-monopoly law to define "anti-competitive practices". For example, China's Patent Law states that a CL may be granted to eliminate or reduce the adverse effects on competition where the exercise of the patent right by the patentee is legally adjudicated to be an act of monopoly.[37] As for the definition of "anti-competitive practice", China's Anti-Monopoly Law provides, among others, that operators who hold a dominant market position shall be prohibited from engaging in the following practices, which may be classified as an abuse of dominant position: (1) selling products at unfairly high or unfairly low prices, (2) selling products at a price lower than cost without legitimate grounds, (3) refusing to conduct transactions with relevant trading partners without legitimate grounds, (4) forcing trading partners to conduct transactions without legitimate grounds, (5) conducing tie-in deals or imposing other unreasonable conditions on a deal without legitimate grounds, (6) discriminating without legitimate grounds, and (7) other practices.[38] Furthermore, the draft Guidelines for the Antimonopoly Law Enforcement Concerning Intellectual Property set more detailed rules on anti-competitive behaviours of patent holders.[39]

Unusually, the Patent Law of Israel provides a broad definition for the "abuse of monopoly". Art. 119 states:

> The exercise of a monopoly conferred by a patent shall be deemed abusive, if one of the following circumstances exists in respect of the invention, the product or the process which is the subject of the patent, and if the patent holder did not provide a reasonable justification for its existence:
>
> (*1*) *all the demand for the product is not satisfied in Israel on reasonable terms*;

[37] Patent Law, as amended in 2008, Art. 48 (2).

[38] Art. 17, China's Anti-Monopoly Law, 2007.

[39] The draft is still in the process of consultation.

[40] Israel Patent Law no. 5727 of 08/08/1967, Art. 119. WIPO CDIP/5/4, Annex I, 2010, p. 95.

(2) *the conditions attached by the patent holder to the supply of the product or to the grant of a license for its production or use are not fair under the circumstances of the case, do not take account of the public interest and arise essentially out of the existence of the patent;*
(3) *exploitation of the invention by way of production in Israel is impossible or restricted by the importation of the product;*
(4) *the product is not produced in Israel and the patent holder refuses to grant to a local producer a license for its production or use on reasonable terms, neither for the requirements of the local market nor for export purposes;*
(5) *the patent holder refuses to grant a license for the production of the product or for the use of the process in Israel on reasonable terms and because of that refusal-*
(a) *the export of a product from Israel is prevented or adversely affected; or*
(b) *the launching or development in Israel of a commercial or industrial activity is prevented.*[40]

The defining of a patentee's "anti-competitive practice" or "abuse of monopoly" in patent law, as that in Israel, does have its virtue, not least because this creates a direct connection between the exercise of an anti-competitive practice and the threat of a CL.

2.6 Summary

The 'prior negotiation' is an important mechanism to make sure the patentee is heard before a CL is sought. As the compromise made by the developed countries and developing countries, Art. 31 (b) of the TRIPS Agreement leaves great flexibility and ambiguity by using terms such as 'commercial' and 'reasonable' to qualify the requirement. Every member state may employ the flexibility to meet the needs of the particular country. As general wisdom, if a member state wishes to apply the CL effectively, it is advisable to clear up the ambiguity by adopting specific rules or guidance on the 'reasonable commercial terms' and 'reasonable period of time'.

---

[41] Some use the term "compensation" instead of "remuneration" in this context. However, considering the goal and nature of the CL system, it is more appropriate to use the term "remuneration", which is neutral, while the term "compensation" implies a punishment for a wrong or injustice.

[42] MTN.GNG/NG11/W/32/Rev. 2, pp. 98–103.

[43] MTN.GNG/NG11/W/32/Rev. 2, p. 98.

3 Adequate Remuneration[41]

Remuneration is a key term of a CL, as it has been a well-established principle that a patentee should be rewarded. As John Stuart Mill put it: "That he, the Inventor, ought to be both compensated and rewarded. . .will not be denied. . .it would be a gross immorality of the law to set everybody free to see (or use) a person's work without his consent, and without giving him an equivalent" (Principles of Political Economy, 1848). Prior to the TRIPS Agreement, almost all countries required the licensee of the CL to pay reasonable or adequate remuneration or compensation to the patentee.[42] One obvious exception was the US law that did not require the payment of remuneration while a CL was granted to remedy an adjudicated violation of antitrust laws.[43] At the international level, the Paris Convention does not require the payment of remuneration for CL. However, Art. 31 (h) of the TRIPS states: "the right holder shall be paid *adequate remuneration* in the circumstances of each case, taking into account the economic value of the authorization". What is the 'adequate remuneration'? What are the 'circumstances of each case'? What is the 'economic value of the authorization'? These questions have been the source of significant contention among academics and practitioners.

3.1 The Meaning of "Adequate Remuneration"

Different terms, including "adequate", "suitable", "proper", "reasonable", "fair", "justifiable",[44] have been used to define the appropriate amount of remuneration payable to the patentee under a CL. For instance, in Australia, sec. 133(5) of the Patents Act states: "this has to be an amount negotiated by the patentee and applicant or an amount determined by the Federal Court as **just and reasonable**, having regard to the economic value of the licence and the desirability of discouraging anti-competitive behaviour". In Singapore, Art. 16.7 of the Patent Act provides that "neither party shall permit the use of the subject matter of a patent without the authorization of the right holder" unless "the patent owner is provided with **reasonable and entire** compensation for such use and manufacture".

What is "adequate remuneration"? The interpretations are highly varied, and there is no single accepted approach. According to the Resource Book, the term "adequate" generally is used to indicate something that is sufficient, or meets minimum standards, but not more than that.[45] This interpretation reaffirms that "adequate remuneration" could be defined differently since it gives no clear guidance on what is "sufficient" or what is "minimum". Others may argue that the remuneration for a patent CL may be considered adequate if it safeguards the **legitimate interests** of the patent owner. The adequacy of remunerations should

[44] Välimäki (2011), p. 1.

[45] Resource Book, p. 475.

be guided by the specific circumstances of each case. If the CL is used for the restoration of the competitive environment or to meet a pubic need, this should be taken into account when deciding on the adequacy of the remuneration. Thus, the term "adequate remuneration" alone carries little meaning unless it is interpreted by taking into account "the circumstances of each case".

3.2 Approaches to Assess "Adequate Remuneration"

3.2.1 Market Approach

The Resource Book mentions several approaches to determine "adequate remuneration". One much-cited approach is to ask what the licensee would have been required to pay as compensation to the patent holder for a voluntary licence under ordinary circumstances. This approach, however, suffers from several defects. Firstly, this approach relies on the assumption that there is a market for licences regarding the type of technology involved in the particular case, and the market rate would provide an indication at least as to what patent holders might expect from licensing their technology. However, this assumption may be unrealistic since the "market rate" may be difficult to determine or misleading.[46] It may be difficult or impossible to find a comparable royalty for the patent to be compulsorily licensed. Secondly, it may not be appropriate to set the remuneration for a CL based on the royalty of a voluntary licence because the granting of a CL implies that the law admits a value (e.g., public health) of higher priority than the exclusive right of a patent holder. This suggests that more weight should be given to the purpose for which a CL is sought.

3.2.2 Cost Approach

The cost approach attempts to assess the "adequate remuneration" based on the research and development cost of the patentee in relation to the technology under the CL. It usually requires the patent holder to present a detailed justification for its royalty request. The patent holder may be asked to provide specific data on his research and development costs (including any offsetting tax or accounting benefits). The granting authority could, on the basis of this data, determine what level of royalty would adequately reflect the patent holder's interest in the country in question.[47] This approach has serious defects because there is little co-relation

[46] Resource Book, p. 476.

[47] Resource Book, p. 476.

[48] Taubman (2008), pp. 927 and 956.

between the value of a CL and the cost of R&D due to the high uncertainty of the scientific research and innovation.

3.2.3 Patent Value Approach

Professor Taubman in his well-cited article explores extensively the different approaches to determine "adequate remuneration". The first one could be categorised as "**the patent value approach**". This viewpoint claims that the adequate remuneration should be based on the "economic value of the patent", i.e. the potential value for the patent owner. This economic value could then be used as a benchmark, which is discounted by certain factors.[48] This approach does not seem to find correct base for calculating adequate remuneration for CL because Art. 31 (h) of the TRIPS Agreement clearly states that the granting authority should "take into account the economic value of the authorization", instead of basing the remuneration on the "value of the patent". Notably, the value of the authorisation is different from the value of the patent.

3.2.4 Income Approach

Under "**the income approach**", the remuneration for the CL should be based on the amount of actual or potential financial income the licensee may gain with the licence.[49] This approach has some force in that it is closer to "the economic **value of the authorization**", as stipulated by Art. 31 (h) of the TRIPS Agreement. However, the actual income of the licensee may not reflect the true value of the CL for a number of reasons. Firstly, more often than not, the price of the products manufactured or sold under a CL is decided by government authorities, not by the market. Secondly, sometimes the products under the CL are not sold in an arm-length transaction.

3.2.5 Infringement Compensation Approach

Under the "**infringement compensation approach**", the adequate remuneration is calculated in the same manner as the commercial damages in patent infringement cases,[50] which is the 'damages adequate to compensate for the injury' caused by a certain infringement as per Art. 45 of the TRIPS Agreement. This approach is problematic since it departs completely from the stipulations of Art. 31 (h) of the

---

[49] Taubman (2008), pp. 927 and 956.

[50] Taubman (2008), pp. 927–970; Oxford University p. 956.

[51] Art. 30 of the TRIPS Agreement.

[52] Taubman (2008), p. 957.

TRIPS Agreement. Moreover, it makes no distinctions between a well-justified CL and a punishable infringement.

3.2.6 Reasonable Reward Approach

Professor Taubman proposes that 'adequate remuneration' for CL under the TRIPS Agreement should be "**the reasonable compensation for the normal exploitation of a patent and the legitimate interest of the patentee**". To Taubman, the remuneration is adequate if it reasonably compensates for any conflict with the regular exploitation of the patent, as well as for any prejudice of legitimate interests.[51] This interpretation would also allow for a punitive approach in cases where CL is used as a penalty for anti-competitive measures.[52] Under this approach, the value of the patent is an important basis for the evaluation of the remuneration. This approach suffers from the same defect as that of "**the patent value approach**". According to Art. 31 (h) of the TRIPS Agreement, the value of a patent is not the basis for determining adequate remuneration.

3.2.7 Dual Approach

Taking a more idealistic approach, Välimäki suggests that the calculation of adequate remuneration for CLs should be divided into two different situations: (1) CL used to resolve social or other such issues and (2) CL used as a penalty for violating existing legislation. In the first scenario, the objective of the CL is mainly to lower the price of drugs[53]; thus, the remuneration is usually lower than regular royalty, but it should not be so low as to prevent parallel trade, decrease incentive to innovate, or decrease economic growth and employment. In the second scenario, where a CL is used as a penalty, the remuneration should be lower than the regular level so as to reflect its corrective or punitive nature. This would mean that adequate (and reasonable) remuneration could be zero in the case of anti-competition.[54] This methodology seems logical. However, this approach cannot be conducted without difficulties. It is not easy to maintain a balance between the need to lower the price of patented products to meet public demand and the goal to prevent upsetting patent holders. Moreover, it is questionable to place the interest of the public and the necessity of maintaining the incentive to innovate at the same priority in this context.

Considering the general principle for interpreting international treaties, the logical conclusion is that the assessment of 'adequate remuneration' should be *co-related* to the "value of the authorization" and should also take into account the

[53] Although this argument focuses on the CL of patented drug, it is equally applicable to other patented products.

[54] Välimäki (2011), p. 17. Taubman (2008), pp. 953–954.

particular circumstances of each case. The objective of the CL should be given significant weight. The adequate remuneration should be set by conducting a comprehensive analysis of the circumstances of each case.

3.3 Particular Circumstances of Each Case

Art. 31 (h) of the TRIPS Agreement states that "the right holder shall be paid adequate remuneration *in the circumstances of each case*, taking into account the economic value of the authorization". These provisions suggest that the remuneration must reflect the circumstances of each case. The remuneration of the CL must not be calculated on the average or the uniform fee that is paid in the same industry. For instance, the Section 88(5) of the Indian Patents Act 1970 provided that "...the royalty and other remuneration reserved to the patentee shall in no case exceed four percent of the net ex-factory sale price in bulk of the patented article (exclusive of taxes levied under any law for the time being in force and any commissions payable)...". This clause was later abolished because it was not considered to be in compliance with Art. 31 (h) of the TRIPS Agreement. The TRIPS Agreement requires member states to decide the quantum of royalty or other remuneration by taking into account the "circumstances" of each case. What are the "circumstances of each case"? Professor Jerome Reichman, based on the Georgia Pacific factors developed in the USA,[55] proposed seven factors for evaluating "reasonable remuneration" for non-voluntary use of patent in developing countries. The seven additional factors (hereafter "Reichman's 7 factors") include

[55] In *Georgia-Pacific Corp.* v. *United States Plywood Corp.*, 318 F Supp 1116, 6 USPQ 235 (SD NY 1970), the court used these 15 factors to determine the monetary payments that would compensate for a patent infringement: (1) royalties the patentee receives for licensing the patent in suit; (2) rates the licensee pays for use of other patents comparable to the patent in suit; (3) nature and scope of licence in terms of exclusivity and territory/customer restrictions; (4) licensor's established policy and marketing program to maintain patent monopoly by not licensing others to use the invention; (5) commercial relationship between licensor and licensee, such as whether they are competitors or inventor and promoter; (6) effect of selling the patented specialty in promoting sales of other products of the licensee, existing value of the invention to the licensor as a generator of sales of his non-patented items, and extent of such derivative or convoyed sales; (7) duration of patent and term of licence; (8) established profitability of the products made under the patent, its commercial success, and its current popularity; (9) utility and advantages of patent property over old modes and devices; (10) nature of the patented invention, character of the commercial embodiment of it as owned and produced by the licensor, and benefit of those who have used the invention; (11) extent to which the infringer has made use of the invention and the value of such use; (12) portion of profit or selling price customarily allowed for the use of the invention; (13) portion of realizable profit attributable to the invention as distinguished from non-patented elements, significant features/improvements added by the infringer, the manufacturing process, or business risks; (14) opinion testimony of qualified experts; (15) outcome from hypothetical arm's-length negotiation at the time infringement began.

[56] Reichman (2003).

(1) Particular social impact of the invention such as the therapeutic value of a pharmaceutical product;
(2) Per capita GDP and the ability of the general population to pay for needed or essential products;
(3) The existence of crises or emergency conditions, such as environmental disasters or epidemics threatening public health;
(4) Vital needs of national economic development, national security, or the like;
(5) The extent to which the underlying research and development was covered by public funds in either the country of origin or the importing country;
(6) The extent to which the investment in research and development was directed at developing countries, or made in the country imposing the CL, which would pull for a higher royalty;
(7) The extent to which imposition of a CL would broaden consumption beyond that likely to occur under an exclusive license, and this broadening of consumption (or of producers) could yield a multiplier or lottery effect that would translate into revenues beyond investment-backed expectations.

Professor Reichman argues that these and other public interest factors should be weighed against the Georgia Pacific factors to arrive at a reasonable royalty tailored to the different circumstances found in developing countries. The royalties resulting from these modifications would normally range from 4 to 8 % of the generic price.[56] Professor Reichman rightly includes the public interest factors in the calculation of CL remuneration, and his methodology would offer great flexibilities to developing countries. However, Professor Reichman's approach has its limitations. Firstly, the 7-factor approach focuses on the CL of pharmaceutical patents and does not necessarily apply to all patents. Secondly, it would not be simple to administrate his "7 factors" method because, according to Professor Reichman, the determining authority would need to balance the 15 Georgia Pacific factors against the 7 public interest factors. Given the complexities of the methodology and the various offsetting factors involved, it may be hard to determine the potential remuneration. What is more, it seems questionable to compare the CL remuneration to the patent infringement compensation to which the Georgia Pacific factors apply.

By viewing the wording of Art. 31 (h) and the purpose of CL, the competent authority should take into account the following "circumstances": (1) the economic value of the authorisation, that is, the amount of economic gain that a compulsory licensee might extract from the market; (2) the purpose of granting CL; this should be given considerable weight since this is the reason for which the system of CL exists; (3) the scope and duration of the CL; (4) the R&D cost of the patentee for making the patented invention;(5) the extent that the governments pay for the underlying R&D in relation to the patented invention; (6) the nature of the compulsorily licensed patent; (7) the normal market rate of patent licenses in the same industry. In the Sorafenib CL case, the Controller of India reached a royalty at 6 % of net sales of the drug by referring to the following situations: the R&D cost for

[57] Application for Compulsory Licence under Section 84 (1) of the Patent Act 1970 in Respect of Patent No. 215758, Compulsory License Application No. 1, 2011, pp. 5–60.

[58] Chatterjee.

making the invention and developing the drug Sorafenib (about 1.8 billion euro), the nature of this particular invention, the possible number of consumers, the royalty rate suggested by international organisations such as the UNDP Guidelines.[57] Upon the appeal of Bayer, the IPAB upheld, on 4 March 2013, the Controller's decision but raised the royalty from 6 to 7 % of net sales of the drug.[58]

3.4 Methods to Determine Remuneration for Pharmaceutical Products

In the post-TRIPS era, especially after the Doha Declaration, most patent CLs are granted in the pharmaceutical industry; thus, the CL of pharmaceutical patents is of particular significance in practice. The methods to determine the payment for pharmaceutical patents are worth special attention.

Theoretically, to achieve the goal of CL, the setting of remuneration should be relatively predictable and easy to administer. There have been a number of guidelines or models for setting CL remuneration for drugs developed by international organisations or national authorities.

3.4.1 WHO Guidelines

In 2005, the World Health Organization issued the Remuneration Guidelines for Non-Voluntary Use of a Patent on Medical Technologies. The WHO Guidelines conclude that different countries may choose different approaches to remuneration based on administrative capacity, resource constraints, and policy objectives concerning access and innovation and other factors. The WHO Guidelines suggest that countries should adopt royalty guidelines to enhance transparency and predictability, and the United Nations Development Programme (UNDP), Japanese Patent Office (JPO), Canadian, and Tiered Royalty Method (TRM) approaches are all viable and appropriate options for establishing royalties in CL cases. Particularly, the Medical Innovation Prize Fund (MIPF) approach offers a viable alternative mechanism for both funding medical R&D and facilitating access to affordable medicines.

3.4.2 2001 UNDP/HDR Guidelines

The 2001 UNDP Human Development Report proposed a simple system of royalty guidelines. The base royalty rate is 4 % of the price of the generic product. This can

[59] Application for Compulsory Licence under Section 84 (1) of the Patent Act 1970 in Respect of Patent No. 215758, Compulsory License Application No. 1, 2011, p. 60.

be increased or decreased by 2 %, depending on such factors as the degree of inventiveness of a particular medicine or the role of governments in paying for R&D. The advantages of this approach include its simplicity, predictability, easiness to administer, and ability to incorporate certain factors particular to a licensed product (e.g., degree to which it is innovative). In the Sorafenib CL case in India, the Controller cited the UNDP Guidelines as a reference before he reached a 6 % royalty of net sales.[59]

3.4.3 The 1998 JPO Guidelines

In 1998, the JPO issued guidelines for setting royalties on government-owned patents. The 1998 JPO guidelines allow for normal royalties of 2–4 % of the price of the generic product and can be increased or decreased by as much as 2 %, for a range of 0–6 %. Also, the 1998 JPO guidelines include a "utilisation factor", of 0–100 %, which is used to allocate royalty payments among patent owners, when the product consists of a combination of multiple inventions. When the invention is the product, the ratio is 100 %. Otherwise, the ratio is the fraction that represents the value of the part compared to the value of the whole product. This is particularly useful when setting remuneration for fixed-dose combinations or other medicines that combine many different patented inventions. This method would reflect the contribution of a given patent more precisely. The "utilisation factor" can be used independently with any of the other methods of setting royalties. However, compared with the 2001/UNDP/HDR guidelines, the JPO guidelines are somewhat more difficult to administer because they incorporate a broader range of relevant factors into the royalty calculation.

3.4.4 2005 Canadian Export Guidelines

In 2005, the Canadian government adopted the guidelines for CL of patents for export to countries that lack the capacity to manufacture medicines. These guidelines are a sliding scale of 0.02–4 % of the price of the generic product based on the country rank in the UNDP Human Development Index (HDI). The formula is one plus the number of countries on the UNHDI minus the importing country's rank on the UNHDI divided by the number of countries on the UNHDI multiplied by 0.04. With 177 countries currently in the UNHDI index, the royalty rate can be expressed as follows:

Royalty rate = 0.04 × [(178) – rank importing country]/177

The Canadian royalty guidelines result in very low royalties, ranging from 0.02 to 4 % of the generic sales price. The average rate is 1.9 %, weighted by global population, and 1 %, weighted by global rates of HIV infection. For most developing countries, the rates are less than 3 %. The Canadian method can be considered a useful norm for those countries facing severe resource constraints in providing access to medicine for all, not least because the rate under this approach is easy to calculate and is relatively low. However, the Canadian method is less useful for middle- or high-income countries since the extremely low royalty would lead to the discouragement of R&D investment.

3.4.5 Tiered Royalty Method (TRM)

Different from the 2001 UNDP/HDR, 1998 JPO, or 2005 Canadian methods, the royalty rate under the TMR is not based on the price of the generic product. Instead, the royalty is based on the price of the patented product in the high-income country. The base royalty is 4 % of the high-income country price, which is then adjusted to account for relative income per capita or the relative income per person with the disease. TRM would result in much higher royalties in middle- and high-income countries with low burdens of disease and the lowest royalties for countries that have the lowest incomes and the highest rates of disease burden.

The TRM provides a more rational framework for sharing the costs of R&D and is particularly useful for countries with low or middle income to deal with prevalent public health concerns. The differences of royalty under the TRM are considerably larger than for the 2005 Canadian method. For instance, the United Kingdom would pay US$149 per year in remuneration for stavudine under the TRM but only US $0.79 under the 2005 Canadian method. For Chile, the remuneration for stavudine would be US$23 under the TRM but US$0.64 under the 2005 Canadian method. Under the TRM, countries with high incidence of HIV would pay much lower royalties. For example, Thailand has about twice the per capita income of the Philippines, but, under the TRM, it would pay less (for stavudine, US$1.80 compared to US$5.49 for the Philippines) due to Thailand's much higher disease burden. The TRM is particularly appropriate for global or regional patent pools that serve countries with very different circumstances in terms of incomes or disease burdens. However, under the TRM, the royalties are independent of manufacturing costs and vary directly with proxies for therapeutic value (the high-income price) and capacity to pay.

3.4.6 Medical Innovation Prize Fund (MIPF)

With the MIPF approach, remuneration is not awarded to pharmaceutical innovators by a sales-based royalty. Rather, the developers of patented products compete to seek a portion of a national budget that rewards medical innovation. The payments from the government to the innovators are allocated according to each product's contribution to the improved health outcomes. The MIPF approach provides the greatest rewards for products that are actually used and that provide incremental health benefits. The MIPF approach can be implemented in countries of different levels of development, incomes, and health care priorities. It is recommended that the overall level of funding for an MIPF approach increases with national income and the level of development. However, in essence, MIPF is not a royalty or remuneration for patent.

The above guidelines and approaches are designed to determine the remuneration of the CL for pharmaceutical products. They are less or not useful for other industries.

4 Conclusion: Prospects and Options

As demonstrated above, we can make a few observations: firstly, Art. 31 (b) of the TRIPS Agreement leaves broad room for countries to implement the requirement of "prior negotiation". Proposing "an offer" or "an invitation to treat" by the applicant would satisfy the test, while the essential terms such as royalty should be contained. Secondly, Art. 31 (h) of the TRIPS Agreement also grants great flexibilities to WTO members to determine the "adequate remuneration" for CL, and thus developing countries are allowed to develop rules and procedures adapted to their own circumstances for setting royalty rates. Thirdly, in order to determine the "adequate remuneration", the granting authority should take into account "all circumstances" of each case, which include the purpose of the CL (to address crises or emergency conditions, such as environmental disasters or epidemics threatening public health), the nature of the invention (e.g., innovativeness of the invention, social impact of the invention, etc.), the role of governments in paying for R&D cost, the R&D cost incurred by the patentee in making the invention or in developing it, the scope of the licence, etc. Among these, more weight should be given to the purpose of the CL. Especially, the authority should make distinction between two different situations: (1) cases where CL is imposed to address a social crisis or other such circumstances and (2) cases where CL is imposed as a penalty to punish the anti-competitive practices. Fourthly, in the case of remuneration for pharmaceutical patents, the basic principle of access to medicines for all should be upheld, and the balance between compensating patent holders and ensuring access to life-saving medicines must be appropriately weighted. Following these principles, the target CL remuneration for pharmaceutical patents should not be very high, and it should be an approximation of the average royalty paid on pharmaceutical products in the granting country. The globally recognised guidelines such as those proposed by the UNDP and the WHO could serve as guidance for setting the CL royalty. Lastly, the rules and procedures for setting the CL remuneration should be simple to administer and easy to predict.

References

Chatterjee P (2013) India's first compulsory licence upheld, but legal fights likely to continue. http://www.ip-watch.org/2013/03/04/indias-first-compulsory-licence-upheld-but-legal-fights-likely-to-continue/

Li S et al (2008) A study report on reforming patent compulsory licensing system. In: Law and Regulation Division, SIPO (ed) A study report on revising "Patent Law Implementing Rules", vol 2. Intellectual Property Press

Liu X (2006a) Proposals on improving China's patent compulsory license system. Chinese J of Law 6

Lin X (2006b) The patent compulsory licensing under the TRIPS Regime. Law Press

Liu X (2009) A study on patent compulsory license system in China—with particular reference to the drafted 3rd amendment to the patent law of the P. R. of China. In: Adelmann M, Brauneis R, Drexl J, Nack R (eds) Patents and technological progress in a globalized world. Springer, Berlin

Love J (2001) Consumer project on technology, "Implementing TRIPS Safeguards with Particular Attention to Administrative Models for Compulsory Licensing of Patents", Attachment 1, Art. 6, WHO meeting in Harare, Zimbabwe, 21 August 2001. http://www.cptech.org/ip/health/cl/harare-aug2001.html

Nolff M (2002) Compulsory patent licensing in view of the WTO ministerial conference declaration on the TRIPS Agreement and public health. J Pat Trademark Off Soc 84(133):3

Reichman JH (2003) Non-voluntary licensing of patent inventions: historical perspective, legal framework under TRIPS, and an overview of the practice in Canada and the USA. UNCTAD-ICTSD Project on IPRS and sustainable development

Sun H (2003) A wider access to patented drugs under the TRIPS Agreement. Boston Univ Int Law J 21(10):3

Taubman A (2008) Rethinking TRIPS: 'Adequate Remuneration' for non-voluntary Patent Licensing. J Int Econ Law 11(4):927

Treitel GH (1995) The law of contract, 9th edn. Oxford University Press, Oxford

Välimäki E (2011) Calculation of royalties in compulsory licensing of pharmaceutical patents in Europe – how much is justified? Nord J Commer Law 1 (special edition)

WIPO CDIP (Committee on Development and Intellectual Property) (2010) Patent related flexibilities in the multilateral legal framework and their legislative implementation at the national and regional levels. CDIP/5/4, p 15, Sec. 49. http://www.wipo.int/meetings/en/doc_details.jsp?doc_id=142068

Ancillary Orders of Compulsory Licensing and Their Compatibility with the TRIPS Agreement

Richard Li-dar Wang

Contents

Abstract Compulsory licensing is a well-recognised institution for striking a balance between patent and copyright protection and social or economic goals in general. For a compulsory licence to work effectively, three conditions must be met at first: competent licensees with sufficient capacities, adequate market size, and access to necessary know-how. If the third condition is missing, the authority granting such licences may issue a know-how transfer order to fill in the gap. Ancillary orders may also direct non-voluntary licensees to address specific harms to public interest, ensuring the attainment of their policy goals. In addition, the granting authority can issue a side effect averting order to alleviate unnecessary impact that the licence may impose on the patent or copyright holders. Given that no exception to the protection of undisclosed

---

R.L.-d. Wang is Associate Professor of Law; S.J.D. 2007, Indiana University Maurer School of Law. This chapter was previously published in Marquette Intellectual Property Law Review, vol. 18, Number 1, pp. 88–105 (March 2014).

R.L.-d. Wang
National Chiao Tung University, Hsinchu, Taiwan, Republic of China
e-mail: rcdwie@gmail.com

R.M. Hilty and K.-C. Liu (eds.), *Compulsory Licensing*, MPI Studies on Intellectual Property and Competition Law 22, DOI 10.1007/978-3-642-54704-1_10,

information is expressly acknowledged in the TRIPS Agreement, there are some doubts about the know how transfer orders' compatibility with the TRIPS. These doubts are not well founded. On the other hand, orders requiring local manufacturing are likely to violate the principle of non-discrimination between imports and local production as enshrined in Article 27.1 of the TRIPS Agreement.

1 Introduction

The Agreement on Trade-Related Aspects of Intellectual Property Rights (TRIPS Agreement) of the World Trade Organization (WTO) is one of the key international conventions in the field of intellectual property (IP). It is the first international treaty that lays down the mandatory minimum standard of patent protection for nations across the world. Given the comprehensive coverage of WTO membership,[1] the TRIPS Agreement has effectively established an international standard for IP protection in member states. With respect to copyright and patents, this Agreement expressly allows for compulsory licence granted by competent authorities, with an aim to facilitate an adjusting mechanism to balance IP protection, on the one hand, and social or economic policy goals in general, on the other.[2]

Specifically, Article 31 of the TRIPS Agreement authorises WTO members to issue compulsory licences on patents to address national emergencies, extreme urgency, or other socio-economic issues arising at the domestic level, subject to the procedures and limitations stipulated in the same article. Through Article 9.1, one of the incorporation clauses in the TRIPS Agreement, the compulsory licence scheme as to the author's translation and reproduction rights for developing countries, as provided in the Appendix of the Berne Convention (1971), essentially merges into and becomes an integral part of the TRIPS Agreement. This involuntary licence regime affords developing countries leeway to adapt the level of copyright protection to address local economic, social, or cultural needs.[3]

In light of the important role that compulsory licensing could play in contemporary IP systems, the WTO reaffirms the member's right to grant such licences in the Declaration on the TRIPS Agreement and Public Health, adopted in November 2001 at the Doha Ministerial Conference (Doha Declaration).[4] One of the main themes in the Declaration is that patent protection should be implemented in a manner that permits WTO members to protect public health and to promote access of the general public to essential medicines. For that purpose, WTO members may

---

[1] As of 2 March 2013, the WTO has 159 members.

[2] *See, e.g.*, Correa (2000), pp. 242–243; Pacón (1996), pp. 339–340; Watal (2001), p. 319.

[3] Article I(1) of the Appendix of the Berne Convention (1971).

[4] Declaration on the TRIPS Agreement and Public Health, para. 5.b, WT/MIN(01)/DEC/2 (20 November 2001).

use, to the full extent, the flexibilities as set forth in Articles 30 and 31 of the TRIPS Agreement.[5]

Following the guidance of the Doha Declaration, WTO members have made use of the compulsory licence scheme to address their domestic issues, particularly in meeting the demands of public health. For instance, Brazil,[6] India,[7] Taiwan,[8] and Thailand[9] have issued compulsory licences on pharmaceuticals essential for treating deadly diseases in recent years. Even so, relative to the large number of patents now in effect in WTO members, the frequency and number of compulsory licences to date have been still low and small.[10]

2 Conditions for Compulsory Licensing to Be Effective

The compulsory licence does not exist in a vacuum. Rather, the success of a compulsory licensing regime depends on the industrial and technological context that the licensee encounters. For a compulsory licence to be effective, a number of conditions must be present. First of all, licensees with sufficient capacities are indispensable.[11] The lack of technical sophistication and ability to learn has been a significant detriment to technological transfer in developing countries.[12] Existing manufacturing capacity also matters with respect to the quantity and speed at which the compulsory licensee could put the patented technology or copyrighted work into production. The more qualified capacity is in place, the faster the licensed IP can come into mass production and fulfil the underlying goal of individual compulsory licences—whether it is local working of the technology, treating a public

[5] *Id.* para. 4.

[6] Brazil issued a compulsory licence against Merck & Co. for its HIV/AIDS drug, efavirenz, in May 2007; Quadir (2009), pp. 437, 459. For more details, see the chapter "The Use of Compulsory Licences in Latin America" by Carlos M. Correa, in this volume.

[7] On 9 March 2012, the Indian patent authority granted generics manufacturer Natco Pharma Ltd. the right to produce and sell Bayer's Sorafenib, a patented medicine that is useful in treating liver and kidney cancers at an advanced stage; Bonadio (2012), pp. 719, 719. For more details, see the chapter "Compulsory Licence Under Indian Patent Law" by N.S. Gopalakrishnan and Madhuri Anand, in this volume.

[8] In the wake of the avian flu crisis, Tamiflu was considered an effective remedy for the H5N1 virus. Failing to secure sufficient supply from F. Hoffmann-La Roche Ltd., the Taiwanese Government granted a compulsory licence on Tamiflu on December 2005. For more details, see the chapter "Compulsory Licence and Government Use in Taiwan: A Regress" by Kung-Chung Liu, in this volume; also Liu (2008), p. 760 n. 12; Kane (2009), pp. 1137, 1167.

[9] Thailand granted a couple of compulsory licences in 2006 and 2007, including the patented HIV/AIDS drugs efavirenz (from Merck) and Kaletra (from Abbott), and Plavix, which is used for treating heart disease; Osenga (2012), pp. 309, 319.

[10] *See* Liu (2012), pp. 679, 681; Mengistie (2010), pp. 175, 178.

[11] Mengistie (2010), p. 178; Wang (2004), pp. 215 and 235–236.

[12] Mengistie (2010), p. 179.

health crisis, disseminating advanced knowledge, and fostering higher education or any other social or cultural needs.

Notably, the required capacity is not limited to those located within the issuing country. If the scope of the compulsory licence includes importation, the issuing government could utilise competent manufacturers located oversees to exploit the licensed IP and produce targeted products to fulfil domestic needs. This practice is allowable under the TRIPS Agreement. No provision in the same Agreement stipulates against non-voluntary import licences. The key is that the expected foreign supplier must have the right to produce in its own country and be able to export the products at issue legitimately. There are a couple of situations where those conditions will be met. When the term of the intellectual property covering the licensed subject matter has expired or no pertinent IP protection has been secured in the specific foreign country, it is entirely lawful to practise the subject matter and export the outcomes there. Supply from abroad may also be possible when a compulsory licence is in place in the exporting country. However, Article 31(f) of the TRIPS Agreement requires each of the non-voluntary licences to be granted predominantly for the supply of the domestic market, which does not prohibit the licensee from exporting so long as the exportation constitutes a minor portion of the total production.

Under the Guidance of the Doha Declaration, the WTO General Council established a waiver system in 2003 to soften the ban on production predominantly for exportation.[13] Under the waiver system, compulsory licences predominantly for exports are permitted on condition that the importing WTO member has no pharmaceutical manufacturing capacity, grants such a waiver, and notifies the WTO Secretariat. In December 2005, the General Council of the WTO formalised the waiver system, adding Article 31*bis* to the TRIPS Agreement.[14] This amendment is now waiting to take effect.[15] This waiver system, however, is limited to exporting pharmaceuticals to WTO members, and to date only Rwanda has filed one request for importation.[16]

The second critical condition is the size of the market, which is a decisive factor for the sales revenue that a licensee may reasonably anticipate if practising the patent or copyright. The potential magnitude of the market closely relates to whether the licensee would recover the necessary cost for employing the IP, benefit from economy of scale, or even make a profit.[17] If the market size is narrowly restrained and only a very limited amount of revenue could be generated from the compulsory licence, even manufacturers or publishers with adequate capacity to practise the patent or copyright may stay away from taking it.

---

[13] General Council (2003).

[14] General Council (2005).

[15] As of now, about 70 WTO members have issued notification that they accept of this amendment. Since less than two-thirds of the WTO members have formally accepted the amendment, Article 31*bis* has not yet taken effect and replaced the 2003 waiver. The deadline for WTO members to accept this revision has been extended to 31 December 2013; General Council (2011).

[16] Rwanda (2007).

[17] Mengistie (2010), p. 178; Wang (2004), p. 236.

In calculating the size of potential market for compulsory licences, the base for assessment in most cases would still be confined by the boundaries of the issuing country. Foreign markets are highly uncertain, depending on the patent status of the targeted products in foreign countries, whether a compulsory licence for importation will be imposed in those countries and whether they would utilise the waiver system to lift the limitation of Article 31(f) of the TRIPS Agreement. Though there might be opportunities for the licensees to export part of their production to countries granting compulsory licences on importation of the same products, the chances are quite unsure and it may seem remote for potential candidates in considering whether to take the compulsory licence or not. As a result, countries that have only small populations or weak buying power will suffer from the constraint of market size,[18] and the function of compulsory licence would be seriously curtailed.

A third precondition for an effective compulsory licence concerns necessary know-how.[19] The patent law surely requires public disclosure of the claimed technology to enable persons skilled in the art to carry out the invention themselves.[20] But from time to time, additional know-how is still necessary for them to put the claimed invention into industrial application at a commercial scale. IP licensing agreements, however, typically do not contain obligations regarding technical assistance or technology transfer from the IP owner.

In the scenario of compulsory licensing, it is implausible to expect right holders to voluntarily provide any technical guidance to the licensee. If the licensee does not possess all the skills that are critical for practising the licensed IP, such as the know-how on commercialisation, improving of the manufacturing process, optimising of the yield rate, etc.,[21] she will still be unable to duplicate the product of the right holder successfully. When this situation arises, the compulsory licence may not work as effectively as expected.

3 Ancillary Orders to Ensure the Effectiveness of Compulsory Licensing

If countries fall short of the essential conditions as set forth above, necessary measures should be made to make up the deficiencies. The first two conditions, however, are not so easy to restore. If competent licensees do not exist, the government could only choose to step in and practise the patent or copyright with its own facilities. Even so, the feasibility of this measure still depends on the

[18] *See* Kettler and Collins (2002), pp. 12–39.

[19] Mengistie (2010), p. 178; Wang (2004), pp. 236–237.

[20] Article 29.1 of the TRIPS Agreement provides: "Members shall require that an applicant for a patent shall disclose the invention in a manner sufficiently clear and complete for the invention to be carried out by a person skilled in the art . . .".

[21] Wang (2004), p. 237.

presence of production facilities and technical sophistication of the country with regard to the licensed IP. Factors affecting the magnitude of the market, such as population and national income, are difficult to change within a short period of time as well.

3.1 Know-How Transfer Orders

The only condition that the authority concerned might be able to create in granting a compulsory licence is the necessary know-how. It may issue an ancillary order to require the right holder to provide additional know-how to the licensee.[22] In order to ensure the transfer of the licensed technologies, the order should obligate the right holder to provide technical assistance and hand over technical documents that contain the know-how or other technologies that the licensee identifies as necessary for implementing the compulsory licence. If the right holder obeys the order and conveys undisclosed know-how, the receiving licensee is obligated to maintain its secrecy and pay reasonable royalty for using the know-how, just as a voluntary trade secret licensee is.

The licensee may encounter difficulties in identifying necessary know-how for transfer, but she does not have to recite the know-how item by item. Rather, the scope and content of the transfer order could be defined in category with reasonable particularity, just as attorneys do in requesting opposing parties to produce documents or records in the discovery process of civil litigations in the United States.[23] In case of doubt, the granting authority of the compulsory licence should adjudicate the dispute through adequate procedures and determine the proper scope and content of the transfer. Where conflicts arise concerning whether the licensee has abused her right in know-how transfer and attained unreasonable advantages over the right holder, the granting agency or the court should have the authority to decide whether the licensee is liable to pay compensation and refrain from further using particular know-how.

Since IP right holders will undoubtedly tend to be reluctant to transfer undisclosed know-how, other sources of such transfers should be secured to facilitate the implementation of compulsory licences. For that purpose, the know-how transfer order could excuse persons who have access to the right holder's technical information or materials from their obligations under any existing non-disclosure agreement, thus enabling the licensee to get possession of necessary know-how. To alleviate possible adverse impact on business honesty and integrity, this immunity

---

[22] Regrettably, the author has not found any national practice that adopts orders similar to what the chapter proposes here.

[23] Rule 34(b)(1) of Federal Rules of Civil Procedure: "The request [to produce any designated documents or electronically stored information]: (A) must describe with reasonable particularity each item or category of items to be inspected; . . .".

can only be triggered at the time when the right holder does not faithfully follow the transfer order and hand over all necessary technical information and through a formal adjudication of the granting authority to confirm that the disobedience surely exists.

Such an exemption of the non-disclosure obligation might seem vulnerable to distortion and abuse, which could be difficult to redress once the trade secret was revealed. The primary function of that exemption, nevertheless, lies in deterrence. It is an enforcement measure of last resort, which should be administered cautiously and conservatively. Countries should not solely rely on the non-disclosure exemption but rather need to establish other remedies, such as fines and injunctive relieves, to enforce the know-how transfer order. Once those remedies have failed and the exemption is granted, the competent authority should set up adequate rules and procedures to monitor the flow of trade secrets and to prevent possible abuse. If executed appropriately, immunity from any existing non-disclosure obligation could confidently be a useful enforcement measure against the right holder's resistance.

3.2 Goal-Attainment Ensuring Orders

In addition to know-how transfer orders, there are still other types of ancillary orders that would help the compulsory licence work effectively towards its contemplated goal. For those non-voluntary licences granted on the ground of unavailability of affordable drugs to the public, the manufacturer undertaking the licence should be directed to distribute those drugs at an affordable price, or even provide them for free to especially needy patients.[24] In the same vein, in the case of compulsory licences on the basis of non- or insufficient local working, the licensee should be required to manufacture the targeted products within the country and not be allowed to import instead from overseas.[25]

4 Side-Effects Preventing Orders

Besides ancillary orders that serve to ensure the effectiveness of compulsory licensing, there is another type of order that is purported to prevent adverse side effects to the rights holder. For example, in the *Bayer-Natco* case of India in 2012,

[24] *In re* Natco Pharma Ltd and Bayer Corp., C.L.A. No. 1 of 2011, at 60–61 (Order item a & h) (Controller of Patents March 9, 2012), *available at* http://www.ipindia.nic.in/ipoNew/compulsory_License_12032012.pdf.

[25] *Id.* at 61 (Order item i). *See also* the chapters "The Use of Compulsory Licences in Latin America" and "Scope and Duration of Compulsory Licensing: Lessons from National Experiences" by Professor Carlos M. Correa and Ida Madieha bt. Abdul Ghani Azmi, in this volume.

the targeted product Sorafenib is a drug for treatment at the advanced stages of kidney and liver cancer. Bayer named it Nexavar and distributed it at a price of Rs. 280,428 (about US$4,600) for 1 month's therapy. Natco applied for compulsory licensing and proposed to sell the drug at one-thirtieth of the price.[26] The Indian government approved the application and required Natco to refrain from representing Sorafenib from its own production as Nexavar of Bayer, or the two companies as associated in any aspect. Furthermore, Natco's Sorafenib had to be visibly different from Bayer's Nexavar in color, shape, trade name, and outside packaging.[27]

Those mandates are quite similar to the special packaging and/or coloring/shaping requirements as stipulated in TRIPS Article 31*bis*.[28] The common goal of those ancillary orders is to prevent possible confusion of the licensee's products with the right holder's and to inhibit the pharmaceuticals manufactured under the license from being diverted into the stream of commerce outside of the granting country.

Another example of side-effect preventing orders can be found in the Berne Convention. Article IV(3) of the Appendix of the Berne Convention requires that copyrighted works translated or reproduced under a compulsory licence have to contain indications of the true author and the title of the work.[29] This requirement protects the author's moral rights, including the right of attribution and the right to the integrity of the work, from being impaired. According to Article 6*bis*(1) of the Berne Convention, the author's right of attribution and the right to integrity of the work shall be independent of the transfer of the author's economic rights. Consequently, they should stay intact even when the author is facing compulsory licences.

5 TRIPS-Compatibility of Ancillary Orders

5.1 Know-How Transfer Orders

The know-how transfer orders described above seem to be an ideal companion of compulsory licence. Whether it is in compliance with the TRIPS Agreement, however, is somewhat problematic. Since there is no general exception in the TRIPS Agreement for all types of IP, a specific exception is necessary for exempting any derogation of IP protection from the level as required in the same Agreement. The first two paragraphs of Article 39 require WTO members to protect

[26] *In re* Natco Pharma Ltd and Bayer Corp., C.L.A. No. 1 of 2011, at 5–6 (Controller of Patents March 9, 2012), *available at* http://www.ipindia.nic.in/ipoNew/compulsory_ License_12032012.pdf.

[27] *Id.* at 61–62 (Order item k); *see also* Bonadio (2012), p. 721.

[28] General Council (2005), Annex to the TRIPS Agreement, para. 2(b)(ii).

[29] Article IV(3) of the Appendix of the Berne Convention (1979).

trade secrets, which cover undisclosed know-know. Meanwhile, the same article, or even the same section of the Agreement, contains no exception to the trade secret protection it demands. This is not a coincidence. National trade secret laws of WTO members usually provide few exceptions as well. The United States' Uniform Trade Secret Act, for example, contains just one exception.[30]

The fact that no relevant exception to trade secret protection currently exists surely casts some doubts on adopting know-how transfer orders. But there is another avenue for justifying such orders under the TRIPS Agreement. In the first sentence of Article 39.1, the TRIPS Agreement articulates that the purpose of protecting trade secrets is to ensure "effective protection against unfair competition as provided in Article 10*bis* of the Paris Convention (1967)". Article 10*bis*(2) of the Paris Convention defines the act of unfair competition as "any act of competition contrary to honest practices in industrial or commercial matters". When a compulsory licence has been issued and the licensee follows the authorisation of the court or granting agency to request the right holder to transfer know-how that is indispensible for fulfilling the licence, this practice should not in itself constitute an act of unfair competition contrary to business honesty. Compulsory licensing is a well-recognised mechanism to introduce adequate exploitation of patents or copyright to achieve public interest in various socio-economic aspects. The licensee here is just an undertaker of such a legitimate mechanism and does not come into competition with the right holder for her own commercial interest. As long as the compulsory licence and ancillary order are based on national laws, granted legally by the authority concerned, and the licensee faithfully secures the secrecy of the know-how, there should be no offense to Article 10*bis*.

Furthermore, laws and measures that compel disclosure of trade secrets usually do exist outside the trade secret law. Mandatory disclosure is commonly seen in the fields of corporate auditing and marketing approval. In the TRIPS Agreement, Article 39.3 authorises WTO members to require submission of undisclosed test data for the purpose of reviewing the marketing application of pharmaceutical or agricultural chemical products that utilise new chemical entities on condition that such data shall be protected against unfair commercial use. The same disclosure requirement is present in the section of civil and administrative procedures and remedies of the TRIPS Agreement as well. In Article 43.1, the Agreement stipulates that national courts shall have the authority to order specific evidence, including confidential information, to be produced by one of the parties subject to conditions that could ensure the protection of its secrecy.[31] The two provisions comprise part

[30] Unif. Trade Secrets Act (1985) § 3(a) & § 3 cmt. The exception excludes from compensation damages accruing after the trade secret has been revealed or otherwise no longer sustains an advantage over competitors.

[31] Article 43.1 of the TRIPS Agreement: "The judicial authorities shall have the authority, where a party has presented reasonably available evidence sufficient to support its claims and has specified evidence relevant to substantiation of its claims which lies in the control of the opposing party, to order that this evidence be produced by the opposing party, subject in appropriate cases to conditions which ensure the protection of confidential information."

of the treaty context that must be taken into consideration when interpreting the scope and content of trade secret protection mandated by the TRIPS Agreement.[32] Consequently, the fact that no exception appears in the trade secret law does not denote that no limitation on the trade secret right is permitted. As long as adequate measures are adopted to warrant its confidentiality, well-grounded disclosure orders from other areas of laws should be reasonably recognised by analogy.

The objective clause of the TRIPS Agreement further fortresses the same position. In Article 7, the Agreement proclaims that the protection of IP rights should contribute to the transfer and dissemination of technology, to the mutual advantage of producers and users of technological knowledge, and in a manner conducive to social and economic welfare. Know-how transfer orders are purported to assist compulsory licensing to balance IP protection and the socio-economic welfare of the public. By requiring transfer of critical know-how, those orders can ensure complete conveyance of all necessary technologies between IP right holders and non-voluntary licensees, thus substantially enhancing the efficacy of technology dissemination that the compulsory licensing regime is aiming to achieve. Taking all the above analyses into consideration, know-how transfer orders in effect could not be sensibly characterised as TRIPS incompatible.

5.2 Local Manufacturing Orders

Article 5A(2) and (4) of the Paris Convention (1967) expressly recognises failure to work a patent and insufficient working as legitimate grounds for granting compulsory licences. This is often regarded as a local working requirement imposed on patent owners. In his famous treatise, Bodenhausen described the prevailing view of the word "working" in the context of the Paris Convention:

> Normally, working a patent will be understood to mean working it industrially, namely, by manufacture of the patented product, or industrial application of a patented process. Thus, importation or sale of the patented article, or of the article manufactured by a patented process, will not normally be regarding as "working" the patent.[33]

In 1995, Article 2.1 of the TRIPS Agreement further incorporates Article 5 of the Paris Convention. WTO members would accordingly grant compulsory licences for the reason of insufficient domestic working from patent owners. In order to achieve the goal of local working, the granting countries might grant additionally an ancillary order requiring the licensees to manufacture the targeted products domestically and forbidding importing instead. This type of goal-attainment ensuring

[32] For the significance of treaty context in construing disputed treaty terms, see *infra* text accompanying footnotes 39–40.

[33] Bodenhausen (1968), p. 71.

orders, however, may be incompatible with the non-discrimination principle as stipulated in Article 27.1 of the TRIPS Agreement. This clause demands that patent rights shall be enjoyable without discrimination as to, *inter alia*, whether products are imported or domestically produced. A WTO panel once ruled that Article 27.1 applies to Article 31 as well. It follows that the granting authority of compulsory licensing might not be able to treat patent owners and the licensees in a different way on the basis of whether the targeted products are imported or locally manufactured.[34]

The idea of non-discrimination and avoiding trade distortion is a cornerstone of WTO. The most-favoured-nation principle and national treatment principle, two overarching doctrines throughout the WTO, vindicate and exemplify the importance of this basic policy.[35] Article 27.1 of the TRIPS Agreement crystallises and enshrines the same idea in the field of patent law. Even though failure to work and insufficient working are explicitly acknowledged as grounds for compulsory licensing in the TRIPS Agreement, the meaning of the terms must be interpreted according to the whole context of the Agreement, including Article 27.1.

Article 3.2 of the Understanding on Rules and Procedures Governing the Settlement of Disputes (DSU) points out that when disputes arise, the provisions of WTO agreements will be clarified in accordance with customary interpretation rules of public international law. The WTO Appellate Body has consistently held that Article 31 of the Vienna Convention on the Law of Treaties (VCLT), as a rule of treaty interpretation, has attained the status of customary international law.[36] Article 31.1 of the VCLT states:

> A treaty shall be interpreted in good faith in accordance with the *ordinary meaning* to be given to the terms of the treaty in their *context* and in the light of its object and purpose (emphasis added).

Even though the requirement of working a patent is understood as a mandate of local manufacturing in the context of the Paris Convention, it may slightly change its meaning when migrating into another treaty context. As a transitive verb with an object, the ordinary meaning of the term "work" may include "to function", "to cause to be in operation", or "to fashion or create a useful or desired product by expending labor or exertion on".[37] The manner in which local working is proceeding, however, has not been specified. In light of the non-discrimination principle as

---

[34] Panel Report, *Canada—Patent Protection of Pharmaceutical Products*, para. 7.91, WT/DS114/R (March 17, 2000).

[35] *See* Article 3 (MFN) and Article 4 (national treatment) of the TRIPS Agreement. *See also*, *e.g.*, Trebilcock and Howse (2005), pp. 28–30.

[36] *E.g.*, Appellate Body Report, *United States—Standards for Reformulated and Conventional Gasoline*, 15, WT/DS2/AB/R (April 29, 1996); Appellate Body Report, *Japan—Taxes on Alcoholic Beverages*, 9, WT/DS8/AB/R, WT/DS10/AB/R, WT/DS11/AB/R (October 4, 1996).

[37] Oxford Dictionaries, Definition of Work, *available at* http://oxforddictionaries.com/definition/english/work?q=work (last visited June 6, 2013); Merriam-Webster, Definition of Work (Transitive Verb), *available at* http://www.merriam-webster.com/dictionary/work (last visited June 6, 2013).

to the place of production, to "work" a patent could and should be construed more broadly as to "practise" a patent. In this way, the local working requirement can avoid direct collision with the non-discrimination principle and fit into the new context of the TRIPS Agreement much more adequately.[38]

In the *U.S.—Copyright Act* case, a WTO panel held that when TRIPS provisions are incorporated from other international conventions, their original contexts in those external instruments could also be integrated into the Agreement as a basis of interpretation.[39] The *acquis* thus introduced from other international instruments, however, constitutes only part of the context when interpreting those provisions. The text of the TRIPS Agreement is undeniably another significant component of the context. For the same reason, the panel in *U.S.—Copyright Act* case recognised that Article 13 of the TRIPS Agreement applies to provisions incorporated from the Berne Convention, though no analogous exception clause to the author's public communication right is present in that Convention.[40]

Professor Carlos Correa has argued that the non-discrimination requirement of TRIPS Article 27.1 is targeted at infringing products rather than the patentee's products. He indicates that since the language of Article 27.1 just states "patent rights enjoyable without discrimination as to . . . whether products are imported or locally produced", it could be interpreted as mandating that inventors shall possess equivalent rights of patents against infringing products whether produced domestically or imported from abroad.[41] When the ordinary meaning of treaty language is vague even in light of its context, the negotiating history could be instrumental in ascertaining its true intention.[42] During the negotiation process of the TRIPS Agreement, the local working requirement aroused heated debates among developed and developing countries. The current language of Articles 2.1 and 27.1 was the compromise that the opposing parties eventually reached to resolve this deadlock when concluding the negotiation.[43] If we consider for now that the non-discrimination requirement as to the place of production is for infringing products rather than the patentee's products, the negotiating history will be neglected and the intention of the drafter will be distorted. Even though Professor

---

[38] For similar conclusion, see Straus (1996), p. 205.

[39] Panel Report, *United States—Section 110(5) of the US Copyright Act*, para. 6.92, WT/DS160/R (June 15, 2000).

[40] *Id.* para. 6.94.

[41] *See* the chapter "The Use of Compulsory Licences in Latin America" by Professor Carlos M. Correa, in this volume.

[42] Article 32 of the Vienna Convention on the Law of Treaties provides for supplemental means of treaty interpretation: "Recourse may be had to supplementary means of interpretation, including the preparatory work of the treaty and the circumstances of its conclusion, in order to confirm the meaning resulting from the application of article 31, or to determine the meaning when the interpretation according to article 31: (a) leaves the meaning ambiguous or obscure; or (b) leads to a result which is manifestly absurd or unreasonable".

[43] Watal (2001), p. 318.

Correa refers to the *U.S.-Section 337* case of the GATT era[44] to illustrate possible discrimination between infringing products from importation and local production, the measure at issue in the same case—border measures that in essence only target imported goods—has been expressly recognised in the text of the TRIPS Agreement as legitimate remedies against IP infringement.[45] It therefore would not be probable for the agreement to institute a prohibition in Article 27.1 against such enforcement measures that are particularly authorised in the same instrument.

According to the analysis above, in light of the non-discrimination principle in Article 27.1, the local working requirement should not be interpreted as a local manufacturing requirement. Similarly, ancillary orders to secure local manufacturing on the side of the licensee may violate the same clause as well. When insufficient practising of a specific patent is found, the non-voluntary licensee should be permitted to import, as well as to produce domestically the targeted products to meet the local demand.[46]

6 Concluding Remarks

Compulsory licensing is a well-recognised regime to strike a balance between patent and copyright protection and socio-economic goals. In order to make it work effectively, some ancillary measures are necessary. When the licensee lacks access to critical know-how for practising the licensed technology, the granting authority of the compulsory licence may require the right holder to transfer such know-how to fill the gap. In addition, we might see the authority requiring the licensee to manufacture the targeted product locally or to provide the licensed medicine to the public at an affordable price so as to ensure that compulsory licensing attains its contemplated goal.

On the other hand, the granting authority can issue a side-effect averting order to alleviate unnecessary impact that compulsory licensing may impose on the right holder so that the licence will not become too intrusive. Those two types of ancillary orders are practical complements to non-voluntary licences and could be beneficial for the current regime of compulsory licensing, both nationally and internationally. They are undoubtedly worthy of consideration to be incorporated into national laws and international conventions.

---

[44] Report of the Panel, *United States—Section 337 of the Tariff Act of 1930*, L/6439 (November 7, 1989).

[45] *See* Section 4 of Part 3 of the TRIPS Agreement: Special Requirements Related to Border Measures.

[46] For a similar view, see Bonadio (2012), p. 723. For an opposing view, see Mercurio and Tyagi (2010), pp. 275, 313 (the differential treatment resulting from local working requirements does not amount to an unjustified disadvantage and hence is not a discrimination under Article 27.1 of the TRIPS Agreement).

The fact that no exception is expressly acknowledged in the trade secret section of the TRIPS Agreement casts some doubts on the legality of know-how transfer orders. These doubts are not well founded. Outside of the trade secret section, the TRIPS Agreement contains at least two provisions demanding submission of undisclosed information. The objective clause of Article 7 also suggests against incompatibility of those orders with the TRIPS Agreement. On the other hand, orders requiring local manufacturing are likely to contravene the TRIPS Agreement by violating the non-discrimination principle between imports and local production in Article 27.1. Even though the TRIPS Agreement expressly incorporates the local working requirement of patent owners from the Paris Convention, the meaning of "working" should be adjusted properly to reflect the change of treaty context and is reasonably construed in this Agreement to encompass importation to avoid direct conflict with Article 27.1.

Acknowledgements The author would like to express his gratitude to Professor Byungil Kim, Mark Janis, Michael Mattioli, Donald Knebel, and Kung-Chung Liu for their invaluable views and comments. The draft of this chapter was presented at the Symposium on International Trade, Technology and Business Law, June 14, 2013, Taipei, Taiwan, jointly organised by the Institute of Technology Law, National Chiao Tung University and Faculty of Law, Chinese University of Hong Kong. Many thanks to Justice Chang-Fa Lo and Professor Bryan Mercurio for their insightful suggestions at that event. Shortcomings of this chapter, if any, should still be attributed to the author.

References

Bodenhausen GHC (1968) Guide to the application of the Paris Convention for the protection of industrial property. WIPO, Geneva

Bonadio E (2012) Compulsory licensing of patents: the Bayer-Natco case. Eur Intellect Prop Rev 34:719

Correa CM (2000) Intellectual property rights, the WTO and developing countries: the TRIPS Agreement and policy options. Zed Books, London

General Council (2003) Implementation of Paragraph 6 of the Doha Declaration on the TRIPS Agreement and Public Health Decision, WT/L/540 and Corr.1, 1 September 2003. http://www.wto.org/english/tratop_e/trips_e/implem_para6_e.htm

Kane EM (2009) Achieving clinical equality in an influenza pandemic: patent realities. Seton Hall Law Rev 39:1137

Kettler HE, Collins C (2002) Using innovative action to meet global health needs through existing intellectual property regimes. Available at http://www.iprcommission.org/papers/word/study_papers/sp2b_kettler_study.doc. Last visited 25 Nov 2012

Liu KC (2008) Rationalising the regime of compulsory patent licensing by the essential facilities doctrine. Int Rev Intellect Prop Comp Law 39:760

Liu KC (2012) The need and justification for a general competition-oriented compulsory licensing regime. Int Rev Intellect Prop Comp Law 43:679

Mengistie G (2010) The patent system in Africa: its contribution and potential in stimulating innovation, technology transfer and fostering science and technology: part 2. Int Trade Law Rev 16:175

Mercurio B, Tyagi M (2010) Treaty interpretation in WTO dispute settlement: the outstanding question of the legality of local working requirements. Minn J Int Law 19:275

Osenga K (2012) Get the balance right! Squaring access with patent protection. Pac McGeorge Global Bus Dev Law J 25:309

Pacón AM (1996) What will TRIPS do for developing countries? In: Beier F-K, Schricker G (eds) From GATT to TRIPS—the agreement on trade-related aspects of intellectual property rights. VCH, Weinheim, pp 329–356

Quadir R (2009) Patent stalemate? The WTO'S essential medicines impasse between pharmas and least developed countries. Rutgers Law Rev 61:437

Rwanda (2007) Notification under paragraph 2(a) of the decision of 30 August 2003 on the implementation of paragraph 6 of the Doha Declaration on the TRIPS Agreement and public health, IP/N/9/RWA/1. http://www.wto.org/english/tratop_e/trips_e/ta_docs_e/3_ipn9rwa1_e.pdf

Straus J (1996) Implications of the TRIPS Agreement in the field of patent law. In: Beier F-K, Schricker G (eds) From GATT to TRIPS—the agreement on trade-related aspects of intellectual property rights. VCH, Weinheim, pp 160–215

Trebilcock MJ, Howse R (2005) The regulation of international trade, 3d edn. Routledge, London, pp 28–30

Wang RL (2004) Functions and restraints of compulsory licensing: perspective from TRIPS Agreement and public health. Technol Law Rev 1:215 (in Chinese)

Watal J (2001) Intellectual property rights in the WTO and developing countries. Kluwer, The Hague

WTO General Council (2005) Amendment of the TRIPS Agreement, WT/L/641. Available at http://www.wto.org/english/tratop_e/trips_e/wtl641_e.htm

WTO General Council (2011) Amendment of the TRIPS Agreement – third extension of the period for the acceptance by members of the protocol amending the TRIPS Agreement, WT/L/829. http://www.wto.org/english/tratop_e/trips_e/ta_docs_e/3_wtl829_e.pdf

Scope and Duration of Compulsory Licensing: Lessons from National Experiences

Ida Madieha bt. Abdul Ghani Azmi

Contents

Abstract The TRIPS Agreement provides significant flexibility to member countries to determine the scope and duration of compulsory licences issued by them. TRIPS mandates, however, that the scope and duration of the licence must not go beyond the purpose for which the licence is issued. For countries that have never invoked compulsory licences before, the lack of detailed provision on this offers little guidance on how to invoke such licences. This chapter examines national experiences on compulsory licences and draws lessons from them by identifying the relevant criteria in setting the scope and duration of compulsory licences. From these experiences, several observations can be made. It is essential that the terms of such non-voluntary licences address the harm to be alleviated. The terms of the licences must be relevant and effective and proportionate to the harm to be alleviated. The chapter ends by suggesting that national authorities have broad

I.M. Azmi is Professor of Law.

I.M. Azmi
Civil Law Department, Ahmad Ibrahim Kulliyyah of Laws, International Islamic University Malaysia, Kuala Lumpur, Malaysia
e-mail: imadieha@iium.edu.my; imadieha@hotmail.com

R.M. Hilty and K.-C. Liu (eds.), *Compulsory Licensing*, MPI Studies on Intellectual Property and Competition Law 22, DOI 10.1007/978-3-642-54704-1_11,

discretion in terms of the scope of the licences. However, such licence must be carefully crafted to reach the specific purpose for which the licence is issued or to cure the harm it seeks to remedy.

1 Introduction

Compulsory licensing has always been economically and politically important to a balanced intellectual property system.[1] Despite the controversy a compulsory licence may evoke, it is a standard, but exceptional, safety measure during national emergencies, instances of public interest, or breaches of antitrust rules.[2] This remedy is available not only for patents but also for copyrights and industrial designs. There is also a view that a compulsory licensing provision furthers the same goal of general patent laws: creating an incentive for new technologies,[3] by encouraging the production and use of patented goods and increasing access to advanced technology.[4]

It has been said that 'controversy over the appropriate scope of compulsory licensing was one of the reasons TRIPS negotiations were initiated'.[5] Earlier, texts such as the Anell Draft and the Brussels Draft tended to limit the issuance of compulsory licences.[6] The final TRIPS text, however, does not purport to limit the grounds on which compulsory licences may be granted. Nevertheless, TRIPS imposes the fulfilment of certain requirements in the event that member countries decide to issue compulsory licences.

In this chapter, the term 'compulsory licence' is used in the context of a third party use of patents without the authorisation of the owner. It includes government use, Crown use, and an order from the court compelling the compulsory licensing of intellectual property without the consent of the owner in infringement proceedings, in an application for injunctive relief, or for anti-competitive conduct. This is in line with the TRIPS Agreement that lumps all these types of compulsory licences as 'other use without authorization of the right holder' under Article 31.

The rationale behind compulsory licensing is that it permits people other than the patent owner to exploit the inventions where the patentee is either unable or unwilling to do so. Traditionally, national governments avail themselves of this

[1] Herz (1946).

[2] Correa (1999, 2000) and Reichman and Hasenzahl (2003).

[3] Fauver (1987–1988).

[4] Or to ensure that the patent system serves its constitutional purpose of promoting the progress of science and useful arts. Herz (1946), p. 902.

[5] UNCTAD-ICTSD (2005), p. 463.

[6] Ibid.

right, but in some instances the order may come from the court or the authorities in charge of antitrust or competition law.[7]

This chapter explores the possible scope and duration of compulsory licences that can be issued by member countries. The term 'scope' here refers to the range of relief that can be granted in a compulsory licence. It also refers to the terms and conditions of the compulsory licence. It precludes any discussion on the recognised ground for the issuance of compulsory licences.

This chapter explores the practice in countries where compulsory licences had been issued. As these practices have not garnered much criticism, arguably they can be considered to have received 'judicial acceptance' or be recognised as a 'customary practice' or 'evolving state practice'. As alluded by Reichman, 'the practical ramifications of Article 31 may ultimately depend on a combination of state practice at the local and regional levels and subsequent legislative or judicial action at the international level'.[8] From these national practices, we derive the criteria that national authorities may consider in determining the scope of the reliefs granted by way of compulsory licences.

2 Must Not Go Beyond the Purpose for Which the Licence Is Issued

The first guidance issued by TRIPS is that the scope and duration must be limited to the purpose for which the compulsory licence is issued.

On this, Article 31 (c) of the TRIPS Agreement provides:

> The scope and duration of such use shall be limited to the purpose for which it was authorized, and in the case of semi-conductor technology shall only be for public non-commercial use or to remedy a practice determined after judicial or administrative process to be anti-competitive.

Article 31 does not set a limit on the scope and duration of the compulsory licence. It only states that the scope and duration must be limited to the purpose for which it was authorised. To that extent, member countries have greater flexibility in determining the kind of reliefs to be granted and their lifespan, depending on the kind of harm that is being alleviated or the public interest that is being pursued. The tenor of this chapter is that the basic purpose behind the issuance of a compulsory licence should be the overriding interest that determines the scope and duration of

[7] Reichman defines 'compulsory licensing' as 'the practice by a government to authorize itself or third parties to use the subject matter of a patent without the authorization of the right holder for reasons of public policy'. Reichman and Hasenzahl (2003), p. 10.

[8] Reichman and Hasenzahl (2003), p. 16.

the licence. It is argued here that both the scope and duration are coterminous with each other, both being defined by the purpose for which the licence is issued.

What is the relevant 'purpose' described in Article 31(c)? Arguably, this relates to the grounds for the issuance of the compulsory licence. In the context of public health reasons such as the occurrence of epidemics or pandemics, the scope of the licence is limited to only 'essential medicines that are necessary to address the health needs'. The licence cannot be issued for 'medicines' in general. It must be limited to specific technology, not an entire class or category.[9] For example, a government can authorise the compulsory licensing of a specific drug but not all anti-retroviral therapy.[10] The production and sale of the drugs will also be limited to the region suffering from the outbreak. There may also be conditions in terms of the markings, colouring, packaging, and labelling of the products. Further, the licence must enable either the production or the importation of the medicines in the shortest time period possible. It is in this regard that some consider the disclosure of the associated production know-how under compulsion on the part of the licensee to enable the speedy production of the drugs. To enable the licensee to enjoy economies of scale, it may be wise to allow the licensee to export excess production to other countries.[11] After all, TRIPS requires that the drugs produced under compulsory licence be predominantly used in the country, but it does not prohibit the exportation of excess supply. All these limitations correspond with the nature of compulsory licences as a safety valve to bridge the gap between public health needs and patent owner rights.

By the same token, in determining the terms of the licence on other grounds besides public health, the issuing authorities must take into account what is needed by the licensee to practice the patented invention and must award the patent owner a reasonable royalty in exchange. The scope of the licence must take into account: (a) the nature of the invention, (b) the ability of the person to whom a licence would be granted under the order to work the invention to the public advantage, (c) the risks to be undertaken by that person in providing capital and working the invention if the application for an order is granted.[12] There may also be a necessity to impose restrictions with regard to the field of application, the territory, or the amount of production.[13] In line with voluntary licences, such compulsory licences can equally be limited to persons, time, place, manufacture, use, or sale.[14]

[9] Osenga (2012), p. 318.

[10] Osenga (2012), p. 318.

[11] Lybecker and Fowler (2009), p. 230.

[12] Lord Mackay of Clashfern (2008), para 397.

[13] Stoll et al. (2009), p. 571.

[14] For voluntary licences, see Lord Mackay of Clashfern (2008), para 380.

3 Must Address the Harm to Be Alleviated

Compulsory licences are issued to remedy certain harm or in pursuance of public interest. The corollary effect is that issuing authorities must ensure that the reliefs granted must be robust enough to alleviate the harm.

In the case of non-working, the scope of the licence must be necessary to work the invention in the country. The notion of 'working' here is in the sense of being put into use or manufactured in the country. Correa views working obligation as a tool to promote local manufacturing and the production of new technologies. In such an instance, the licensee must not be allowed to use the licence for importation. Instead, it is for the purpose of manufacture of the product in the country where the patent is issued.[15] In fact, in the UK, a compulsory licence can be issued if a patented technology and products are not worked in the country to the fullest extent that is reasonably practicable. In *Extrude Hone Corp's Patent*,[16] it was considered whether the demand for a method, apparatus, and material for honing using abrasive particles suspended in a semisolid plastic medium was being met by importation. The learned Mr. Justice Whitford of the Chancery Division was of the opinion that 'the patentees made no real effort in the early years to exploit their invention or to introduce it commercially into the United Kingdom'. He thus concluded that 'the invention although capable of being commercially worked in the United Kingdom had not been and was not being so worked to the fullest extent that was reasonably practicable'. The usual assumption that importation meets the economic demand of a patented product does not apply in all circumstances. Besides the UK, the experience in India also exemplifies this line of thinking. The Comptroller of Patents in *Natco Pharma Limited v Bayer Corporation* was of the view that 'worked in India' means 'manufactured to a reasonable extent in India'.[17]

The other harm sought to be remedied in Nexavar's case in India is the non-availability of the drug.[18] As a result, the licensing terms must ensure that the drugs produced under compulsory licence reached their target audience. Thus, we see the licence issued by the Patent Registrar containing explicit conditions that the price must be affordable to normal members of the public and made available for free to certain groups of people so that the drugs must reach the patients. In some circumstances, the term can also include the importation of the goods from overseas

[15] Correa (2012).

[16] [1982] R.P.C. 361.

[17] *Natco Pharma Limited v Bayer Corporation*, http://www.ipindia.nic.in/iponew/compulsory_license_12032012.pdf Accessed 11th April 2013. For more details, see the chapter "Compulsory Licence Under Indian Patent Law" by N.S. Gopalakrishnan and Madhuri Anand, in this volume.

[18] It was argued by Natco Pharma that Nexavar was available in India in limited amount and at an excessively high price. Therefore, the reasonable requirements of the public with respect to the patented invention had not been satisfied. The patented invention was not available to the public at an affordable price, and the patented invention was not worked in India.

by the licensee if local production is not feasible or economical. One view is that "working as requiring actual assembly in the country" no longer coincides with the reality of production of goods in the world today. "If it is cheaper to manufacture elsewhere and then import, the product will be available at a more reasonable price in the importing country".[19] Numerous examples can be found where a compulsory licence has been issued for the purpose of importation of generic drugs from other countries. The availability of cheaper imported drugs offers an easy solution to non-working and non-availability of patented drugs at affordable prices. The experiences of Malaysia, Ecuador, Ghana, Indonesia, Rwanda, and Thailand are a testimony to this notion.

The order may also include the power to export to enable the patent to be worked to the fullest extent that is reasonably practicable. By allowing exports, public interest is served to the maximum,[20] as the licensee is able to enjoy economies of scale, which in turn reduces the cost of production and ensures sufficient supply of products in the market. In such instances, however, the issuing authorities must be mindful not to allow exports to countries where the patent owner is already operating so as to avoid unnecessary harm to his pecuniary interest. In a UK case, *Penn Engineering and Manufacturing Corporation's Paten*t,[21] the applicant sought a compulsory licence under a patent relating to self-anchoring studs, in which there had been no manufacture in the UK. A compulsory licence was granted, including the power to export.[22]

Needless to say, the lifespan of the compulsory licence must correspond to the nature of harm alleviated or public interest pursued. The time period will depend on the nature of the invention and the urgency of the problem. For more complex technology, a longer time is needed to work out the invention. It is therefore usual for the non-voluntary licence to be for the remaining duration of the patent term. The redress needed to remedy life-threatening epidemics must be of a sufficiently long period in order to effectively contain the spread of the disease. At the same time, it must be long enough to enable the licensee to recoup his expenses,[23] otherwise there will be no incentive for him to undertake the project. For these reasons, a number of compulsory licences for communicable and non-communicable diseases have been for the remaining period of the patent

[19] Fauver (1987–1988).

[20] Per Justice Graham, [1972] F.S.R. 533; [1973] RPC 233.

[21] [1972] F.S.R. 533; [1973] RPC 233.

[22] It was held by Justice Graham that the public interest demanded that exports from the country should be on as large a scale as possible. At the same time, it would not be right to deprive an inventor of such reasonable remuneration as he might be able himself to get from his own exploitation. If a patentee was already manufacturing in the United Kingdom and exporting to foreign countries, it might well be reasonable for him to ask that the grant of a compulsory licence should be restricted so as to prevent export by the licensee to those countries to which the patentee was already exporting. *Penn Engineering and Manufacturing Corporation's Paten*t [1972] F.S.R. 533; [1973] RPC 233.

[23] UNCTAD-ICTSD (2005), p. 470.

term. An excellent example of this can be found in the experience of India in the compulsory licences of 'Nexavar', which was for the remaining lifespan of the patent. Another striking example is Indonesia, with respect to the compulsory licence of retroviral drugs in 2005 and of a drug for hepatitis B in 2012. However, in some instances, despite the urgency of health problems, countries issue compulsory licences with a rather short lifespan. An excellent example of this is Malaysia, in the issuance of government use licences for retroviral drugs in 2003 for only 5 years. Meanwhile, Thailand issued a compulsory licence for retroviral drugs in 2006 and 2007 for a short period, but this was renewed in 2010.[24]

By the same token, there may be a necessity to set the time frame for which the licensee is expected to begin the project. If the harm to be alleviated is non-working, a compulsory licence must include the time period in which the invention should be worked "without undue delay" and "to the fullest extent that is reasonably practicable".[25]

4 Must Be Relevant and Effective

As a corollary to addressing the harm addressed, the terms of the licence must equally be relevant and effective. So far, we have ventured into the compulsory licences of drugs for public health purposes where the issues are clear cut and the harm can be remedied by a simple compulsory licensing of the patented technology. The remaining discussion forays into the issuance of compulsory licences to remedy anti-competitive practices, where more wide-ranging compulsory licences can be issued. In the US, compulsory licensing is a standard remedy to address anti-competitive effects caused in these situations:

(1) anti-competitive mergers,
(2) cases in which the harm arises from an anti-competitive use of IP rights, and
(3) cases in which the harm arises from activities that do not involve IP rights.[26]

As explained by the representative from the US in a WIPO survey on compulsory licences:

> The scope of such a license is limited to the extent that is necessary to remedy the competitive harm. For example, in some cases licenses should be made available to a limited number of licensees only. In other cases, licenses must be made available to any willing licensee. A license must be confined to permitting the use of the IP right in question in the markets in which competition has been harmed. Attaching a reasonable royalty requirement to use the IP right may preserve incentives to innovate by continuing to

[24] For more, see the chapter "Compulsory Licences: Law and Practice in Thailand" by Jakkrit Kuanpoth, in this volume.

[25] See the views of Justice Graham in *Penn Engineering and Manufacturing Corporation's Patent*, [1972] F.S.R. 533; [1973] RPC 233 on this.

[26] WIPO (2001), p. 14.

compensate the patent owner for its invention. The duration of such licenses is limited to the period of time necessary to remedy the harm to competition.[27]

One of the prime thrusts in an antitrust case is to 'pry open to competition a market that has been closed' and 'to restore competition'.[28] As the purpose of the relief is to restore competition in the market, the terms of the licence must be not only relevant but also effective to reduce the anti-competitive effects.[29] In essence, this requires not only the simple prohibition on the anti-competitive practices but also 'broader structural relief where necessary to restore competition'.[30]

On that score, the judicially compelled licences are the broadest in terms of scope,[31] as they do not only deal with the disputed patented technology but may also extend to other associated intellectual property such as copyright, trade secrets, and, possibly, trademarks. This is justifiable, as 'only the existence of IP rights was protected without restrictions, not their exercise'.[32] Furthermore, the objectives of compulsory licensing as a remedy to iron out anti-competitive practices are seen as an alternative to complete patent forfeiture when necessary to restore the market to normalcy.[33] The basic thrust for the conferral of a compulsory licence is that although the patent holder is entrusted with exclusive rights, he cannot 'overreach his privilege as to intrude upon the right of the public'.

In some cases, effective reliefs involve the divestiture of the patent owner and licensing of certain intellectual property that was critical to the particular technology. In *Dow Chemical*, the harm that needed to be addressed was a merger that would significantly reduce competition in the development of new consumer plastic products and polythene process technology (LLDPE). To avoid a possible anti-competitive effect, Dow was required by the US Fair Trade Commission to divest and license certain IP that was critical to the production of LLDPE. The compulsory licence involved "all formulations, patents, trade secrets, technology, know-how,

---

[27] WIPO (2001), p. 33.

[28] Corbett (2001).

[29] Further analysis of the use of compulsory licences to remedy anti-competitive practices can be found in Correa (2007).

[30] Holmes (1980–1981).

[31] The term 'judicially compelled' is derived from Nunnenkamp (1993–1994), p. 408.

[32] Germany reported that compulsory licenses were appropriate means to combat anti-competitive practices in individual cases. Germany emphasised that in accordance with the EU Court of Justice, only the existence of IP rights was protected without any restriction, not their exercise. Therefore, the exercise of IP rights was subject to the same control under competition law as other forms of property, above all tangible property. When abuse control under antitrust law is applied in connection with IP rights, particular importance is attached to striking a balance between the interests of the holder of the protected right in preventing the market entry of a party seeking to obtain a licence by means of the protected right and the interests of free competition. The "essential facilities doctrine" within the framework of abuse control in Article 102 of the Treaty on the Functioning of European Union was particularly mentioned by Germany. WIPO (2001), p. 33.

[33] Lauroesch (1990–1991) citing *National Lead*, 332 U.S. at 328–35; *General Electric*, 125 F. Supp. 844.

specifications, designs, drawings, processes, quality control data, research materials, technical information, management information systems, software, the Drug Master File, and all information relating to the United States Food and Drug Administration Approvals".[34] The compulsory licence was in the form of a non-exclusive, irrevocable, royalty-free use of the technology, including future developments in the US, as well as other parts of the world.[35]

It is thus possible that in order to eliminate anti-competitive effects, the compulsory licensing must address not only patented technology but also associated know-how[36] and copyright. In the celebrated *Microsoft* case, the final judgment required Microsoft to license all of its IP for client–server interoperability (including copyright, trade secrets, and patents) in the server software field of use on reasonable terms.[37] The Consent Decree compelled Microsoft to make available the documentation for the communication protocols to prospective licensees for evaluation prior to signing a licence. It also requires Microsoft to enlarge the scope of licence to permit use of the communication protocols both to communicate with a larger variety of Windows client operating systems and to operate on clients that are functioning as servers.[38]

What is relevant and effective differs from case to case. In *Intergraph Corp v Intel Corp*,[39] in order for Intergraph to have access to Intel's chips and technical know-how that has been regarded as essential standards, the US District Court for the Northern District of Alabama ordered the compulsory licensing of its proprietary information and pre-release product that is covered under patents, copyright,

---

[34] Correa (2007), p. 7.

[35] Decision and Order dated April 3, 2009 http://www.ftc.gov/os/caselist/0810214/index.shtm Accessed 11th April, 2013.

[36] The US stated that there is no requirement to include "know-how" transfer provisions in the IP licence if the licence can be successfully drafted without them. However, if "know-how" is necessary to remedy the identified competitive harm, such provisions are included in the licence. See WIPO (2001), p. 20.

[37] Microsoft Consent Decree Compliance Advisory—August 1, 2003, www.justice.gov/atr/cases/f0200/0233.htm accessed 11th April 2013.

[38] Microsoft Consent Decree Compliance Advisory—August 1, 2003, www.justice.gov/atr/cases/f0200/0233.htm accessed 11th April 2013.

[39] The District Court Order was:

a. Intel shall supply Intergraph with all Intel product information, including but not limited to technical, design, development, defect, specification, support, supply, future product, product release or sample data, whether existing in product data books, "yellow backs," Confidential Information Transmittal Records, email or other mediums . . ., whether it is on an advance basis for the development of motherboards, graphics subsystems or workstations utilizing Intel's existing, or future generation products (hereinafter "Product Development"), or current products as needed for support of such products. . . .

c. Intel shall supply Intergraph with an allocation, and set aside a supply of microprocessors, semiconductors, chips, and buses (hereinafter "Chips") on an advance basis for product development ("Chips Samples"), in such quantities as forecasted by Intergraph in the same manner and the same terms as is done by Intergraph's similarly situated competitors.

See 195 F.3d 1346. (Fed Cir. 1999).

and trade secrets to Intergraph on reasonable and non-discriminatory terms.[40] Intel argued that if the compulsory licence is enforced, it will disclose technical information that is not generally known, samples of new products before they are available to the public, and individualised technical assistance. The decision was, however, reversed on appeal.[41]

More contentious is the compulsory licensing of trademarks.[42] Two exceptional examples can be found on this, i.e. *FTC v Cereal Companies* and *FTC v Borden Company*. However, this practice has been abandoned, as Article 21 of the TRIPS Agreement prohibits the compulsory licensing of trademarks.[43]

In sum, with regard to compulsory licences to remedy anti-competitive practices from the experience of the US that has been discussed earlier, the lesson that we can derive is that the scope of such a licence is strictly discretionary as long as it is 'necessary' and bears 'reasonable relationship' to the alleged violations and is confined to the 'least drastic' alternatives.[44] Finally, the relief imposed must not be prescribed as a form of "punishment" but must instead be for the remedial purpose of offsetting the proven law violations. Finally, although the examples given have been US cases, it is argued here that the same considerations will face countries that allow the issuance of compulsory licences on anti-competitive grounds such as China, Taiwan,[45] and Germany.[46]

5 Must Be Proportionate to the Purpose of Issuing the Compulsory Licence Without Unreasonably Harming the Patent Owner

The breadth of the discretionary powers to issue non-voluntary licence for abuse of monopoly raises concerns about whether it is in violation of Article 13 and Article 30 of the TRIPS Agreement, which set the limitations and exceptions of intellectual

[40] Correa (2007) p. 9.

[41] 195 F.3d 1346. (Fed Cir. 1999). In the words of the Federal Circuit at para 85, "The remedy of compulsory disclosure of proprietary information and provision of pre-production chips and other commercial and intellectual property is a dramatic remedy for antitrust illegality, and requires violation of antitrust law or the likelihood that such violation would be established. In the proceedings whose record is before us, Intergraph has not shown a substantial likelihood of success in establishing that Intel violated the antitrust laws in its actions with respect to Intergraph, or that Intel agreed by contract to provide the benefits contained in the injunction. The preliminary injunction is vacated".

[42] Holmes (1980–1981), pp. 63–75.

[43] Correa (2007), p. 21.

[44] Holmes (1980–1981), p. 45.

[45] For more, see the chapter "Compulsory Licence and Government Use in Taiwan: A Regress" by Kung-Chung Liu, in this volume.

[46] For more, see the chapter "Compulsory Licensing in Germany" by Philipp Maume, in this volume.

property. Such limitations and exceptions must be confined to special cases that do not conflict with a normal exploitation of the work and do not unreasonably prejudice the legitimate interest of the right holder. An objection along this line has been raised in *Microsoft Corp (The Computing Technology Industry Association Inc. and Others, intervening) v Commission of the European Communities (Software & Information Industry Association and Others, intervening)*.[47]

Such concerns arise, as in this case the compulsory licence issued carried broad implications on a whole gamut of intellectual property, including copyright, patent, trade secret,[48] and even future patents. In this case, Microsoft was faced with the allegation that it had abused its dominant position in the relevant markets by (1) refusing to supply interoperability information to its competitors related to the work group server operating systems and (2) tying its Windows Media Player software in with its Windows operating system. The Commission ordered that Microsoft pay a hefty fine. What was more controversial is that Microsoft was compelled to disclose a detailed description of the design and operation of the communications protocols that would allow a competitor to use it in its own server operating system. Microsoft claimed that allowing that would have the effect of disclosing a great deal of information about the internal design of the Windows operating systems.

When the case came to appeal before the Court of First Instance of the European Union, it was found that "the scope of the remedy must be assessed in the light of the abusive conduct in which Microsoft was found to have engaged, which depended in particular on the degree of interoperability envisaged by the Commission in the contested decision".

With respect to compulsory licences, the Court of First Instance commented that the disclosure of the communication protocols is 'justified by the need to put the infringement to an end'.[49] On the argument that the compulsory licensing may be against the TRIPS Agreement, the Court of First Instance rejected Microsoft's

[47] [2007] 5 C.M.L.R. 11. The decision of the Court of First Instance. See also *Microsoft Corp v Commission of the European Communities*, [2005] E.C.D.R. 19.

[48] In the UK as well, in the context of Crown use, contractors may be allowed to use technical information other than that relating to a patented invention. Lord Mackay of Clashfern (2008), para 405.

[49] At para 288 of [2007] 5 C.M.L.R. 11, the European Court of First Instance commented, "Furthermore, the Commission confirmed, in answer to one of the written questions put by the Court, that the contested decision did not establish that the interoperability information was not covered by a patent or by copyright or, on the contrary, that it was. There was no need to decide that issue since, in any event the conditions for finding an abuse and for imposing the remedy [prescribed by Art. 5 of the contested decision] were satisfied whether or not the information is protected by any patent or copyright". See also para 289 of the judgement [2007] 5 C.M.L.R. 11. "It follows from the foregoing considerations that the appraisal of the merits of the first part of the plea must proceed on the presumption that the protocols in question, or the specifications of those protocols, are covered by intellectual property rights or constitute trade secrets and that those secrets must be treated as equivalent to intellectual property rights".

arguments that the compulsory licensing "goes further than is necessary to achieve interoperability and, consequently, violates the condition that limitations or exceptions can be applied to intellectual property rights only in special cases". The Court of First Instance found the scope of the compulsory licence to be proportionate to the Commission's stated objective of eliminating the effects of Microsoft's anti-competitive conduct. The Commission's new balancing test appears to legitimise compulsory licensing whenever a dominant undertaking's competitors would benefit from access to the applicant's intellectual property, regardless of whether such a measure is necessary to remedy anti-competitive conduct or not.[50]

The terms of the licence set by the European Commission and endorsed by the European Court of the First Instance were bound to be controversial, but the remedy appears to be a standard compulsory licensing requirement necessary to bring an end to the abusive refusal to disclose information covered by IP rights.[51]

The same approach has been taken with respect to copyright materials that are regarded as essential facilities or de facto industry standard[52] as in *IMS Health*.[53] In this case, IMS was ordered to share its database system with two companies that have been alleged to have infringed its system, which is known as the 'bricks' model. The decision has been lauded as illustration of how, in rare circumstances, the European Commission will resort to compulsory licences to remedy abuse of copyright.[54]

In sum, the scope of remedy must be assessed in the light of the abusive conduct. When the harm that needs to be reduced is wide ranging and complex and when the technology involved is immersed in layers of intellectual property, it may be necessary to bundle all the associated intellectual property in the compulsory licence. The breadth of the issuing authorities' discretion in crafting the terms of the non-voluntary licence is also the practice in other countries, including the UK.[55] However, it must be cautioned that whatever reliefs are crafted into the non-voluntary licensing terms, they must be proportionate to the harm remedied.

[50] Para 780 of the judgment [2007] 5 C.M.L.R. 11.

[51] Nazzini (2008).

[52] Correa (2007), p. 11.

[53] Case COMP D3/38.044, *NDC Health v. IMS Health*: Interim Measures, 2002 O.J. (L 59) 18 (July 3, 2001) [hereinafter *IMS*], *suspended*, Cases T-184/01 R(1), *IMS Health v. Commission*, [2001] E.C.R. II-2349, and T-184/01 R(2), IMS Health v. Commission, Order of the President of the Court of First Instance of Oct. 26, 2001, *aff'd*, Case C-481/01 P(R), *NDC Health v. IMS Health*, Order of the President of the Court of Apr. 11, 2002.

[54] Fine (2002).

[55] Similarly, the practice in the UK is that the possible relief for abuse of monopoly falls within the discretion of the Comptroller. He is free to set the terms of the licence as he sees fit. Lord Mackay of Clashfern (2008), para 398–399.

6 Conclusion

In interpreting Article 31 (c) of the TRIPS Agreement, one has to be mindful of the underlying purpose for which a compulsory licence has been issued. Past experiences in the US, the EU, and Germany have illustrated that this may cover not only existing patents but also future patents, related know-how, and copyright. The licence may implicate reasonable royalty or even nominal or free royalty.[56] It may allow importation or be restricted to local manufacture depending on the harm to be alleviated.

National experiences have shown the latitude of discretion possessed by authorities in issuing compulsory licences. Reichman suggested that there is a more expansive concept of public interest dimensions that would shape the discourse on compulsory licences.[57] The notion of compulsory licences must take into account all the noble aspirations contained in the preamble of the TRIPS Agreement, particularly Articles 7, 8(1), and 8(2). In his viewpoint, 'all these provisions arm developing and least-developed countries with legal grounds for maintaining a considerable degree of domestic control over intellectual property policies in a post-TRIPS environment, including compulsory licences'.

Such a licence must be carefully crafted to reach the specific purpose for which the licence is issued or cure the harm it seeks to remedy. If the main purpose is access to essential medicines in an emergency, the licence must enable either the production or the importation of the medicines in the shortest time period. In the context of abuse of patent rights, the scope of the licence may be broad ranging, This is however justifiable, as in the US, many of today's most frequently granted non-voluntary licenses are part and parcel of consent decrees, whether they emanate from the Department of Justice, from the Federal Trade Commission, or from the courts.[58] In Europe, the non-voluntary licences were brought for review before the Court of First Instance.

As 'compulsory licensing' is a two-edged sword,[59] the limitations in the scope and duration of the compulsory licence will ensure that a balance is maintained between the competing interests of patentees and the public[60] and to guarantee the efficient use of inventions.[61]

[56] Holmes (1980–1981).

[57] Reichman and Hasenzahl (2003), p. 11.

[58] Reichman and Hasenzahl (2003), p. 22.

[59] As viewed by Reichman, in Reichman and Hasenzahl (2003), p. 23.

[60] Osenga (2012), p. 320.

[61] Yosick (2001).

References

Corbett RJT (2001) Protecting and enforcing intellectual property rights in developing countries. Int Law 35:1083
Correa CM (1999) Intellectual property rights and the use of compulsory licences: options for developing countries, trade-related agenda, development and equity. Working papers, South Centre, Geneva
Correa CM (2000) The strengthening of IPRs in developing countries and complimentary legislation. www.eldis.org/vfile/upload/1/document/0708/DOC9368.pdf. Accessed 11 Apr 2013
Correa CM (2007) Intellectual property and competition law: exploration of some issues of relevance to developing countries. ICTSD IPRs and sustainable development programme issue paper no 21, International Centre for Trade and Sustainable Development, Geneva
Correa CM (2012 u.p) The use of compulsory licences in Latin America. In: The fifth conference on European and Asian Intellectual Property, Academic Sinica, 3–5 December 2012
Fauver C (1987–1988) Comment, compulsory patent licensing in the US: an idea whose time has come. Northwestern J Int Law Bus 8:666
Fine F (2002) Responses and replies: NDC/IMS: in response to Prof Korah. Antitrust Law J 70:247
Herz A (1946) Compulsory licensing. J Patent Office Soc 28:889
Holmes WC (1980–1981) Compulsory patent and trademark licensing: a framework for analysis. Loyola Univ Chic Law J 12:43
Lauroesch MW (1990–1991) General compulsory patent licensing in the United States: good in theory, but not necessary in practice. Santa Clara Comput High Technol Law J 6:41
Lord Mackay of Clashfern (ed) (2008) Halsbury laws of England. Reed Elsevier, UK
Lybecker KM, Fowler E (2009) Compulsory licensing in Canada and Thailand: comparing regimes to ensure legitimate use of the WTO rules. J Law Med Ethics 37:222
Microsoft Consent Decree Compliance Advisory (2003) www.justice.gov/atr/cases/f0200/0233.htm. Accessed 11 Apr 2013
Nazzini R (2008) The Microsoft case and the future of Article 82. Antitrust ABA 22:59
Nunnenkamp KJ (1993–1994) Compulsory licensing of critical patents under CERCLA. J Nat Resources Environ Law 397
Osenga K (2012) Get the balance right! Squaring access with patent protection. Pac McGeorge Global Bus Dev Law J 25:309
Reichman JH, Hasenzahl C (2003) Non voluntary licensing of patented inventions: historical perspective, legal framework under TRIPS and an overview of the practice in Canada and the USA. Issue paper no 5. ICTSD-UNCTAD, Geneva
Stoll PT, Busche J, Arend K (2009) WTO trade related aspects of intellectual property rights. Martinus Nijhoff Publishers, Leiden
UNCTAD-ICTSD (2005) Resource book on TRIPS and development, UNCTAD-ICTSD project on IPRs and sustainable development. Cambridge University Press, Cambridge
WIPO (2001) Survey on compulsory licences granted by WIPO Member States to address anti-competitive uses of intellectual property rights. CDIP/4/4 Rev./Study/Inf/s. http://www.wipo.int. Accessed 11 Apr 2013
Yosick JA (2001) Compulsory patent licensing for efficient use of inventions. Univ Illinois Law Rev 1275

The Requirements for Compulsory Dependency Licences: Learning from the Transformative Use Doctrine in Copyright Law

Matthias Leistner

Contents

Abstract Under the TRIPS regime, compulsory licences for the exploitation of dependent patents are governed by the specific provision of Art. 31 (l) TRIPS. Hitherto, this provision is of very limited practical relevance; in fact, there is almost no case law and only a little amount of literature on Art. 31 (l) TRIPS. Essentially, the paper argues in favour of a functional and relative approach to the interpretation of the main Art. 31 (l) TRIPS condition, i.e. that "(i) the invention claimed in the second (dependent) patent shall involve an important technical advance of considerable economic significance in relation to the invention claimed in the first patent". The chapter draws on copyright law doctrine of transformative use to argue that both substantive conditions of Art. 31 (l) (i) TRIPS should be interpreted consistently with regard to the relation to the primary patent, i.e. a lower threshold should apply if the primary patent embodies only an incremental technical advance.

M. Leistner is Professor of Law.

M. Leistner
Institut für Handels- und Wirtschaftsrecht, Rheinische Friedrich-Wilhelms-Universität Bonn, Bonn, Germany
e-mail: leistner@jura.uni-bonn.de

R.M. Hilty and K.-C. Liu (eds.), *Compulsory Licensing*, MPI Studies on Intellectual Property and Competition Law 22, DOI 10.1007/978-3-642-54704-1_12,

1 Introduction

Under the TRIPS regime, compulsory licences for the exploitation of dependent patents are governed by the specific provision of Art. 31 (l) TRIPS. The provision foresees three cumulative conditions that apply in addition to the general conditions of Art. 31 (a)–(k) TRIPS. Compared to the previous regime under the Paris Convention,[1] this constitutes a restriction of the freedom of the TRIPS Members to grant compulsory licences in dependency cases (see below Sect. 2). Accordingly, the global situation with regard to dependency licences, which had always been characterised by an extremely limited practical significance of this instrument, has not changed in this regard; as a consequence, there is almost no case law and only little literature on Art. 31 (l) TRIPS (see below Sect. 3). This chapter argues from the specific perspective of a comparison to the treatment of free derivative use in copyright law and reaches the conclusion that Art. 31 (l) TRIPS should be interpreted in a "relative" and flexible manner, resulting in a broader field of application of this provision (see below Sects. 4 and 5).

2 Art. 31 (l) TRIPS as a Restriction Compared to the Previous International Regime

2.1 The Situation Before Art. 31 (l) TRIPS

Before the entry into force of Art. 31 (l) TRIPS, there was considerable leeway for national legislators to grant compulsory licences in situations of dependent patents. The previous regime was governed only by Art. 5A Paris Convention, which left PC Members wide liberty to foresee compulsory licences for dependent patent holders.[2] Consequently, in some national legislations, such as the Netherlands or Japan, compulsory dependency licences could (and partly still can) be granted upon the sole condition of the dependent patent holder requiring a licence for the exploitation of his patent and the refusal of the holder of the first patent to grant a licence. In many other PC Member States, such as Belgium, Denmark, Finland, France, the United Kingdom, and Sweden, the sole condition of an important technical advance (or substantial contribution to the arts) applied without the additional condition of "considerable economic significance".[3] Partly, reservation periods of 3 years after the grant of the first patent were and are foreseen in national

[1] Paris Convention for the Protection of Industrial Property of March 20, 1883, as revised and amended (PC), available at http://www.wipo.int/treaties/en/ip/paris/trtdocs_wo020.html.

[2] See Straus (1996), pp. 207 et seq. with further references.

[3] See Straus (1996).

laws as an additional restriction, such as in the UK.[4] In Germany, the general condition of sufficient public interest in the grant of a compulsory licence also applied to the case of dependency licences. At first glance, this previous legal situation with regard to the grant of dependency licences has been "restricted severely vis-à-vis the previous regime" by Art. 31 (l) TRIPS.[5]

2.2 *Art. 31 (l) TRIPS: Important Technical Advance of Considerable Economic Significance*

Compared to the general conditions of Art. 31 (a)–(k), in the case of dependency licences, Art. 31 (l) (i) TRIPS provides for the double *additional* condition that "the invention claimed in the second patent shall involve an important technical advance of considerable economic significance in relation to the invention claimed in the first patent".[6] Furthermore, according to Art. 31 (l) (ii), "the owner of the first patent shall be entitled to a cross-licence on reasonable terms to use the invention claimed in the second patent", and according to Art. 31 (l) (iii), "the use authorized in respect of the first patent shall be non-assignable except with the assignment of the second patent". Thus, essentially, Art. 31 (l) TRIPS adds the condition of "considerable economic significance of the invention claimed in the second patent in relation to the invention claimed in the first patent" to the established and widespread condition of an important technical advance in relation to the first patent.

As a consequence, a number of TRIPS Member States have amended their national Patent Acts to include the condition of an "important technical advance of considerable economic significance in relation to the invention claimed in the first patent".[7] Particularly, in Europe, partly also in reaction to Art. 12 Biotech Directive,[8] which foresees a specific compulsory dependency licence with regard to the relationship between prior or secondary patents and plant variety rights under the Art. 31 (l) TRIPS conditions,[9] many Member States have implemented the

[4] See Straus (1996); Leitzen and Kleinevoss (2005), pp. 199, 204.

[5] See Straus (1996), p. 207; Correa (2007), p. 317.

[6] These two qualifications apply cumulatively to each other and to the general conditions of Art. 31 (a)–(k); cf. Eikermann (2009), Art. 31, note 50; Hoehne (2013), Art. 31, note 39.

[7] See the summary report of the answers of the AIPPI national groups to Question 202 "The impact of public health issues on exclusive patent rights", I 6), 2008, Congress in Boston, USA, available at https://www.aippi.org/download/commitees/202/SR202English.pdf.

[8] Directive 98/44/EC of the European Parliament and of the Council of 6 July 1998 on the legal protection of biotechnological inventions, OJ L 213/13-21 of 30.7.1998 (Biotech Directive).

[9] In the German statute, originally, the new specific conditions of Art. 31 (l) TRIPS had been cumulated with the "old" general condition of the sufficient public interest. This was criticised in parts of literature as over-restrictive (cf., e.g., Straus 1998, pp. 314, 316 et seq.). At the occasion of the implementation of Art. 12 Biotech Directive, the German legislator corrected this mischief and implemented the TRIPS-identical conditions for compulsory licences under Art. 12 Biotech

TRIPS conditions identically into their national laws. Accordingly, e.g., Sec. 48A (1) (b) UK Patent Act 1977, Art. L 613-15 & 613-15-1 French *Code de la Propriété Intelectuelle*, as well as Sec. 24 (2) No. 2 German Patent Act, now provide for the essential condition of an important technical advance of considerable economic significance in relation to the invention claimed in the first patent. Other TRIPS Members, such as Japan,[10] however still provide for a broader possibility of compulsory dependency licences.[11]

Against this background, the interpretation of the flexible and cumulative conditions of (1) important technical advance of (2) considerable economic significance in relation to the invention claimed in the first patent becomes of crucial importance as to the "practicability and chances of success of the TRIPS regulation".[12]

3 Case Law and Literature on Art. 31 (l) TRIPS

Comparative law analyses under the old regime have revealed that there was almost no case law on the respective national provisions regulating compulsory dependency licences.[13] This situation has not changed under Art. 31 (l) TRIPS.[14]

As far as can be seen, the only important case on compulsory dependency licences in national law is the German Federal Court of Justice's (*Bundesgerichtshof*) *Polyferon*-case, which was decided under the (old) German general "public interest" condition in 1995.[15] The case involved a new and inventive therapeutical use of an existing and patented medical substance. The new use was of relevance for the medical treatment of the general public and thus, arguably, in the public interest.

Directive across the board for all categories of inventions; cf. Explanatory Memorandum, BT-Drs. 15/1709, p. 13; Leitzen and Kleinevoss (2005), pp. 198, 199.

[10] In Japan, under the condition that the compulsory licence must not unreasonably prejudice the legitimate interests of the right holder or exclusive licensees, see Art. 92 Japanese Patent Act (Act No. 121 of 1959). In Switzerland, a literal implementation of the Art. 31 (l) TRIPS conditions in Art. 36 Swiss Patent Act (for compulsory dependency licences in the strict sense) is combined with a particularly developed system of further possible compulsory licences (partly also applicable in dependency situations, such as namely for biotechnological research tools, Art. 40b Swiss Patent Act).

[11] Cf. further on the comparative law perspective Leitzen and Kleinevoss (2005), 199, 204 et seq.

[12] Straus (1996), p. 208; Correa (2007), pp. 317 et seq.; cf. also Eikermann (2009), Art. 31, note 51: "subjective judgment that necessarily involves a range of discretion".

[13] Cf. Straus (1996), p. 208 with reference to the reports of the national groups of AIPPI in the AIPPI Yearbook 1988/IX.

[14] Cf. summary report of the answers of the AIPPI national groups to Question 202 "The impact of public health issues on exclusive patent rights", I 6), 2008, Congress in Boston, USA, available at https://www.aippi.org/download/commitees/202/SR202English.pdf.

[15] Federal Court of Justice (BGH) GRUR 1996, 190—Polyferon (X ZR 26/92, 5.12.1995); cf. also Kern (1996).

Accordingly, the German Federal Patent Court had granted a compulsory licence in favour of the holder of the dependent patent on the grounds stated under the former Sec. 24 (1) German Patent Act. The Federal Court of Justice nullified this judgment. While the public interest test, according to the Federal Court of Justice, did not demand an outright abusive behaviour of the right holder of the first patent as a precondition of a compulsory licence under Art. 31 TRIPS,[16] still the mere general public interest in the provision of the drug for the new therapeutical use was not sufficient, as it had not been proven that the respective therapeutical need could not be satisfied with existing "more or less equivalent alternative substances". For this reason, according to the Federal Court of Justice, the principle of proportionality guiding the balancing of interests of the right holder of the first patent, on the one hand, and the general public, on the other, demanded the denial of a compulsory licence.[17] This also followed from the underlying principle of absolute substance protection (*absoluter Stoffschutz*) for substance patents that showed the general objective of the legislator to extend patent protection for new and inventive substances to all future uses of such substances.[18] In addition, the burden of proof for the—difficult to establish—negative fact that there was no alternative substance with more or less equivalent medical effects was put on the applicant for the compulsory licence.[19]

While this case is an example in point for the overall very restrictive approach to compulsory dependency licences, it still applied the old general public interest test under German law, which has now been replaced for dependency licences by the specific Art. 31 (l) (i) TRIPS condition of an important technical advance of considerable economic significance in relation to the invention claimed in the first patent (now in Sec. 24 (2) German Patent Act). Therefore, the *ratio decidendi* should not be transposed identically to the interpretation of the new Sec. 24 (2) German Patent Act. To sum up, as far as can be seen, recently there has been no specific relevant case law of national supreme courts on Art. 31 (l) TRIPS (or its respective

[16] Federal Court of Justice (BGH) GRUR 1996, 190, 192—Polyferon (X ZR 26/92, 5.12.1995), note 47 et seq. In cases of abusive behaviour of the holder of an upstream essential patent, German and European antitrust laws apply independently of Sec. 24 Patent Act; cf. further chapters "Compulsory Licensing in Germany" by Phillip Maume and "Refusal to Licence as an Abuse of Market Dominance—from Commercial Solvents to Microsoft" by Matthias Lamping, in this volume.

[17] Federal Court of Justice (BGH) GRUR 1996, 190, 193—Polyferon (X ZR 26/92, 5.12.1995), note 50: ("... ist bei der Interessenabwägung der Grundsatz der Verhältnismäßigkeit zu beachten. Deshalb kann eine Zwangslizenz an einem Arzneimittel nicht zugesprochen werden, wenn das öffentliche Interesse mit anderen mehr oder weniger gleichwertigen Ausweichpräparaten befriedigt werden kann").

[18] Federal Court of Justice (BGH) GRUR 1996, 190, 193—Polyferon (X ZR 26/92, 5.12.1995), note 52 et seq.

[19] Cf. Federal Court of Justice (BGH) GRUR 1996, 190, 194—Polyferon (X ZR 26/92, 5.12.1995), notes 59 and 65.

implementing provisions in national law) at all and only very little case law of national higher courts.[20]

The comments on Art. 31 (l) TRIPS in the established textbooks and commentaries on the TRIPS Agreement more or less reflect the hitherto extremely limited practical relevance of the provision. Most authors limit their comments to an explanation of the cumulative character of the conditions in Art. 31 (l) (i)–(iii) TRIPS and the general structure of the provision.[21] At least, some authors emphasise the flexible character of the test and the resulting range of discretion of the TRIPS Members[22] and correctly point out the relative character of the concept of "considerable economic significance", which might be differently evaluated in "developing and developed countries, as well as for small and large companies".[23] In addition, it has always been emphasised (already for the former national provisions on compulsory licences in cases of dependency under the PC regime) that in spite of the extremely limited practice, the mere existence of such provisions might have implications, acting as a psychological 'hammer on the wall' to lead the way to successful negotiation of contractual licences for dependent improvement[24] and use inventions.[25] In particular, with regard to genetic inventions—where the principle of absolute substance protection leads to significant dependency problems concerning innovations in the field of functional genome analysis and genetic diagnostic methods—an *effective* application of the provision on dependency licences could arguably at least contribute to a better balancing of interests between holders of patents on genetic sequences and dependent patents on new functions of

[20] In more recent case law, the only detailed and substantially relevant judgment on the conditions of dependency licences that could be identified in relevant national higher courts' case law is the judgment of the Commercial Court of Berne (Handelsgericht Bern) sic! 2006, 348 (HG 03 9024, 6.7.2005—Anschlaghalter III, where a compulsory licence on the grounds mentioned under Art. 36 Swiss Patent Act was denied in a case of minor technical and economic importance. The court emphasised the interdependency and flexibility of the two elements of "important technical advance" and "considerable economic significance" but held that both elements were not present in the case. As for the important technical advance, a relative assessment was applied; nonetheless—insofar similar to the Polyferon case—the claimant could not establish the need for his purely alternative solution. As for the considerable economic significance, the court applied a subjective yardstick, assessing the economic significance from the perspective of the claimant, as well as from the perspective of the consumers. However, according to the court, under both perspectives, the condition of economic significance was not fulfilled as the sales figures of the secondary product were remarkably insignificant. A "relative" yardstick, comparing the economic significance for the claimant to the economic harm for the defendant, as it will be proposed here, was not applied.

[21] Cf., inter alia, Eikermann (2009), Art. 31, note 50 et seq.; Hoehne (2013), Art. 31, note 38 et seq.

[22] Cf. Eikermann (2009), Art. 31, note 51.

[23] Correa (2007), p. 318; Correa and Yusuf (1998), p. 212.

[24] Cf. on the particular (potential) importance of Art. 31 (l) TRIPS for improvement inventions Correa and Yusuf (1998), p. 212.

[25] Cf. Schieble (2005), p. 181; Straus (1996), 208.

such sequences.[26] However, the effectiveness of the existing provisions to reach this goal (directly or as an indirect incentive for successful licence negotiations) has to be doubted if a restrictive construction of the new two-element test, rooted in the old restrictive public interest criterion, prevails.[27] In particular, the test should not be interpreted in light of a general (absolute) public interest criterion, requiring a preeminent public interest, thus limiting possible compulsory licences to certain cases of exceptional economic impact measured by absolute standards. Instead, in what follows it is argued that a comparatively broad, "relative" construction of the two elements of the test of "important technical advance of considerable economic significance in relation to the invention claimed in the first patent" is preferable, drawing some inspiration from a comparison to the copyright free (transformative) use doctrine. Fundamental justification for this flexible approach can also be found in the TRIPS guiding principles of Art. 7 and 8, which provide for some leeway of manoeuvre of the Member States in interpreting the substantive TRIPS provisions.

4 Arguments for a "Relative" and Flexible Interpretation of Art. 31 (l) TRIPS

4.1 Comparison to Copyright Law

Compulsory licences for derivative works or new "value-added" uses of copyrighted works in derivative markets are generally not foreseen in existing international, regional, and national copyright laws.

Instead, for derivative works, which substantially derogate from the original work, thus leaving the overall impression of an independent creation (behind which the original entirely fades into the background) and which therefore are no longer a mere adaptation, Continental European copyright law traditionally provides for a doctrine of "free derivative use".[28] Under the U.S. fair use doctrine, a similar case

[26] This was one of the explicit goals of the European Biotech Directive and its implementation in the new Sec. 24 (2) German Patent Act; cf. the Explanatory Memorandum of the German legislator, BT-Drs. 15/1709, pp. 11, 13; Schieble (2005), p. 179; Straus (1998), pp. 314, 317 et seq.; cf. further on the role of obligatory non-exclusive licences to solve the dependency problem with regard to genetic diagnostic methods van Overwalle (2010), p. 1630; Huys et al. (2012), pp. 441, 446.

[27] See the justified concern of Schieble (2005), pp. 178 et seq.; on the potential of broad and differentiated mechanisms of compulsory licensing in national laws, such as in Switzerland, to prevent unduly restrictive licensing behaviour indirectly, van Overwalle (2010), p. 1630; van Zimmeren and van Overwalle (2011), pp. 4 et seq.; cf. with a rather restrictive attitude in German doctrine, e.g. Rogge (2006), § 24, note 22, with further references.

[28] Apart from this general approach to derivative works, certain specific derivative uses, such as quotations, are of course also exempted in copyright law; cf., e.g., for quotations Art. 10 (1) Berne Convention.

group of transformative fair use has been established by the courts in the framework of the four fair use factors of 17 U.S.C. § 107.[29] In general, a *relative yardstick* is applied (under the Continental European doctrine, as well as under the first and third fair use factor in the U.S.) comparing the creativity of the used parts of the original work to the degree of transformative character of the derivative work.[30] Thus, under Continental European doctrine, the more creative the original is, the higher the necessary degree of transformation would have to be to consider the derivative work a "free use" of the original.

In line with the utilitarian concept of U.S. copyright law, the case group of free transformative use is broader. Even certain uses of a work in identical form, but in a completely new context for a product or service in a new market, for which there is a public interest, but where the original right holder has no existent, substantive licensing activity, can be justified as free transformative use.[31] The main factor to evaluate these situations is the question of whether there is substantial harm from the derivative use in question to a potential market (namely, the licensing market) for the exploitation of the original copyrighted work by the right holder;[32] the element of harm to a potential market is assessed rather strictly by the U.S. courts in the most recent cases: specific proof of actual harm to existing licensing activities seems to be required from the right holder.[33]

4.2 Consequences

4.2.1 Consequence for Patent Law: Relative and Flexible Interpretation of Art. 31 (l) TRIPS

Firstly, as for Art. 31 (l) TRIPS, comparison to copyright law doctrine indirectly strengthens the argument for a relative and flexible construction of the two elements

---

[29] See Campbell v. Acuff-Rose, 510 U.S. 569, 579 ff. (1994); cf. on the different concept of transformation in patent law in the wake of In re Bilski (and meanwhile applied beyond computer-related inventions and namely in the field of genetic inventions) Huys et al. (2011), pp. 1104 et seq.

[30] As an example for the Continental European approach, see the German Federal Court of Justice (BGH) GRUR 1958, 500, 502—Mecki-Igel (I ZR 49/57, 1.4.1958) for the traditional authority on the "fade into the background" test (*Verblassenstheorie*); under the first three elements of the U.S. fair use doctrine, a similar approach can be identified, e.g. in Campbell v. Acuff-Rose, 510 U.S. 569, 579 ff. (1994) (on transformative use through parody).

[31] Cf. Núñez v. Caribbean Int'l News Corp., 235 F.3d 18, 22 f. (1st Cir. 2000); Kelly v. Arriba Soft, 336 F.3d 811, 818 f. (9th Cir. 2003); Bill Graham Archives v. Dorling Kindersley Ltd., 448 F.3d 605, 608 ff. (2d Cir. 2006); Field v. Google, Inc., 412 F.Supp.2d 1106, 1118 ff. (D. Nev. 2006); Perfect 10, Inc. v. Amazon.com, Inc., et al., 508 F.3d 1146, 1155 (9th Cir. 2007).

[32] Cf. also Harper & Row v. Nation Enterprises, 471 U.S. 539, 566 (1985): "undoubtedly the single most important element of fair use".

[33] See Perfect 10, Inc. v. Amazon.com, Inc., et al., 508 F.3d 1146, 1168 (9th Cir. 2007): potential harm that is not actually proven remains hypothetical and thus irrelevant for the fourth factor.

of an important technical advance of considerable economic significance in relation to the invention claimed in the first patent.

As for the element of an important technical advance, certain differences between the innovative processes regulated in copyright law on the one hand and patent law on the other make a direct and concrete comparison difficult and unsuitable.[34] Thus, while copyright law protects individual personal creations, patent law regulates the field of applied technical inventions and their exploitation, which is very often characterised by an incremental development of inventions and their further application in comparatively small iterative and interconnected steps. However, the general guiding principle that a *relative* (i.e., comparative) assessment between the creativity/inventive step involved in the first work/invention to the creativity/technical advance embodied in the second work/invention is adequate to balance the interests of the involved parties in cases of derivative creativity can certainly be transposed from established copyright doctrine to the interpretation of the element of "an important technical advance in relation to the invention claimed in the first patent".[35] Thus, the comparison to copyright law strengthens the prevailing opinion in legal doctrine on Art. 31 (1) TRIPS, as well as its implementing provisions in national laws, that a relative assessment is necessary with regard to the element of an important technical advance and that the old and restrictively interpreted general condition of an imminent public interest must not be read into this concept.[36] Instead, compliant with the wording of the provision and the general principles of TRIPS, a relative and flexible yardstick should be applied, due to which the inventive step embodied in the invention, claimed in the first patent, should be compared to the inventive step embodied in the invention, claimed in the second patent: if the second invention, compared to the first invention, constitutes an important, i.e. comparatively substantive, technical advance, this should be sufficient to fulfil the first element of Art. 31 (1) (i) TRIPS. Consequently, when the first patent involves only a comparatively small inventive step, this will proportionally lower the threshold for the necessary degree of technical advance of the invention, claimed in the second patent.

As for the element of a "considerable economic significance in relation to the invention claimed in the first patent", the comparison to the interpretation of the first and fourth elements of the U.S. fair use test, concerning the character of the use and the effect of the use upon the potential market for or value of the copyrighted work, can provide for some indirect guidance. With regard to the fourth element, more recent judgments have required *actual proof* of a possible concrete damage to existing licensing activities of the copyright holder of the original work.[37] At the

[34] Cf. also the attempts to compare the doctrines in German literature by Wegmann (2013), pp. 360 et seq.; Wolff (2005), pp. 37 et seq.

[35] With an even more direct parallel to copyright law, Wolff (2005), p. 41; recently with a justified qualification and adaptation of this position to the specifics of patent law, Wegmann (2013), p. 368.

[36] Cf. in literature Correa (2007), p. 317; Correa and Yusuf (1998), p. 212.

[37] See above footnote 33.

same time, as for the public interest in certain new use forms, which might be considered in favour of an admissible dependent transformative use (first element), the general public interest in socially useful services was regarded as sufficient by the courts without requiring a particularly overwhelming or imminent public interest.[38] Again, this shows that the old restrictive assessment of the public interest criterion with regard to the *general* conditions of compulsory licences in many national Patent Acts, requiring an imminent public interest of particular importance, should clearly not be transposed to the new and *specific* criteria for dependency licences in patent law. Typically, the important technical advance brought by the second invention should be regarded as a sufficient public interest. As for the additional assessment of the relative economical effects of the dependent use, a *concrete* economic analysis of the impact of this use upon the potential market for or value of the dominant patent should be carried out. As a matter of course, this assessment has to consider the fact that in the case of Art. 31 (l) TRIPS and its implementations in national law, the right holder shall be paid adequate remuneration, taking into account the economic value of the authorisation (Art. 31 (h) TRIPS). When this is considered, the economic analysis of potential harm to the economic exploitation interest of the holder of the original patent boils down to the assessment of the question as to whether the potential welfare gain through the use of the invention, claimed in the dependent patent, is larger than the potential harm to the holder of the first patent. This is because if the holder of the second patent can realise the welfare gain embodied in the underlying improvement or use of the invention, this gain will be larger than the potential harm to the holder of the first patent, who could therefore—in the specific case of dependency licences—be fully compensated for his loss under the terms of an adequate remuneration.

Of course, such concrete assessment will often be hard for the competent authority or the courts to make, and therefore such interpretation of the element of a considerable economic significance will not necessarily make the national provisions on compulsory licences in cases of dependent inventions more effective in practice. Also, transaction costs have to be taken into account and ex ante effects of a too broadly framed provision on possible compulsory licences in dependency situations have to be borne in mind.[39] Therefore, even on the basis of the proposed concrete economic analysis, the instrument of compulsory dependency licences will presumably remain of comparatively limited practical relevance with regard to the future grant of such compulsory licences through the competent authorities or the courts.

However, on principle, the *relative* and concrete economic approach to the element of considerable economic significance, which has been proposed here instead of a more restrictive approach (interpreting the element as a limitation to

[38] Perfect 10, Inc. v. Amazon.com, Inc., et al., 508 F.3d 1146, 1155, 1165 (9th Cir. 2007): "search engine provides social benefit by incorporating an original work into a new work, namely, an electronic reference tool", thus making the use by the search engine "highly transformative".

[39] Cf. generally on the relationship between compulsory dependency licences and the economic rationale behind patent law Pohl (2000), p. 244, with further references.

certain cases of exceptional economic impact by absolute standards),[40] would certainly improve the indirect (psychological) ex ante effects of the instrument of compulsory dependency licences and would thus at least make the instrument gradually more effective in order to reach the goal of an efficient patent law framework, especially with regard to genetic and biotechnological inventions.[41]

4.2.2 Consequence for Copyright Law: Introduction of Compulsory Licence Provisions

The comparison of copyright and patent laws, *secondly*, highlights that while in patent law compulsory licences at least exist as a potential means to balance the interests of right holder and secondary user in cases of dependent inventions, the general copyright law approach to derivative works is characterised by a "black-and-white" picture of either a (more or less limited) exemption for free transformative use or an extension of the exclusive adaptation right of the copyright holder to such innovative uses.[42] A middle category, i.e. a copyright *internal* provision on possible compulsory licences for innovative uses, does not exist; instead (insofar as regards patent law[43]), only general competition law will provide for the possibility to grant compulsory licences under certain strict conditions when the right holder is in a dominant position and the denial to license is deemed abusive.

In fact, it might be argued that a compulsory licence provision in copyright law for certain dependent uses, in particular to enhance competition on derivative markets, would at least set indirect incentives for the copyright holders to force them into negotiations in dependency situations.[44] Compared to patent law, this is

[40] Cf., e.g., Rogge (2006), § 24, note 22: important technical advance of considerable economic significance even more restrictive than the general public interest. However, this overlooks the relative character of the new two-element test.

[41] Cf. Schieble (2005), pp. 179 et seq. (although sceptical as to whether such more flexible interpretation will prevail in future practice).

[42] Of course, a similar mechanism exists in patent law with regard to the scope of patents in cases of dependent inventions, where under certain circumstances *independent inventive activity* can be raised as an objection by the user of an equivalent solution to get out of the scope of the patent claims (at least under German law, see Federal Court of Justice (BGH) GRUR 1994, 597—Zerlegvorrichtung für Baumstämme (X ZR 16/93, 17.3.1994)). However, the instrument of compulsory licences exists in patent law on top of this balancing of interests with regard to the construction of the patent claims; a similar additional instrument does generally not exist in copyright law yet.

[43] General competition law applies with regard to abusive refusals to license by dominant undertakings notwithstanding the *additional* specific patent law provisions on compulsory licences; cf. further chapters "Compulsory Licensing in Germany" by Philipp Maume and "Refusal to Licence as an Abuse of Market Dominance—from Commercial Solvents to Microsoft" by Matthias Lamping, in this volume.

[44] Cf., as an example in a more general sense, the specific compulsory licences for cable retransmission in the German copyright act that gave rise to a recent judgment of the Federal Court of Justice. According to this judgment, the service providers of Online-VCRs may have a

particularly obvious for those categories of works that are of rather technical or applied character, such as scientific works, industrial designs, news articles, or computer programs and databases. The extremely limited practice with regard to compulsory licences in patent law is not necessarily an argument against the implementation of this instrument for such categories of works in copyright law. This is because the institutional framework, namely in Continental European and partly Asian copyright laws, with established collective rights management organisations, might provide for a more effective application (or at least indirect psychological effect) of instruments, such as compulsory or statutory licences in copyright law. Accordingly, for news articles, scientific works, industrial designs, computer programs, and databases, the recent academic proposal for a European Copyright Code by the WITTEM group[45] provides for a compulsory licence for uses of such works that are indispensable to compete on a derivative market if the right holder has refused to license the use on reasonable terms and the use does not unreasonably prejudice the legitimate interests of the right holder.[46]

5 Conclusion

To sum up, this chapter argues that Art. 31 (l) TRIPS should be interpreted in a relative and flexible manner. *Both* cumulative elements, i.e. the important technical advance and the considerable economic significance, should be assessed in concrete relation to the invention claimed in the first patent.

As for the element of important technical advance, this results in a comparative assessment of the inventive step involved in the second invention compared to the inventive step embodied in the first invention. In particular, no predominant or imminent public interest in the dependent use or improvement should be required. In fact, this would significantly lower the threshold of important technical advance in cases where the first patent involves only a small inventive step. This might be particularly helpful with regard to the dependency problem concerning genetic patents because typically the identification of a new function of a DNA sequence will have to be considered an important technical advance compared to the invention underlying the substance patent on the sequence as such.[47]

The element of considerable economic significance, if assessed in relation to the first patent, requires a concrete economic analysis of the potential gain through the

right to a compulsory licence with regard to the cable retransmission right of the broadcasting organisations; cf. Federal Court of Justice (BGH) ZUM-RD 2013, 314 (I ZR 151/11, 11.4.2013). This clearly shows the direct potential of compulsory licences to enable the opening of new markets in copyright law.

[45] See the Proposal for a European Copyright Code by the WITTEM Group (WITTEM Proposal for a European Copyright Code; available at http://www.copyrightcode.eu/).

[46] See Art. 5.4 (2) WITTEM Proposal for a European Copyright Code.

[47] Schieble (2005), p. 180.

use of the second patent compared to the potential harm through the limitation of the licence market or value of the first patent. Again, the yardstick should be a purely relative economic analysis of the concrete markets in question. No particularly important (absolute) economic significance should be required. This is because specifically in dependency situations, the mere economic interest of the holder of the first patent in an adequate share of the profits through the use of the second patent can be fully considered in the framework of setting the adequate remuneration according to Art. 31 (h) TRIPS.

References

Correa CM (2007) Trade related aspects of intellectual property rights: a commentary on the TRIPS agreement. Oxford University Press, Oxford

Correa CM, Yusuf A (eds) (1998) Intellectual property and international trade: the TRIPS agreement. Wolters Kluwer, London

Eikermann A (2009) In: Stoll P-T, Busche J, Arend K (eds) WTO – trade-related aspects of intellectual property rights. Martinus Nijhoff, Leiden

Hoehne F (2013) In: Busche J, Stoll P-T, Wiebe A (eds) TRIPS, Internationales und europäisches Recht des geistigen Eigentums – Kommentar. Carl Heymanns, Köln

Huys I, van Overwalle G, Matthijs G (2011) Gene and genetic diagnostic method patent claims: a comparison under current European and US Patent Law. Eur J Hum Genet 19:1104–1107

Huys I, Matthijs G, van Overwalle G (2012) The fate and future of patents on human genes and genetic diagnostic methods. Nat Rev Genet 13:441–448

Kern M (1996) Recent Federal Supreme Court decisions on experimental use and compulsory licensing. CASRIP Newsl 3(2). http://www.law.washington.edu/Casrip/Newsletter/default.aspx?year=1996&article=newsv3i2eu

Leitzen M, Kleinevoss T (2005) Renaissance der patentrechtlichen Zwangslizenz? – Die Neuregelung des § 24 Abs. 2 PatG. Mitteilungen der deutschen Patentanwälte 5:198–205

Pohl C (2000) Die Voraussetzungen der patentrechtlichen Zwangslizenz – Eine Untersuchung unter besonderer Berücksichtigung ihrer europarechtlichen Vorgaben, der Pariser Verbandsübereinkunft und des TRIPS-Abkommens. Peter Lang, Frankfurt a. M.

Rogge R (2006) In: Benkard G (ed) Patentgesetz. C.H. Beck, München

Schieble A-M (2005) Abhängige Genpatente und das Institut der Zwangslizenz. Nomos, Baden-Baden

Straus J (1996) Implications of the TRIPS Agreement in the field of patent law. In: Beier F-K, Schricker G (eds) From GATT to TRIPS – the agreement on trade-related aspects of intellectual property rights. VCH, Weinheim, pp 160–215

Straus J (1998) Abhängigkeit bei Patenten auf genetische Information – ein Sonderfall? GRUR 3/4:314–320

van Overwalle G (2010) Turning patent swords into shares. Science 330:1630–1631

van Zimmeren E, van Overwalle G (2011) A paper tiger? Compulsory license regimes for public health in Europe. Int Rev Intellect Prop Comp Law 1:4–40

Wegmann K (2013) Der Rechtsgedanke der freien Benutzung des § 24 UrhG und die verwandten Schutzrechte. Nomos, Baden-Baden

Wolff C (2005) Zwangslizenzen im Immaterialgüterrecht. V&R unipress, Göttingen

Compulsory Licences of Pharmaceutical Patents to Remedy Anti-Competitive Practices Under Article 31(k) of the TRIPS Agreement: Can Competition Law Facilitate Access to Essential Medicines?

Burton Ong

Contents

Abstract While the TRIPS Agreement has been amended, through the introduction of the Article 31*bis* system, to enable patented pharmaceuticals manufactured under a compulsory licence to be exported to patients in less-developed countries upon satisfaction of specific criteria, it is unclear whether this mechanism provides a satisfactory legal framework to enable sufficient life-saving drugs to reach those who are unable to pay the full prices charged by the major pharmaceutical companies in their home markets. This chapter examines the possibility of relying, as an alternative, on another exception within the TRIPS Agreement—the Article 31 (k) provision, which permits compulsory patent licences to be granted to remedy anti-competitive practices—to facilitate access to essential medicines by enabling

---

B. Ong is Associate Professor.

B. Ong
Faculty of Law, National University of Singapore, Singapore
e-mail: burton@nus.edu.sg

R.M. Hilty and K.-C. Liu (eds.), *Compulsory Licensing*, MPI Studies on Intellectual Property and Competition Law 22, DOI 10.1007/978-3-642-54704-1_13,

generic versions of patented drugs to be exported to, and imported by, less-developed countries without having to seek the prior consent of the relevant pharmaceutical patent proprietors. It is submitted that, in the hands of courageous and inventive competition authorities who are able to surmount various tricky political, jurisdictional, and doctrinal hurdles, competition law principles may be able provide the means of facilitating such an endeavour.

1 Introduction

Pharmaceutical patents confer upon their respective owners legal monopolies that enable them to control who may make, use, sell, offer for sale, or import these patented medicines. This puts pharmaceutical patent owners in extremely influential positions that enable them to determine which markets are supplied with these patented medicines, in what quantities, and, subject to the operation of other regulatory mechanisms, at what price levels they deem appropriate. However, the exclusive rights granted to patent holders under national patent laws are qualified by provisos drawn from the World Trade Organization's (WTO) Trade Related Aspects of Intellectual Property (TRIPS) Agreement that make compulsory licences of patents available to the government or third parties in specifically defined circumstances. These include situations of "national emergency or other circumstances of extreme urgency or in cases of public non-commercial use", as provided for in Article 31(b) of the TRIPS Agreement, which could apply to a public health crisis where generic drug manufacturers are authorised to supply low-cost generic versions of patent-protected medicines necessary to treat life-threatening diseases and illnesses. While this proviso allows for use of the patented subject matter without the authorisation of the patent holder, it is also subject to an additional constraint imposed by Article 31(f) of the TRIPS Agreement—that "any such use shall be authorised predominantly for the supply of the domestic market of the Member authorising such use". This means that an Article 31(b) compulsory licence that authorises a generic drug manufacturer to make, sell, and offer to sell generic versions of the patented medicine is circumscribed in its geographical scope. Such a compulsory licence can lawfully authorise patented medicines to be made for, and sold to, domestic consumers predominantly. Exports of these generic drugs in significant quantities, produced in such dire situations by generic drug manufacturers under a compulsory licence issued on Article 31(b) grounds, to patients in other jurisdictions would exceed the terms of such a compulsory licence and could attract liability for patent infringement.

This impediment to the flow of potentially life-saving drugs to people located in Member states, particularly in the world's least developed countries, with insufficient or no pharmaceutical manufacturing capacity to produce the medicines needed to address their own public health problems, prompted the international community to agree to amend the TRIPS Agreement.[1] A Protocol amending the TRIPS Agreement, issued by the General Council at the WTO on 6th December 2005, introduced a specific mechanism in the new Article 31*bis* for Member states to allow patented medicines manufactured under a compulsory licence to be exported to countries faced with such public health issues. This amendment essentially sets out the circumstances in which the preexisting obligation found in Article 31(f) of the TRIPS Agreement should be waived such that patented pharmaceuticals made under a compulsory licence in one Member state might be lawfully exported to another that does not have the requisite drug-manufacturing technologies to satisfy its own domestic public health needs. Despite the good intentions behind this amendment, experience has shown that the Article 31*bis* waiver mechanism has only been utilised once in practice,[2] and it has been criticised for the administrative burdens it places on exporting Member states that might want to use the system to produce pharmaceutical products for export to eligible importing Member states.[3]

It has been argued that Member states ought to consider exploring *other* legislative mechanisms as alternatives to the Article 31*bis* system[4] to facilitate the exportation of patented pharmaceuticals made under a compulsory licence—alternatives that they are clearly permitted to pursue under the preexisting flexibilities of the TRIPS Agreement and explicitly reaffirmed by the General Council. In particular, attention has been focused on Article 31(k) of the TRIPS Agreement, which envisages Member states being free to allow their courts and tribunals to grant compulsory patent licences "to remedy a practice determined after judicial or administrative process to be anti-competitive", as a possible legal route to enable generic drugs made in one country to be shipped to afflicted patients in another jurisdiction. One of the core legal issues lies in the scope of the concept of an "anti-competitive practice" that is used in this part of the TRIPS Agreement—to what extent should it be interpreted consistently with conventional and contemporary competition law jurisprudence, and should this criterion be given exactly the same meaning in the context of the patent law framework as the phrase is understood in competition or antitrust law circles? Or is there room to adopt a more

[1] For a comprehensive account of the series of events directly connected to the efforts to amend the TRIPS Agreement to facilitate the export of patented pharmaceuticals produced under a compulsory licence (starting from the Doha Declaration on the TRIPS Agreement and Public Health 2001 and spanning the TRIPS Council Decision of 30 August 2003 implementing paragraph 6 of the Doha Declaration and the 2005 General Council Decision on the Article 31*bis* amendment of the TRIPS Agreement), see Gervais (2012), at pp. 54–75.

[2] The "Paragraph 6" waiver mechanism for the export of patented pharmaceuticals made under a compulsory licence, which requires both importing and exporting countries to formally notify the WTO of their intentions, has only been utilised by Rwanda (importing country) and Canada (exporting country) in a transaction notified on 30 August 2003. See http://www.wto.org/english/tratop_e/trips_e/public_health_e.htm and n 26 below.

[3] See Sect. 4 of this chapter below.

[4] See Ng-Loy (2009), p. 162.

flexible definition of what constitutes an "anti-competitive practice", incorporating a wider range of public policy considerations that are not typically employed in conventional modes of competition law analysis?

In this chapter, I propose to examine the viability of using Article 31(k) of the TRIPS Agreement as part of an alternative mechanism to facilitate the exportation of compulsorily licensed patented pharmaceuticals to alleviate the public health problems facing those Member states that were the intended beneficiaries of the 2005 Protocol Amending the TRIPS Agreement. I start by looking briefly at the compulsory licensing framework for patents under Article 31 of the TRIPS Agreement, followed by an explanation of the mechanics behind the Article 31*bis* amendment and its deficiencies. This will be followed by an assessment of the contrasting views expressed by legal scholars on the feasibility of relying on a compulsory licence granted under the auspices of Article 31(k) as a substitute for the approach set out in Article 31*bis*. The discussion below will then analyse how conventional and contemporary competition law principles might be applied to a typical hypothetical scenario involving generic drug manufacturers operating in one country trying to export their life-saving medicines, made under a compulsory patent licence, to patients located in another country with no pharmaceutical sector or drug-manufacturing capacity of its own.

2 Compulsory Patent Licences Under Article 31 of the TRIPS Agreement

National patent laws of WTO Member states are required to comply with the minimum standards of protection articulated in Articles 27–34 of the TRIPS Agreement. Article 28, for example, requires Member states to confer on patent owners the exclusive right to prevent unauthorised persons from "making, using, offering for sale, selling, or importing for these purposes" a patented product.[5] Among these provisions are restrictions on the freedom of Member states to include exceptions to the exclusive rights enjoyed by patent holders within their domestic patent law frameworks.[6] Furthermore, Article 31 sets out a series of conditions that Member states must satisfy before their national patent laws may allow for governmental or third party use of the subject matter of a patent without the

[5] See Article 28(1)(a) of the TRIPS Agreement. Article 28(1)(b) covers patented processes and requires owners of such patents to enjoy the right to prevent unauthorised third parties from "using the process" and from acts of "using, offering for sale, selling or importing for these purposes at least the product obtained directly by that process".

[6] The most notable of which is Article 30 of the TRIPS Agreement, which only allows Member states to "provide limited exceptions to the exclusive rights conferred by a patent, provided that such exceptions do not unreasonably conflict with a normal exploitation of the patent and do not unreasonably prejudice the legitimate interests of the patent owner, taking account of the legitimate interests of third parties".

authorisation of the right holder. In other words, these criteria essentially demarcate the limits for when a compulsory licence can be issued under national patent laws to deal with patented subject matter protected under such laws. These provisions give Member states some leeway in crafting legislative exceptions, defences, and provisos in their national patent laws to further various larger public policy goals and national interests, such as protecting public health and furthering other humanitarian objectives.

Under Article 31(b), a Member state may allow for the compulsory licensing of patented subject matter only if the proposing user "has made efforts to obtain authorisation from the right holder on reasonable commercial terms and conditions and that such efforts have not been successful within a reasonable period of time", though this requirement may be waived "in the case of a national emergency or other circumstances of extreme urgency or in cases of public non-commercial use". In a public health crisis when access to a patented medicine is necessary to save lives or to contain an epidemic, it is not difficult to envisage a Member state relying on Article 31(b) as a basis for justifying the grant of a compulsory licence to generic drug manufacturers to make and sell patent-protected medicines without the patent holder's authorisation.

However, Article 31(b) is subject to a significant qualifier in Article 31(f), which requires that "any such use shall be authorised predominantly for the supply of the domestic market of the Member authorising such use". This means that any compulsory licence to make and sell a patented pharmaceutical that is granted under a Member state's patent regime must be primarily limited to meeting the needs of its domestic market and that the medicines made under such a licence cannot be exported predominantly to patients abroad. Making such excessive exports of patented pharmaceuticals made under a compulsory licence would exceed the scope of the authorisation given to the licensee and would entitle the patent owner to seek injunctive relief. As such, this flexibility is only of practical value to Member states that have their own domestic pharmaceutical production capacity and access to the relevant technology necessary to manufacture the patent-protected medicines they require.[7] The least developed countries, on the other hand, would lack the means to domestically produce generic versions of the patented medicines they needed even if compulsory patent licences to manufacture such drugs could be granted under their respective national patent laws.

In contrast, Article 31(k) of the TRIPS Agreement offers an additional flexibility to Member states by allowing them to permit compulsory licences under their national laws on completely different grounds—"to correct anti-competitive practices"—that are not subject to the constraints identified above.[8] This limb of

---

[7] This was one of the principal reasons for setting up the import-and-export mechanism for patented pharmaceuticals via Article 31*bis* of the TRIPS Agreement. See n 15 and 16 below and accompanying text.

[8] Article 31(k) provides that "(m)embers are not obliged to apply the conditions set forth in subparagraphs (b) and (f) where such use is permitted to remedy a practice determined after judicial or administrative process to be anti-competitive...".

Article 31 allows Member states to use competition law principles as a basis for granting a compulsory licence to a third party, where the conduct of the patent holder has been held by a domestic court or tribunal, such as a national competition authority or regulator, to be anti-competitive in character. What is not clear is the exact breadth of this provision and, in particular, whether it is possible to grant a compulsory licence on these grounds as a means for facilitating the manufacture and export of patent-protected medicines, free from the geographical constraints imposed by Article 31(f), to meet the health care needs of those in the least developed countries and other Member states that lack the technological infrastructure to avail themselves of other compulsory-licence-related flexibilities found elsewhere in Article 31 of the TRIPS Agreement.

National patent laws that have implemented Article 31(k) of the TRIPS Agreement differ in the degree of legislative specificity used to describe the type of conduct by the patent holder that would qualify as an eligible "anti-competitive" practice. In Singapore, for example, the relevant provisions of the Singapore patent statute provide that "any interested person may apply to the court for the grant of a licence under a patent on the ground that the grant of the licence is necessary to remedy an anti-competitive practice" and that, "without prejudice to the generality" of this section, the court may determine that the grant of a licence is necessary to remedy an anti-competitive practice if there is a market for the patented invention in Singapore that is "not being supplied" or "not being supplied on reasonable terms" without valid reason.[9] This provision has never been litigated before the courts, but it appears, from a literal reading of the statute, that the Singapore courts have considerable discretion as to how they might interpret and apply this provision.

In other jurisdictions, the national patent statute might set out instances of "anti-competitive" conduct by the patent holder in greater detail that would trigger the availability of a compulsory licence on Article 31(k) grounds. In Argentina, the national patent statute provides that the following forms of conduct shall be considered "anti-competitive practices"[10]:

(a) comparatively excessive pricing, compared to the average market or being discriminatory of patented products, in particular when there are offers of supplying the market at prices significantly lower than those offered by the patentee for the same product;
(b) refusal to supply the local market on reasonable commercial terms;
(c) interference with commercial or production activities;
(d) any other act that enters into the behaviours considered punishable by Law No. 22.262 or its replacement or substitute.

[9] *Patents Act 1994*, sections 55(1) and 55(2).

[10] See Article 44 of the Patent and Utility Models Law No. 24.481, amended by Law No, 24.572 (T. O. 1996) (translated from Spanish).

This aspect of Argentinean patent law was the subject of a WTO trade dispute initiated by the United States, which wanted to clarify that a prior determination of anti-competitive conduct by the national competition authority was required before a compulsory licence could be issued. Both countries eventually reached a mutually agreed solution confirming that if any of the above practices were found to exist, "such a finding will not in and of itself warrant an automatic determination that a patent owner is engaging in an 'anti-competitive' practice" and that "in order to justify the granting of a compulsory licence ... a prior decision must have been handed down by the National Commission on the Defense of Competition" after analysing the practice using Law No. 25.156 (Law of Defense of Competition), which requires "the existence of an abuse of a dominant position in the market ... in order for a practice to be considered 'anti-competitive'".[11] By interpreting its patent statute in this way, Argentina has declared that compulsory licences issued on Article 31(k) grounds can only be issued if its national competition authority has established that the patent holder has committed an infringement of Argentina's competition laws prohibiting conduct that amounts to an abuse of a dominant position.

3 The Doha Declaration on the TRIPS Agreement and Public Health and the Article 31*bis* Protocol

Following the Doha Ministerial Conference in 2001, Member states of the WTO issued a Declaration on the TRIPS Agreement and Public Health (the Doha Public Health Declaration),[12] which recognised "the gravity of the public health problems afflicting many developing and least-developed countries, especially those resulting from HIV/AIDS, tuberculosis, malaria and other epidemics", and affirmed that the TRIPS Agreement "can and should be interpreted and implemented in a manner supportive of WTO Members' right to protect public health and, in particular, to promote access to medicines for all".[13] The Doha Public Health Declaration reaffirmed "the right of WTO Members to use, to the full, the provisions in the TRIPS Agreement, which provide flexibility for this purpose" and made specific reference to the following flexibilities:

> (b) Each Member has the right to grant compulsory licences and the freedom to determine the grounds upon which such licences are granted.
> (c) Each Member has the right to determine what constitutes a national emergency or other circumstances of extreme urgency, it being understood that public health crises,

---

[11] *Argentina—Patent Protection for Pharmaceuticals and Test Data Protection for Agricultural Chemicals* (WT/DS171). WTO Documents WT/DS171/3, WT/DS196/4, IP/D/18/Add.1, IP/D/22/Add.1 (20 June 2012).

[12] WT/MIN(01)/DEC2, Adopted by the WTO on 14 November 2001.

[13] At paragraphs 1 and 4 of the Doha Public Health Declaration.

> including those relating to HIV/AIDS, tuberculosis, malaria and other epidemics, can represent a national emergency or other circumstances of extreme urgency.[14]

However, it was reported that some governments at the Doha Ministerial Conference were unsure of how these flexibilities would be interpreted and how far their right to use them would be respected. They called for further clarification, and this resulted in paragraph 6 of the Doha Public Health Declaration, which "assigned further work to the TRIPS Council – to sort out how to provide extra flexibility, so that countries unable to produce pharmaceuticals domestically can import patented drugs made under compulsory licensing".[15] Paragraph 6 of the Doha Public Health Declaration contained the following exhortation:

> We recognize that WTO Members with insufficient or no manufacturing capacities in the pharmaceutical sector could face difficulties in making effective use of compulsory licensing under the TRIPS Agreement. We instruct the Council for TRIPS to find an expeditious solution to this problem and to report to the General Council before end of 2002.[16]

In 2003, the General Council agreed upon a system to facilitate the export of patented pharmaceuticals made under a compulsory licence to importing countries facing health crises by setting out criteria for when the export restriction set out in Article 31(f) of the TRIPS Agreement could be justifiably waived.[17] This system was eventually translated into an amendment of the TRIPS Agreement via a Protocol that introduced Article 31*bis*, which provides that "(t)he obligations of an exporting Member under Article 31(f) shall not apply with respect to the grant by it of a compulsory licence to the extent necessary for the purposes of production of a pharmaceutical product(s) and its export to an eligible importing Member(s) in accordance with the terms set out in . . . the Annex to this Agreement".[18]

Under the Article 31*bis* system, an eligible importing Member[19] must notify the TRIPS Council of the specific names and expected quantities of the patented

[14] At paragraph 5 of the Doha Public Health Declaration.

[15] 'Decision removes final patent obstacle to cheap drug imports', WTO Press Release on 30 August 2003, Press/350/Rev.1, which announced the decision reached by the TRIPS Council following a 2-year deadlock between WTO member governments on how to implement the instructions of the 2001 WTO Ministerial Declaration.

[16] See n 12 above.

[17] 'Implementation of paragraph 6 of the Doha Declaration on the TRIPS Agreement and public health', WT/L/540 and Corr.1, Decision of the General Council of 30 August 2003.

[18] 'Amendment of the TRIPS Agreement', WT/L/641, Decision of the General Council of 6 December 2005, Article 31*bis* (1).

[19] Paragraph 1(b) of the Annex to the TRIPS Agreement defines "eligible importing Member" to mean any least developed country Member or any Member state that has notified the TRIPS Council of its intention to use the Article 31*bis* system. The developed countries have voluntarily declared that they will not use the system as an importing country, while other countries—namely Hong Kong China, Israel, Korea, Kuwait, Macao China, Mexico, Qatar, Singapore, Chinese Taipei, Turkey, and the United Arab Emirates—have announced that they will only use the system in situations of national emergency or other circumstances of extreme urgency. See WTO Press Release, Press/350/Rev.1, n 15 above.

pharmaceutical product(s) needed and confirm with the TRIPS Council that it satisfies the requisite qualifying criteria[20] and that, where the pharmaceutical product is patented in its territory, it has granted or intends to grant a compulsory licence in accordance with Article 31 and 31*bis* of the TRIPS Agreement.[21] Exporting Member states that use this system to issue a compulsory licence for the manufacture of patented pharmaceuticals for foreign patients can only do so if the licence issued contains the following conditions:

> (i) only the amount necessary to meet the needs of the eligible importing Member(s) may be manufactured under the licence and the entirety of this production shall be exported to the Member(s) which has notified its needs to the Council for TRIPS;
> (ii) products produced under the licence shall be clearly identified as being produced under the system through specific labelling or marking. Suppliers should distinguish such products through special packaging and/or special colouring/shaping of the products themselves, provided that such distinction is feasible and does not have a significant impact on price; and
> (iii) before shipment begins, the licensee shall post on a website the following information:
> – the quantities being supplied to each destination as referred to in indent (i) above; and
> – the distinguishing features of the product(s) referred to in indent (ii) above.[22]

Furthermore, the exporting Member is required to notify the TRIPS Council of the grant of such a compulsory licence under this system and the conditions attached to the licence.[23] Other noteworthy features of the Article 31*bis* system include the imposition of an obligation on importing Members to "take reasonable measures within their means, proportionate to their administrative capacities . . . to prevent re-exportation of the products that have actually been imported into their territories under the system",[24] as well as an obligation on all Member states to "ensure the availability of effective legal means to prevent the importation into, and sale in, their territories of products produced under the system and diverted to their markets inconsistently with its provisions".[25]

The Article 31*bis* system thus provides Member states with a framework for introducing an additional TRIPS-compliant exception to their national patent law regimes that have been specifically designed to overcome the application of the export restriction in Article 31(f) to patented pharmaceuticals made under a

---

[20] In the Appendix to the Annex to the TRIPS Agreement, Member states can only use the Article 31*bis* system if they lack the necessary manufacturing capacities in the pharmaceutical sector. If they are least developed country Members, they are deemed to have insufficient or no manufacturing capacities in the pharmaceutical sector. Otherwise, it must be established that the importing Member state has no manufacturing capacity or insufficient capacity for the purposes of meeting its own needs.

[21] Subparagraphs 2(a)(i), (ii) and (iii) of the Annex to the TRIPS Agreement.

[22] Subparagraphs 2(b)(i), (ii) and (iii) of the Annex to the TRIPS Agreement.

[23] Subparagraph 2(c) of the Annex to the TRIPS Agreement, which also requires disclosure of information relating to the identity of the licensee, the products for which the licence has been granted, the quantity for which it has been granted, and the country where they will be exported to, as well as the duration of the licence.

[24] Paragraph 3 of the Annex to the TRIPS Agreement.

[25] Paragraph 4 of the Annex to the TRIPS Agreement.

compulsory licence. What about the preexisting flexibilities available elsewhere in the TRIPS Agreement? One might infer from the TRIPS Council's implementation of paragraph 6 of the Doha Public Health Declaration via a tailored amendment to the TRIPS Agreement, in the form of the Article 31*bis* system, that *rather* than providing Member states with more detailed guidance about how to use the preexisting flexibilities to create exceptions to the patent rights of pharmaceutical patent holders, the new system was regarded as a *necessary* amendment to the TRIPS Agreement. One could take the view that the preexisting flexibilities found in the TRIPS Agreement may have been construed as inadequate and not capable of being deployed effectively to facilitate access to patented medicines needed by Member states facing public health crises. However, it would seem that in developing the Article 31*bis* system, the TRIPS Council did not consider the new system it was proposing to be the *only* possible solution to the public health problems faced by Member states. The liberty of Member states to pursue *other* TRIPS-compliant options was clearly preserved. Article 31*bis* (5) of the Protocol amending the TRIPS Agreement explicitly recognises that the preexisting flexibilities could still potentially be used by Member states to achieve the public health goals identified in the Doha Public Health Declaration:

> This Article and the Annex to this Agreement are without prejudice to the rights, obligations and flexibilities that Members have under the provisions of this Agreement other than paragraphs (f) and (h) of Article 31, including those reaffirmed by the Declaration on the TRIPS Agreement and Public Health . . . It is also without prejudice to the extent to which pharmaceutical products produced under a compulsory licence can be exported under the provisions of Article 31(f).

4 Criticism of the Article 31*bis* System and Alternative Legal Mechanisms to Facilitate Access to Essential Medicines

The export restriction waiver system housed within the Article 31*bis* provisions was clearly the product of a political compromise between WTO Member countries and the various interest groups and stakeholders they represented during the meetings of the TRIPS Council. It is thus unsurprising that there are imperfections in the system that has only been used once since the waiver system was announced by the TRIPS Council in 2003.[26] The fact that the international community is less than

[26] Rwanda is the only country to have used the export restriction waiver system as an importing Member state, in 2007, to gain access to generic anti-retroviral drugs (a triple combination AIDS therapy drug, TriAvir) produced and exported by Apotex under a corresponding compulsory licence granted in Canada. See Rwanda, Notification Under Paragraph 2(a) of the Decision of 30 August 2003 on the Implementation of Paragraph 6 of the Doha Declaration on the TRIPS Agreement and Public Health, IP/N/9/RWA/1, 19 July 2007 and Canada, Notification Under Paragraph 2(a) of the Decision of 30 August 2003 on the Implementation of Paragraph 6 of the Doha Declaration on the TRIPS Agreement and Public Health, IP/N/10/CAN/1, 8 November 2007.

enthusiastic about this mechanism is reflected by the fact that this mechanism, approved by WTO Member countries on 6 December 2005, has yet to be formally accepted by two-thirds of these Member countries, whose governments must submit official instruments of acceptance before this amendment to the TRIPS Agreement can actually take effect.[27] While it is not the purpose of this chapter to evaluate all the deficiencies of the Article 31*bis* mechanism, some of the more significant criticisms that have been made about the system are worth highlighting before examining the viability of developing alternative legal mechanisms that could also be used to facilitate access to essential medicines.

For instance, legal commentators have described the waiver system as an "administratively complex regime" that has been loaded up with "bureaucratic requirements", though they may ultimately believe "there is not much room in the present global political environment for negotiating a different deal" and that the Article 31*bis* system "can play a positive role from the standpoint of public health, even if it is not the optimal solution from the perspective of any interested stakeholder".[28] Chief among the obstacles to the effective use of the system are the fears that eligible importing countries might harbor about making general notifications to the WTO of their intent to make use of the system. This is a political barrier that diminishes the attractiveness of the system because potential importing Members might believe that they might draw hostile reactions from patent-holding industries that could direct their foreign direct investments elsewhere.

Another practical obstacle lies in the requirement that manufacturers of compulsorily licensed generic versions of patented drugs seeking to export their products to importing Members under the system are only allowed to produce on a "drug-by-drug, country-by-country and case-by-case" basis, making it difficult for these exporters to make long-term supply capacity planning decisions due to the uncertainties relating to the size of foreign markets.[29] Exporting Member states that use this system are required to impose limits to the scope of the compulsory licence granted to generic drug manufacturers who can only produce a quantity of medicines that meet the needs of the specific eligible importing Member and must ensure that the entirety of this production is exported to the importing Member.[30]

In light of these criticisms, legal commentators have canvased the possibility of using alternative TRIPS-compliant legal frameworks to achieve the same goals

[27] As of 5 November 2012, only 45 countries have submitted these instruments of acceptance, far short of the 102 formal acceptances (out of 153 members) required. WTO Member countries appear to have dragged their feet in this matter, even though these amendments proposed in 2005 simply codified the "waiver" system adopted by the TRIPS Council in 2003, which, in turn, emerged from paragraph 6 of the Doha Public Health Declaration in 2001. The General Council had originally contemplated a deadline of 1 December 2007 for the Article 31*bis* amendments to formally take effect, but this deadline has since been shifted thrice to 31 December 2009, 31 December 2011, and 31 December 2013.

[28] Abbott and Reichman (2007), pp. 921, 933 and 936–938.

[29] Medecins Sans Frontieres (2006).

[30] See paragraph 2(b)(i) of the Annex, n 22 above and accompanying text.

without resorting to the administratively cumbersome legal machinery created by the Article 31*bis* system. These include the possibility of a *sui generis* exception allowing for the export of generic versions of essential medicines established within a framework permitted by Article 30 of the TRIPS Agreement,[31] an option that was specifically raised by developing counties as a possibly straightforward and expeditious solution during the negotiations that preceded the Doha Public Health Declaration.[32] The other option highlighted by legal commentators is the use of compulsory licensing under the domestic competition laws of importing and exporting countries,[33] as explicitly permitted under Article 31(k) of the TRIPS Agreement, to circumvent the constraints imposed by Articles 31(b) and 31(f).

Using the flexibility found in Article 31(k), which is premised on the application of national competition laws to remedy anti-competitive practices, to facilitate the import and export of essential medicines to least developed countries facing shortages of affordably priced medicines has both advantages and disadvantages. It requires a judicial or administrative process to determine that the patent holder has engaged in anti-competitive conduct, which could take a significant amount of time in some legal systems. However, taking this route frees the Member state from the requirement of attempting to obtain prior authorisation from the right holder on reasonable commercial terms and conditions, as provided for in Article 31(b), or from having to pay "adequate remuneration" for the compulsory licence, as required under Articles 31(h) and 31*bis* (2). Article 31(k) provides that "[t]he need to correct anticompetitive practices may be taken into account in determining the amount of remuneration in such cases"—a language that suggests that the remuneration rates payable, if payable at all, to the patent holder might be reduced to reflect the unlawful character of its anti-competitive conduct that might even attract fines or penalties imposed by the national competition authority over and above the issuance of a compulsory licence.

4.1 Competition Law as a Basis for Issuing Compulsory Licences to Manufacture and Export Patented Pharmaceuticals Under Article 31(k)

Competition policies are explicitly identified within the provisions of the TRIPS Agreement as valid counterweights to the rights of intellectual property holders, including patent holders, with Member states empowered to take "appropriate

[31] See n 6 above. The possibility of devising an exception to exclusive rights of the patent holder under the national laws of an exporting country that is consistent with Article 30 of the TRIPS Agreement is an alternative that is strongly endorsed by Abbott and Reichman (2007), at pp. 957–958. See also Matthews (2004), pp. 73, 89.

[32] Abbott and Reichman (2007), at p. 935.

[33] See Cottier (2007), p. 173.

measures, provided that they are consistent with the provisions of this Agreement ... to prevent the abuse of intellectual property rights by right holders or the resort to practices which unreasonably restrain trade".[34] However, the national competition laws of Member states have not been harmonised in the same way as their domestic intellectual property regimes have converged upon the standards enshrined within the TRIPS Agreement. There is significant room for diversity between the competition laws and policies adopted by the different Member states, with developed countries having considerably more sophisticated competition law regimes compared to the least developed countries, which might not even have such laws in place as yet. While Article 31(k) acknowledges that compulsory licences may be issued by Member states under their national competition law regimes without being constrained by Article 31(f), it is silent on the substantive legal principles that ought to be used by each Member state to determine the availability of a compulsory licence that overrides the rights of a patent holder. Academic commentators have reached varying conclusions about the feasibility of relying on flexibility found within Article 31(k) of the TRIPS Agreement to facilitate the movement of patented medicines via compulsory licensing to address the public health crises facing developing and the least developed countries. Two different approaches towards the potential of competition law as a basis for issuing such compulsory licences will be examined and contrasted below, with the views of their respective proponents illustrated within the context of the following hypothetical scenario[35]:

(a) Pharma A is the patent holder for a drug that is protected in developed and developing countries but not in Country B, one of the least developed countries in the world. The patented drug is new and highly efficient in treating a particular disease that threatens public health in Country B, which lacks the necessary technology or manufacturing technology to produce the patented drug for the benefit of its citizens. There are no effective substitutes for this drug.
(b) Country B is unsuccessful in its attempts to negotiate with Pharma A to supply sufficient quantities of the drug to Country B at an affordable price. Pharma A is concerned that lowering its prices to the level requested by Country B would adversely affect the profitability of its drug sales in other countries. Parallel imports of the drug are not available in the quantities required by Country B, and whatever drugs that are available through parallel trade are still too expensive for the average pandemic victim in Country B. Moreover, Pharma

[34] Article 8(2) of the TRIPS Agreement. These competition-policy-related concerns, which Member states are entitled to act upon, are elaborated upon in Section 8 of the Agreement ('Control of Anti-Competitive Practices in Contractual Licences'), where examples of "licensing practices or conditions that may in particular constitute an abuse of intellectual property rights having an adverse effect on competition in the relevant market" are identified in Article 40(2).

[35] This hypothetical scenario is a modified and condensed version of the fact pattern set out by Cottier (2007), at p. 188.

A strictly controls the quantities of the drug it supplies to its wholesalers and distributors and places comprehensive contractual restrictions on their freedom to sell these drugs outside of specifically defined territories.

(c) Country C protects this drug under its patent regime, which also allows for compulsory licences to be issued against the patent holder in line with the parameters set out in the TRIPS Agreement. Generics C is a manufacturer of generic versions of drugs in Country C and produces this patented drug under a compulsory licence for its home market but is prevented, under the terms of the licence that implement the restraints articulated in Article 31(f) of the TRIPS Agreement, from exporting substantial quantities of the drug to meet the health care needs of Country B.

(d) Generics C is unable to negotiate a voluntary export licence between itself and Pharma A for the purposes of supplying Country B because of Pharma A's concerns about increasing the available supply of low-priced generic versions of the drug in Country B that may be re-exported to its other markets in developed countries. The legal question is whether a case can be made for the invocation of domestic competition law principles in Country C as a basis for issuing a compulsory licence to Generics C, as allowed under Article 31(k) of the TRIPS Agreement, which could permit the licensee to export the generic version of the drug to Country B. Would Pharma A's conduct in (i) refusing to supply or significantly restricting the supply of the drug to Country B and (ii) refusing to grant a voluntary licence to its competitor in Country C that allows Generics C to export generic versions of the drug to Country B amount to an anti-competitive practice that could justify a compulsory licence remedy from the courts or competition authority in Country C?

In the hypothetical situation above, getting the generic medicines manufactured by Generics C to patients in Country B would also require the importers in Country B to be lawfully permitted to import such patented products into the country. If the patented drug is not protected in Country B, then no such legal impediment exists. On the other hand, if Pharma A has secured patent protection for the drug in Country B, then importers in Country B may have to obtain a compulsory licence to import the drugs from Generics C via either the domestic patent law framework[36] or competition law regime.[37]

---

[36] Such a compulsory licence could be issued under the national patent framework of Country B, by either its courts or national patent authority, on grounds such as to address a "national emergency or other circumstances of extreme urgency" and would be "predominantly for the supply of the domestic market of the Member authorising such use".

[37] Both Country B and Country C need to issue compulsory licences (to respectively import and export the patented drug) under their respective domestic competition law regimes. National competition authorities will have to first establish a competition law infringement—most likely an abuse of a dominant position by the patent holder—before deciding if a compulsory licence is an appropriate antitrust remedy. Some have taken THE view, which will be elaborated upon below... if a compulsory licence is issued from within the patent regime ON Article 31(k) grounds,

4.1.1 The Doha Waiver Solution and Article 31*bis* System as a Necessary Substitute for Underdeveloped Domestic Competition Policies

While acknowledging that this is a relatively unsettled area of the law, Cottier has argued that it would be difficult to obtain a compulsory licence against the wishes of a patent holder under European Community competition law principles because "innovation and added value is an important requisite for the justification of expropriating intellectual property rights against the will of the right holder".[38] The handful of cases involving attempts to acquire compulsory licences from intellectual property owners alleged to have abused their dominant positions in violation of Article 82 EC of the Treaty of Rome has shared this common theme: the party seeking the compulsory licence must show that the intellectual-property-owning dominant undertaking's refusal to grant him a licence has prevented a new product from emerging in the market.[39] In the context of patented medicines, any drugs produced by generic manufacturers under a compulsory licence from the patent holder would not satisfy this requirement. In Cottier's analysis, competition policy in Europe "aims at fostering innovation, rather than distribution, in line with strategies to provide incentives in competition law and policy for creativity".[40] As such, if these competition law policies were applied in Country C, a patent holder that refuses to license his patent to a competitor for strategic or commercial reasons would not, without anything more, be regarded as having engaged in anti-competitive conduct that could provide a basis for the grant of a compulsory licence in Country C that would enable Generics C to manufacture and export the patented drug to Country B.

This analysis of the position taken within the European competition law framework is consistent with the conspicuous reluctance of the European courts to embrace a general principle along the lines of the American "essential facilities" doctrine,[41] which has been given a lukewarm reception by the US Supreme Court

---

then the organ of state granting that licence must be satisfied that the patent holder has engaged in a conduct that would have equally attracted liability under the competition law regime.

[38] Cottier (2007), at p. 190.

[39] Joined Cases C-241/91P and C-242/91P, *RTE and ITP v Commission* (*Magill*) [1995] ECR I-743; Case C-7/97, *Oscar Bronner v Mediaprint* [1998] ECR I-7791; Case C418/01, *IMS Health v NDC* [2004] ECR I-5039; Case T-201/04, Microsoft v Commission [2007] ECR II-000.

[40] Cottier (2007), at p. 191, citing Ullrich (2005), pp. 726–757.

[41] The phrase "essential facilities" has only been explicitly used by the European Commission to justify its decisions in a line of infrastructure-related cases starting from *Sealink/B&I Holyhead: Interim Measures* [1992] 5 CMLR 255, [41]. In Case C-7/97, *Oscar Bronner v Mediaprint* [1998] ECR I-7791, Advocate General Jacobs, at [65–66], opined the need to strictly confine the limits of the concept of essential facilities, while the ECJ, despite agreeing with the position set out by AG Jacobs, carefully avoided using the term "essential facilities" in its judgment.

itself,[42] suggesting that a dominant firm's mere refusal to supply (or, in the hypothetical scenario above, to license its intellectual property to) its competitor will not be regarded as an abuse of dominance within the scope of European competition law principles. US antitrust law is similarly regarded as having a relatively limited role as a counterweight against increasingly expansive intellectual property protection.[43] Cottier thus concludes that, as far as the US and EC competition law principles are concerned, "it is fair to say that the refusal to market a technology for strategic or commercial reasons does not per se amount to uncompetitive conduct, as much as the refusal to share technology or a facility with a competitor per se amounts to an abuse of a dominant position" and that "[i]n applying predominant concepts of anti-competitive conduct, domestic courts are unlikely to find conditions of Article 31(k) fulfilled which, in return, would allow generic producers located in industrialized countries to step into the market in need".[44]

As such, if Country C were an industrialised country whose competition law regime applied these competition law principles highlighted above, then the pursuit of a compulsory licence against Pharma A (to allow Generics C to export generic versions of the patented drug to Country B) on competition law grounds—to "remedy a practice determined after judicial or administrative practice to be anti-competitive"—would not be a real option. However, Country C's competition law regime may not adopt Euro-American competition law principles because of its different socio-economic and developmental priorities. With no international consensus as to what substantive standards or legal principles ought to be applied by the many different countries that have their own competition law and policy frameworks, commentators like Drexl have pointed out that there is room for divergence between states at different stages of economic development in the way their respective competition laws are interpreted and applied, particularly when this branch of the law is used in juxtaposition with intellectual property laws to further their respective national public welfare goals.[45] Cottier thus suggests that Country C could, at least in theory, "adopt rules which treat denial of a voluntary license for the purpose of exportation to Country B [as] a case of anti-competitive conduct, if Pharma A refuses to provide essential drugs to Country B at reasonable costs at the very same time ... [on the basis that] such conduct amounts to an abuse of a dominant position of Pharma A with negative effects in countries B and C alike".[46]

---

[42] See *Verizon Communications Inc v Trinko LLP* 124 S.Ct 872 (2004), 880–881, where the US Supreme Court described the essential facilities doctrine as something "crafted by some lower courts", with the court finding "no need to either recognize it or to repudiate it" in this case.

[43] Fox (2005), at pp. 758–769.

[44] Cottier (2007), at p. 192.

[45] Drexl (2005), at pp. 702–725. Competition law is not limited to producer interests and efficiency goals. It equally and foremost protects consumer interests and has to serve the public at large.

[46] Cottier (2007), at pp. 193–194.

In Cottier's view, for Generics C to be able to obtain a compulsory licence to export the generic versions of the patented drugs it manufactures under Country C's competition law rules, Country C would have to tweak the competition law jurisprudence of developed industrial economies and incorporate an international human rights dimension into its domestic competition law framework. Cottier argues that "competition law does not exclude taking into account external effects" and that the TRIPS Agreement "does not prevent Members from defining the concept of anti-competitive practices in a way so as to take into account competitive relations abroad"; moreover, where "what is at stake [is] the right to health and life of people affected ... these rights can and should be linked to the protection of intellectual property and to competition policies by means of the rule of reason" because "[c]onsiderations as how best to achieve human rights concerns should be considered in defining, and responding to, anti-competitive practices" as "[i]t is necessary to expand the relationship of IPRs and competition policy and to form a regulatory triangle, including human rights".[47] Ultimately, in Cottier's view, the rule of reason underlying the competition law provisions of the TRIPS Agreement "offers the portal to introduce human rights concerns in shaping appropriate rules on competition in domestic law".[48]

However, this approach suggested by Cottier for Country C to take advantage of the flexibility afforded to it by Article 31(k) of the TRIPS Agreement comes with a caveat that, when compared against the Doha waiver solution and the Article 31*bis* system, invoking competition law principles to issue compulsory licences is "somewhat more restrictive and only applies on constellations of anti-competitive conduct" because "it is limited to the abuse of a dominant position, effective only if the right holder refuses to engage in business at reasonable terms while preventing third parties from doing so", while the Doha waiver solution and the Article 31bis system simply allow "granting export licensing if so requested by an importing country (and if efforts at a voluntary license fail)" without needing the exporting country to demonstrate that anti-competitive conduct has occurred.[49] In Cottier's final analysis, the Doha waiver solution and the amendment to the TRIPS Agreement were "legally necessary" steps taken by the international community to facilitate access to essential patented medicines because of the inherent limitations of relying on alternative domestic competition law principles and policies via the Article 31 (k) flexibility:

> Firstly, established doctrines of competition policy in developed countries are essentially limited to promoting and protecting innovation in industrialised countries, in particular the US and EU... Short of a waiver, generic producers in the US and EU could not obtain compulsory licences. Secondly, competition doctrines responsive to the needs of developing countries, taking into account distributional goals, are not yet sufficiently developed and established... Short of an agreed waiver, the state of play in competition policies would have given [rise] to legal insecurity and complex dispute settlement. The waiver brought

[47] Cottier (2007), at pp. 194–195.

[48] Cottier (2007), at p. 195.

[49] Cottier (2007), at p. 196.

> appropriate clarifications. It was a proper answer, at this stage. It offers a surrogate for distributive competition policies which developing countries should have developed in their own domestic competition policy and laws, but have largely failed to do so up to this point in time.[50]

As Cottier admits, his suggested approach for Country C to develop its domestic competition law regime to permit it to grant a compulsory licence to Generics C on the ground that Pharma A has abused its dominant position "will not be a matter of simply expanding established doctrines of US or EU law . . . it will also be a matter of reviewing these doctrines and policies in the new triangle of human rights, intellectual property and competition law in the process of globalization and enhanced mutual responsibility for human well-being on this globe".[51]

4.1.2 Bypassing the Doha Waiver Solution and the Article 31*bis* System via Alternative Competition-Law-Driven Compulsory Licensing Provisions Found in Domestic Patent Statutes

A more optimistic view of the potential for countries in the position of Country C to utilise the flexibility of Article 31(k) to make compulsory licences available to Generics C on competition law grounds, which would circumvent the Doha waiver solution and the Article 31*bis* system altogether, is taken by those legal commentators who advocate the freedom of developing countries to take full advantage of the options given to them under the TRIP Agreement. With reference to the carefully crafted legislative provisions found within the domestic patent law statutes of India and Singapore, Ng-Loy has argued that it is a very real option for TRIPS Member states to fully utilise the flexibility found in Article 31(k) of the TRIPS Agreement to allow pharmaceutical products produced under a compulsory licence to be exported in circumstances falling outside the Doha waiver solution or the Article 31*bis* system.[52]

Both Singapore and India have accepted the proposed amendments to the TRIPS Agreement and committed themselves towards implementing the Article 31*bis* system within their respective national patent statutes.[53] However, as Ng-Loy has observed, both Singapore and India have *also* amended their respective patent law

---

[50] Cottier (2007), at p. 198.

[51] Cottier (2007), at p. 199. This tripartite approach towards analysing the web of difficult policy issues relating to access to patented pharmaceuticals is reflected in the more recent works of other legal scholars. See Brown (2012).

[52] Ng-Loy (2009), at pp. 179–184.

[53] India's acceptance of the TRIPS Amendment took place on 26 March 2007, while Singapore's acceptance was dated 28 September 2007. India has amended its patent legislation accordingly, with Section 92A(1) of the Indian *Patents Act 1970* providing that "[c]ompulsory licence[s] shall be available for manufacture and export of patented pharmaceutical products to any country having insufficient or no manufacturing capacity in the pharmaceutical sector for the concerned product to address public health problems. . .".

regimes to explicitly preserve for themselves the option of allowing compulsory licences to be issued against patent owners on *alternative* competition law grounds that could permit licensees to export the patented products they have manufactured under such licences without having to rely on the mechanics of the Article 31*bis* system.

In Singapore, section 55(1) of the Singapore *Patents Act 1994* provides that "[a] ny interested person may apply to the court for the grant of a licence under a patent on the ground that the grant of the licence is necessary to remedy an anti-competitive practice". This is the sole ground on which a compulsory licence may be obtained from the patent holder and was introduced in the 2004 amendments to the Act. Ng-Loy has also pointed out that the introduction of the current compulsory licensing provision was accompanied by the deletion of another provision in the Act, the former section 55(4)(c), which required any compulsory licence to be "limited to the supply of the patented invention predominantly in Singapore". Taking these simultaneous legislative amendments to Singapore's patent system together, she argues that "[t]he implication ... must be that it is now possible, when a compulsory licence is issued in Singapore to remedy an anti-competitive practice, for the licence to permit exportation of the products under the compulsory licence".[54]

In India, section 84(1) of the Indian *Patents Act 1970* states that one of the grounds on which an interested third party like Generics C could apply for a compulsory licence to manufacture Pharma A's patented medicine would be where "the reasonable requirements of the public with respect to the patented invention have not been satisfied". Section 84(7) goes on to explain that the "reasonable requirements of the public shall be deemed not to have been satisfied –

(a) if, by reason of the refusal of the patentee to grant a licence or licences on reasonable terms, –

  (i) an existing trade or industry or the development thereof or the establishment of any new trade or industry in India or the trade or industry of any person or class of persons trading or manufacturing in India is prejudiced; or
  (ii) the demand for the patented article has not been met to an adequate extent or on reasonable terms; or
  (iii) *a market for export* of the patented article manufactured in India is not being supplied or developed; or
  (iv) the establishment or development of commercial activities in India is prejudiced...."[55]

When compulsory patent licences are issued, section 90(1) sets out the following conditions that may be attached to the compulsory licence:

In settling the terms and conditions of a licence under section 84, the Controller shall endeavour to secure – ...

[54] Ng-Loy (2009), at p. 184.

[55] These provisions were introduced via section 39 of *The Patents (Amendment) Act*, 2002 (No. 38 of 2002) (emphasis added).

(vii) that the licence is granted with a predominant purpose of supply in the Indian market and that the licensee *may also export the patented product*, if need be in accordance with the provisions of [section 84(7)(a)(iii)]; ...

(ix) that in case the licence is granted to remedy a practice determined after judicial or administrative process to be anti-competitive, the licensee *shall be permitted to export the patented product*, if need be.[56]

Ng-Loy regards these compulsory licensing provisions within the Indian patent statute as examples of how competition law and policy considerations might be infused into the patent system to facilitate the manufacture and export of generic versions of patented drugs. In her analysis, sections 90(1)(vii) and 90(1)(ix) would enable the Indian Patent Office to grant compulsory licences to generic drug manufacturers on competition law grounds in a manner consistent with the flexibility found in Article 31(k) of the TRIPS Agreement. Reading in conjunction with each other sections 84(7)(a)(iii) and 90(1)(vii) would enable an interested third party like Generics C to apply for a compulsory licence to make and export generic versions of Pharma A's patented drug on the basis that Pharma A has refused to license, or refused to license on reasonable terms, Generics C such that the export market for these generic drugs (in Country B, for example) is not being supplied or developed. Pharma A's refusal to license its patent may thus be regarded as anti-competitive because it raises a barrier to market entry into a foreign market (the importing country) that is, in all likelihood, undersupplied by the patent holder. Ng-Loy argues that the language used in section 90(1)(ix), which replicates the exact phrase used in Article 31(k) of the TRIPS Agreement, is an even clearer example of how anti-competitive conduct by the patent holder might provide a legal basis to obtain a compulsory licence for Generics C to manufacture patented drugs for export:

> If the patentee refuses to supply patented drugs at an affordable price to the public in another country (one which may have the drug manufacturing capacity and therefore does not qualify for the waiver system in the 2003 WTO decision) and this refusal is determined by the other country's judicial or administrative body to be anti-competitive, a generic drug company in India could potentially apply for the grant of a compulsory licence to manufacture the drugs and, under the authority of s.90(1)(ix), the compulsory licence could permit export of these drugs to this other country.[57]

What is extraordinary about this line of analysis is the argument that a judicial or administrative determination of anti-competitive conduct in *another* country that needs to import the generic drugs (Country B) can be used by the Indian Patent Office as a justification for awarding a compulsory licence to an applicant (Generics C) within its own territorial jurisdiction (Country C) to manufacture and export these generic drugs. Such an interpretation of the legal basis for a compulsory licence to use a patented invention is probably unjustifiable insofar as it would involve a court in one country curtailing the exclusive intellectual property rights of a patent holder within that country on the basis of a judicial or administrative determination made in

[56] These provisions were introduced via section 54 of *The Patents (Amendment) Act*, 2005 (No. 15 of 2005) (emphasis added).

[57] Ng-Loy (2009), at p. 183.

another country about the patent holder's anti-competitive conduct in that foreign territory. Competition authorities are highly unlikely to assert jurisdiction over anti-competitive conduct abroad unless there are adverse economic effects on competition domestically.[58] Courts that purport to apply competition law principles to determine if a compulsory patent licence is justifiable are unlikely to depart from this "effects-based" principle. So unless the anti-competitive conduct taking place outside of Country C (in Country B) results in anti-competitive effects on a relevant market within Country C or if a transnational market spanning Countries B and C could be constructed,[59] it would be difficult to support Ng-Loy's position.

However, in the right factual matrix, it *may* be possible to re-characterise the conduct of the patentee *within* Country C as an "anti-competitive" practice, which better resonates with conventional competition law principles, which could then provide a legitimate basis for granting a compulsory licence to Generics C to manufacture and export the patented drugs to Country B. At the same time, Country B would have to clear the way for these pharmaceutical products to enter its territory through the grant of a separate compulsory licence to import them. Using the Article 31(k) compulsory licence as an alternative, the Article 31*bis* mechanism would thus require two Member states (Countries B and C) to simultaneously grant two compulsory patent licences (one to manufacture and export and one to import) in a coordinated way. The next section will attempt to set out an analytical framework that may be developed to facilitate this process.

4.2 Circumscribing the Patent Monopoly: "Anti-Competitive" Conduct as a Justification for Granting Compulsory Pharmaceutical Patent Licences

While the goals of competition law are aligned with patent law to the extent that both are concerned with promoting innovation and dynamic efficiency, competition law principles may still be employed as tools to counterbalance the short-term excesses of the patent system where there are concerns that the scope of the exclusive rights enjoyed by patent holders is too wide.[60] This is reflected in various parts of the TRIPS

[58] The so-called effects-based approach to extraterritorial jurisdiction, as applied within the context of competition law infringements, can be traced back to the seminal American antitrust decision in *US v Aluminum Co. of America*, 148 F.2d 416 (1945) which is congruent with the public international law principle of "objective territoriality". See Akehurst (1972–1973), p. 145.

[59] This is highly unlikely because of the national regulatory barriers to market entry for pharmaceuticals and legal restrictions on the movement of such products between countries. See discussion below in Sect. 4.2.1.

[60] It has been argued that competition policy can be used to achieve other broader policy goals as well—that "TRIPS provides significant scope within which competition policy may be employed to advance a public health agenda that may be compromised if IP protection is left unchecked". See Berger (2006), at p. 183.

Agreement, particularly in the Article 31(k) option of permitting Members to grant compulsory patent licences to remedy "anti-competitive" practices, though it does not define exactly what qualifies as the sort of conduct that could justify such an incursion into the patent holder's exclusive rights. Neither is there any complete consensus between national competition authorities in developed nations, much less among developing and the least developed countries, on when specific forms of conduct by patent holders should be regarded as anti-competitive, if at all.[61]

A conservative approach towards interpreting the language in Article 31(k) of the TRIPS Agreement is to insist that what qualifies as an "anti-competitive" practice for the purposes of granting a compulsory patent licence must be assessed using *exactly* the same general competition law principles found elsewhere in a Member state's national legal framework. From the perspective of a developed country with a mature competition law framework, this would typically entail establishing a conduct that has an actual or likely direct adverse effect on the competitive process in a properly defined relevant market, resulting in economically inefficient anti-competitive market foreclosure effects. This would explain why Cottier has expressed the view that it is highly doubtful whether the competition law jurisprudence of the European Community and the United States would make a compulsory patent licence available to Generics C on the basis that Pharma A has engaged in anti-competitive conduct by abusing its position of market dominance. A compulsory licence could only be available on substantially modified competition law grounds if Country C's domestic laws deviated from the competition law principles and policies embraced by the courts in developed countries and cultivated its own competition rules that incorporated human rights considerations within its competition law regime.

A more liberal approach might accept a broader view of what should count as an "anti-competitive" practice, at least as far as patents are concerned, particularly in the context of the conduct of a pharmaceutical patent holder with the ability to control the supply of life-saving drugs. Adopting such a perspective might involve questionable assessments of the reasonableness of the patent holder's conduct, the moral implications of its decisions to restrict the availability or increase the price of the patented drug, and an impressionistic evaluation of whether it has violated social or ethical norms that could undermine the legitimacy of its exclusive proprietary interests. It may be argued that countries with patent statutes containing such compulsory licensing provisions that do not explicitly define what an "anti-competitive" practice is could have the flexibility of taking this more liberal approach. The lack of judicial experience in applying these compulsory patent

[61] These include intellectual property-competition law interface issues such as market definition, refusals to licence IPRs, the applicability of the essential facilities doctrine in relation to IPRs and IPR licensing restraints imposed by dominant firms. See United Nations Conference on Trade and Development (UNCTAD) (2002), at p. 26.

licensing provisions also contributes to the lack of certainty in this issue.[62] This uncertainty, however, could be used to lend support to those who argue that jurisdictions with such provisions in their patent statutes should be given the opportunity to preserve for themselves the freedom to interpret the criterion of "anti-competitive" conduct more broadly.[63] This is probably where Ng-Loy is coming from when she argues that developing countries such as India and Singapore are at liberty to adopt, and have in fact already adopted, internal checks within their respective domestic patent systems to make compulsory patent licences available on competition law grounds when Pharma A's conduct, in refusing to voluntarily license Generics C on terms that would enable Generics C to export generic versions of the patented drug to patients in Country B, or when its conduct within the market in Country B itself amounts to anti-competitive practice.

Despite the divergent attitudes taken by commentators towards the feasibility of using the Article 31(k) compulsory licensing mechanism as a substitute for Article 31*bis* to facilitate access to life-saving drugs, it might be worth exploring how conventional competition law principles—those commonly understood and broadly accepted by the international competition law community—might be sensibly applied to the hypothetical scenario involving Pharma A's conduct in Country B and Country C. Even though there is no international consensus about what precise legal standards ought to be applied by states that have enacted their own domestic competition law regimes, particularly when evaluating the legality of unilateral conduct by undertakings in possession of significant market power, it is submitted that all states should evaluate allegations of anti-competitive practices within a market-based framework that focuses on how structural, legal, and economic conditions in the market affect the competitive process and the impact of the patent holder's conduct on that process. Establishing an infringement of the competition

---

[62] For example, even though such compulsory licensing provisions have been present in the Singapore patent statute for almost two decades, the courts have not had the chance to give a judicial interpretation of its scope of application. The same can be said of the experience in South Africa (see Berger 2006, at p. 199). In contrast, the Indian patent authority recently issued its first compulsory licence to a generic drug manufacturer on the grounds that the reasonable requirements of the public had not been satisfied, that the patented invention had not been made available to the public at a reasonable price, and that the patented invention had not been worked in India. See *Natco Pharma Limited v Bayer Corporation*, Compulsory License Application No. 1 of 2011 (Controller of Patents, Mumbai) (9 March 2012). See http://www.ipindia.nic.in/ipoNew/compulsory_License_12032012.pdf.

[63] As one pro-patient pharmaceutical patent skeptic has put it, "[w]hile Members have significant flexibility to determine what they consider to be anti-competitive, the failure of TRIPS to provide a definition cannot be understood as providing a blank cheque to determine what practices may be considered anti-competitive... [i]t seems appropriate... that the concept of anti-competitive conduct must in some ways be linked to... expressly identified and potentially problematic outcomes. However, given the... appropriate role for the use of competition policy as a means for indirectly increasing access to essential medicines, what may be considered as anti-competitive for the purposes of compulsory licences issued in accordance with the provisions of Article 31 is almost certainly broader than conduct that has a direct anti-competitive effect". (See Berger 2006, at p. 185.)

rules by a pharmaceutical patent holder that could trigger the grant of an Article 31 (k) compulsory licence involves at least two analytical steps:

(1) establishing that the patent holder occupies a position of dominance in the relevant market for the patented pharmaceutical product; and
(2) establishing that the conduct of the patent holder—in the exporting country, the importing country, or in *both* countries—infringes the competition law prohibition against the abuse of a dominant position that justifies the grant of compulsory licences.

4.2.1 Market Definition: Establishing Dominance of the Pharmaceutical Patent Holder in the Relevant Market(s)

The reliance of the pharmaceutical industry on patent protection for the various major drugs available in different territorial markets creates multiple legal monopolies for their respective patent holders. These legal monopolies are likely to also translate into economic monopolies where there are no effective product substitutes to be found, thereby conferring upon these patent holders enough market power to be considered dominant undertakings. In the hypothetical scenario described earlier, it would not be too difficult to define the relevant market as the market comprising a single drug for the treatment of a particular disease. As the owner of a patent monopoly, Pharma A is prima facie at liberty to decide who to license its intellectual property to and on what terms, if at all. This gives Pharma A very significant control over the volume of the drug that is supplied to the market, to whom such supplies are made, and the price to be paid for these supplies. This substantial degree of market power enjoyed by Pharma A may be tempered, to some extent, by the legal and regulatory framework of each country it does business in, where, for example, restrictions may be imposed on its ability to charge above certain price levels.

Establishing that Pharma A occupies a position of market dominance for the purposes of conducting a competition law analysis of its conduct is thus probably not too difficult.[64] The more challenging question is the geographical extent of the relevant market—does the relevant market extend beyond the national boundaries of each state in which it sells the drug? If Pharma A is the holder of a valid product patent that has been registered multiple times in different jurisdictions, then it is the sole supplier of the patented drug in all these territories (along with any patent licensees it has selected to manufacture and distribute its medicinal product). However, national patent laws in many jurisdictions give patent holders the

[64] In addition to the market power derived from having patent monopolies, pharmaceutical companies have also consolidated and strengthened their market positions through strategic transnational mergers and acquisitions over the years. See Rosenberg (2006), at pp. 65–78.

exclusive right to control imports of the patented product, with limited exceptions for parallel imports in narrowly defined circumstances, thereby making it difficult to define the relevant market as one that is transnational or international in scope. Thus, establishing anti-competitive conduct that amounts to an abuse of a dominant position must involve evaluating the behavior of these dominant firms within the territorial limits of each national market.

4.2.2 Abuse of Dominance: Establishing "Anti-Competitive" Practices by the Dominant Patent Holder in the Relevant Market(s)

If Pharma A has secured patent protection for its drug in both Country B and Country C, where Pharma A has chosen to pursue a high-price, low-volume commercial strategy while refusing to license generic drug manufacturers such as Generics C (or subjecting its licences to contractual restraints preventing exports of the patented drugs made by Generics C), then *two* types of compulsory licences are necessary to facilitate the supply of these patented drugs, made in Country C by Generics C, to patients in Country B. Since Country B has no pharmaceutical manufacturing capacity of its own, any compulsory licence issued by Country B would simply permit the import of foreign-manufactured patented drugs into Country B. On the other hand, any compulsory licences granted by legal institutions in Country C to Generics C would have to go further—Generics C would have to be permitted to manufacture *and* export these patented drugs to Country B.

Anti-Competitive Conduct Within Country B (the Importing Country)

If the strength of the patent protection it enjoys, coupled with the lack of effective substitutes for the patented drug, puts Pharma A in a position of market dominance akin to a monopolist in a single-drug market, then all the competition-related problems and economic inefficiencies associated with the conduct of monopolists are likely to be present: supply is reduced, and prices are raised above competitive levels in such a way as to enable the monopolist to capture for itself as much of the consumer surplus as it can. The highly inelastic nature of the demand for life-saving pharmaceuticals means that it would be economically rational for the profit-maximising monopolist to undersupply the market and charge higher prices. Consumer welfare is thus adversely affected, at least for the duration of the patent protection before generic manufacturers may enter the market, if at all, or until an effective substitute that does not infringe upon the monopolist's patent is developed, if at all.

Pharma A's high-price and low-volume sales strategy could, in theory, provide a basis for a competition law infringement premised on excessive pricing within Country B. There are established precedents from the competition laws of developed countries for regarding excessive pricing as an unlawful abuse of an undertaking's dominant position.[65] However, simply establishing a competition law infringement will not guarantee the desired remedial outcome of a *compulsory licence to import* generic versions of the patented drug. The relevant legal institution handling the complaint must also be persuaded that such a compulsory licence is also *necessary* to remedy the anti-competitive practice—that financial penalties or behavioural remedies imposed upon the dominant patent holder would not be sufficient to address the problem. In any case, a compulsory licence to import generic versions of the patented drug into Country B can be secured without even having to rely on competition law grounds—Country B could simply invoke one of the *other* justifications for allowing compulsory licences,[66] such as the case of a national emergency or other circumstance of extreme urgency, in response to its public health crisis.

For some who believe that competition law principles can be used to facilitate access to life-saving patented drugs in Country B, the possibility of securing a compulsory licence to import such products in Country B on grounds of anti-competitive conduct (excessive pricing in undersupplied markets in Country B) is a crucial step in triggering the availability of a compulsory licence in Country C—the source of the generic versions of these drugs that can only be exported to Country B if a compulsory licence is granted in Country C on Article 31(k) grounds. Ng-Loy has argued that Pharma A's anti-competitive conduct in Country B could provide a legal basis for legal institutions in Country C to grant a compulsory licence to Generics C to produce (in Country C) and export (to Country B) generic versions of the patented drug.[67] However, for the reasons already discussed earlier, it would *not* be defensible for a competition authority to exercise extraterritorial jurisdiction in this manner, given the separate and distinct character of the two national markets (Country B and Country C) and the absence of any nexus between the foreign conduct of the dominant patent holder (in Country B) and harmful effects on competition in Country C.

[65] See, for example, Article 82(a) of the Treaty of Rome, which prohibits, *inter alia*, "directly or indirectly imposing unfair purchase or selling prices or other unfair trading conditions". This example of conduct that amounts to an abuse of a dominant position was also imported into the UK legislative framework in Section 18(2)(a) of the *Competition Act 1998*. Within the European competition law framework, the European Court of Justice has held, in *Case 27/76 United Brands v Commission* [1978] ECR 207 at [250], that "charging a price which is excessive because it has no reasonable relation to the economic value of the product supplied is . . . an abuse", a proposition that was accepted by the UK Court of Appeal in *Attheraces Ltd v The British Horseracing Board* [2007] EWCA Civ 38 at [204]. More pertinently to the context of this chapter, the UK Competition Appeal Tribunal has upheld a decision of the Office of Fair Trading that a pharmaceutical company had abused its dominant position in the UK by charging excessive prices. See *Napp Pharmaceutical Holdings v Director General of Fair Trading* [2002] CAT 1, [392].

[66] See discussion above in Sect. 2.

[67] See n 57 above and accompanying text.

Anti-Competitive Conduct Within Country C (the Exporting Country in Which Generics C Is Located)

Since Country C is the source of the generic versions of the patented drug and the place from which they are exported to patients abroad, the availability of a *compulsory licence to manufacture and export* these products will play a pivotal role in determining the feasibility of an alternative mechanism to the Doha waiver solution and Article 31*bis* system for facilitating access to life-saving medicines based on the Article 31(k) exception to patent protection. Country C must grant the remedy of a compulsory licence to Generics C to produce and export generic versions of Pharma A's patented drug in response to Pharma A's anti-competitive practices *within* Country C.

When analysing the conduct of Pharma A to determine if it has abused its market dominance, it may be helpful to think of two broad categories of abusive conduct. One category would comprise conventional varieties of anti-competitive conduct also associated with non-patent-owning dominant undertakings—such as excessive pricing, exclusive dealing, and refusals to supply (or deal with, or license to, competitors).[68] The other category would comprise "bad" behaviour where the patent holder specifically exploits the patent system to obtain the greatest possible commercial advantage for itself—such as extending of duration of patent protection, sham patent litigation against generic-manufacturing rivals, patent evergreening, and seeking of excessively broad patents to block research by competitors.[69] Even if they may produce exclusionary effects in the market, none of these sorts of conduct in the latter category have been consistently condemned by competition authorities in developed countries with mature competition law systems, making it difficult—and it is beyond the scope of this chapter—to assess the viability of establishing competition law infringements from any of these practices. In any case, even if such practices were regarded as anti-competitive under Country C's competition law regime, it may not follow that awarding a compulsory patent licence to Generics C to manufacture *and* export the patented drug would be a necessary or appropriate remedial response to such anti-competitive conduct.

What if Generics C were to approach Pharma A for a patent licence to manufacture generic versions of the patented drug in Country C with a view to exporting these medicines to Country B and Pharma A turned down this request to avoid making low-cost versions of its patented drug available in the market? Would Pharma A's refusal to license Generics C, or refusal to license except on very restrictive terms, amount to an anti-competitive practice that could justify the grant

[68] See Berger (2006), at pp. 188–194, which explores how the conduct of dominant-patent-owning pharmaceutical companies might be analysed as conventional species of abusive conduct. It should be noted, however, that the focus of Berger's analysis is to evaluate the possibility of using the competition law regime to facilitate *domestic* access to patented pharmaceuticals—that is, for compulsory licences to be granted to local generic drug manufacturers to supply generic drugs to patients within *that* jurisdiction.

[69] See, for example, Rosenberg (2006), at p. 74.

of a compulsory patent licence to Generics C to make generic versions of the medicine for export purposes?

As a patent holder with proprietary rights in its pharmaceutical invention, Pharma A is *prima facie* entitled to decide the terms on which it is prepared to grant a licence to Generics C, if at all. If Pharma A wants to contractually prevent Generics C from exporting the generic versions of the drug it has manufactured to patients in Country B, then it should be at liberty to do so—a bare refusal to license, without anything more to substantiate an allegation of anti-competitive exclusionary effects on a relevant market for the patented drug in Country C, should not qualify as an unlawful anti-competitive practice. Moreover, the competition law regimes may also be sensitive to the innovation-incentivisation rationales[70] that underpin national intellectual property statutes and the exclusive rights they confer on patent holders such as Pharma A. Such a regulatory posture might translate into a general attitude of deference towards the patent holder's decision not to license a third party or to only grant licences with restrictive contractual restraints and a instinctive reluctance to regard such conduct as competition law infringements.

Within the European Community, the courts have held that a dominant undertaking's refusal to license its intellectual property rights to a third party is an abuse of its dominant position only in "exceptional circumstances".[71] Refusing to license intellectual property rights to a third party that needs it to develop a new product, despite evidence that there is consumer demand for such a product that is unmet by the dominant undertaking that owns these intellectual property rights, has been regarded as one such exceptional circumstance. In the present context where life-saving drugs protected by patents are concerned, Pharma A may choose not to license its pharmaceutical patent to Generics C to manufacture drugs for export to Country B because Pharma A is already selling the drug in Country B, and the availability in Country B of the lower-priced generic versions of the drug manufactured by Generics C would erode Pharma A's bottom line. What sort of additional factors could be raised for Pharma A's conduct to cross the "exceptionality" threshold in order to justify the grant of a compulsory licence to Generics C? One possibility would be if Generics C required a patent licence from Pharma A to produce fixed-dose combination medicines, which combine multiple drugs (both patented and unpatented) into a single product that simplifies the treatment of serious chronic diseases. Pharma A's refusal to license could thus be characterised

[70] The policy dilemma at the heart of the intellectual property-competition law interface lies in the difficulty of determining what is the optimal level at which competition policy should be deployed to curtail abuses of the intellectual property regime, particularly when there is the potential to upset the endogenous balance struck within the patent system between the innovation-promoting incentives and the exclusionary impact of granting exclusive legal monopolies to patent holders. However, as one commentator has observed, the innovation-incentive argument in favour of robust protection for patent holders is weaker in the developing world, particularly in the least developed countries that lack the necessary infrastructure to engage in high-level innovation activities. See Berger (2006), at pp. 187 and 192.

[71] See *Magill*, n 39 at [50].

as anti-competitive because it stymies innovation and prevents the emergence of a product for which there is consumer demand, thereby undermining a key rationale for having patent protection in the first place.[72] Another possibility would be if Generics C can show that it is able to profitably produce and sell generic versions of Pharma A's drug, perhaps by adopting a low-cost high-volume sales strategy that Pharma A is unable or unwilling to pursue, to a targeted group of patients in Country B who would not otherwise be able to afford anything supplied by Pharma A. In theory, where the lives of patients in Country B are at stake because the supply of essential medicines into that country has been curtailed by the actions of the patent holder, there is likely to be more room for the passionate public health advocate in Country C to advance persuasive arguments to support the view that Pharma A's refusal to license ought to be construed as an "exceptional" circumstance that qualifies as an abuse of a dominant position and triggers the availability of a compulsory licence to manufacture and export these patented medicines to Country B.

5 Conclusion

The potential for Article 31(k) compulsory patent licences to be used as a vehicle to facilitate access to life-saving patented medicines in lieu of the Article 31*bis* mechanism has not been fully explored by those who have pushed for stronger exceptions to the exclusive rights of patent holders on public health grounds. This is perhaps not surprising, given the substantial economic influence wielded by the pharmaceutical industry on governments around the world and the political pressures faced by TRIPS signatories to avoid upsetting their trading partners in the developed economies. In any case, the option for Member states in the position of Country B and Country C to cooperate with each other, by granting compulsory licences to remedy anti-competitive practices by patent holders like Pharma A, remains a possible course of action subject to three final observations.

Firstly, the likelihood of using competition policy as a basis to grant compulsory licences in the manner described above will hinge almost entirely on whether or not the relevant authorities in Country C have the requisite institutional capacity to deploy these legal tools, particularly when navigating the conceptually challenging jurisdictional issues to avoid illegitimate extraterritorial applications of Country C's competition law regime to Pharma A's activities in Country B.

Secondly, the impact of facilitating access to patented medicines through compulsory licensing may be limited if the importing country does not implement corresponding legal reforms in its domestic drug approval regulatory regimes. Regulatory regimes that include features of data exclusivity for clinical data submitted by pharmaceutical companies seeking registration and marketing

---

[72] See Berger (2006), at p. 192.

approval for their medicines, perhaps through trade secret laws or other legal frameworks, are likely to raise additional obstacles for importers of generic versions of patented drugs (manufactured under a compulsory licence abroad) to introduce these medicines to the domestic market.[73]

Thirdly, the *actual* grant of compulsory patent licences on grounds of anti-competitive conduct may not even be necessary to facilitate the process of making drugs manufactured in Country C available to patients in Country B. The mere *possibility* of such action by Country C's legal institutions, or the *threat* that such a remedy could result from a complaint made by a public health advocate,[74] may be sufficient to motivate Pharma A to enter into a voluntary licensing agreement with Generics C that permits the latter to export generic versions of the drug manufactured in Country C to markets abroad such as Country B.

References

Abbott F, Reichman J (2007) The Doha Round's public health legacy: strategies for the production and diffusion of patented medicines under the amended TRIPS provisions. J Int Econ Law 10 (4):921

Akehurst M (1972–1973) Jurisdiction in international law. Br Year B Int Law 46:145

Berger J (2006) Advancing public health by other means: using competition policy. In: Roffe P, Tansey G, Vivas-Eugui D (eds) Negotiating health: intellectual property and access to medicines. Earthscan, London

Brown AEL (2012) Intellectual property, human rights and competition: access to essential innovation and technology. Edward Elgar, Cheltenham

Cottier T (2007) The Doha Waiver and its effects on the nature of the TRIPS system and on competition law: the impact of human rights. In: Govaere I, Ullrich H (eds) Intellectual property, public policy and international trade, college of Europe studies No. 6. P.I.E. Peter Lang, Brussels

Drexl J (2005) The critical role of competition law in preserving public goods in conflict with intellectual property rights. In: Maskus KE, Reichman JH (eds) International public goods and transfer of technology under a globalized intellectual property regime. Cambridge University Press, Cambridge

Fox E (2005) Can antitrust policy protect the global commons from the excesses of IPRs? In: Maskus KE, Reichman JH (eds) International public goods and transfer of technology under a globalized intellectual property regime. Cambridge University Press, Cambridge

Gervais D (2012) The TRIPS Agreement: drafting history and analysis, 4th edn. Sweet & Maxwell, London

Matthews D (2004) WTO decision on the implementation of paragraph 6 of the Doha Declaration on the TRIPS Agreement and public health: a solution to the access to essential medicines problem? J Int Econ Law 7:73

---

[73] See Pugatch (2006), at pp. 97–132.

[74] This seems to have been the lesson learnt from the complaint lodged with the South African competition authority by civil society organisations against two pharmaceutical giants that led to favourable settlement agreements involving voluntary licensing arrangements with generic drug manufacturers on less onerous terms. See Berger (2006), at pp. 197–200.

Medecins Sans Frontieres (2006) Neither expeditious, nor a solution: the WTO August 30th decision is unworkable. In: Prepared for the XVI international AIDS conference, Toronto, August 2006. http://www.doctorswithoutborders.org/news/hiv-aids/WTO_chretien.pdf

Ng-Loy WL (2009) Exploring flexibilities within the global IP standards. IPQ 2:162

Pugatch MP (2006) Intellectual property, data exclusivity and market access. In: Roffe P, Tansey G, Vivas-Eugui D (eds) Negotiating health: intellectual property and access to medicines. Earthscan, London

Rosenberg B (2006) Market concentration of the transnational pharmaceutical industry and the generic industries: trends on mergers, acquisitions and other transactions. In: Roffe P, Tansey G, Vivas-Eugui D (eds) Negotiating health: intellectual property and access to medicines. Earthscan, London

Ullrich H (2005) Expansionist intellectual property protection and reductionist competition rules: a TRIPS perspective. In: Maskus KE, Reichman JH (eds) International public goods and transfer of technology under a globalized intellectual property regime. Cambridge University Press, Cambridge

United Nations Conference on Trade and Development (UNCTAD) (2002) Competition policy and the exercise of intellectual property rights. UNCTAD, TD/B/COM.2/CLP/22/Rev.1, 19 April 2002

Denial of Injunctive Relief on Grounds of Equity: Situation in the U.S. and Japan

Ichiro Nakayama and Yoshiyuki Tamura

Contents

Both authors are Professors of Law.

I. Nakayama
Kokugakuin University, School of Law, Tokyo, Japan
e-mail: nakayama@kokugakuin.ac.jp

Y. Tamura
Hokkaido University, School of Law, Sapporo, Hokkaido, Japan
e-mail: ytamura@juris.hokudai.ac.jp

R.M. Hilty and K.-C. Liu (eds.), *Compulsory Licensing*, MPI Studies on Intellectual Property and Competition Law 22, DOI 10.1007/978-3-642-54704-1_14,

Abstract In common law nations such as the United States, injunctions are categorised as remedies in equity and theoretically it is supposed to be an exceptional remedy that courts may grant in their discretion in cases where common law remedies like damages fail to provide effective protection. However, the courts in the United States had almost automatically granted injunctions until the 2006 Supreme Court decision in *eBay*, which has dramatically changed the landscape. While the ratio of denial of injunctive relief has drastically increased after the *eBay* case, Federal Trade Commission in 2011 provides useful framework in discussing whether to grant injunction: ex ante transaction versus ex post transaction. Based on this analytical tool, FTC proposes insightful recommendations to modify some court practices. On the other hand, in Japan, the patentee has the "right" to seek injunction and the Japanese courts rarely deny the injunction. However, since the exclusivity of patents is merely a means to achieve the prosperity of industry, the goal of patent law, a patent "right" just after the examination and registration by the Patent Office could be conceived as a provisional one because it can be viewed as a mere transit point within the broader process in which the requirements for excluding others from using the invention are reviewed step by step.

1 Introduction

Patents give exclusive power to patentees. Article 28 of Trade-Related Aspects of Intellectual Property Rights (TRIPS) stipulated that "[a] patent shall confer on its owner the following exclusive rights.... to prevent third parties not having the owner's consent from" working the patented invention. The patentee's exclusive power is closely related to remedies against infringement. Given that inventions are intangibles and no one can keep inventions under physical control, injunctive relief is quite important because it enables patentees to keep their inventions under legal control by enjoining the alleged infringers from using them. There is no doubt that injunctive relief plays a critical role in securing exclusivity. Accordingly, conventional wisdom is that patentees usually obtain injunction in case of patent infringement (e.g., Article 44 of TRIPS). Patent acts in some civil law nations provide that the patentee is entitled to request that the court grant injunctive relief. The Japanese Patent Act is one such example and will be discussed later.

In contrast, common law nations are in a unique situation. They have two different legal origins: common law and equity. As explained later, an injunction is a remedy in equity and is generally considered an exception. Another characteristic in equity is the broad judicial discretion. Taken together, the courts in common law nations inherently have greater power to deny injunctive relief. Nonetheless, the courts in the United States have rarely exercised such power historically. Rather, they have paid more attention to securing the exclusivity of the patent right. However, the U. S. Supreme Court changed the landscape in 2006. Since then, the denial of injunctive relief has increased.

It is quite interesting to see why and how the U.S. courts' decision on injunction changed, especially from the perspective of a civil law nation, such as Japan. In addition, these changes pose not only practical but also theoretical questions.

This chapter consists of five parts. After the introduction, Sect. 2 makes a general survey of how the courts in the U. S. have granted or denied injunctive relief and how they have changed their practice. Section 3 then analyses the theoretical aspects of such court practices, referring to the report of the Federal Trade Commission. Section 4 deals with the denial of injunctions under the Japanese Patent Act. Section 5 summarises the findings in previous sections.

Putting aside other common law nations, the subject of this chapter is limited to the U. S. because it is the nation where the changes have been taking place and drawing so much attention worldwide.

2 Injunctions in the U.S. Patent Law

2.1 Statutory Provision

35 U.S.C. § 283 provides an injunctive relief as follows:

> The several courts having jurisdiction of cases under this title may grant injunctions in accordance with the principles of equity to prevent the violation of any right secured by patent, on such terms as the court deems reasonable.

The statutory language makes two things clear. First, injunctions under U.S. patent law are remedies in equity. Second, the courts have discretion on whether to grant injunctions, as shown in the statutory language of "may".

These characteristics are interrelated. The Supreme Court in an older case described the characteristics of equity as follows: "The essence of equity jurisdiction has been the power of the Chancellor to do equity and to mould each decree to the necessities of the particular case. Flexibility rather than rigidity has distinguished it. The qualities of mercy and practicality have made equity the instrument for nice adjustment and reconciliation between the public interest and private needs as well as between competing private claims".[1]

In terms of remedies, injunctions are remedies in equity, whereas damages are remedies in common law. Thus, the Supreme Court recognised "the fundamental principle that an injunction is an equitable remedy that does not issue as of course".[2] Rather, it describes an injunction as an "extraordinary remedy".[3] It means that

[1] Hecht Co. v. Bowles, 321 U.S. 321, 329–330 (1944).

[2] Amoco Production Co., v. Gambell, 480 U.S. 531, 542 (1987) [citing Weinburger v. Romero-Barcelo, 456 U.S. 305, 311 (1982) and Harrisonville v. W.S. Dickey Clay Mfg. Co., 289 U.S. 334, 337–338 (1933)].

[3] *Weinburger*, 456 U.S. at 312 [citing R.R. Comm'n Pullman Co., 312 U.S. 496, 500 (1941)].

injunctions in equity may be granted only when certain conditions are met, which will be discussed in the next subsection.

2.2 Four-Factor Test

In 2006, the Supreme Court in *eBay*[4] reconfirmed "well-established principles of equity", namely a four-factor test to be satisfied before a court may grant injunctive relief. It held that a plaintiff seeking a permanent injunction must satisfy the following four-factor test.

(1) It has suffered an irreparable injury.
(2) Remedies available at law, such as monetary damages, are inadequate to compensate for that injury.
(3) Considering the balance of hardships between the plaintiff and defendant, a remedy in equity is warranted.
(4) The public interest would not be disserved by a permanent injunction.[5]

The Supreme Court also held that the district court had an equitable discretion in deciding the grant or denial of injunctive relief.[6]

It further contended that the four-factor test should be applicable to patent cases.[7] That was not surprising because it was well recognised, as mentioned above, that an injunction was an equitable remedy. The problem is how the courts should apply the four-factor test, given their broad discretion. Before discussing the *eBay* case itself, the next subsection briefly illustrates a situation before *eBay*.

2.3 Injunctions Before eBay

While recognising the equitable nature of injunctive relief, the courts before the *eBay* decision tended to put more focus on the exclusivity of the patent right. For instance, the Court of Appeals for the Federal Circuit (CAFC) stated that "[a] lthough the district court's grant or denial of an injunction is discretionary depending on the facts of the case", "injunctive relief against an adjudged infringer is usually granted".[8] CAFC was of the belief that, given that "[t]he very nature of the patent right is the right to exclude others", "where validity and continuing infringement have been clearly established, ... immediate irreparable harm is

[4] eBay Inc., v. MercExchange L.L.C., 547 U.S. 388, 391 (2006).
[5] *Id.* at 391.
[6] *Id.* at 391.
[7] *Id.* at 391.
[8] W.L. Gore & Assoc., Inc. v. Garlock, Inc., 842 F. 2d 1275, 1281 (Fed. Cir. 1988).

presumed" (footnotes omitted) and that "[t]o hold otherwise would be contrary to the public policy underlying the patent laws".[9] It further explained that "presumption [of irreparable harm] derives in part from the finite term of the patent grant, for patent expiration is not suspended during litigation, and the passage of time can work irremediable harm".[10]

Based upon these arguments,[11] CAFC's 1989 decision stated that it was "the general rule that an injunction will issue when infringement has been adjudged, absent a sound reason for doing it".[12] Consequently, the courts granted injunctions almost automatically in patent infringement cases until the Supreme Court changed this practice, as discussed below.

2.4 eBay *Decision*

In 2006, *eBay* clarified the four-factor test as explained earlier. In addition, it changed then-prevailing practices developed by CAFC.

In this case, the district court denied an injunction, even though it acknowledged a presumption of irreparable harm. In rebutting the presumption, the district court argued that the patent holder would not suffer irreparable harm without an injunction because it did not practise its inventions and was willing to license its patented inventions.[13] Its decision was reversed by CAFC. CAFC granted an injunction, reiterating that "the general rule is that a permanent injunction will issue once infringement and validity have been adjudged".[14]

The Supreme Court rejected both the district court's categorical denial of injunctive relief and CAFC's categorical grant of such relief.[15] However, all the Supreme Court held was that equitable discretion under a four-factor test "must be exercised consistent with traditional principles of equity, in patent disputes no less

[9] Smith International, Inc. v. Hughes Tools Co. 718 F. 2d 1573, 1581 (Fed. Cir. 1983).

[10] H.H. Robertson Co. v. United Steel Deck, Inc., 820 F.2d 384, 390 (Fed. Cir. 1987).

[11] CAFC in both *Smith* and *Robertson* discussed presumption of irreparable harm in the context of preliminarily injunctions. Standards of preliminary injunctions were explained as follows: "[a] plaintiff seeking a preliminary injunction must establish that he is likely to succeed on the merits, that he is likely to suffer irreparable harm in the absence of preliminary relief, that the balance of equities tips in his favor, and that an injunction is in the public interest". Winter v. Natural Res. Def. Council, Inc., 555 U.S. 7, 20 (2008). In other words, "[t]he standard for a preliminary injunction is essentially the same as for a permanent injunction with the exception that the plaintiff must show a likelihood of success on the merits rather than actual success". *Amoco*, 480 U.S. at 546 n. 12. Thus, CAFC cited both *Smith* and *Robertson* in the context of permanent injunctions. Richardson v. Suzuki Motor. Co. Ltd. 868 F. 2d. 1226, 1247 (Fed. Cir. 1989). *See infra* note 58 and accompanying text.

[12] *Richardson*, 868 F. 2d. at 1247.

[13] MercExchange, L.L.C. v. eBay, Inc., 275 F. Supp. 2d 695, 712 (E.D. Va. 2003).

[14] MercExchange, L.L.C. v. eBay, Inc., 401 F. 3d 1323, 1338 (Fed. Cir. 2005).

[15] *eBay*, 126 S. Ct. at 393.

than on other cases".[16] It avoided taking any position on whether to grant an injunction in the particular case. Instead, two concurring opinions seem to illustrate different views among Justices.

Justice Roberts' concurring opinion, joined by Justice Scalia and Justice Ginsburg, stated that the traditional practices of granting injunctive relief "in the vast majority of patent cases" were "not surprising" because "the difficulty of protecting a right to *exclude* through monetary remedies" "often implicates the first two factors of the traditional four-factor test".[17] While it attached an importance to exclusive power of the patent right, it seemed to recognise that there is no need to change the long-standing practices.

In contrast, Justice Kennedy's concurring opinion, joined by Justice Stevens, Justice Souter, and Justice Breyer, stressed the changing circumstances. Pointing out the emergence of the industry "in which firms use patents not as a basis for producing and selling goods, but, instead, primarily for obtaining licensing fees", it expressed concern that these firms might use injunction "as a bargaining tool to charge exorbitant fees" or use the threat of an injunction "simply for undue leverage in negotiation", especially when "the patented invention is but a small component" of the allegedly infringing products.[18] In such cases, it suggested that monetary damage would be sufficient as a remedy for patent infringement and warned district courts not to follow blindly the historical practice of issuing an injunction.[19]

2.5 *After* eBay

2.5.1 Overview

As mentioned above, it used to be a general rule to issue injunctions in patent infringement cases. It is no longer so after *eBay*. According to the survey by the University of Houston Law Center, among 230 district courts' rulings after *eBay* until 5/26/2013, permanent injunctions were granted in 168 cases, and denied in 62 cases.[20] The granting rate is about 73 %. Injunctions were denied in about one-fourth of the cases. This shows clearly the changing application of the four-factor test. A question is how it has changed.

---

[16] *Id.* at 394.

[17] *Id.* at 395.

[18] *Id.* at 396.

[19] Id. at 396–397.

[20] University of Houston Law Center, *Post-eBay Permanent Injunction Rulings By District Courts – to 5/26/2013*, available at http://www.patstats.org/Patstats2.html. The Center updates case lists every several months. However, the latest version of 5/26/2013 seems to delete by mistake six cases listed in the previous version of 11/30/2012, which can be also downloaded in the same URL. All of the six cases denied injunctions from 1/9/2012 to 12/3/2012. So we added these six cases to the latest version and calculated the figures in the text.

2.5.2 FTC's Analysis of Post-eBay Cases

The Federal Trade Commission (FTC) analysed how courts had applied the four-factor test after *eBay* in its 2011 report entitled "The Evolving IP Marketplace: Aligning Patent Notice and Remedies with Competition" (hereinafter Report).[21] Although theoretical aspects of the Report are discussed later in this chapter, the following is a brief summary of its findings.

First, the first factor (irreparable harm) of the four-factor test and the second one (inadequate monetary damage) are closely related because injuries suffered by the patentees are often considered irreparable when monetary damages are inadequate to compensate for that injury.[22] Although injunctions are typically granted in cases where patentees and infringers compete in a goods market, the courts may require the patentees to prove irreparable harm concretely with supporting evidence such as lost market share, lost customers, and price erosion.[23] Market definition matters in deciding whether customers would be lost due to infringement.[24] If the market is so narrowly defined that the infringer is the sole competitor, then lost market share would be easily established and so would be irreparable harm. On the other hand, if the market is so broadly defined that non-infringing third parties supply alternative goods in the market, it would be hard to establish lost market share and irreparable harm. Damages to a patentee's reputation may be considered to be inadequately compensated by money damages because they cannot be quantified.[25]

Second, injunctions are not necessarily denied even when patent holders are non-practising entities (NPEs) and do not compete with the infringers. The courts may grant injunctions to NPEs such as universities and research organisations, taking into account the existence of their exclusive licensees, damages to their reputation, or lost licensing revenues.[26] This means that the courts do not categorically deny injunctions simply because the patent holders were NPEs. Instead, the courts examine, on a case-by-case basis, whether NPEs could prove irreparable harm. Consequently, when the courts find that NPEs fail to show concrete evidence

---

[21] FEDERAL TRADE COMMISSION, THE EVOLVING IP MARKETPLACE: ALIGNING PATENT NOTICE AND REMEDIES WITH COMPETITION (2011), available at http://www.ftc.gov/os/2011/03/110307patentreport.pdf.

[22] *Id.* at 260. Rather, the first and the second factors seem to overlap, which led to criticism that the Supreme Court in eBay "erred by separating the two factors". DONALD S. CHISUM, CHISUM ON PATENT § 20.04 [2][c][iii] (2013).

[23] FTC, *supra* note 21 at 261.

[24] *Id.* at 262.

[25] *Id.* at 263. However, some commentators cast doubt on whether the fact of the infringement would "injure" a patentee's reputation. Rather, they assert, the infringer's use of the patented invention would enhance the patentee's reputation. Chien and Lemley (2012), p. 1, 13 n. 65.

[26] FTC, *supra* note 21 at 264–265. But see *supra* note 25 for arguments against damages to reputation. The argument that lost licensing revenues diminished a patentee's abilities to invest in R&D was also criticised as retrospective by another court on the ground that such harm was a past harm that may be recovered by damages and ongoing royalty would not harm the patentee in future. Hynix Semiconductor, Inc. v. Rambus Inc., 609 F. Supp. 2d 951, 983 (N.D. Cal. 2009).

of irreparable harm such as lost market share or lost opportunities of licensing, they deny injunctions to NPEs.[27] As Justice Kennedy's concurring opinion in *eBay* suggests,[28] the fact that the patented invention is a non-core, small component of the alleged infringer's product may be considered against injunctive relief.[29]

Third, in analysing the third factor (balance of hardships) of the four-factor test, the courts often rejected the infringers' claim by citing CAFC's statement that "[o] ne who elects to build a business on a product found to infringe cannot be heard to complain if an injunction against continuing infringement destroys the business so elected".[30] Balance of hardship weighs in the infringer's favour when the patentee fails to prove irreparable harm and injunction would have severe impact on the infringer.[31] Taking the infringer's hardship into account, the court sometimes delays the start of injunction for certain period of time so that infringers may design around the patent.[32]

Fourth, the fourth factor of the four-factor test (public interest) does not draw the attention of many courts. Courts often grant injunction, recognising that a strong patent system would serve the public.[33] On the other hand, courts discuss public interest extensively when the cases deal with health care products (e.g., drugs and medical devices) or computer security software.[34] This does not necessarily mean, however, that courts deny injunctions in these cases.

2.5.3 Chien and Lemley's Analysis of Post-eBay Cases

Chien and Lemley also reviewed post-eBay cases. Their findings are, in general, similar to those of FTC.[35] Moreover, their review of 192 district court decisions revealed an interesting result that grant rates of injunctions vary by type of

---

[27] FTC, *supra* note 21 at 265–267.

[28] *See supra* note 18 and accompanying text.

[29] FTC, *supra* note 21 at 267. In spite of Justice Kennedy's suggestion, a commentator pointed out that district court decisions have often rejected "small component" arguments. CHISUM, supra note 22 at § 20.04 [2][c][vi][C]. But *see infra* note 69 and accompanying text.

[30] FTC *supra* note 21 at 268. The cited text is in Windsurfing Int'l, Inc. v. AMF, Inc., 782 F.2d 995, 1003 (Fed. Cir. 1986).

[31] FTC *supra* note 21 at 269.

[32] FTC, *supra* note 21 at 270.

[33] *Id.* at 270.

[34] *Id.* at 271. A commentator points out that to protect valid patents is just one public interest and that "[t]he proper question on the public interest should be: will an injunction harm a specific public interest that 'outweigh[s] the public's interest in a robust patent system'?", even though he seems to have no objection to the conclusion of most cases that the public interest would not be disserved. CHISUM, *supra* note 22 § 20.04 [2][c][vii].

[35] Chien and Lemley (2012) at pp. 11–13.

patentee.[36] They classified the patent holders in four different categories: university/research organisation, individual, practising company, and patent assertion entities (PAEs).

"PAE" is the term proposed by Chien[37] to replace such terms as "NPE" or "patent troll". "Patent troll" may be the most commonly used term to accuse some patent holders of causing the hold-up problems described in Justice Kennedy's concurring opinion.[38] According to the then assistant general counsel at Intel who was said to begin using it, "[a] patent troll is somebody who tries to make a lot of money off a patent that they are not practicing and have no intention of practicing and in most cases never practiced".[39] "Patent troll" is, however, a vague notion. On the other hand, "NPE" means, by its term, an entity that does not practise the patented invention. It is relatively clear, but it includes universities. Arguing that universities engaging in technology transfer should be distinguished from other types of NPEs that may cause the above-mentioned problem, Chien proposed the term "PAE" in order to exclude universities from NPE. Chien defined PAEs as "entities that use patents primarily to get licence fees rather than to support the development or transfer of technology".[40]

Based upon this definition, Chien and Lemley identified PAEs, by using internet research and case pleadings, among patentees subject to investigation. Then they discovered that courts had denied injunctions more often to PAEs than the other three types of patentees. The injunction grant rate of PAEs is 26 %, whereas that of university/research organizations, individuals, and practising companies is 100, 90, and 79 %, respectively.[41] In addition, they found that the defendant did not contest injunction in four out of five cases where the court granted it to PAEs. Therefore, they concluded that PAEs "tend to succeed in their request [of injunction] only when the defendants failed to object".[42]

---

[36] *Id.* at pp. 10–11. 192 cases were taken from the above-mentioned survey by the University of Houston Law Center, *supra* note 20. It should be noted that Chien and Lemley used case lists in the survey until August 5, 2011. *Id.* at 9 n. 46. The case lists have been updated thereafter. *See supra* note 20 and accompanying text.

[37] Chien (2010), p. 297.

[38] *See supra* note 18 and accompanying text.

[39] *See* an interview with Mr. Peter Detkin in Sandburg (2001). In the article, Mr. Detkin also said, "[w]e were sued for the use of the term 'patent extortionists' so I came up with 'patent trolls'".

[40] Chien (2010) at p. 300. "Patent-assertion entities are focused on the enforcement, rather than the active development or commercialization of their patents." *Id.* at 328. FTC also used PAE in its report to "refer to firms whose business model focuses on purchasing and asserting patents that they typically purchase". FTC, *supra* note 21 at 50 n. 2. *See also* Lemley (2008), p. 611.

[41] Chien and Lemley (2012) at p. 10. Although the grant rate of university/research organisation is 100 %, it should be noted that there are only three cases.

[42] *Id.* at p. 11.

2.5.4 Causal Nexus Between Infringement and Harm

Recent CAFC decisions seem to impose a heavier burden on the patentee seeking a preliminary injunction, especially when the patented feature is just one of many features of the allegedly infringing product. One of the requirements for a preliminary injunction is to prove irreparable harm.[43] Whether the patentee successfully proved irreparable harm was one of the issues in both cases litigated between Apple and Samsung (*Apple I*,[44] *Apple II*[45]).

In *Apple I*, CAFC held that "a showing of some causal nexus" was required between infringement and the harm to the patentee "as part of the showing of irreparable harm", arguing that "[s]ales lost to an infringing product cannot irreparably harm a patentee if consumers buy that product for reasons other than the patented feature".[46] This means that the patentees must show that the patented feature drove the demand for the product.

However, it was not so easy to do so in this case, given that the products in question were smartphones and tablets. They had many features, and each of the asserted patents did not cover all of them. In fact, CAFC upheld the district court's denial of a preliminary junction with respect to three patents, including one utility patent and two design patents. The main reason for one of the design patents was that "smartphone design in general was not a determinative factor in consumer decision making".[47] The reason for the utility patent was that the patentee failed to show that it was either necessary to or a core functionality of the smartphone and that consumers' purchasing decisions were based on the existence of the feature protected by the patent.[48]

On the other hand, CAFC affirmed the district court's analysis of a likelihood of irreparable harm with respect to the second design patent on tablets.[49] Several factors were taken into account. One factor was that the patentee and the infringer were two big competitors in the tablet market. Therefore, the district court stated that "it is arguably more likely that market share lost by Apple [the patentee] will be lost to Samsung" (footnotes omitted), and CAFC endorsed this finding.[50] The other factors included the findings that "design mattered more to customers in making

[43] *See supra* note 11 for the other requirements.

[44] Apple, Inc. v. Samsung Elecs. Co., 678 F.3d 1314 (Fed. Cir. 2012) (hereinafter *Apple I*).

[45] Apple, Inc. v. Samsung Elecs. Co., 695 F.3d 1370 (Fed. Cir. 2012) (hereinafter *Apple II*).

[46] *Apple I*, 678 F.3d at 1324.

[47] Apple, Inc. v. Samsung Elecs. Co., 2011 U.S. Dist. LEXIS 139049, *67 (N. D. Cal., Dec. 2, 2011). *See* also *Apple I*, 678 F.3d at 1324.

[48] *Apple*, 2011 U.S. Dist. LEXIS 139049 at *124. *See* also *Apple I*, 678 F.3d at 1327.

[49] In spite of its support for the district court's analysis of irreparable harm, CAFC reversed its conclusion to deny injunctive relief. In doing so, CAFC held that the district court erred in finding that substantial questions were raised as to the validity of the patent. *Apple I*, 678 F.3d at 1328.

[50] *Apple*, 2011 U.S. Dist. LEXIS 139049 at *94. *See* also *Apple I*, 678 F.3d at 1328.

tablet purchases" and that the patentee "had claimed all views of the patented device".[51]

In *Apple II*, CAFC reiterated the causal nexus requirement. After referring to *Apple I*, CAFC in *Apple II* held that "to satisfy the irreparable harm factor in a patent infringement suit, a patentee must establish both of the following requirements: 1) that absent an injunction, it will suffer irreparable harm, and 2) that a sufficiently strong causal nexus relates the alleged harm to the alleged infringement".[52] *Apple II* seems to have followed *Apple I*, but it went one step further. *Apple I* stated that "some causal nexus" was required. On the other hand, *Apple II* stated that "a sufficiently strong causal nexus" was necessary. CAFC seems to have raised the bar for causal nexus.

Applying this standard to the specific facts of the case, CAFC reversed the district court's grant of a preliminary injunction. An asserted patent in *Apple II* was related to a unified search feature used in smartphones. Since the patentee's smartphone implemented the patented unified search feature in its application called "Siri", he argued that Siri was core to the functioning and sales of his smartphone, thanks to its search function. The district court agreed with the patentee and found the causal nexus requirement satisfied because the patentee successfully showed that "the '604 Patented feature is core to Siri's functionality and is thus a but-for driver of demand for Siri".[53]

However, CAFC rejected these arguments. CAFC criticised that the patentee's argument was based on circumstantial evidence of the popularity of Siri, which incorporated the unified search feature, and that such an argument did not directly tie consumer demand to the patented feature.[54] Instead, CAFC required the patentee to show that consumers bought the infringing product because it was equipped with the apparatus claimed in the patent.[55] Nonetheless, according to CAFC, the district court's findings indicated that some consumers who bought the patentee's smartphones liked Siri's search feature because of its comprehensive search function, and thus it did not mean that the patented unified search feature was the driver of consumer demand.[56] It further pointed out: "unified search is not one of the top five reasons consumers select Android smartphones".[57] CAFC concluded that the district court's findings were insufficient to satisfy the causal nexus requirement.

CAFC made the above-mentioned arguments in the context of preliminary injunctions. Thereafter, the district court in *Apple I* extended them to permanent injunctions. It held that the causal nexus requirement was applicable to permanent injunctions because the irreparable harm requirement was common in both

---

[51] *Apple I*, 678 F.3d at 1328.

[52] *Apple II*, 695 F.3d at 1374.

[53] Apple, Inc. v. Samsung Elecs. Co., 877 F. Supp. 2d 838, 909 (N. D. Cal. 2012).

[54] *Apple II*, 695 F.3d at 1375.

[55] *Id.* at 1376.

[56] *Id.* at 1376.

[57] *Id.* at 1376.

preliminary and permanent injunctions and "there is nothing in the *Apple II* opinion suggesting that its discussion of irreparable harm should be limited to the preliminary injunction context".[58]

The district court further contended that the patentee should establish causal nexus on a patent-by-patent basis, not on an aggregate basis.[59] Then, the court analysed each of the asserted patents and found the causal nexus for none of them. It listed several reasons: (1) the general importance of design in consumer choice of smartphones did not prove that the specific element of design covered by each of the asserted design patents drove consumer demand[60]; (2) quotations from consumer surveys and industry review to show the importance of particular designs were not "specific enough to clearly identify actual patented designs" and were anecdotal[61]; (3) the demonstration of the importance of ease of use in customer choice was too general, not specific to each of the asserted utility patents[62]; (3) individual consumers' voices did not represent the broader picture of consumer choice in the market[63]; and (4) the survey of willingness to pay for the patented feature among consumers who already purchased the product did not establish that the patented feature drove consumer demand for the product.[64] Accordingly, the district court found that the irreparable harm requirement was not established.

In this case, the patentee directly competed with the infringer in the market, which usually weighs in favour of issuing injunctions as explained above. While recognising this fact, the district court did not consider it determinative, arguing that "[w]ithout the required causal nexus, the parties' status as direct competitors simply does not justify an injunction".[65]

As a series of cases illustrate, the causal nexus inquiry makes it harder to grant injunction, especially when the infringing product has not only the patented features but also many other features. However, one may notice that *eBay* did not explicitly mention the casual nexus inquiry. It may raise a question of how it relates to the four-factor test. CAFC *in Apple II* explained: "the causal nexus inquiry is indeed part of the irreparable harm calculus: it informs whether the patentee's allegations of irreparable harm are pertinent to the injunctive relief analysis, or whether the patentee seeks to leverage its patent for competitive gain beyond that which the inventive contribution and value of the patent warrant".[66]

[58] Apple, Inc. v. Samsung Elecs. Co., 2012 U.S. Dist. LEXIS 179532, *31 (N. D. Cal., Dec. 17, 2012). *See also supra* note 11.

[59] *Apple*, 2012 U.S. Dist. LEXIS 179532 at *39.

[60] *Id.* at *41–42.

[61] *Id.* at *42–44.

[62] *Id.* at *44–45.

[63] *Id.* at *45–47.

[64] *Id.* at *48–50.

[65] *Id.* at *70.

[66] *Apple II*, 695 F.3d at 1375. *See also Apple I*, 678 F.3d at 1324.

In addition, in finding no irreparable harm caused by infringement of the patent that covered non-core technology of the product, the district court found it persuasive that Justice Kennedy, in his concurring opinion in *eBay*,[67] suggested a denial of an injunction based on the patent that covers a small component of the entire product.[68] The district court may have considered that Justice Kennedy's "small component" arguments supported the causal nexus inquiry. On the other hand, as a commentator observed, in many cases prior to *Apple I* and *Apple II*, the courts rejected "small component" arguments.[69] Thus, *Apple I* and *Apple II* imply that "small component" arguments in the context of the causal nexus inquiry may become more influential than ever.

2.6 Summary

The U.S. patent law makes it clear that an injunction is a remedy in equity and that the courts have discretion whether to grant or deny injunctive relief.

The courts are obliged to exercise such discretion in accordance with well-established equity principles, namely the four-factor test clarified in *eBay*. The four-factor test is, however, flexible enough to give the court broad discretion.

Historically, the U.S. courts have been applying the four-factor test in different ways. Before the *eBay* decision was made, CAFC tried to establish a general rule that injunction automatically followed the findings of infringement. However, such a general rule was rejected by the Supreme Court in *eBay*.

After eBay, the denial of injunction has increased. Although various factors have been taken into consideration, it turns out that some types of patentees such as PAEs hardly obtained injunctions.

Moreover, recent CAFC decisions seem to impose a heavier burden on the patentee to prove causal nexus between infringement and harm to the patentee, which may make it harder for the patentee to prove irreparable harm. It is not so clear whether the causal nexus inquiry will prevail. If it does, injunction may be denied more often than ever when the patented feature is just one of many features of the infringing product.

In sum, equity is characterised by its flexibility, and the four-factor test is no exception. The fact that injunction is a remedy in equity has nothing to do with the patent system. However, it gives the U.S. patent system the flexibility to take various policy considerations into account in granting or denying injunctions. Then what policy considerations should be taken into account in the current patent system? This is discussed in the following section.

---

[67] *See supra* note 18 and accompanying text.

[68] *Apple*, 2011 U.S. Dist. LEXIS 139049 at *124.

[69] CHISUM, supra note 22 at § 20.04 [2][c][vi][C]. *See also supra* note 29 and accompanying text.

3 Theoretical Analysis of Denial of Injunctive Relief

3.1 2011 FTC Report[70]

When analysing the theoretical aspects of denying an injunction, it will be helpful to refer to the analysis in the 2011 FTC Report, thanks to its comprehensiveness.[71] This Report proposes the improvement of patent notice and the coordination of remedies against patent infringement.

3.2 Ex Ante Patent Transactions vs. Ex Post Patent Transactions

When analysing the current state of the patent system, the FTC Report suggests drawing a distinction between ex ante patent transactions and ex post patent transactions. According to this Report, an ex ante patent transaction is a transaction that occurs before the purchaser has obtained the technology through other means and is accompanied by a technology transfer.[72] This Report makes the assessment that ex ante patent transactions are desirable because they advance innovation, create wealth, and increase competition among technologies.

By contrast, an ex post patent transaction is defined as a transaction that occurs after the firm has invested in creating, developing, or commercialising the technology.[73] Such ex post transactions occur because patent infringement is a strict liability offense, and firms need ex post licences to avoid liability even if they invented or obtained the technology independent of the patentee.

According to the FTC Report, strict liability for patent infringement is a necessary evil associated with the patent system. The threat of a patent infringement suit

[70] *See supra* note 21.

[71] At the request of the U.S. Congress to conduct research for the amendment of the patent law, this Report was prepared by the FTC in cooperation with the Patent and Trademark Office (PTO) and the Department of Justice (DOJ). The preparation of this Report was an ambitious undertaking in which 8 days of hearings (December 2008) and a workshop (May 2010) that involved more than 140 participants (businesses, start-ups, independent inventors, patent practitioners, economists, and patent law scholars) were held, and over 50 written submissions were received.

[72] FTC, *supra* note 21 at 40. The definition of an ex ante patent transaction under the FTC Report is as set forth in the main text, but when considering the subsequent discussions regarding patent notice, it may be more accurate to say that this term refers to a transaction for a patented invention (including the licensing and assignment of patent rights) that occurs before a (relationship-specific) investment is made for the exploitation of the patented technology.

[73] FTC, *supra* note 21 at 40 n. 43, 50. In the case of ex post patent transactions as well, when considering the subsequent discussions, it may be more accurate to say that this term refers to a transaction for a patented invention that occurs after a (relationship-specific) investment is made for the exploitation of the patented technology without any knowledge of the patent right.

deters infringement and safeguards the exclusivity that is at the heart of the patent system. A business model that is based on invention followed by technology transfer will only succeed if a firm can prevent copying and recoup its investment in R&D.

On the other hand, ex post transactions against independent developers distort competition in technology markets and deter innovation because the failure of ex ante transfer results in duplicated R&D effort. In addition, because relationship-specific investment and sunk costs have already been put into using the technology, the patentee can use such investment as negotiation leverage for a higher royalty, and as a result the increased uncertainty and higher costs can deter innovation.

3.3 Notice Problems

According to the FTC Report, the goal of the patent system is to facilitate ex ante transactions while making ex post transactions less necessary or frequent.[74] However, the status quo in certain industries (the IT industry in particular) is that the notice function of patents, which informs the public of what technology is protected and what is not ("patent notice"), is deteriorating.[75] Firms are forced into ex post transactions due to poor patent notice, which causes an excessive number of ex post transactions.

Accordingly, the source of this problem lies with notice problems or notice failure. According to the FTC Report, there are multiple factors that contribute to notice failure, such as overly broad and/or vague claims, the pendency of patent applications in the PTO, and the large number of patents that are potentially relevant to IT products.[76]

Viewed from this perspective, the existence of PAEs is considered to be particularly problematic. The FTC Report explains that the business model of PAEs, which focuses on purchasing and asserting patents against manufacturers already using the technology rather than developing and transferring technology, has amplified concerns about the effects of ex post patent transactions on innovation and competition.[77] This is because PAEs are mainly engaging in ex post transactions, and thus, the FTC argues, their activity can cause harm associated with ex post transactions.[78] The FTC further analyses notice problems as one of the

---

[74] FTC, *supra* note 21 at 9.

[75] *See, generally*, FTC, *supra* note 21 at 74–92.

[76] FTC, supra note 21 at 51, 81–91. The third factor is a phenomenon referred to as patent thickets or anti-commons.

[77] FTC, *supra* note 21 at 50–51.

[78] FTC, *supra* note 21 at 67–70.

conditions that make it easier for patentees like PAEs to pursue ex post patent transactions.[79]

3.4 Recommendations Made by the FTC Report

According to the FTC Report, clear patent notice can increase innovation by encouraging collaboration, technology transfer, and design around. Therefore, to facilitate ex ante transactions while minimising the frequency and risks of ex post transactions, it is imperative to make direct improvements to patent notice and to coordinate the remedies against patent infringement in order to mitigate the problems that are caused by poor patent notice, especially in the IT industry. This chapter will discuss the latter (i.e., the coordination of remedies against patent infringement) with a particular emphasis on injunctions.

Based on the analytical framework of *eBay*, it is necessary to restrict the right to seek an injunction in order to mitigate the adverse effects caused by the notice problem. The FTC Report provides recommendation on how the lower courts should apply these factors.

3.4.1 Recommendation Regarding Irreparable Harm and Inadequacy of Money Damages

The FTC Report points out that much discussion with respect to the first factor (irreparable harm) and the second factor (inadequacy of money damages) tends to focus on whether the patentee practises the invention, which may lead to a conventional assumption of both the categorical denial of injunctions for non-practising patentees and the categorical grant of injunctions for practising patentees.

However, as mentioned earlier,[80] the FTC considers such a conventional assumption inaccurate. Moreover, the FTC criticises categorical rules for neglecting the diversity of non-practising patentees, ranging from PAEs to universities and semiconductor design houses.[81] The FTC argues that since universities and semiconductor design houses compete in a technology market, infringement makes them suffer harm such as lost customers and disregard of their patents by the industry and that, thus, this harm is analogous to that suffered by manufacturing

[79] FTC, *supra* note 21 at 72. Although it is not clearly stated in the FTC Report, the high royalties that are realised through opportunistic behaviour, relationship-specific investment, and network externalities are arguably excessive as incentives for the contribution of technology.

[80] *See supra* note 23–29 and the accompanying text.

[81] FTC, *supra* note 21 at 228.

patentees.[82] Therefore, while acknowledging that the denial of an injunction may certainly prevent PAEs from engaging in opportunistic behaviour, the FTC stresses the importance of injunctions for universities and semiconductor design houses, which encourage ex ante transactions and also rely on the threat of injunctive relief against infringement to secure ex ante transactions.[83] Accordingly, the FTC Report makes the following recommendation:

> Courts should not presume irreparable harm based on a finding of infringement or the patentee's use of the patent. Conversely, courts should recognize that infringement can irreparably harm the ability of patentees that primarily engage in technology transfer through licensing to compete in a technology market.[84]

3.4.2 Recommendation Regarding Balance of Hardships Between the Parties

With regard to the third factor in the *eBay* decision (balance of hardships), the FTC Report states that when considering the extent of the hardship to the patentee, the first issue to look at is whether the invention is a minor component for which acceptable alternatives are available. The reason for this is that the contribution of the patented invention would be small in such cases.

Even though the invention covers just a small component of the whole product, the infringer has invested in the development of the whole product before ex post transaction occurs, which means that the infringer incurs the sunk costs. Taking advantage of this sunk cost, the patentee can capture hold-up value that it would not earn ex ante. Accordingly, the FTC Report concludes as follows:

> Courts should consider the hardship of an infringer facing hold-up under this prong. . .except in those instances where an infringer "elects" to infringe by copying a patented invention with knowledge of the patent.[85]

FTC explains that the proviso aims to limit the application of the argument that an infringer cannot be heard to complain if an injunction destroys its business,[86] assuming that many infringers may have no knowledge of the patent in question due to notice problems and, thus, may not truly "elect" to infringe it.[87] In addition, the proviso may be justifiable based on the reasoning that if an infringement is committed with the knowledge of the patent right, it was possible for the infringer to enter into an ex ante transaction, and there are no notice problems, so there is no need to restrict injunctive relief.

---

[82] FTC, *supra* note 21 at 229.

[83] FTC, *supra* note 21 at 229.

[84] FTC, *supra* note 21 at 230–231.

[85] *Id.* at 233.

[86] *See supra* note 30 and the accompanying text.

[87] FTC, *supra* note 21 at 232.

3.4.3 Recommendation Regarding Public Interest

As explained earlier, with regard to the fourth factor in the *eBay* decision, courts often cite the public interest in the ability of the patent system to promote innovation as supporting an injunction.[88] However, the FTC Report is skeptical of this approach because, while public interest is important, an injunction in some circumstances such as those involving hold-up based on a patent for a minor component could unduly raise the prices charged to consumers and deter rather than promote innovation. Accordingly, the FTC Report's recommendation regarding this issue is as follows:

> When warranted by the facts, courts should consider the public's interest in avoiding patent hold-up, which can increase costs and deter innovation.[89]

4 Denial of Injunctions Under the Japanese Patent Law

4.1 Status Quo

The Japanese Patent Act stipulates that "a patentee or exclusive licensee may demand a person who infringes or is likely to infringe the patent right or exclusive license to stop or prevent such infringement" [Article 100 (1)]. The conventional understanding of this provision is that once infringement is found, the patentee is entitled to demand permanent injunction. Thus, many seem to oppose restricting the availability of injunctions based on the ground that such restriction would contravene the purpose of the law, which is to grant full rights for patents that have been granted through examination by the Patent Office.[90] As a result, the effort to introduce legislation restricting the right to seek an injunction was abandoned by the Patent System Subcommittee in the Intellectual Property Policy Group of the Industrial Structure Council, which decided in February 2011 that it would not deal with this issue through new legislation due to the fact that there were arguments both for and against it.[91]

---

[88] *See supra* note 33 and the accompanying text.

[89] FTC, *supra* note 21 at 233.

[90] There has not been much debate regarding the restriction on the right to seek an injunction. But the type of attitude referred to in the main text may reflect the negative views concerning the active use of compulsory licences under Article 93 of the Patent Act, and the traditional view that sanctifies the exercising of the right to exclude, in principle, does not consider it to be a violation of Article 21 of the Antimonopoly Act, which provides that the exercising of patent rights is exempted from the application of the Antimonopoly Act.

[91] Industrial Structure Council, Intellectual Property Policy Group, Patent System Subcommittee Report "The Legislative Challenges regarding the Patent System" (draft) (2011) pp. 56–57, http://www.jpo.go.jp/shiryou/toushin/shingikai/pdf/tokkyo_syiryou034/01.pdf.

4.2 *Possibility of Abuse of Rights*

When courts believe that seeking injunctive relief constitutes an abuse of rights, they may, in theory, dismiss a claim for injunction under the current provision. In practice, they seldom do so. However, a recent decision implied a possibility that injunction may be denied on the ground of an abuse of rights.

This case was one of the worldwide litigations between Apple and Samsung.[92] It involved a Standard-Essential-Patent (SEP) concerning UMTS (Universal Mobile Telecommunications System) standards. The UMTS standards were developed by 3GPP (3rd Generation Partnership Project), which was organised by standard setting organisations such as ETSI (European Telecommunications Standards Institute). ETSI's IPR policies required their members to make reasonable efforts to disclose SEPs in a timely manner. They also provided that once SEPs were disclosed, ETSI asked SEP owners to guarantee that they were willing to grant irrevocable licences on FRAND (fair, reasonable, and non-discriminatory) terms.

In June 2005, the technologies proposed by the patentee in suit were adopted as UMTS standards. In May 2006, the patentee filed a Japanese patent application with prior date of May 2005, which led to SEP in suit subsequently. In August 2007, the patentee submitted disclosure of its patent application, as well as its FRAND declaration. In July 2011, the patentee sent the user of SEP a letter saying that it was willing to grant worldwide, non-exclusive licence with a certain royalty rate (the specific royalty rate was not disclosed in the judgment). The user's counterargument was that the royalty rate demanded by the patentee was unreasonably high. Then the user filed this suit to request confirmation of the non-existence of the patentee's right to seek damages based on FRAND-encumbered SEPs. Even after filing the suit, the user (plaintiff) made a counteroffer with a different royalty rate (again, the specific number was not disclosed in the judgment). Negotiation continued. However, no agreement had been reached.

The court first confirmed the general principle that parties in preparation for concluding contracts might bear an obligation to disclose critical information and negotiate in good faith even though it was not explicitly provided in the Japanese Civil Code. The court also noted that, given the FRAND declaration under ETSI's IPR policies, the patentee in suit owed an obligation to negotiate in good faith a licence on FRAND terms with anyone who seeks a FRAND licence. The court further continued that by the time the user in suit made a concrete counteroffer asking for a FRAND licence, the patentee and the user were in preparation for concluding a licence contract and, therefore, both parties were obliged to disclose critical information and negotiate in good faith. Based on this understanding, the court found that the patentee in this case violated the obligation to negotiate in good faith because he had never disclosed relevant information necessary for the user to decide whether either party's licence proposal was in compliance with FRAND terms. In addition, the court pointed out that the patentee kept filing petitions for

[92] Tokyo District Court, February 28, 2013, 2011 (Wa) No. 38969 (Apple v. Samsung).

preliminary injunction in different proceedings and that he disclosed the patent application of SEP in suit 2 years after the technologies covered by such SEP were adopted as standards. Taking these factors into account, the court held that exercising a right to demand damages without fulfilling an obligation to negotiate in good faith constituted an abuse of rights and, therefore, the patentee was not allowed to seek damages.[93]

Although only damages were disputed in this case, the court's argument may be extended to the issue of whether to grant injunction in a similar situation. In fact, the courts applied an abuse of rights doctrine to preliminary injunction. Intellectual Property High Court in its latest decisions held that it would be an abuse of rights for the patentees who made FRAND declaration to seek injunction against a willing licensee.[94] Consequently, as far as SEP is concerned, it is likely that a claim for injunction based on FRAND-encumbered SEP may constitute an abuse of rights and may accordingly be dismissed.

4.3 Denial of Injunction in Copyright Cases

In copyright law, there are two exceptional court decisions that appeared to introduce the *eBay* doctrine into infringement cases.

The first case concerned a photo book comprising 95 pages of B5 paper and a total of 177 photos. One of the nine photos located on the last page, which was 4 cm × 3 cm in size and occupied only a small area of the total page, was found to infringe copyright.[95] The court awarded damages but denied injunctive relief on the grounds that the amount of the loss was small and an injunction would prevent the defendant from selling this photo book in which it had already made a large investment. In addition, this was a case where the infringer was reusing a photograph that had appeared in an earlier edition, and the court also took into consideration the fact that there was a misunderstanding over whether or not the photographer was employed when the photo was taken and, thus, whether or not the work-for-hire doctrine may be applicable. Reference to such facts implies that the court dismissed a claim for an injunction not only because the infringer had made a significant relation-specific investment but also because it had a plausible reason to do so.

---

[93] This conclusion was modified by the appellate court. It held that seeking damages more than FRAND-royalties might constitute an abuse of rights. It further calculated the amount equivalent to FRAND-royalties. Intellectual Property High Court, May 16, 2014, 2013 (Ne) 10043.

[94] Intellectual Property High Court, May 16, 2014. 2013 (Ra) 10007, 10008.

[95] Naha District Court, September 24, 2008, *Hanrei Jiho* No. 2042, p. 95 [*Shashin De Miru Shuri-jo* Case].

The second case[96] was related to a book about a famous murder case. The plaintiff was the defendant in the murder case and sought both damages and an injunction to prevent publication of the book on the grounds of infringements of the right to privacy, the right of portrait, copyright, moral right of an author, etc. The defendant in this case included the author who wrote the book after a series of interviews and exchange of letters with the plaintiff, who was the defendant in the murder case. The book included copies of two letters from the plaintiff.

While admitting that publication and sale of the book, on the face of it, infringed the copyright and the moral right, the court denied an injunction, arguing that the acts of the defendants were not substantially illegal enough to justify an injunction. In reaching such a conclusion, the court took into consideration the following facts: the plaintiff gave his consent to a request from the author for quotation from two letters in her book; the murder case had a tremendous impact on society due to its cruelty and viciousness, as well as the plaintiff's age and his social status; the publication of the book concerned the legitimate interest of society and dealt with facts relating to public interest; and Article 41 of the Copyright Act exempted from infringement reproduction and exploitation for the purpose of reporting current events of a work involved in the event or seen or heard in the course of the event to the extent justified for purposes of news reporting.

On the other hand, the court awarded damages for emotional injury caused by reproduction of one of two letters that infringed the right to privacy, copyright, and moral rights, even though it denied the illegality of the reproduction of the other letter and, accordingly, dismissed a claim for damage.

In this case, copyright and moral rights were among a bunch of rights (e.g., the right to privacy and the right of portrait) that the plaintiff alleged were infringed, and the court might not have focused on IPR issues. Nevertheless, it is still a case in which the court denied an injunction while awarding damages against copyright infringement.

4.4 Summary

The Japanese Patent Act is considered to entitle patentees to injunction. Unlike the U.S. patent law, the statutory language of the Japanese Patent Act acknowledges no judicial power to deny injunction. Moreover, the statutory language supports the policy consideration that patent right should be protected to secure exclusivity. As a result, Japanese courts grant injunction almost automatically after finding infringement.

---

[96] Hiroshima District Court, May 23, 2011 *Hanrei Jiho*, No. 2166, p. 92. However, the findings of copyright infringement was overturned in the appellate court[Hiroshima High Court, May 30, 2013, 2012(Ne) 354].

However, this does not mean that the patentee's "rights" to demand injunction have no limit. They are subject to general civil law principles such as abuse of rights. The Japanese Civil Code Article 1 (3) stipulates that "No abuse of right is permitted". While Japanese courts may be able to use such general doctrine to deny injunctions, they have rarely done so except in a few cases.

Will we see more court decisions that follow these exceptional cases? At the present time, we don't think so. Not only the statutory language but also the policy consideration for strong property right may continue to be obstacles to the flexible approach in the U.S. In fact, in a case where just two lines in the defendant's book were found to infringe on a copyright, the court approved the suspension of the printing, publication, and distribution of the defendant's book in its entirety unless the infringing portion was deleted.[97] Thus, the prospects regarding the adoption of the *eBay* doctrine do not look very promising.

4.5 Analysis

As described above, there is a deep-set sense of discomfort in Japan with the flexible approach to injunctions that are set out in the *eBay* decision. In this regard, we must keep in mind that there are differences between the respective frameworks of Japanese law and U.S. law. The basic structure of the U.S. patent law falls under the common law system, and damages take precedence over injunctions. An injunction based on equity is granted only when monetary damages fail to provide adequate compensation. Therefore, as a matter of legal structure, it is natural for only monetary damages to be awarded in cases where injunctive relief is not considered to be appropriate as a matter of equity.

By contrast, the basic structure of the Japanese patent law falls under the continental law (civil law) system, and injunctions take precedence over damages. It is commonly recognised that the exclusive right of a patent comes first, followed by damages when such exclusive right is infringed. Accordingly, under Japanese law, it makes logical sense that injunctions precede damages.

However, if the ultimate goal of patent law is the prosperity of industry,[98] the exclusivity of patents is not an end in itself but merely a means to achieve this goal. Thus, if it is the case that the full enforcement of injunctions somehow hampers the achievement of this goal, necessary restrictions should be placed on this exclusivity.

Moreover, if the 2011 FTC Report is correct in its assessment that the patent system must take ex post factors (e.g., relationship-specific investments,

[97] Tokyo District Court, January 29, 2010, 2008 (*Wa*) 1586. However, the finding of copyright infringement was overturned in the appellate trial [Intellectual Property High Court, July 14, 2010, 2010 (*Ne*) 10017].

[98] Article 1 of the Japanese Patent Act provides as follows: "The purpose of this Act is to encourage inventions through promoting the protection and the utilization of inventions, and thereby contribute to the development of industry".

asymmetric bargaining powers, and opportunistic behaviour) into consideration, such factors should be considered somewhere in the system. However, in the ex ante examination by the Patent Office, consideration of anti-competitive effects is limited to technical matters (i.e., patentable subject matter, novelty, and non-obviousness). It is difficult for the Patent Office to consider ex post factors (e.g., relationship-specific investments, asymmetric bargaining powers, and opportunistic behaviour) in its ex ante examination because it cannot predict such factors in advance. The problem here relates to the ex post execution of rights, so it is more effective to rely on ex post adjustment by courts rather than on prior screening by the Patent Office.

From this perspective, we can see that a patent "right" at the stage where it has passed the examination and registration by the Patent Office is nothing more than a provisional right because it can be viewed as a mere transit point within the broader process in which the requirements for excluding others from using the invention are reviewed step by step. The scope of the patent "right" (or, more precisely, "restriction against the acts of others") gradually takes shape through this process.[99] The fact that the Patent Office granted a patent right does not mean that the patent right is exempt from scrutiny of other factors at a later time, such as in an infringement suit. The following chart summarises the whole process:

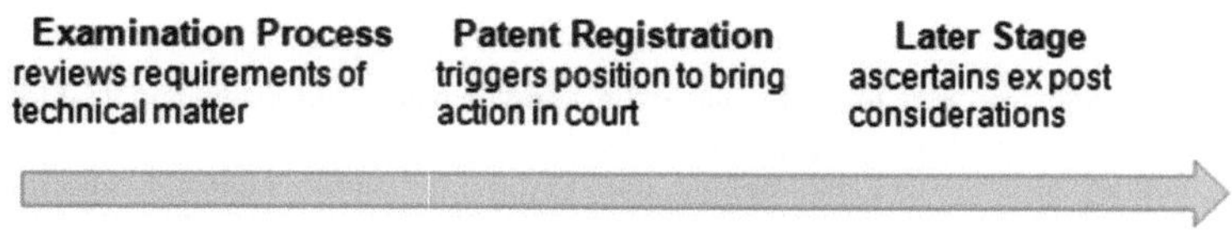

There are three possible institutions that can conduct an ex post examination at this later stage: the Patent Office, courts, and the Fair Trade Commission.

The Patent Office would employ a compulsory licence. The advantage of the Patent Office is that it has expertise in technical matters. The courts would employ the denial of injunctions discussed in this chapter. Courts are adept at gathering evidence regarding the situation of both parties. The Fair Trade Commission would rely on anti-monopoly regulations. The Fair Trade Commission is adept at assessing the market situation. In this way, each institution has its strengths and weaknesses. Accordingly, from an institutional design perspective, it is desirable to leave open the possibility of filing a claim under any of these methods instead of limiting the forum to any one of these institutions.

[99] Tamura (2013), p. 35.

5 Conclusion

We believe cases where the right to seek an injunction should be denied in infringement lawsuits can be broadly divided into the following three types.

The first type can be referred to as the "ex post factors type", where it is desirable to deny an injunction when taking into consideration the ex post factors that could not be considered at the time of examination by the Patent Office but need to be considered to achieve the goal of the patent system.

The second type can be referred to as the "public interest type". An example of this type is where a public health issue is involved.

The third type can be referred to as the "bona fide type". An example of this type is where patented technology is inserted into a standard in a concealed manner.

This chapter focused its theoretical analysis on the first type, which requires considerations that are unique to patent law. This is not in any way intended to negate the theories and possibilities for restricting the right to seek an injunction in the other two types.

References

Chien C (2010) From arms race to marketplace: the complex patent ecosystem and its implications for the patent system. Hastings Law J 62:297

Chien CV, Lemley MA (2012) Patent holdup, the ITC, and the public interest. Cornell Law Rev 98:1

Lemley MA (2008) Are universities patent trolls? Fordham Intellect Prop Media Ent Law J 18:611

Sandburg B (2001) You may not have a choice. Trolling for Dollars, 30 July 2001. http://www.phonetel.com/pdfs/LWTrolls.pdf

Tamura Y (2013) Innovation To Tokkyoseido (Innovation and patent system). Nihon Kogyo Shoyuken Hougakkai Nenpo (Annual Report of Japan Association of Industrial Property Law) 36:35

Review of Granted Compulsory Licences

Chung-Lun Shen and Jyh-An Lee

Contents

Abstract Legislators recognise that exceptions and limitations may be established to help the achievement of the ultimate goal under patent law. However, exceptions and limitations are made to keep the interest balance between the patentee and the public, including the potential competitors of the patentee. Such interest balance would be obtained when patentees are restrained from asserting their exclusive rights against some acts that have no substitution effects on the patented products and, at the same time, are conducive to the disclosure of and access to the patent to enhance the technological development. This inference is supported by Art. 30 of the TRIPS Agreement, after which limited exceptions can be allowed in patent law provided that they "do not unreasonably conflict with a normal exploitation of the

---

C.-L. Shen is Associate Professor of Law. J.-A. Lee is Assistant Professor of Law.

C.-L. Shen
College of Law, National Chengchi University, Taipei, Taiwan
e-mail: clshen@nccu.edu.tw

J.-A. Lee
Faculty of Law, The Chinese University of Hong Kong, Hong Kong
e-mail: jyhan.lee@gmail.com

R.M. Hilty and K.-C. Liu (eds.), *Compulsory Licensing*, MPI Studies on Intellectual Property and Competition Law 22, DOI 10.1007/978-3-642-54704-1_15,

patent and do not unreasonably prejudice the legitimate interests of the patent owner, taking account of the legitimate interests of third parties".

In our opinion, "a normal exploitation" and "the legitimate interests" of the patent should be subject to the substitution effects of the products made under compulsory licence, and the legitimate interests of third parties should be measured by whether such interests benefit the ultimate goal of patent law. When the infringing acts have no substitution effects, "a normal exploitation" and "the legitimate interests" of the patent are not negatively impacted, and such acts may justifiably be named as exceptions and limitations.

The granting of a compulsory licence functions through the waiver of specific exclusive rights, to an extent. Therefore, the granting of a compulsory licence is among the exceptions and limitations under patent law. Based on our arguments about the exceptions and limitations, the granting of a compulsory licence should be tested by the criteria of Art. 30 TRIPS Agreement to secure its justification.

1 Introduction

A compulsory licensing provision is common in most countries' patent laws.[1] Nevertheless, compulsory licensing is not often instituted in these countries.[2] The practice of compulsory licensing varies from country to country. For example, in Brazil compulsory licensing is occasionally used by the government as a tool to threaten drug companies to reduce prices.[3]

In recent years, a number of Asian countries have granted compulsory licences, leading to considerable international controversy among local governments, patent holders, and their home countries. Most of these compulsory licences concern citizens' access to essential medicines, pharmaceutical companies' incentive to invest in research and development for new drugs, and the correct interpretation of relevant international treaties, especially the Agreement on Trade-Related Aspects of Intellectual Property Rights (TRIPS), a fundamental set of game rules established by the World Trade Organization (WTO) members. Because the practice of compulsory licence significantly affects patent owners' profits from the domestic market and control over their inventions, most of them are against such practices. On the other hand, increasing drug prices have troubled governments in

---

[1] Dutfield and Suthersanen (2008), p. 127; Correa (1994), p. 330; See chapter "The Use of Compulsory Licences in Latin America" by Carlos M. Correa, in this volume. It should be noted that the United States is one of the few countries that do not include compulsory licensing provisions in its patent law, and it has continuously discouraged other countries from resorting to compulsory licensing. *See id*, pp. 127, 314–316; Ford (2000), pp. 953–354.

[2] See chapter "The Use of Compulsory Licences in Latin America" by Carlos M. Correa, in this volume; Goldstein (2008), p. 476; Dutfield and Suthersanen (2008), p. 127; Ho (2009a), p. 1071.

[3] Dutfield and Suthersanen (2008), p. 319; Emilio (2011), pp. 69–70.

developing countries where lack of access to affordable medicines imperils the health and lives of their citizens.

According to Art. 31 (i) and (j) of TRIPS, the "legal validity of any decision relating to the authorization" of compulsory licensing and "any decision relating to the remuneration" of such licence should be "subject to judicial review or other independent review by a distinct higher authority". Among the patent law of most countries, compulsory licensing and any decision relating to the remuneration of such licence are subject to judicial review. Very few of them have "other independent review by a distinct higher authority". Therefore, this chapter will start with a short note on the meaning of "other independent review by a distinct higher authority" (Sect. 2) and focuses mainly on judicial review of compulsory licensing cases by two Asian countries, namely India and Taiwan (Sect. 3). Then an inquiry into Art. 30 of the TRIPS Agreement for criteria for judicial review will be made (Sect. 4), which will be followed by the conclusion (Sect. 5).

2 The Meaning of "Other Independent Review by a Distinct Higher Authority"

According to Art. 31 of TRIPS, in additional to judicial review, compulsory licensing and any decision relating to the remuneration of such licence may also be subject to "other independent review by a distinct higher authority". However, TRIPS does not provide a clear definition of what "other independent review by a distinct higher authority" is. We argue that "other independent review by a distinct higher authority" is supposed to be made by entities other than judicial bodies. But does that mean that such "higher authority" is an administrative agency? We believe so. Having said so, and acknowledging that members have flexibility in implementing the review scheme,[4] the design of such "distinct higher authority" should be different from that of a typical administrative body. The "distinct higher authority" should maintain a certain degree of institutional independence to prevent interference from the administrative body that grants compulsory licensing. Therefore, the "independent review" is not purely administrative in nature but rather comes with a "quasi-judicial" characteristic so that the legislative purpose of Art. 31 can be achieved.

In Taiwan, the Taiwan Intellectual Property Office (TIPO) is under the Ministry of Economic Affairs (MOEA), which has oversight over the legality and appropriateness of decisions made by the TIPO via the Administrative Appeal Review Committee (AAPC). According to Article 52(2) of the Administrative Appeal Act, the members of the AAPC under the MOEA shall be chosen from the agency's

[4] Gervais (2008), p. 390; Ho (2009a), p. 688 ('In addition, the negotiating history confirms that there should be no restrictions on the type of subject matter considered permissible since such restrictions were actually contemplated and specifically rejected').

senior staff, righteous gentlemen in the society, scholars, or experts; inter alia, the ratio of the righteous gentlemen, scholars, and experts shall be not less than one half. We therefore argue that the AAPC is "a distinct higher authority" as required by Art. 31 of TRIPS.[5] The AAPC of the MOEA upheld the decision made by the TIPO, which granted a compulsory licence against Philips (for more, see Sect. 3.2).

3 Judicial Review of Granted Compulsory Licence in Certain Asian Countries

The Paris Convention and the TRIPS Agreement have not identified the legal substantive grounds upon which compulsory licences function, to allow flexibility for the granting authorities under national laws.[6] While Art. 5(A) of the Paris Conventions seems to position the prevention of abuse of patents as the justification for launching the compulsory licensing system,[7] Art. 31 of the TRIPS Agreement concentrates on the procedures that shall be followed prior to the grant of compulsory licences.[8] As a matter of fact, the Paris Convention attempts to exemplify "abuses of the patent" by using the terms "failure to work" or "insufficient working". However, the Paris Convention doesn't define what situations constitute the patentee's "failure to work" or "insufficient working". Furthermore, the assertion of the aforesaid two grounds shall be subject to "a grace period" for the patentee to work the patent to avoid the grant of compulsory licences.[9] It should also be noted that the grounds of "failure to work" or "insufficient working" merely form a prima facie of abuses of the patent. If the patentee could provide legitimate reasons for his inaction, "failure to work" or "insufficient working" would be justified.[10]

As we understand it, the possible grounds for the issue of compulsory licensing under the Paris Convention and the TRIPS Agreement should be read together with Art. 2(1) of the TRIPS Agreement.[11] Compulsory licensing functions as an exception or limitation to the exclusive rights enjoyed by the patentee. To secure the

[5] Mueller (2006), p. 583.

[6] Gervais (2008), p. 390; Ho (2009a), p. 688 ('In addition, the negotiating history confirms that there should be no restrictions on the type of subject matter considered permissible since such restrictions were actually contemplated and specifically rejected').

[7] *See* Art. 5(2) of the Paris Convention.

[8] *See* Art. 31(b) of the TRIPS Agreement.

[9] *See* Art. 5(4) ('A compulsory licence may not be applied for on the ground of failure to work or insufficient working before the expiration of a period of four years from the date of filing of the patent application or three years from the date of the grant of the patent, whichever period expires last; it shall be refused if the patentee justifies his inaction by legitimate reasons') of the Paris Convention.

[10] Bonadio (2012), p. 722.

[11] Art. 2(1) of the TRIP Agreement states: 'In respect of Parts II, III and IV of this Agreement, Members shall comply with Articles 1 through 12, and Article 19, of the Paris Convention (1967)'.

correctness of the grant of a compulsory licence, a review by court is indispensable according to Article 31 of the TRIPS Agreement. Under the judicial review, the legal validity of and remuneration for a granted compulsory licence should be examined.[12] The review of the legal validity of a compulsory licence is conducted to ensure that such licence complies with the interest measure established by Art. 31 of the TRIPS Agreement, namely to balance the conflict of interests between the patentee and the public, including competitors of the patentee. Therefore, the legal grounds for a compulsory licence, the scope and duration of the licence, and the properties of the licence should be thoroughly reviewed to justify the grant of a compulsory licence. It is worth noting that the Doha Declaration and the pending Article 31*bis* of the TRIPS Agreement were proposed to take into consideration the lack of pharmaceutical manufacture capability in some members. In this aspect, the review of the legal validity of a compulsory licence, especially on the occasions where public health is threatened by an epidemic, shall factor in the new norms under the Doha Declaration and Article 31bis of the TRIPS Agreement.

Generally speaking, the grounds for a compulsory licence have often drawn the most attention during review. Other aspects of review in accordance with the TRIPS Agreement have generally been incidental to the authority's ultimate decision as to whether a compulsory licence should be granted.

3.1 *India*

According to Art. 84(1) of the Patents Act 1970, there are three legal and substantive grounds for the application for a compulsory licence on specific patents, which are that "the reasonable requirements of the public with respect to the patented invention have not been satisfied", that "the patented invention is not available to the public at a reasonable affordable price", and that "the patented invention is not worked in the territory of India", respectively. In addition, Art. 84(1) complies with the Paris Convention by setting up the time limitation for application for such a licence, namely the application must be filed at the earliest on the expiration of 3 years from the date of the grant of a patent.[13] These three grounds created the main disputes in the following case, namely whether they are endorsed by the Paris Convention.

[12] *See* Art. 31(i) and (j) of the TRIPS Agreement.

[13] Art. 84(1) of the Patents Act 1970 states: 'At any time after the expiration of three years from the date of the grant of a patent, any person interested may make an application to the Controller for grant of compulsory licence on patent on any of the following grounds, namely:—(a) that the reasonable requirements of the public with respect to the patented invention have not been satisfied, or (b) that the patented invention is not available to the public at a reasonably affordable price, or (c) that the patented invention is not worked in the territory of India'.

The patentee, Bayer Corporation (hereinafter "Bayer"), owns a patent on a drug "Sorafenib" used in treating liver and kidney cancers at an advanced stage.[14] Bayer was granted the "Sorafenib" patent in India on March 3, 2008.[15] Bayer also had the regulatory approval for importing and marketing this drug under the trade name "Nexavar", which is subject to the protection of the "Sorafenib" patent in 2008.[16]

An Indian generic drug manufacturer, Natco Pharma Ltd. (hereinafter "Natco" or "the applicant"), applied for the grant of a compulsory licence on the "Sorafenib" patent on July 29, 2011.[17] Basically, Art. 84(1) of the Patents Act 1970 is stipulated as the legal grounds for the grant of a compulsory licence. The time limitation is obviously not the issue the two parties would like to argue in this case. The applicant in this case negotiated with the patentee to seek a voluntary licence on the patented drug and failed to conclude the licence due to disagreement on the price.[18] Such negotiation for a voluntary licence on a patent will be taken into account in determining whether a compulsory licence will be granted under Art. 84 (1) of the Patents Act 1970.[19] From this point, it seems that the requirement of Art. 31(b) of the TRIPS Agreement that the applicant negotiated a voluntary licence first is also satisfied in this case.

Based on Art. 84(6)(i) and 84(7)(a)(ii),[20] the Indian Controller of Patents favoured the applicant's arguments and thought that the insufficient quantum of the patented drug provided by the patentee through importation to the Indian market had never met the needs of patients despite the market statistical data supplied by the patentee.[21] The Controller also questioned whether infringing drugs marketed by M/s. CIPLA, another generic drug manufacturer in India, could effectively supplement the lack of the patented drug in market. After observing that the

[14] *See* Decision about Application for Compulsory License under Section 84(1) of the Patents Act, 1970 in respect of Patent No. 215758, at 4, the Controller of Patents, Mumbai, Compulsory License Application No. 1 of 2011, the 9th of March 2012 (hereinafter "Natco/Bayer C.L. decision").

[15] Natco/Bayer C.L. decision, at 5.

[16] *Id.*

[17] *Id.* On the review about the impact of compulsory licences on Indian markets and foreign investment, please see chapter "Economic and Procedural Constraints of Compulsory Licences for Medicines" by *Yugank Goyal*, in this volume.

[18] Natco/Bayer C.L. decision, at 6.

[19] *See* Art. 84(6)(iv) of the Patents Act, 1970.

[20] Art. 84(6)(i) of the Patents Act, 1970 states: (6) In considering the application filed under this section, the Controller shall take into account (i) the nature of the invention, the time which has elapsed since the sealing of the patent and the measures already taken by the patentee or any licensee to make full use of the invention. Art. 84(7)(a)(ii) of the Patents Act, 1970 states:(7) For the purposes of this chapter, the reasonable requirements of the public shall be deemed not to have been satisfied (a) if, by reason of the refusal of the patentee to grant a licence or licences on reasonable terms, (ii) an existing trade or industry or the development thereof or the establishment of any new trade or industry in India or the trade or industry in India or the trade or industry of any person or class of persons trading or manufacturing in India is prejudiced.

[21] Natco/Bayer C.L. decision, at 21–24.

patentee sought remedies against the infringement of the patented drug, the Controller found that the infringing drugs were actually facing the risk of having an injunction sought by the patentee, and it was not suitable to ignore the limited distribution to the patients.[22] The Controller then emphasised that even by adding the volume of the infringing drugs into calculation of the availability of the patented drug, the reasonable requirement of the public for the patented drug had not been satisfied.[23]

Although the Controller agreed with the patentee's argument about the interpretation of "the public" under Art. 84 (1)(b) of the Patents Act,[24] he also desired that the patentee should have implemented price discrimination on the patented drug to ensure affordability to the public.[25] The failure to use price discrimination seems to affect the interpretation of "reasonable affordable price". Additionally, the Controller affirmed his position again that the infringing drug products have no influence over the determination of the reasonable affordable price for the patented drug.[26] Finally, based on the fact that the price of the patented drug was prohibitive for the public, the Controller concluded that the second ground for the grant of a compulsory licence had been satisfied.[27]

The third ground for the grant of a compulsory licence is whether the patented drug has not been worked in the territory of India. After hearing the arguments made by the parties concerned, the Controller supported the applicant's position to limit the interpretation of "is worked" to the supply of the patented drug by local manufacture in India. There are three main reasons to justify the decision of the Controller. Firstly, the Controller rebuked the patentee over the amendment, in its submitted materials, of the text of Art. 84(7)(a)(ii). The Controller especially noted that the elimination of the requirement of local manufacture was made merely to shift implicitly this requirement into Art. 84 (1)(a) for determination of "the reasonable requirements of public", having nothing to do with the interpretation of Art. 84 (1)(C).[28] Moreover, the Controller recognised that the development of international patent law tends to authorise the states to establish the legal grounds for the grant of a compulsory licence to cope with public health threats.[29] Reading

---

[22] *Id.* at 21.

[23] *Id.* at 23.

[24] *Id.* at 30–31. In respect of "the public" stipulated under Article 84 (1)(b) of the Patents Act, the patentee argued that "reasonable affordable price" of the patented drug should be subject to the paying capacity of specific public sections rather than that of all public sections. The patentee claimed that the grant of a compulsory licence doesn't purport to make the lower class of patients on the paying capacity afford the patented drug to have the treatment of liver or kidney cancer.

[25] *Id.* at 30–35. The patentee further argued that the grant of a compulsory licence doesn't purport to make the lower class of patients on the paying capacity afford the patented drug to have the treatment of liver or kidney cancer.

[26] *Id.* at 36.

[27] *Id.*

[28] *Id.* at 39–40.

[29] *Id.* at 41.

the text of the Paris Convention on compulsory licence, the Controller also found that "failure to work" is not defined. As a consequence, without any contradiction with the Paris Convention, the Indian legislators had the discretion to set up the special requirement of local manufacture of the patented products to define "failure to work" in order to assuage the effects of patent abuses.[30] Finally, the Controller stated that the requirement of local manufacture is conducive to transfers of technology promoted by the TRIPS Agreement, and its benefits would be palpable, especially when the term of the patent expires.[31]

After the decision of compulsory licence was made by the Controller of Patents, Bayer moved its appeal to the Intellectual Property Appellate Board (hereinafter "IPAB"[32]). The appellant mainly raised six points to question the legality of the grant of compulsory licences, among which there are at least four questions connected with the substantive issues of compulsory licence.[33] Firstly, the appellant

---

[30] *Id.* at 41–43.

[31] *Id.* at 43–45.

[32] According to Section 120 (1) of the Patents Act, the Appellate Board established under section 83 of the Trade Marks Act 1999 shall be the Appellate Board for the purposes of this Act. Indian Trademark Act, section 92: (1) The Appellate Board Shall not be bound by the procedure laid down in the code of civil procedure, 1908 but shall be guided by principles of natural justice and subject to the provisions of this Act and the rules made thereunder, the Appellate Board shall have powers to regulate its own procedure including the fixing of places and time of its hearing. (2) The appellate Board shall have, for the purpose of discharging its functions under this Act, the same powers as are vested in a civil court under the Code of Civil Procedure 1908 while trying a suit in respect of the following matters, namely: (a) receiving evidence, (b) issuing commissions for examination of witnesses, (c) requisitioning any public record and (d) any other matter which may be prescribed. (3) Any proceeding before the Appellate Board Shall be deemed to be a judicial proceeding within the meaning of section 193 and 228, and for the purpose of section 196, of the Indian Penal Code and the Appellate Board Shall be deemed to be a civil court for all the purposes of section 195 and Chapter XXVI of the Code of Criminal Procedure 1973. The IPAB is therefore judicial in nature.

[33] Review Order about Decision of Compulsory License under Section 84(1) of the Patents Act, 1970 in respect of Patent No. 215758, at ¶4, Intellectual Property Appellate Board, Chennai, Order No. 45 of 2013, OA/35/2012/PT/MUM, the 4th day of March 2013 (hereinafter "Natco/Bayer C.L. Review Order"):

Learned senior counsel Mr. P.S. Raman appearing for the appellant submitted that the compulsory licence order was vitiated by several errors;

(i) Under Section 87(1) where the Controller should have arrived at prima facie satisfaction that a case has been made out, notice was not given to the appellant herein, which is a grave miscarriage of justice;
(ii) (The compulsory licence application is not supported by any evidence;
(iii) The appellant had sought for adjournment to enable the invention to be worked to the fullest extent and this was not granted, which is against the law;
(iv) While deciding whether the reasonable requirement of the public has been satisfied, the Controller ought to have taken into reckoning the presence of another player, CIPLA (not before us) and the supply made by CIPLA and by totally ignoring its presence, injustice has been caused;
(v) The Controller ought to have ascertained what is the reasonable price and thereafter, decided the issue of granting compulsory licence; and

argued that it is necessary to consider the existence of the patentee's competitors in the market of the patented medicine to decide if the reasonable requirement of the public has been satisfied.[34] The competitors mentioned by the appellant included the infringer in this case. Since another firm, CIPLA, was an infringer of the patent, and marketed the infringing medicine with an affordable price, the appellant thought that the infringing medicines sufficed to meet the urgent needs of the public for treating the cancers specified in the case. However, this argument was rejected by the IPAB.[35] Affirming the position of the Controller on this issue, the IPAB emphasised that the grant of compulsory licence is merely relevant to patented inventions. Further, in terms of systematic interpretation on patent law, the meaning of patented invention indicates an invention protected by a patent that is reflected in the products the patentee or its licensees will sell in the market.[36] Under such interpretation, the infringing products never came from the patented invention, so the reasonable requirement of the public should not be considered. Certainly, even though CIPLA's infringing products might deal with the need of the public for treatment of cancers specified in the case, the risk of judicial injunction sought by the patentee over the infringing medicine should not be ignored.[37] As long as such an injunction was made, CIPLA's infringing products would be forced to leave the market.[38] The uncertainty of legal risk of injunction strengthened IPAB's conclusion that CIPLA's infringing products are not a leeway for the patentee to escape the responsibility of marketing sufficient medical products for the public.[39]

Secondly, the appellant contended that the requirement of working under Section 84(1)(c) of the Indian Patents Act that constitutes a ground for the grant of compulsory licence wouldn't be satisfied merely by the manufacture of the patented products in the territory of India.[40] According to the appellant's opinion, the importation of the patented products may also meet with the aforesaid requirement of working. The IPAB adopted a more flexible interpretation on the require-

(vi) The controller was in error in concluding that the manufacture in India was necessary to meet the "working" requirement under Section 84(1)(c) of the Act.

[34] The substantive issue is "(iv) While deciding whether the reasonable requirement of the public has been satisfied, the Controller ought to have taken into reckoning the presence of another player, CIPLA (not before us) and the supply made by CIPLA and by totally ignoring its presence, injustice has been caused", mentioned in note 1. *See* also Section 84 of the Patents Act 1970.

[35] Natco/Bayer C.L. Review Order at ¶¶23–29.

[36] Natco/Bayer C.L. Review Order at ¶28 ("Therefore, the words 'patented invention' can only mean what the patentee or his licensee markets and nothing else").

[37] Natco/Bayer C.L. Review Order at ¶29.

[38] Natco/Bayer C.L. Review Order at ¶29 ("While it is true that the injunction application was closed, if CIPLA had failed to file the accounts as undertaken, it was open to the appellant to move the Court for modification of the order").

[39] It's the author's observation in this case.

[40] The substantive issue is "(vi) The controller was in error in concluding that the manufacture in India was necessary to meet the "working" requirement under Section 84(1)(c) of the Act", mentioned in note 1.

ment of working than the Controller did in the first instance.[41] The IPAB never thought that the working of the patented products merely goes through manufacturers, nor did it give a necessary interpretation of "working" to include importation.[42] Based on the practical need for the patented products in the Indian market,[43] as the authors observe to have been the case, the IPAB seemed to prioritise the interpretation of working as local manufacture. If the patented products weren't made in the local market and were instead imported, the patentee should have provided sufficient evidence to show the reason why the importation occurred in the place of manufacture in India.[44] Otherwise, the requirement of working would not be satisfied, and thus the grant of compulsory licence was justified under patent law. Obviously, the patentee in this case failed to disclose the grounds for the importation of the patented medicine, so IPAB concluded that Section 84(1)(c) is applied to grant a compulsory licence.

On the third substantive issue, the appellant questioned the interpretation of Section 84(1)(a) and (b) about "the reasonable requirement of the public" and "a reasonable affordable price".[45] On the "the reasonable requirement of the public", the appellant argued that the postponed marketing of the patented medicine resulting from compliance with the related statutory requirements should be recognised in its definition.[46] In addition, it further argued that the Patient Assistance Program, a social benefit program in India, also contributes to the fulfilment of the reasonable requirement of the public and is among the factors influencing the requirement.[47] Shifting the focus to "a reasonable affordable price", the appellant thought that "a reasonable affordable price" should be decided as one reasonable to

---

[41] Natco/Bayer C.L. Review Order at ¶52.

[42] Natco/Bayer C.L. Review Order at ¶52 ("Therefore, we cannot decide that 'the working' totally excludes import, or that 'working' is synonymous to "import" and that if there is no manufacture in India, then there is no working").

[43] Natco/Bayer C.L. Review Order at ¶51 ["Section 84(7)(e) which refers to the working of invention in the territory of India and importation from abroad of the patented articles, clearly indicates different activities. In a given case there may be an invention which cannot be manufactured in India and it is also possible that there is an invention where the reasonable requirement of public itself is small in number and setting up a factory just for the said purpose is not practicable"].

[44] Natco/Bayer C.L. Review Order at ¶52 ("In any event, we are not furnished with any evidence regarding this aspect viz., whether the appellant in its facility in India, which admittedly the appellant does not deny, could not have manufactured this drug. So, with regard to Section 84(1)(c), we find that the word 'worked' must be decided on a case to case basis and it may be proved in a given case, that 'working' can be done only by way of import, but that cannot apply to all other cases. The patentee must show why it could not be locally manufactured. A mere statement to that effect is not sufficient there must be evidence").

[45] The substantive issue is "(ii) The compulsory licence application is not supported by any evidence", mentioned in note 1.

[46] Natco/Bayer C.L. Review Order at ¶¶31–32.

[47] Natco/Bayer C.L. Review Order at ¶32.

the patentee and the public[48] and, consequently, that the R&D expenditure involved in the patent should be a significant factor in deciding what is a reasonable, affordable price for the patented medicine.[49] At the same time, the appellant was also concerned about distorting the market and opposed fixing the price for the patented medicine by the Controller through the grant of compulsory licence.[50]

The IPAB disagreed with the appellant on this issue and declared that the grant of compulsory licence is completely in accordance with public interest rather than exclusively with the patentee's interest or the licensee's interest.[51] The concept of public interest is a lever to check the affordability of the patented medicine. As to whether the reasonable requirement of the public was satisfied, IPAB resorted to assessing whether the commercial scale of the practising of the patented products had reached an adequate extent that is reasonably expected in the market.[52] Moreover, IPAB affirmed the Controller's position that the Patient Assistance Program would not work to satisfy the reasonable requirement of the public.[53] After considering the prohibitive price and insufficient quantity of the patented medicine in this case, the IPAB supported the Controller's opinion on the issue and held that Section 84(1)(a) and (b) applies to the grant of compulsory licence in this case.

According to the reviews about the aforesaid substantive issues, the IPAB affirmed the grant of compulsory licence in the appeal stage, except that IPAB modified the original order issued by the Controller about the royalty rate.[54] The case is worth observing further to see whether a motion of appeal will be made to the Indian Supreme Court.

---

[48] Natco/Bayer C.L. Review Order at ¶33 ("According to the appellant, the price of any product must be reasonable to the public and to the manufacturer/innovator").

[49] Natco/Bayer C.L. Review Order at ¶31 ("The affordability has to be decided considering the nature of the product and reasonably affordable price should be fixed taking into account the price at which the appellant can sell the product considering the expenditure incurred by them").

[50] Natco/Bayer C.L. Review Order at ¶35 ("Learned counsel submitted that in no case of compulsory licence anywhere, the authority had fixed the price and that fixing the price would actually distort the competition").

[51] Natco/Bayer C.L. Review Order at ¶43 ("Therefore, we must bear in mind that these proceedings are in public interest; they are neither against the inventor, nor in favour of the compulsory licensee").

[52] Natco/Bayer C.L. Review Order at ¶38 ("The reasonable requirements of the public would not be deemed to have been satisfied, if the patented invention was not being worked in the territory of India on a commercial scale to an adequate extent or on reasonable terms and was not being so worked to the fullest extent that is reasonably practicable [vide: Section 84(7)(d)]. The failure to meet the demand on reasonable terms must logically mean both quantity and price").

[53] Natco/Bayer C.L. Review Order at ¶42.

[54] Natco/Bayer C.L. Review Order at ¶54.

3.2 Taiwan

There were three recorded compulsory licences in Taiwan,[55] two of which had gone through judicial review, namely the Nippon Soda Topsin case and the CD-R case. The Tamiflu case was never appealed. However, the Nippon Soda Topsin case was based on a deleted provision and has no bearing on the current law. The following discussion will be limited to the CD-R case.

The TIPO raised five key reasons to justify its granting a compulsory licence in the proceedings before the Taipei High Administrative Court. Firstly, the TIPO asserted that "failure to conclude a licensing agreement having reasonable commercial terms and conditions in due time" can't be interpreted to have the precondition of "technological blocking" where the patentee fails to work the invention protected by the patent or to work the invention to the fullest extent in the market.[56] In the TIPO's position, "failure to conclude the licensing agreement" functions as an independent ground for the grant of a compulsory licence. Secondly, even though the applicant had practised the five CD-R patents prior to the grant of a compulsory licence, the TIPO opined that such practice never stops the applicant from applying for the compulsory licence over the same patents according to Art. 31(b) of the TRIPS Agreement, and as a consequence the compulsory licence granted by the TIPO doesn't contradict Art. 31(b).[57] Moreover, the TIPO concentrated solely on the calculation of royalties for the five CD-R patents to determine if the applicant had proposed reasonable commercial terms and conditions to the patentee for negotiation of the licensing agreement. The TIPO also set up the test of "a considerable period of time" by considering both the duration and terms of negotiation. After the interpretation of "the reasonable commercial terms and conditions" and "a considerable period of time", the TIPO concluded that the grounds for the compulsory licence have occurred in this case.[58]

Fourthly, the TIPO emphasised that the wording "such practice [under the compulsory licence] shall be mainly to supply the requirements of the domestic market" constitutes a condition attached to a compulsory licence rather than a ground for determining if a compulsory licence would be legally granted.[59] The applicant's exports involving the patented CD-Rs prior to the grant of a compulsory licence in this case seem to have nothing to do with the decision on a compulsory

[55] For more details, see the chapter "Compulsory Licence and Government Use in Taiwan: A Regress" by Kung-Chung Liu, in this volume.

[56] "The defendant's arguments (1)" under "the issues", Taipei Gao Deng Xing Zheng Fa Yan 95 Nian Du Su Zi Di 2783 Hao Pan Jue.

[57] "The defendant's arguments (2)" under "the issues", Taipei Gao Deng Xing Zheng Fa Yan 95 Nian Du Su Zi Di 2783 Hao Pan Jue.

[58] "The defendant's arguments (3)" under "the issues", Taipei Gao Deng Xing Zheng Fa Yan 95 Nian Du Su Zi Di 2783 Hao Pan Jue.

[59] "The defendant's arguments (4)" under "the issues", Taipei Gao Deng Xing Zheng Fa Yan 95 Nian Du Su Zi Di 2783 Hao Pan Jue.

licence made by the TIPO. Finally, the TIPO clarified that although the TRIPS Agreement has no self-executing effects over Taiwanese patent law, the ground for a compulsory licence under Art. 76(1) of Taiwan Patent Act doesn't violate Art. 31 of the TRIPS Agreement and Art. 5(A) of the Paris Convention.[60]

As a matter of fact, in this case, the real issue should be whether Philips's refusal to conclude a licensing agreement under Gigastorage's proposal of reasonable commercial terms and condition in due time would constitute an independent ground for the grant of a compulsory licence. This issue may be recognised further as whether failure to conclude a reasonable licensing agreement in due time would be considered a substantive ground for third parties to apply for a compulsory licence or just a necessary procedural step for the applicant to express its best efforts to seek a voluntary licence to avoid the distortion of compulsory licences, when the substantive grounds have been satisfied.

Unfortunately, the Taipei High Administrative Court didn't respond to the above-mentioned issue; instead, following the text of Art. 76(1) of the Patent Act, it merely reviewed what "reasonable commercial terms and conditions" means according to the provision. The Court found that the TIPO erred in evaluating "reasonable commercial terms and conditions" exclusively by royalty calculation and stated that it should be evaluated as a whole if the terms and conditions under a licensing agreement are reasonable.[61] As a consequence, the Court held that the compulsory licence granted by the TIPO should be revoked because the applicant failed to provide sufficient and convincing evidence to prove that the terms and conditions proposed are reasonable in the market.[62]

4 Criteria for Judicial Review of Compulsory Licence Under Art. 30 TRIPS

4.1 Whether There Is Deterioration of the Values Respected by Patent Law

Under the theory of utilitarianism,[63] there is a social contract between the patentee and the government on behalf of the public under patent law. On one hand, the government grants exclusive rights to the patentee to secure his future incentives for

[60] "The defendant's arguments (7)" under "the issues", Taipei Gao Deng Xing Zheng Fa Yan 95 Nian Du Su Zi Di 2783 Hao Pan Jue.

[61] *See* "the substantive issue (1)", paragraph 4, "the opinion", Taipei Gao Deng Xing Zheng Fa Yan 95 Nian Du Su Zi Di 2783 Hao Pan Jue.

[62] *See* "the substantive issue (1)", paragraph 6–21, "the opinion", Taipei Gao Deng Xing Zheng Fa Yan 95 Nian Du Su Zi Di 2783 Hao Pan Jue.

[63] *See* Dinwoodie et al. (2002), p. 49 ('Patent laws are intended to encourage the introduction of new technology and the public disclosure of new technological information by giving the owner of

innovation through adequate recovery of R&D expenditures and reasonable returns in practising the invention protected by the patent. On the other, the patentee shoulders the duty to provide the public with high-quality inventions such that the public can access those inventions for the purposes of learning, technological improvement, and even re-innovation. "High-quality" inventions are reflected in the eligibility and requirements of a patent under patent law, which include the subject matter of a patent, novelty, non-obviousness, utility, enablement, and written description.[64] It is worth noting that the requirements of enablement and written description further address the significance of invention disclosure for public notice due to intangible properties of a patent. According to the utilitarian theory, the granting of exclusive rights is merely the means to achieve the ultimate goal of enhancing technological development under patent law that is rooted in the disclosure of and access to the invention to be enjoyed by the public.

Certainly, legislators also recognise that exceptions and limitations may be established to help the achievement of the ultimate goal under patent law. However, exceptions and limitations are made to keep the interest balance between the patentee and the public, including the potential competitors of the patentee. Such interest balance would be obtained when patentees are restrained from asserting their exclusive rights against some acts that have no substitution effects on the patented products and, at the same time, are conducive to the disclosure of and access to the patent to enhance the technological development.[65] This inference is

the patent a limited right to exclude others from making, using, selling, or importing a product covered by the patent, in exchange for the patent owner disclosing the invention to the world').

[64] "Written description" came from the necessity of patent disclosure and public notice, the main purpose of which is to determine the scope and boundary of claims. This requirement has been admitted by U.S. patent case law. *See Regents of the University of California* v. *Eli Lilly & Co.*, 119 F.3d 1559 (Fed. Cir. 1997); *Ariad Pharms., Inc.* v. *Eli Lilly & Co.*, 598 F.3d 1336 (Fed. Cir. 2010); Crouch (2010), pp. 385–387; Schuster (2007), p. 491.

[65] For example, the exhaustion doctrine and the experimental exception under patent law. The substitution effects result from the infringer's unauthorised practice of a patent without any justified ground under patent law. Since patent infringement occurs through unauthorised practice of a patent, the marketing of infringing products often produces unexpected and unnecessary competition with patented products in the market. Such illegal competition launched by the infringer goes with the advantages of price due to lower cost sunk into patent infringement than new innovation. Therefore, as long as the quality of infringing products can follow that of patented ones, incentives may be created to attract consumers in the market to purchase the infringing products rather than the patented ones. This is called "substitution effects". The assessment of substitution effects has been playing a key role in the calculation of "lost profits" as patent damages. Substitution effects are also considered when the court interprets "fair use" under copyright law. Further, substitution effects are pivotal in the application of Art. 30 of the TRIPS Agreement. Canada—Patent Protection of Pharmaceutical Products, Report of the panel, WTO document WT/DS114/R, 17 March 2000, para. 7.55: The normal practice of exploitation by patent owners, as with owners of any other intellectual property right, is to exclude all forms of competition that could detract significantly from the economic returns anticipated from a patent's grant of market exclusivity. The specific forms of patent exploitation are not static, of course, for to be effective exploitation must adapt to changing forms of competition due to technological development and the evolution of marketing practices. Protection of all normal exploitation

supported by Art. 30 of the TRIPS Agreement, after which limited exceptions can be allowed in patent law provided that they "do not unreasonably conflict with a normal exploitation of the patent and do not unreasonably prejudice the legitimate interests of the patent owner, taking account of the legitimate interests of third parties".[66]

4.2 Whether There Are Substitution Effects

In our opinion, "a normal exploitation" and "the legitimate interests" of the patent should be subject to the substitution effects of the products made under compulsory licence, and the legitimate interests of third parties should be measured by whether such interests benefit the ultimate goal of patent law. When the infringing acts have no substitution effects, "a normal exploitation" and "the legitimate interests" of the patent are not negatively impacted, and such acts may justifiably be named as exceptions and limitations.

The granting of a compulsory licence functions through the waiver of specific exclusive rights, to an extent. Therefore, the granting of a compulsory licence is among the exceptions and limitations under patent law. Based on our arguments about the exceptions and limitations, the granting of a compulsory licence should be tested by the criteria of Art. 30 to secure its justification.[67]

Art. 5 of the Paris Convention, which was incorporated into the legal system under the TRIPS Agreement, is to be interpreted according to Art. 30 of the TRIPS Agreement. Under Art. 5(A) of the Paris Convention, the granting of a compulsory licence is to alleviate the effects resulting from abuses of a patent. "Abuses of a patent" may be understood as the occasions where the execution of exclusive rights over the subject matters has very limited economic benefits to the patentee but hinders the achievement of the ultimate goal under patent law, violates fundamental values in human society, or restrains third parties from competing with the patentee in the market.[68] However, on attempting to cure the negative effects due to patent

practices is a key element of the policy reflected in all patent laws. Patent laws establish a carefully defined period of market exclusivity as an inducement to innovation, and the policy of those laws cannot be achieved unless patent owners are permitted to take effective advantage of that inducement once it has been defined.

[66] *See* Art. 30 of the TRIPS Agreement ('Members may provide limited exceptions to the exclusive rights conferred by a patent, provided that such exceptions do not unreasonably conflict with a normal exploitation of the patent and do not unreasonably prejudice the legitimate interests of the patent owner, taking account of the legitimate interests of third parties').

[67] Gervais (2008), p. 381 ("Given the specific mention of this type of use in art. 31, art. 30 should not apply to those cases. Otherwise, there would have been no need to list specific conditions to be met in art. 31") (omitted note 612). But Art. 30 seems to be flexible in establishing the exceptions of the exclusive rights to achieve a balanced interest between the patentee and the public under patent law. See the chapter "Limiting Patents" by Lionel Bently and Brad Sherman, in this volume.

[68] *See* Liu (2012), pp. 690–692; Liu (2008), pp. 772–774.

abuse through the grant of a compulsory licence, Art. 30 of the TRIPS Agreement reminds us of the substitution effects of the products produced under compulsory licence in the markets. In other words, the grant of a compulsory licence works as interference into the marketing scheme of the patentee who is protected by exclusive rights, merely through supplementing the patented products to keep the public from the harm of patent abuse. It was never the original expectation of legislators that the Paris Convention or the TRIPS Agreement should allow the products made under a compulsory licence to compete directly with the patented products in the market. From this point, "failure to work" and "insufficient working" would be recognised as a necessary threshold to apply compulsory licensing to cure patent abuses even though such wording hasn't been presented in the TRIPS Agreement.

As a consequence, the judicial review over the legal validity of a compulsory licence should establish clear grounds justifying its granting, connected with the abuses of a patent, and make sure that the products under a compulsory licence work as complements to cure the patent abuses.

Taking the *Natco* case in India as an example, the interpretation of Art. 84(1) of the Patents Act ought to seek the real grounds on which the values pursued by the legislators are deteriorated by patent abuse, and secure that the compulsory licence will not substantially influence the normal exploitation and legitimate interest enjoyed by the patentee due to substitution effects in the market. In fact, Art. 84 (1) (a), (b), and (c) of the Patents Act merely cite inadequate or insufficient supplies of the patent products caused by abuses of a patent, which hinder attainment of a specific value that the legislators cherish and wish to ensure through patent law. The granting of a compulsory licence under such circumstances is expected to lead to more patented products to resolve the aforesaid inadequate or insufficient supplies. As mentioned above, the Doha Declaration authorises members to establish the grounds for granting a compulsory licence. And the legal ground in the case of *Natco* is undoubtedly related to public health. The Indian Controller's decision to grant a compulsory licence on the patented drug treating liver and kidney cancers does not seem to run counter to the TRIPS Agreement and the Paris Convention. However, the patented drug in *Natco* was not used to respond to an emergency in the form of a pandemic in India but was a long-term treatment to extend the lives of patients. Based on the therapeutic effect of extension of lives, the Controller in *Natco* did not seem to question further whether there were any alternatives having similar therapeutic effect, as well as acceptable price in the market.

On the contrary, if there are other similar qualified drugs serving as alternatives to the patented drug, the failure to ascertain the market share of the patented drug inevitably distorted the decision on granting a compulsory licence. Under such circumstances, the alternatives might work with the patented drug as complements to satisfy the adequate and sufficient requirement for patients suffering from liver or kidney cancer. As a consequence, when the compulsory licence was granted on the patented drug, the licensed products would compete directly with the patented drugs, rather than supplementing the inadequate and insufficient supplies to secure specific value protected under patent law. The substitution effects resulting from the direct competition with the patented drug do not justify the grant of a compulsory licence. It is worth noting that in determining the market share of the patented drug, the infringing drug in the market should be ignored. The infringing drug could bring in a competitive and affordable price, but it is vulnerable to the risk of an injunction by the court and may lack sufficient authorised tests of its safety and therapeutic effect. Consequently, the infringing drug should not be counted into the assessment of the market share of the patented drug. Additionally, irrespective of importation from foreign markets or manufacture in India, the availability of the patented drug in the market should be evaluated in the overall market. Distinguishing the origin of the patented drug when deciding the grant of a compulsory licence might violate the principle of technological neutrality expounded by Art. 27(1) of the TRIPS Agreement.[69]

The "Tamifu" case in Taiwan involved the issue of public health. As the purpose of grant of a compulsory licence was to combat the threat of Avian Influenza H1N1 under the circumstance of insufficient supplies of the patented drug, the ground for the grant of the compulsory licence is justified in terms of the Paris Convention and the TRIPS Agreement. The order issued by TIPO to use the patented drug as a priority over compulsorily licensed one may be inferred that the TIPO seemed to have recognised the substitution effects in determining whether a compulsory licence would be granted.[70]

Compared with the "Tamifu" case, the CD-R case in Taiwan was more controversial in terms of the grounds for the grant of a compulsory licence. In spite of never being addressed by the Taipei High Administrative Court, the issue should have been whether the refusal to issue a voluntary licence, or the failure to conclude a voluntary licence in due time, constituted an independent ground for the grant of a compulsory licence under Taiwanese patent law even though reasonable terms and conditions had been offered. As we discussed in this chapter, the grant of a compulsory licence is to assuage the negative effects caused by patent abuses. Prior to applying for a compulsory licence, the applicant is obliged to prove that a specific value that patent law is intended to foster has been deteriorated by patent abuses.[71] Then the applicant also needs to raise evidence that the products under a compulsory licence will work as complements, rather than substitutions, to secure the aforesaid value from the impact of patent abuses. However, in this case, it seems that the applicant neither clarified what value behind patent law is susceptible to patent abuses nor ensured that a compulsory licence will be indispensable to restore such value against patent abuses without delivering any unfair substitution effects on the patented products. We firmly believe that the simple refusal to grant a voluntary licence or the failure to conclude a voluntary licence in due time never constitutes an independent ground for the grant of a compulsory licence under

[69] *See* Bonadio (2012), pp. 722–724.

[70] TIPO, the decision of a compulsory license, Zhi Fa Zi no. 09418601149 (智法字第0941860114號).

[71] de Carvalho (2005), p. 320 ('Refusals to license patents violate the law only when they are accompanied by an otherwise unlawful conduct').

Taiwanese patent law. Otherwise, the provisions about the compulsory licence will forestall any possibility of voluntary licence. To grant a compulsory licence in place of a voluntary licence without any justification is certainly not the value the legislators sought.

5 Conclusion

The issue of compulsory licence has been among the most controversial ones under patent law. In view of the developments on the grant of compulsory licence in the global community, the grounds for the application of a compulsory licence usually are the basis for much dispute between the applicant and the patentee. While the textual indication of Art. 5(A) of the Paris Convention seems to consider "failure to work" the invention protected by the patent or "insufficient working" of such invention an independent ground for the grant of a compulsory licence, the TRIPS Agreement does not even clarify the grounds for the grant of a compulsory licence but merely addresses the negotiation obligation prior to applying for a compulsory licence. This chapter attempts to probe into the relation between patent abuses and the substantive grounds for a compulsory licence. We find that the real grounds result from the deterioration of the values behind patent law by patent abuses, for example anti-competitive effects, threats to public health, obstruction of the achievement of the ultimate goal of patent law, and so on. This is the first step for the judiciary to take when reviewing the justification for the grant of a compulsory licence.

Moreover, based on Art. 30 of the TRIPS Agreement, this chapter also argues that the judicial review should ascertain that the products made under a compulsory licence work as complements, rather than substitutions, to cure the negative effects caused by patent abuses. This is the second step for the judicial review to take when probing the justification for the grant of a compulsory licence. Ignoring these two steps of a review would deprive a compulsory licence of its justification and even impair the function of a voluntary licence under patent law. At the same time, such neglect will also run the risk of hindering compulsory licence from the adequate role of exceptions and limitations under patent law.

References

Bonadio E (2012) Compulsory licensing of patents: the Bayer/Natco case. Eur Intellect Prop Rev 34(10):719–728

Correa CM (1994) The GATT agreement on trade-related aspects of intellectual property rights: new standards for patent protection. Eur Intellect Prop Rev 16(8):327–335

Crouch D (2010) An empirical study of the role of the written description requirement in patent examination. Northwestern Univ Law Rev Colloquy 104:382–397

de Carvalho NP (2005) The TRIPS regime of patent rights. Kluwer Law International, Frederick

Dinwoodie GB et al (2002) International and comparative patent law. Lexisnexis, Newark
Dutfield G, Suthersanen U (2008) Global intellectual property law. Edward Elgar, Cheltenham
Emilio AB (2011) Tripping over TRIPS and the global HIV/AIDS epidemic: legislation and political decisions in Brazil and the United States. J Contemp Health Law Policy 28:57–85
Ford SM (2000) Compulsory licensing provisions under the TRIPS Agreement: balancing pills and patents. Am Univ Int Law Rev 15:941–974
Gervais DJ (2008) The TRIPS Agreement: drafting history and analysis, 3rd edn. Sweet & Maxwell, London
Goldstein P (2008) International intellectual property law: cases and materials. Foundation Press, New York
Ho CM (2009a) Unveiling competing patent perspectives. Houston Law Rev 46:1048–41114
Ho CM (2009b) Current controversies concerning patent rights and public health in a world of international norms. In: Takenaka T (ed) Patent law and theory: a handbook of contemporary research. Edward Elgar publishing, Cheltenham, pp 673–711
Liu KC (2008) Rationalising the regime of compulsory patent licensing by the essential facilities doctrine. Int Rev Intellect Prop Comp Law 39(7):757–774
Liu KC (2012) The need and justification for a general competition-oriented compulsory license regime. Int Rev Ind Prop Comp Law 43(6):679–699
Mueller JM (2006) Note: the tiger awakens: the tumultuous transformation of India's patent system and the rise of Indian pharmaceutical innovation. Univ Pittsburgh Law Rev 68:491–640
Schuster MI (2007) Sufficient disclosure in Europe, is there a separate written description doctrine under European Patent Convention? Univ Missouri-Kansas City Law Rev 76:491–504

Part III
Doctrinal Discussions

Limiting Patents

Lionel Bently and Brad Sherman

Contents

Abstract Drawing on the 2010 WIPO Study into patent exclusions and exceptions, the chapter examines the limits that are placed on patents in different countries around the world. After looking at some of the problems that arise in undertaking a global study of this nature, we then look at some of the key reasons given for the existence of different exclusions and exceptions. This is followed by a wide-ranging historical account of the fate of exclusions and exceptions over the last century. The chapter ends by speculating on possible future developments and a plea to ensure that the flexibility in international law is not constrained unnecessarily.

L. Bently is Herchel Smith Professor of Intellectual Property; Director of CIPIL.
B. Sherman is Professor of Law.

L. Bently
Faculty of Law, University of Cambridge, Cambridge, UK
e-mail: lb329@cam.ac.uk

B. Sherman
Law School, University of Queensland, Brisbane, Australia
e-mail: b.sherman@griffith.edu.au

R.M. Hilty and K.-C. Liu (eds.), *Compulsory Licensing*, MPI Studies on Intellectual Property and Competition Law 22, DOI 10.1007/978-3-642-54704-1_16,

1 Introduction

After a period of time at the end of the twentieth century that was dominated by an overriding concern with strengthening patent rights, over the last two decades or so there has been a renewed interest in the limits of patent protection. Concerns about the protection of inappropriate subject matter (notably genes, computer-related inventions, and business methods), worries that a fall in the standards used to determine patentability (particularly in relation to inventiveness), and a growing interest in the adverse impact that patent protection has on science have given rise to a range of different questions: where should the boundaries of protection be, what are the appropriate thresholds for protection, and what type of subject matter should be protected? Building on the lesson that what is not protected may be as important as what is, there has been a renewed interest in many countries around the world in re-examining the limits of patent protection.

This renewed interest in the limits of patent protection has also been present at the international level. After a period of discussion and debate in a number of international fora, it was decided at the 13th session of WIPO's Standing Committee on the Law of Patents, held on March 2009, that a study would be commissioned on exclusions, exceptions, and limitations that 'focused on, but not limited to, issues suggested by members such as public health, education, research and experimentation and patentability of life-forms, including from a public policy, socio-economic development perspective, bearing in mind the level of economic development'.[1] The resulting study, which was submitted at the 15th session of the Standing Committee on the Law of Patents on October 2010 and discussed at the 15th, 16th, and 17th sessions, is a wide-ranging and detailed review of exceptions and exclusions in patent law around the world. This chapter builds upon the WIPO Study to examine some of the ways that patents have been limited and how they have changed over time.

2 Problems in Studying Patent Limitations

Undertaking a global study of the limitations to patent protection gives rise to a number of challenges. One problem, which is endemic to comparative studies of this nature, is the question of how to ensure that we are comparing like with like. In some cases, the problem may be that two countries may use the same term to describe what, in practice, may be very different things. In other cases, a limitation that achieves similar results may be called different things in different countries. Another problem that needs to be taken into account when thinking about patent limitations—which we return to in more detail later in the chapter—is that the

[1] WIPO (2010), para. 9(c)(i).

relative effectiveness of particular limitations will always be influenced by an array of different factors, which may differ between countries and change over time.

Another problem that needs to be confronted when thinking about the way that patents are limited relates to the question of where the boundaries of the project should be set. While this is an issue in all projects, it is particularly acute here, given that patents are limited geographically, temporally, and qualitatively. In addition to limiting the types of subject matter that are potentially protectable, applicants must also show that their invention is industrially applicable, useful, new, and non-obvious (or some similar requirement). Applicants must also disclose their inventions in such a way that they can be repeated. Patents are also only granted for a 20-year period in the territory in which they are registered. While they are very wide ranging, the types of uses that fall within a patent owner's control are also limited, both in terms of the types of uses that are protected and the situations where third party use is excused from prosecution. The fact that patents are limited in a variety of different ways means that a study of limitations is potentially coextensive with a general study of patent law. These problems are made worse by the fact that some of the different limitations are interchangeable. For example, in some jurisdictions, the subject matter exclusion has been interpreted in such a way that it overlaps with the inventive step requirement. In other cases, the policy goals of exclusions can sometimes be performed equally well by exceptions. To some extent, many of these problems were resolved in the WIPO Study as a result of the fact that it was limited to a study of exclusions and exceptions in patent law. In the study, *exclusions* were defined to mean exclusions from the subject matter of patents, no matter how novel or inventive something may have been. This would include, for example, the exclusion of abstract theories, discoveries, and methods of treatment. In turn, an *exception* was defined to mean limitations that are imposed on patentees' rights such as a limitation excusing from liability uses that would otherwise violate a patentee's rights because they are used for research or education. These are referred to as 'exceptions', 'defences', 'permitted acts',[2] 'free uses', 'restrictions', or 'users' rights'. Exceptions were also defined to include situations where a person is able to use the subject matter of a patent on payment of a fee. These are usually referred to as 'compulsory licences', 'non-voluntary licences', or 'statutory licences'.

In studying patent exceptions and exclusions as part of a broader inquiry into the appropriate limits of patent protection, it is important to understand the rationales or goals that lie behind particular limitations. For various reasons, this is a problematic but essential exercise. Given the vast number of exceptions and exclusions and the fact that these have changed considerably over time, it is not surprising that the Study found that the explanations given for the existence of different exceptions and exclusions were often inconsistent, changing, and controversial. In many cases, the Study found very little material to explain the exclusions from patentability or exceptions to patentees' rights. In part, this is because there has rarely been a

[2] Cook et al. (2010).

careful analysis of when and why limits are drawn or how incommensurable values are to be weighed against one another. Indeed, as the law of patents has become more globalised and underpinned by increasingly detailed international norms, it seems that less and less thought is given to the justification for individual legal provisions and more and more to questions of adequate compliance. In many ways, the problems encountered in the Study are not that surprising, given that lawmakers rarely provide clear explanations as to what their provisions are intended to achieve. These problems are exacerbated by the fact that exceptions and exclusions are often introduced to deal with a specific problem or issue. Despite this, however, and this is particularly the case with legislative limitations, when a solution is developed it is often recast in abstract neutral language (rather than referring to the specific issue that may have instigated the reform in the first place).

These problems are exacerbated by the fact that different justifications are sometimes given to explain the same exclusion or exception in different countries. For example, while animals are excluded in Europe on the basis of public policy, in Canada the Supreme Court excluded animals from patentability on the basis that they did not fall within the definition of invention.[3] In turn, the countries of the Andean Community exclude '[a]ny living thing, either complete or partial, as found in nature, natural biological processes, and biological material, as existing in nature, or able to be separated, including the genome or germplasm of any living thing' from patentability because these are not inventions. The situation is much the same in relation to 'discoveries'. In Europe, for example, discoveries are excluded because they are 'abstract', 'intellectual', and 'non-technical' in character: in short, they are not inventions. In contrast, the explanation for the exclusion in the United States is more explicitly policy oriented. In *Gottschalk v Benson* (1972), for example, the Supreme Court explained that the exclusion from patentability of natural phenomena, mental processes, and abstract intellectual conceptions was explicable because these are the 'basic tools of scientific and technological work'.[4] While the explanation for the exclusion of discoveries in the EPO is ontological—discoveries are by their very nature not inventions—in the United States the question of whether discoveries of naturally occurring phenomena are inventions is not a key concern: rather, discoveries are excluded because of the consequences that would arise if they were protected.[5]

Despite these problems, the WIPO Study was able to identify a number of different rationales or explanations for the existence of different exclusions. One of the most common reasons given for excluding subject matter is because it does

---

[3] *Harvard College v. Canada (Commissioner of Patents)* 2002.

[4] But cf. *In re Meyer* 1982, citing *Leroy v Tatham* 1852, 'scientific principles and laws of nature, even when for the first time discovered, have existed throughout time, define the relationship of man to his environment, and, as a consequence, ought not to be the exclusive rights to any one person'.

[5] The exclusion of discoveries (where the use of the discovery is unknown) has also been explained on the related ground that the subject matter lacks utility or industrial applicability. See *Brenner v. Mason* 1966.

not qualify as an invention. In many jurisdictions, this was the reason for not protecting biological innovations, computer programs, mathematical methods, and discoveries.[6] In other situations, more pragmatic and practical reasons have been offered to explain the reason why certain types of subject matter have been excluded from protection. This is the case, for example, in relation to the exclusion of computer programs that was initially justified, at least in some cases, on the basis that the patent offices were not set up to deal with this new technology. As the U.S. President's Commission on the Patent System said in 1966, the 'Patent Office now cannot examine applications for programs because of a lack of a classification technique and the requisite search files'. These problems were exacerbated by the fact that 'even if these were available, reliable searches would not be feasible or economic because of the tremendous volume of prior art being generated. Without this search, the patenting of programs would be tantamount to mere registration and the presumption of validity would be all but non-existent'.[7]

Another common and relatively uncontroversial reason for excluding subject matter from patent protection is because it is already (adequately) protected by some other form of intellectual property. This is often the case with literary and artistic works (which are protected by copyright)[8] and plant varieties (which are protected by plant breeders' rights legislation). The Eurasian Patent system seems to take a similar approach to subject matters that could be protected by trademarks (symbols) and designs law. In a limited number of situations, certain types of inventions have been excluded on the basis that there are certain categories of invention that are undesirable to encourage. In such cases, it would be odd to offer incentives to produce such inventions by granting patents. The most obvious example of such subject matter relates to inventions the exploitation of which would be contrary to public policy or accepted principles of morality.

A number of other inventions have been excluded on the basis that the benefits that flowed from patenting were outweighed by countervailing principles that demanded that the subject matter in question should not be protected. Historically, this was the case, for example, in relation to medicines and food (which are no longer able to be excluded under TRIPS). Some countries do, however, maintain

[6] The EPC defines a non-exhaustive list of matters that are deemed not to be inventions. The 'exclusions' from patentable subject matter, in effect, clarify the 'positive' side of what is protectable. Other examples of this approach can be seen in the Andean Pact (Art 15 of decision 486), as well as the national laws of Algeria and South Africa. Article 6 of the Algerian Patents Ordinance 19/07/2003 – 1424, No. 03–07; South Africa Patents Act No 57 of 1978.

[7] Quoted in *Gottschalk v Benson* 1972.

[8] European Patent Convention (1973), Art 52(b). The United States has operated a 'printed matter' exception': In re Ngai, (2004) (printed matter teaching new use for an existing product does not render otherwise unpatentable use protectable, the court observing that if the position was otherwise 'anyone could continue patenting a product indefinitely provided that they added a new instruction sheet to the product'). Some laws, particularly those of countries that are parties to the Eurasian Patent Convention, go further and specify that integrated circuits, buildings, and aesthetic designs are not protectable by patents. Law on Inventions, Utility Models and Designs 2008, Art 10(1)(g), (h), (i) (Armenia).

the possibility of operating such exclusions. The patent law of Ghana, for example, excludes 'products and processes excluded by law for national security, economy, health or any other national concern', while Jordan and Moldova exclude inventions necessary to protect the life and health of humans. Kenya similarly excludes 'designated methods for the prevention or treatment of serious health hazards and life threatening diseases'. These systems recognise that in certain circumstances, where the free exploitation of an invention is necessary to promote public health (etc.), there should be no property rights over those subjects. In these situations, the logic of patent law should give way to the greater social good.

The WIPO Study also identified a number of different overarching rationales that were used to justify and explain the various exceptions to patentee's rights. In many cases, the exceptions from a patentee's rights were explained by reference to the core rationale for the provision of patents: namely, to provide an incentive to invest in research and to disclose information by the provision of short-term monopoly rights. In principle, patents should only be granted where and to the extent that such monopolies are required to rectify market failure. They should also not be granted where to do so would restrict further invention. Essentially, this is a cost-benefit analysis: can the same incentive be provided with less social cost? Or would a marginal reduction in the incentive lead to a significant reduction in social cost? Some limitation on patentee's rights can be explained by the fact that extending protection to cover the permitted act would not enhance incentives significantly (or appropriately). This is a common explanation for exceptions relating to private use (or the corollary, the limitation of the patentee's rights to commercial, trade, or business uses.) Many countries exclude from liability either de minimis uses[9] or uses that are non-commercial. The Egyptian law permits 'Acts not prejudicial to normal exploitation of the patent, or the interests of patent owner and third parties'. The Community Patent Convention—which never came into operation but influenced the drafting of the laws of many European countries—provided that acts that are done privately *and* for non-commercial purposes do not infringe.[10] In the United Kingdom, this has been interpreted as meaning that while private uses need not be secret or confidential, they must be 'for the person's own use'.[11] Where an activity has both commercial and non-commercial benefits, it is necessary to ascertain the subjective intention of the user. If the infringer was motivated by commercial interests, the defence would not apply. However, if the subjective purposes were non-commercial, the defendant could rely on the immunity. This is the case even if the resulting information has a commercial benefit.[12]

A number of other exceptions exist because they are needed to ensure that the patent system doesn't undermine the very goals that it is attempting to achieve. The

[9] See, e.g., *Finney v. United States* 1975. The experimental use exception was sometimes viewed as part of the de minimis rule: *Byam v. Bullard* 1852.

[10] Community Patent Convention (1979), Art. 31.

[11] *SKF Laboratories v. Evans Medical* 1989; *McDonald v. Graham* 1994.

[12] *SKF Laboratories v. Evans Medical* 1989.

most obvious of these is the experimental use exception. As it is a universal premise of modern patent systems that the patentee discloses the invention so that the public can perform the invention, it is necessary that third parties are able to experiment with the invention to ascertain whether it in fact works (and is sufficiently disclosed). As patent offices do not undertake this task, this freedom must be conferred on competitors, as it is they who have the incentive to investigate and ultimately challenge the validity of the patent. Moreover, this capacity to investigate the invention must be given from the moment the patent is granted. After all, there would be no point in requiring competitors to wait until after the patent had lapsed before they could challenge the patent. This justification for the experimental use exception would, of course, only justify a narrow exception to experiment on the subject matter of the invention. It would, however, be compatible with experiments that ultimately have a commercial purpose, given that a competitor's motivation is to compete.

Other exceptions reflect the fact that while the incentive to invest offered by a patent is an important goal, it sometimes conflicts with other goals or interests, and the latter are regarded of a higher rank or importance. The most obvious examples are the exceptions and compulsory licences relating to national security and emergencies, such as the exception in the Bangui Accord that permits exploitation by an administration or organisation authorised by the Minister of the Member State concerned for the purposes of 'vital economic interest, public health, defence or the country's needs', subject to remuneration.[13] Other countervailing public interests include free competition, education, and privacy. Education seems to be prioritised over patentees' interests in the countries (mostly from South America) that expressly except use in teaching from the patentee's rights.[14] Arguably, privacy interests also justify the exception for 'private use' (though this exception can also be justified on the basis of market failure).

Exceptions may also operate to reconcile patents with private interests. One such interest is the 'right of property' in tangible objects (and the social interest in the alienability of such property). The conflict between the scope of intellectual property rights and property rights can be seen most obviously in the doctrine of 'first sale' or 'exhaustion of rights'. Here, the presumption in the free alienability of tangible property prevents patentee's rights reaching beyond the first marketing of patent products. In Europe, the principle of exhaustion of rights also represents a prioritisation of the goal of creating a single Community. Sometimes, exceptions are also deemed to be desirable in order to maintain existing social practices and expectations. One obvious example relates to the farmers' privileges.

---

[13] Ukraine (use in emergency conditions such as natural disaster, accident, epidemic and use by a person authorised by the Cabinet of Ministers to protect the health of population, ecological safety, or other public interests), Uzbekistan (use in cases of natural calamities, disasters, epidemics, and other exceptional circumstances).

[14] Argentina, Bolivia, Columbia, Costa Rica, Ecuador, Guatemala, Mexico, Nicaragua, Peru, and Uruguay. The two other countries are Poland and Switzerland.

The preservation of expectations also provides a convincing rationale for the US exception for use of certain methods by medical practitioners.

3 Towards a History of Exceptions and Exclusions

The WIPO Study was underpinned by a broad-ranging historical review of exclusions and exceptions adopted in countries around the world and an examination of how they have changed over time. The historical analysis showed that while exclusions from patentability have a lengthy history, the existence of exceptions was a more recent phenomenon. Historically, exclusions and exceptions have arisen in one of two ways. One approach that has been adopted in many countries has been expressly to exclude subject matter or types of inventions in the relevant patent legislation (or occasionally in related statutes). The French Law of 1844, for example, excluded 'pharmaceutical compositions or medicines of all kind' and 'schemes and combinations relating to credit and finance' from protection. The second way that exclusions and exceptions have arisen is a result of judicial innovation and interpretation. This approach has been widely adopted in common law countries, which have tended to operate with a general rubric as to patentability, which has been flexibly interpreted over the centuries. For example, for many years patentability in the United Kingdom turned on the interpretation of the Jacobean phrase 'manner of new manufacture', the domain of monopoly grant preserved for the Crown by the famous Statute of Monopolies of 1623. Over time, this phrase was interpreted by the courts to exclude an array of different types of subject matter, such as 'principles'[15] (which has been excluded from the late eighteenth century). The United States offered a slightly different model but again built around a similar rubric, echoed in slightly different form in the offered patents to 'any person who has invented or discovered any new and useful art, machine, manufacture or composition of matter, or any new and useful improvement thereof'.[16] Over time, the broad definition was qualified by judicially developed doctrines that covered an array of aberrant subject matter, including the 'moral utility doctrine',[17] aspects of the 'natural world', 'discoveries',[18] 'unembodied inventions', the 'handiwork of nature', medical inventions,[19] and business methods. A similar fate also befalls exceptions.

One of the general findings of the WIPO Study was that the history of exclusions and exceptions could be divided into two periods. The first, which spanned the period from around the 1883 Paris Convention until the late 1990s (when TRIPS

---

[15] Boulton v. Bull 1795; Pila (2010), pp. 25–108.

[16] Patent Act of 1793, ch 11, s. 1 (US); Patent Act of 1870, ch 230, s. 24 (US).

[17] *Lowell v Lewis* 1817; *Evans v. Eaton* 1818; *Juicy Whip Inc v Orange Bang* 1999.

[18] *Morton v. NY Eye Infirmary* 1862.

[19] See Duffy (2009–2010), pp. 634–637; Anon (2007–2008), pp. 303–304.

was implemented in Member States), was marked by the growth in the number of exceptions and exclusions and by the absence of international norms. The second period, from TRIPS until the present day, saw a number of changes, including the development of international norms, a decline in the number of exclusions, and the beginning of a migration towards exceptions. We will look at each in turn.

4 Exclusions and Exceptions Pre-TRIPS

There are a number of notable characteristics of the law that related to exclusions and exceptions in the pre-TRIPS period. One of which was that exclusions and exceptions were primarily a question for national law. In part this occurred because while the Paris Convention provided a framework for international patenting, it did not impose any significant limitations on what a Member State could deem to be patentable or what could be excluded. As long as there was no discrimination on the grounds of nationality, the Paris Convention gave members of the Union freedom to adopt the exceptions they considered to be appropriate in their national law. The one notable limitation on subject matter is found in Article 4 quarter. This provides that

> The grant of a patent shall not be refused and a patent shall not be invalidated on the ground that the sale of the patented product or of a product obtained by means of a patented process is subject to restrictions or limitations resulting from domestic law.

Just as the Paris Convention did not control the exclusions from patentability, so too it set no positive requirements about what the exceptions needed to look like. With the exception of forfeiture, compulsory licensing, and ships, aircraft, or land vehicles that temporarily or accidentally visited a country, the Convention did not—and still does—limit national law. Instead, national laws were left with the freedom to limit rights as they saw fit.

While there may have been a lacuna in international patent law in relation to exceptions and exclusions, this does not mean that national laws were developed in isolation. Indeed, one of the findings of the WIPO Study was the impact that traditions of colonisation and other historical networks of influence had on the adoption and adaptation of patent law in many countries. The Study also found that many national patent laws were shaped by regional agreements (notably the 1973 European Patent Convention, the 1994 Eurasian Patent Convention, and the 2000 Andean Agreement) and by WIPO model laws.

Another notable characteristic of the law in the pre-TRIPS period was that there was a gradual but consistent proliferation in the number of exclusions and exceptions. The Study also found that there was also a degree of standardisation in the types of things that were excluded—or at least the way that these were expressed. This was particularly the case in relation to methods of medical treatment, animal varieties, plant varieties, biological processes, nuclear technologies, and computer programs.

The proliferation and standardisation was particularly notable in relation to exclusions to patentable subject matter. Thus, while at the time of the Paris Convention (1883) there were only a handful of different types of things that were excluded in a limited number of countries, a century later there had been a rapid increase both in the types of things that were excluded and the number of countries that applied these exclusions. While the exceptions to patentee's rights have a less impressive history in the pre-TRIPS period than exclusions, nonetheless the overall picture is very similar. Thus, while there were very few exceptions in 1883, a very different picture emerged over the following century. Over this time, a number of statutory exceptions have become more common. For example, 'exhaustion' and 'prior use' now appear in the laws of many countries. The exception on experimental use, which was all but non-existent at the end of the nineteenth century, is now one of the most common exceptions.

There are a number of reasons for the increase in the number of exclusions and exceptions that occurred in the pre-TRIPS period. One simple reason was the expansion in what was *potentially* patentable, which, in turn, was a consequence of shifts in technological capacity following breakthrough inventions and discoveries, most obviously in the fields of atomic energy, electricity, computing, and biology.

While the incremental expansion in the types of things that are potentially patentable led to an increase in the categories of subject matter that were excluded, there are a number of notable changes: one of which was the gradual extension of patent protection across the twentieth century to biological materials, including plants, microorganisms, genetically modified organisms, animals, and (potentially) to humans. While various types of inventions such as letter bombs, contraceptives, and abortifactants have already been excluded because to protect and thus to sanction them was seen to be immoral, the specter of patent protection for living things galvanised political opposition. Drawing on a range of ethical and religious arguments, opponents of patents on life successfully lobbied for the introduction and/or expansion of the types of inventions that should be excluded from patent protection because, put simply, it would be wrong to grant them protection. In Europe, this led to a list of inventions that were excluded such as processes for cloning human beings, processes for modifying the germ line genetic identity of human beings, and uses of human embryos for industrial or commercial purposes.[20] In a similar vein, the fear that the extension of patent law to biological inventions would restrict access to food and undermine food security prompted many countries to exclude 'food' and 'food processing' from patent protection.

In the same way in which the patenting—whether real or threatened—of new types of subject matter was a key motivation behind the development of a number of new exclusions, the increase in patentable subject matter also led to an increase in the number of exceptions to protection. This was one of the consequences of the extension over the latter part of the twentieth century of patent protection into areas

[20] EU Biotech Directive (1998), Art. 6.

of basic science, which was particularly evident in relation to biotechnology. Concerns over the negative consequences of this expansion led many to ask whether the parameters of the exclusions should be strengthened (for example, so that the exclusion of discoveries are made more robust) or whether the goal of keeping basic science free could be accommodated through exclusions. Many countries have acted on these concerns and introduced or strengthened private use and experimental use exceptions to ensure ongoing access to the basic building blocks of science.

Yet another explanation for the proliferation in the number of exclusions and exceptions is the changing standing of patents in the eyes of policymakers and economists. The broad ranging resistance to patenting that was exhibited in the name of economic liberalism and free trade in the nineteenth century has given way to a much wider acceptance of the benefits of patenting. However, limits to patenting emerged in relation to activities that were not regarded as economic or that countries sought to insulate from market mechanisms.

The growth in the number of exceptions is also an indirect product of the increase in the number of regulatory mechanisms that pharmaceutical companies now have to meet before they can place a new drug on the market. One of the unintended consequences of this was that it eroded the time patentees had to exploit their inventions (which has been compensated by the development of a range of supplementary protection schemes). The flipside of this was the question of whether patent protection could be used to prevent a competitor who intended to market a generic drug once the patent term for the drug had expired from gathering the information needed for regulatory approval during the patent term. While in many countries this is possible under the research exception, there were doubts in the United States that the existing defences could be relied upon for this to occur. To overcome this problem, the so-called Bolar exception was introduced, which allows third parties to experiment on patented inventions in order to acquire the data needed to gain regulatory approval on generic inventions.[21,22]

In many cases, the increase in the number of exclusions can also be attributed to the growing number of countries that have signed up to regional agreements that mandated that Member States exclude certain subject matter or provide limits to patent owner's rights. For example, Article 52 of the 1973 European Patent Convention contained a non-exhaustive list of things that were deemed not to be inventions and thus not to be patentable: discoveries, scientific theories, mathematical methods, methods of performing a mental act, playing a game or doing business, aesthetic creations, presentations of information, and computer program. The European Patent Convention also includes exclusions in relation to biological subject matter, immoral inventions,[23] and methods of medical treatment.[24]

[21] *Roche Products Inc. v Bolar Pharmaceuticals* 1984.

[22] Heath (1997).

[23] Article 53.

[24] WIPO (1979), Art. 112.

The model law for developing countries developed by WIPO in 1979, which contained a similar list of things that were not to be protected, also had a degree of influence.

While regional mechanisms played an important role in expanding the reach of the exclusions and in standardising the form that these took, the same cannot be said about the role that the regional agreements played in relation to exceptions. This is because with the notable exception of the WIPO Model Law of 1979, the regional agreements were much less concerned with exceptions than they were with the granting of rights. We have already seen how the menu of exclusions embodied in the European Patent Convention directly limited the options of members of the European Patent Convention (and associated territories). However, because the Convention is only concerned with the regulation of the grant of rights, it contains no provisions on exceptions. That is not to say that regional standardisation of exceptions has not occurred in Europe. Rather curiously, there has been some standardisation via the Community Patent Convention (1975), which contained provisions in relation to a range of exceptions, including acts done privately and for non-commercial purposes, acts done for experimental purposes,[25] exhaustion,[26] and provision for 'prior users' to retain personal rights.[27] While the Convention never made it into force, nevertheless it provided a model for European countries that was widely adopted. Indeed, most European countries (apart from Austria) incorporated these provisions into their national law in anticipation of the Convention coming into force.[28] For various reasons, this never occurred.

While the growth in the number of exceptions occurred in an environment of relatively limited international norms, nonetheless international patent law played an important role in reinforcing a particular way of thinking about exceptions. Specifically, the Patent Co-operation Treaty played a role in building an international consensus and the de facto standardisation of the type of things that were excluded. Although the Treaty did not require substantive harmonisation of national laws, the Treaty appears to have indirectly standardised a bundle of exclusions. This is because Rule 39.1 of the Patent Co-operation Treaty declares that the International Search Authorities are not required to search an international application if the subject matter falls within any of the following categories:

(i) scientific and mathematical theories;
(ii) plant or animal varieties or essentially biological processes for the production of plants and animals other than microbiological processes and the products of such processes;
(iii) schemes, rules, or methods of doing business, performing purely mental acts, or playing games;

[25] Art. 31.
[26] Art. 28.
[27] Art. 37.
[28] Holzapfel and Sarnoff (2008).

(iv) methods of treatment of the human or animal body by surgery or therapy, as well as diagnostic methods;
(v) mere presentations of information;
(vi) computer programs to the extent that the International Search Authority is not equipped to search prior art concerning such programs.

The fact that the International Search Authorities are not required to search in these areas reinforced a specific way of thinking about patents and the types of things that should be excluded from protection that is now reflected in the patent laws of many countries.

5 Exclusions and Exceptions After TRIPS

The period from the 1980s to present has seen a number of changes in relation to exceptions and exclusions. One of most notable, which was a direct consequence of the TRIPS Agreement, was that for the first time international norms came to play an important role in this area of patent law. As well as changing the forum of influence, TRIPS also reversed the process of expansion that had occurred over the last century. In part this was because one of the goals of TRIPS was the substantive harmonisation of patentable subject matter, which was implemented through the principle that patents should, with one or two exceptions, be available 'in all fields of technology'. TRIPS also aimed to ensure that countries no longer excluded pharmaceutical products and processes from patent eligibility.[29] The effect, not surprisingly, was to dramatically alter the number of exclusions at the domestic level.

That said, TRIPS contains a number of explicit and implicit flexibilities; one of the findings of the WIPO Report was that these have been adopted widely. The most obvious flexibility is that while Article 27(1) requires Member States to ensure that patents are available in all fields of 'technology', the Agreement does not define what is meant by 'technology'. While many important questions about Article 27 (1) remain unresolved, contracting parties seem to have considerable room to exclude subject matter from patentability on the basis that it is not an invention or an invention in a field of technology.[30] It appears that parties can exclude discoveries, scientific theories, mathematical methods, aesthetic creations, methods of performing mental acts, and methods of doing business from patentability on the basis that they are not 'technical' or are not 'inventions'.[31]

Given that technology is an evolving concept, the better view must be that the requirement should not preclude an exclusion being adopted in a national or

[29] Correa (2007), p. 271.

[30] Correa (2007), pp. 271–272.

[31] *Cf Classen Immunotherapies Inc v. Biogen Idec, GlaxoSmithKline and Merck & Co, Inc* 2006.

regional law unless and until there is international consensus on what is meant by 'technology'. For the moment, there could not be said to be agreement that computer programs, animals, higher life forms, or isolated genes and cells fall within the definition of technology. In these fields, the WTO should offer Member States a wide margin of discretion to define patentability in line with their own conceptions of technology. In addition to the flexibility in Article 27(1), Article 27 (2) and (3) contains explicit exceptions for morality, methods of treatment, and certain biological inventions, while Article 73 allows exclusions in the field of armaments and nuclear technology.[32]

While there is some flexibility in the TRIPS Agreement, its impact on exclusions in national law has been profound. The overall effect of TRIPS was to alter dramatically the number and things that were excluded from patentability. For example, in contrast to the situation in 1980, very few laws now contain exceptions relating to food or medicines. In part these changes were reinforced by (and also a product of) the growing acceptance in the 1980s and 1990s of economic liberalism and neoliberalism by many policymakers, legal scholars, and judges. One of the consequences of this was that it created doubts about some subject matter that had traditionally been excluded from patentability. If the economic argument that patents incentivise investment in research and development was correct, why have restrictions on the patenting of computer programs or methods of medical treatment? Following this logic, some commentators went so far as to argue that everything that reaches the threshold of novelty and inventiveness should be patentable. Some courts, famously the United States Supreme Court in *Diamond v Chakrabarty*, came close to adopting that view.[33]

Although the position in relation to exclusions post-TRIPS is relatively straightforward, the situation in relation to exceptions is somewhat more complicated. While there has been a growth in international norms limiting exclusions from patentability, there are much fewer provisions that restrict the exceptions that countries can use in their patent laws. As a result, Member States still have considerable room in terms of the exceptions to patentee's rights that they wish to implement in their patent laws.

The TRIPS Agreement introduced the first significant limitations on the exceptions that could exist in the patent laws of Member States. These are found in Article 30 and in the principle of non-discrimination as to the field of technology. Article 30, which has become known as the three-step test, has three requirements: the exception must be 'limited', it must not 'unreasonably conflict with the normal exploitation of the patent', and it must not 'unreasonably prejudice the legitimate interests of the patent owner, taking account of the legitimate interests of third parties'.[34] The meaning of Article 30 was considered in 2000 by the WTO Panel in Canada-Pharmaceutical Products, which concerned exceptions in Canadian patent

[32] Applied in Albania, Brazil, China, India, Mozambique and Portugal.

[33] Risch (2008), p. 658.

[34] Echoing Art. 9(2) of the Berne Convention and Art. 13 of TRIPS.

law: the so-called regulatory review exception and the stockpiling exception. Although the Panel decision has been criticised by some and needs to be read in the light of further developments within TRIPS (in particular, the emphasis on public health in the Doha Declaration),[35] it suggests that Member States have a reasonable degree of flexibility in relation to the exceptions to patentee's rights. While it is not clear that some exceptions—such as an experimental use defence that allows experiments *with* (rather than merely *on*) the invention[36] or that allows experimental use even though there is a commercial purpose—would meet the Article 30 standard,[37] the Panel hinted that experimental use exceptions would be regarded as 'limited exceptions'.[38]

TRIPS also provides Member States with the freedom to decide on the precise form of exhaustion that they wish to adopt. Article 6 specifies that provisions in the Agreement do not extend to exhaustion of rights (except for Articles 3 and 4, which deal with discrimination based on citizenship). In some countries, exhaustion is 'international': that is, it extends to articles placed on the market 'in any country'.[39] Others apply regional or national exhaustion.[40] TRIPS also leaves scope for Member States to adopt 'consistently with the other provisions of this Agreement, appropriate measures to prevent or control' the abuse of intellectual property rights that have an adverse effect on competition. A number of countries expressly include exceptions permitting the exploitation of patents by an authorised third party to counter anti-competitive practices, often conditioned on payment of remuneration.[41]

The post-TRIPS period has also seen a continuation of the process of standardisation that had taken place across the course of the twentieth century. In addition to the ongoing expansion of existing agreements (such as the European Patent Convention), a number of new regional agreements were entered into that helped to standardise exclusions and exceptions, including the Andean Agreement (2000), the Eurasian Patent Convention (1994), the Cooperation Council for the Arab States of the Gulf (1998), and the Bangui Agreement (1999). Some further standardisation of exclusions can be attributed to the post-TRIPS deployment of bilateral treaties, particularly free trade agreements setting TRIPS-plus standards. The major players in promoting such arrangements have been the United States, the European Union, and Japan. Free trade agreements championed by the United States, for example, have sought to limit exclusions from patentability. Many free trade agreements ritually reaffirm the obligation to provide patents for inventions in

---

[35] Declaration on the TRIPS Agreement and Public Health (2001).

[36] Belgian Patent Act 2005, Art 28(1)(b). See van Overwalle (2006), pp. 906 ff.

[37] Prinz zu Waldeck und Pyrmont (2008), p. 304.

[38] See Gilat (1995).

[39] Andean Pact, Art 54; Antigua, s. 11(4)(1)(a).

[40] The countries of the European Union, for example, apply regional exhaustion.

[41] See, in particular, the laws of Argentina, Australia, Barbados, Belize, Dominica, Pakistan, Papua New Guinea, the Philippines and Trinidad and Tobago.

all fields of technology,[42] require that plants are not excluded from patentability,[43] remove the possibility (available under TRIPS) of exclusions for animals,[44] and require recognition of new medical use patents.[45] Some also set a maximum standard for the industrial applicability requirement (reflecting the US notion of specific, substantial, and credible use).[46]

Another (nascent) trend that has developed in recent years that was identified in the study that seems set to increase in the future is the growing reliance on exceptions as a way of limiting patent rights. It seems that policymakers who feel the need to limit patent rights are increasingly doing so by creating new defences (or exceptions) to protection rather than by excluding subject matter. The increased reliance on exceptions as a way of limiting patent rights can be seen, for example, in relation to the Bolar exceptions and in the compulsory licensing provisions that have been introduced in many countries (most notably to allow the supply of pharmaceuticals to developing countries). There has also been a shift away from exclusions towards exceptions to deal with concerns that have arisen in relation to methods of medical treatment and business methods. Although the exception is not common, section 287(c) of the United States Patent Act is of interest because it is indicative of what may become a more popular way of limiting patent rights in the future. The provision indicates that a patent is unenforceable against a medical practitioner (or a related health care entity) where the infringement occurs during 'a medical practitioner's performance of medical activity'. The provision was introduced in 1997, largely in response to the controversy that arose from the case of *Pallin v Singer*,[47] where a surgeon sought to enforce a patent he had obtained for a particular method of performing eye surgery characterised by making a particular shaped incision in a specific point on the eye. Following the controversy, it was suggested that medical treatment should be excluded from patentability, but this was opposed by the biotechnology industry. Senator Bill Frist came up with the idea of utilising an exception instead, and, despite objections, the compromise was accepted.[48] In a similar vein, section 273 of the US Patent Act (as amended by the First Inventor Defense Act of 1999) offers a defence to infringement of business method patents where a defendant can show that he used the business method at least one year before the application was filed. Similar changes may also occur in

---

[42] US-CAFTA-DR, Art 15.9(1)l US-Chile FTA, Art 17.1; US-Jordan, art 4.17; US-Peru FTA Art 16.9; US-Singapore, Art 16.7.

[43] US-Bahrain, Art 14.8(2); US-Chile FTA, Art 17.9 (2); US-CAFTA-DR, Art 15.9(2); US-Jordan Art 4.17 (implicitly); US-Morocco, Art 15.9(2); US-Oman FTA, Art 15.8; US-Peru FTA Art 16.9 (2).

[44] US-Morocco FTA, Art 15.9(2).

[45] US-Bahrain, Art 14.8(2); US-Oman, Art 15.8(1).

[46] US-CAFTA-DR Art 15.9; US Peru, Art 16.9(11).

[47] *Pallin v Singer* 1995.

[48] Omnibus Consolidated Appropriations Act, Limitation on Patent Infringements Relating to a Medical Practitioner Performance of a Medical Activity 1997. See Havins (1999); Anon (2007–2008).

the future in relation to computer-implemented inventions. As the consequences of patenting in this field become clear, commentators argue that it may be necessary to broaden existing exceptions (perhaps introducing a fair use concept), particularly to give full effect to the rights of free speech.[49]

In many cases, the increased reliance on exceptions is a consequence of the fact that TRIPS limits the extent to which exclusions can be used to implement policy goals. This situation is exacerbated in some countries by the narrow and overly restrictive way that TRIPS is interpreted by policymakers. In other situations, it seems that for various reasons policymakers simply prefer to use exceptions to limit patent rights. In Europe, frustration with subject matter has seen a shift away from exclusions towards inventive step as a way of reining in patent protection. It is possible to imagine this renewing interest in patent exceptions. Unlike the blunt all-or-nothing nature of exclusions—which remove rather than balance or reduce incentives—exceptions can be fine-tuned to ensure that an appropriate compromise is made within the patent system. As exceptions can be tailored to specific conditions, they allow policymakers to develop more nuanced ways of reconciling conflicting interests. Exceptions can be conditioned, for example, to require users to pay remuneration or to ensure that a patent is only used when specified conditions are met.

Whether it is a consequence of many exclusions not being available or simply because exceptions are a preferred way of implementing a particular policy goal, it seems clear that exceptions will play an increasingly important role in setting the limits of patent protection in the future. It is important to note that the effectiveness of a specific exception will always be influenced by the environment in which it operates. What works in one country may not work in another. The effectiveness of an exception could be influenced, for example, by the propensity of patent agents to formulate claims to avoid exclusions, the capacity of the patent offices to screen ex ante, the accessibility of the legal system (for those wishing to challenge granted patents), the interpretive traditions of a particular country (such as whether exclusions are interpreted narrowly), the availability of alternative forms of protection (such as the use of trade secrets and confidentiality), and the extent to which licensing is a realistic option. One of the lessons from copyright law is that the value of an exception depends on how risk averse the relevant gate keepers are: whether it is a librarian interpreting library-copying provisions or an in-house lawyer for a publishing company that construes fair dealing very narrowly (and against the interests of authors). Similar issues also arise in relation to patent exceptions. Another factor that potentially undermines the effectiveness of patent exceptions is the possibility that statutory exceptions are overridden by private contracts. It is easy to foresee, for example, a situation where the supply of patented materials is coupled with detailed contractual restrictions that interfere with statutory exceptions. If greater reliance is placed on exceptions, particularly in effecting the careful balance between owners and the public, this issue will need to be

[49] Burk (2000).

confronted. Given the significant role that exceptions play in preserving the public domain of science, and the fact that this is only likely to increase in the future, it is also particularly important that international norms are not allowed to stifle this important avenue for calibrating national patent policy.

References

Algerian Patents Ordinance 19/07/2003 – 1424, No. 03–07

Andean Pact

Anon (2007–2008) Revisiting the compromise of 35 USC §287(c). Texas Intellect Prop Law J 16:299

Belgian Patent Act (enacted on April 25, 2005)

Burk D (2000) Patenting speech. Texas Law Rev 79:99

Community Patent Convention (1979)

Cook T, Johnson P, Roughton A (2010) The modern law of patents, 2nd edn. Lexis Nexis, London

Correa C (2007) TRIPS: a commentary. Oxford University Press, Oxford

Declaration on the TRIPS Agreement and Public Health (2001) (WT/MIN(01)/DEC/2), 14 November 2001

Duffy J (2009–2010) Rules and standards on the forefront of patentability. William & Mary Law Rev 51:609

European Patent Convention (1973)

European Union Biotech Directive (1998) Directive 98/44/EC of the European Parliament and of the Council of 6 July 1998 on the legal protection of biotechnological inventions

Gilat D (1995) Experimental use and patents. IIC Stud 16

Havins W (1999) Immunizing the medical practitioner 'Process' infringer: greasing the Squeaky Wheel, good public policy or what? Univ Detroit Mercy Law Rev 77:51

Heath C (1997) The patent exemption for 'Experimental Use' in clinical trials, Germany, Japan and the US compared. AIPPI J 22:267

Holzapfel H, Sarnoff J (2008) A cross-Atlantic dialog on experimental use and research tools. American Law on Inventions, Utility Models and Designs (2008) (Armenia)

Omnibus Consolidated Appropriations Act: Limitation on Patent Infringements Relating to a Medical Practitioner Performance of a Medical Activity, 1997, Pub L No 104–208, 110 State 3009, s. 616 (codified as 35 USC s. 287(c))

Pila J (2010) The requirement for an invention in patent law. Oxford University Press, Oxford

Prinz zu Waldeck und Pyrmont W (2008) Special legislation for genetic inventions: a violation of Article 27(1) TRIPS. In: Prinz zu Waldeck und Pyrmont, W., Adelman, M.J., Brauneis, R., Drexl, J., Nack, R. (Eds.) Patents and technological progress in a globalized world: Liber Amicorum Josef Straus. Springer, p 289

Risch M (2008) Everything is patentable. Tennessee Law Rev 75:591

South Africa Patents Act No 57 of 1978

Statute of Monopolies (1623)

van Overwalle G (2006) The implementation of the biotechnology directive in Belgium and its after effects. IIC 37:860

WIPO (1979) Model law for developing countries on inventions. WIPO, Geneva

WIPO (2010) Standing Committee on the Law of Patents, *Exclusions from Patentability and Exceptions and Limitations to Patentees' Rights*. Document SCP/13/7 (prepared by Lionel Bently, Brad Sherman, Denis Borges Barbosa (with Karin Grau-Kuntz), Shamnad Basheer (with Shashwat Purohit and Prashant Reddy), Coenraad Visser, and Richard Gold (with Professor Yann Joly). WIPO, Geneva

Decisions

Boulton v. Bull (1795) *ER* 126:651
Brenner v. Mason (1966) 383 US 519 (US S Ct)
Byam v. Bullard (1852) 4 F. Cas 934, 935 (CCD Mass) (No 2262)
Classen Immunotherapies Inc v. Biogen Idec, GlaxoSmithKline and Merck & Co, 2006 (USCAFC)
College v. Canada (Commissioner of Patents) (2002) *SCC* 76 (Supreme Court of Canada)
Evans v. Eaton (1818) 16 U.S. (3 Wheat.) 454
Finney v. United States (1975) 188 USPQ 33 (CCTD)
Gottschalk v Benson (1972) 409 US 63
Harvard College v. Canada (Commisioner of Patents) 2002 4 SCR 45, 2002 SCC 76
Harvard Oncomouse (2004) T 315/03, para 4.4
In re Meyer (1982), 688 F.2d, 789, 795 (CCPA)
In re Ngai (2004) 367 F. 3d 1336, 1338 (Fed Cir)
Juicy Whip Inc v Orange Bang Inc, (1999) 185 F.3d 1364 (Fed Cir)
Leroy v Tatham (1852) 55 US 155
Lowell v Lewis (1817) 15 F Cas 1018 (CCCD Mass)
McDonald v. Graham (1994) *RPC* 407
Morton v. N.Y. Eye Infirmary (1862) 17 F Cas 879 (CCSDNY)
Pallin v Singer (1995) 36 USPQ 2d 1050 (D Vt)
Roche Products Inc. v Bolar Pharmaceuticals Co (1984) 733 F. 2d 858 (Fed Cir)
SKF Laboratories v. Evans Medical (1989) *FSR* 513

Mandatory Licensing Under Patent Law and Competition Law: Different Concerns, Complementary Roles

Hanns Ullrich

Contents

Abstract The purpose of this chapter is limited to defining the differences of the functions and of the operation of compulsory licences, which typically are available under patent law, on one hand, or, on the other, are imposed as a matter of enforcing the antitrust laws. The thesis of this contribution is that each of patent law's compulsory licensing rules does (and ought to) follow its own distinct rationale. Their common denominator is that they are specific to the systematic operation of patent protection as an incentive mechanism for innovation. By contrast, competition law constitutes part of the framework regulation of the market. Where its application results in imposing licensing obligations on patentees, it does so in order to correct an unjustified restriction of competition. This remedial function of antitrust-related licensing obligations is complementary to but different from patent law's rules on compulsory licensing. The different functions of system-supportive

H. Ullrich is Prof. Dr. iur., em., MCJ (NY Univ.), Research Affiliate, Max Planck Institute for Innovation and Competition, Munich; Visiting Professor, College of Europe, Bruges.

H. Ullrich
Max Planck Institute for Innovation and Competition, Munich, Germany
e-mail: hanns.ullrich@ip.mpg.de

R.M. Hilty and K.-C. Liu (eds.), *Compulsory Licensing*, MPI Studies on Intellectual Property and Competition Law 22, DOI 10.1007/978-3-642-54704-1_17,

or system-intrinsic mandatory licensing rules and competition-related obligations also mean that before introducing new or broadening existing provisions on compulsory licences a proper diagnosis has to be made of the ill that they are supposed to cure.

1 Introduction

Imposing an obligation on a patentee to share her/his exclusivity with third parties by granting licences to exploit the protected invention seems to be in conflict with the notion of patents as rights of individual property.[1] The patent statutes of some major jurisdictions, such as the U.S. Patent Act, do not know of such an obligation. In Europe and most parts of the world, however, it has a long tradition and takes various forms.[2] In terms of the number of grants, compulsory licences rarely have had great importance. As a matter of policy, however, they have raised considerable controversy at all times[3] precisely because they affect the property rationale of patent protection. More recently, the debate has again gained momentum due to concerns about affordable access to patented medicines[4] and, more generally, about the proper operation of an ever-expanding system of protection. It is, indeed, mainly in regard of the latter aspect that the proper definition of the interface between patent protection and competition is discussed so widely and vividly from opposing standpoints. On one side are the advocates of introducing more considerations of competition policy in the patent system itself[5]; on the other are those who seek to defend the patent exclusivity against the application of the law against restraints of competition (or antitrust laws) that would result in imposing licensing duties on patentees, be the patentee market dominant.[6]

---

[1] See the opening sentence of the section on compulsory licences in Cornish et al. (2010), pp. 7–40.

[2] *WIPO*, Committee on Development and Intellectual Property (CDIP), 7th sess., May 2-I, 2011, Patent-related flexibilities in the multilateral legal framework and their legislative implementation at the national and regional levels, Annex I and II (CDIP/5/4 “Provisions of Law on Compulsory Licensing”; *WIPO* Questionnaire on Exceptions and Limitations to Patent Rights (www.wipo.int/scp/en/exceptions/index.html).

[3] See Cornish et al. (2010), sub 7–41 et seq., referring also to the USA accepting the failure of the Nairobi Conference of 1981 on the Revision of the Paris Convention for the Protection of Industrial Property rather than a modification of its rules on compulsory licensing (Art. 5A), see Kunz-Hallstein (1982), p. 45; Stoll (1994), pp. 235 et passim.

[4] See *C. Visser*, Patent Exceptions and Limitations in the Health Context, Annex V of *WIPO*, Standing Committee on the Law of Patents, Exclusions from Patentability and Exceptions and Limitations to Patentees' Rights, Study by *L. Bently* et al., Geneva 2010, passim; Boschek (2012), p. 621 82012; Cottier (2007), pp. 173 et passim, Cornish et al. (2010), pp. 7–43; Godt (2010), pp. 25 et passim.

[5] Liu (2012), p. 679.

[6] See only Shelanski (2009), p. 369; Geradin (2004), p. 1519.

It is not the objective of this chapter to re-enter into a general patent/competition policy debate. Rather, its purpose is limited to defining the differences of the functions and of the operation of compulsory licences, which typically are available under patent law, on one hand, or, on the other, are imposed as a matter of enforcing the antitrust laws. Clearly, the legislator may always introduce competition-related rules on mandatory licensing into patent law.[7] The thesis of this contribution, however, is that each of patent law's compulsory licensing rules does (and ought to) follow its own distinct rationale. Their common denominator is that they are specific to the systematic operation of patent protection as an incentive mechanism for innovation, which rests on the transformation of knowledge into an object of private property. By contrast to these compulsory licensing rules, which are built into patent law as a matter of smoothing, controlling, or counterbalancing the operation of the system of protection, competition law constitutes part of the framework regulation of the market, within which patent protection is supposed to produce its innovation-enhancing effects. Where its application results in imposing licensing obligations on patentees, it does so in order to correct an unjustified restriction of competition. This remedial function of antitrust-related licensing obligations is complementary to but different from patent law's rules on compulsory licensing. Not every friction within or limit of the system of patent protection, which the latter rules seek to prevent or to overcome, is due to an absence of sufficient competition or rests upon it being unlawfully restricted. However, most structural deficits of competition[8] and any restriction of competition, which runs afoul of the antitrust laws, distort the proper functioning of patent protection in general or at least in the particular case.

The different functions of system-supportive or system-intrinsic mandatory licensing rules on one hand, and, on the other, of competition-related obligations, which are of a regulatory nature or aim at correcting antitrust torts, also mean that before introducing new or broadening existing provisions on compulsory licences a proper diagnosis has to be made of the ill that they are supposed to cure. In this regard, no more than it can aim at discussing the patent/competition interface in general, this contribution cannot discuss all the potential that the rules on compulsory patent licensing may have for mitigating the various problems of patent

[7] See, e.g., Art. L 613-16 French code de la propriété intellectuelle (c.prop.int.), Art. 40c Swiss Patent Act, Sect. 50A, 51 UK Patents Act. Typically, such rules provide for the grant of compulsory licences as a remedy to anti-competitive practices that a competent competition authority has found to exist. An exception is Sect. 48A (1)(c), 48B(1)(c) UK Patents Act. Conversely, the grant of compulsory licences may be limited to remedying anti-competitive practices a competition authority has found to exist; see Art. 31 lit.c) TRIPS Agreement.

[8] Such structural deficits may be a result of altogether (failing) market mechanisms or of inherited market deficits or market distrust. Control by market (de-/re-)regulation may require intervention into the price mechanism or specific access rules, which are outside the scope of this contribution.

protection or for enhancing its operation.[9] Instead, an examination of the principles commonly governing compulsory licences in a few European jurisdictions must suffice for illustration (Sect. 2). They will then be put in contrast to obligations to licence, which are imposed on patentees as a matter of remedying anti-competitive conduct (Sect. 3).

2 Compulsory Licences Under Patent Law

2.1 Preliminary Points

2.1.1 The International Framework

Commonly, national laws provide for the grant of compulsory licences either expressly or implicitly by the administrative or judicial implementation of often enough vaguely worded rules[10] in three particular situations:

- where a (second) patent cannot be exploited without infringing another (the "first" or "head") patent (remedying dependence),
- where the patented invention is not (or not sufficiently) put to use by the patentee (remedying "non-working"),
- where the public interest so requires (remedying a policy conflict).[11]

These grounds for granting compulsory licences do not mirror an international consensus, nor is compulsory licensing limited to these grounds by international

[9] More particularly, the contribution will not address the issues raised, on one hand, by the introduction of a general system of licensing obligations or, on the other, by policy-specific concepts of compulsory licensing, e.g. rules on compulsory licensing in the interest of environmental protection or energy saving. Ultimately, such approaches require examining the effects of system changes, which cannot be done here; see infra Sect. 2.2.2, text following n. 48.

[10] Art. 5A Paris Convention provides in general terms that "Each country of the Union shall have the right to take the legislative measures providing for the grant of compulsory licenses to prevent abuses which might result from the exercise of the exclusive right conferred by the patent, for example failure to work". Thus, it is for the countries of the Union to determine "abuse" (see BGH of 5 December 1995, GRUR 1996, 190 = 28 IIC 24 (1997)—"*Polyferon*". They may do so in similarly unspecific terms, referring to specific forms only by way of illustration or, conversely, by specifying only particular grounds for compulsory licences. The latter approach is taken by many European countries; see § 24 German Patent Act (PatG), Arts. L.613-11, L 613-15, L 613-16 French Code de la propriété intellectuelle (c.prop.int.), and generally *WIPO*, Flexibilities, loc. cit., Annex II (1).

[11] Alternatively, States may rely on their privilege of government use or "Crown use"; see Sect. 55–59 UK Patents Act; Cornish et al. (2010), pp. 7–50 et seq; for the USA Reichman (2003), p. 19; Rushing (2012), p. 879.

convention law.[12] International conventions, in particular Art. 5A Paris Convention and Art. 31 TRIPS Agreement, only put some constraints on the substance of compulsory licences—e.g., it must be non-exclusive, proportionate to its purpose in terms of scope and duration, limited to domestic markets,[13] and subject to adequate remuneration. They also predetermine the granting procedure: compulsory licences may only be granted on the merits of the particular case and only once negotiations for a voluntary licence have failed; there is a "period of grace" for the patentee, and judicial review of the granting decision and of the remuneration must be available.[14]

These rules of international law leave some leeway for national patent policy regarding compulsory licences but obscure the differences between the various situations asking or allowing for the grant of compulsory licences.

2.1.2 National Policy

The diversity of national[15] laws is not only one of details, which cannot be presented here. Typically, compulsory licences are granted only upon request to be made by any (interested) person.[16] In dependency cases, however, by definition

---

[12] See supra n. 10. Art. 31 TRIPS Agreement does not control the grounds supporting the grant of compulsory licences; see UNCTAD/ICTSD (2005), sub 1 (p. 462).

[13] Art. 31 lit.f): "any such use shall be authorized predominantly for the supply of the domestic market of the Member authorizing such use"; for an exception, see Art. 31bis TRIPS (resulting from the Doha Declaration, see Cornish et al. 2010, pp. 7–43; Cottier 2007, 4). For the rationale of this limitation, see infra Sect. 2.2.2.

[14] See UNCTAD/ICTSD (2005), loc. cit., Chapter 24. For the limitations put on the grant of compulsory licences by TRIPS, compare the distinction made by Secs. 48A, 48B, 50, and 54 UK Patents Act between compulsory licences to be imposed on patentees of WTO Members and patentees of non-WTO Members, respectively.

[15] In the European Union, originally proposed rules on compulsory licences (see Art. 21 et seq. Proposal for a Council Regulation on the Community patent—General Approach, Council Doc. 16113/09 of 27 November 2009) have been abandoned in favour of national law when the Union authorised a group of Member States to introduce unitary patent protection by way of enhanced cooperation; see recital 10 Reg. (EU) Nr. 1257/2012 of the European Parliament and the Council of 17 December 2012 implementing enhanced cooperation in the area of the creation of unitary patent protection, OJ EU 2012 L 361, 1. The validity of this approach is controversial.

[16] Explicitly "any person", Sect. 481(1) UK Patents Act; implicitly, § 24 PatG (see *R. Rogge* in Benkard 2006, § 24, annot. 10). National laws of other countries distinguish between, on one hand, compulsory licences on grounds of non-use [Art. L 613-11 c.prop.int.: "toute personne"; § 36 (4) PatG Austria: "jedermann"; Art. 70 Italian Codice della propriéta industriale (c.prop.ind.): "ogni interessato"; but see Art. 37 Swiss Patent Act requiring a showing of sufficient interest] and, on the other, compulsory licences on grounds of dependency, where only the holder of the dependent patent may request or claim the licence (see Art. L 613-14 c.prop.int.; Art. 71 c.prop. ind.; § 36(1) PatG Austria; Art. 36 Swiss Patent Act). The latter approach seems to be the more appropriate, if not the only practicable in view of the grant-back obligation of the compulsory licensee; see Art. 31 lit. l) (ii) TRIPS Agreement and infra Sect. 2.2.1, text following n. 34, "Relationship to Competition Policy".

such interest may only lie with the owner of the dependent patent. Conversely, as regards the grant of compulsory licences in the public interest, more particularly the grant of licences, which are commanded by major health policy concerns, in some jurisdictions public authorities may ex officio intervene to facilitate the general availability of licences by way of opening up licence-of-right mechanisms.[17] A more general difference exists between countries that entrust the grant of compulsory licences to their patent offices and those that attribute such authority to courts and do so even as regards compulsory licences in the public interest.[18] This difference may be relevant for the organisation of judicial review, which is particular to every country anyway. More importantly, the choice of a judicial administration of compulsory licensing system favours a transition from granting compulsory licences by the exercise of some discretionary power to granting them as a matter of right, i.e. it favours the introduction of a right or a claim to obtain a compulsory licence; at least it tends to narrow the margin of discretionary power.

2.2 Principles

2.2.1 Dependent Patents: Frictions Inherent in the System

Generally, a subjective right of individuals to obtain a compulsory licence is recognised as regards dependency licences.[19] The reasons are twofold. For one thing, there can be no more and no other applicant/claimant than the holder of a

[17] While this is a general option under Sect. 48 UK Patents Act, in other jurisdictions public interest licences may be applied for by any person anyway [e.g., § 24 PatG; § 36(5) PatG Austria; Art. 40 Swiss Patent Act]. By contrast, Arts. L 613-16 and L 613-18 c.prop.int. provide for a system of licences of right, where public health interests (Art. L 613-16) or a general interest of the national economy (Art. L 613-18) so demands, but subject the operation of such a system of licence of rights to prior regulatory intervention by the competent Minister.

[18] The former attribution of competence characterises the systems in the UK (see Sect. 48 et seq. UK Patents Act) and in Austria (§ 37 PatG Austria), the latter the systems in Germany (§ 24 PatG) and in Switzerland (Art. 36–46 Swiss Patent Act). Arts. L 61-13, L 613-15 c.prop.int. attribute to the courts the authority to grant compulsory licences for non-use and in dependency cases, respectively, whereas Arts. L 616-16–L 613-18 c.prop.int. attribute to the Minister concerned the authority to establish the system of licences of right, which then are to be obtained from the Minister in charge of intellectual property, with, however, the determination of royalties being reserved to the courts, should parties not agree. Italy (Arts. 73, 80, c.prop.ind.) and Belgium attribute the competence generally and directly to the interested ministries. For the complex Belgian system, see Arts. 31–38 Belgian Patent Act; Van Overwalle (2006), pp. 889,908 et seq.

[19] Expressly § 24(2) PatG; § 36 PatG Austria; Art. 36 Swiss Patent Act; a matter of interpretation as regards Sect. 48 in conjunction with Sect. 48A (1) lit. b (i) UK Patents Act; Art. L 613-15 c.prop. int.; Art. 31 § 1er, para. 2 Belgian Patent Act; Art. 71 c.prop.ind. In French patent law, this is mirrored by the distinction between "licences obligatoires judiciaires" and "licences obligatoires administratives"; see Pollaud-Dulian (2011), no. 618 et seq.

dependent patent.[20] For another, the dependency link in and of itself establishes the interest in the grant of the licence.

Dependence as a Matter of Patent Law

Indeed, dependency is defined not in terms of technical feasibility or economic opportunity but strictly in terms of patent law. It occurs where and to the extent that the use of an invention as protected by a second patent infringes the first patent in that it comes within the scope of the latter's claims, either entirely or in part.[21] Typical cases are presented by improvement patents, and also by application patents, e.g. those relating to chemical compounds[22] or to gene-technological inventions.[23] Since the second patent covers an invention that has been recognised to merit protection by a patent,[24] its owner has a legitimate interest in exploiting it. However, the mere fact that she/he obtained a patent for the second invention is not enough to entitle her/him to infringe the head patent. She/he needs a licence. Generally, obtaining such licence is a matter of contractual arrangement between the parties in accordance with their mutual interests and market conditions.[25] It is only where, in relation to the first patent, the second invention involves an

[20] See supra n. 16. Contra *Rogge*, in: Benkard (2006), § 24, annot. 10, who fails to take account of the fact that § 24 (2) PatG entitles the owner of the head patent to a grant-back licence for the dependent patent. § 24 (2) PatG addresses a bilateral relationship between two (or more) patentees.

[21] See the definition in Art. 31(1) lit. l) TRIPS Agreement and in the national rules mentioned supra n. 19. Only Sect. 48 A lit.(b)(i) UK Patents Act seems to follow a broader concept (exploitation of "any other patented invention ... prevented or hindered").

[22] See Kraßer (2009), § 33, I. lit. c), no. 8 (p. 748), and the recognition of a cascade of dependencies by Art. 54(4), (5) EPC, regarding application patents for new and inventive medical indications.

[23] For details, see Schieble (2005), pp. 95 et seq., 153 et seq.; Koikkara (2010), pp. 84 et seq.

[24] Protection by a utility model will not qualify in Germany (see *Rogge* in Benkard 2006, § 24 annot. 22), which appears to be questionable, where the criteria for obtaining protection are equivalent to those of patents. With respect to dependent plant variety protection, a right to obtain a compulsory licence on a first biotechnological patent has been introduced by Art. 12 Dir. 98/44/EC of the European Parliament and the Council on the protection of biotechnological inventions of 6 July 1998 (OJEC 1998 L 213, 13—"Biotech Dir."). Art. 12(2) provides for the grant of a compulsory licence in the reverse hypothesis.

[25] This is a general rule of compulsory licensing, as expressed by the fact that failure of contract negotiations is a condition precedent to the grant of compulsory licences; see Art. 31 lit. b) TRIPS Agreement. The interest of the owner of the head patent in recouping her/his investment in the making of the first invention will be taken care of by the fact that the grant of the compulsory licence must be subject to remuneration that takes account of the economic value of the compulsory licence; see Art. 31 lit. h) TRIPS Agreement, § 24 (6, 4th sent.) PatG, § 37(1) PatG Austria, § 40e(5) Swiss Patent Act; Sect. 48 (6) (d) UK Patents Act; not explicit, Art. L 613-12(2) c.prop.int. However, deduction must be made of the value that the second patents add to the first by way of the improvement made or the application patent offered.

important technical advance that is of considerable economic significance[26] that under the TRIPS Agreement the national legislator does not need to accept that the achievement of the patent system's objective of promoting innovation risks being blocked by the owner of the first patent refusing to grant such licence. Rather, the legislator may provide for the grant of a compulsory licence to the owner or to the owners of (a) second patent(s).[27]

The Threshold: Important Technical Advance of Considerable Economic Significance

A public interest additionally justifying the grant of a licence to use the first patent is not (or no longer[28]) required. Nor may the threshold requirement that the dependent patent must involve an important technical advance of considerable economic significance be read as by itself illustrating the public interest in the grant of the compulsory licence.[29] The rationale underlying the threshold requirement is to maintain for either party the patent system's operation as an incentive also for incremental innovation.[30] Therefore, Art. 31 lit. l),(i) expressly puts the contribution to be made by the second invention in relation to the first invention. This first invention may or may not be a "fundamental" one.[31] What matters is whether beyond its mere qualification for patent protection the second invention adds to technical innovation by the advance it presents and by its economic

[26] Art. 31 lit.l),(i) TRIPS Agreement. Generally, national laws adopt this threshold requirement literally, albeit in varying translations.

[27] As there may exist several dependent patents (for improvements and application inventions) belonging even to different patentees, the head patent may become subject to several compulsory licences.

[28] See § 24(2) PatG, which following its amendment by the Act of 21 January 2005 transforming the Directive on biotechnological inventions (supra 24) into German patent law (BGBl 2005 I 146) refers only to para. 1, no. 1 of § 24 PatG. For the impact of the amendment, see Schieble (2005), pp. 160 et seq., 178 et seq.

[29] Contra: Pollaud-Dulian (2011), no. 649. Compare also the contradictory annotation by *Rogge* in Benkard (2006), § 24, annot. 14 and 22 respectively and the caveat by Schieble (2005), pp. 179 et seq. The 2005 amendment is misinterpreted by Gruss (2011), pp. 382 et seq. There is no reason to distinguish between dependent patents and dependent plant variety rights. For the latter, plant breeders may obtain a compulsory licence without having to demonstrate a public interest. The same holds true for patents depending on a plant breeder's right, Art. 12(2) Biotechnology Directive (supra n. 24).

[30] For a discussion of the vertical dilemma, which cumulative (or incremental) innovation creates for the proper operation of patent protection see only Scotchmer (2004), pp. 132 et seq.

[31] This follows from determining dependence by reference only to patent law criteria. Art. 31 lit l) TRIPS Agreement rightfully uses the terminology of "first" and "second" patents rather than a misleading characterisation of the patents as "principal" or "dominant" v. dependent.

significance. This it may do even if—and sometimes in particular—where the first invention appears to be small in terms of inventiveness or economic use.[32] It may also exist—and possibly again particularly so—where the first invention appears to be fundamental or is cast in broad, unspecific claims but where its innovation potential is fully activated only subsequently by improvement or application inventions that satisfy the condition of patentability by their own merits. These merits need not be fundamental in their turn. It is enough that they substantially contribute to making the first invention work properly and/or efficiently or that they substantially broaden its utility. The point really is to overcome a stalemate where the incremental step made by the second invention actually represents a leap forward in terms of innovation.[33]

Relationship to Competition Policy

Since the dependence of the second patent on the head patent is defined in terms of patent scope alone,[34] the need for compulsory licences will vary with the design of patent protection and the traditions and methods of claim construction. Absolute instead of purpose-bound protection of chemical compounds or of gene-technological inventions[35] or broad rather than literal construction of claims will extend the field of compulsory licensing. However, patent dependencies may also be the result of the individual business and patenting strategies of firms.[36] They might then raise concerns of competition policy.[37] Yet, such concerns may not affect in any way the interpretation and application of patent law's rules on

[32] More particularly, patent dependence may exist even where there are substitutes to the first patent in terms of competition or where there are ways to invent around the first invention. The problem of dependent inventions is less one of the unavailability of a way to escape the first patent than one of affording a viable way to improve on it.

[33] The threshold requirement may not be confused with an "advance in the art", as required under German patent law up to 1968. However, it shares the latter's problems of definition. At any rate, it must be assessed objectively by reference to the existing technological knowledge and the technological value added to the first invention. By contrast, the economic significance may be determined by reference to the relevant (national?) markets.

[34] But see supra n. 21. Note also that Sect. 48A (1)(b)(ii) UK Patents Act allows to grant a compulsory licence in case "the establishment or development of commercial or industrial activities in the United Kingdom is unfairly prejudiced" by a refusal to grant a licence on reasonable terms. This rule seems to express a patent-related industrial rather than a competition policy.

[35] For a discussion, see Schieble (2005), pp. 95 et passim, Gruss (2011), pp. 221 et passim.

[36] See Weber et al. (2007), pp. 123 et seq., 163 et seq.; Granstrand (1999), pp. 218 et seq., Granstrand (2010), pp. 220 et seq. Typically, such strategies aim at access to (cross-)licensing arrangements, which, as such, may present problems for competition policy.

[37] See, generally, Ullrich (2009), p. 399; Ullrich (2013). Dependence strategies must, however, be distinguished from various other types of strategies, such as cluster building or defensive patenting.

compulsory licensing on grounds of patent dependency. Such dependency may exist independently of any competitive relationship between the owners of the first and the second patent, respectively. Also, patent law defines dependency quite differently from the way the concept of dependence is used in competition law.[38] Moreover, while competition law is concerned with particular anti-competitive practices existing on specifically defined relevant markets, the concern of patent law is with unblocking innovation for whatever markets, be they part of the relevant markets of the head invention, in some way related to these markets, or entirely separate. Finally, while imposing obligations on patentees to license their patents represents one among many ways to remedy an anti-competitive practice, typically as an *ultima ratio* remedy specifically tailored to undo the anti-competitive features of a practice, patent law's rules on compulsory licensing do not provide for flexibility but only for a binary decision to grant or not to grant a licence compulsorily.[39] This is so because the raison d'être of these rules is twofold. On one hand, they serve to overcome the inefficiencies that for patent protection as an incentive mechanism systematically result from the combined effects of the cumulative nature of the innovation process and of the fragmentation of technologies into selective bits of invention-based exclusivities.[40] On the other, they help maintain patent protection's principle of operating as a system of property rights.

The systematic rationale of the rules on the grant of compulsory licences in favour of dependent patents, which is to enable rather than only to incentivise innovation, is confirmed by some complementary provisions. First, the holder of the head patent is entitled to a cross-licence on the dependent patent [Art. 31 lit.l), (ii) TRIPS Agreement].[41] This is less a matter of fairness than one of innovation policy, given that the dependent patent must involve an important technical advance of considerable economic significance, while the head patent need not be of such nature. The idea simply is that in the interest of broadest innovation the mandatorily non-exclusive character of the compulsory licence (Art. 31 lit.d) TRIPS Agreement) should be so effectively, i.e. the owner of the first patent is invited to act as "co-innovator" in all regards. Second, the compulsory licence may be assigned to a third party only together with the dependent patent. As poorly

[38] See § 20(2) German Act Against Restraints of Competition (GWB).

[39] However, considerations of competition law may come in when determining whether negotiations for a voluntary licence failed because the holder of the first patent made the grant of the licence subject to unreasonable commercial terms and conditions [Art. 31(b) TRIPS Agreement], such as unduly restrictive or discriminatory conditions.

[40] For this effect of selective fragmentation, see Ullrich (2009), at pp. 424 et seq.

[41] See § 24 (2, 2nd sent.) PatG; § 36 (1, 2nd sent.) PatG Austria; Art. 36(3) Swiss Patent Act; Art. L 613-15(4) c.prop.int.; Sect. 48A (4) UK Patents Act; Art. 71(2) c.prop.ind.; Art. 32, § 3(3) Belgian Patent Act unduly limits the right to a cross-licence to cases where the first and the second patents relate to the same industry. § 36(1), 2nd sent. PatG Austria requires the cross-licence to be non-exclusive. This seems to be a matter of reciprocity rather than required by Art. 31 lit. d) TRIPS Agreement (the cross-licence is a condition for the grant of the compulsory licence for the head patent, not itself a compulsory licence). At any rate, it also follows from principles of competition law.

conceived as it is, the provision is intended to make sure that the compulsory licence for the first patent will in fact be used for working the second—by definition important—patent rather than be exploited separately and independently.[42]

2.2.2 The Working Requirement: A Matter of Policy and Perspective

The interest in having the patent system's incentive to innovate result in actual innovation also underlies the rules on the grant of compulsory licences for patents that are not exploited in the country of protection. However, national laws differ as much as the grounds for making compulsory licences available on account of non-exploitation vary. Given the historical root of patents in privileges granted for the introduction of new technologies, mostly technologies originating from abroad,[43] the core concept is that the "monopoly" must benefit the domestic economy in terms of not only the importation of new goods but the establishment of production capacities on the domestic market as well.[44] The aim was not only to create more employment but also to introduce new technologies into the domestic production process, i.e. to achieve knowledge learning and capacity building.[45] This explains why Art. 5A Paris Convention illustrates the "abuses" justifying the grant of compulsory licensee by referring to "failure to work" the patent domestically, meaning failure to actually manufacture on the domestic territory. Non-supply or insufficient supply of the domestic market, in particular in case it concerns elementary or otherwise essential goods, is but an additional aspect of the "failure to work", which then brings in a different notion of public interest needs as a qualifying criterion.

The Shift from Domestic Manufacturing to Sufficient Supply

In accordance with the principle of territoriality, the rules on compulsory licensing governing non-exploitation of patents tend to be designed with a view to the interests of the national economy of the country of protection. This perspective may or may not be that of an international division of labor, depending on how other

---

[42] For a similar analysis, see De Carvalho (2010), sub. 31.9.9. This effect will be achieved more adequately and safely by limiting the compulsory licence to its use for the working of the second patent as required by Art. 31 lit c) TRIPS Agreement and expressly provided for by, e.g., Art. 36 (1) Swiss Patent Act. Art. 32 § 4 Belgian Patent Act provides for such a limitation only in respect of dependencies existing between plant breeders' rights and biotechnological patents.

[43] See only Silberstein (1961), passim, who retraces the different strands of (mercantilist) State privileges and inventor entitlement of patent protection.

[44] See Kohler (1900), pp. 613 et seq., examining all of the arguments for or against the working requirement; Pollaud-Dulian (2011), loc. cit., at nos. 619, 623.

[45] This is at the core of the debate on technology transfer to developing countries, which has been going on for more than half a century; see, for an assessment, Sampath and Roffe (2012).

countries see the respective competitive advantages in international trade. Often enough, therefore, there may be a conflict between or a convergence of patent policy and trade policy of a State or among the patent policies and trade policies of States. As a matter of law, it is the rules on the free movement of goods[46] and the principle of non-discrimination[47] that in the EU and on the WTO level, respectively, have led States to distinguish more clearly between non-working of the invention (on the domestic territory)[48] and non-supply or insufficient supply of the domestic market. The distinction is not always as explicit as it is in Sect. 48 a (1) (a) UK Patent Act[49] since frequently the term used is that of non-working, to which "importation" simply is assimilated.[50] Yet the substantive modification of the rules on compulsory licences is always profound. While on the level of distribution/dissemination the innovation rationale of patent protection may remain intact or, in terms of a reward function, even be amplified, compulsory licensing may no longer be used to make the expectations materialise, which are more deeply at the root of relying on "monopoly" rights for stimulating innovative economic activity, namely the prospect of technological development within the respective territories granting and protecting such rights. Instead, there is a shift from promoting innovation to protecting it in the interest only of sufficiency of supply, i.e. of satisfying demand.

This shift is evidenced by the fact that importation of patented products or of the products resulting from a patented process is not merely an alternative to but a substitute for domestic manufacturing, thus an absolute defence against the impo-

[46] See ECJ of 18 February 1992, cases C-30/90, Commission/UK and case C-235/89, Commission/Italy, Rep. 1992 I 829 resp. 858; of 27 October 1992, case C-191/90, Generics/Smith Kline and French Laboratories, Rep. 1992 I 5335.

[47] See Art. 27 (1, 2nd sent. in fine) TRIPS Agreement; UNCTAD and ICTSD (2005), loc. cit., pp. 372 et seq., 481 et seq.; Gervais (2012), pp. 2.358 et seq., both pointing to controversies about whether local working requirements effectively amount to unjustified discrimination. The issue tends to be obscured by concerns about compliance with additional public interests (e.g., affordable access to medicines); see also de Carvalho (2010), sub 27.59 et seq.; Correa (2007), pp. 284 et seq.

[48] As follows from the very rationale of—territorially defined!—patent protection, contra De Carvalho (2010), sub 27.59.

[49] Sect. 48A(1)(a): "... where the patented invention is a product that a demand in the United Kingdom for that product is not being met at reasonable terms"; comp. Sect. 48B(1)(a),(b), which, in respect of patents held by proprietors not coming under WTO rules, provides for a strict domestic manufacturing requirement ("not being ... worked to the full extent that is reasonably practicable" [lit (a)] and for the grant of compulsory licence in case supply of the domestic market with a patented product is "to a substantial extent" made by way of importation [lit. (b)].

[50] § 24(5) PatG; § 36(4) PatG Austria; Art. 37(1) Swiss Patent Act; Art. 31 § 1er, para. 1 Belgian Patent Act; Art. L 613-11(3) c.prop.int.; Art. 70 (1) c.prop.ind; Art. L 613-11(2) c.prop.int. and Art. 70(2) c.prop.ind. also provide expressly for the grant of a compulsory licence in case supply has been interrupted for more than 3 years, thus stressing that the concern is with supply rather than with innovation (see following text).

sition of a compulsory licence.[51] In fact, the concern of compulsory licensing is not with spreading an innovation (or, for that matter, with inciting the patentee to do so by herself/himself) but only with satisfying an existing demand.[52] Pursuant to Art. 31 lit. c) TRIPS Agreement, the licence must be limited accordingly, i.e. to what satisfies demand "sufficiently".[53] By the same token, the qualification of the applicant[54] for the compulsory licence need not be other than that of a reliable distributor.[55]

The Impact of Additional Public Interest Criteria

To the difference of non-working the patented invention within the territory of the State of protection, failure to supply at least sufficiently its market more easily justifies exposing the patentee to a judicially enforceable claim to the grant of a compulsory licensee, as do most States. Additionally, requiring the applicant to show the existence of a public interest in the grant[56] means that the patentee is not

---

[51] This is made evident by Art. L 613-11 c.prop.int., which in para. 1 distinguishes between working (lit. a): "exploitation") and supplying (lit. b) "commercialiser") and in para. 3 assimilates "importation" to "exploitation". This seems to imply that there is no working requirement for patented processes at all. Thus, Sect. 48A(1) UK Patents Act provides for no working requirement but in lit. (a) requires only sufficient supply "where the patented invention is a product". Read literally, this would not even cover products resulting from a patented process even though they enjoy full patent protection [Sect. 60(1)(c); generally Art. 64(2) EPC].

[52] See Sect. 48A(1)(a) UK Patents Act; somewhat broader Art. L 613-11(1)(b) c.prop.int. ("satisfaire aux besoins du marché français"). As under UK law the "demand" criterion is not qualified, one may assume that the demand must be more than de minimis but less than substantial. It is also not evident whether and how the "demand" or "les besoins du marché" may be determined irrespective of prices and, therefore, what "reasonable" royalties may be.

[53] § 24(5) PatG; § 36 PatG Austria; Art. 37(1) Swiss Patent Act. The terms used vary (Germany: "ausreichend", Swiss: "in genügender Weise", both mean sufficient; Austria: "angemessen" = reasonably or adequately). A problem of these criteria is that they lend themselves to being interpreted and applied differently depending on whether the supply is insufficient in view of a demand for (new) goods of generally merchandisable character (consumer goods or industrial supplies) or in view of a concurrent public interest, such as health care or energy saving. Yet, with the exception of § 24(5) PatG and Sect. 50(1) UK Patents Act (with respect only to non-WTO patent proprietors), the national patent laws considered here do not ask for such a qualification.

[54] This criterion is made explicit only by Art. L 613-12(1) c.prop.int. and Art. 31§ 2(2) Belgian Patent Act.

[55] See, as regards domestic manufacturing, Art. L 613-12(1), Art. L 613-17 c.prop.int. ("toute personne qualifiée"); Art. 31 § 2(2) Belgian Patent Act; Sect. 50(2)(b) UK Patents Act. The limitation of the transfer of the compulsory licence by Art. 31 lit.e) TRIPS Agreement (only "with that part of the enterprise or good will which enjoy such use") makes more sense in regard of a working requirement than in regard of a supply requirement.

[56] The main example is Germany (see supra n. 52, 53) since § 24(5) PatG is to be applied within the limits of § 24(1) PatG; see also Art. 21 (1) of the proposed Community Patent Regulation (supra n. 15). Such public interest must be more than a general interest in innovation; typically, it is one of

held to satisfy any demand but only qualified needs. The assumption is that markets will work well enough, but the result is that compulsory licensing rules operate selectively.[57] A corresponding approach underlies national laws, which specifically require the invention to be worked domestically in case non-working "porte gravement préjudice au développement économique et à l'intérêt public" (Art. L 613-18 c.prop.int.).[58] Since the French legislator has provided for special rules regarding compulsory licensing in the interest of public health (Art. L 613-16 et seq. c.prop.int.), the regime of administratively imposed licences of right as provided for by Art. L 613-18 c.prop.int. seems to be aimed at a serious market failure that may only be remedied by the systematic grant of (non-exclusive) compulsory licences.[59] The public interest then could not only be one of satisfying particular public needs but one mirroring a distinct industrial policy,[60] which is important enough to impose on patentees a duty to actually work the protected invention in the interest of a national economy. Art. L 613-18 c.prop.int, therefore, raises not only a problem of compatibility with free trade principles[61] but also the more fundamental one of its relationship to the operation of patent protection as a market-based system of promoting innovation by way of incentives.

Ultimately, however, this is a problem of any working requirement. Whereas imposing duties on the use—or the non-use[62]—of property is by no means inconsistent with the (constitutional) concept of property as a private right,[63] such imposition necessarily is in conflict with the way patent protection is supposed to achieve its purpose. As analysed and accepted nowadays, patents are neither privileges nor monopoly rights, which carry with them duties to actually innovate, let alone to do so on administratively predetermined markets. Rather, the idea is to stimulate innovation by providing for incentives, namely for rights of exclusivity, which allow capturing market opportunities in competition with both existing

---

specific public needs, such as access to new medicines; see BGH of 5 December 1995, GRUR 1996, 190 = 28 IIC 242(1997)—*Polyferon*; *Rogge* in Benkard (2006); § 24 annot. 27. Due to the assimilation of imports to domestic manufacturing, the relationship between paras. 1 and 5 of § 24 PatG is unclear; see Kraßer (2009), § 34 IV.a), 5 (p. 831).

[57] On one hand, this means more autonomy for patentees, and, on the other, it may mean more reluctance of courts to "select" a particular patentee and to charge her/his patents with a public interest burden; see infra Sect. 2.3.2.

[58] To the difference of Art. L 613-11(3) c.prop.int., here importation is not assimilated to exploitation. Compare also Sect. 48 a(1)(b)(ii) UK Patents Act.

[59] Neither the law nor the literature suggests that the failure must be due to non-working of the patents concerned. Rather, Art. L 613-18 c.prop.int. is understood as enabling market intervention by the State; see Pollaud-Dulian (2011), at no. 661.

[60] Such as inciting enterprises by the threat of opening a regime of licences of right to invest in the production of climate-friendly or energy-saving products, in interoperable communication devices, etc.

[61] See supra n. 47.

[62] E.g. of farm land or of urban land under zoning law.

[63] See Ullrich (2012b), p. 425 (=ssrn 2179511).

and—mainly—with other innovative technologies.[64] Such an understanding does not at all exclude binding the exercise of these exclusive rights in knowledge to the purpose they are granted for.[65] There is, however, a long way to go from such limitation of the exercise of the right to affirmatively imposing a duty to actually use it as expected by an authority having the power to grant compulsory licences. For one thing, such an affirmative approach too easily loses sight of the advantage that typically will result from the autonomous use of property rights by their owners.[66] That autonomy not only expresses a freedom right but also characterises the operation of the patent system as a market mechanism, more particularly as a system relying on the discovery process resulting from competitive markets. As such, it is not supposed to direct innovation to specific directions a State might wish to favour as a matter of industrial policy.[67] The downside, of course, is that, in the real world, such a "one size fits all" approach may fit some industries better than others.

For another thing, a strict domestic working requirement tends to overshoot the objective that its proponents generally have in mind, i.e. avoiding the risk that, instead of enabling innovation by preventing imitation, patents are used to block that very innovation and/or its dissemination.[68]

Relationship to Competition Policy

Indeed, as legitimate as they are, these concerns essentially are a matter of competition policy in that they mainly relate to real or perceived dangers of (national) markets being foreclosed and/or market power being used abusively. Leaving the matter to competition policy would appear to be the more opportune as, in the absence of market power, the practices in question are unlikely to occur and as patent law's use requirement does not address them adequately. For one thing, the shift from compulsory licensing as a way to remedy non-working to granting compulsory licences only when market supply is refused or insufficient precisely allows patentees to maintain strategies of defensive patenting of all kinds. Competition law may be designed to assess them as to their specific anti-competitive effects on territorially affected relevant markets.[69] For another, even a strict

[64] For details, see Ullrich (2009), pp. 407 et seq., Ullrich (2001), pp. 367, 371 et seq.

[65] See Ullrich (2012b), passim; for a fundamental discussion see Drahos (1996), pp. 220 et seq.; also Van Overwalle and van Zimmeren (2009), pp. 415, 421 et seq.

[66] See references supra n. 64. For the consequences of the curtailment of that autonomy by compulsory licences, compare, e.g., ECJ of 9 July 1985, case 19/84, *Pharmon/Hoechst*, Rep. 1985, 2281.

[67] A goal-oriented framework regulation of markets or well-targeted subsidies, possibly granted at an early stage of the innovation process, may better suit industrial policy. In fact, interference and frictions with the patent system constitute one of the problems of state-funded industrial R&D.

[68] See reference supra n. 44.

[69] See reference supra n. 37.

(domestic) manufacturing requirement, while per se outlawing defensive patenting based on non-use of the protected invention, would still not prevent blocking strategies, which, on the basis of the patentee using the invention herself/himself, are aimed at hindering market entry by rivals.[70] Frequently enough, compulsory licensing under patent law is not even a useful remedy, given its prerequisites and limitations and given also that, as such, a compulsory licence may not be the proper remedy in the first place.[71]

2.2.3 Overriding Public Interests: A Complementary, Not a Corrective, Measure

The Requirements to Sufficiently Supply Market Demand and to Satisfy Public Needs

In addition to compulsory licensing as a remedy to insufficient supply of their markets, most States provide for compulsory licences in the public interest, to be granted by courts or upon a specific administrative procedure.[72] Under these rules, either any public interest in the provision of patented products or the use of patented methods[73] may justify the grant of a compulsory licence, or only specific public interests may do so, typically public health concerns.[74] Whatever the qualification may be, there is an overlap with the rules on compulsory licensing relating to insufficient supply of the domestic market, as the latter also covers any demand, i.e. any need whose satisfaction is in the public interest. Moreover, insufficient supply is not or need not be defined with respect only to quantity or quality but also with respect to the reasonableness of the commercial terms of supply.[75]

[70] Such as patent clustering or evergreening strategies; see references supra n. 37.

[71] Instead of granting third parties a compulsory licence under the narrow conditions set by Art. 31 TRIPS Agreement, it may be both more effective and proportionate to order a (market-dominating) patentee to resume supply or to reduce prices to competitive levels. Even if there is an interested licensee, it might be more appropriate to order the patentee to negotiate the licence on fair terms rather than to impose administratively or judicially a compulsory licence.

[72] As to the former, see § 24(1) PatG; §§ 36, 37 PatG Austria, Art. 40 Swiss Patent Act; for the latter, Art. L 613-17 c.prop.int. (see Pollaud-Dulian 2011, no. 653 et seq.); Art. 31bis Belgian Patent Act; Van Overwalle (2006), at pp. 908 et seq. Note that a broad concept of government or Crown use, such as in the UK (Sect. 55 UK Patents Act, see Cornish et al. 2010, pp. 750 et seq.) may diminish the use of, if not the need for, compulsory licences in the public interest.

[73] Typically diagnostic methods, see Art. L 613-16 (1), lit. a) and lit. c) 3) c.prop.int.; Art. 31bis § 1 lit.a) Belgian Patent Act; Art. 40c Swiss Patent Act (only in case of anti-competitive conduct).

[74] See supra n. 72. The different approaches tend to coincide with the distinction between judicially and administratively granted licences; see supra n. 19.

[75] To this effect, expressly, Sect. 48A(1)(a) UK Patents Act, also Art. 21(1) Proposed Community Patent Regulation (supra n. 15). A criterion that supply must be on reasonable commercial terms may also be read into the "sufficiency" requirement (but see Art. L 613-11, lit. b c.prop.int.): "quantité suffisante") or might be derived from the fact that general law or competition rules

Consequently, the rules on compulsory licensing in the public interest mainly need to come in where sufficient supply of the domestic market cannot be ensured by the grant of compulsory licences on the ground of non-exploitation of the patented invention, be it because the grounds for the grant of such licences are defined narrowly[76] or be it because the patentee has a valid excuse for non-exploitation.[77] Since the working or the supply requirements generally are cast in the same broad terms, the latter situation may occur more frequently. It also reveals best the specific function of the public interest as a prerequisite to the grant of the compulsory licences: the patentee must (voluntarily[78]) grant a licence or else accept the compulsory licence irrespective of the fact that she/he acts in perfect conformity with patent law, the reason being precisely that there is an overriding public interest in market supply.[79] Such may be the case not only where the patentee is excused from supplying the market but also where her/his insufficiently supplying the market is to be excused. Thus, the compulsory licence may establish not only a way of substitute supply but also a second source of supply.[80] The concern then is not with sufficient supply of the market but with adequate, if not full, satisfaction of the public interest.[81]

The Patent v.Public Interest Dilemma

While this chapter is not the place to examine the political need and the legal framework of compulsory licensing in the public interest,[82] the distinction between sufficient supply of the market with patented products or processes needed in the

exclude abusive prices anyway. Such overlap of considerations of patent law and competition law or general principles is made explicit with regard to public interest licences by Art. L 613-16(2) c. prop.int., unusually high prices being even a separate ground for the grant of the licence.

[76] Whereas the shift from the domestic manufacturing requirement to sufficient supply of the domestic market by importation typically saves process patents from compulsory licences, public interest licences will cover them; see, expressly, Art. L 613-16(1) c.prop.int., Art. 31bis § 1 Belgian Patent Act.

[77] The grounds justifying or excusing non-supply or insufficient supply mostly are not made explicit by national rules relating to non-working; see Art. L 613-11(1) c.prop.int.; Art. 31 § 1 (1) Belgian Patent Act; Art. 37(1) Swiss Patent Act. The principle seems to be that the patentee is held only to her/his best efforts; see § 36(4) PatG Austria. Sect. 50(2)(a) UK Patents Act; Pollaud-Dulian (2011), at no. 632.

[78] See Art. 31 lit. b) TRIPS Agreement. Under the circumstances discussed here, "voluntarily" is a euphemistic term, of course.

[79] Compare BGH of 5 December 1995, GRUR 1996, 190 = 27 IIC 242, 245 (1993)—"Polyferon" (no abuse of the patent required).

[80] In the interest of public health, Art. L 613-16 c.prop.int. and Art. 31bis Belgian Patent Act allow to establish a system of licences of right.

[81] But see, as regards § 24 (1) PatG, BGH of 5 December 1995, GRUR 1996, 190 = 27 IIC 242 (1997)—"Polyferon".

[82] The discussion generally focuses on public health, in particular in developing countries and in the TRIPS framework as developed during negotiations of the (ongoing) Doha Round; see

public interest and adequate or even full satisfaction of a public interest deserves particular attention. There is, indeed, not only a risk that the pursuit of the public interest is allowed to override the right of exclusivity of the patentee and its autonomy, a matter that appears to be acceptable at least where the patentee by her/his own failure or for legitimate grounds is not willing or able to meet the public interest needs. Rather, there is also the risk that the operation of the patent system, as defined by law, is distorted. The reason is that many of the public interest needs, which may justify compulsory licences, in particular those relating to public health, represent a dilemma for the design of a patent system. Their satisfaction asks for both at the same time, stimulating enhanced and advanced innovation, on one hand, and, on the other, allowing broad and generally affordable access to the protected innovative products and processes. By affording the incentive of market exclusivity, the patent system may promote the former, but it may not equally support the latter, at least not where the relevant markets are imperfect, as they are almost by definition in public interest situations. National patent laws seek to mitigate the dilemma by designing protection in accordance with a State's perception of its societal needs, although they may do so only within the framework of their international obligations of protection.[83] More particularly, they provide for specific exclusions from patentability, define exceptions from protection more or less broadly, and include countervailing rights, such as precisely rules on compulsory licensing.[84] To a certain extent, these elements of the system of protection are interchangeable and/or interdependent.[85] This means that they may not be put in practice independently from each other or else the operation of the system, as intended by the legislator, its coherence and consistency will be put in jeopardy. Thus, the application of the rules on compulsory licensing in the public interest must take account of the fact that these rules are part of the system, i.e. it must accept the logic of protection, not undermine it. More particularly, where by way of a broad definition of patentable subject matter innovation in public need products has been made a matter of the patent system, the pursuit of the public interest may be seen not as being in conflict with patent protection but as being part of it. As a result, it is not only the royalties due under a compulsory licence that may not be set below incentive levels.[86] Rather, the very decision of whether and when to grant a compulsory licence in the public interest ought to be taken in accordance with the

references supra n. 4 and, inter alia, Van Overwalle and van Zimmeren (2011), p. 4; Koikkara (2010), pp. 82 et passim; Reichman (2010), p. 589.

[83] The difference between sovereign national policy and its limitations by international obligations is mirrored by the differences between Sect. 48A and Sect. 48B UK Patents Act; see also supra n. 49.

[84] See for a broad international comparison the studies by *L. Bently* et al. in WIPO (2011); for the revision of Belgian law, see Van Overwalle (2006), p. 889; for Swiss law, Art. 9, Art. 37-40e Swiss Patent Act (as compared to §§ 11, 24 PatG).

[85] See Bently (2011), p. 1; Burk and Lemley (2003), pp. 1575, 1630 et seq.; Van Overwalle (2011), p. 435.

[86] See infra Sect. 2.3.1.

fact that patents are a tool of competition in and for markets.[87] If the production of innovation in public need goods is expected to result from the operation of patent protection, the operation of markets must be respected to the extent this is compatible with the public interest.[88] This is the more true as the compulsory licence in the public interest is granted upon request by a private party, typically a commercial firm and (potential) rival of the patentee, who necessarily pursues her/his private profit interests when articulating the public need.

2.3 Practical Problems

There are more grounds for granting compulsory licences than the three major ones dealt with here. However, the rationales are similar to those explained above; if not, they tend to be problematic. A good, albeit still rare example of compulsory licensing rules serving the patent system's incentive function for innovation are those that seek to make research tools available in the field of biotechnology.[89] An example of a problematic ground for granting compulsory licences, which has been generally outlawed by Art. 31 lit. f) TRIPS Agreement,[90] is the (industrial) policy of States to defend their foreign trade interests against blocking domestic patents by the threat of granting compulsory licences.[91] Due precisely to the TRIPS Agreement, the practical importance of these problematic grounds is rather limited. However, the TRIPS Agreement has also contributed to generally limiting the practical importance of the better established grounds of compulsory licensing. More particularly, instead of mitigating the development controversy surrounding Art. 5A Paris Convention,[92] Art. 31 TRIPS Agreement reaffirmed and reinforced its limits. An example of this is the rule of non-exclusivity of the compulsory licence,[93] which exposes the compulsory licensee to the risk that the patentee might step into the market whenever she/he thinks fit, in particular as soon as the licensee has "developed" the local market. This is not the place to comment on the catalogue of

[87] See references supra n. 64.

[88] Starting from the assumption of a conflict between private property and the public interest BGH of 5 December 1995, GRUR 1996, 190 = 27 IIC 242, 246, 248 et seq. (1997)—"Polyferon" comes to a similar conclusion.

[89] See, e.g., Art. 40b Swiss Patent Act.

[90] For the exception, see Art. 30bis TRIPS Agreement and supra n. 4, 13; Reichman (2010), pp. 591 et seq.

[91] See, with respect to non-WTO patents, Sect. 48B(1)(d)(i), UK Patents Act.

[92] See reference supra n. 3.

[93] Art. 5A(4) Paris Convention as regards compulsory licences to remedy non-working; Art. 31 lit. d) TRIPS Agreement with respect to any compulsory licence. A case-by-case approach would have made more sense. While non-exclusivity generally fits compulsory licences (and cross-licences) well in dependency cases, it may deter firms from applying for public interest licences where these require high investments.

limits established by Art. 31 TRIPS Agreement.[94] However, a proper determination of the remuneration, i.e. generally of the royalties, which the compulsory licensee has to pay to the patentee, may depend on the grounds upon which the licence is granted. In this regard, therefore, a brief remark seems to be in point.

2.3.1 The Remuneration Issue

Unlike in the case of an expropriation, the remuneration that the licensee has to pay to the licensee is not meant to compensate the patentee for the loss or impairment of the property right she/he suffers by an act of State.[95] Rather, it represents a compensation for the use that a third party, the compulsory licensee, may make of the patented invention in her/his own private interest as a matter of realising the concomitant public interest underlying the ground for the grant of the compulsory licence.[96] For this reason, the legislator may and sometimes expressly does leave the fixing of the remuneration to settlement between the parties.[97] In the absence of such ex post understanding,[98] the granting authority—typically a court, at least by way of judicial review—will have to determine the remuneration in accordance with standards, which in most countries have been set, if at all,[99] only in vague terms borrowed from Art. 31 lit.h) TRIPS Agreement.[100] According to this

[94] Art. 31 TRIPS Agreement frequently is understood as a catalogue of "safeguards" (see, e.g., Gervais 2012, 2.409, page 492), namely, of the patentee's interests. A countervailing concern for a list of generally legitimate grounds of compulsory licences is missing. While it is true that such grounds are not the subject of Art. 31, they are not absent from the TRIPS Agreement; see Art. 2 (incorporating the Paris Convention) and Arts. 7 and 8(1). Therefore, they need to be respected in interpreting and applying Art. 31 TRIPS Agreement.

[95] See the separate rules on expropriation as provided for by Art. 32 Swiss Patent Act; Art. L 613-20 c.prop.int. (as distinguished from Art. L 613-19 c.prop.int.); see also *Rogge* in Benkard (2006), § 24, annot. 3.

[96] See *Rogge* in Benkard (2006), § 24, annot. 3. It does not follow that the level of the remuneration ought to be determined by analogy to the damages an infringer would have to pay (contra de Carvalho 2010, at 31.64, p. 496 et seq.). The award of damages presupposes tort-like conduct; the licensee does not have to disgorge profits or to compensate for profits lost, the less so as the patentee is in conflict with the rationale of patent protection or with a public interest.

[97] To this effect, expressly, Art. 34 § 1 Belgian Patent Act; for the "licence d'office", Art. L 613-17, (3) and Art. L 613-18(6) c.prop.int.; Sect. 46(3) UK Patents Act.

[98] Compulsory licences will be granted only once licence negotiations have failed; see. Art. 31 lit. b) TRIPS Agreement.

[99] Art. L 613-12(3) c.prop.int. does not give any indication as to the level of remuneration, just as Art. L 613-12(1) c.prop.int. is silent as to the reasons for the failure of contract negotiations. In respect of both concerns, Art. 72(1), (2) c.prop.ind. hardly is more explicit ("eque condizioni", "equo compenso", respectively).

[100] § 24 (6, 4th sent.) PatG; § 37(1, 2nd sent.) PatG Austria; Art. 34 § 1, 3^{e} al. Belgian Patent Act; Art. 40(5) Swiss Patent Act; Sect. 48A(6)(d) UK Patents Act [but see for non-WTO patents Sect. 50(1)(b)]. Literature mostly refers to criteria developed by case law or by experts with respect to

provision, the remuneration must be adequate in the circumstances of each case, taking into account the economic value of the authorisation to use the patented invention.

These two criteria need to be put in relation to the reasons leading to the grant of a compulsory licence, namely, first, the failure of negotiations between the parties on the voluntary grant of a licence "on reasonable commercial terms and condition-s"(Article 31 lit. b) TRIPS Agreement) and, second, the substantive justification of the grant of a compulsory licence.[101] Thus, in dependency cases, the grant of the compulsory licence typically serves to overcome a commercial stalemate between holders of (eventually) blocking patents. Therefore, the remuneration ought to be fixed by reference precisely to reasonable commercial terms as would result from an arm's-length dealing in competitive markets. Due regard will have to be given to the possibility that the dependent patent may be more valuable than the head patent and that it may even enhance the latter's value.[102] Given the licensee's own patent position, these commercial terms will hardly ever be affected by the non-exclusive character of the compulsory licence (Art. 31 lit. d) TRIPS Agreement). Non-exclusivity would even seem to be appropriate in view of the patentee's right to obtain a licence to use the dependent invention since competition policy favours non-exclusivity of cross-licensing arrangements.

By contrast, as regards compulsory licences on grounds of non-working the patented invention and/or of insufficient supply of the domestic market, the mandatorily non-exclusive character of the licence is likely to affect its economic value. This is so whenever the licensee has to make considerable investments in production and/or distribution and, therefore, normally would ask for exclusivity as a matter of reasonable commercial terms.[103] Moreover, the very reason for assimilating importation to domestic manufacturing, i.e. economies of scale and optimal geographic allocation of resources,[104] may stand in the way of effectively sanctioning insufficient supply by the grant of compulsory licences where the domestic market is not large enough to allow the licensee to match the patentee's competitive advantage. There simply will be no sufficient private interest in the grant of a compulsory licence to satisfy a public interest in a supply that the patentee does not sufficiently provide.

---

the general assessment of the value of patents and licences; see, e.g., Correa (2007), pp. 322 et seq., and the references infra n. 107.

[101] The relevance of the ground justifying the compulsory licence is not generally recognised, but see Gervais (2012), at no. 2.409 (p. 496); Correa (2007), p. 322.

[102] See Art. 31 lit. b)(i) TRIPS Agreement. Not infrequently, it is this improvement that makes the head patent commercially viable. If so, the interest of the holder of the head patent first to recoup her/his investment alone will be diminished, and so it will be generally by the availability of the cross-licence for the dependent patent.

[103] See the justification of exclusivity clauses in licence agreements under competition law ever since ECJ of 8 June 1982, case 258/78, *Nungesser/Commission*, Rep. 1982, 2015.

[104] See supra Sect. 2.2.2, text following n. 48.

This mismatch may not be a matter of primary concern where, for one reason or another, the patentee's interest in supplying herself/himself a given geographic market is limited and where, therefore, the availability of compulsory licences only serves to overcome her/his unwillingness to grant a voluntary licence. However, the mismatch will be of great concern in case it contributes to the non-satisfaction of specific public interests, such as a State's concern about making essential medicines generally available at affordable prices. The problem is broadly discussed[105] but is not the subject of this chapter. The only point to be made here is that the availability of compulsory licences in the public interest, more particularly in the interest of specific public needs, represents a compromise made to have TRIPS Members accept the principle that patent protection must be made available for inventions in whatever field of technology [Article 27(1) TRIPS Agreement]. Consequently, compulsory licences are supposed to mitigate the dilemma between setting market-based incentives for innovation and the State's concern for catering for the public interest.[106] This, however, also means that they may not be used to undercut the system of protection, let alone to suspend its operation altogether.

In the latter respect, the dividing line does not run along the patentee's interest not to be held to subsidise, be it indirectly, a public policy by accepting non-rewarding prices because that much of a respect for patent protection is generally recognised, at least in theory. Nor is the concern with the licensee's interest in having to pay as little of a royalty as her/his business can bear at the margin because she/he may abstain from requesting or taking the compulsory licence in the first place. Rather, the demarcation line is between, on one hand, controlling the patentee's supply strategies, which ought to be a matter of competition policy, and, on the other, imposing an obligation on the patentee, be it indirectly, as to whose demand she/he has to meet. This then is a matter of interventionist market regulation. Such, indeed, is the very characteristic that distinguishes compulsory licences in the public interest from the other types of compulsory licences. The specificity of the public interest informs the interventionist reach of the grant of the compulsory licence. However, the problems that such public interest licences produce are not so much linked to their specific interventionist features. Rather, they result from the discrepancy that exists between, on one hand, the territoriality of patent protection and of the grant and the terms of compulsory licences and, on the other, the global availability of precisely such territorially defined protection for worldwide markets and business activities. All the parties concerned tend to shift the benefits and burdens of patent protection around strategically according to where globalisation and/or territoriality of markets operate to their advantage or disadvantage.[107]

[105] See references supra n. 4 and, inter alia, Karres (2007), pp. 87 et passim.

[106] See supra Sect. 2.2.2, text following n. 56, Sect. 2.2.3

[107] See, for a discussion triggered by recent practices in India of granting compulsory licences in the pharmaceutical sector, Boschek (2012), p. 612; comp. also Taubman (2008), p. 927.

2.3.2 A Remedy of No Avail?

In addition to a mismatch of private and public interests, which affects the availability of compulsory licences where the grant depends on the concomitant existence of a public interest,[108] there are quite a number of other obstacles impeding access to compulsory licences or even nullifying any interest in applying for them. In the first regard, most frequently named are the difficulties of concretising the vague grounds justifying the grant of a compulsory licence into a justification under the circumstances of a given case. Thus, predicting what will actually constitute, e.g., "insufficiency" of supply or an "excuse légitime", or overcoming the procedural hurdles,[109] may make filing an application unattractive in terms of costs and time lost on innovation markets. In the latter respect, the most mentioned obstacle is the non-exclusive character of the compulsory licence and its limitation to the technology as patented, i.e. its non-extension to the concomitant, invention-specific know-how. These difficulties might even be exacerbated by the fact that the grant of a compulsory licence precisely does not embrace an entire technology but only the patent right. This, indeed, means that access to technologies that are covered by more than one patent, as typically is the case for most technologies with the exception precisely of patents on chemical compounds,[110] must be sought patent by patent, thus increasing the number of the already existing hurdles.[111]

However, as serious as these problems are, they do not affect all categories of compulsory licences to the same degree. Non-exclusivity, non-extension to invention-specific know-how, and the need to apply for a compulsory licence patent by patent will only rarely frustrate the interest of the owner of a dependent patent in obtaining access to the head patent. As she/he masters the technology, her/his concern is with the procedural hurdles, with their costs, and the time lost. More particularly, what matters for the holder of dependent patents is that her/his claim to a compulsory licence may not be presented as a defence in infringement proceedings relating to the

[108] While the private interest in the grant of a compulsory licence needs to be supported by a public interest where the law so requires, the public interest may be satisfied in many ways other than by the grant of compulsory licences. To take again the market for pharmaceuticals, price regulation and collective bargaining between health care institutions and pharmaceutical industry are typical forms, yet another one is facilitating and, in particular, speeding up market entry of generics.

[109] For the infinite complexity of the granting procedure provided for by Belgium law with respect to compulsory licences in the interest of public health, see Art. 31bis Belgian Patent Act; Van Overwalle (2006), loc. cit., at pp. 911 et seq.; Arts. L-613-17 and L 613-18 c.prop.int. separate the settlement of non-agreement or royalties by a court from the administrative procedure for the introduction of a system of licences of right.

[110] As chemical compounds, more particularly base compounds of pharmaceuticals, may be protected by only one or a few patents, they are particularly vulnerable to compulsory licensing. This contributes to both the tense controversies and the attempt to obtain additional protection for inventive variations and applications; see references supra n. 4 and, generally, European *Commission*, Pharmaceutical Sector Inquiry, Final Report 8 July 2009 sub. C.

[111] Note that Art. 31 lit. a) TRIPS Agreement requires a case-by-case, not a patent-by-patent, analysis; see Gervais (2012), loc. cit., sub 2.406.

head patent.[112] Instead, it must be enforced by separate action. Possibly, it may not even be brought as a counterclaim, where the grant lies within the competence of an administrative authority rather than within the jurisdiction of a (patent infringement) court.[113] This difficulty is compounded by her/his need to go through as many—and diverse!—national procedures as there are territorially defined national patents covering the economically and geographically relevant market for the head invention and the dependent invention. This difficulty exists even in the internal market of the European Union. For one thing, the European patent with unitary effect produces unity only as regards protection but not with respect to countervailing rights.[114] For another, the European bundle patent, which still prevails and will remain generally available, is national in character and territorial in its geographic scope. Thus, whatever the applicable patent law will be, the result is always that, contrary to the purpose of patent protection,[115] compulsory licences are largely ineffective as a means to support independent incremental innovation whenever the improvement represents, as it typically does, an invention whose exploitation depends on approval by the holder of a first patent.

Similar problems affect the effective availability and functionality of compulsory licences to remedy insufficient supply of the market, be it by importation or local working. Whatever the conceptual and practical importance of such compulsory licences may be, in the internal market of the EU insufficient supply may not be defined by reference to single national markets. Yet, given the national character and scope of the patents forming the European bundle patent, it is only in national terms that compulsory licences on grounds of insufficient supply will be admitted, and so they will be in respect of unitary patent protection, should they be available at all.[116] Indeed, while any applicable national law must admit supply by importation, in either case the application of national law means that sufficiency of supply will be determined with respect to the needs of national markets rather than with respect to the internal market. It is, however, not for patent law but for the rules on the free movement of goods and the rules on competition to ensure that patented products are adequately distributed throughout the entire Union and its Member States. This it is irrespective of the form of patent protection, unitary or (inter)nationally bundled, because in the internal market the territory of the patentee's responsibilities cannot be narrower than that which she/he is offered and may access for exploitation.[117]

---

[112] Concerning the difference of mandatory licensing as a remedy to violation of the rules of competition (antitrust) law, see BGH of 6 May 2009, case KZR 39/06—Orange Book Standard, 41 IIC 337 (2010); Ullrich (2010a), p. 369.

[113] As is the case in the UK, for the difference of many other European jurisdictions, see supra n. 18.

[114] For details, see Ullrich (2012a), sub. 2.3.2. with references.

[115] See Ullrich (2012b), loc. cit. sub II.2.b) (II) et passim.

[116] See reference supra n. 114.

[117] This is the principle underlying Union-wide exhaustion of national patent protection; see *H. Ullrich* in Immenga and Mestmäcker (2012), Band 1, EU/Teil 2, pp. 1634 et seq. (annot. 74 et seq). As Union-wide exploitation of national patents does not rest only on the autonomy they

And again, it is also access to the entire internal market that a compulsory licensee may need to act as an efficient supplier, be it by default or as a second source.

3 Mandatory Licensing Under Competition Law

3.1 Principles of Controlling a Patentee's Unilateral Conduct

As noted earlier, the criteria determining the grant of compulsory licences under patent law rest upon system-intrinsic considerations of patent protection alone.[118] However, patents, like any property,[119] may be used and exploited only in conformity with competition law, the more so since, as an innovation incentive, the patent exclusivity will work properly under conditions of competition only.[120] While at least all the major jurisdictions do have more or less similar, well-developed sets of competition rules regarding bilateral licensing transactions,[121] competition policies relating to unilateral practices of patentees vary considerably both as regards their orientation and their implementation.[122] Therefore, the following presentation will be limited to the "European" competition rules as enshrined in Article 102 of the

confer upon their respective owners but rests also on the rules on free movement inside the Union, such autonomy may not be turned against the latter; see ECJ of 20 January 1981, cases 55/80 and 57/80, *Musik Vertrieb Membran/GEMA*, Rep. 1981,147.; of 14 July 1981, case 187/80, *Merck/ Stephar*, Rep. 1981, 2063; of 5 December 1996, cases C-267/95 and 268/95, *Merck/Primecrown*, Rep. 1996 I 6285. Likewise, the duties that the autonomy entails for the patentee under national law may not be used to limit in their turn the free movement of goods, at least not where the autonomy results from EU unitary patent protection and possibly not even where it rests on protection by a European bundle of national patents. After all, due to the principle of optionality between unitary protection and protection by a bundle of patents, and due also to the latter being upgraded to pan-European protection by the Agreement on a Unified Patent Court, the European patent has become a legitimate form of patent protection throughout the Union, which must conform to the Union's standards; see also reference supra n. 114.

118 See Sect. 2.2.1, text following n. 37; Sect. 2.2.2, text following n. 68.

119 See (EU) General Court of 23 October 2003, case T-65/98, *Van den Bergh Foods/Commission*, Rep. 2003 II 4653; BGH of 4 March 2008, case KVR 21/07—Soda-Club II, WuW DE-R 2268, 2274 et seq.; Shelanski (2009), loc. cit.

120 See references supra n. 64; *H. Ullrich, A. Heinemann*, in: Immenga and Mestmäcker (2012), Bd. 1, EU/Teil 2, pp. 1694 et seq. with references.

121 See for a recent comparison of U.S. practice and EU practice, Früh (2012), pp. 317 et passim; Feil (2009), passim.

122 See, for a comparison of U.S. and EU approaches, Schweitzer (2008), p. 59; Patterson (2008), at pp. 35 et passim; Gifford and Kuderle (2011), p. 694; Früh (2012), loc. cit., at pp. 387 et passim; Conde Gallego (2008), p. 215.

Treaty on the Functioning of the European Union (TFEU).[123] These do also control competition policies in EU Member States to the extent inter-EU trade is concerned.[124]

3.1.1 The Threshold to Control: Market Dominance

Relevant Product and Technology Markets

Unilateral conduct, such as refusals to deal or, for this matter, refusals to license[125] or any autonomous act of use or non-use of the patent right, comes within the purview of the competition rules only if it is that of an enterprise dominating the market.[126] Dominance is defined as a market position allowing an enterprise to determine its market conduct to a substantial degree independently from the

---

[123] Art. 102 TFEU reads: "Any abuse by one or more undertakings of a dominant position within the internal market or in a substantial part of it shall be prohibited as incompatible with the internal market in so far as it may affect trade between Member States. Such abuse may, in particular, consist in:

(a) directly or indirectly imposing unfair purchase or selling prices or other unfair trading conditions;
(b) limiting production, markets or technical development to the prejudice of consumers;
(c) applying dissimilar conditions to equivalent transactions with other trading parties, thereby placing them at a competitive disadvantage;
(d) making the conclusion of contracts subject to acceptance by the other parties of supplementary obligations which, by their nature or according to commercial usage, have no connection with the subject of such contracts".

[124] Article 3 para 1 Regulation (EC) No. 1/2003 of the Council on the implementation of the rules on competition laid down in Article 81 and 82 of the Treaty (now Article 101, 102 TFEU), OJEC 2003 L 1, 1; Article 3 para. 2, 2nd sent. Reg. 1/2003, allows Member States to apply stricter national law to unilateral conduct; for examples, see infra n. 126.

[125] As distinct from refusals to licence resulting from concertation within or among (a group of) licensees, which come under Article 101 TFEU. The typical case of an agreement not to grant (additional) licences is presented by exclusive licences; for an example of concertation among licensees on the exercise of a veto right, see *Commission decision* of 25 July 1975, *Bronbemaling/ Heidemaatschippij*, OJEC 1975 L 249/27.

[126] Some national laws additionally allow controlling unilateral conduct of firms that do not dominate a market but do have relational market power vis-à-vis other enterprises, typically small or medium-sized ones, which as to their offer or supply depend on the former. Such control, however, will be limited to discriminatory or disruptive and to predatory practices; see e.g. § 20 German Act Against Restriction of Competition (GWB), Article L 420 Code de commerce. Such control of relational market power has always been politically controversial, in particular as regards its potential for protectionist implementation. The matter cannot be discussed here; see, generally, *K. Markert* in Immenga and Mestmäcker (2007), § 20, annot. 7 et seq., with references; for a summary comparison of national laws, Lamping (2010), pp. 169 et seq.; Këllezi (2008), pp. 55, 61 et passim.; with respect to licensing practices, Jung (2004), pp. 379, 400 et seq.

reactions of its competitors, suppliers, or clients.[127] Dominance, therefore, is not tantamount to monopoly but results from non-exposure to effective competition, whatever the reasons may be.[128] As such, the patent exclusivity does not confer market power, let alone market dominance.[129] Rather, it must result from the competitive position a patented subject matter holds as a product on a relevant market. It is, indeed, only by reference to identical and to substitute products that the reactivity of customers and of competitors and, thus, dominance, can be ascertained. The reach of a "relevant" market or its limits in terms of products belonging to the same market, of the geographic area covered, and of the pertinent periods of time generally is defined from the demands' perspective. Thus, the test is whether by their utility in terms of quality and price the available offers are reasonably interchangeable or substitutable.[130]

With respect to the exploitation of patented subject matter, two — interdependent — market levels are generally distinguished, that of the product market, where goods made pursuant to the patent's technical teaching are traded, and that of the technology market, where licences for the use of the patent's technical teaching are traded.[131] While with respect to the former the general concept of market definition applies, in particular the criteria of price/quality substitutability, the latter market is more difficult to define, inter alia, because the utility of a technology for a licensee largely depends on her/his specific technological needs and receptive or absorptive capacity.[132] Ultimately, determination of the relevant technology market tends to be complex and fact specific. What matters in the context of the chapter presented here is that relevant product and/or technology

---

[127] Generally recognised criterion since ECJ of 14 February 1978, case 27/26, *Hoffmann-La Roche*, Rep. 1979, 468 at nos. 38 at seq.; for details, see *A. Fuchs* in Immenga and Mestmäcker (2012), loc. cit., EU/Teil 1, at pp. 592 et seq. (Art. 102 AEUV annot. 73 et seq.).

[128] Superior performance, entry barriers of all sorts (economic or political), natural monopoly, past predatory practices, persistent market position after market deregulation, etc.

[129] Uncontroversial, see already ECJ of 29 February 1968, case 24/67, *Parke Davis/Proebel*, Rep. 1968, 85 at p. 112; of February 1971, case 40/70, *Sirena/Eda*, Rep. 1171, 69, 84 (no. 16); of 8 Juni 1971, case. 78/0, *Deutsche Grammophon/Metro-SB-Großmärkte*, Rep. 1971, 487 at pp. 500 et seq. (nos. 14 et seq.); see also *Ullrich, Heinemann* in Immenga and Mestmäcker (2012), loc. cit., EU/Teil 2, at pp. 1719 et seq. (nos. 42 et seq.), 1724 et seq. (no. 49) with references.

[130] See, generally, Früh (2012), loc. cit., at pp. 154 et passim; *Fuchs, Möschel* in Immenga and Mestmäcker (2012), loc. cit., EU/Teil 1, at pp. 581 et passim (nos 48 et seq.), with references to case law.

[131] Product markets include products directly resulting from a patented process (see Article 64 (2) EPC); technology markets are particularly relevant for patented processes. For the distinction between and interdependence of product and technology markets, see European Commission (2004), p. 2 at nos. 19 et seq., 26 et seq.; European Commission (2011), pp. 1, 26 et seq. (nos. 112 et seq.) *Ullrich, Heinemann* in Immenga and Mestmäcker (2012), loc. cit., EU/Teil 2, at pp. 1722 et seq. (nos. 46 et seq.), Früh (2012), loc. cit., at pp. 214 et passim, with respect to technology transfer agreements, pp. 274 et seq., with particular emphasis on R&D-related innovation markets, which *Commission*, ibid. at no. 25 will consider only exceptionally.

[132] For a detailed criticism of EU administrative practice, see Früh (2012), loc. cit., at pp. 256 et seq.

markets only rarely coincide with patent exclusivity.[133] They may be narrower, where the patented invention has broad and/or different fields of techno-economic application, or they may be broader, when there are patented or non-patented (non-patentable or no longer patented, i.e. generic) substitutes on the market. Moreover, technology markets are defined precisely by reference to technologies rather than by reference to patents, and technologies typically embrace several, if not a multitude of patents and also technological know-how, at least the invention-specific know-how, often enough held as a trade secret.[134]

Criteria of Market Dominance

However difficult, the proper definition of the relevant market is crucial for ascertaining whether a patentee or, for that matter, the holder of a technology, dominates a market or is exposed to competition, which effectively subjects her/his conduct to control by the reactions of competitors and consumers or suppliers rather than only to some more or less noticeable residual competition. The reason is that, with respect to (too) narrowly defined relevant markets, the indicia of dominance gain as much presumptive force as they lose if applied to (too) broadly defined markets. This effect is obvious for relevant geographic and for product markets since the market shares held by the alleged "monopolist" and by her/his rivals respectively are generally considered to represent prima facie indicia of the existence or the absence of dominance.[135] It also holds true for the assumption that the number of existing technologies may indicate the existence of substantial competition on technology markets.[136] More generally, the assessment of the intensity of competition or, conversely, of its absence in view of a dominant firm is the easier the narrower the markets are defined and vice versa. There is, indeed, a complex

[133] In which case the patentee would enjoy a monopoly.

[134] See Früh (2012), loc. cit., at p. 259. Note in this context that trade secret protection contributes to non-transparency of technology markets.

[135] See *Fuchs, Möschel*, in Immenga and Mestmäcker (2012), loc. cit., EU Teil 1, at pp. 599 et seq. (nos. 87 et seq.), pointing to the fact that market shares are only indicative of market power and need to be put into relation to the market shares held by other market actors and to their number, etc. The indicative strength of market shares increases with their size, 40–75 %, being sufficient only if additional factors also indicate dominance (ibid at no. 91). A rule of thumb still is that '30 % is not enough, 60 % may or may not indicate monopoly, over 90 % do establish "monopoly"' [Judge *Learned Hand*, in *U.S. v. Aluminium Company of America* (*Alcoa*) 148 F. 2d.416 (2nd Cir. 1945)].

[136] *Commission*, Guidelines on technology transfer agreements, loc. cit., at no. 131 (four or more technologies); see, for a critique, Früh (2012), loc. cit., at pp. 205 et seq.

analysis to be carried out[137] regarding not only the strength or weakness of residual competition resulting from substitute products or technologies and the relative potential and strength of the dominant firm, both of which are difficult enough to assess.[138] Rather, account must be taken of the existence and effect of entry barriers and of potential competition (including the dynamics of the market[139]), of the presence and strength of network effects,[140] of the dependence of suppliers or customers on the alleged "monopolist" as a customer or as a supplier,[141] and of the supportive effects that the portfolio of exclusive rights held by the owner of the technology may produce by stabilising her/his position in the market.[142] All in all, it has to be determined whether a firm's conduct is sufficiently controlled by competition or needs to be controlled by law.[143] Such determination is more easily made with respect to narrowly defined markets than it is with respect to broader markets. Moreover, market definitions and — possibly as a result — the determination of dominance risk being result driven,[144] with the ensuing risk of subjecting powerful firms to either too much or insufficient control.

---

[137] See, for the following only, *Fuchs, Möschel*, in Immenga and Mestmäcker (2012), loc. cit., EU/Teil1, at pp. 604 et passim (nos. 97 et passim), with references to administrative and judicial practices.

[138] In terms of access to resources or financing, established supply and distribution chains, diversification (including cross-subsidisation), locational advantages, etc.

[139] For a critical assessment, see Früh (2012), loc. cit., at pp. 306 et passim.

[140] Generally discussed in the context of controlling the exercise of patents reading on industrial standards, see Wielsch (2008), pp. 135 et seq.; Picht (2013), pp. 445 et seq., both with references.

[141] See *Fuchs, Möschel*, in Immenga and Mestmäcker (2012), loc. cit., EU/Teil 1, at p. 580 (no. 46), 598 (no. 85); Lamping (2010), loc. cit., at pp. 177 et seq. (proposing at pp. 180 et seq. to extend control to relational market power in general); Këllezi (2008), loc. cit., at pp. 82 et seq. There is an overlap with the concept of abuse relating to the exploitation of a situation of dependence; see e.g. *Commission* of 22 December 1987, case IV/30.787 *Eurofix-Bauco/Hilti*, OJEC 1988 L. 65, 19, confirmed by Court 1st Inst. of 12 December 1991, case T-30/89 *Hilti/Commission*, Rep. 1991 II 1439.

[142] See *Ullrich, Heinemann*, in Immenga and Mestmäcker (2012), loc. cit., EU/Teil 2, at pp. 1724 et seq. (no. 49); *Fuchs, Möschel* in Immenga and Mestmäcker (2012), EU/Teil 1, at pp. 606 et seq. (no. 103) all with references.

[143] *Fuchs, Möschel* in Immenga and Mestmäcker (2012), loc. cit., EU/Teil 1, at pp. 580 et seq. (no. 47), 593 et seq. (no. 77).

[144] See Lamping (2010), loc. cit., at p. 179 (narrow definition to bridge gap of control over relational market power); *H. Ullrich* in Immenga and Mestmäcker (1997), pp. 1250 et seq. (no. 39), criticising ECJ of 6 April 1995, cases C-241/91-P and C-247/91-P, RTE and ITV/Commission, Rep. 1995 I 743 at no. 47, for disregarding competition for access to information. See also *Fuchs, Möschel* in Immenga and Mestmäcker (2012), loc. cit., EU/Teil 1, at p. 580 (no. 40), 594 (no. 78), arguing that market dominance may need to be defined in relation to the suspected abuse, i.e. the more anti-competitive the alleged abuse is, the less intensive dominance needs to be (which compares to the assumption that some abuses might occur only in the absence of competition).

3.1.2 Abusive Refusals to Licence

Anti-competitive Access Foreclosure

When controlling whether the conduct of market-dominating holders of intellectual property actually amounts to an abuse within the meaning of Article 102 TFEU, the above-mentioned risk is frequently articulated as a dilemma between, on one hand, the danger that excessive control might produce chilling effects on IPR owners' or firms' willingness to innovate and, on the other, the risk that insufficient control could prevent other market actors from engaging in follow-on innovation or dissemination of innovation.[145] However, to the extent that this risk is realistic, it is unrelated to the so-called incentive function of intellectual property protection. The connecting factor for control is not the exclusivity afforded by intellectual property right(s) but the market dominance of its owner as established by the above-mentioned criteria. Also, the abuse does not consist in the exercise of the right as such but in the anti-competitive objective or effect of the practice she/he pursues on the relevant market, in particular its innovation-inhibiting effect.[146] It is, indeed, well established that, as any owner of intellectual property, market-dominating firms may acquire intellectual property rights and rely on the protection that these rights provide against infringement by imitation,[147] just as they may resort to any form of competition on the merits of their lawful achievements and of their superior performance. However, market-dominating enterprises may not deviate from such standards by conduct "which is such as to influence the structure of a market, where, as a result of the very presence of the undertaking in question, the degree of competition is weakened, and which, through recourse to methods different from those which condition normal competition in products or services on the basis of transactions of commercial operators, has the effect of hindering the maintenance of the degree of competition still existing or the growth of that competition".[148] While the European Court of Justice has made it clear that the market power need not be the means used to bring about the anti-competitive (abusive) practice,[149] it is

[145] The problem has been most vividly discussed in relation to the Microsoft case (infra n. 166); see only Geradin (2004), p. 1519; Heinemann (2006), pp. 704, 713; more generally Govaere (2008), p. 541; for a different approach, see Früh (2012), loc. cit., at pp. 408 et passim.

[146] See Article 102 lit. b) TFEU.

[147] Well established principle; see only ECJ of 29 February 1968, case 24/67, *Parke Davis/ Proebel*, Rep. 1968, 85 at p. 112; of 5 October 1988, case 54/87, **CICRA/Renault**, Rep. 1988, 6039 at nos. 15 et seq.; of 5 October 1988; case 238/87, *Volvo/Veng*, Rep. 1988, 6211 at no. 8; *Ullrich, Heinemann*, in Immenga and Mestmäcker (2012), loc. cit., EU/Teil 2, at p. 1726 (no. 50) with references. See also Drexl (2007), p. 647; Ullrich (2014), p. 241.

[148] ECJ of 13 February 1979, case 85/76, *Hoffmann-La Roche/Commission*, Rep. 1979, 461 at no. 91; see also *Fuchs*, *Möschel*, in Immenga and Mestmäcker (2012), loc. cit., EU/Teil 1, at pp. 619 et seq. no. 128 et seq., with references.

[149] ECJ of 13 February 1979, case 85/76, *Hoffmann-La Roche/Commission*, Rep. 1979, 461 at no. 91.

also clear that it is because of it dominating the market that a firm is held to abstain from anti-competitive conduct[150] and is held even to a "special responsibility" to respect any remaining or "residual" competition.[151] Nevertheless, the concept of abuse is of an objective nature.[152] The concern is with restrictions of competition additionally affecting a dominated (or a related)[153] market and not with the way they are brought about or the legal form into which they are cast, let alone their intentional or non-intentional character.[154]

The types of abuses, in part listed in the illustrative catalogue of Article 102 TFEU, are generally classified into the two categories of exploitative and exclusionary practices,[155] the former being essentially directed at customers or suppliers, the latter—directly or indirectly—at competitors on the relevant or on a related (upstream or downstream) market. There is, however, considerable controversy and uncertainty regarding the details of the definition and the assessment of the subgroups of these categories, in particular as regards exclusionary practices, which cannot be re-examined here.[156] For a systematic comparison between compulsory licensing rules of patent law and obligations to licence under competition law, it is enough to consider those exclusionary practices, which are aimed at foreclosing market actors from access to the dominated or to a related market.

---

[150] While a causal link between dominance and the abuse need not be established, it is the dominance that makes the anti-competitive practice constitute an abuse under Article 102 TFEU; see for the somewhat artificial controversy *Th. Eilmannsberger* in Hirsch et al. (2007), Article 82 EG annot. 124 et passim; *Fuchs, Möschel* in Immenga and Mestmäcker (2012), loc. cit., EU/Teil 1, at pp. 623 et seq. (nos. 136 et seq.), with references.

[151] Ever since ECJ of 9 November 1983, case 322/81, *Michelin/Commission*, Rep. 1983, 3461 at no. 57 ("special responsibility not to allow its conduct to impair genuine undistorted competition on the Common Market"/"responsabilité particulière de ne pas porter atteinte à une concurrence effective et non faussée"); see also *Fuchs, Möschel*, in Immenga and Mestmäcker (2012), loc. cit., EU/Teil 1, at pp. 619 et seq. (no. 130), with references.

[152] Well-established rule; see ECJ of 13 February 1979, case 85/76, *Hoffmann-La Roche/Commission*, Rep. 1979, 461 at no. 91; for details, see *Eilmannsberger* in Münchener Kommentar (2007), loc. cit., Article 82 EG, annot. 150 et passim.

[153] For the problem of "leveraging" market power into not (yet) dominated but related markets, see *Fuchs, Möschel*, in Immenga and Mestmäcker (2012), loc. cit., EU/Teil 1, at pp. 624 e seq (nos. 138 et seq.), with references.

[154] As distinguished from the purpose, aim, and effect of a practice, see *Fuchs, Möschel*, in Immenga and Mestmäcker (2012), loc. cit., EU/Teil 1, at pp. 628 et seq. (nos. 149 et seq.), with references.

[155] Leaving aside a third category, namely abuses that result in deterioration of market structures. Since the introduction of merger control, this category has become sort of subsidiary. Where applicable outside structural changes of markets, this category does not add much to that of exclusionary practices; see *Fuchs, Möschel*, in Immenga and Mestmäcker (2012), loc. cit., EU/Teil 1, at pp. 728 et passim (nos. 383 et passim, no. 391).

[156] For details, see *Fuchs, Möschel*, in Immenga and Mestmäcker (2012), loc. cit., EU/Teil 1, at pp. 635 et passim, 645 et passim; *Eilmannsberger* in Münchener Kommentar (2007), loc. cit., annot. 150 et passim, 169 et passim, following more closely the catalogue of Art. 102 lit. a)–d) throughout the presentation.

Since literature covering the matter is both abundant and diverse,[157] a summary of the principles must suffice.

Access foreclosure is not intellectual property specific but a matter of general concern for competition policy. Practices cover such diverse matters as are absolute refusals to supply competitors,[158] discriminatory non-admission to — selective or exclusive — distribution systems[159] and/or territories, exclusions from the use of proprietary infrastructures (essential facilities), non-admission to trade associations,[160] and so forth. While the assessment of these practices requires substantial differentiation, they have in common the fact that they are based on freedom of contract as the way to exploit proprietary assets or to realise shared interests and that they will be remedied by obligations to grant access by way of contract whenever they produce more anti-competitive effects than beneficial results. Therefore, it comes as a surprise that, as regards general refusals to contract out intellectual property, courts and doctrine quasi-unanimously start from the premise that, even when an owner of intellectual property dominates the market, subjecting her/him to an obligation to license must remain an exception requiring the presence of particular circumstances.[161] Obviously, this "exceptional circumstances" credo rests on of intellectual property with a exclusive right, a fallacy, which equales the "right to exclude" of as if that were an entitlement to market control rather than one to prevent unlawful appropriation of the protected subject matter. This fallacy obscures the true problems. For one thing, what is at stake is not the property but the quite normal and general freedom to contract. For another, the issue simply is which "circumstances" stand for an anti-competitive practice since there is no preestablished and limited number of such "circumstances".

---

[157] See, among the monographs, only Lamping (2010), loc. cit., at pp. 147 et passim; Früh (2012), loc. cit., at pp. 406 et passim; Koikkara (2010), loc. cit., at pp. 121 et passim; Anderman and Schmidt (2011), pp. 73 et passim, and see the chapter by *M. Lamping*, Refusal to Licence as an Abuse of Market Dominance: from Commercial solvents to Microsoft, this volume.

[158] The leading EU case is ECJ of 6 March 1974, Case 6/73 *Commercial Solvents/Commission*, Rep. 1974, 223. The prohibition of refusals to deal has a long history in French competition law relating to "refus de vente", which Art. 420 para. 1 code de commerce still lists as an example of abuse of market power (originally the refus de vente was prohibited in general, subject to narrow exceptions).

[159] Discriminatory refusals to supply with a view to protect distribution systems against (often enough innovative) outsiders represent a major type of cases of control of relational market power; see, for Germany, § 26 para. 2 GWB until amended so as to protect only small and medium-sized enterprises, *K. Markert* in Immenga and Mestmäcker (1981), § 26, annot. 115 et seq.

[160] § 19 para. 5 GWB even provides for particular rules reaching beyond mere antitrust concerns.

[161] ECJ of 5 October 1988, case 238/87 *Volvo/Veng*, Rep. 1988 I 6211 at no. 8, and explicitly in the leading **Magill** case of ECJ of 6 April 1995, cases C-241/91 P and C-242/91 P, *RTE and ITV Publications*, Rep. 1995 I 743 at no. 50. The test is assumed to (have to) be stricter than that applicable to refusals to supply in general (as if contractual autonomy were a different one when it comes to IPR); see Court of 1st Instance of 17 September 2007, case T-201/04, *Microsoft/ Commission*, Rep. 2007 II 3601, at n. 284.

Thus, in *Volvo/Veng*,[162] the Court indicated that the owner of design protection covering spare parts for automobiles may be under a duty to license independent spare part manufacturers in case she/he no longer produces such spare parts herself/himself while many of the automobiles she/he produced are still in use. The hypothesis, thus, is one of a refusal to license competitors on an after-market, which becomes unlawful when the protected products become old products and the owner of the design disinterested.[163] By contrast, in the leading *Magill* case,[164] the Court held the owners of copyright in the listings of the owners' own TV broadcast programs to a duty to license a newcomer who needed the listings as indispensable information for introducing a new product (an all-program weekly magazine) in a separate, neighbouring market (for all-program weekly magazines), which the copyright owners did not supply (but in which they were obviously interested, at least in part). However, the discrepancy between the two cases is only superficial. They simply follow two different but equally legitimate rationales, consumer protection, on one hand, and, on the other, promoting innovation. The former is absent from design protection (as it is from most IPR), while the latter in a way resonates with the creativity paradigm underlying the grant of copyright protection but is not a pervasive concept nor specifically articulated in any of its rules.[165] That is why, in both cases, competition law had to step in.

Only the innovation rationale has been further developed. In the *Microsoft* case,[166] the General Court (then the Court of 1st Instance), assuming arguendo that Microsoft enjoyed protection for the information regarding the interoperability of its operating programs under both the laws of patents or copyright and of trade secrets,[167] held that *Magill*'s a "new market" rules did not require a showing that the applicant actually had a new product to offer for a demand existing in a related market (nor, a fortiori, what the new product might be). Rather, the Court held that it would suffice to show the existence of a realistic and considerable potential for innovation by the introduction of products different from those of the market-

---

[162] Supra n. 161, at no. 9.

[163] *Eilmannsberger* in Münchener Kommentar (2007), loc. cit., Art. 82, annot. 193, suggests that a dominant firm that abstains from further developing and offering improved versions of the market-dominating product commits a sort of exploitative abuse, since the harm essentially affects consumers.

[164] Supra n. 161 at no. 51 et seq.

[165] To the difference of patent protection, copyright protection is not subject to a working requirement. For the transposition of patent law considerations to copyright and, conversely, for the applicability of the case law of the ECJ to patents, see only Koikkara (2010), loc. cit., at pp. 165 et seq.

[166] Court of 1st Instance of 17 September 2007, case T-201/04 *Microsoft/Commission*, Rep. 2007 II 3601 at no. 283 et seq., 312 et seq.

[167] For the issue of whether and to what extent secret technological know-how may be subject to the control of refusals to license on grounds of withholding indispensable information from innovating firms operating on different markets, in particular of information relating to interfaces within system technologies, see Koikkara (2010), loc. cit., at pp. 181 et passim; Surblyte (2011), passim.

dominating firm, for which there is potential demand in a then-arising neighbouring market.[168] It is an open question just how far these extensions of the *Magill* precedent may be stretched. It is equally unsettled whether the criterion of indispensability of access to the protected information — meaning access to use it — may be assimilated to the "essential facility" doctrine[169] and, on this basis or another, support claims for access to "sole source" goods more generally.[170]

The next cases coming to the Court of Justice concern the relationship between intellectual property rights and technological standards.[171] It already has held rightfully that the losing party in a competition for the establishment of a standard and for its acceptance by the market is not entitled to obtain a licence from the winning firm on grounds of an abuse of it dominating the market as a result of its victory.[172] Licences for patents reading on standards, however, while in principle concerning the vertical relationship of technology and product markets,[173] frequently are needed by firms acting in both markets. The reason is that the standards relate to interfaces of system technologies, where many firms may both hold patents covering the interface and be dependent on licences for complementary patents reading on the same or an interdependent interface. Frequently enough also, it is not the refusal of a licence as such that becomes the object of litigation but the terms of the licence, the patentee being strongly interested in royalty income based on the — typically broad — use of the standard. Yet the terms of the licence depend on whether or not there is an obligation to license and on what its basis is.[174] One case that is pending before the Court of Justice[175] precisely demonstrates this ambivalence.

---

[168] Court of 1st Inst. supra n. 166 at nos. 335, 643 et seq.

[169] For the criterion of indispensability, see Sasinowska (2013), p. 539 with references; as to the differences between indispensability of access to information and the essential facility doctrine, see Koikkara (2010), loc. cit., at pp. 160 et seq. However, rejecting a priori the application of the essential facility doctrine in case the "facility" is the subject matter of an intellectual property right, as is done under German competition law (§ 19 II no. 2 GWB), might not be helpful either; see Lamping (2010), loc. cit., at pp. 236 et seq. with references.

[170] See Wielsch (2008), loc. cit., at pp. 132, et seq. Examples may come from various fields: spare parts protected by design rights, patented research tools, or medical or other data held in protected databases.

[171] For the following, see, inter alia, Picht (2013), loc. cit., at pp. 375 et passim; Körber (2013), pp. 183 et passim; Tapia (2010), passim; Ullrich (2010b), p. 14, all with references.

[172] ECJ of 29 April 2004, case C-418/01, *IMS Health/NDC Health*, Rep. 2004 I 5039.

[173] As in BGH of 6 May 2009, case KZR 39/06, "*Orange Book Standard*", GRUR 2009, 694 = 41 IIC 369 (2010).

[174] Thus, in case of institutionalised standardisation, the licence terms typically have to conform to the RAND/FRAND benchmark of fair, reasonable, and non-discriminatory contract conditions. This benchmark need not be that of the general criteria for non-abusive (non-exploitative, non-predatory) prices or royalties since the standard's contribution to the value of the patent, as well as the licensees' contribution to the propagation of the standard, have to be taken into account; see Ullrich (2010b), loc. cit., at pp. 76, 80; Ullrich (2007), p. 817; for details, Körber (2013), loc. cit., at pp. 228 et passim.

[175] See pending case C-170/13, *Huawei/ZTE*, concerning the request for a preliminary ruling by LG Düsseldorf of 21 March 2013, case 4b O 104/12, GRUR RR 2013, 196 = WuW DE-R3922.

The Remedies

The cases cited represent no more than an illustration of possibly abusive refusals to license, not a classification, let alone a comprehensive one. However, they should suffice to show that competition law only allows controlling specific refusals to license, which, as acts of a market-dominating firms, produce qualified anti-competitive effects under the circumstances of a given case. In accordance with general principles of competition law, the remedies will be equally specific, namely tailored to undo precisely the anti-competitive effect of a refusal.[176] This means, on one hand, that the remedy will cover the technology of the information to the full extent that access is indispensable.[177] On the other, however, it also means that the patentee will only be ordered to cease the anti-competitive conduct and to desist from resuming it. In case the refusal to license is anti-competitive as such, the patentee may be ordered to grant a licence upon request, typically a licence limited to what is necessary to obtain the indispensable information or the indispensable right of use.[178] If, however, the refusal to license is anti-competitive only because it is discriminatory or predatory, or discriminatory or predatory only as to the conditions of the grant of a licence, the patentee may only be enjoined from that specific practice.[179] Moreover, unless there is but one way of granting a reasonable licence, the patentee will only be ordered to grant a licence at reasonable (meaning competitive) conditions to be agreed upon in negotiation with the licensee. In any

---

The request must be seen against the backdrop of the Commission investigating cases of patent hold-ups of the use of standards; see *Commission*, press releases, IP/14/48 (Motorola), IP/14/490 (Samsung) of 29 April 2014.

[176] See, generally, *M. Bauer* in Münchener Kommentar (2007), loc. cit., Vol. 1, Art 7 VO 1/2003, annot. 13 et seq., 24 et seq; *J. Keßler*, ibid., Vol. 2, GWB, § 32 GWB, annot. 38 et seq. Thus, in cases of licences offered only in bundled form (tie-ins) or at discriminatory conditions, only the tying in or the discriminatory practice will be prohibited; see also infra n. 179.

[177] See supra n. 167. Typically, technologies are covered by several patents, and so are standardised interfaces of system technologies. To the extent that the patented inventions are technically "essential" for the working of the (standardised) technology, the patents will all be covered by an order to cease and desist from a refusal to license. As to the concept of essentiality, see *Commission*, Guidelines on technology transfer agreements, loc. cit., at nos. 215 et seq. (regarding pools exploiting patented standards); Commission (2011), C 11,1 at nos. 277 et passim (regarding access to (patented) standards).

[178] See *Commission* of 21 December 1988, case IV/31.851—*Magill TV Guide/ITP, BBC and RTE*, OJEC 1989 L74, 43, at no. 27 (with Art. 2 of the order), as confirmed by Court 1st Inst. of 10 July 1991, case T-70/89, *BBC* et al./*Commission*, Rep. 1991 II 485 at no. 78 et seq; conf'd by ECJ of 6 April 1995, cases C-241/91 P and C-242/91 P *RTE and ITP/Commission*, Rep. 1995 I 743 at nos. 90 et seq.; *Commission* of 24 March 2004, case COMP/C-3.37792 — *Microsoft*, OJEC 2007 L 32, 23 with Art. 5 of the order relating to the disclosure of interoperability information), as confirmed by Court 1st Inst. of 17 September 2007, case T-201/04, Rep. 2007 II 3601.

[179] See, e.g., *Commission* of 22 December 1987, cases IV.30.787 and 31.488, *Eurofix-Bauco/Hilti*, OJEC 1988 L. 64, 19 (Art. 1, 3 of the order), conf'd by Court 1st Inst. of 12 December 1991, case T-30/89, *Hilti/Commission*, Rep. 1991 II 1439; more complex Art. 6 of the order of the Commission's Microsoft decision, supra n. 178, as confirmed by Court 1st Inst. supra n. 178 at no. 1194 et seq.

case, it is never the competition authority that grants the licence by way of an administrative act. Rather, the patentee is ordered to abstain from her/his anti-competitive conduct.

Remedies to anti-competitive conduct by a market-dominating patentee do not only exist as a matter of administrative action but are also available as a matter of private enforcement of the competition rules. They may take the form of injunctive relief; more often, however, only that of claims for damages.[180] In the former case,[181] the market-dominating patentee again will be held only to abstain from what has been found to constitute the anti-competitive conduct. Therefore, a direct claim to obtain a licence on given terms will be difficult to establish. Even if it can be established, it may not necessarily help as a defence[182] against an action for patent infringement brought against the candidate licensee unless courts become willing to recognise that, where there is an obligation to licence, the patentee is no longer entitled to injunctive relief.[183] Indeed, instead of serving as a remedy to prevent an illegitimate use of the patented invention, injunctive relief simply becomes a means of hold-up and of imposing on the candidate licensee the patentee's preestablished contract terms.

3.2 Mandatory Licensing Under Patent Law and Competition Law: Which Relationship?

3.2.1 Patent Law as Lex Specialis?

It is also the conflict between the exclusivity resulting from patent protection and the principle for general access underlying open standardisation for systems innovation that has brought the question to the fore whether patent law's rules on compulsory licences ought not to preclude the application of competition law's

[180] Even as regards a violation of Art. 102 TFEU, private enforcement essentially is a matter of national law, see § 33 GWB; for the impact of Union law, see *Eilmannsberger* in Münchener Kommentar (2007), loc. cit., Vol. 1, Art. 82 EG, annot. 592 et passim. As of recent, the Commission has submitted a proposal for a Directive on certain rules governing actions for damages under national law for infringements of the competition law provisions of the Member States and of the European Union of 11 June 2013, Doc. COM (2013) 404 final, which if adopted would harmonise national law as regards damage claims only.

[181] See *Th. Lübbig*, in Münchener Kommentar (2007), Vol. 2, § 33 GWB annot. 34, *V. Emmerich* in Immenga and Mestmäcker (2007), loc. cit., § 33 annot. 101 et seq.

[182] Possibly, however, if brought as a counterclaim. This is a matter of national procedural law.

[183] See supra n. 174, 175; Körber (2013), loc. cit., at pp. 251 et passim; Ullrich (2010a), loc. cit.; Ullrich (2010b), loc. cit., at pp. 643 et passim. Under the Orange Book case law, the position of the owner of patents reading on standards is particularly advantageous because she/he may hold up market actors using the standard as infringement suits go patent by patent separately. In addition, the antitrust defence may be brought only upon the defendant foregoing the defences of non-infringement and of invalidity of the patent.

rules on mandatory licensing.[184] The legal argument for this proposition is that the existence of a particular mechanism for the grant of compulsory licences under patent law testifies to the lex specialis character of patent law's provisions on compulsory licensing. A more practical reason is that at least the specialised patent infringement courts consider themselves to be over-asked by the no less special issues a competition law defence raises.[185] However, since such a proposition tends to give patent law precedence over competition law, it has not met with much approval. In Germany, the Federal Supreme Court[186] rightfully insisted on the different objectives of both sets of rules. It even admitted, at least as a matter of principle, that in infringement proceedings the defendant may defend herself/himself against the grant of injunctive relief by invoking her/his right to obtain a licence if the patentee's refusing it would amount to a violation of competition law. While the Federal Supreme Court has not given full effect to the defence,[187] the principle ought to be beyond doubt. As has been explained throughout this contribution, the rules of patent law, which provide for the grant of compulsory licences, do pursue purposes that are different from those at which competition law aims when it is applied with a view to prevent a patentee from practising anti-competitive refusals to license.

More importantly, there is a systemic difference between the two sets of rules. Whereas the former is intended to ensure the intrinsic functionality of exclusive patent rights as a support to innovation or to accommodate patent protection with other public policy concerns, the latter serves to ensure that a market-dominating patentee does not use her/his exclusive rights to undermine the operation of the system, within which patent protection is embedded and supposed to produce its benefits, namely within a system of competitive markets. After all, patents are granted to overcome a market failure. Therefore, they may not be used by patentees to create just another one. As a means of transforming information as a public good into a private merchandisable good, patents deploy their functionality only under conditions of competition.[188] It is, indeed, the market, not the patent, that provides the opportunities for innovation, and it is competition that ensures that these opportunities are used optimally by market actors in that it determines the value of the patent, i.e. the reward an efficient patentee may obtain on the basis of her/his exclusive right. Since, by definition, competition is weakened in case a patentee

[184] For a discussion, see Jung (2004), loc. cit., at pp. 383 et seq.; Lamping (2010) loc. cit., at pp. 125 et seq.; both with references.

[185] While there is some substance to this concern, courts possibly may overcome it by relying on information and advice from the competition authorities; see §§ 90 et seq. GWB, Commission (2004) C 101, 54. However, this will slow down infringement proceedings, which probably is why German courts shun taking the antitrust defence or seek to reduce its impact (see supra n. 183).

[186] BGH of 13 July 2004, case KZR 40/02—*Standard-Spundfass II* (*Standard Tight Head Drum*), GRUR 2004, 966 (sub A III 1., 2.) = 36 IIC 741 (2005) comment *M. Leistner*.

[187] See supra n. 173, 183.

[188] See Lamping (2010), loc. cit., at pp. 109 et seq., Ullrich (2001), loc. cit., at pp. 367 et seq., both with references.

dominates the market, both the discovery process and the price mechanism for innovative technologies and goods, as normally resulting from competition on the merits, are in jeopardy. It is for this reason that competition policy must intervene so as to maintain and stabilise residually existing and potentially developing competition by holding the dominating patentee to a particular responsibility.[189] This responsibility toward residual competition in no way diminishes the dominating firm's legitimate interest in her/his own innovation. Patentees are entitled to obtain full protection for their innovative technologies and goods. However, they are not entitled to appropriate for themselves the entire market(s) with all its(their) opportunities for (substitute or complementary) innovations.[190]

3.2.2 Competition Law as Lex Specialis?

Conversely, there is no principle to the effect that the grant of compulsory licences under patent law may not be based upon considerations of competition policy. While with respect to specific subject matter, such as semiconductor technology or diagnostic methods, Art. 31 lit. c) TRIPS Agreement or the patent laws of some States make the grant of a compulsory licence dependent on a competent authority having first determined the existence of an anti-competitive practice,[191] these particular rules hardly provide an argumentum e contrario. Clearly also, if applied properly, competition law may help to overcome problems that narrowly defined compulsory licensing rules of patent law do not solve adequately.[192]

However, suggestions to read considerations of competition policy into existing grounds for the grant of a compulsory patent licence with a view to extend the scope of such authority[193] should be considered with caution. It is true that, to some extent, compulsory licensing rules relating to non-working/insufficient supply or to patent dependencies concern situations where there is little competitive pressure on the patentee. It is also true that, as a general proposition, maintaining competitive markets is in the public interest. However, it is the very purpose of competition

[189] See supra n. 151.

[190] Quite another question is whether, as a matter of legislative design and/or statutory interpretation, the scope of an exclusive right, as granted, may extend to all derivative products [e.g., a trademark for cars also to the car's embodiment as a toy or a design of the body of a car also and independently to its (spare) parts]; see for a discussion Dreier (2001), p. 51. Such, in fact, was the assumption underlying, e.g., the cases of *Volvo/Veng* and of *Magill*, supra n. 161.

[191] For the latter example, see Art. 40c Swiss Patent Act, Art. L 613-16 c.prop.int.

[192] As suggested with respect to Art. 31bis TRIPS Agreement by *B. Ong*, Compulsory licences of pharmaceutical patents to remedy anti-competitive practices under Art. 31(k) of the TRIPS Agreement: Can competition law facilitate access to essential medicines? This volume at p. XXX.

[193] See, inter alia, Jung (2004), loc. cit., at pp. 404 e seq. with references. A different matter is whether the efficient operation of the patent system itself may be enhanced by a competition-oriented system of compulsory licensing. At least in part, this would amount to an interventionist or regulatory liability rule; for recurrent proposals to this effect, see inter alia already Prahl (1989), passim; Scherer (1977), passim.

policy and law to define how and to what extent this particular public interest is to be implemented with respect to a given national or a regionally integrated economy. Certainly, by providing for property rights allowing market actors to exploit exclusively market opportunities for their inventions/innovations and by defining the thresholds for acquiring such exclusivities and their scope, including the exclusions, limitations, and exceptions,[194] as well as by the conditions for the grant of compulsory licences, patent law itself constitutes a framework regulation for innovation markets. However, it does so in its own systemic terms. Whether well conceived or not, these must be interpreted and applied in conformity with their purpose and in conformity with the system of protection, which they are supposed to serve and support.[195]

Conversely, competition policy, as expressed in national or supranational competition law, rests on specific, rather sophisticated and complex terms and concepts, which need to be respected as such, because, in their turn, they serve and support a policy purpose and a system of rules. Transposing them into another context, that of patent law, without transforming them does not change anything except competences.[196] Yet, transforming them through adaptation to the other environment would not only raise the question of just what such adaptation should be but also risk producing system friction. In fact, such transformation would require legislative support. There are, however, good reasons for reserving for each set of rules its distinct functionality. Patent law and competition law, each in its own way, define the exclusive powers of the patentee and her/his contractual autonomy, respectively, as to their core and scope. Both systems interact, but competition law will intervene only to control for anti-competitive practices. It is not designed simply to introduce "more competition"[197] into the patent system, certainly not more than the latter allows by its own design to take place inside its operation. An example in point of the two systems operating at a functional distance is presented by the existence of cumulative, possibly defensive, or even blocking patents.[198] Although, prima facie, they seem to be at least in part in conflict with the patent system itself

[194] See Bently (2011), loc. cit., pp. 1 et passim (=doi:10.1093/clp/cur011).

[195] Ullrich (2012b), loc. cit., at pp. 433 et passim.

[196] Which in itself poses a problem.

[197] While there is a large body of theoretical concepts of competition, the question of what kind of competition and just how much of it will provide the necessary and sufficient support to a given or to some given objectives, in particular that of enhancing innovation, rarely finds an uncontroversial answer. For a broad overview of concepts of competition and of competition policy objectives, see *W. Kerber*, *D. Schwalbe*, Ökonomische Grundlagen des Wettbewerbsrechts, in Münchner Kommentar (2007), vol. 2 sub H.III. and IV. (pp. 248 et passim), with extensive references. In fact, the task of negatively determining what represents an (unreasonable) restriction of competition is difficult enough, and such approach may be enough anyway as a paradigmatic matter of maintaining precisely the open-ended nature of the process of competition and of its multidimensional operation.

[198] For the following, see European *Commission*, Pharmaceutical Sector Inquiry—Final Report of 8 June 2009, passim (http://ec.europa.eu/competition/sectors/pharmaceuticals/inquiry/index.html); Ullrich (2013), loc. cit., passim.

and raise "obvious" problems for competition policy, they are not simply the result of illegitimate patenting strategies but are largely due to the fragmentary character of patent protection of new technologies. Whether outlawing non-use altogether, and thereby defensive patents, would by itself result in broader competition for innovation is anything but certain. Moreover, whether and under which circumstances such practices or their combination produces anti-competitive effects is a matter of highly complex analysis and assessment. It needs to be done, but shifting it from competition authorities to patent authorities is hardly a promising route to take. Rather, both ought to do "their" job properly.

4 Conclusion

In sum, the conclusion of this contribution must be a confirmation of its title. The availability of compulsory licences under patent law and the control of anti-competitive refusals to license under competition law serve different concerns, but complementary functions. In essence, the former may help bridge systemic deficits or dilemmas of patent protection, whereas the latter seeks to maintain the operation of the system of competition, within which patent protection is embedded. In a broader perspective, the former approach is affirmative. It can be used at an early stage of the innovation process and irrespective of market power considerations. The latter is corrective and intervenes only once an abuse of market power has been committed. Yet within its purpose, which also is to promote innovation, competition policy may be more effective than is patent policy. The technicalities, to which the grant of compulsory licences is commonly subject, do weaken it more than does the complexity of market analysis and of conduct evaluation with respect to the control of abuses of market dominance.

References

Anderman S, Schmidt H (2011) EU competition law and intellectual property rights, 2nd edn. Oxford

Benkard G (2006) Patentgesetz, 10th edn. Munich

Bently L (2011) Exclusions from patentability and exceptions to patentees' rights: taking exceptions seriously, Current Legal Problems is the name of a legal periodical in the U.K., p 4

Boschek R (2012) Intellectual property rights and compulsory licensing, the case of pharmaceuticals in emerging markets. World Comp 35(4)

Burk D, Lemley M (2003) Policy levers in patent law. Va Law Rev 89:1575

Commission (2004) Notice on the co-operation between the Commission and the courts of the Member States in the application of Art. 81 and 82 EC (new Art. 101, 102 TFEU). OJEU C 101:54

Commission (2011) Guidelines on the application of Art. 101 of the TFEU to horizontal cooperation agreements. OJEU C 11:1

Conde Gallego B (2008) Unilateral refusals to license indispensable intellectual property rights – U.S. and EU approaches. In: Drexl J (ed) Research handbook on intellectual property and competition law. Cheltenham, p 215

Cornish W, Llewllyn D, Aplin T (2010) Intellectual property, 7th edn. Sweet & Maxwell, London

Correa C (2007) Trade related aspects of intellectual property rights. Oxford

Cottier T (2007) The Doha waiver and its effect on the nature of the TRIPS-system and on competition law – the impact of human rights. In: Govaere I, Ullrich H (eds) Intellectual property, public policy and international trade. Brussels, p 173

De Carvalho N (2010) The TRIPS regime of patent rights. 3rd edn. Austin

Drahos P (1996) A philosophy of intellectual property. Aldershot

Dreier T (2001) Primär- und Folgemärkte. In: Schricker G, Dreier T, Kur A (eds) Geistiges Eigentum im Dienste der Innovation. Baden-Baden, p 51

Drexl J (2007) Abuse of dominance in licensing and refusal to license: a more economic approach to competition by imitation and to competition by substitution. In: Ehlermann K, Atanasiu I (eds) The interaction between competition law and intellectual property law. European Competition Law Annual 2005. Oxford, p 647

European Commission (2004) Guidelines on the application of Article 81 of the E.C. Treaty to technology transfer agreements. OJEC C 101:2

European Commission (2011) Guidelines on the application of Article 101 TFEU to horizontal cooperation agreements. OJEU C 11:1

Feil M (2009) Lizenzkartellrecht – US-amerikanische und europäische Entwicklungen. Cologne

Früh A (2012) Immaterialgüterrechte und der relevante Markt. Cologne

Geradin D (2004) Limiting the scope of article 82 of the EC treaty, what can the EU learn from the U.S. Supreme Court's judgment in Trinko in the wake of Microsoft, IMS, and Deutsche Telekom? Common Mark Law Rev 41:1519

Gervais D (2012) The TRIPS Agreement, 4th edn. London

Gifford D, Kuderle R (2011) Antitrust approaches to dynamically competitive industries in the United States and the European Union. J Comp Law Econ 7(3):694

Godt C (2010) Differential pricing of patent protected pharmaceuticals for life-threatening infectious diseases inside Europe – can compulsory licenses be employed. In: Godt C (ed) Differential prizing of pharmaceuticals inside Europe. Baden-Baden

Govaere I (2008) In pursuit of an innovation policy rationale: stakes and limits under article 82 TEC. World Comp 31(4):541

Granstrand O (1999) Economies and management of intellectual property. Cheltenham (paperback 2000)

Granstrand O (2010) Industrial innovation, economies and intellectual property, 5th edn. Gothenburg

Gruss D (2011) Patentrechtliche Abhängigkeit und funktionsgebundener Stoffschutz bei biotechnologischen Erfindungen. München

Heinemann A (2006) Gefährdung von Rechten des geistigen Eigentums durch Kartellrecht? Der Fall "Microsoft" und die Rechtsprechung des EuGH. GRUR 704, 713

Hirsch G, Montag F, Säcker FJ (eds) (2007) Münchner Kommentar zum Europäischen und Deutschen Wettbewerbsrecht/Kartellrecht. Munich

Immenga U, Mestmäcker E-J (1981) Gesetz gegen Wettbewerbsbeschränkungen. Munich

Immenga U, Mestmäcker E-J (1997) EG-Wettbewerbsrecht. Munich

Immenga U, Mestmäcker E-J (2007) Wettbewerbsrecht, GWB, 4th edn. Munich

Immenga U, Mestmäcker E-J (eds) (2012) Wettbewerbsrecht, 5th edn. Band 1, EU/Teil 2, Munich

Jung P (2004) Die Zwangslizenz als Instrument der Wettbewerbspolitik. ZWeR

Karres N (2007) Der Spannungsfeld zwischen Patentschutz und Gesundheitsschutz aufgezeigt am Beispiel der patentrechtlichen Zwangslizenz. Frankfurt

Këllezi P (2008) Abuse below the threshold of dominance? Market power, market dominance, and abuse of economic dependence. In: Mackenroth M-O et al (eds) Abuse of dominant position: new interpretation, new enforcement mechanisms. Berlin, p 55

Kohler J (1900) Handbuch des deutschen Patentrechts in vergleichender Darstellung. Mannheim
Koikkara S (2010) Der Patentschutz und das Institut der Zwangslizenz in der Europäischen Union. Tübingen
Körber T (2013) Standard essential patents, FRAND commitments and competition law. Baden-Baden
Kraßer R (2009) Patentrecht, 6th edn. C.H. Beck, Munich
Kunz-Hallstein H-P (1982) Die Ergebnisse der Konferenz von Nairobi zur Revision der Pariser Vebandsübereinkunft. GRUR Int 45
Lamping M (2010) Patentschutz und Marktmacht. Cologne
Liu K-C (2012) The need and justification for a general competition-oriented compulsory licensing regime. Int Rev Intellect Prop Comp Law 43:679
Patterson M (2008) Intellectual property and sources of market power. In: Govaere I, Ullrich H (eds) Intellectual property, market power and the public interest. Bruxelles
Picht P (2013) Strategisches Verhalten bei der Nutzung von Patenten in Standardisierungsverfahren aus der Sicht des Europäischen Kartellrechts. Bern
Pollaud-Dulian F (2011) La propriété industrielle. Paris
Prahl K (1989) Patentschutz und Wettbewerb. Göttingen
Reichman J (2003) Non-voluntary licensing of patented inventions. ICTSD/UNCTAD, Issue Paper No. 5, Geneva, p 19
Reichman J (2010) Compulsory licensing of patented pharmaceutical inventions: evaluating the options. In: Correa C (ed) Research handbook on the protection of intellectual property under WTO rules. Cheltenham, p 589
Rushing S (2012) Plugging the leak in §1498: coercing the United States into notifying patent owners of government use. Vanderbilt J Transnatl Law 45:879
Sampath P, Roffe P (2012) Unpacking the international technology transfer debate: fifty years and beyond. In: ICTSD discussion paper, International Centre for trade and sustainable development, Geneva, June 2012
Sasinowska B (2013) Refusal to supply – is indispensability still indispensable. EUZW 539
Scherer F (1977) Economic effects of compulsory patent licensing. NY University, Monograph 1977-2 of Graduate School of Business Administration Monograph Series in Finance and Economics, New York
Schieble A-M (2005) Abhängige Genpatente und das Institut der Zwangslizenz. Baden-Baden
Schweitzer H (2008) Controlling the unilateral exercise of intellectual property rights – a multitude of approaches, but no way ahead? In: Govaere I, Ullrich H (eds) Intellectual property, market power and the public interest. Bruxelles, p 59
Scotchmer S (2004) Innovation and incentives. Cambridge
Shelanski H (2009) Unilateral refusals to deal in intellectual property and other property. Antitrust Law J 76:369
Silberstein M (1961) Erfindungsschutz und merkantilistische Gewerbeprivilegien. Zürich
Stoll P (1994) Technologietransfer – Internationalisierungs- und Nationalisierungstendenzen. Berlin
Surblyte G (2011) The refusal to disclose trade secrets as an abuse of market dominance – Microsoft and beyond. Berne
Tapia Cl (2010) Industrial property rights, technical standards and licensing practices (FRAND) in the telecommunication industry. Cologne
Taubman A (2008) Rethinking TRIPS. "Adequate Remuneration" for non-voluntary patent licensing. J Int Econ Law 11:927
Ullrich H (2001) Intellectual property, access to information, and antitrust: harmony, disharmony, and international harmonization. In: Dreyfuss R et al (eds) Expanding the boundaries of intellectual property. Oxford, p 365
Ullrich H (2007) Patente, Wettbewerb und technische Normen: Rechts- und ordnungspolitische Fragestellungen. GRUR 817

Ullrich H (2009) Propriété intellectuelle, concurrence et régulation – limites de protection et limites de contrôle. Rev.int.dr.écon (RIDE) 399

Ullrich H (2010a) Comment on the German Federal Supreme Court Decision Orange Book. Int Rev Intellect Prop Comp Law 41:369

Ullrich H (2010b) Patente and technische Normen: Konflikt und Komplementarität in patent- und wettbewerbsrechtlicher Sicht. In: Leistner M (ed) Europäische Perspektiven des Geistigen Eigentums. Tübingen, p 14

Ullrich H (2012a) Intellectual property: exclusive rights for a purpose – the case of technology protection by patents and copyright. In: Klafkowska-Wasniowska K et al (eds) Problemy Polskiego i Europejskiego Prawa Prywatnego. Warsaw, p 425

Ullrich H (2012b) Enhanced cooperation in the area of unitary patent protection. ERA Forum 13. p 589, doi:10.1007/s 12027-013-0275-2

Ullrich H (2013) Strategic patenting by pharmaceutical industry – towards a concept of abusive practices of protection. In: Drexl J, Lee N (eds) Pharmaceutical innovation, competition and patents. Cheltenham, p 241

UNCTAD and ICTSD (2005) Resource book on TRIPS and development. Cambridge University Press, Cambridge

Van Overwalle G (2006) The implementation of the biotechnology directive in Belgium and its after-effects – the introduction of a new research exemption and a compulsory license for public health. Int Rev Intellect Prop Comp Law 37:889, 908 et seq

Van Overwalle G (2011) Policy levers tailoring patent law to biotechnology: comparing U.S. and European approaches. UC Irvine Law Rev 1:435

Van Overwalle G, van Zimmeren E (2009) Functions and limits of patent law. In: Claes E et al (eds) Facing the limits of the law. Berlin, p 415

Van Overwalle G, van Zimmeren E (2011) A paper tiger? Compulsory license regimes for public health in Europe. Int Rev Intellect Prop Comp Law 42:4

Weber G, Hedemann G, Cohausz H (2007) Patentstrategien. Cologne

Wielsch D (2008) Zugangsregeln. Tübingen

WIPO (2011) Standing Committee on the law of patents, exclusions from patentability and exceptions and limitations to patentees' rights. In: WIPO Doc. SCP/15/3, Geneva

Legal Remedies Against Abuse, Misuse, and Other Forms of Inappropriate Conduct of IP Right Holders

Reto M. Hilty

Contents

Abstract The abuse (or misuse) defence against various forms of dysfunctional enforcements of IP rights appears to be, at first glance, an efficient remedy, which surely entails faster effects than the lengthy prosecution of a compulsory licence. At a closer look, however, the legal consequences of an abuse defence are quite unclear. International law—to the extent that it addresses issues of abuse—does not offer guidance. Furthermore, it's questionable whether approaches of equity, primarily known in common law countries (notably the denial of an injunctive relief in case of an inappropriate lawsuit), provide convincing results—apart from the fact that civil law systems mostly lack such approaches anyway. We rather need an intermediate solution between unrestricted enforcement and non-injunction. Particularly, more balance may be achieved through monetary compensation to the right holder: In case enforcement of an IP right proves to be abusive, this right should still not become valueless to its holder by denial of injunctive relief; rather, a

R.M. Hilty is Professor of Law and Director of the Max Planck Institute for Innovation and Competition.

R.M. Hilty
Max Planck Institute for Innovation and Competition, Munich, Germany
e-mail: hilty@ip.mpg.de

R.M. Hilty and K.-C. Liu (eds.), *Compulsory Licensing*, MPI Studies on Intellectual Property and Competition Law 22, DOI 10.1007/978-3-642-54704-1_18,

downgrade of the right in terms of a "liability regime" may be justified. Indeed, the compulsory licence permits usage against payment to the right holder. If its current conception is deemed to be too complex in practice, and if it is illusory that the abuse defence constitutes a convincing alternative, the legal setting of the compulsory licence should be modified.

1 Introduction

The legal instrument of the compulsory licence doubtlessly remedies certain imbalances inherent in the IP system in view of possibly conflicting interests of the parties involved—specifically, the interests of the right holder, on one hand, and those of the general public, on the other. In particular, the effect of compulsory licence is to limit (but not to eliminate) the exclusivity of an IP right by permitting the use of the subject matter of protection by an independent market participant. The preconditions to acquire a compulsory licence, however, are complex, and the whole procedure may be time consuming and costly, with ambiguous prospects for the plaintiff. Therefore, in some situations, the compulsory licence will hardly be an appropriate approach to pursue certain interests of a third party. For instance, if a right holder enforces his rights without comprehensible gains or traceable intentions, the defendant should be in the position to react instantly based on other appropriate measures.

One such conceivable appropriate measure and alternative to the compulsory licence could be a "misuse" or "abuse defence" against situations in which the enforcement of an IP right unduly affects the interests of the defendant. In fact, at first glance, such approaches are not uncommon. On the contrary, 35 U.S.C. § 271 addresses "patent misuse" explicitly,[1] and international law also recognises the option of Member States to take appropriate measures "to prevent the abuse of intellectual property rights by right holders" (Art. 8.2 TRIPS). A second view, however, suggests deeper reflections, at least for two reasons.

- Firstly, the misuse or abuse defence risks leading to unintended outcomes of a judicial proceeding. Based on this argument, the defendant unavoidably concedes the existence of a (valid) legal title. Therefore, the discretion of the judge is limited to either affirming or denying inappropriate conduct on the part of the plaintiff.

  Instead, an alleged infringer of an IP right first of all should claim the legal conformity of his own action by denying the existence of any enforceable right. This defense strategy—irrespective of whether or not the assertion is true—in the first instance lies in the general public interest because it leads to crucial

[1] For the range of this provision, see Sect. 4.2 below.

findings of the court. In particular it sheds light on the question of whether or not the legal title at stake (e.g. a patent or a trademark) was granted lawfully. In fact, invalidation during the judicial proceeding reveals to competitors that there is no need to respect the concerned IP right further—a tremendously important piece of information for all market participants which ultimately lies in the core interest of the general public.

If the court affirms the IP right, the defence strategy of the alleged infringer should be to challenge the assertion that his action actually lies within the scope of protection of that legal title. Again, this defence may or may not be true in substance. However, it is of paramount—also public—interest to know the range of a concrete IP right. For it lies in the nature of the IP system that right holders tend to go to the outermost limit to defend their rights—or even beyond. Thus, an injunction accepted by the alleged infringer risks extending the scope of protection beyond the intended legal exclusivity—and in turn overly limits the freedom of all other parties.

- Secondly, the misuse or abuse defence promises more than it can deliver. At least in civil law jurisdictions, it is by no means clear what such inappropriate conduct of a right holder leads to. In other words, the defence as such is not a remedy for inadequate injunctions of IP rights. Rather, imbalances within the IP system provoked by such conduct need to be corrected based on other—concrete—legal measures a judge may apply. This issue shall be discussed more extensively hereinafter.[2]

First, the rather confusing terminology related to "misuse" and "abuse" shall be addressed (Sect. 2). Hereafter, some examples will outline the practical impacts of such behaviour (Sect. 3). An analysis of the legal framework of both international and national laws (Sect. 4) will be followed by reflections on different legal remedies with a special focus on the denial of injunctive relief (Sect. 5), which approach is of particular interest in view of the legal situation in Europe (Sect. 6). These considerations will lead to the conclusion that the concept of the compulsory licence is one of the most promising approaches to balance different interests involved.

2 Terminology

It seems quite problematic to describe the aforementioned specific forms of inappropriate conduct. Although the US patent law in 35 U.S.C. § 271 explicitly uses the term "patent misuse", this seems not to be very accurate. We hardly would speak of the "misuse" of a right; rather, a "right", a "legal position", etc. may be

[2] See Sect. 5 below.

"abused", whereas "misuse" may be understood as a particular, narrower meaning of "abuse".

Ironically, the German language only has one term, which is "Missbrauch"; intuitively (but wrongfully), one might tend to translate this as "misuse". In the Romance languages, in contrast, only the term "abuse" exists; it derives from the Latin "abusus", modified, e.g., in "abuso" (Spanish and Italian) or "abus" (French). Subject to other—in particular, non-European—languages that may or may not make such distinctions, it primarily seems to be a problem of the English language to have at its disposal two terms expressing similar concepts, albeit without congruent meanings—even though in English literature both terms often are used combined: "misuse or abuse of . . .".

In fact, the delimitation of the two terms is not easy; it is rather a "felt" distinction, which therefore seems to be somehow fuzzy. "Misuse" refers to an improper, inappropriate, incorrect use of something, divergent from its intended use (or understanding). In the legal language, this is reflected in expressions like "misconception", "misappropriation", etc. "Abuse", in contrast, has a stronger negative connotation; it reflects a more deliberate intention (e.g., "abuse of a child"). The difference between the two terms becomes more easily perceptible in the case of medication (in which field the primary discussion seems to take place[3]):

1. Drug misuse is the improper use of medications for purely therapeutic gains but does not include the improper use of drugs taken for pleasure and the like.

2. Drug abuse is a more repetitive and willful habit of taking drugs for the purpose of pleasure, ecstasy and euphoria but does not include the repeated use of drugs for therapeutic purposes.

Such comparisons relating to one subject matter and thereby clarifying that both terms may be correct depending on the context are hardly conceivable in the legal context. Specifically, the field of IP law proves rather the opposite, namely the inaccuracy of the legal language. In fact, as we have seen in the introduction, both terms can be found—in the US patent legislation, it is the term "misuse" (35 U.S.C. § 271), whereas in the international legislation, the term "abuse" is common (Art. 8.2 TRIPS). Neither regulation, however, provides for definitions, and any dissociation from the other term is missing.

Nevertheless, the term "patent misuse" not only from a linguistic point of view justifies doubts concerning its accuracy. Beyond that, it foremost relates to a rather singular US patent law doctrine, which shall not further be discussed at present. However, it is important to note that this US doctrine—as far as can be seen—has neither been transplanted to other jurisdictions nor is its scope uncontested within the US doctrine—or even worse, it is disputed whether "patent misuse" may play an independent role except in antitrust law.[4]

---

[3] The following differentiation can be found at www.differencebetween.net/language/difference-between-abuse-and-misuse.

[4] Heinemann (2002), pp. 53–54; for a critical view on the relation between patent and antitrust law, see also Lemley (1990), pp. 1599–1632; see also note 25 below.

If instead we aim at a more general—a "global"—perspective, the term "abuse" might be more appropriate, although even this term risks being too narrow with respect to "other forms of inappropriate conduct", which are also mentioned in the title. In fact, viewed from a greater distance, we may distinguish two major fields of uses of IP rights (or conduct of rights holders):

- uses (or conduct) in line with the functions of the IP system, reflecting the objectives for which IP rights are granted; to some extent, these objectives are mirrored in Art. 7 TRIPS;
- uses (or conduct) conflicting with the functions of the IP system and insofar with Art. 7 TRIPS; regarding such uses (or conduct), the term "dysfunctional" might describe best why such uses (or conduct) may not be tolerated: they ultimately risk perverting the objectives for which IP rights are granted—patents might impede new innovation, copyrights may hinder access to protected works, etc.

At the same time, it is important to clarify that the evaluation of a concrete use of an IP right (or conduct of the right holder) obviously depends on the circumstances of the individual case. Under certain circumstances, a specific use (or conduct) may fulfil the function of the IP system in question, whereas in other cases the same behaviour may turn out to be dysfunctional. This observation makes it obvious that the legal framework needs to be flexible enough to find the appropriate balance on a case-by-case basis.

3 Forms of Dysfunctional Uses or Conduct

Dysfunctional uses or conduct may be observed in different areas and contexts. A demarcation between such areas and contexts is hardly possible, particularly since certain uses or conduct unavoidably—or even intentionally—overlap. For the present purpose, a comprehensive and exhaustive identification of all possible uses or conduct would not help the discussion. The sole purpose of this chapter shall be to accentuate some typical examples in order to demonstrate that dysfunctional uses or conduct are not just doctrinal fantasy but increasingly are noticed in practice. More important than the following exemplification, however, will be the subsequent question of how to (legally) deal with dysfunctional uses or conduct.

Basically, we may observe dysfunctional uses or conduct in the following areas and contexts:

- Judicial proceedings may be used abusively, meaning that individual IP rights—although as such appropriately acquired or granted—are exploited in a dysfunctional way. In that respect, one can observe random law suits against competitors by which right holders attempt to extend the actual scope of protection, to weaken the competitor's market position etc.[5] Such observations can be made not only in the field of technology, but also, among others, in that of trademarks.[6] Specifically, based on new trademark forms—like abstract colors or 3D shapes—competitors easily may be urged to stop certain activities, although such activities may lie outside the scope of protection.[7]

- Dysfunctional uses are found in application and granting procedures with the purpose of acquiring "doubtful" IP rights, such as by making use of a low quality of patent examination or the entire lack of any substantial examination.[8] Examples are so-called evergreening patents[9] (which is particularly a concern in the pharmacy industry, where such practices are common, e.g., to hinder the market entrance of generic drugs),[10] divisional applications for one single product (a strategy primarily observed in the IT sector),[11] vague claim drafting, etc.
- The IP system as such may be operated in a dysfunctional way. In that case, patents in particular—but possibly also IP rights in shapes, colours, and so on—may have been acquired appropriately; however, they are used to "monopolise" key technologies (one example being standards[12]), protect technology-overarching building blocks (in that respect, the field of nanotechnology

---

[5] Kesselheim (2007), pp. E307–E308; cf. Judge Posner's backlash against patent misuse: Roberts (2012), http://www.washingtonpost.com/business/technology/famous-judge-spikes-apple-google-case-calls-patent-system-dysfunctional/2012/06/08/gJQAM1bQOV_story.html; another famous problem of exploiting IP rights is "patent trolls": Hilty (2012), p. 25; Chien (2009), pp. 1573–1615.

[6] E.g. Leo Stoller, called "Mr. Trademark Abuse", Moynihan (2005), http://www.nytimes.com/2005/07/04/business/04stealth.html?pagewanted=all&_r=0. Especially problematic are trademark applications that are just made to file suit against a future applicant. Cf. German Federal Supreme Court (BGH) 2001, GRUR, p. 242—*Classe E*. Article 52(1) b of Council Regulation (EC) No 207/2009 is a possible tool against such behaviour.

[7] Cf. Case C-529/07—*Lindt & Sprüngli/Franz Hauswirth* [2009], ECR I-04893.

[8] Cf. the curious practice of the U.S. Patent and Trademark Office (PTO): Lemley and Moore (2004), p. 63.

[9] This is an attempt to extend the period of a patent protection beyond its actual term. There are some different forms of "evergreening" (cf. Darrow 2010, p. 132; Mueller and Chisum 2008, p. 1106), but generally a patent holder files an ancillary variation of the already patented innovation. Such variations often cannot be deemed an invention in terms of Art. 27(1) TRIPS; however, if a nearly identical patent is granted (e.g., due to insufficient examination), the effect is a "reset of the clock" as regards the protection period; Chalmers (2007), pp. 31–32.

[10] Although "evergreening" does not lead to a temporal extension of the old patent (Darrow 2010, p. 131), it decreases, especially for generic companies, the possibility of stepping into the market of a special product: Kesselheim (2007), pp. E308–E309.

[11] Lemley and Shapiro (2007), p. 1992; Ohly (2008), p. 791.

[12] Industry standards become problematic if they cannot be practised without using a related patent (essential patent) and if the patentee asks for excessive royalty rates; thus, the industry standard is commercially blocked: von Meibom and Nack (2009), p. 511. Notable examples of dysfunctional use of "standard-essential" patents can be found in the mobile phone industry, e.g. in litigations between Samsung and Apple (see only BBC News Technology 2012, http://www.bbc.co.uk/news/technology-20812871) or between Motorola and Apple (see Kanter 2013, http://www.nytimes.com/2013/05/07/technology/07iht-google07.html?_r=0); see also Lemley and Shapiro (2007), pp. 1994–1998; related to Standard-Setting Organizations, Lemley (2002), pp. 1889–1980.

provides good examples), and control derivative markets (notably for spare parts) and also to acquire legal protection for business-method patents.[13]

- The picture would be incomplete without mentioning a broad variation of IP strategies having the sole purpose of fostering the right holder's own market position, irrespective of the actual functions of IP rights, notably the function of protecting innovation and creation to the proper extent to prevent market failure. Such strategies may lack transparency for third parties and thus reduce legal certainty.
- Apart from that, a further field of uses or conduct may be observed, namely multiple forms of exclusionary conduct, which—subject to the abuse of a dominant market position—as a matter of principle need to be dealt with in antitrust law.[14] Antitrust law as such, however, shall not be discussed at present.[15] Rather, a broader perspective needs to be taken—one not limited to antitrust law, but also not excluding it, since this may be a partial aspect of the greater picture. This is especially important in view of the fact that antitrust law is by no means sufficiently developed in a number of countries. In addition, the range of remedies against dysfunctional uses or conduct outside of antitrust law differs.

All these forms of use or conduct are discussed increasingly in practice and theory. Consequently, calls for remedies against such uses and conduct hardly may be ignored anymore. The question, however, is whether the legal institution of a "misuse" or an "abuse defence" would help. This question cannot be answered before we have given account of currently existing legal norms that might apply.

---

[13] The "boom" of "junk patents"-related business methods mainly occurred during a period of one decade, after the *State Street* decision (*State Street Bank & Trust Co. v. Signature Financial Group, Inc.*, 149 F.3d 1368 [Fed. Cir. 1998]), leading to lots of legal conflicts; see Liu (2011), pp. 401–406. The *Bilski* decision (*in re Bilski*, 545 F.3d 943, 88 U.S.P.Q.2d 1385 [Fed. Cir. 2008]), however, raised the bar again, Liu (2011), p. 405.

[14] Leading cases on the European level were Case C-241/91 P and 242/91 P—*RTE* (*Magill*) [1995], ECR I-743; Case T-201/04—*Microsoft* [2007], ECR II-3601; Case C-418/01—*IMS Health* [2004], ECR I-5039. More recently, the German Federal Supreme Court (BGH) stated that the assertion of an injunctive relief may—under specific circumstances—constitute an abuse of a dominant market position: BGH 2009, GRUR, pp. 694–698 para. 27; for further details, see Körber (2013), pp. 185–188, 221. According to the European Commission, the threat of injunction (or an enforcement) may impede effective competition and therefore may be considered as an abuse (COMM., 13.2. 2012, COMP/M.6381, para. 107). As to the differences between EU antitrust law and the four-factor test according to the US jurisdiction (point 5, below), see Körber (2013), pp. 225 et seq.

[15] See, however, chapter "Mandatory Licensing Under Patent Law and Competition Law: Different Concerns, Complementary Roles" by Hanns Ullrich and chapter "Refusal to License as an Abuse of Market Dominance: From Commercial Solvents to Microsoft" by Matthias Lamping (in this volume).

4 Legal Framework

4.1 International Law

Art. 8 TRIPS authorises Member States to apply "appropriate measures ... to prevent the abuse of IP rights by the right holders...". Further provisions dealing with "abuse" can be found in TRIPS, though none of these directly focus on the abuse of IP rights as such. Rather, three additional contexts of abusive use or conduct are addressed in TRIPS:

- Art. 40, para. 2, TRIPS relates to "licensing practices or conditions that may in particular cases constitute an abuse of intellectual property rights having an adverse effect on competition in the relevant market"; in respect to such uses or conduct, Member States are free to provide for legal remedies consistent with the other provisions of TRIPS.
- A number of provisions are directed at enforcement procedures, including provisional measures and boarder measures. More concretely, Art. 41 TRIPS not only requires Member States to ensure that enforcement procedures "permit effective action against any act of infringement of intellectual property rights", but also that such procedures "shall be applied in such a manner as to avoid the creation of barriers to legitimate trade and to provide for safeguards against their abuse". In return, Art. 48 TRIPS allows Member States (but does not oblige them) to "order a party at whose request measures were taken and who has abused enforcement procedures to provide to a party wrongfully enjoined or restrained adequate compensation for the injury suffered because of such abuse". Likewise, Art. 50 TRIPS (and similarly Art. 53 TRIPS) allows Member States "to order the applicant to provide a security or equivalent assurance sufficient to protect the defendant and to prevent abuse".
- Art. 63 TRIPS provides for transparency by obliging Member States to publish or make publically available the laws, the regulations, final judicial decisions and administrative rulings with a view not only to the availability, the scope, the acquisition and the enforcement of IP rights, but also related to the prevention of the abuse of such rights. As regards technical cooperation, Art. 67 TRIPS requires developed country Members to assist developing and least-developed country Members (amongst others) in the preparation of laws and regulations on the prevention of the abuse of IP rights.

The second aspect, related to the abuse of procedural measures, deserves particular attention. More details shall be explained later.[16] First, however, one fundamental question needs to be answered—namely, what exactly does "abuse of IP rights by the right holder" mean? In fact, the scope of the statement made in Art. 8 TRIPS is not further defined by international law. Consequently, this provision is

---

[16] See Sect. 5 below.

subject to the interpretation of each Member State. On one hand, this openness provides for a promising outset in that it seems to leave room for far-reaching balancing measures within the national legislation. However, on the other hand, a related question needs to be answered at the same time: what does the term "appropriate measures" mean?

In that respect, we have to recall that according to Art. 2 TRIPS, the Paris Convention (PC), and in particular its Art. 5 unavoidably applies as well.[17] This is important when it comes to understanding the scope of Art. 8 TRIPS. In fact, the PC historically responded to far-reaching provisions in national legislations which were related in particular to a "patent abuse" in terms of non-working of the invention. Such conduct of the patent holder quite often led to the forfeiture of the patent in question (e.g., Austria[18] and Belgium,[19] both laws from the 1850s). In the light of such national provisions, the PC aimed at a limitation of the permissible sanctions; the particular intention was to avoid the forfeiture of the patent. In several steps (1883, 1900, 1925), the PC was amended, and Art. 5 A PC ultimately limited possible sanctions in two paragraphs as follows:

> (2) Each country of the Union shall have the right to take legislative measures providing for the grant of compulsory licenses to prevent the abuses which might result from the exercise of the exclusive rights conferred by the patent, for example, failure to work.
>
> (3) Forfeiture of the patent shall not be provided for except in cases where the grant of compulsory licenses would not have been sufficient to prevent the said abuses. No proceedings for the forfeiture or revocation of a patent may be instituted before the expiration of two years from the grant of the first compulsory license.

Having that historical background in mind, it becomes obvious that the PC did not aim at a positive authorisation of the Member States to take measures against an abuse of IP rights (in that case, patent rights) but solely limited the catalogue of such measures in their national legislations. Basically, one measure remained allowed, namely the compulsory licence, although subject to certain conditions. Forfeiture, in contrast, was subjected to even narrower conditions.[20]

Read in this light, TRIPS does not provide for an open-ended catalogue of "appropriate measures"; rather, if such measures need to be "consistent with the provisions of this Agreement", Art. 5 PC has to be considered as well. In other words, Art. 5 PC limits the freedom of Member States to take measures in relation to TRIPS as well.

---

[17] Further information: Pflüger (2011), Paris Convention, introductory remarks 7.

[18] Art. 29(2)a Österreichisches Patentgesetz 1852, reproduced in von Kleinschrod (1855), pp. 151–152; the rule has its origin in Art. 21d, e Kaiserliches Patent vom 31. März 1832, reproduced in Alex Historische Rechts- und Gesetzestexte Online, available at http://alex.onb.ac.at/cgi-content/alex?aid=jgs&datum=1019&page=14&size=45.

[19] Art. XXIII Law of May 24, 1854 (Belgium), reproduced in Abbott (1886), p. 46; Trimble (2012), p. 514 note 6.

[20] See Bodenhausen (1968), p. 69; Pflüger and Prüfer-Kruse (2011), p. 232.

4.2 National Laws

The limitation imposed by Art. 5 PC to take "appropriate measures" only, however, does not limit the national legislature's freedom to determine independently what use or conduct by right holders shall constitute an "abuse". To define such acts, a national legislature basically has three options:

- Specific provisions on the "abuse" might be introduced in the IP legislation. Subject to further research on the situation in different national systems, this seems not to be a widely applied approach.[21]

  Notably, 35 U.S.C. § 271 (addressing "patent misuse" explicitly) should not be misunderstood as a directly applicable rule. Instead, this provision reflects the limits of the misuse doctrine developed by case law in 1917[22] and 1942[23] and in further cases.[24] The scope of this doctrine, however, is the subject of heated discussion in the US, also in view of newer cases in which certain antitrust considerations have been introduced.[25] This US legislation, however, is a special case in the first place and shall not further be debated at present.
- Provisions on "abuse" may be—and typically are—introduced in the antitrust legislation, which, however, should also not be misunderstood. Antitrust law, by definition, addresses not the abuse of a right but necessarily the abuse of a dominant market position. Whether or not that dominant position is due to IP rights involved, ultimately, is not relevant.
- The "abuse" of a right may be regulated in the general legislation.[26] It may be assumed that in a constitutional legal regime, such provisions are common practice; in doctrinal terms, however, such approaches widely vary in detail. In particular, the question arises as to whether such general provisions would apply either if an IP right as such (meaning the lawfully granted legal title and,

[21] A few examples can be found in the French Copyright Law (Art. L. 121-3, L. 122-9, L. 111-3 Code de la Propriété), Carré (2012), p. 397.

[22] *Motion Picture Patents Co. v. Universal Film Co.*, 243 U.S. 502.

[23] *Morton Salt Co. v. G.S. Suppinger Co.*, 314 U.S. 488.

[24] E.g., The United States Court of Appeals for the Federal Circuit defines patent misuse as to "impermissibly broaden the 'physical or temporal scope' of a patent grant with anticompetitive effect"; *Windsurfing Int'l, Inc. v. AMF, Inc.*, 782 F.2d 995, 1001 (Fed. Cir. 1986). For more on the history of the misuse doctrine, see Gordon and Hoerner (2000), pp. 1–35; Feldmann (2003), pp. 402–421; Bohannan (2011), pp. 479–486.

[25] The question basically is whether the misuse doctrine applies in case of anti-competitive effects of behaviour only; cf. Feldmann's title "The Insufficiency of Antitrust Analysis for Patent Misuse", Feldmann (2003), pp. 399–449; Cotter (2011), pp. 460–468; Bohannan (2011), pp. 490–495; Trimble (2012), pp. 516–517.

[26] E.g., § 242 German Civil Code. But related to IP, only few cases are known. Once, however, the Jena Court of Appeal denied injunctive relief because of dysfunctional conduct of the right holder based on § 242 German Civil Code. OLG Jena (Court of Appeal), MMR 2008, 408, 413.

with it, the legally protected market position) is used (e.g., exerted) abusively or if abusive prosecution procedures or the like occur.

Yet even if the last-mentioned general approaches towards the abuse of a right theoretically may apply to dysfunctional uses or conduct in connection with IP rights, not much is gained. At the end of the day, the decisive question is what remedies apply against such uses or conduct. In fact, as we have stated in the introduction already, the abuse (or possibly misuse) defence as such does not constitute a workable remedy.

5 Possible Remedies: In Particular the Denial of Injunctive Relieve

If therefore concrete legal instruments have to apply, a number of approaches might be considered. Namely, the forfeiture of the IP right might be conceivable (however, subject to the limitations set by Art. 5 PC[27]). Alternatively, the grant of a compulsory licence could help in certain constellations.[28] More generally speaking, other forms of what are called "liability approaches" might apply—in other words, legal instruments may provide for a compensation of the right holder in case of certain use activities by third parties, on one hand, but may not prevent them from such uses, on the other hand. However, all these remedies will hardly help a third party that believes that the use of an IP right or the conduct of a right holder is abusive—simply because they are not geared to such behaviour. Therefore, if the currently existing legal provisions are not amended in a way that helps the concerns of such a third party, the path it will have to take will be stony, time consuming, and of unsure outcome.

In contrast, the denial of injunctive relief promises to be an easy, time- and cost-efficient remedy that may bring back sufficient balance to the system. In fact, in certain special cases, it seems adequate that an IP right remains unenforceable—although from a substantive point of view it may be infringed. Such denial of injunctive relief seems to be justifiable under comparatively narrow conditions. Specifically, in cases in which (full) injunction risks harming legitimate interests of the (unauthorised) user of the protected subject matter, whereas legitimate interests of the right holder would not outweigh that harm, an unlimited injunctive relief

[27] See Sect. 4.1 above.

[28] It should be noted, however, that the grant of a compulsory licence does not depend on the abuse of an IP right by its right holder in the narrow sense of the term. Rather—and typically—compulsory licences are intended to avoid dysfunctional effects of the IP systems, regardless of the conduct of the right holder—whose non-use of a patent, e.g. as a matter of principle, may not be deemed an abuse.

might overshoot the mark.[29] This situation may occur, for example, if the use in question does not cause any disadvantage to the right holder. However, one still may argue that there is no need for the right holder to justify why he wants his IP rights to be fully enforced—whether or not the injunctive relief objectively meets his interests. Therefore, an additional premise for the denial of an injunctive relief derives from the requirement that an IP right is used abusively or that the conduct of the right holder constitutes an abuse.

In fact, in common law, the judges have certain flexibilities at their disposal to balance the interests involved in a particular case—flexibilities deriving from considerations of "equity", with which to "correct" a detected inadequateness of (written) law. Based on that, the US case law has developed comparatively concrete rules. Notably confirmed by the famous *eBay v. MercExchange* case,[30] the US jurisdiction has designed a tool (the "four-factor test") to recalibrate the patent system so as to achieve an appropriate equilibrium. According to that jurisdiction, it has to be taken into account (1) whether a plaintiff in case of non-injunction would face irreparable injury, (2) whether an alternative adequate remedy (such as damages) can meet the plaintiff's concern, (3) whether the injunction lies in the public interest, and (4) which party in view of a balance of harms should be favoured.

However, from a civil law perspective, it is not obvious that this path is trodden at all. On the contrary, the idea that an IP right, although infringed, shall not be enforceable sounds weird to the ears of a Continental European lawyer. At least it would amount to a heavy burden to find legally sound arguments as to why a claim granted by law—namely, injunctive relief in case of an infringement of an IP right—should be denied without a statutory basis to do so. Although it seems not entirely inconceivable that in case of an abuse of an IP right or abusive conduct on the part of a right holder a judge would be tempted to reach that result, it is hardly imaginable that he would weigh the legitimate interest of the right holder, on one hand, and those of the (unauthorised) user, on the other hand.[31]

[29] This ultimately leads to "over-protection" of the right holder to the detriment of competitors: Hilty (2012), pp. 12, 13.

[30] 547 U.S. 388 (2006). In 2007, the District Court, E.D. Virginia, to which the case returned, finally denied the injunctive relief, 500 F. Supp. 2d 556 (2007). More about this case and its impacts: Elrefaie (2010), pp. 221–242; Phillips (2009), pp. 416–434; Petersen (2008), p. 23; Trimble (2012), pp. 518–520; O'Melinn (2008); pp. 119–131. Cf. the discussion about the subject matter: Ohly (2008), pp. 789–790.

[31] Nevertheless, also in civil law countries, it is disputed whether a judge should weigh interests of parties in an IP case under special circumstances, in particular if an IP right is inflexible and can therefore be used abusively, e.g. in the German copyright law, Hoeren and Herring (2011), pp. 502–503.

6 The European Law Perspective

From a European law perspective, however, one might be tempted to find ways leading to a similar direction as the common law is able to go.[32] The following considerations focus on the so-called Enforcement Directive,[33] which the EU Member States were required to implement in their national laws. These considerations hardly reflect the common doctrinal understanding of that Directive—but it receives impetus from the aspiration not only to seek more flexibility in the EU civil law systems but also to challenge the question to what extent European law actually obliges Member States to balance their IP systems in cases of abuse.

Foremost, Recital 17 of the Enforcement Directive calls for a case-by-case approach: "The measures, procedures and remedies provided for in this Directive should be determined in each case in such a manner as to take due account of the specific characteristics of that case, including the specific features of each intellectual property right and, where appropriate, the intentional or unintentional character of the infringement".[34] Further, Art. 3, para. 2 obliges Member States to provide for the measures, procedures, and remedies that shall "be effective, proportionate and dissuasive[35] and shall be applied in such a manner as to avoid the creation of barriers to legitimate trade and to provide for safeguards against their abuse". In stating this, the Directive corresponds to Art. 41 and Art. 48 TRIPS; these provisions are focusing not on the abuse of an IP right as such, but (in the case of the Directive) on the abuse of "measures, procedures and remedies".

Beyond that, Art. 11 and Art. 13 of the Directive address injunctions and damages, respectively. Article 11 reads as follows: "Member States shall ensure that, where a judicial decision is taken finding an infringement of an intellectual property right, the judicial authorities *may* issue against the infringer an injunction".[36] Art. 13, para. 1, in contrast, reads: "Member States shall ensure that the competent judicial authorities, on application of the injured party, *order* the infringer ... to pay the right holder damages". In other words, the judicial

[32] See also Ohly, seeking a proportional approach to injunctive relief in patent law in order to avoid economic damages, Ohly (2008), p. 796. Although infringement should generally trigger an injunction, there may be exceptions: Ohly (2009), p. 266; see also Kraßer (2009), p. 875, calling for a denial of injunctive relief under special circumstances. Also in competition law, proportional remedies (including injunctive relief) are postulated: Köhler (1996), pp. 82, 89.

[33] Directive 2004/48/EC of the European Parliament and of the Council of 29 April 2004 on the enforcement of intellectual property rights.

[34] Relating to the case-by-case approach, see also Sect. 2 above, last part. In addition, according to Recital 24 of the Enforcement Directive, measures, procedures, and remedies against further infringements depend on the particular case and must be justified by the circumstances: Ohly (2009), p. 265.

[35] For further reflections on these three criteria, see Ohly (2009), pp. 257–274.

[36] Emphasis added. Art. 11 refers to Art. 44 I TRIPS: Walter and Goebel (2010), para. 13.11.4. Furthermore, it calls to mind 35 U.S.C. § 283, to which the Supreme Court referred in the *eBay v. MercExchange* case.

authorities have discretion as to whether or not to grant injunction, whereas damages (as the case may be) must always be ordered.[37]

Having in mind that Directives need to be implemented in different European jurisdictions and considering the fact that the English legislation, among others, is based on common law principles, the wording of Art. 11 may be understood as nothing but a concession to the "equity approach".[38] However, one might go one step further and ask whether Art. 11 does not provide for a kind of a "ceiling". In other words, does a Member State infringe EU law if the "may" provision in Art. 11 of the Directive is replaced by a "must" provision in the national legislation? At least indirectly, the above-quoted Recitals 17 and 24 of the Directive advocate the balancing of the system by urging a case-by-case approach. Beyond that, Art. 3, para. 1 *expressis verbis* requires "safeguards" against the abuse of "measures, procedures and remedies". This is not the same as the abuse of the IP right as such, but at closer look an abuse of "measures, procedures and remedies" may result in indirect forms of abuse of the right as well.

Read in that light, one might argue that Art. 11—related to injunctions—at least implicitly envisages dysfunctional uses of IP rights or conduct of right holders. One may shy away from the conclusion that Member States were obliged to limit injunctive relief to cases in which the enforcement of an IP right would meet the functions of the related IP system. In addition, Art. 11 relates to Art. 12, which—very narrowly—defines the requirements to order pecuniary compensation instead of injunction (namely, that the infringer acted "unintentionally and without negligence", that "execution of the measures in question"—e.g. injunction—"would cause him disproportionate harm", and that "pecuniary compensation to the injured party appears reasonably satisfactory"). In view of this provision, a certain reluctance of the European legislature to accept alternatives to an injunction can hardly be ignored.[39] Nevertheless, read together with Art. 3, para. 1 of the Directive, according to which "measures, procedures and remedies shall be fair and equitable", the way to an equity-based approach seems to be passable. From that perspective, it is at least not conflicting with the Directive to argue that a Member State that does not provide for sufficient flexibility—even if this means allowing for inequitable enforcement against certain users of the subject matter of protection—disregards the overall aim of the Enforcement Directive. Admittedly, that aim is

[37] Emphasis added. von Mühlendahl (2007), p. 377.

[38] Another view refers to Art. 102(1) Council Regulation (EC) No 207/2009 of 26 February 2009 on the Community trade mark (former Art. 98(1) Council Regulation [EC] No 40/94 of December 1993), which requires injunction in case of an infringement of the Community trademark "unless there are special reasons for not doing so". According to the ECJ, however, this exception must be interpreted strictly; cf. case C-316/05—*Nokia v. Wärdell*, [2006] ECR I-12083, para. 30; Ohly (2009), p. 266.

[39] One may even argue, based on the Latin phrase *expressio unius est exclusio alterius*, that the denial of injunctive relief would *only* be possible under the narrow conditions of Art. 12—without alternatives; see Ohly (2009), p. 264; Bently and Sherman (2009), p. 113 note 105.

disputable, especially in the light of Recital 10, which emphasises the aspiration to a high level of IP protection.

7 Conclusions

As we have seen, focusing on an abuse (or possibly misuse) defence related to dysfunctional uses of IP rights or conduct of right holders without further reflection on the legal consequences falls short of the mark. The legal consequences of such uses or conduct, however, are not addressed by international law. Likewise, the EU Enforcement Directive—inherently aiming at a harmonisation of the effects of national provisions only without providing for a unified (European) legal basis—does not provide concrete answers on how to deal with dysfunctional uses or conduct.

Therefore, the national legislatures are in charge of establishing remedies to ban such uses or conduct. Subject to further research, however, we may assume that in a majority of national legislations and practices, certain weaknesses can be detected:

- First of all, the problem of abusing (or possibly misusing) IP rights, or the problem of other forms of inappropriate conduct of right holders, in certain legislations may be reflected from a theoretical point of view. However, the more concrete challenges of dysfunctional effects potentially emanating from the IP system under certain conditions will hardly explicitly be responded to in the IP legislation.

  Instead, most countries will likely address the issue of an abuse of rights in the general legislation only. It is, however, hardly imaginable that a court would apply such general provisions in the case of an abusive exertion of an IP right or similar constellations that increasingly occur in practice. At least those (Civil Law) countries that lack the balancing instruments of equity might face difficulties making use of such unspecified legislation.

  What should be established, in other words, is a sort of "interface" between such general provisions on the abuse of rights—understood in a very broad sense, including dysfunctional uses of an IP right or conduct of the right holder—on one hand, and an application of concrete legal remedies to recalibrate the IP system in order to achieve an appropriate equilibrium, on the other hand.

  The currently observable shortcomings in national legislations counteract other interests involved. Consequently, the interests of the right holders tend to prevail, possibly to the detriment of the general interests.
- Certain legal remedies to counter abuses of rights or other dysfunctional conduct might exist in most national legislations—at least to some extent. But the impact of such legislation in practice is hardly traceable since only a comparatively small number of case decisions are available. Beyond that, it seems questionable

how appropriate remedies codified in the general legislation are to recalibrate the IP system in order to achieve an appropriate equilibrium.

What usually is missing in civil law countries, however, is the remedy of the denial of injunctive relief.[40] As was shown before, this lack may result in a potentially imbalanced legislation. In view of that, it seems questionable whether the requirements set out by the EU Enforcement Directive[41]—but ultimately also the requirements of TRIPS—can be met with such an arrangement.

However, even if the denial of an injunctive relief should be admissible—on whichever legal basis—the question arises as to whether the legal consequences would be convincing in individual cases. More concretely, if a use activity either can or cannot be stopped, this would per se not entail any kind of compensation to the right holder as an alternative to injunction. Insofar, the denial of an injunctive relief as such ends up in an undifferentiated black and white picture. "Grey scales" only can be introduced if the non-injunction is compensated on a monetary basis. One can consider such compensation as damages. In the result, however, this construction ends up in the formula "use permission against payment" which stands for the basic characteristics of the compulsory licence.

- In view of that, the compulsory licence seems to be most promising. This remedy has been stipulated from the outset in most national IP legislations since the international legislation (foremost the PC) allowed Member States to do so. However, only very recently has the compulsory licence been "rediscovered", so to speak, by some developing countries in order to balance certain issues within the IP system.

  In fact, the compulsory licence might be at the beginning of a "new career", at least in patent law. According to the international legislation (especially Art. 31 TRIPS), however, compulsory licences need to meet comparatively strict requirements. Thus, the compulsory licence currently primarily responds to domestic needs, rather than to dysfunctional uses of an IP right or dysfunctional conduct of a right holder in general.

  Therefore, the potential of compulsory licences has not yet been sufficiently capitalized on. Its value—to some extent—lies in its capability of basically carrying into effect the "liability regime" approach,[42] which ultimately downgrades the "property regime".[43] This is particularly relevant in constellations of dysfunctional uses of the IP right or dysfunctional conduct of a right holder.

[40] See Sect. 5 above.

[41] See Sect. 6 above.

[42] See Sect. 5 above.

[43] See "eBay's effect on copyright injunctions: When property rules give way to liability rules", Phillips (2009), pp. 411–416. Fundamental on property and liability rules were Calabresi and Melamed (1972), pp. 1089–1128; see also Merges (1996), pp. 1293–1393; Lemley (2012), pp. 463–486.

In view of its balancing effect, a compulsory licence regime seems to be a truly appropriate measure, especially when compared to an (uncompensated) denial of injunctive relief. However, this insight hardly helps if the instrument of the compulsory licence is not applied in practice in order to remedy dysfunctional uses or conduct. To foster its application, one should consider the establishment of flanking measures, particularly with a view to the transaction costs the potential licensee has to bear, including the legal uncertainty and the time required to obtain the use allowance. This, however, is another topic that shall not be further explored at this point.[44]

References

Abbott B (1886) The patent laws of all nations, vol 1 (Algeria-Turkey). Brodix, Washington

ALEX Historische Rechts- und Gesetzestexte Online/Österreichische Nationalbibliothek, Kaiserliches Patent vom 31. März 1832. http://alex.onb.ac.at/cgi-content/alex?aid=jgs&datum=1019&page=14&size=45. Accessed 7 June 2013

BBC News Technology (21 December 2012) EU accuses Samsung of patent abuse in Apple Lawsuits. http://www.bbc.co.uk/news/technology-20812871. Accessed 4 June 2013

Bently L, Sherman B (2009) Intellectual property law, 3rd edn. Oxford University Press, Oxford

Bodenhausen G (1968) Guide to the application of the Paris Convention for the protection of industrial property as revised at Stockholm in 1967. BIRPI, Geneva

Bohannan C (2011) IP misuse as foreclosure. Iowa Law Rev 96:475–527

Calabresi G, Melamed D (1972) Property rules, liability rules and inalienability: one view of the cathedral. Harv Law Rev 85:1089–1128

Carré S (2012) France. In: Hilty R, Nérisson S (eds) Balancing copyright – a survey of national approaches. MPI studies on intellectual property and competition law, vol 18. Springer, Heidelberg, pp 387–429

Chalmers R (2007) Evergreen or deciduous? Australian trends in relation to the 'evergreening' of patents. Melbourne Univ Law Rev 30:29–61

Chien C (2009) Of Trolls, Davids, Goliaths, and Kings: narratives and evidence in the litigation of high-tech patents. N C Law Rev 87:1571–1615

Cotter T (2011) Four questionable rationales for the patent misuse doctrine. Minn J Law Sci Technol 12:457–489

Darrow J (2010) Debunking the "Evergreening" patents Myth. Harv Law Rec 6:131–133

Differencebetween.net, Difference between abuse and misuse. www.differencebetween.net/language/difference-between-abuse-and-misuse. Accessed 6 June 2013

Elrefaie E (2010) Injunctive relief post eBay and the various applications of the four-factor test in differing technological industries. Hastings Sci Technol Law J 2:219–242

Feldmann R (2003) The insufficiency of antitrust analysis for patent misuse. Hastings Law J 55:399–449

Gordon G, Hoerner R (2000) Overview and historical development of the misuse doctrine. In: ABA Section of Antitrust Law, intellectual property misuse: licensing and litigation. American Bar Association, Chicago, pp 1–35

Heinemann A (2002) Immaterialgüterschutz in der Wettbewerbsordnung. Mohr Siebeck, Tübingen

[44] For more on this, see chapter "Ancillary Orders of Compulsory Licensing and Their Compatibility with the TRIPS Agreement" by Richard Li-dar Wang, in this volume.

Hilty R (2012) Keynote. In: Liu K, Hilty R (eds) The enforcement of patents. Kluwer Law International, Alphen aan den Rijn, pp 9–31
Hoeren T, Herring E (2011) WikiLeaks und das Erstveröffentlichungsrecht des Urhebers. Informationsfreiheit als externe Schranke des Urheberrechts? MMR 500–504
Kanter J (6 May 2013) New York Times: Europe rules against patent move by Google's Motorola Unit. http://www.nytimes.com/2013/05/07/technology/07iht-google07.html?_r=0. Accessed 9 June 2013
Kesselheim A (2007) Intellectual property policy in the pharmaceutical sciences: the effect of inappropriate patents and the market exclusivity extensions on the health care system. AAPS J 9(3):E306–E311
Köhler H (1996) Die Begrenzung wettbewerblicher Ansprüche durch den Grundsatz der Verhältnismäßigkeit. GRUR 82–92
Körber T (2013) Standard essential patents, FRAND commitments and competition law. Nomos, Baden-Baden
Kraßer R (2009) Patentrecht, 6th edn. Beck, München
Lemley M (1990) The economic irrationality of the patent misuse doctrine. Calif Law Rev 78:1599–1632
Lemley M (2002) Intellectual property rights and standard-setting organizations. Calif Law Rev 90:1889–1980
Lemley M (2012) Contracting around liability rules. Calif Law Rev 100:463–486
Lemley M, Moore K (2004) Ending abuse of patent continuations. Boston Univ Law Rev 84:63–118
Lemley M, Shapiro C (2007) Patent holdup and royalty stacking. Tex Law Rev 85:1991–2049
Liu Y (2011) Patenting business methods in the United States and Beyond – globalization of intellectual property protection is not always an easy game to play. Int Rev Intellect Prop Comp Law 42:395–416
Merges P (1996) Contracting into liability rules: intellectual property rights and collective rights organizations. Calif Law Rev 84:1293–1393
Moynihan C (4 July 2005) New York Times: He says he owns the word 'Stealth' (actually, he claims 'Chutzpah,' too). http://www.nytimes.com/2005/07/04/business/04stealth.html?pagewanted=all&_r=0. Accessed 4 June 2013
Mueller J, Chisum D (2008) Enabling patent law's inherent anticipation doctrine. University of Pittsburgh Legal Studies Research Paper No. 2008-19, pp 1102–1164
O'Melinn L (2008) Effects of eBay: discretion, statutory damages, and private attorneys-general. Akron Intellect Prop J 2:119–132
Ohly A (2008) "Patenttrolle" oder: Der patentrechtliche Unterlassungsanspruch unter Verhältnismäßigkeitsvorbehalt? Aktuelle Entwicklung im US-Patentrecht und ihre Bedeutung für das deutsche und europäische Patentsystem. GRUR Int 787–798
Ohly A (2009) Three principles of European IP enforcement law: Effectiveness, proportionality, dissuasiveness. In: Drexl J, Hilty R, Boy L, Godt C, Remiche B (eds) Technology and competition. Contributions in honour of Hanns Ullrich. Larcier, Brussels, pp 257–275
Petersen B (2008) Injunctive relief in the post-eBay world. Berkeley Technol Law J 23:193–218
Pflüger M (2011) In: Cottier T, Véron P (eds) Concise international and European IP law, 2nd edn. Wolters Kluwer, Alphen aan den Rijn, pp 191–210
Pflüger M, Prüfer-Kruse T (2011) In: Cottier T, Véron P (eds) Concise international and European IP law, 2nd edn. Wolters Kluwer, Alphen aan den Rijn, pp 210–241
Phillips J (2009) eBay's effect on copyright injunctions: when property rules give way to liability rules. Berkeley Technol Law J 24:405–435
Roberts J (8 June 2012) Washington Post: Famous judge spikes Apple-Google case, calls patent system 'dysfunctional'. http://www.washingtonpost.com/business/technology/famous-judge-spikes-apple-google-case-calls-patent-system-dysfunctional/2012/06/08/gJQAM1bQOV_story.html. Accessed 2 June 2013

Trimble M (2012) Injunctive relief, equity, and misuse of rights in U.S. patent law. GRUR Int 514–522

von Kleinschrod C (1855) Die international Patentgesetzgebung nach ihren Prinzipien nebst Vorschlägen für ein künftiges gemeines deutsches Patentrecht. Enke, Erlangen

von Meibom W, Nack R (2009) Patents without Injunction? – Trolls, Hold-ups, Ambushes and Other Patent Warfare. In: Zu Waldeck und Pyrmont Prinz W, Adelmann M, Brauneis R, Drexl J, Nack R (eds) Patents and technological progress in a globalized world. MPI studies on intellectual property, competition and tax law. Springer, Heidelberg, pp 495–517

von Mühlendahl A (2007) Enforcement of intellectual property rights – is injunctive relief mandatory? Int Rev Intellect Prop Comp Law 38:377–380

Walter M, Goebel D (2010) In: Walter M, von Lewinski S (eds) European copyright law. A commentary. Oxford University Press, Oxford, pp 1193–1364

Crown Use and Government Use

Celeste C. Yang

Contents

Abstract Throughout the course of patent law development, compulsory licence has been one of the most discussed topics around the world. Recently, Crown use or government use in the Commonwealth countries has drawn much attention and became an important addition to the discussion. This chapter first looks into the legislative history and provisions in both the U.K. and the U.S. and further introduces some landmark case laws in these two countries that shape the rules respectively. The Crown use in the U.K. has played a vital role in the line of development of this legal concept. The U.S. embodies a similar rule known as government use in

---

C.C. Yang is Assistant Professor.

C.C. Yang
Institute of Law for Science and Technology, National Tsing Hua University, Hsinchu, Taiwan
e-mail: cyang525@yahoo.com

R.M. Hilty and K.-C. Liu (eds.), *Compulsory Licensing*, MPI Studies on Intellectual Property and Competition Law 22, DOI 10.1007/978-3-642-54704-1_19,

28 USC §1498. In the conclusion, this chapter differentiates Crown use from government use and finds that the legal theories supporting the rules are different and the U.S. is much more relaxed in terms of the scope of use and method recognised for authorisation; this chapter also points out the procedural difference between the civil law compulsory licence and the Crown use and government use.

1 Introduction

Patent compulsory licence has long been studied throughout the course of patent law development around the world. Under the WTO, during the negotiation of the TRIPS Agreement, there had been extensive discussion of compulsory licence. Recently, the topic of Crown use or government use has drawn much attention and has become an important addition to the discussion.[1] Countries of the Commonwealth have primarily employed this rule. The history of Crown use in the U.K. has played a vital role in the line of development of this legal concept. While the U.S. does not explicitly provide compulsory licence rules, it does however embody a rule known as government use in 28 USC §1498. Even though government use in the U.S. has retained some of the traits from Crown use, it has also evolved into a kind of its own.

This chapter will first look into the legislative history and provisions in both the U.K. and U.S. and further introduce some landmark case laws in these two countries. In the conclusion, the chapter will differentiate the two by their respective features and also compare the two.

2 The Development of Crown Use Under UK Law

2.1 Crown Use Under 1883 Act

The origin of compulsory licence has been subject to heated debate. Some believe it began in the preparatory work of the Patents, Design and Trade Marks Act of 1883 in Britain, while others point to the resolutions of the 1873 Patent Congress in Vienna.[2] However, most scholars agree that compulsory patent licence spontane-

[1] For more details concerning Thailand, Taiwan, and Latin America, see the chapters "Compulsory Licences: Law and Practice in Thailand" by Jakkrit Kuanpoth; "Compulsory Licence and Government Use in Taiwan: A Regress" Kung-Chung Liu; and "The Use of Compulsory Licences in Latin America" by Carlos M. Correa, in this volume.

[2] Brand (2007), p. 218.

ously arose in the late nineteenth century.[3] The emergence of Crown use has been somewhat less controversial. The Crown's privilege against patentees was first introduced in some earlier British cases,[4] and thereafter the term Crown use was included in the 1883 Act, which prompted many Commonwealth countries to implement like provisions.[5] The framers were concerned that patent might turn into unreasonable monopoly and thus placed some limitations on the patent rights to assure the reasonableness of patent power.[6] Under Section 22 of the 1883 Act, there were three grounds for compulsory licence, including when (a) the patent was not being worked in the United Kingdom, (b) the reasonable requirements of the public with respect to the invention cannot be supplied, or (c) any person is prevented from working or using to the best advantage an invention of which he is possessed.[7] The compulsory licence provision is different from Crown use, as this chapter will elaborate in the following section. For compulsory licence, under any of the circumstances described above, the Board of Trade may order the patentee to grant licence on such terms as to the amount of royalties, securities for payment or otherwise as the Board having regard to the nature of the invention and the circumstance of the case may deem just. The precondition for compulsory licence mainly focused on extracting the most economic and social value of the patent. The 1883 Act recognised that every patentee was entitled to an award, however not an award of unreasonable amount, especially if it could destroy a whole industry. The President of the Board of Trade took the chemical industry as an example and explained that if Germany refused to license to England the patent of a chemical reaction needed for a hot blast furnace in the iron industry, the whole iron industry would be destroyed. From this perspective, it appears that the initial intent to include compulsory licence was to protect the proper development of domestic industries.[8]

The provision of Crown use was not included in Section 22 but rather stipulated in Section 27 as an individual clause. Many consider Crown use to be a type of compulsory licence.[9] Section 27 of the 1883 Act provided that (1) A patent shall have to all intents the like effect as against her Majesty the Queen, her heirs and successors, as it has against a subject. (2) But the officers or authorities administering any department of the service of the Crown may, by any time after the application, use the invention for the services of the Crown on terms to be before or after the use thereof agreed on, with the approval of the Treasury, between those officers or authorities and the patentee, or, in default of such agreement, on such

[3] See *Id.*

[4] *Feather v. The Queen*, 6 Best and Smith 257, 1865, and affirmed in *Dixon v. The London Small Arms Company Limited*, L.R. 1 App. Cas. 632.

[5] 1883 Patents, Design and Trade Marks Act, S.27.

[6] Brand (2007), p. 218.

[7] 1883 Patents, Design and Trade Marks Act, S.22.

[8] Crawford Munro (1884).

[9] Cornish (2004), p. 26.

terms as may be settled by the Treasury after hearing all parties interested. It clearly states the patent's binding force against the Crown as well as patentee's right to remuneration. However, this was not always the case. Compared to some earlier case laws, the courts have consistently recognised that patents had no binding effect on the Crown.

2.2 *Case Law Before 1883 Act:* Feather v. the Queen *Case*

In *Feather v. The Queen*,[10] the court was confronted with the issue of whether the Crown needs to obtain a licence to use a patent for its service. The patentee in this case, Robert Bernard Feather, obtained a patent on the "improvement in the construction of ships or vessels" on 26th of November 1852. Feather claimed that the Commissioners executing the office of Lord High Admiral of the United Kingdom infringed his patent in constructing and using of a ship called the "Enterprise". Commissioners explained that the construction and use of the patent in building the ship was in the exercise of their office and on behalf of the Crown, thus for the service of the Crown. The court rejected Feather's contention based on several grounds.[11]

Firstly, the Court reasoned that a different rule of construction prevails when interpreting grants from the Crown. The grant should not operate in derogation of the prerogative of the Crown. The court explained that "there are no express words to take away from the Crown the right of using the invention. In construing grants from the Crown, a different rule of construction prevails from that by which grants from one subject to another are to be construed. In a grant from one subject to another, every intendment is to be made against the grantor, and in favour of the grantee, in order to give full effect to the grant; but in grants from the Crown an opposite rule of construction prevails. Nothing passes except that which is expressed. And in no species of grant does this rule of construction more especially obtain than in grants which emanate from, and operate in derogation of, the prerogative of the Crown".

Secondly, the court rejected the ground that a patent is a contract between the Crown and patentee because the grant was simply an exercise of prerogative. It illustrated this point by referring to the Crown granting toll collection to fairs and markets but not agreeing to pay toll to these private vendors: "...however general and universal by the terms of the grant the right to take toll may be as against the rest of the world, the Crown will nevertheless be exempt from toll; This appears strong to show that in granting a privilege, otherwise of universal application, the

[10] See *Feather v. The Queen*, 6 Best and Smith 257, at 265.

[11] See *Id.* at 283.

Crown will not be bound unless it expressly declares its intention to that effect; and that grants of privilege, however general in their terms, can, in the absence of express words to bind the Crown, be taken only as conferring the privilege as against the subject, exclusive of the Crown".

Thirdly, the court analysed the wording of the patent and found that the subjects listed out did not include the Crown. The court explained, "there are parts of the letters patent from which it is to be inferred that the Crown was not to be bound. The grant is of 'special license, full power, sole privilege and authority,' terms which appear referable to a right conferred as against the *fellow subjects of the grantee, rather than as against the Crown*. This is followed by a prohibition to "*all and every person and persons, bodies politic and corporate, and all other our subjects whatsoever*," against making, using or practicing the invention...It is obvious that none of these provisions, by which the exclusive right of the patentees are protected, can be applicable to the Crown: all tend to show that the privilege was intended to be against fellow subjects".

Lastly, the patentee does not enjoy a remedy against the Crown even if the court found infringement. The court relied on the reason that the dignity of the Crown needs to be upheld. Patent was not granted against the Crown; therefore, no tort or wrong was constituted, "as the infringement of a patent right constitutes a tort or wrong, in the proper sense of the term, and as no wrongful act can be alleged against the Crown,... even if our decision on the first question had been in favour of the suppliant, a petition of right to the Crown would not be open to him as a means of redress. Our judgment must therefore be for the Crown".

Section 27 of the 1883 Act later repealed these views. We will take a look below.

2.3 Section 27 of 1883 Act Repealed the Case Law: Patentee Has Like Effect Against the Crown

Section 27(1) provides that "a patent shall have to all intents the like effect as against her Majesty the Queen, her heirs and successors, as it has against a subject". This provision overturned *Feather v. the Queen*'s point of view as to the binding force of patent on the Crown. Enforcing patent against the Crown is no longer considered derogating the prerogative of the Crown, and a patent will have the like effect against the Crown as it has against a subject. The provision does not say that a patent has the "same" effect but only a "like effect", namely the force of the patent against the Crown is limited. Patent is now valid against the Crown, subject to provision of subsection 2. The differences particularly lie in the enforcement of the patent and the royalty terms, where the Crown will still be able to use the patent as long as it pays the terms of the agreement. The royalty rate shall be decided by all parties interested, which shall be approved by the Treasury.

Section 27 (2) stipulates that "the offices or authorities administering any department of the service of the Crown may, by themselves, their agents, contractors, or others, at any time after the application, use the invention for the services of the Crown *on terms to be before or after the use thereof agreed on, with the approval of the Treasury*, between those officers or authorities and the patentee, or, in default of such agreement, on such terms as may be settled by the Treasury after hearing all parties interested". This provision not only extended patent's binding force on the Crown but also extended that on their agents, contractors and others, as long as they are working in the service of the Crown. The Crown's privilege extends to third parties, and the scope of the application extends to any service of the Crown. This third party privilege thus became the distinct trait of Crown use provisions.[12] And in the event of patentees refusing to comply with the Crown's request, their patents may be void.

Note that private contractors are not always protected by the privilege attached to the Crown;[13] their protection would depend on the nature of the contract or relationship between the Crown and the private entity. In the case of *Dixon v. The London Small Arms Company*,[14] the Secretary of War issued a notice requiring the defendants to provide and deliver rifles made in accordance with patent claims. The private parties who undertook this project were later sued by the patentee. The Queen's Bench Division held that they had infringed the patents because the nature of the contract is one of sale or manufacture, not one of employment by the Crown; hence, the defendants were not protected by the privilege. The Queen's Bench explained that whether the contract is one of sale or manufacture does not alter the outcome of the case because the court found no distinction between the two. They reasoned that under a contract of sale, the seller may tender products that are already made, either purchased from another party or manufactured by himself. Hence, a contract for sale can reasonably entail manufacture. However, the Court of Appeals had a different point of view. They made a distinction between a contract of sale and a contract of manufacture. If the contract is seen as a contract of sale, then the Crown did not authorise the use of the patent, so the defendants would not be protected by the privilege. But if the contract is seen as a contract of manufacture, then the defendants would be doing the same work as the agents in the Crown's workshop, who are protected by the privilege. Since the rifle company was a private contractor and was deemed not to be doing the work for the Crown, they are liable for patent infringement. It shows that a mere contract cannot fulfil the writing authorisation requirement.

[12] de Carvalho (2010), pp. 428–429.

[13] Wallace (1884).

[14] *Dixon v. The London Small Arms Company* 1 Q.B.D. 384, (1876).

2.4 *Subsequent Development in the Patents Acts of 1907, 1949, and 1977*

2.4.1 The Patent Act of 1907: Assignment to Secretary for War or the Admiralty of Certain Inventions

Art. 29 of the Patents and Designs Acts 1907 continues to affirm that patent has binding power over the Crown—"A patent shall have to all intents the like effect as against the Crown. His Majesty the King as it has against a subject: Provided that any Government department may, by themselves, their agents, contractors, or others, at any time after the application, use the invention for the services of the Crown on such terms as may, either before or after the use thereof, be agreed on, with the approval of the Treasury, between the department and the patentee, or, in default of agreement, as may be settled by the Treasury after hearing all parties interested".

In the Patents and Designs Act of 1907, the Crown use provision was supplemented by Article 30 (1), which required that certain inventions relating to war be assigned to the Crown.[15] The "certain inventions" refer to the improvements of instruments or munitions of war. The patentee may assign the patent to the Secretary of State for War or Admiralty either for or without valuable consideration.[16] This provision differs from the 1883 Act, in that the Crown needed to enter into an agreement with royalty terms approved by the Treasury, whereas in the 1907 Act, when the use was for war purposes, the Crown may use the patent for a consideration, which does not need to reflect the true value of the patent.

2.4.2 The Patents Act of 1949: Authorisation from Crown Needs to Be in Writing, Rights of Third Parties and Other Emergency Circumstances That Allow Crown Use Are Regulated

The Patents Act of 1949 had more elaborate provisions on Crown use. Section 46 listed in detail the circumstances for and obligations the government needs to bear under Crown use. It required that "any government department, and any person authorized *in writing* by a government department, may make, use and exercise any patented invention for the services of the Crown". The authority of the government in terms of timing and subjects are also stipulated. Section 46(4) provides that "The authority of a government department in respect of an invention may be given under this Section either before or after the patent is granted and either before or after the

[15] The Patents and Design Acts, 1907, S. 29–30.

[16] *Id*, Art. 30: (1) The inventor of any improvement in instruments or munitions of war may (either for or without valuable consideration) assign to the Secretary of State for War or the Admiralty on behalf of His Majesty all the benefit of the inventions and of any patent obtained or to be obtained for the invention; and the Secretary of State or the Admiralty may be a party to the assignment.

acts in respect of which the authority is given are done, and *may be given to any person whether or not he is authorized directly or indirectly by the patentee to make, use, exercise or vend the invention*". The government also has the obligation to notify the patentee as soon as practicably possible of the use of the invention and provide information regarding the extent of such use and the use it may require from time to time. The notification obligation can be exempted if it is against the public interest.

Section 46(6) further stipulates that "service of Crown" includes foreign governments working with the UK for defence purposes. The applicability of Crown use became more specific as time evolved. Rights of third parties in respect to Crown use are also provided in Section 47, in which the Act eliminated third parties' right against the government even if they have obtained patent rights under licence or assignment from the patentee. The provisions shall have no effect on the governments if they restrict or regulate the use of the invention. Third parties, such as exclusive licensees, were entitled to recover from patentees the royalties they had agreed with the government.

There is also a list of emergencies that qualify government and persons authorised by government to make, use, exercise, and vend the invention, including (1) efficiently prosecuting any war in which His Majesty may be engaged; (2) maintaining supplies and services essential to the life of the community; (3) securing sufficiency of supplies and services essential to the well-being of the community; (4) promoting the productivity of industry, commerce, and agriculture; (5) fostering and directing exports and reducing imports, or imports of any classes, from all or any countries and for redressing the balance of trade; (6) ensuring that the whole resources of the community are available for use, and are used, in a manner best calculated to serve the interests of the community; or (7) assisting the relief of suffering and the restoration and distribution of essential supplies and services in any part of His Majesty's dominions or any foreign countries that are in grave distress as the result of war. The definition of "period of emergency" should be defined by Order in Council.

The case *Pfizer Corporation Appellants v Ministry of Health Respondents 1965* illustrated the scope of "service of the Crown" and "use/sale" under the 1949 Act.[17] Pfizer was the registered legal owner of letters patent in respect of a drug used in treatment under the National Health Service. In 1961, the Minister of Health decided to use the powers conferred by Section 46 of the 1949 Patent Act and invited tenders for the supply of the drug to National Health Service hospitals. The purpose was to obtain certain drugs from sources other than the patentee and its licensees. Prior to the announcement, supplies of the drug in National Health Service hospitals were procured from Pfizer's licensees manufacturing the drug in the United Kingdom. Through advertisements, the Minister promised the protection of an authorisation under Section 46 of the Act. Fraser Chemicals Ltd., a British importer, accepted the tender and obtained supplies of the drug manufactured

[17] *Pfizer Corporation Appellants*; *v Ministry of Health Respondents 1965* case 2 W.L.R. 387.

abroad. Fraser was not a licensee of Pfizer and did in fact meet the requirements of the Ministry by the mere importation of tetracycline made by Messrs in Italy, where the drug enjoyed no patent protection. Fraser sold the drug to the Ministry and National Health Service hospital, and it was subsequently used in the treatment of inpatients and outpatients in the National Health Service hospitals. Outside these hospitals, the drug might also be used under the National Health Service Act in the treatment of patients. In such case, the drug was normally obtained on the prescription of a National Health Service general practitioner. It was supplied by a local chemist or pharmacist. At the relevant time, the patient was liable to pay to the supplying pharmacist a National Health Service charge of 2s. (originally 1s.). A similar charge was payable by outpatients supplied with drugs by the hospital pharmacy. The drug was also provided and used in the administration of the general medical services by general practitioners and chemists who were not servants or agents of the Crown.

Among other declarations, Pfizer contended in this action that the Minister was not empowered under the section to authorise any person to make, use, and exercise the invention for the purpose of making and/or supplying medicines to National Health Service hospitals for use in the treatment of inpatients and outpatients because the employment of such medicines is not a use of the patented invention "for the services of the Crown" but "for the benefit of the patients" and that the supply of such medicines to outpatients in such hospitals on payment of a charge or to private inpatients paying hospital maintenance charges was a sale of the invention that is not authorised by Crown use.

The first issue was whether the use of this drug in National Health Service hospitals or under prescription by doctors working under the National Health Service can be said to be within section 46 (1) as being "for the services of the Crown". Pfizer pointed out that the drug was used for the benefit of the patient, not for the benefit of the service of the Crown. The court agreed with this argument and referred to the statutory wording "for" the service of the Crown, which should benefit the department of the Crown or the persons employed by the Crown. However, that was not the case here because the beneficiaries were the general public. The court refused to give a wide interpretation.

The second issue involves whether the "use" of the drug under Section 46 includes "sale". The court traced the line of explanation on the scope of service of the Crown and concluded that a sale is not protected under the Crown use privilege. It looked into the case of *Dixon v. London Small Arms Co. Ltd.* case, in which the court affirmed that a sale would be an infringement. The subsequent development of legislation, including the Patents and Designs Act 1907, Defence Regulations, the Patents Act 1949, and Atomic Energy Act 1946, has also confirmed this finding. Section 46 was never intended to enable the Crown to use an invention by distributing it to third parties for their use and benefit because such a use would be for the subjects of the Crown and not for the services of the Crown.

The court then considered the essential issue: does the supply by the Minister of drugs to outpatients of National Health Service hospitals who pay the National Health Service charge of 2s. amount to a sale by the Minister? The court found the answer to be in the affirmative. Supplies of drugs under charge are all sales since the patients can be required to pay the charge before the drug is supplied. Section 46 (1) of the Act of 1949 does not authorise such a sale by a government department, its servants, or agents.

The last issue talked about whether importation enjoyed Crown use privilege, and since Section 46 expressly referred to using, making and exercising the patented invention. Thus, the court refused to include importation as a Crown use right. However, this is no longer the case in the Patents Act of 1977.

2.4.3 The Patents Act of 1977: Crown Use Includes Research in Atomic Energy or Other Important Fields and for Foreign Defence Purposes

The 1977 Act continued the extensive provision on Crown use. Authorisation still needs to be in writing for government departments or individuals working for the Crown. Section 55 stipulates the scope, including making, using, importing, or keeping the product arising out of the invention. Sale was not included in the 1907 Act but is now open to the sale or offer to sell where to do so would be incidental or ancillary to making, using, importing, or keeping the patented invention. Sale or offer to sell for foreign defence purposes, production or supply of specified drugs and medicines, or disposal or offer to dispose of it are also within the scope of Crown use. The foreign defence purposes include to help the Crown fulfil its obligation under an agreement with another country regarding defence matters or to help the United Nations or its members to carry out armed actions under resolution. The Crown is also privileged to use process patents. If the invention or any product obtained directly by means of the invention is a specified drug or medicine, the Crown may sell or offer to sell the drug or medicine. Rights of third parties that restrict or regulate the use of the patented invention are still void against the Crown. Section 59 also listed out the emergency situations that are similar to the 1907 Act.

The time to give authorisation is very flexible. Section 55(6) provides: "The authority of a government department in respect of an invention may be given under this section either before or after the patent is granted and either before or after the use in respect of which the authority is given is made, and may be given to any person whether or not he is authorised directly or indirectly by the proprietor of the patent to do anything in relation to the invention". The government has a duty to notify the patentee unless it would appear contrary to the public interest to do so.

The 1977 Act gives a specific definition on the "service of the Crown", which includes (a) the supply of anything for foreign defence purposes, (b) the production or supply of specified drugs and medicines, and (c) such purposes relating to the production or use of atomic energy or research into matters connected therewith as the Secretary of State thinks necessary or expedient, and "use for the services of the Crown" shall be construed accordingly.

In terms of compensation, Section 58(10) provides, "in considering the amount of any compensation for the use of an invention for the services of the Crown after publication of an application for a patent for the invention and before such a patent is granted, the court shall consider whether or not it would have been reasonable to expect, from a consideration of the application as published under section 16 above, that a patent would be granted conferring on the proprietor of the patent protection for an act of the same description as that found to constitute that use, and if the court finds that it would not have been reasonable, it shall reduce the compensation to such amount as it thinks just".

In *Dory v Sheffield Health Authority*,[18] the court confirmed that authorisation can be applied retrospectively. The patent is related to machines known as lithotriptors for treating stones in kidneys under the National Health Service Act 1977. The defendants sought to dismiss Dory's claim on the ground that the use and keeping of the machines were a use by the Crown "for the services of the Crown" under Section 55 of the Patents Act 1977. Note that the appropriate government department had authorised the supplier of the machines retrospectively under Section 55 (6) of the Patents Act 1977. The plaintiff argued that the action should be stayed and not dismissed because at the time the writ was issued, the health authority had not been authorised and was therefore an infringer, and therefore Section 55 cannot apply. Dory contended that Sheffield and the Lothian Health Board were only entitled to the protection of Sec. 55(8) of the Patents Act 1977 after authorisation had been given. The health authority contended that it was a government department for the purpose of Section 55 of the Patents Act 1977, exercising the powers of the Secretary of State on his behalf. The plaintiff, however, argued that the health authority acted only as an agent and became entitled to the protection of Section 55 (8) of that Act after the authorisation was given.

The court dismissed the action with costs on the following grounds: first, a health authority exercised the functions of the Secretary of State, devolved through the provisions of the National Health Service Act 1977 and regulations made under it, and any use of a patented invention by the health authority was and always had been Crown use for the purpose of section 55 of the Patents Act 1977. Second, retrospective authority given under subsection (6) took away any cause of action that the proprietor of the patent might have had against that person before the authority was given and substituted a right of remuneration under the subsection.

In a more recent case, *MMI Research Ltd v Cellxion Ltd and others*,[19] the court was again asked to determine the scope of Crown use. The case involved an undisclosed user who later claimed to be a government official and thus should be granted the Crown use. The patent at issue is related to a method of breaking through mobile telephone network security so that the identification numbers of a mobile telephone and its user could be obtained. On 11 March 2009, the court found

[18] *Dory v Sheffield Health Authority*, 1991 F.S.R. 221.

[19] *MMI Research Ltd v Cellxion Ltd and others*, Chancery Division (Patents Court), 2009 EWHC 1938 (Pat).

that the patent was valid and the defendants infringed that patent. At a subsequent hearing, the defendant inquired into whether the sales of its infringing device amounted to Crown use under Section 55 of the Patents Act 1977, as the sales had been made to a number of police forces, as well as a government department, anonymously named as Customer. The defendant hoped to obtain an authorisation in respect of its device.

The court reasoned that before any act that would otherwise be an infringement ceased to be so by virtue of Section 55 of the 1977 Act, it had to be established that the person doing the act was a government department or a person authorised in writing by a government department. However, there was no evidence as to what steps had been taken by the defendants to obtain an authorisation, whether the authorisation was intended to be of the defendant or the police forces and whether prospective or retrospective authorisation was being sought. The question in relation to Crown use had therefore become hypothetical because no such authorisation had been obtained. The court felt it would be wrong for the court to attempt to deal with points that might in the future arise if the defendants or the police obtained an authorisation to use the invention from a government department. The court did however reaffirm the Pfizer case on the two requirements: (1) it is for the service of the Crown, and (2) there is authorisation in writing.

Under emergency or expedient circumstances, the Crown or government department may also use the patent, and these national emergencies or expedient circumstances are (a) for the efficient prosecution of any war in which Her Majesty may be engaged; (b) for the maintenance of supplies and services essential to the life of the community; (c) for securing a sufficiency of supplies and services essential to the well-being of the community; (d) for promoting the productivity of industry, commerce, and agriculture; (e) for fostering and directing exports and reducing imports, or imports of any classes, from all or any countries and for redressing the balance of trade; (f) generally for ensuring that the whole resources of the community are available for use, and are used, in a manner best calculated to serve the interests of the community; or (g) for assisting the relief of suffering and the restoration and distribution of essential supplies and services in any country or territory outside the United Kingdom that is in grave distress as the result of war. The definition of period of emergency still needs to be defined by the Council of Order, and the draft of Order cannot be submitted to the Queen if it has not been approved by each house of the Parliament. It shows that there are restricted circumstances to use patent under emergencies, and the regulations to issue the Order are also burdensome since each house of Parliament needs to approve it.

3 Governmental Use in the United States

Unlike the British law, the U.S. does not have a general provision on compulsory licence. There are three broad categories that permit the use of patent and are deemed to be the exceptions to a patentee's exclusivity. They are statutory exceptions, sovereign immunity for governmental entities under the Eleventh Amendment of the US Constitution, and judicial remedies.[20] The concept of government use can be explained by the sovereign immunity category or by the eminent domain theory.

3.1 *Statutory Exceptions*

Congress explicitly provides some limited compulsory licence under specific bodies of law.[21] The U.S. Congress has made particular efforts to serve the public interest, especially in the field of technology. For example, the Plant Variety Protection Act mandates a compulsory licence if it concerns the adequate supply of food. Another example is the Atomic Energy Act (AEA),[22] in which §2183 (c) provides that (1) whenever any patent has been declared to affect the public interest, the Commission is licensed to use the invention or discovery covered by such patent in performing any of its powers under this chapter and (2) any person may apply to the Commission for a non-exclusive patent licence to use the invention or discovery covered by such patent, and the Commission shall grant such patent licence to the extent that it finds that the use of the invention or discovery is of primary importance to the conduct of an activity by such person authorised under this chapter.

3.2 *Government Use*

28 U.S.C. § 1498 embodies the concept of "government use" for patent and copyright cases and provides:

> Whenever an invention described in and covered by a patent of the United States is used or manufactured by or for the United States without license of the owner thereof or lawful right to use or manufacture the same, the owner's remedy shall be by action against the United States in the United States Court of Federal Claims for the recovery of his reasonable and entire compensation for such use and manufacture. Reasonable and entire compensation shall include the owner's reasonable costs, including reasonable fees for expert witnesses and attorneys, in pursuing the action if the owner is an independent inventor, a nonprofit organization, or an entity that had no more than 500 employees at any time during the 5-year period preceding the use or manufacture of the patented invention by or for the United States.
>
> For the purposes of this section, the use or manufacture of an invention described in and covered by a patent of the United States by a contractor, a subcontractor, or any person,

[20] Lee (2003), pp. 175, 182.

[21] Yosick (2001), p. 1276.

[22] Lee (2003), p. 182.

> firm, or corporation for the Government and with the authorization or consent of the Government, shall be construed as use or manufacture for the United States.

The doctrine of sovereign immunity prohibits suit against the government unless it has consented thereto by an express and unequivocal statute and requires that such statute be narrowly construed in the government's favour.[23] As such, the United States is not liable under 28 U.S.C.A. § 1498 for inducing patent infringement or for inducing copyright infringement. However, the United States or a federal agency department does not enjoy sovereign immunity in a patent infringement case when the alleged infringer brings a declaratory judgment action for patent invalidity and inequitable conduct. The Federal Circuit has held:[24] "That Congress has consented to an action for money damages for patent infringement by the government does not in any way imply that Congress intended to bar equitable actions related to the validity of government-owned patents". It shows that the government only enjoys partial sovereign immunity and is not immune from monetary damage.

Other scholars base government use on eminent domain theory. Many U.S. case laws rely heavily on this doctrine. The Fifth Amendment of the U.S. Constitution entitles individuals to compensation when government appropriates their real property. The same reasoning should apply by analogy to government's use on patent. The patent infringement amounts to a "taking" under the Fifth Amendment, and thus the patentee is entitled to compensation for the infringing use. In a suit against the federal government for unlicensed use of a patent, a patent holder may recover "reasonable and entire compensation". This is confirmed in the legislative history in the House Report 1910.[25]

The Supreme Court revisited this issue within a patent infringement context in *Florida Prepaid Postsecondary Education Expense Board v. College Savings Bank and United States*.[26] College Savings Bank had patented a method of guaranteeing sufficient funds to cover college tuition costs. It sued a Florida state agency, Florida Prepaid Postsecondary Education Expense Board (Florida Prepaid), claiming violation of the Patent and Plant Variety Protection Remedy Clarification Act. Florida Prepaid challenged the validity of the Patent and Plant Variety Protection Remedy Clarification Act because it tried to abrogate the state's sovereign immunity in patent infringement cases. The Supreme Court reversed the holdings of two lower courts and held that Congress had improperly annulled the states' sovereign immunity by passing this act. It explained that under the Fourteenth Amendment of the U.S. Constitution, the authorisation for "appropriate legislation" to protect against deprivations of property without due process of law did not provide Congress with authority to abrogate state sovereign immunity from claims of patent infringement

[23] *Office of Personnel Management v. Richmond*, 496 U.S. 414, 1990.

[24] *Delano Farms Co. v. California Table Grape Com'n*, 655 F.3d 1337, 2011.

[25] H.R.Rep. No. 61-1288, at 1, 1910.

[26] *Florida Prepaid Postsecondary Education Expense Board v. College Savings Bank and United States*, 527 U.S. 627, 1999.

in the Patent and Plant Variety Protection Remedy Clarification Act. Absent identification of a historical pattern of states infringing patents and then providing inadequate remedies or pleading sovereign immunity from infringement claims so as to deprive patentees of property without due process of law, and absent limits to confine its scope to remedy acts of state infringement, the act has significant likelihood of being unconstitutional. The Court went on to reaffirm that patent falls in the definition of "property" and thus no person shall be deprived of it without due process of law. The patent infringement by government will only be considered depriving without due process of law when no remedy or inadequate remedy is provided.

3.2.1 Eminent Domain Theory

28 U.S.C. § 1498(a) grants the government the right to use or manufacture an invention covered by patent and gives the patentees only the right to sue the United States government for reasonable and entire compensation. This statute and its predecessors have long been viewed as an exercise of eminent domain over patent property.

The Fifth Amendment protects against abuse of government authority in a legal procedure. Eminent domain requires a showing of two elements: a property right and a proper venue to bring suit against the government. This limitation does not prohibit the taking of private property but instead places a condition on the exercise of that power.[27] In *Advanced Software Design* Case, the court explained that § 1498 (a) "is more than a waiver of immunity and affects an assumption of liability by the government".[28]

3.2.2 The Use of Patent and the Notion of Taking

The Fifth Amendment bars the government from forcing some people alone to bear public burdens and thus mandated the government to provide "just compensation" to the injured property owner.[29] In other words, the Amendment obligates the federal government to pay a property owner just compensation whenever a state actor, duly authorised by law, effects a taking of private property for a public use. The more difficult problem is trying to discern whether the type of conduct in which the government has engaged can be characterised as a taking.[30] In a series of decisions involving the Patent Act of June 25, 1910, the lower federal courts have shown sufficient legislative authorisation as takings. The language found in these

[27] Miller (2010–2011), pp. 2–3.

[28] *Advanced Software Design Corp. v. Fed. Res. Bank*, 583 F.3d 1371, 1375 (Fed.Cir.2009).

[29] Reese (2006–07), p. 117.

[30] Cotter (1998), pp. 535–536.

opinions can be traced back to some Supreme Court decisions from the late nineteenth and early twentieth centuries, in which the Court on several occasions appeared to endorse this view.[31]

However, many scholars have argued that the use of patent does not have the same effect as appropriating a real property. One main difference lies in the fact that when using a patent, the patentee still retains the right to use the technology, whereas when a real property is appropriated, the owner of the property can no longer enjoy all the privilege the law bestows upon him. As such, the ground to analogise patent use and eminent domain is weak. Some argue that the reason to compensate the patentee lies not on the ground of eminent domain but on tort liability.[32] This issue was recently discussed in the Zoltek case and, referring back to an old case, the Schillinger case.

In the Schillinger case,[33] the issue was to determine whether the Court of Claims had jurisdiction over the case. Until the creation of the Court of Claims in 1855, the only recourse of claimants when the United States had wronged them was to appeal to Congress. The jurisdictional statute defined the jurisdiction of the Court of Claims as: "the Court of Claims shall have jurisdiction to hear and determine all claims founded upon the Constitution of the United States or any law of Congress . . .or upon any contract, expressed or implied, with the Government of the United States, or for damages . . .in cases not sounding in tort, in respect of which claims the party would be entitled to redress against the United States . . . if the United States were suable".

In the recent Zoltek case,[34] the court followed the Schillinger case, stating that the court recognised that by enacting the Patent Act 1910, the Congress "added the right to sue the United States in the court of claims" for patent infringement. Under this case law, patent infringement by the government is analogised to "taking" a "compulsory license". The view is consistent with the text of the Patent Act of 1910, which provided for reasonable compensation for patent infringement, and with the legislative history, which provided that the purpose of the bill was "to enlarge the jurisdiction of the Court of Claims so that said court may entertain suits against the United States for the infringement or unauthorised use of a patented invention, in certain cases, and award reasonable compensation to the owner of the patent".

The court went further to point out Congress' intention of legislating the sovereign immunity waiver in 1948, which stated, "in response to *Schillinger*, Congress provided a specific sovereign immunity waiver for a patentee to recover for infringement by the government. Had Congress intended to clarify the dimensions of the patent rights as property interests under the Fifth Amendment, there would have been no need for the new and limited sovereign immunity waiver. The

[31] *Id.*

[32] *Zoltek v. U.S.*, 442 F.3d 1345, 2006.

[33] *Schillinger v. U.S.*, 155 U.S. 163, 1894.

[34] See *Zoltek v. U.S.* 442 F.3d 1345, 2006.

manner in which Congress responded to *Schillinger* is significant. The life of the law has not been logic; it has been experience. Neither the Court of Federal Claims nor this court can ignore the path of the patent law as it has evolved under § 1498".

3.2.3 Contractors and Consent

28 U.S.C. § 1498 (a) also provides immunity to any other persons authorised by the government to use the patent: "for the purposes of this section, the use or manufacture of an invention described in and covered by a patent of the United States by a contractor, a subcontractor, or any person, firm, or corporation for the Government and with the authorization or consent of the Government, shall be construed as use or manufacture for the United States". The Supreme Court in the *Richard Screw* case[35] has stated that §1498(a) was meant to "relieve the contractor entirely from liability of every kind for the infringement of patents in manufacturing anything for the government" in order "to stimulate contractors to furnish what was needed for the war, without fear of becoming liable themselves for infringements. This purpose survives today".

In the Schillinger case,[36] it was also contended whether the contractor or person is a properly authorised agent of the government. The Court of Claims stated that the government never acknowledged the plaintiffs' rights in the Schillinger patent. The court found no infringement or reasons to invalidate the patent; therefore, no compensation was justified because the government did not act through its "competent agent" to take or use private property while acknowledging explicitly or tacitly that the property was individual property. The general principle the court relied on was that on a policy imposed by necessity, governments should not be held liable for unauthorised wrongs inflicted by their officers on the citizen, though occurring while discharging their official duties. Here the claimants never authorised the use of the patent right by the government, never consented to but always protested against it, threatening to interfere by injunction or other proceedings to restrain such use.

There was no act of Congress in terms of directing, or even by implication suggesting, the use of the patent. There was no recognition by the government or any of its officers of the fact that in the construction of the pavement there was any use of the patent or that any appropriation was being made of claimants' property. The mere fact of the use of a patented process in the construction of a pavement by a contractor with the government did not justify a claim that the government, by accepting and using the completed structure, had appropriated any property of the patentee.

§ 1498(a) provides total immunity to third parties who are not government entities, including government contractors or subcontractors. They are allowed to

[35] *Richard Screw Anchor v. United States*, 275 US 343, 1928.

[36] See *Schillinger v. U.S.*, 155 U.S. 163, 1894.

use or make the subject matter of a private patent with minimal government consent or authorisation. In *Molinaro v. Watkins-Johnson CEI Division*, although the court found apparent ambiguity in the statutory requirement of consent, it found that government consent is satisfied both by a contract between the government and a third party involving an allegedly infringed item and by the government's acceptance of an item as stipulated in a third party contract.[37] Therefore, it appears that the government may implicitly give consent or authorisation under § 1498(a).

3.2.4 Compensation

In the Schillinger case, the Supreme Court heard the appeal and affirmed the lower court's decision that the plaintiffs lacked a cause of action against the government. The court believed that the taking of intangible property differed from the taking of tangible property because the government's use of a patent right does not "per se" cause the patentee's loss, whereas should a tangible article be appropriated, the owner instantly becomes so much poorer.

However, the Supreme Court must have presumed that Congress, in passing § 1498 and depriving a patent owner of remedy against an infringing government contractor, intended to give the owner the equivalent of what it took away. By requiring "reasonable and entire compensation" for the use of the patent, the United States has acknowledged that it cannot take away a patent holder's right to reparation. § 1498 requires the government to waive sovereign immunity to reparation when a contractor has used a patent, and the reason for reparation rests on tort liability.

Therefore, § 1498 encourages patent use because contracting companies know they can reduce bids on government contracts since they can use patents without fear of liability.[38]

In *TVI Energy Corp. v. Blane*,[39] the court took the notion of implied consent or authorisation one step further. The court extended § 1498(a) protection by including bidders (yet to become contractors) who were demonstrating to the government use of the allegedly infringed product under specific government guidelines. Based on the legislative history of § 1498(a), the court concluded that Congress intended "to allow the Government to procure whatever it wished regardless of possible patent infringement, which is a broad scope of 1498(a). Therefore, even when the defendant in this case was a bidder and not yet a government source, the court nevertheless held that the defendant was immune from infringement liability".

In *Leesona Corp. v. U. S.*,[40] the Court set out several rules in determining the "complete and reasonable compensation". It first explained that damages were to be

[37] Molinaro v. Watkins-Johnson Cel Division, *359 F.Supp. 474 (1973)*.

[38] Rushing (2012), pp. 883–886.

[39] *TVI Energy Corporation v. Milton C. Blane and Blane Enterprises, Inc.*, 806 F.2d 1057, 1986.

[40] *Leesona Corp. v. U. S.*, 220 Ct.Cl. 234, 1979.

measured on an eminent domain rather than a 'tort' theory; multiple damages and attorney fees were not recoverable; savings to the government could not be awarded in addition to a reasonable royalty; comparative royalty technique is the preferred method of determining just compensation, although unpatented, original equipment anodes, cathodes, and battery covers were to be included in the compensation base; and by virtue of taking, the plaintiff lost his exclusive right to domestic manufacture of the batteries, which was a factor to be considered in fixing a reasonable royalty.

The court explained that the theory of recovery against the government for patent infringement is not analogous to that in litigation between private parties; when the government has infringed, it is deemed to have "taken" the patent licence under an eminent domain theory, and just compensation is required by the Fifth Amendment. It went on to say that it was a fundamental error to base recovery on a tort theory, rather than on an eminent domain theory, because there was no clear indication that the government intended to assume responsibility for any payment other than the just compensation required by the Fifth Amendment, and absent an express assumption of such a duty, no further liability other than that which was constitutionally mandated could be assumed.

In terms of payment calculation, the proper measure in eminent domain is what the owner has lost, not what the taker has gained. The eminent domain is necessary to protect the public, and the compensation must be just. If the government infringes a patent, the patentee is only entitled to reasonable and entire compensation, rather than entitled to the increased damages heaped on other parties as punishment or deterrence, as he/she would have acquired were the infringer a private party. As such, lost profits in addition to royalty could not be awarded against the United States in patent infringement action. Actual value of the subject patent was the proper measure of just compensation for a government's infringement rather than the total loss suffered by the entire corporate patentee as a consequence of losing both the exclusive domestic manufacturing rights and the procurement contract that was to usher the patentee into the battery-manufacturing field, although some elements of business injury might be weighed in determining what the owner might have sold for, if willing to sell.

For purpose of determining reasonable and entire compensation due to government's infringement of a patent, there is a need to differentiate between evaluating the value of the property taken in light of the patentee's business needs and granting compensation for loss of business due to taking or for any incidental losses. The former is proper; the latter is not.

3.3 *Judicial Action Resulting in Compulsory Licensing Arrangements*

The third type of de facto compulsory licence is when a judicial decision required the patentee to do so. Even when an infringing party cannot find relief in statutory infringement exceptions or within sovereign immunity concerns, the federal court system may craft remedies for the patent holder that result in a compulsory licensing relationship. In patent infringement cases, when a court finds that patent infringement has occurred, the patentee usually requests a prayer for the remedy. While considering the proper remedy, the courts may consider the aspects of equity.[41]

4 Conclusion

From the previous sections on the provisions on Crown use and government use, we can see they share similarities but certainly are not the same. We will next compare the two in more detail. Also, this chapter finds that the notion of Crown use or government use is quite different from the idea of "compulsory licence" even though many have categorised them as a type of compulsory licence.

4.1 Differences Between Crown Use and Government Use

Crown use in the UK initially relied on the belief that the grant in Crown use should not operate in derogation of the prerogative of the Crown. The Crown has the privilege to use the patent. The later development in legislation has established patentee's right against the Crown for such use. The US, on the other hand, relies on the sovereign immunity and eminent domain theory. It believes that a patentee cannot sue the United States unless it has consented to it. This was no longer the case when legislators expressly in 28 U.S.C. 1498 affirmed patentees' right to sue, which is seen as a waiver to the sovereign immunity. The courts have later relied on eminent domain theory to explain that government use of a patent is a taking, and patentees should be compensated. As such, based on the different theories that developed the laws, we can distinguish that Crown use is a "privilege" of the Crown, whereas the US enjoys its "sovereign immunity".

4.1.1 Scope of Use

In the UK, the use is limited to "for the service of the Crown". The 1977 Act includes a detailed definition of this term, which refers to defence, medicine, and research purposes. In the Pfizer case, the court pointed out that the drug was used for the benefit of the patients, not for the benefit of the service of the Crown, because the beneficiary was not the department of government but the general public; thus,

[41] Lee (2003) at 186–88.

the use was not for the service of the Crown. The US usage is much broader, in the sense that as long as it is for the government's benefit, then it may exercise its government use power under 1498(a), which is an easy test to satisfy.

UK allows Crown use to include the right to manufacture, use, sell and supply, and also use during national emergencies or for foreign defence purposes. There is strict requirement regarding the declaration of national emergency and detailed regulations on invoking the foreign country defence purposes. The US limits it to use or manufacture and did not set out all the requirements or regulations on national emergency and foreign defence purposes.

4.1.2 Method in Authorisation

In the UK, the Crown needs to be authorised in writing. However, the Dixon case shows that a mere contract does not satisfy the "in writing" requirement. The authorisation can be given before or after the use. The Dory case reaffirmed that an authorisation may apply retrospectively. In the US, in the Molinaro case, the court found ambiguity in the form of consent and held that a contract or implied authorisation would satisfy the authorisation requirement. Given the loose requirement to recognise the existence of an authorisation, the US government use can be invoked more easily than Crown use in the UK.

4.1.3 Who Are Authorised

The UK allows any government department and any person authorised in writing to enjoy the privilege. The US, under 1498(a), covers a contractor, a subcontractor, or any person, firm, or corporation for the government. As such, both countries provide broad scope for those protected. As the US Supreme Court in the *Richard Screw* case has stated, §1498(a) was meant to "relieve the contractor entirely from liability of every kind for the infringement of patents in manufacturing anything for the government".

4.2 Differences Between Civil Law Compulsory Licence and Crown Use/Government Use

4.2.1 Process Initiation

In most civil law jurisdictions, compulsory licence can be initiated in two ways, either by government order or upon individual requests. A compulsory licence needs to be *issued* before the use of the patent. This procedural requirement raises the bar for a government to use a patent. Without an order from the government or a request from an individual or private company, the government will not be able to issue a compulsory licence. Under Crown or government use, there is no need for the government to wait for an individual to bring up a request. Specifically, the requesting party needs to submit an application to the administrative agency, usually the Patent & Trademark Office. The PTO would examine whether the use conforms to the preconditions, such as use for public health, before a compulsory licence can be issued. The preconditions are examined beforehand, whereas in Crown use or government use, there is no such proceeding before using the patent.

4.2.2 All Users Need to Obtain a Licence from the Licensee

The Crown or the government has the power to use the patent without obtaining a licence from the patentee. This is true in both the U.K. and the U.S., while the former enjoys the privilege and the latter has sovereign immunity. As such, there is no need to obtain a licence from the patentee.[42] In the case of compulsory licence, even if the government wishes to use the patent, a compulsory "licence" needs to be obtained. The individuals using the patent need to obtain a licence from the patentee as well because they do not enjoy the privilege or immunity like that of the Crown or the US government.

4.2.3 Conditions That May Invoke This Use

In terms of the circumstance in which the Crown or government may invoke this right, the two countries are somewhat different. Under U.K. law, the 1883 Act gave a detailed explanation on what "service of the Crown" means. It includes the use for defence purposes, both national defence and defences carried out to fulfil international organisation obligations. The service also includes the production and supply of medicine and drugs and the development of atomic energy. However, the U.S. government is not subject to the limited purpose as the U.K. law prescribes. Unless it falls under the statutory exceptions, the §1948(a) allows the government to use all patents. For the compulsory licence regulations, the applicable circumstance is usually limited to specific circumstances, such as war or medicine for undeveloped countries. And only when all the requirements are fulfilled can the administrative agency issue a compulsory licence. Thus, the applicable condition is much narrower than Crown or government use. So in a sense the Crown use or government use gives the government much more power and freedom in using patents to advance the public interest.

[42] de Carvalho (2010), p. 428.

References

Brand O (2007) The dawn of compulsory patent licensing. IPQ 2:218

Cornish WR (2004) Intellectual property-omnipresent, distracting, irrelevant? Oxford University Press, Oxford, p 26

Cotter TF (1998) Do federal uses of intellectual property implicate the fifth amendment? Florida Law Rev 50(529):535–536

Crawford Munro JE (1884) The Patents, Designs, and Trade Marks Act, 1883, with rules and instructions. http://archive.org/stream/patentsdesignsa01britgoog#page/n106/mode/2up. Last visited 25 Oct 2013

de Carvalho NP (2010) The trips regime of patent rights, 3rd edn. Kluwer, Amsterdam, pp 428–429

Lee KW (2003) Permitted use of patented inventions in the United States: why prescription drugs do not merit compulsory licensing. Ind Law Rev 36(175):182

Miller JI (2010–2011) 28 U.S.C. § 1498(A) and the unconstitutional taking of patents. Yale J Law Technol 13(1):2–3

Reese BE (2006–2007) Do as i say, not as i do: an international and comparative study of governments' rights to "Infringe" patents in light of the Federal Circuit's recent interpretation of 28 U.S.C. § 1498 and a call for congress to modernize the statute. Buffalo Intellect Prop Law J 4:84, 117

Rushing S (2012) Plugging the leak in §1498: coercing the United States into notifying patent owners of government use. Vanderbilt J Transnatl Law 45(879):883–886

Wallace R (1884) The Patents, Designs and Trade Marks Act, 1884, with introductory chapter, explanatory notes and decided cases. http://archive.org/stream/patentsdesignsa00britgoog#page/n128/mode/2up. Last visited 10/8/2013

Yosick J (2001) Compulsory patent licensing for efficient use of inventions. Univ Illinois Law Rev 1276

Fair Use: A Workable Concept in European Patent Law?

Geertrui Van Overwalle

Contents

Abstract Over the last decade, the patent system has sparked significant controversy worldwide. Concerns have been expressed about the expansion of the patent system, both in terms of patentable subject matter and of the numbers of patents granted. Irritation has equally been voiced with regard to certain (inadequate or unfair) uses of the patent system. As to the latter, various remedies have been put forward to deal with inadequate licensing practices (Sect. 2). However, patent law's toolbox may not be sufficient to redress restrictive licensing behaviour in all its facets. Recalling to mind the rationale of patent law and the underlying 'social contract' (Sect. 3), an alternative and seemingly more flexible remedy to deal with unreasonable behaviour is examined: the fair use exception (Sect. 4). We explore whether the fair use exception from US copyright law may be implemented in European patent law, and provide a tool to extend the 'social contract' to the post-grant phase. We field test the fair use doctrine in Europe by applying the doctrine on the Myriad case, a prime example of problematic licensing in the field of human genetics (Sect. 5). The fair use approach may equally be tested in other

---

G. Van Overwalle is Professor of IP Law at the University of Leuven.

G. Van Overwalle
Centre for Intellectual Property Rights, University of Leuven, Leuven, Belgium
e-mail: Geertrui.VanOverwalle@law.kuleuven.be

R.M. Hilty and K.-C. Liu (eds.), *Compulsory Licensing*, MPI Studies on Intellectual Property and Competition Law 22, DOI 10.1007/978-3-642-54704-1_20,

technological areas, such as the ICT or telecom sector, in order to learn to what extent the concept can apply to all fields of technology (Sect. 6).

1 Introduction

In the past decade, the patent system has been seriously criticised. For quite some time, academics have been rather critical about the patent system.[1] Nowadays, also newspapers comment on patent cases and often portray patents as a negative story.[2] A first trend that has received a lot of criticism relates to the unbridled *expansion* of the patent system, both in terms of patentable subject matter and the number of patents granted.[3] The scope of patentable subject matter has been stretched considerably to adapt patent law to the new realities of ICT and genetics by extending protection to computer-related inventions and biological material. Concerns are raised about the potentially harmful effect of such expansion on the freedom to operate and on follow-on innovation. Patent law has expanded not only in respect to scope but even more so in respect to the number of patents granted.[4] Recent years have seen a remarkable increase in patents in the fields of ICT technology and biotechnology.[5] Concerns have been voiced about the impact of the current patent surge on the quality of patents and the fluent exchange of ICT and genome-related technology in a landscape of patent thickets. At present, technological areas such as ICT technology and biotechnology are so crowded with patents that the freedom to use protected inventions may be considerably limited.

A second trend that has become visible over the last few years is the growing sensitivity to unreasonable *behaviour* of patent rights holders.[6] In recent years, some companies have either refused to license some inventions or have licensed them exclusively at relatively high prices. The current *Zeitgeist* seems to be more

---

[1] There is a wide array of US scholarly literature expressing discontent with the current patent system. See Bessen and Meurer (2008), Boldrin and Levine (2008), Burk and Lemley (2009), and Jaffe and Lerner (2004). The author of the present paper also looked into the shortcomings of the patent system from an international perspective; see Van Overwalle and van Zimmeren (2009), pp. 415–442.

[2] For an example in the genetics area, see Caulfield et al. (2007), pp. 850–855.

[3] See Van Overwalle and van Zimmeren (2009), and the references cited there.

[4] Patent filings worldwide grew by 7.2 % in 2010, after having fallen by 3.6 % in 2009. That growth was driven by a steep filing increase in China and the US, which accounted for four-fifths of worldwide growth. An all-time high of 1.98 million applications were filed globally, consisting of 1.23 million resident applications and 0.75 million non-resident applications. See World Intellectual Property Indicators (2011).

[5] For some details in genetics, see Hopkins et al. (2007), p. 185; Jensen and Murray (2005), p. 239. For some details in other sectors, see Sheehan et al. (2003).

[6] See Van Overwalle and van Zimmeren (2009), and the references cited there.

sensitive to such uses of the patent system. One saga that made the headlines worldwide is the Myriad case, a case in the field of genetics where restrictive licensing policies have been widely applied. Myriad, a US company owning a suite of US and European patents covering breast and ovarian cancer (BRCA) genes,[7] demanded fees of $2,400[8] or more for carrying out its own test at a few licensed centres and tried to stop all other tests involving the BRCA genes in public health genetic laboratories. It was this behaviour, rather than the patents themselves, that led to wide controversy. At first sight, other sectors such as ICT and telecom may seem to be less prone to restrictive licensing behaviour. Due to the nature of the products, and to the importance of interoperability and compatibility, there is a recurrent need among companies to (cross-)license their patents. However, when dealing with standard essential patents, companies such as Apple and Samsung endlessly debate on the exact scope and level of FRAND (fair, reasonable, and non-discriminatory) licensing terms. Concerns are being expressed on how time-consuming negotiations and restrictive and/or unreasonable licensing practices can frustrate access to technology and opportunities for further research and development.

In summary, the growing discontent with patent law manifests itself in relation to patentable subject matter and the coming into *existence* of patent rights. Recent events illustrate that the irritation is also orientated towards the *exercise* of patent rights. Our chapter deals with the growing unease with regard to the exercise of patent rights, in particular with restrictive and/or unreasonable licensing behaviour. We kick off by looking at the various remedies in current patent law to deal with such behaviour.

2 Patent Law's Toolbox

A first instrument to limit the rights of restrictive patentees is the *research exception*.[9] Although the European-style research exception may provide protection against infringement for many (university or private sector) scientists involved in

[7] See Matthijs et al. (2013), pp. 704–710; Huys et al. (2012), pp. 441–448; Huys et al. (2011), pp. 1104–1107.

[8] Matthijs and Hodgson (2008), pp. 58–60; Matthijs (2007), pp. 27–44.

[9] In Europe, a list of limitations to the right of a patentee was suggested for the first time in the Community Patent Convention (CPC) of December 15, 1975, and reintroduced as Article 9 of the Proposal for a Council Regulation on the Community Patent of August 1, 2000. In the meantime, the Unitary Patent Package (UPP) saw the light and formally adopted the research exception in Article 27 (b) of the Agreement on a Unified Patent Court, Brussels, January 11, 2013 ("The rights conferred by a patent shall not extend to any of the following: acts done for experimental purposes relating to the subject matter of the patented invention"). Anticipating the implementation of the CPC, the 'mother' provision on the research exception was introduced in many EPO member states.

basic research,[10] it is doubtful whether it can constitute a safe harbour for researchers concentrating on applied research with a commercial finality. As a possible remedy against restrictive licence behaviour, critical analyses have also been prepared on the *compulsory licence* mechanism in patent law. In most countries, a government or a court can usually compel a patent holder to license his rights for reasons of dependency or insufficient exploitation. Recently, compulsory licences have been provided to address the potential hindering effects of patents in public health care.[11,12] One might argue that there is yet another instrument in patent law, namely *patent term duration*. However, the patent term duration defence is too limited to deal with the problems discussed here.

Measures have also been contemplated outside patent law, more particularly in competition law. Even though European competition law leaves considerable freedom to the patentees to set up their licensing agreements and does not prohibit exclusive licensing as such, a measure is available to deal with cases of extreme monopolistic licensing behaviour of patent holders: the *abuse of dominant position*.[13]

The line of research on restrictive licensing behaviour has taught, however, that those instruments, either internal or external to patent law, may well not be sufficient to meet the growing concern regarding the hindering effects of patents. Alternative and more flexible remedies to redress unreasonable patent rights behaviour may be necessary. One idea that struck our attention and whetted our curiosity is implementing the fair use exception from copyright into the patent law arena.

3 The Social Contract

To appreciate the plea for an introduction of a fair use concept in patent law, it is necessary to dig into patent law legitimation theories and the patent law rationale.[14] The debate on the legitimation of the patent system has a long and turbulent history

[10] See van Zimmeren and Van Overwalle (2014).

[11] In France, Switzerland, and Belgium, such a compulsory licence 'for public health' has been introduced. For more, see van Zimmeren and Van Overwalle (2011).

[12] Compulsory licences for European patents are regulated by national law. Compulsory licences for European patents with unitary effect are governed by the laws of the participating Member States as regards their respective territories (see Recital 10 Regulation (EU) 1257/2012 of the European Parliament and of the Council of 17 December 2012 implementing enhanced cooperation in the area of the creation of unitary patent protection, *Official Journal of the European Union*, L 361/1, 31 December 2012).

[13] Article 102 Treaty on the Functioning of the European Union (TFEU), *Official Journal of the European Union*, C 83/47, March 30, 2010. For more details, see van Zimmeren (2011).

[14] This section mainly reiterates some of the thoughts I have expressed in Van Overwalle (2007); Van Overwalle and van Zimmeren (2009). Under the heading 'Signs of the Times: Evolving Reasons for Patent Fair Use' Katherine Strandburg provides additional, interesting rationales for the introduction of a fair use exception in patent law (see Strandburg 2011, at pp. 281–289).

in both academic and political circles. The present consequentialist justification, focusing on both the 'incentive to invent and innovate' and on the 'incentive to disclose' argument,[15] is probably most accepted to date, as it reconciles both the private and public interests. The private interest of the inventor is served through the grant of a limited exclusionary right as an incentive to further creativity and inventiveness (including necessary investments in research and development). The public interest benefits through the development of accessible goods and services and the dissemination of technical knowledge, thanks to the disclosure requirement. The TRIPS Agreement equally reflects this utilitarian approach, balancing two objectives: rewarding compensation for creators and inventors for innovation, on one hand, and promoting the interests of the public at large in securing access to science and technology, on the other hand. Articles 7,[16] 8,[17] and 30[18] of the TRIPS Agreement confirm this effort for achieving an equilibrium,[19] in other words, a "social contract".[20] A patent right cannot be viewed as a title giving (almost) complete freedom of action but rather as temporary permit to exploit monopoly rights under fair and reasonable conditions, in other words, as a duty-bearing privilege.[21] In the light of the many controversies surrounding gene and disease

---

[15] For more on this theory, as well as the other justifications theories, see Burk and Lemley (2009); Drahos (1996); Machlup (1959); Penrose (1951); Sterckx (2005); Van Overwalle and van Zimmeren (2009).

[16] Article 7 stipulates that "The protection and enforcement of intellectual property rights should contribute to the promotion of technological innovation and to the transfer and dissemination of technology, to the mutual advantage of producers and users of technological knowledge and in a manner conducive to social and economic welfare, and to a balance of rights and obligations".

[17] Article 8 equally stipulates that "(1) Members may, in formulating or amending their laws and regulations, adopt measures necessary to protect public health and nutrition, and to promote the public interest in sectors of vital importance to their socio-economic and technological development, provided that such measures are consistent with the provisions of this Agreement. (2) Appropriate measures, provided that they are consistent with the provisions of this Agreement, may be needed to prevent the abuse of intellectual property rights by right holders or the resort to practices which unreasonably restrain trade or adversely affect the international transfer of technology".

[18] Article 30 sets forth that "Members may provide limited exceptions to the exclusive rights conferred by a patent, provided that such exceptions do not unreasonably conflict with a normal exploitation of the patent and do not unreasonably prejudice the legitimate interests of the patent owner, taking account of the legitimate interests of third parties". According to the drafters of the *Copyright Declaration—A Balanced Interpretation of the "Three-Step Test" in Copyright Law* (available at http://www.ip.mpg.de/de/pub/aktuelles/declaration-threesteptest.cfm, last visited June 18, 2013), the fact that third party interests are not explicitly mentioned in the three-step test as applied in copyright law does not detract from the necessity of taking such interests into account. Rather, it indicates an omission that must be addressed by the judiciary.

[19] Similarly Gervais (2003), p. 81, point 2.10.

[20] The term "social contract" is used by Lord Hoffman in the House of Lords' Decision of 21 October 2004 (*Kirin-Amgen and others v. Hoechst Marion Roussel and others*) [2004] *UKHL* 46, § 77; the term "implicit social contract" is set forth by Baldwin (2007).

[21] "If the purpose in creating the privilege is to fulfil some approved goal then it should also follow that the privilege [patent] holder is subject to duties not to exercise the privilege in a way that defeats the purpose for which the privilege [patent] was granted", Drahos (1996), at p. 220. Similarly,

patents and the growing discontent with some undesirable effects and undesired excrescences of the current patent system, there is an urgent need to re-explore this concept.

The social contract underlying the patent system is embedded in patent rules that are being put to the test day by day at the event of the *grant*, the coming into *existence* of patent rights. In view of the many concerns with regard to the potential hindering effects of the restrictive licensing behaviour of patent holders in genetics, the social contract test should be extended to the *post-grant* level and should also be challenged with regard to the *exercise* of patent rights.

At present, patent holders have wide discretion on how to exercise their rights, and European patent law hardly provides rules with regard to exploitation and licensing. Such tools, either internal or external to patent law, should definitely be used to meet the growing concern regarding the hindering effects of patents. However, does that suffice? Are a number of exceptions and a mechanism aimed at limiting cases of *extreme* restrictive licensing behaviour sufficient to balance private and public interests with regard to the exercise of rights? Does the social contract not require that *all un*reasonable or *un*fair licensing behaviour detrimental to public health be forbidden? In genetics, it was not the grant of the BRCA patents as such that led to a worldwide commotion but rather the exorbitant fees and the refusal to license to public genetic labs that aroused emotions. From a pure competition law perspective, it is questionable whether the Myriad business model would infringe competition law and could be qualified as an abuse of dominant position. From a wider perspective, however, one could argue that the Myriad licensing behaviour is a threat to the social contract embedded in patent law and should therefore be forbidden.

Further concrete efforts from the legislator to design institutional and legal responses to monitor the exercise of patent rights in an attempt to safeguard an adequate balance between private and public interests in the *post-grant* phase might be considered. And that is where the fair use exception might step in.

4 Fair Use

Studying the plasticity of the fair use concept is not totally new. In a pioneering article, Maureen O'Rourke already examined the introduction of a doctrine of fair use in patent law.[22] O'Rourke argues that patent law should adopt a fair use doctrine. The fair use concept eases some of the tensions created by strong patent rights and may play a valuable role in balancing exclusive rights and public welfare.

"Holders of intellectual property privileges are subject to those duties that maximize the probability that the purpose for which the privilege was first created is achieved" (Drahos 1996, at p. 221); "The grant of these monopolies would be tied to the idea of duty. Duty-bearing privileges would form the heart of an instrumentalism of intellectual property" (Drahos 1996, at p. 223).

[22] O'Rourke (2000).

Building on the work of O'Rourke, Katherine Strandburg equally takes the view that a fair use type infringement exception should take its place in patent law's toolbox.[23] A fair use exception can carve out specific types of uses, using a scalpel rather than a cleaver to shape a socially beneficial patent scope.[24] Infringement exceptions can account for the fact that different uses of patented technology have different social costs and benefits.[25]

The efforts of O'Rourke and Strandburg, as well as writings from other scholars such as De Larena,[26] have mainly focused on the particular US context. The present analysis aims at widening the conversation and theorising on the implementation of the US fair use copyright concept in European patent law. On the other hand, the present article is more limited in scope and far more modest than previous scholarly writings on this topic. Different from the aim of O'Rourke and Strandburg to establish a fully fletched doctrine of fair use in patent law and to contemplate *new* factors,[27] the current chapter mainly aspires to test to what extent the prevailing copyright fair use theory and the *incorporated* four factors can be operationalised. The underlying question is whether fair use can provide relief for some of the (alleged) harmful consequences of patent rights. The present chapter looks at the Myriad case, a prime example of a problematic patent case in the field of human genetics, to field test the fair use doctrine in Europe.[28] Further research could elaborate on this approach and complement this first assessment by putting restrictive and/or unreasonable licensing cases in other technological areas, such as ICT or telecom, to test.

Let us now turn to the origin of fair use, more particularly US copyright law. Copyright law (US) and *droit d'auteur* (Europe) fundamentally differ in their conceptual approach on the protection of creations of the mind.[29] The main

---

[23] Strandburg (2011).

[24] Strandburg (2011), at p. 277.

[25] Strandburg (2011), at p. 277.

[26] De Larena (2005).

[27] Strandburg (2011).

[28] Even though the Myriad saga may well have come to a standstill on June 13, 2013, in the US with the decision of the Supreme Court, the current legal framework in Europe remains quite cumbersome, as European and national patent legislation and case law widely allow patenting of isolated genomic DNA and complementary DNA (c-DNA). See article 5 of Directive 98/44/EC of 6 July 1998 of the European Parliament and of the Council on the legal protection of biotechnological inventions (*Official Journal L* 213, 30/07/1998 p. 0013) and the legislation in the various EU Member States, having copied (more or less) article 5. Article 5 sets forth that the human body, at the various stages of its formation and development, and the simple discovery of one of its elements, including the sequence or partial sequence of a gene, *cannot* constitute patentable inventions (par. 1) and that an element isolated from the human body or otherwise produced by means of a technical process, including the sequence or partial sequence of a gene, *may* constitute a patentable invention, *even if the structure of that element is identical to that of a natural element* (par. 2—my Italics). Par. 3 adds that the industrial application [read: function] of a sequence or a partial sequence of a gene must be disclosed in the patent application.

[29] See Strowel (1993).

difference between the two regimes relates to the very nature of the granted rights. US copyright law looks at the rights of authors as mainly economic rights, the author being seen as a provider of a product. In contrast, European *droit d' auteur* is rather based on natural law theory and focuses on the non-patrimonial dimension of the author's creation. Notwithstanding the different approaches, both copyright law and *droit d'auteur* grant an exclusive right to the author to reproduce or authorise the reproduction of her/his work, in any manner and form she/he wishes, be it direct or indirect, temporary or permanent, in part or in whole.

Equally, both regimes have developed exceptions to the main right(s) in an attempt to safeguard the balance between public and private interests. However, the US and Europe substantially differ in the way the exceptions have been conceptualised. The US has introduced a flexible, open regime through the development of a doctrine of fair use, whereas Europe has established a rather rigid, closed regime through the implementation of a limited list of exceptions.

The US doctrine of fair use is a statutory codification of a hundred years of judicial decisions, excusing certain "salutary" uses from infringement liability meeting certain assessment criteria.[30] Article 107 of the Copyright Act provides that certain uses are fair and non-infringing depending on a calculus of four factors.[31] Article 107 stipulates:

> Notwithstanding the provisions of sections 17 U.S.C. § 106 and 17 U.S.C. § 106A, the fair use of a copyrighted work, including such use by reproduction in copies or phonorecords or by any other means specified by that section, for purposes such as criticism, comment, news reporting, teaching (including multiple copies for classroom use), scholarship, or research, is not an infringement of copyright. In determining whether the use made of a work in any particular case is a fair use the factors to be considered shall include:
>
> 1. the purpose and character of the use, including whether such use is of a commercial nature or is for nonprofit educational purposes;
> 2. the nature of the copyrighted work;
> 3. the amount and substantiality of the portion used in relation to the copyrighted work as a whole; and
> 4. the effect of the use upon the potential market for or value of the copyrighted work.

In European *droit d'auteur*, the concept of fair use is not present as such. Unlike US copyright law and their open approach, European copyright law permits only a limited list of exceptions[32] and does not have the open-ended authority to resolve

---

[30] Goldstein (2001), at p. 293.

[31] Goldstein (2001), at p. 293. Some scholars have argued that there is a fifth factor at play: "Empirically, it can be demonstrated that judges also invoke other factors, especially a hidden fifth factor—namely, the extent to which the claimed fair use serves the public interest—without which few, if any, major federal appellate decisions affirming fair use are likely to be found"; see Reichman and Okediji (2012). Examining whether a fifth factor is really at play, and to what extent the notion of "public policy" differs from the concept of "public interest" is very important, but goes beyond the scope of the current paper. See Van Overwalle (2000).

[32] Guibault (2002); Hugenholtz and Okediji (2008).

cases outside the specifically listed categories.[33] The list is laid down in Directive 2001/29 on Copyright and Related Rights in the Information Society,[34] more in particular in article 5. The exceptions listed in article 5 (1) are mandatory, whereas the exceptions laid down in article 5 (2) and (3) are optional.

Consequently, European Member States had to remove exceptions that did not appear in article 5 (2) and (3) and amend exceptions that conflicted with them.[35] Moreover, Member States were not allowed to enact exceptions outside the list provided in article 5 (2) and (3). However, they could keep "traditional" exceptions of lesser importance as long as they only concerned analogue uses.

Thoughtful observers set forth that the strength of the US fair use doctrine is the considerable flexibility it provides in balancing the interests of copyright owners, subsequent authors, and the public. Fair use, however, is often unfavourably judged for its unpredictability and case-by-case nature.[36] Comparing the US open list approach with the European closed list approach leads experts to believe that an advantage of the closed list over fair use is that a list of exceptions is more specific and predictable, whereas an advantage of fair use over an exceptions list is that an open list is more flexible and adaptable over time.[37]

5 Fair Use and European Patent Law

Can the fair use doctrine be implemented in European patent law? The legal basis to introduce a fair use test in patent law might be found in the TRIPS Agreement, in particular in Article 30, stating that "Members may provide limited exceptions to the exclusive rights conferred by a patent, provided that such exceptions do not unreasonably conflict with a normal exploitation of the patent and do not unreasonably prejudice the legitimate interests of the patent owner, taking account of the legitimate interests of third parties". Article 30 is considered to legitimise the closed list exceptions in current European patent law. Is there a good reason why the same Article 30 could not be employed to introduce new hypotheses to the closed list or—more radically—to switch to an open list and apply the US fair use factors as parameters to assess whether certain uses could be exempted from patent infringement?

---

[33] Goldstein and Hugenholtz (2010), at p. 364. Cf. Goldstein (2001), at p. 293.

[34] Directive 2001/29/EC of the European Parliament and of the Council of 22 May 2001 on the Harmonization of Certain Aspects of Copyright and Related Rights in the Information Society, *OJ. L* 167, 22/06/2001 pp. 10–19 (see http://eur-lex.europa.eu/LexUriServ/LexUriServ.do?uri=CELEX:32001L0029:en:NOT, last visited September 24, 2013).

[35] See Hart (1998), at p. 169.

[36] Samuelson (2008–2009), at pp. 2540–2541 and the authors cited there.

[37] Samuelson (2008–2009), at pp. 2540–2541 footnote 17.

On the other hand, one could easily think of various objections against the introduction of a fair use concept in European patent law. Foremost, there is wide disagreement in academic scholarship about the feasibility of 'legal transplants'. The same legal rule will operate quite differently in different countries, with differing traditions.[38] Furthermore, the argument has been raised that the fair use doctrine can only be invoked as a 'defense' on the side of the alleged infringer and cannot prescribe the behaviour of the patent holder. Last but not least, litigation costs are likely to be very expensive.[39]

Let us, for a moment, put the pros and cons of transplanting a known legal concept to a new legal environment aside and limit ourselves to testing the fair use concept in a prime case of restrictive licensing behaviour, namely the Myriad case, and evaluate to what extent the four conditions are fulfilled in this setting.

(1) The purpose and character of the use

In order for the fair use exception to apply and in line with US copyright law, the *intent of the alleged infringer* should be taken into account, on a case-by-case basis. It seems to be generally accepted that the use, in order to be exempted, has to lie between two extremes. The first extreme is the case where a third user employs the patented product or method to sell his/her own products on the market, which does not appear to be fair at all. The second extreme is the case where a university researcher uses the patent in order to test whether the invention works the way it is claimed in the patent, which can be considered fair use of the patented invention.[40]

In the Myriad case, most of the third users were clinicians in public or private non-profit hospitals. Even though the intent of this type of institutional users is non-commercial in nature, it remains to be seen whether the use of the patented invention against the payment of a nominal fee will be qualified as commercial or not. So it is doubtful whether the first criterion would be fulfilled.

(2) The nature of the patented work

In order to be exempted under the fair use doctrine and in line with US copyright law, the amount of time, money, and *effort of the inventor/patent holder* should be taken into account on a case-by-case basis.[41] Use of the patent would appear not to be fair use if the protected technology is revolutionary or disruptive, requires millions of dollars (or Euros) for its development, or is owned by small companies or independent inventors. On the other hand, use of patent would appear 'fair' if the patented technology only offers a minimal improvement in a crowded field, if the investment is minimal, or if the patent is held by large companies or universities.[42]

---

[38] For more on the discussion on legal transplants, see Legrand (1997); Pintens (1998); Watson (2000); Watson (1993); Zweigert and Kötz (1996).

[39] See O'Rourke (2000), at p. 1243.

[40] De Larena (2005), at p. 811.

[41] De Larena (2005), at pp. 811–812.

[42] De Larena (2005), at pp. 811–812.

In the Myriad case, it has been repeatedly argued that the 'discovery' of the BRCA genes was the result of perseverant, yet routine work,[43] as was the establishment of the association between the gene and the disease. In light thereof, the second criterion might well be fulfilled.

(3) The amount and substantiality of the portion used—the nature of the advance of the infringing work—transformative use

The third factor appears to be the most important condition of the fair use test in US copyright law. This factor would focus on the *type* and manner rather than on the pure *volume* of the use by the alleged infringer on a case-by-case basis.[44] It may be argued that an exact use of the invention would constitute an infringement, whereas a transformative use could constitute a 'fair' use of the patented invention.

In the Myriad case, the lab clinicians use the (knowledge about) the patented BRCA genes in their own, 'home brewn' methods.[45] Even though such use is not identical to the work performed by the inventor who isolated and characterised the relevant gene(s), establishing a link between those genes and a disease can probably not be qualified as transformative either. So it remains uncertain whether the third criterion would be fulfilled.

(4) The effect of the use upon the potential market

The fourth and last criterion relates to the effect of the use upon the market. Copyright protection aims at providing (economic) incentives to promote creations. This is even truer for patent law, as (scientific) experiments can be significantly more costly.[46] An infringement would clearly exist if a reasonably priced research licence is easily accessible to all who qualify. Conversely, a fair use of the invention would be accepted when even non-competitors are denied access to a licence, particularly when the technology would not be commercialised by the patentee.[47]

In the Myriad case, this last condition is fulfilled in the most convincing way. There is wide evidence that Myriad was not willing to provide reasonably priced licences. On the other hand, the fact that public and private non-profit hospitals offered in-house tests at nominal cost diminished the potential market share of Myriad for the BRCA tests.

It is often suggested that the fair use test does not require that *all* four factors be present, but rather requires a comprehensive *overall* assessment, where one factor is not prioritised over another. With that in mind, measuring the Myriad case against the four factors of the fair use doctrine leads us to believe that an unambiguous answer to the question whether the four conditions are clearly, indisputably, and

[43] Baldwin (2007); Matthijs (2007).

[44] De Larena (2005), at pp. 811–812.

[45] Matthijs (2007).

[46] De Larena (2005), at p. 813.

[47] De Larena (2005), at p. 813.

overall met in this controversial case is difficult to give. It is not sure at all whether the current behaviour of clinicians would be shielded under a fair use exception. Applying the fair use concept does not allow prediction of the outcome of a dispute in advance, and the 'concept' can therefore not be regarded as a 'standard'. One will not only have to wait for the decision of the court, but it should be borne in mind that the decision pattern of a court may vary over the years. Hence, the fair use test does not simply and (recti)linearly contribute to legal certainty. Conversely, it is by no means certain whether the current restrictive licensing behaviour of Myriad would be considered unlawful, unreasonable, and 'unfair' under the fair use doctrine.

6 Conclusion

Our conceptual analysis of the US fair use exception leads us to conclude that the fair use concept may inspire European legislators in designing institutional and legal responses to monitor the exercise of patent rights in an attempt to safeguard an adequate balance between private and public interests and operationalise the 'social contract' in the post-grant phase.

However, our exploration of the application of the US fair use concept in one contentious real life case, namely the Myriad (breast cancer genes) case, brings us to believe that the introduction of a fair use doctrine in European patent law is not very helpful in remedying restrictive and exorbitant licensing behaviour and preserving the 'social contract' on which patent law is based in the area of genetics. Further research is needed to explore to what extent our limited conclusion holds when testing the US fair use concept in other technological sectors, such as ICT or telecom. At first sight, these sectors seem less prone to restrictive licensing behaviour. Due to the nature of the products, and to the importance of interoperability and compatibility, there is a recurrent need among companies to (cross-)license their patents. However, when dealing with standard essential patents, endless debates on the exact scope and level of FRAND licensing terms arise. The fair use concept might prove to be a valuable instrument in this context.

Future research could also provide a more advanced comparison of the US fair use exception and European functional look-alikes, such as the research exception and the compulsory licence. An investigation of the similarities and differences between the four fair use components in US patent law and the seven research exception parameters in European patent law[48] could shed some new light on the various motivations and approaches in Europe and the US in dealing with

[48] The first of those parameters relates to the *direct* goal of the research: is the research carried out *on* or *with* the patented device? A second parameter focuses on the *indirect* goal of the experiment: is the research performed with a commercial or non-commercial (fundamental) goal in mind? Especially this last criterion highly resembles the first fair use factor (*intent*). The seven parameters were the result of a comparative and in-depth analysis of the research exceptions in Germany, the

limitations in patent law. A study of the distinction between fair use and compulsory licence may trigger interesting discussions on the conditional/unconditional nature of use by third parties. In case of fair use, unconditional use by third users is allowed, whereas in the regime of compulsory licences, remuneration for the patent holder is often contemplated. The comparison becomes more challenging when one imagines that a fee would be charged for the fair use as well.[49]

Last but not least, future research might go beyond testing to what extent the current fair use factors may be operationalised in European patent law and might field test Strandburg's Patent Fair Use 2.0 Proposal. In case this research leads to the conclusion that the fair use doctrine is not amenable to European patent law, yet other alternatives will have to be contemplated to maintain the equilibrium between exclusive rights and public welfare in cases of unreasonable licensing behaviour.

Acknowledgements The author wishes to thank the International Association for the Advancement of Teaching and Research in Intellectual Property (ATRIP) for the opportunity to present a first draft of this paper at the annual conference organised in Vilnius in September 2009 on *Horizontal issues in IP law—Uncovering the matrix*. The author also wishes to express her gratitude to Reto Hilty, Marie-Christine Janssens, Kung-Chung Liu, Jerome H. Reichman, and Esther van Zimmeren for helpful comments and Anneleen Straetemans and Nicolas Van Aken for their research assistance. The author also gratefully acknowledges the support of the Vancraesbeeck Fund.

References

Baldwin T (2007) Ethics and patents for genetic diagnostic tests. In: Van Overwalle G (ed) Gene patents and public health. Bruylant, Brussel

Bessen J, Meurer M (2008) Patent failure: how judges, bureaucrats and lawyers put innovators at risk. Princeton University Press, New Jersey

Boldrin M, Levine DK (2008) Against intellectual monopoly. Cambridge University Press, Cambridge

Burk DL, Lemley MA (2009) The patent crisis and how the courts can solve it. The University of Chicago Press, Chicago

Caulfield T, Bubela T, Murdoch CJ (2007) Myriad and the mass media: the covering of a gene patent controversy. Genet Med 9:850–855

De Larena LR (2005) What copyright teaches patent law about "Fair Use" and why universities are ignoring the lessons. Oreg Law Rev 84:779

Drahos P (1996) A philosophy of intellectual property. Dartmouth Publishing Group, Aldershot

Gervais D (2003) The TRIPS Agreement. Drafting history and analysis. Sweet & Maxwell, London

Goldstein P (2001) International copyright. Principles, law and practice. Oxford University Press, Oxford

---

Netherlands, and Belgium; see Van Overwalle (2000). A somewhat more simplified approach—in terms of parameter analysis—can be found in van Zimmeren and Van Overwalle (2014).

[49] O'Rourke already reflected on *conditional* fair use, where a fee would be demanded; see O'Rourke (2000), at pp. 1234–1235.

Goldstein P, Hugenholtz PB (2010) International copyright. Principles, law and practice. Oxford University Press, Oxford
Guibault LMCR (2002), Copyright limitations and contracts. In: Information law series. Kluwer Law International, The Hague
Hart M (1998) The proposed directive for copyright in the information society: nice rights, shame about the exceptions. Eur Intellect Prop Rev 20:169
Hopkins M et al (2007) DNA patenting: the end of an era? Nat Biotechnol 25:185
Hugenholtz PB, Okediji RL (2008) Conceiving an international instrument on limitations and exceptions to copyright, 06 March 2008
Huys I, Van Overwalle G, Matthijs G (2011) Gene and genetic diagnostic method patent claims. A comparison under current European and US patent law. Eur J Hum Genet (EJHG) 19 (10):1104–1107
Huys I, Matthijs G, Van Overwalle G (2012) The fate and future of patents on human genes and genetic diagnostic methods. Nat Rev Genet 13(6):441–448
Jaffe AB, Lerner J (2004) Innovation and its discontents: how our broken patent system is endangering innovation and progress. Princeton University Press, Princeton
Jensen K, Murray F (2005) Intellectual property landscape of the human genome. Science 310:239
Legrand P (1997) The impossibility of legal transplants. Maastricht J Eur Comp Law 4:111ff
Machlup F (1959) Review of the patent system. Study for the United States Senate, Washington D.C.
Matthijs G (2007) DNA diagnostics in practice. In: Van Overwalle G (ed) Gene patents and public health. Bruylant, Brussel
Matthijs G, Hodgson S (2008) The impact of patenting on DNA diagnostic practice. Clin Med 8:58–60
Matthijs G, Huys I, Van Overwalle G, Stoppa-Lyonnet D (2013) The European breast cancer gene patent oppositions and appeals: coloring in the lines. Nat Biotechnol 31:704–710
O'Rourke MA (2000) Toward a doctrine of fair use in patent law. Columbia Law Rev 100:1117
Penrose ET (1951) The economics of the international patent system. John Hopkins Press, Baltimore
Pintens W (1998) Inleiding tot de rechtsvergelijking. Universitaire Pers, Leuven
Reichman JH, Okediji RL (2012) When copyright law and science collide: empowering digitally integrated research methods on a global scale. Legal studies research paper series. Research Paper No. 13-03, University of Minnesota Law School
Samuelson P (2008–2009) Unbundling fair uses. Fordham Law Rev 2537
Sheehan J, Guellec D, Martinez C (2003) Business patenting and licensing: results from the OECD/BIAC survey. In: Patents, innovation and economic performance, proceedings of the OECD conference on IPR, Innovation and economic performance, 28 August 2003
Sterckx S (2005) The ethics of patenting – uneasy justifications. In: Drahos P (ed) Death of patents. Lawtext Publishing, Oxon, pp 175–211
Strandburg KJ (2011) Patent fair use 2.0. Univ Calif (UC) Irvine Law Rev 265
Strowel A (1993) Droit d'auteur et copyright – Divergences et convergences. Bruylant, Brussels
Van Overwalle G (2000) Klinische proeven en volksgezondheid. Naar een herijking van het algemeen belang in het octrooirecht [Clincial trials and public health. Reassessing the notion of public interest in patent law]. Tijdschrift voor Privaatrecht (TPR) [J Priv Law] 899–968. http://ssrn.com/abstract=1718619
Van Overwalle G (2007) Gene patents and public health. Setting the scene. In: Van Overwalle G (ed) Gene patents and public health. Bruylant, Brussel, pp 11–24
Van Overwalle G, van Zimmeren E (2009) Functions and limits of patent law. In: Claes E, Devroe W, Keirsbilck B (eds) Facing the limits of the law. Springer, Heidelberg, pp 415–442
van Zimmeren E (2011) Towards a new patent paradigm in the biomedical sector? Facilitating access, open innovation and social responsibility in patent law in the US, Europe and Japan. PhD Thesis, University of Leuven, 16 May 2011
van Zimmeren E, Van Overwalle G (2011) A paper tiger? Compulsory license regimes for public health in Europe. Int Rev Intellect Prop Competition Law (IIC) 42:4–40

van Zimmeren E, Van Overwalle G (2014) A false sense of security offered by zero-price liability rules? Research exceptions in the US, Europe and Japan in an open innovation context. In: Okediji R, Bagley M (eds) Global perspectives on patent law. Oxford, Oxford University Press, 379–417

Watson A (1993) Legal transplants. Edinburgh, 1974 – Athens

Watson A (2000) Legal transplants and European private law (Ius Commune Lectures on European Private Law). Electronic J Comp Law 4.4. http://www.ejcl.org/ejcl/44/44-2.html. Last visited 18 June 2013

World Intellectual Property Indicators (2011) WIPO economics & statistics series. World Intellectual Property Organization, Geneva

Zweigert K, Kötz H (1996) Einführung in die Rechtsvergleichung auf dem Gebiete des Privatrechts. Mohr, Tübingen

Economic and Procedural Constraints of Compulsory Licences for Medicines

Yugank Goyal

Contents

Abstract The chapter argues that since there is no conclusive evidence for a causal relationship between the issuance of compulsory licences (CL) for medicines and any fall in innovation or foreign direct investment (FDI) inflow, various other factors like predictability and market potential need to be taken into account for understanding the after-effects of a grant of CL. The chapter examines the trends in CLs after the Doha Declaration and carves out a case for adhering to transparent procedures for imparting some predictability to the process in order to mitigate losses from possible repercussions.

Y. Goyal is Associate Professor. Ph.D. Candidate at the University of Hamburg, Germany.

Y. Goyal
Honorary Research Fellow, Jindal Global Law School. University of Hamburg, Hamburg, Germany
e-mail: ygoyal@jgu.edu.in; yugank.goyal@edle-phd.eu

R.M. Hilty and K.-C. Liu (eds.), *Compulsory Licensing*, MPI Studies on Intellectual Property and Competition Law 22, DOI 10.1007/978-3-642-54704-1_21,

1 Compulsory Licensing

Intellectual property rights (IPR) awards temporary exclusivity to the right holder with a view to providing incentives to innovate. However, this very exclusivity drives the prices up, resulting in shrinking of the market. Designing an optimal IPR framework therefore demands a compromise between the costs of deadweight losses against benefits of increased investments in innovation.

The case of pharmaceutical inventions is particularly tricky. While the innovation in pharmaceutical products is highly expensive in the form of R&D costs, the social costs of these patents are also very high.[1] Patents on pharmaceutical drugs, while crucial for inventing new drugs, create monetary barriers to access to medicines. In cases that invoke normative principles of health policies, therefore, one can imagine the role of the state. Whenever the value of the deadweight loss becomes unaffordable (as it happens in the case of life-saving medicines), the government may need to step in and mandate the right holder to license its intellectual property to a third party, which can then make the invention accessible to people outside its reach. In other words, a compulsory licence (CL) provides a national government with the authority to practise an invention covered by a patent (or copyright) or authorise another party to do so without permission from the patent holder.[2] Since the structure of IPR rests squarely within the domain and principle of property rights,[3] such licensing structures bring liability rules into the game.[4] CL has been incorporated in the international regulatory framework, in the Trade Related Aspects of IP Rights (TRIPS) Agreement, with certain terms and conditions spelt out therein.

2 Impact on Incentives to Innovate and Foreign Direct Investment

The idea linking CL with incentives to innovate has been studied, with no conclusive result. While some scholars have argued the conventional wisdom that CLs induce inefficiency in the form of reduced incentives to innovate,[5] there are many results that dispute such conclusions. Fisch (1994) has tried to establish that CL reduces investments into research by comparing innovation activities in Canada and

[1] See, for e.g., Balasubramaniam (2002).

[2] See Cahoy (2008), p. 141.

[3] Mazzoleni and Nelson (1998), p. 273, show that conventional thinking among economists, lawyers, and many public officials is heavily weighted towards the proposition that 'patent rights are conducive to economic progress'.

[4] For a very interesting study on this, see Reichman and Lewis (2005).

[5] Gilbert and Shapiro (1996), pp. 12753–12754, briefly mention how compulsory licence may reduce efficiency.

the USA in a period when the former was going through an intense programme of CL and had much lower investment in research. Bird and Cahoy (2008) and, much earlier, Lee and Mansfield (1996) argued that CL will reduce the flow of FDI in the country. Yet as the Eastman Commission reveals, if compared to other developed countries, CL did not significantly erode the innovation in Canada.[6] This was largely because Canada's market was rather insignificant to the worldwide market for pharmaceuticals.[7]

In a classic study of 700 companies (various industries, including pharmaceuticals), 42 of which were subject to CL, Scherer (1977) notes that these 42 companies actually spent more on R&D. Evidence on the impact of CL on FDI is primarily anecdotal, and it is difficult to derive anything out of it. A very interesting study by Moser and Voena (2012) uses an exogenous event of CL after World War I, under the 'Trading With the Enemy Act', to examine the effect of CL on domestic innovation. Analysing around 130,000 chemical inventions, Moser and Voena conclude that compulsory licensing increased innovation by about 20 %.[8] Stephenie Lee (2011) does a similar study for World War II and again finds a positive correlation between CL and domestic innovation activities. Indeed, the economic literature suggests that learning by doing plays an integral role in increasing productivity.[9]

There is no conclusive correlation that CL hurts incentives to innovation and affects FDI negatively. In fact, predominantly, the factors on which the correlation depends are (a) predictability of imposition of CL and (b) relative importance of the market.[10] Uncertain licences will have high social costs indeed because companies will engage in wasteful precautions against the uncertainties. Having no idea about the patent protection regime, and having understood that CLs will be granted at the whims of the government, a company may not even enter the market at all. But this will hurt only smaller economies and is unlikely to affect countries where companies will have a lot to lose. This result cannot be conclusive universally, and even in poor nations robust analysis needs to be done. As I show below, the reactions of the pharmaceutical industry towards specific instances of issuance of CLs was not consistent across a range of countries. Rather, it was a response towards capriciousness of the government's decisions and was more pronounced when the country in question was an insignificant market. In many of these countries, the market shows great promise, and hence costs of CL are internalised in the discounted future profits that the market promises to the international firms.

---

[6] See, for this study, McFetridge (1998).

[7] Ibid, p. 84 (McFetridge reports that with the exception of Merck, 1994, Canadian R&D expenditures as a percentage of worldwide expenditures were less than 2 %; e.g. 1.3 % for Glaxo, 1.0 % for Hoffman LaRoche, 0.7 % for Pfizer, 1.2 % for Sandoz, 1.4 % for Ciba, 1.7 % for Eli Lilly, and 6.1 % for Merck).

[8] Moser and Voena (2012), p. 404. They also conclude that this increase of 20 % took 8 to 9 years to set in and remained statistically significant throughout the 1930s (p. 409).

[9] Foster and Rosenzweig (1995), p. 1205.

[10] Chien (2003), pp. 891–892.

It may be worthwhile to model these intuitions. The structure is clear from the diagram below. Consider, for example, that π_m is profit earned by the patent holder in the event there is no CL and let π_{CL} be the profits earned when CL is imposed. Consider also T as the discounted value of time, and let L be the licence fee (royalty). For simplicity, we assume that royalty is per period and not fixed. All the above values (except T) are in any modern currency that retains the same value throughout the length of the patent, and all values are per year values. Therefore, the value of T is as follows.

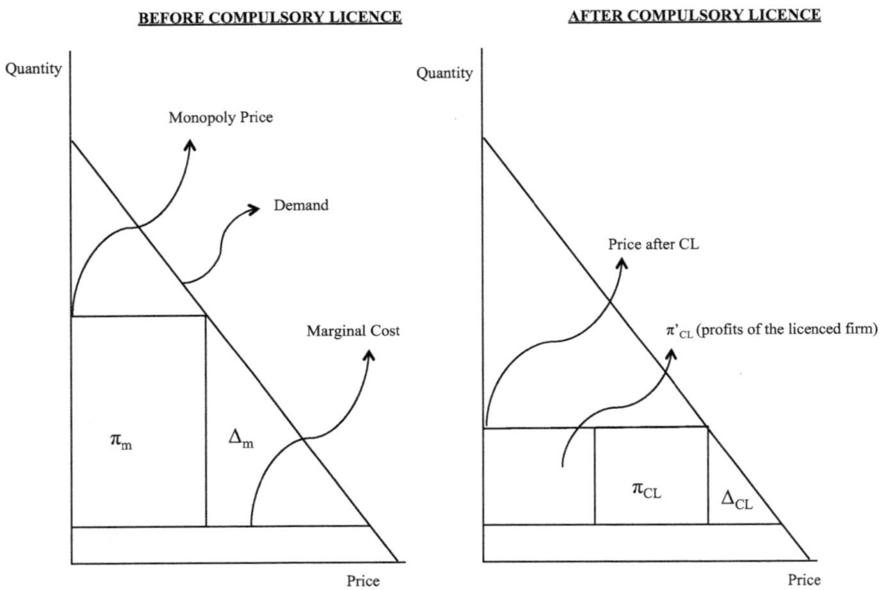

Graphs showing change in values of monopoly revenues and deadweight losses before and after CL grant

Let the present discounted value for the duration of the CL be h_{CL} and the same value for perpetuity be h. We then compare the social gain of CL discounted with h_{CL} and the loss in FDI and incentives to innovate, discounted with h. Let the value of the loss by either reduction in incentives to innovate or lower FDI be denoted by F.

For the CL to be socially desirable,

$$(\Delta_m - \Delta_{CL})h_{CL} \geq hF$$

$$h_{CL} \geq \left(\frac{F}{\Delta_m - \Delta_{CL}}\right)h$$

Assuming T is continuous,

Then, $h_{CL} = \int_{t=0}^{t=\infty} e^{-rt}dt$ and $h = \int_{t=0}^{t=\infty} e^{-rt}dt$, where r is the discount rate and x is the duration of the CL.

For perpetuity, $h = \frac{1}{r}$.

Hence,

$$\int_{t=0}^{t=x} e^{-rt}dt \geq \frac{F/r}{(\Delta_{\mathrm{m}} - \Delta_{\mathrm{CL}})},$$

$$F \leq (\Delta_{\mathrm{m}} - \Delta_{\mathrm{CL}})r \int_{t=0}^{t=x} e^{-rt}dt.$$

The equation shows that loss due to falling FDI inflow increases with increasing discount rates. For developing nations, the value of r is usually higher. Therefore, as income levels and market sizes of countries increase, their FDI falls less.

Note that the value of F also depends on the probability of imposition of CL. As forthcoming cases will show, companies that choose to impose a cost of F over countries that grant the CL do so only after the licence has been imposed, but the countries need to expect this *ex ante*. In other words, countries have a probability estimate of imposition of trade sanctions, loss of FDI, or drop in the innovation rate for diseases particularly germane to their countries, and their actions that result in F are dependent upon that probability estimate. Hence $F = f(\theta)$ and $f'(\theta) > 0$ (I denote the probability by $\theta \in [0, 1]$, and F is increasing in θ).

This is easy to understand intuitively. If the loss of future profits accruing from a drop in either innovation or FDI is huge, the government would want to reduce the expected probability of issuing a CL, and if one were issued, it would aim to diminish the losses. This can be achieved by crystallising the legal conditions and provisions through which the CL decision and implementation are carved out.

3 Observing the Post-Doha Trends

It has been almost two decades since CL was institutionalised in the international regulatory framework. In the beginning, it was felt that this tool would be employed frequently by developing nations since the gap between demand and low-price supply was huge in such countries.[11] It is interesting to note that, except for few systematic assessments of the impact of Doha,[12] there is hardly any research on the pattern of CL activities around the world.

One effort, however, conducted by Beall and Kuhn (2012) deserves special mention. It concludes that the occurrence of CL has been rather modest. They

[11] See, e.g., Banta (2001), p. 2656; see also Kanth (2003).

[12] See, generally, Smith et al. (2009); see also Chaves and Oliveira (2007), pp. 51–54 (focus on Latin American and Caribbean countries).

study 24 international CL episodes from 1 January 1995 through 6 June 2011, involving 40 drug patents of 22 pharmaceutical products. They found that almost half of the CLs were transformed into voluntary licensing or discounted prices.[13] Two-thirds of the total licences were declared for AIDS/HIV.[14] Although the period between 1995 and 2000 saw no activity of CL,[15] this pattern—as expected—was reversed in 2003–2005, when the greatest number of CL programs was implemented, mostly on anti-retroviral drugs.[16] Surprisingly, however, the period between 2006 and 2011 has seen a fair drop in these numbers.[17] Through a quick glance at recent cases of CL, it may be pertinent to view qualitatively the extent to which CL has been invoked in the past 10 years.

Indeed, even though we know that global access to medicines has increased in the last decade, a large chunk of it has actually been on account of bilateral aid, public–private partnership, or increased philanthropic activity.[18] There is a need to assess the sociopolitical factors through which CL is implemented. For purposes of this section, I attempt to briefly categorise and elaborate on the CLs that have been declared from 2000 onwards on pharmaceutical products. I prepare a working inventory of the same and propose key points of each of the cases very briefly, laying open the idea of its impact on HIV prevalence (Table 1) and FDI (Table 2).

The table illustrates the CLs, their specific scope, and the FDI inflow after the grant of CL in the country. While the tables do not exhibit any causal relation between the incident of CL and impact on FDI and HIV prevalence, they do present the extent to which they can be correlated. Indeed, the net FDI inflow is a factor of several sectors and not just pharmaceuticals. Yet fears surrounding CLs' adverse impact on net FDI are examined in the second table. The results do not support the claim that CLs reduce FDI. The table also shows, for each country where anti-retroviral (ARV) drugs were granted CLs, patterns in HIV instances and deaths. The data on HIV prevalence serve two purposes. Firstly, they show the gravity of the problem, justifying the use of CL, and, secondly, they help build a case for whether the change in HIV-related deaths (mentioned in the next column) is attributable to reduction in HIV prevalence or is because of availability of cheaper drugs through CL. While this table fails to show the contribution of CL as one factor in the reduction of HIV, as there could be many others (like increased information, literacy, use of contraceptives, and the like), it is powerfully instructive in gauging the prevalence of the disease. The number of HIV-related deaths (in the last

[13] Beall and Kuhn (2012), p. 3. Note that through compulsory licensing, countries can threaten pharmaceutical companies to discipline their pricing behaviour. These disciplining strategies have been discussed (for Thailand and Brazil) in Feldman (2009), pp. 151–155.

[14] Ibid, p. 4.

[15] Ibid.

[16] Ibid.

[17] Ibid.

[18] Beall and Kuhn (2012), p. 3.

Table 1 Brief illustration of events that invoked CL around the world, from 2000 until 2012

Year	Country	Firm/Drug/Disease	Remarks	FDI inflow[a]	HIV prevalence[b]	HIV-related deaths[c] (in '000)		
						2001	2006	2011
2002	Egypt	Pfizer/Sildenafil/erectile dysfunction	Only 2 months after Pfizer's entry into Egypt's market, the government granted CL citing interests of the poor. Pfizer stopped investments into the proposed production facility in Egypt	Increased from 2003–2007, fell thereafter	NA	NA		
2002–2003	Zimbabwe	Varichem Pharma/ARVs/AIDS	Licence was issued after a period of emergency on AIDS was declared, and patent protection of ARVs was suspended.[d] The CL allowed this local manufacturer to produce the drug during this emergency period (initially imposed for 6 months, then extended to 5 years).[e] It was a precedent for low-income countries, but Zimbabwe's international isolation did not carry the inspiration forward in Africa	Increased since 2003 (except for minor a fall in 2005–2006)	Fell consistently from 22.5 to 15 % of the population from 2003 until 2011	20	20	20

(continued)

Table 1 (continued)

Year	Country	Firm/Drug/Disease	Remarks	FDI inflow[a]	HIV prevalence[b]	HIV-related deaths[c] (in '000)		
						2001	2006	2011
2003	Malaysia	Bristol Myers Squibb and GlaxoSmithKline/ Didanosine, Zidovudine, and Lamivudine +Zidovudine/AIDS	Authorisation for CL was granted to import generics from India, valid for 2 years and 4 % royalties, reducing prices by more than 80 %,[f] which increased patient reach from 1,500 to 4,000. Companies threatened withdrawal and argued they would create an international precedent, but to no avail	Increased, except between 2008 and 2009	Remained almost constant at 0.4 % of the population	4.9	6	5.9
2004	Zambia	Boehringer-Ingelheim and Bristol-Myers Squibb/ various/AIDS	The CL was issued for a domestic company to manufacture the drug with royalties of 2.5 % of total turnover but prohibited export[g]	Increased, except in 2007–2009	Declined from 2003 until 2011, from 14.2 to 12.5 % of the population	72	67	31
2004	Mozambique	Bristol Myers Squibb, GlaxoSmithKline and Boehringer Ingelheim/ Lamivudine, Stavudine and Nevirapine/Various/AIDS	The CL announced royalties reaching 2 % of the sales, and licence was given to a local manufacturer. The reason for issuing the licence was inaccessibility of the ARVs at an affordable	Fell slightly between 2003 and 2005 but has increased rapidly since then	Slightly increased (10.8 to 11.3 % of the population) from 2003 until 2007 and has remained constant since then	46	79	74

			price to a country where close to 11 % of the population suffered from HIV[h]					
2005	Ghana	Various/ARVs/AIDS	Government use licence was issued by the Ministry of Health. A Canadian-based manufacturer decided to supply the drug after CL, but later an Indian generic manufacturer did so[i]	Increased since 2005, except a slight fall in 2008–2009	Fell from 2 to 1.5 % of the population between 2005 and 2011	18	22	15
2005	Indonesia	Boehringer Ingelheim/Lamivudine and Nevirapine/AIDS	In 2004, the government intended to increase access to ARVs but the price of the medicine was too high. A Presidential Decree was issued authorising 0.5 % royalty CL until the end of patent term	Decreased between 2005 and 2006 and 2008 and 2009 but increased during other years	Increased slightly from 0.1 to 0.4 % of the population between 2005 and 2011	<0.2	3.3	15
2005	Taiwan	Roche/Osetamivir/Avian Flu	Owing to the threat of the avian flu, and unsure of Roche's plans to make the drug accessible to Taiwan's population, the government issued a licence to allow the local manufacture of the drug[j]	Fell between 2006 and 2008 but peaked by 2010[k]	NA	NA		

(continued)

Table 1 (continued)

						HIV-related deaths[c] (in '000)		
Year	Country	Firm/Drug/Disease	Remarks	FDI inflow[a]	HIV prevalence[b]	2001	2006	2011
2006–2007	Thailand	Merck/Efavirenz/AIDS	The generics coming from India were half the price of patented medicine. Royalty was 0.5 %. The CL was renewed in 2010. The second wave of CLs came for drugs used for treatments of various kinds of cancers. The new government planned to revoke the licence but, owing to public and civil society pressures, was unable to do so. This was the first time a developing country used CL for a non-communicable disease, attracting a lot of criticism. The CL was renewed in 2010. Industry response was aggravated[1]	Dipped between 2007 and 2009	Fell from 1.4 to 1.1 % of the population between 2005 and 2011	62	34	23
		Novartis, Sanofi-Aventis and Roche/various/Cancers			NA	NA		
		Abbott and Sanofi-Aventis/Lopinavir +ritonavir and Clopidogre/AIDS and cardiovascular			NA	NA		
2007	Brazil	Merck/Efavirenz/AIDS	After threats in 2001, Merck agreed to offer huge discounts. In 2007, however, Brazil issued the CL to buy the drug from an Indian	Minor drop only in 2008–2009	Slight drop from 0.4 to 0.3 % between 2008 and 2011	11	12	15

			generic manufacturer at further reduced price. Merck reacted furiously. The US expressed concern, yet Brazil's tactful diplomatic dealing avoided any major repercussions. Brazil has achieved frequent successes in compelling firms to reduce their prices using CL as a threat[m]					
2007	Rwanda	Apotex/Lamivudine+Nevirapine+Zidovudine/AIDS	CL was granted for importing the drug from Canada through para 6 of Doha Declaration. The CL was valid for 2 years, but delivery of the drug was delayed due to procedural bottlenecks[n]	Increased significantly from 2006–2009 but suffered a drop in 2009–2010	Fell from 3.0 to 2.9 % of the population between 2007 and 2011	21	16	6.4
2010	Ecuador	Abbott/Lopinavir+ritonavir/AIDS	CL was given to an Indian generic manufacturer until the patent's expiry. The prices were slashed by 27 %[o]	Increased in 2010–2011	Consistent through 2003 until 2011 at 0.4 % of the population	2.6	2.2	2
2012	India	Bayer/Sorafenib/Cancer	The CL was granted by the judiciary, and it gave licence to Natco to manufacture the drug at 6 % royalty and licence to last until the end of patent term[p]	NA	NA	NA		

(continued)

Table 1 (continued)

Year	Country	Firm/Drug/Disease	Remarks	FDI inflow[a]	HIV prevalence[b]	HIV-related deaths[c] (in '000)		
						2001	2006	2011
2012	Indonesia	Various/Various/AIDS and Hepatitis B	Six licences in one decree were granted. The royalty rate was set at 0.5 % and licenses until patent's expiry[q]	NA	NA	NA		

[a]Unless specified, data available at http://data.worldbank.org/indicator/BX.KLT.DINV.CD.WD/countries?display=graph last accessed on 1 June 2013

[b]This column reflects population percentage infected with HIV between 15 and 49 years of age. Collected from World Bank Data Repository, http://data.worldbank.org/indicator/SH.DYN.AIDS.ZS/countries?display=graph last accessed on 20 May 2013

[c]Data collected from Global Health Data Repository, World Health Organisation, available at http://apps.who.int/gho/data/node.main.623?lang=en. Table shows average values

[d]The General Notice for Declaration of Emergency can be found at http://www.cptech.org/ip/health/c/zimbabwe/zim05242002.html. During an emergency, the State has rights and powers as espoused in their Patents Act, Section 35, available at http://www.cptech.org/ip/health/c/zimbabwe/art35.html (all these webpages were last accessed on 20 May 2013)

[e]Bucknell (2007)

[f]Authorisation document available at http://www.cptech.org/ip/health/c/malaysia/arv-license.html last accessed on 20 May 2013

[g]The Compulsory License Order is available at http://www.cptech.org/ip/health/c/zambia/zcl.html last accessed on 20 May 2013

[h]Licence copy available at http://www.cptech.org/ip/health/c/mozambique/moz-cl-en.pdf last accessed on 1 June 2013

[i]Notification of the CL is available at http://www.cptech.org/ip/health/cl/Ghana.png last accessed on 1 June 2013

[j]See Leonard (2006)

[k]Data for Taiwan collected from http://unctadstat.unctad.org/ReportFolders/reportFolders.aspx?sCS_referer=&sCS_ChosenLang=en last accessed on 20 May 2013

[l]Fuller (2007)

[m]Petersen and Rohter (2011)

[n]Tsai (2009)

[o]Saez (2010)

[p]David (2007)

[q]Text of Indonesia compulsory licence is available at http://lists.essential.org/pipermail/ip-health/2004-December/007233.html last accessed on 1 June 2013

Table 2 The Pattern of in rise and fall of FDI after CL (source of FDI calculation: World Development Indicators, World Bank)

Country	Year of CL grant	Change in FDI, net inflows (in % terms, with falls in FDI mentioned in parenthesis)									
		2002–2003	2003–2004	2004–2005	2005–2006	2006–2007	2007–2008	2008–2009	2009–2010	2010–2011	2011–2012
Egypt	2002	(0.63)	4.28	3.29	0.87	0.15	(0.18)	(0.29)	(0.05)	(1.08)	(0.63)
Zimbabwe	2002–2003	(0.85)	1.29	10.82	(0.61)	0.72	(0.25)	1.03	0.58	1.33	(0.85)
Malaysia	2003	(0.23)	0.87	(0.15)	0.96	0.18	(0.17)	(0.98)	78.95	0.31	(0.23)
Zambia	2004	0.16	0.12	(0.08)	0.73	1.15	(0.29)	(0.26)	1.49	0.15	0.16
Mozambique	2004	(0.03)	(0.27)	(0.50)	0.51	1.25	0.34	0.60	0.12	1.07	(0.03)
Ghana	2005	1.32	0.02	0.04	3.39	1.17	0.96	(0.13)	0.07	0.27	1.32
Thailand	2006–2007	0.57	0.12	0.37	0.17	0.20	(0.25)	(0.43)	0.88	(0.15)	0.57
Brazil	2007	(0.39)	0.79	(0.15)	0.25	1.30	0.14	(0.38)	0.69	0.34	(0.39)
Rwanda	2007	0.78	0.65	0.05	0.40	4.98	0.54	0.15	(0.64)	1.50	0.78
Ecuador	2010	0.11	(0.04)	(0.41)	(0.45)	(0.28)	4.18	(0.68)	(0.51)	2.59	0.11
India	2012	(0.23)	0.34	0.26	1.76	0.26	0.72	(0.18)	(0.26)	0.21	(0.23)
Indonesia	2012	(5.11)	(4.18)	3.40	(0.41)	0.41	0.34	(0.48)	1.82	0.32	(5.11)
World		(0.09)	0.25	0.93	0.23	0.46	(0.11)	(0.47)	0.16	0.23	(0.09)

column) is not only correlated but also causal. Prevention of deaths is largely because of access to ARVs, which prolong patient's life.

A few important points emerge:

a. There is no reason to believe that CLs will usually result in loss of total FDI into a country. In fact, most of the countries that witnessed loss in FDI during 2008–2009 were actually suffering from the impact of the financial recession that rocked the world during that time (see the last row of the second table, which shows the change in FDI around the world).
b. Attributing reduced FDI to CL is unfounded because, firstly, the FDI is not necessarily decreasing and, secondly, the loss is general across all countries during the time of global economic slowdown.
c. Mozambique and Indonesia suffered a loss in FDI immediately after issuing the CL (which is not attributable to the 2008–2009 financial meltdown). Mozambique has little market potential, and one can expect this. The reduction in Indonesia compels us to dig deeper into what was different about CL in Indonesia.
d. There is a significant impact in reducing the HIV-related deaths due to CL as witnessed in Zambia, Ghana, Thailand, and Rwanda.
e. Zimbabwe experienced a drop in HIV incidence, yet there is no difference in HIV-related deaths in the country. Perhaps this only shows poor supply chain management of drugs. That said, this is only a cursory glance, and more detailed analysis needs to be undertaken.

Overall, the tables reveal that net FDI inflow practically remains immune to CL imposition. CL definitely has a positive effect on public health. The differing experiences in post-CL scenarios are illustrated by how firms react to the issuance of CL. This, in turn, raises important questions in cases of whimsical attitudes towards procedural scrupulousness and predictability. In other words, by being procedurally inappropriate, governments attract a lot more ire from firms than if they had followed principles prescribed in the domestic and international legal framework. I will discuss some cases that explain this in greater detail.

3.1 Egypt

Egypt's law on CL is vague and ambiguous, giving its huge scope.[19] Merely 2 months after Pfizer's entry in 2002, the Ministry granted an authorisation to produce Viagra (which is not a life-saving drug) to all Egyptian companies that applied to do so, citing interests of the poor.[20] This led to Pfizer stopping all future

[19] For a discussion of Egypt's CL statute in the copyright context, see International Intellectual Property Alliance 2006: Special 301 Report Egypt.

[20] Castellano (2006), p. 289.

FDIs to Egypt and scrapping the plan to set up a manufacturing plant in Egypt.[21] Trade sanctions followed shortly after Egypt was put on the 'Priority Watch List'.

Indeed, such reckless use and thoughtless application may do more harm than good. Bird has argued that efforts to reduce the prices of any medicines in the interest of public health must be accompanied by a scrupulous approach that aims to distribute drugs not only at the lowest profitable prices but also with fair and adequate compensation to the patentees.[22] The issue in Egypt was "tainted by the appearance of impropriety and self dealing",[23] which deserves serious attention. The Pharmaceutical Research and Manufacturers Association of American (PhRMA) informed Egypt that its weak intellectual property laws deterred PhRMA from investing US$300 million in Egypt's pharmaceutical sector.[24]

As of today, however, Egypt's pharmaceutical industry is expected to enjoy a compound annual growth rate of more than 11 % by 2014, which has been truly unprecedented.[25] And this growth is largely attributed to the drug pricing reform, which makes generics a more viable option, with numerous drug makers already setting up their units in the country.[26] The 2002 event is unlikely to have a sustained impact on Egypt's economy in the long run. However, we should not miss the fact that Egypt did refrain from granting any further CL in the same manner after that. There is a need to proceed with the exercise with caution, in particular viewing CL as a last resort vis-à-vis life-saving drugs.

3.2 India

India followed a scrupulous procedure to grant its first CL, craftily invoking relevant sections in the Indian Patents Act 2005. The licence was granted for Sorafenib tosylate, an anti-cancer medicine for the treatment of primary kidney and advanced primary liver cancer. India has been called a 'pharmacy for the developing world'[27] due to its generic drug production and yet has one of the lowest levels of access to medicines. Keeping this in mind, and invoking Section 84 (1), the Court decided to grant CL at a royalty of 6 % (based on United Nations

[21] Bird (2009), p. 212.

[22] Ibid, p. 214.

[23] Reichman (2009), p. 254.

[24] Aziz (2003), p. 22.

[25] *See* "Egypt Pharmaceutical and Healthcare Report Q3 2010," *Business Monitor International,* May 2010; available at http://www.researchandmarkets.com/research/d4a32f/egypt_pharmaceutic last accessed on 1 June 2013.

[26] Ibid.

[27] See, for example, Médecins Sans Frontières Campaign for Access to Essential Medicines, background paper, "Examples of the Importance of India as the 'Pharmacy for the Developing World'," available at http://www.doctorswithoutborders.org/news/access/background_paper_indian_generics.pdf last accessed on 1 June 2013.

Development Programme guidelines) until the patent's expiry, leading to a reduction in the price by 97 %.

The procedure that India had adopted involved the judiciary, which came out with a coherent judgment for a complex case that ran for more than 2 years. The faith in the judiciary in India appears to have justified the way problem was confronted. The royalty rate was set at the upper limit of the UNDP's guidelines. Indeed, since the Indian pharmaceutical market is huge, and multinationals are going to suffer enormous losses if they pack up and leave, the Indian programme has an edge over smaller economies. The Indian case therefore involved both the adoption of the right procedure and a heavyweight economy that promises large future returns, in contrast to a minor drop in revenues in the short term. This is the most effective utilisation of CL.

3.3 Brazil

Brazil became TRIPS compliant in 1996.[28] Then between 2002 and 2006, it issued repeated threats to issue CLs.[29] Coupled with a strong local generic industry, the prices of anti-retrovirals were substantially brought down. Of particular interest was the case of granting CL for an anti-retroviral drug (efivarenz) manufactured by Merck at 1.5 % royalty for 5 years, with a price reduction of 93 %.

This resulted in a lot of diplomatic pressure on Brazil. However, Brazil handled the problem quite well and showed remarkable skills of negotiating around the social costs of CL. Brazil embedded CL provisions in its Intellectual Property Law in 1997 (Law number 9279). The statute covering CL is quite broad, which, inter alia, requires the patentee to begin manufacturing the drug in Brazil within 3 years of grant of patent, unless it can show that it reasonably can't.[30] When the USA responded harshly to this move and complained to the WTO, Brazil filed its own complaint challenging the USA's patent code that had similar undertones.[31] Brazil also made efforts to secure access to AIDS treatment as a human rights issue at the UNHRC.[32] It is no surprise therefore that no trade sanctions were pursued against Brazil.[33]

---

[28] For a detailed treatment of Brazil's history of use of compulsory licensing in expanding access, see Marques et al. (2005).

[29] See ibid, pp. 474–476.

[30] See, for e.g., Articles 68 and 71. Article 68 requires that, within 3 years of obtaining a patent, the patent holder must manufacture the subject matter of the patent in Brazil, unless the patent holder can show that local production is not economically feasible or reasonable. Article 71 states that, through an act of the Federal Executive Authorities, a compulsory licence may be granted in cases of "national emergency or public interest".

[31] Bird and Cahoy (2008), p. 313.

[32] Passarelli and Terto (2002), p. 42.

[33] See chapter "The Use of Compulsory Licences in Latin America" by Carlos M. Correa in this volume.

Brazil, interestingly, has also made successful attempts to negotiate with the pharmaceutical companies to lower prices in a series of events. Long before the CL was awarded, Merck had reduced the prices of its drugs in 2001. Through negotiations over invoking CL, Brazil also brought Roche to reduce the prices of nelfinavir (for HIV) by 40 %.[34] In similar way, in 2005, Abbott[35] and Gilead[36] also reduced prices of their HIV drugs to 40–50 %. So it was only when these negotiations failed that Brazil imposed the CL. Brazil is a case worth emulating. It not only carefully selected its target drugs and firms, and concluded successful rounds of negotiation, but also developed an international perception of its image as a health- and patent-friendly nation. Indeed, the response in terms of FDI in Brazil has shown very healthy signs.

3.4 Indonesia

In 2004, Indonesia issued a government use CL on lamivudine and nevirapine until the end of the patent term in 2011 and 2012, respectively, with 0.5 % royalty.[37] However, in September 2012, the government of Indonesia made headlines by granting a set of government use CLs[38] on six drugs (manufactured by five companies) that are used for the treatment of HIV and hepatitis B. The decree licenses patents for a slate of HIV medicines and may represent the broadest single use of the power to grant CL by a country since 1995. All the licences are issued until the end of the patent term, with a royalty rate at 0.5 %.[39]

Indonesia is the largest pharmaceutical market in Southeast Asia. It has been attracting the attention of foreign drug makers for several years. It has the fourth largest population in the world at 250 million, and this is growing at 4 % every year. It is no surprise then that the Economist Intelligence Unit expects pharmaceutical sales to rise by over 11 % a year over the next 5 years in local currency terms, from an estimated US$6.8 billion in 2011.[40] Yet there are criticisms from the industry on

[34] Rich (2001).

[35] For details of this case, see Bjornberg (2006).

[36] Palermo (2008).

[37] van Gelder and Stevens (2010), pp. 5–6.

[38] There are certain advantages of government use licences over CLs procedurally under the TRIPS Agreement, the most notable of which is the ability to proceed with the issuance of the government use licence in the absence of failed prior negotiations with the patent holder, and they are thus easier to issue in the face of a medical emergency, for example. At the same time, a government use licence would limit the choice of firms that could import or produce using that licence to government ministries and state-owned enterprises.

[39] A rough English translation can be found at http://www.citizen.org/documents/PresidentalDecree20121.pdf last accessed on 1 June 2013.

[40] "Indonesia generics: a broad license," *The Economist Intelligence Unit*, 17 October 2012.

how CL may lead to a reduced investment in pharmaceuticals in Indonesia.[41] The FDI inflow in Indonesia fell after the grant of CL, and both HIV instances and deaths have increased in the last 10 years. Clearly, there is a need for Indonesia to re-articulate its strategy of increasing access to medicines through the use of CL in such a way that its efforts translate into reality. The reason why Indonesia was able to consider the issuance of CL confidently is because of its bargaining power vis-à-vis firms. Surprisingly, it has been documented that previously licensed drugs have become ineffective or less effective because the disease has gained resistance.[42] It is unclear whether the impact on FDI and innovation has been positive, but clearly policies towards access to medicines need to be streamlined.

3.5 Thailand

Between November 2006 and January 2007, Thailand issued CLs for three AIDS drugs, at 5 % royalty and varying durations. This allowed Thailand to import, distribute, and sell generic versions manufactured in India, where the three drugs are not patented. The generics were to be produced locally when the state-owned Government Pharmaceutical Organisation has developed the capacity to do so.[43]

In 2007, Thailand came under the Priority Watch List due to lack of transparency and due process regarding the grant of CL. The process followed by Thailand was rather opaque and whimsical. The decrees failed to give any justifiable reason for granting CL and were not preceded by a noticeable demand for such a move. The justification hinged on the high number of people affected by the disease, but analysis on the pricing mechanisms and adherence to the international framework was disturbingly brief. There was no negotiation with the patent holder before the issuance. The CL also didn't meet the requirements of 'public non-commercial use' when the CL was issued to a for-profit enterprise under the Ministry of Public Health.[44] It's no surprise then that shortly after the issuance of the CLs, in March 2007, Abbott Laboratories responded by electing not to launch any new products in Thailand.[45] There have been a number of international controversies surrounding the CL, and serious concerns remain with regard to the quality of medicines provided.[46]

---

[41] Ibid.

[42] Ibid.

[43] *See* original decrees available at http://www.cptech.org/ip/health/c/thailand/thai-cl-kaletra_en.pdf; http://www.cptech.org/ip/health/c/thailand/thaicl4efavirenz.html; http://www.cptech.org/ip/health/c/thailand/thai-cl-clopidogrel_en.pdf last accessed on 1 June 2013.

[44] See, for greater detail, the chapter "Compulsory Licences: Law and Practice in Thailand" by Jakkrit Kuanpoth in this volume.

[45] Fuller (2007).

[46] Lybecker and Fowler (2009), p. 234.

4 Conclusion

There is no conclusive evidence that CL hurts incentives to innovate. This perception is largely drawn from the reactionary approach taken by big multinational pharmaceutical companies, whose patents are bypassed through CLs. However, whether these firms actually end up withdrawing their investments is dependent more on the economic forces than their attitude of 'teaching governments a lesson'. Investments in R&D are huge sunk costs, and once undertaken, it is very difficult to turn back. *Ex ante*, therefore, what matters is the predictability of CL being issued. A procedurally sound implementation of CL acts as a device of credible commitment from the State to the firm. The firms that have made huge investments need to be sure that the State will credibly commit itself to protecting the investments. When States are compelled to breach this commitment, it has to be accompanied by a very strong and robust legal mechanism to provide an unbiased logic towards undermining the investments. In cases of CLs, states take a conscious decision to erode some investments of the firms, which need to be satisfied by providing ample grounds for taking such a step rather than implementing the decision whimsically. Firms also understand their role in access to medicines (and have therefore slashed prices of their drugs on States' insistence or threat). But if they feel that a country has proceeded in an irresponsible manner, ignoring procedural guidelines and acting on political fancy, they will rethink their future investments.

CL is a common resource. This means that consumption of that resource by one person or entity has very high private benefit, but costs (in the form of depletion of the resource) are shared thinly between all constituent members. In other words, there are incentives to overuse the tool (even though there have been very few instances of CLs, such possibilities cannot be ignored). And this creates what Hardin (1968) called the tragedy of the commons. If a country imposes a licence, the benefits accruing to the country concerned are immense. But if (at all) it results in diluted incentives to innovate, the costs are borne by those countries that have higher incidence of that disease, and for which R&D activities are stalled. These countries may also use CL. But before that, they would need innovations in medicines for diseases prevalent in their region. Indeed, pharmaceutical companies often invest in lifestyle drugs rather than life-saving drugs like malaria since the latter affect impoverished countries.[47] These very countries therefore bear the brunt of reduced innovation due to whimsical application of CL in other countries.

Therefore, reckless and frequent implementation of the tool will only blunt its sharpness in the long run. There is thus a need to understand and implement a framework for collaborative action that hinges on a pooled procurement strategy.[48] Consider a case when countries pool their demand for a certain drug and coordinate the usage of CL on that drug. This can encourage the patent holder to consider reducing the prices to affordable levels since the volume is enormous, enabling the

---

[47] Stiglitz (2009), p. 364.

[48] Abbott and Reichman (2007), pp. 969–981. Also see, generally, Reichman (2009).

patent holder to venture into new markets with its trademark and develop long-term investment plans. Incentives can be *calibrated* to companies' willingness to invest.[49]

The world has come a long way from the Paris Convention of 1883. And on this journey, the patent system around the world has gone through radical changes, at multiple levels. CL is a recent battle that the world of IPR seems to be fighting. There are powerful conflicting impulses that invoke different views of morality and philosophy. Exploring the silences in all these debates, I remain skeptical of the efficacy of the patent system that has abused the concept of innovation in the past two decades. Yet I am hopeful that with solidarity, the world's view will become clearer in the long run. We may have ended a journey with Article 31 of TRIPS and the Doha Declaration, but in this ever-changing world, where new meanings are derived from age-old concepts every day, a longer voyage remains.

References

Abbott FM, Reichman JH (2007) The Doha Round's public health legacy: strategies for the production and diffusion of patented medicines under the amended TRIPS provisions. J Int Econ Law 10:921–987

Aziz S (2003) Linking intellectual property rights in developing countries with research and development, technology transfer, and foreign direct investment policy: a case study of Egypt's pharmaceutical industry. ILSA J Int Comp Law 10(1)

Balasubramaniam K (2002) Access to medicines: patents, prices and public policy – consumer perspectives. In: Drahos P, Mayne R (eds) Global intellectual property rights: knowledge, access and development. Palgrave MacMillan, Hampshire

Banta D (2001) Public health triumphs at WTO conference. J Am Med Assoc 286:2655–2656

Beall R, Kuhn R (2012) Trends in compulsory licensing of pharmaceuticals since the Doha Declaration: a database analysis. PLoS Med 9(1):e1001154. doi:10.1371/journal.pmed.1001154

Bird RC (2009) Developing nations and the compulsory license: maximizing access to essential medicines while minimizing investment side effects. J Law Med Ethics 37:209–221

Bird R, Cahoy D (2008) The impact of compulsory licensing on foreign direct investment: a collective bargaining approach. Am Bus Law J 45:283–330

Bjornberg J (2006) Brazil's recent threat on Abbott's patent: resolution or retaliation? Northwestern J Int Law Bus 27:199–226

Bucknell D (2007) The global IP scorecard for Pharma and Biotech compulsory licences. Mondaq Business Briefing, 22 October. http://www.mondaq.com/australia/article.asp?articleid=53442. Last accessed 20 may 2013

Cahoy DR (2008) Confronting Myths and Myopia on the road from Doha. Georgia Law Rev 42:131–192

Castellano RA (2006) Note, patent law for new medical uses of known compounds and Pfizer's Viagra Patent. IDEA 46:283

Chaves GC, Oliveira MA (2007) A proposal for measuring the degree of public health-sensitivity of patent legislation in the context of the WTO TRIPS Agreement. Bull World Health Organisation 85:49–56

[49] Ibid, pp. 973–980.

Chien CV (2003) Cheap drugs at what price to innovation: does the compulsory licensing of pharmaceuticals hurt innovation? Berkeley Technol Law J 18:853–907

David R (2007) Novartis set back in India patent fight over Glivec. Forbes, 7 August. http://www.forbes.com/2007/08/07/novartis-glivec-generics-markets-equity-cx_rd_0807markets02.html. Last accessed 1 June 2013

Feldman J (2009) Compulsory licensing: dangers behind current practices. J Int Bus Law 8:137–167

Fisch AM (1994) Compulsory licensing of pharmaceutical patents: an unreasonable solution to an unfortunate problem. Jurimetrics 34:295–315

Foster AD, Rosenzweig MR (1995) Learning by doing and learning from others: human capital and technical change in agriculture. J Polit Econ 103:1176–1209

Fuller T (2007) Thailand takes on drug industry and may be winning. New York Times 11 April. http://www.nytimes.com/2007/04/11/world/asia/11iht-pharma.4.5240049.html?_r=1&pagewanted=1. Last accessed 1 June 2013

Gilbert R, Shapiro C (1996) An economic analysis of unilateral refusals to license intellectual property. Proc Acad Sci 93:12749–12755

Hardin G (1968) The tragedy of the commons. Science 162:1243–1248

Kanth R (2003) WTO drug deal to spark competition. Business Times, 2 September, Singapore

Lee S (2011) Compulsory licensing and domestic innovation: evidence from the Trading with the Enemy Act after World War II. Economics Department, Stanford University. http://economics.stanford.edu/files/Lee_HThesis2011.pdf. Accessed 1 June 2013

Lee J, Mansfield E (1996) Intellectual property protection and U.S. Foreign Direct Investment. Rev Econ Stat 78:181–186

Leonard A (2006) Adventures with Tamiflu. Salon, 7 September. http://www.salon.com/2006/09/06/taiwan_tamiflu/. Last accessed 1 June 2013

Lybecker KM, Fowler E (2009) Compulsory licensing in Canada and Thailand: comparing regimes to ensure legitimate use of the WTO rules. J Law Med Ethics 37:222–239

Marques URQ, Guimarães VS, Sternberg C (2005) Brazil's AIDS controversy: antiretroviral drugs, breaking patents, and compulsory licensing. Food Drug Law J 60:471–477

Mazzoleni R, Nelson R (1998) The benefits and costs of strong patent protection: a contribution to the current debate. Res Policy 27:273–284

McFetridge DG (1998) Intellectual property, technology diffusion, and growth in the Canadian economy. In: Anderson RD, Gallini NT (eds) Competition policy and intellectual property rights in the knowledge based economy. University of Calgary Press, Calgary, pp 64–104

Moser P, Voena A (2012) Compulsory licensing: evidence from the trading with the enemy act. Am Econ Rev 102:396–427

Palermo MP (2008) Brazil may reject Gilead's AIDS drug patent. Reuters, 10 April. http://www.reuters.com/article/2008/04/10/brazil-aids-gilead-idUSN1034936120080410/. Last accessed 25 May 2013

Passarelli C, Terto V (2002) Good medicine: Brazil's multifront war on AIDS. NACLA Rep Am 35:35

Petersen M, Rohter L (2011) Maker agrees to cut price of 2 AIDS drugs in Brazil. New York Times, 31 March. http://www.nytimes.com/2001/03/31/world/maker-agrees-to-cut-price-of-2-aids-drugs-in-brazil.html. Last accessed 1 June 2013

Reichman JH (2009) Compulsory licensing of patented pharmaceutical inventions: evaluating the options. J Law Med Ethics 37:247–263

Reichman J, Lewis T (2005) Using liability rules to stimulate local innovation in developing countries: application to traditional knowledge. In: Maskus KE, Reichman J (eds) International public goods and transfer of technology under a globalized intellectual property regime. Cambridge University Press, Cambridge, pp 337–366

Rich JL (2001) Roche reaches accord on drug with Brazil. New York Times, 1 September. http://www.nytimes.com/2001/09/01/business/roche-reaches-accord-on-drug-with-brazil.html. Last accessed 30 May 2013

Saez C (2010) Ecuador grants first compulsory licence for HIV/AIDS drug. Intellectual Property Watch, 22 April. http://www.ip-watch.org/weblog/2010/04/22/ecuador-grants-first-compulsory-licence-for-hivaids-drug/. Last accessed 1 June 2013

Scherer FM (1977) The economic effects of compulsory patent licensing (no. 2). New York University, Graduate School of Business Administration, Center for the Study of Financial Institutions, 1977, New York

Smith R, Correa C, Oh C (2009) Trade, TRIPS, and pharmaceuticals. Lancet 373:684–691

Stiglitz J (2009) Trade Agreements and health in developing countries. Lancet 373:363–365

Tsai G (2009) Canada's access to medicines regime: lessons for compulsory licensing schemes under the WTO Doha Declaration. V J Int Law 49:1063–1097

van Gelder A, Stevens P (2010) The compulsory license red herring. International Policy Network. http://www.minimalgovernment.net/media/compulsory-201011.pdf. Last accessed 1 June 2013

World Development Indicators, World Bank. http://data.worldbank.org/indicator/BX.KLT.DINV.CD.WD/countries/BR?display=graph

MIX
Papier aus verantwortungsvollen Quellen
Paper from responsible sources
FSC® C105338

If you have any concerns about our products,
you can contact us on
ProductSafety@springernature.com

In case Publisher is established outside the EU,
the EU authorized representative is:
Springer Nature Customer Service Center GmbH
Europaplatz 3, 69115 Heidelberg, Germany

Printed by Libri Plureos GmbH
in Hamburg, Germany